THE TEEN'S
TOPICAL BIBLE

THE
LIVING BIBLE

HONOR

Tulsa, Oklahoma

Presented By:
Wisdom International
P. O. Box 747
Dallas, Texas 75221
214/518-1833

Published by
Honor Books
P. O. Box 55388
Tulsa, Oklahoma 74155

ISBN 1-56292-018-9

THE
TEEN'S
TOPICAL BIBLE

THE
LIVING BIBLE

Contents

I. How Can You Develop Your Relationship With God?

II. Relationship With Your Parents

III. Relationship With Friends

IV. Dating Relationships

V. What To Do When:

VI. When You Need:

VII. How To Be an Overcomer

VIII. How To Overcome:

IX. God's Purpose for Your Life

X. Scriptural Prayers

XI. The Salvation Experience

I. How Can You Develop Your Relationship With God?

Knowing Jesus as Your Savior

And as Moses in the wilderness lifted up the bronze image of a serpent on a pole, even so I must be lifted up upon a pole, so that anyone who believes in me will have eternal life.

For God loved the world so much that he gave his only Son so that anyone who believes in him shall not perish but have eternal life.

God did not send his Son into the world to condemn it, but to save it.

There is no eternal doom awaiting those who trust him to save them. But those who don't trust him have already been tried and condemned for not believing in the only Son of God.

John 3:14-18

Jesus replied, "With all the earnestness I possess I tell you this: Unless you are born again, you can never get into the Kingdom of God."

John 3:3

For it is my Father's will that everyone who sees his Son and believes on him should have eternal life — that I should raise him at the Last Day.

John 6:40

How earnestly I tell you this — anyone who believes in me already has eternal life! Yes, I am the Bread of Life!

John 6:47,48

The Father loves this man because he is his Son, and God has given him everything there is.

And all who trust him — God's Son — to save them have eternal life; those who don't believe and obey him shall never see heaven, but the wrath of God remains upon them.

John 3:35,36

He will even raise from the dead anyone he wants to, just as the Father does.

And the Father leaves all judgment of sin to his Son, so that everyone will honor the Son, just as they honor the Father. But if you refuse to honor God's Son, whom he sent to you, then you are certainly not honoring the Father.

I say emphatically that anyone who listens to my message and believes in God who sent me has eternal life, and will never be damned for his sins, but has already passed out of death into life.

And I solemnly declare that the time is coming, in fact, it is here, when the dead shall hear my voice — the voice of the Son of God — and those who listen shall live.

The Father has life in himself, and has granted his Son to have life in himself, and to judge the sins of all mankind because he is the Son of Man.
John 5:21-27

Then he said to them, "You are from below; I am from above. You are of this world; I am not.

That is why I said that you will die in your sins; for unless you believe that I am the Messiah, the Son of God, you will die in your sins."
John 8:23,24

The thief's purpose is to steal, kill and destroy. My purpose is to give life in all its fullness.
John 10:10

My sheep recognize my voice, and I know them, and they follow me.

I give them eternal life and they shall never perish. No one shall snatch them away from me, for my Father has given them to me, and he is more powerful than anyone else, so no one can kidnap them from me.

I and the Father are one.
John 10:27-30

Jesus told her, "I am the one who raises the dead and gives them life again. Anyone who believes in me, even though he dies like anyone else, shall live again.

He is given eternal life for believing in me and shall never perish. Do you believe this, Martha?''
John 11:25,26

That God is on one side and all the people on the other side, and Christ Jesus, himself man, is between them to bring them together, by giving his life for all mankind. This is the message that at the proper time God gave to the world.
1 Timothy 2:5,6

Jesus shouted to the crowds, ''If you trust me, you are really trusting God.

For when you see me, you are seeing the one who sent me.

I have come as a Light to shine in this dark world, so that all who put their trust in me will no longer wander in the darkness.
John 12:44-46

Jesus told him, ''I am the Way — yes, and the Truth and the Life. No one can get to the Father except by means of me.''
John 14:6

But anyone who asks for mercy from the Lord shall have it and shall be saved.
Acts 2:21

And Peter replied, ''Each one of you must turn from sin, return to God, and be baptized in the name of Jesus Christ for the forgiveness of your sins; then you also shall receive this gift, the Holy Spirit.''

Acts 2:38

Now change your mind and attitude to God and turn to him so he can cleanse away your sins and send you wonderful times of refreshment from the presence of the Lord.

Acts 3:19

Let me clearly state to you and to all the people of Israel that it was done in the name and power of Jesus from Nazareth, the Messiah, the man you crucified — but God raised back to life again. It is by his authority that this man stands here healed!

For Jesus the Messiah is (the one referred to in the Scriptures when they speak of) a "stone discarded by the builders which became the capstone of the arch."

There is salvation in no one else! Under all heaven there is no other name for men to call upon to save them.

Acts 4:10-12

Don't you believe that all are saved the same way, by the free gift of the Lord Jesus?

Acts 15:11

Because of his kindness, you have been saved through trusting Christ. And even trusting is not of yourselves; it too is a gift from God.

Salvation is not a reward for the good we have done, so none of us can take any credit for it.

Ephesians 2:8,9

For if you tell others with your own mouth that Jesus Christ is your Lord and believe in your own heart that God has raised him from the dead, you will be saved.

For it is by believing in his heart that a man becomes right with God; and with his mouth he tells others of his faith, confirming his salvation.
Romans 10:9,10

Christ also suffered. He died once for the sins of all us guilty sinners although he himself was innocent of any sin at any time, that he might bring us safely home to God. But though his body died, his spirit lived on.
1 Peter 3:18

But to all who received him, he gave the right to become children of God. All they needed to do was to trust him to save them.

All those who believe this are reborn! — not a physical rebirth resulting from human passion or plan — but from the will of God.
John 1:12,13

Knowing the Holy Ghost (as Your Baptizer)

John answered the question by saying, "I baptize only with water; but someone is coming soon who has far higher authority than mine; in fact, I am not even worthy of being his slave. He will baptize you with fire — with the Holy Spirit."
Luke 3:16

If you love me, obey me; and I will ask the Father and he will give you another Comforter, and he will never leave you.

He is the Holy Spirit, the Spirit who leads into all truth. The world at large cannot receive him, for it isn't looking for him and doesn't recognize him. But you do, for he lives with you now and some day shall be in you.

John 14:16,17

But when the Father sends the Comforter instead of me — and by the Comforter I mean the Holy Spirit — he will teach you much, as well as remind you of everything I myself have told you.

John 14:26

But I will send you the Comforter — the Holy Spirit, the source of all truth. He will come to you from the Father and will tell you all about me.

And you also must tell everyone about me because you have been with me from the beginning.

John 15:26,27

But the fact of the matter is that it is best for you that I go away, for if I don't, the Comforter won't come. If I do, he will — for I will send him to you.

John 16:7

When the Holy Spirit, who is truth, comes, he shall guide you into all truth, for he will not be presenting his own ideas, but will be passing on to you what he has heard. He will tell you about the future.

He shall praise me and bring me great honor by showing you my glory.

All the Father's glory is mine; this is what I mean when I say that he will show you my glory.
John 16:13-15

And you no doubt know that Jesus of Nazareth was anointed by God with the Holy Spirit and with power, and he went around doing good and healing all who were possessed by demons, for God was with him.
Acts 10:38

In one of these meetings he told them not to leave Jerusalem until the Holy Spirit came upon them in fulfillment of the Father's promise, a matter he had previously discussed with them.

"John baptized you with water," he reminded them, "but you shall be baptized with the Holy Spirit in just a few days."
Acts 1:4,5

But when the Holy Spirit has come upon you, you will receive power to testify about me with great effect, to the people in Jerusalem, throughout Judea, in Samaria, and to the ends of the earth, about my death and resurrection.
Acts 1:8

And everyone present was filled with the Holy Spirit and began speaking in languages they didn't know, for the Holy Spirit gave them this ability.
Acts 2:4

"In the last days," God said, "I will pour out my Holy Spirit upon all mankind, and your sons and daughters shall prophesy, and your young men shall see visions, and your old men dream dreams.

Yes, the Holy Spirit shall come upon all my servants, men and women alike, and they shall prophesy."

Acts 2:17,18

And now he sits on the throne of highest honor in heaven, next to God. And just as promised, the Father gave him the authority to send the Holy Spirit — with the results you are seeing and hearing today.

Acts 2:33

And Peter replied, "Each one of you must turn from sin, return to God, and be baptized in the name of Jesus Christ for the forgiveness of your sins; then you also shall receive this gift, the Holy Spirit."

Acts 2:38

Even as Peter was saying these things, the Holy Spirit fell upon all those listening!

The Jews who came with Peter were amazed that the gift of the Holy Spirit would be given to Gentiles too!

But there could be no doubt about it, for they heard them speaking in tongues and praising God.

Peter asked, "Can anyone object to my baptizing them, now that they have received the Holy Spirit just as we did?"

So he did, baptizing them in the name of Jesus, the Messiah. Afterwards Cornelius begged him to stay with them for several days.

Acts 10:44-48

Then, when Paul laid his hands upon their heads, the Holy Spirit came on them, and they spoke in other languages and prophesied.

Acts 19:6

And so it is with prayer — keep on asking and you will keep on getting; keep on looking and you will keep on finding; knock and the door will be opened.

Everyone who asks, receives; all who seek, find; and the door is opened to everyone who knocks.

You men who are fathers — if your boy asks for bread, do you give him a stone? If he asks for fish, do you give him a snake?

If he asks for an egg, do you give him a scorpion? [Of course not!]

And if even sinful persons like yourselves give children what they need, don't you realize that your heavenly Father will do at least as much, and give the Holy Spirit to those who ask for him?

Luke 11:9-13

With water I baptize those who repent of their sins; but someone else is coming, far greater than I am, so great that I am not worthy to carry his shoes! He shall baptize you with the Holy Spirit and with fire.

Matthew 3:11

For the Scriptures declare that rivers of living water shall flow from the inmost being of anyone who believes in me.

(He was speaking of the Holy Spirit, who would be given to everyone believing in him; but the Spirit had not yet been given, because Jesus had not yet returned to his glory in heaven.)

John 7:38,39

Don't drink too much wine, for many evils lie along that path; be filled instead with the Holy Spirit and controlled by him.

Talk with each other much about the Lord, quoting psalms and hymns and singing sacred songs, making music in your hearts to the Lord.

Always give thanks for everything to our God and Father in the name of our Lord Jesus Christ.

Honor Christ by submitting to each other.

Ephesians 5:18-21

Knowing God's Character
Through the Word

Oh, put God to the test and see how kind he is! See for yourself the way his mercies shower down on all who trust in him.

Psalm 34:8

The Lord is my strength, my song, and my salvation. He is my God, and I will praise him. He is my father's God — I will exalt him.

The Lord is a warrior — Yes, Jehovah is his name.

Exodus 15:2,3

Who else is like the Lord among the gods? Who is glorious in holiness like him? Who is so awesome in splendor, A wonder-working God?

You reached out your hand and the earth swallowed them.

You have led the people you redeemed. But in your loving-kindness You have guided them wonderfully to your holy land.

Exodus 15:11-13

Then the Lord descended in the form of a pillar of cloud and stood there with him, and passed in front of him and announced the meaning of his name.

"I am Jehovah, the merciful and gracious God," he said, "slow to anger and rich in steadfast love and truth.

I, Jehovah, show this steadfast love to many thousands by forgiving their sins; or else I refuse to clear the guilty, and require that a father's sins be punished in the sons and grandsons, and even later generations."

Exodus 34:5-7

The Lord is my light and my salvation; he protects me from danger — whom shall I fear?
Psalm 27:1

All who are oppressed may come to him. He is a refuge for them in their times of trouble.

All those who know your mercy, Lord, will count on you for help. For you have never yet forsaken those who trust in you.

Psalm 9:9,10

[This song of David was written at a time when the Lord had delivered him from his many enemies, including Saul.]

Lord, how I love you! For you have done such tremendous things for me.

The Lord is my fort where I can enter and be safe; no one can follow me in and slay me. He is a rugged mountain where I hide; he is my Savior, a rock where none can reach me, and a tower of safety. He is my shield. He is like the strong horn of a mighty fighting bull.

All I need to do is cry to him — oh, praise the Lord — and I am saved from all my enemies!

Psalm 18:1-3

He is my strength, my shield from every danger. I trusted in him, and he helped me. Joy rises in my heart until I burst out in songs of praise to him.

Psalm 28:7

Oh, how great is your goodness to those who publicly declare that you will rescue them. For you have stored up great blessings for those who trust and reverence you.

Hide your loved ones in the shelter of your presence, safe beneath your hand, safe from all conspiring men.

Psalm 31:19,20

You are my hiding place from every storm of life; you even keep me from getting into trouble! You surround me with songs of victory.

Psalm 32:7

But the eyes of the Lord are watching over those who fear him, who rely upon his steady love.

He will keep them from death even in times of famine!

We depend upon the Lord alone to save us. Only he can help us; he protects us like a shield.

No wonder we are happy in the Lord! For we are trusting him. We trust his holy name.

Yes, Lord, let your constant love surround us, for our hopes are in you alone.

Psalm 33:18-22

In a great antiphonal chorus they sang, "Holy, holy, holy is the Lord Almighty; the whole earth is filled with his glory."

Isaiah 6:3

Stay away from the love of money; be satisfied with what you have. For God has said, "I will never, never fail you nor forsake you."

That is why we can say without any doubt or fear, "The Lord is my Helper, and I am not afraid of anything that mere man can do to me."

Hebrews 13:5,6

God will surely do this for you, for he always does just what he says, and he is the one who invited you into this wonderful friendship with his Son, even Christ our Lord.

1 Corinthians 1:9

Yes, the Lord hears the good man when he calls to him for help and saves him out of all his troubles.

The Lord is close to those whose hearts are breaking; he rescues those who are humbly sorry for their sins.

Psalm 34:17,18

The Lord saves the godly! He is their salvation and their refuge when trouble comes.

Because they trust in him, he helps them and delivers them from the plots of evil men.

Psalm 37:39,40

How greatly to be envied are those you have chosen to come and live with you within the holy tabernacle courts! What joys await us among all the good things there.

Psalm 65:4

He is like a father to us, tender and sympathetic to those who reverence him.

For he knows we are but dust.

Psalm 103:13,14

For Jehovah God is our Light and our Protector. He gives us grace and glory. No good thing will he withhold from those who walk along his paths.

O Lord of the armies of heaven, blessed are those who trust in you.

Psalm 84:11,12

We live within the shadow of the Almighty, sheltered by the God who is above all gods.

This I declare, that he alone is my refuge, my place of safety; he is my God, and I am trusting him.

For he rescues you from every trap and protects you from the fatal plague.

He will shield you with his wings! They will shelter you. His faithful promises are your armor.

Psalm 91:1-4

All who are thankful should ponder them with me.

For his miracles demonstrate his honor, majesty, and eternal goodness.

Who can forget the wonders he performs — deeds of mercy and of grace?

He gives food to those who trust him; he never forgets his promises.

He has shown his great power to his people by giving them the land of Israel, though it was the home of many nations living there.

All he does is just and good, and all his laws are right, for they are formed from truth and goodness, and stand firm forever.

He has paid a full ransom for his people; now they are always free to come to Jehovah (what a holy, awe-inspiring name that is).

Psalm 111:2-9

Again I say, we are telling you about what we ourselves have actually seen and heard, so that you may share the fellowship and the joys we have with the Father and with Jesus Christ his son.

And if you do as I say in this letter, then you, too, will be full of joy, and so will we.

1 John 1:3,4

But if we are living in the light of God's presence, just as Christ does, then we have wonderful fellowship and joy with each other, and the blood of Jesus his Son cleanses us from every sin.

1 John 1:7

He is for me! How can I be afraid? What can mere man do to me?

Psalm 118:6

Yet they say, "My Lord deserted us; he has forgotten us."

Never! Can a mother forget her little child and not have love for her own son? Yet even if that should be, I will not forget you.

See, I have tattooed your name upon my palm, and ever before me is a picture of Jerusalem's walls in ruins.

Isaiah 49:14-16

The high and lofty One who inhabits eternity, the Holy One, says this: I live in that high and holy place where those with contrite, humble spirits dwell; and I refresh the humble and give new courage to those with repentant hearts.

Isaiah 57:15

And don't you know that if a man joins himself to a prostitute she becomes a part of him and he becomes a part of her? For God tells us in the Scripture that in his sight the two become one person.

But if you give yourself to the Lord, you and Christ are joined together as one person.

That is why I say to run from sex sin. No other sin affects the body as this one does. When you sin this sin it is against your own body.

1 Corinthians 6:16-18

But this is the new agreement I will make with the people of Israel, says the Lord: I will write my laws in their minds so that they will know what I want them to do without my even telling them, and these laws will be in their hearts so that they will want to obey them, and I will be their God and they shall be my people.

And no one then will need to speak to his friend or neighbor or brother, saying, "You, too, should know the Lord," because everyone, great and small, will know me already.

Hebrews 8:10,11

And so it happened just as the Scriptures say, that Abraham trusted God, and the Lord declared him good in God's sight, and he was even called "the friend of God."

James 2:23

I will walk among you and be your God, and you shall be my people.

Leviticus 26:12

He isn't really being slow about his promised return, even though it sometimes seems that way. But he is waiting, for the good reason that he is not willing that any should perish, and he is giving more time for sinners to repent.

2 Peter 3:9

For he longs for all to be saved and to understand this truth: That God is on one side and all the people on the other side, and Christ Jesus, himself man, is between them to bring them together, by giving his life for all mankind. This is the message which at the proper time God gave to the world.

I Timothy 2:4-6

Fellowshipping With God Through Prayer

Again I say, we are telling you about what we ourselves have actually seen and heard, so that you may share the fellowship and the joys we have with the Father and with Jesus Christ his son.

1 John 1:3

For I cried to him and he answered me! He freed me from all my fears.

Others too were radiant at what he did for them.
Theirs was no downcast look of rejection!

This poor man cried to the Lord — and the Lord
heard him and saved him out of his troubles.

For the Angel of the Lord guards and rescues
all who reverence him.

Psalm 34:4-7

Come and hear, all of you who reverence the
Lord, and I will tell you what he did for me:

For I cried to him for help with praises ready
on my tongue.

He would not have listened if I had not
confessed my sins.

But he listened! He heard my prayer! He paid
attention to it!

Blessed be God, who didn't turn away when
I was praying and didn't refuse me his kindness
and love.

Psalm 66:16-20

I, yes, I alone am he who blots away your sins
for my own sake and will never think of them
again.

Oh, remind me of this promise of forgiveness,
for we must talk about your sins. Plead your case
for my forgiving you.

Isaiah 43:25,26

And we are sure of this, that he will listen to
us whenever we ask him for anything in line with
his will.

And if we really know he is listening when we talk to him and make our requests, then we can be sure that he will answer us.

1 John 5:14,15

Hungering and Seeking for God With All Your Heart

The one thing I want from God, the thing I seek most of all, is the privilege of meditating in his Temple, living in his presence every day of my life, delighting in his incomparable perfections and glory.

Psalm 27:4

My heart has heard you say, "Come and talk with me, O my people." And my heart responds, "Lord, I am coming."

Oh, do not hide yourself when I am trying to find you. Do not angrily reject your servant. You have been my help in all my trials before; don't leave me now. Don't forsake me, O God of my salvation.

Psalm 27:8,9

If you belong to the Lord, reverence him; for everyone who does this has everything he needs.

Even strong young lions sometimes go hungry, but those of us who reverence the Lord will never lack any good thing.

Psalm 34:9,10

As the deer pants for water, so I long for you,
O God.

I thirst for God, the living God. Where can I
find him to come and stand before him?

Psalm 42:1,2

O my people, trust him all the time. Pour out
your longings before him, for he can help!

Psalm 62:8

[A Psalm of David when he was hiding in the
wilderness of Judea.]

O God, my God! How I search for you! How
I thirst for you in this parched and weary land
where there is no water. How I long to find you!

How I wish I could go into your sanctuary to
see your strength and glory, for your love and
kindness are better to me than life itself. How I
praise you!

I will bless you as long as I live, lifting up my
hands to you in prayer.

Psalm 63:1-4

The humble shall see their God at work for
them. No wonder they will be so glad! All who
seek for God shall live in joy.

Psalm 69:32

But even so, you love me! You are holding my right hand!

You will keep on guiding me all my life with your wisdom and counsel, and afterwards receive me into the glories of heaven!

Whom have I in heaven but you? And I desire no one on earth as much as you!

My health fails; my spirits droop, yet God remains! He is the strength of my heart; he is mine forever!

But those refusing to worship God will perish, for he destroys those serving other gods.

But as for me, I get as close to him as I can! I have chosen him, and I will tell everyone about the wonderful ways he rescues me.

Psalm 73:23-28

I long, yes, faint with longing to be able to enter your courtyard and come near to the Living God.

Psalm 84:2

The Lord looks down from heaven on all mankind to see if there are any who are wise, who want to please God.

Psalm 14:2

Only those with pure hands and hearts, who do not practice dishonesty and lying.

They will receive God's own goodness as their blessing from him, planted in their lives by God himself, their Savior.

These are the ones who are allowed to stand before the Lord and worship the God of Jacob.

Psalm 24:4-6

Glory in the Lord; O worshipers of God, rejoice.

Search for him and for his strength, and keep on searching!

Psalm 105:3,4

O Lord, we love to do your will! Our hearts' desire is to glorify your name.

All night long I search for you; earnestly I seek for God; for only when you come in judgment on the earth to punish it will people turn away from wickedness and do what is right.

Isaiah 26:8,9

But all these things that I once thought very worthwhile — now I've thrown them all away so that I can put my trust and hope in Christ alone.

Yes, everything else is worthless when compared with the priceless gain of knowing Christ Jesus my Lord. I have put aside all else, counting it worth less than nothing, in order that I can have Christ, and become one with him, no longer counting on being saved by being good enough or by obeying God's laws, but by trusting Christ to save me; for God's way of making us right with himself depends on faith - counting on Christ alone.

Now I have given up everything else - I have found it to be the only way to really know Christ and to experience the mighty power that brought him back to life again, and to find out what it means to suffer and to die with him.

So, whatever it takes, I will be one who lives in the fresh newness of life of those who are alive from the dead.

I don't mean to say I am perfect. I haven't learned all I should even yet, but I keep working toward the day when I will finally be all that Christ saved me for and wants me to be.

Philippians 3:7-12

Since you became alive again, so to speak, when Christ arose from the dead, now set your sights on the rich treasures and joys of heaven where he sits beside God in the place of honor and power.

Let heaven fill your thoughts; don't spend your time worrying about things down here.

You should have as little desire for this world as a dead person does. Your real life is in heaven with Christ and God.

And when Christ who is our real life comes back again, you will shine with him and share in all his glories.

Colossians 3:1-4

And he will give them [food and clothing] to you if you give him first place in your life and live as he wants you to.

Matthew 6:33

And when you draw close to God, God will draw close to you. Wash your hands, you sinners, and let your hearts be filled with God alone to make them pure and true to him.

James 4:8

You must love him with all your heart, soul, and might.

> *Deuteronomy 6:5*

So be very careful to keep on loving him.
> *Joshua 23:11*

I have tried my best to find you — don't let me wander off from your instructions.
> *Psalm 119:10*

Give Him Love Through Praise and Worship

Oh, that these men would praise the Lord for his loving-kindness, and for all of his wonderful deeds!

For he satisfies the thirsty soul and fills the hungry soul with good.

> *Psalm 107:8,9*

Put your trust in the Lord, and offer him pleasing sacrifices.
> *Psalm 4:5*

O Lord, I will praise you with all my heart and tell everyone about the marvelous things you do.

I will be glad, yes, filled with joy because of you. I will sing your praises, O Lord God above all gods.

> *Psalm 9:1,2*

Accept our praise, O Lord, for all your glorious power. We will write songs to celebrate your mighty acts!

Psalm 21:13

Oh, love the Lord, all of you who are his people; for the Lord protects those who are loyal to him, but harshly punishes all who haughtily reject him.

So cheer up! Take courage if you are depending on the Lord.

Psalm 31:23,24

Let all the joys of the godly well up in praise to the Lord, for it is right to praise him.

Play joyous melodies of praise upon the lyre and on the harp.

Compose new songs of praise to him, accompanied skillfully on the harp; sing joyfully.

Psalm 33:1-3

I will praise the Lord no matter what happens. I will constantly speak of his glories and grace.

I will boast of all his kindness to me. Let all who are discouraged take heart. Let us praise the Lord together and exalt his name.

Psalm 34:1-3

But true praise is a worthy sacrifice; this really honors me. Those who walk my paths will receive salvation from the Lord.

Psalm 50:23

Oh, come, let us sing to the Lord! Give a joyous shout in honor of the Rock of our salvation!

Come before him with thankful hearts. Let us sing him psalms of praise.

For the Lord is a great God, the great King of all gods.

Psalm 95:1-3

Always be full of joy in the Lord; I say it again, rejoice!

Philippians 4:4

If you love me, obey me; and I will ask the Father and he will give you another Comforter, and he will never leave you.

John 14:15,16

"Sing, Jerusalem, and rejoice! For I have come to live among you," says the Lord.

Zechariah 2:10

II. Relationship With Your Parents

Maintaining a Godly Attitude
to Parents' Authority

Obey the government, for God is the one who has put it there. There is no government anywhere that God has not placed in power.

So those who refuse to obey the laws of the land are refusing to obey God, and punishment will follow.

Romans 13:1,2

Children, obey your parents; this is the right thing to do because God has placed them in authority over you.

Honor your father and mother. This is the first of God's Ten Commandments that ends with a promise.

And this is the promise: that if you honor your father and mother, yours will be a long life, full of blessing.

Ephesians 6:1-3

My son, listen to me and do as I say, and you will have a long, good life.

Proverbs 4:10

Listen, son of mine, to what I say. Listen carefully.

Keep these thoughts ever in mind; let them penetrate deep within your heart, for they will mean real life for you and radiant health.

Above all else, guard your affections. For they influence everything else in your life.

Proverbs 4:20-23

A wise youth accepts his father's rebuke; a young mocker doesn't.

Proverbs 13:1

I would have you learn this great fact: that a life of doing right is the wisest life there is.

If you live that kind of life, you'll not limp or stumble as you run.

Proverbs 4:11,12

If you profit from constructive criticism, you will be elected to the wise men's hall of fame.

But to reject criticism is to harm yourself and your own best interests.

Proverbs 15:31,32

Little children, let us stop just saying we love people; let us really love them, and show it by our actions.

1 John 3:18

Only fools refuse to be taught.

Listen to your father and mother. What you learn from them will stand you in good stead; it will gain you many honors.

Proverbs 1:8,9

Samuel replied, "Has the Lord as much pleasure in your burnt offerings and sacrifices as in your obedience? Obedience is far better than sacrifice. He is much more interested in your listening to him than in your offering the fat of rams to him."

1 Samuel 15:22

And he humbled himself even further, going so far as actually to die a criminal's death on a cross.

Philippians 2:8

Happy are those who strive for peace — they shall be called the sons of God.

Happy are those who are persecuted because they are good, for the Kingdom of Heaven is theirs.

Matthew 5:9,10

Servants, you must respect your masters and do whatever they tell you — not only if they are kind and reasonable, but even if they are tough and cruel.

Praise the Lord if you are punished for doing right!

Of course, you get no credit for being patient if you are beaten for doing wrong; but if you do right and suffer for it, and are patient beneath the blows, God is well pleased.

This suffering is all part of the work God has given you. Christ, who suffered for you, is your example. Follow in his steps.

1 Peter 2:18-21

You children must always obey your fathers and mothers, for that pleases the Lord.

Fathers, don't scold your children so much that they become discouraged and quit trying.

You slaves must always obey your earthly masters, not only trying to please them when they are watching you but all the time; obey them willingly because of your love for the Lord and because you want to please him.

Work hard and cheerfully at all you do, just as though you were working for the Lord and not merely for your masters, remembering that it is the Lord Christ who is going to pay you, giving you your full portion of all he owns. He is the one you are really working for.

Colossians 3:20-24

And even though Jesus was God's Son, he had to learn from experience what it was like to obey when obeying meant suffering.

Hebrews 5:8

The wicked live for rebellion; they shall be severely punished.

Proverbs 17:11

Only a fool despises his father's advice; a wise son considers each suggestion.

Proverbs 15:5

Winning Parents to the Lord
(How to Win Unsaved Loved Ones)

You are the world's light — a city on a hill, glowing in the night for all to see.

Don't hide your light! Let it shine for all; let your good deeds glow for all to see, so that they will praise your heavenly Father.

Matthew 5:14-16

But thanks be to God! For through what Christ has done, he has triumphed over us so that now wherever we go he uses us to tell others about the Lord and to spread the Gospel like a sweet perfume.

As far as God is concerned there is a sweet, wholesome fragrance in our lives. It is the fragrance of Christ within us, an aroma to both the saved and the unsaved all around us.

To those who are not being saved, we seem a fearful smell of death and doom, while to those who know Christ we are a life-giving perfume. But who is adequate for such a task as this?

Only those who, like ourselves, are men of integrity, sent by God, speaking with Christ's power, with God's eye upon us. We are not like those hucksters — and there are many of them — whose idea in getting out the Gospel is to make a good living out of it.

2 Corinthians 2:14-17

Don't let anyone think little of you because you are young. Be their ideal; let them follow the way you teach and live; be a pattern for them in your love, your faith, and your clean thoughts.

1 Timothy 4:12

Keep a close watch on all you do and think. Stay true to what is right and God will bless you and use you to help others.

1 Timothy 4:16

When I am with those whose consciences bother them easily, I don't act as though I know it all and don't say they are foolish; the result is that they are willing to let me help them. Yes, whatever a person is like, I try to find common ground with him so that he will let me tell him about Christ and let Christ save him.

1 Corinthians 9:22

So pray to the one in charge of the harvesting, and ask him to recruit more workers for his harvest fields.

Matthew 9:38

But if you stay in me and obey my commands, you may ask any request you like, and it will be granted!

John 15:7

Godly men are growing a tree that bears life-giving fruit, and all who win souls are wise.

Proverbs 11:30

For it won't be you doing the talking — it will be the Spirit of your heavenly Father speaking through you!

Matthew 10:20

Most important of all, continue to show deep love for each other, for love makes up for many of your faults.

1 Peter 4:8

For God is at work within you, helping you want to obey him, and then helping you do what he wants.

In everything you do, stay away from complaining and arguing so that no one can speak a word of blame against you. You are to live clean, innocent lives as children of God in a dark world full of people who are crooked and stubborn. Shine out among them like beacon lights, holding out to them the Word of Life. Then when Christ returns, how glad I will be that my work among you was so worthwhile.

Philippians 2:13-16

All the special gifts and powers from God will someday come to an end, but love goes on forever. Someday prophecy and speaking in unknown languages and special knowledge — these gifts will disappear.

1 Corinthians 13:8

And may the Lord make your love to grow and overflow to each other and to everyone else, just as our love does toward you.

1 Thessalonians 3:12

For I am not ashamed of this Good News about Christ. It is God's powerful method of bringing all who believe it to heaven. This message was preached first to the Jews alone, but now everyone is invited to come to God in this same way.

This Good News tells us that God makes us ready for heaven — makes us right in God's sight — when we put our faith and trust in Christ to save us. This is accomplished from start to finish by faith. As the Scripture says it, "The man who finds life will find it through trusting God."

Romans 1:16,17

Don't you realize how patient he is being with you? Or don't you care? Can't you see that he has been waiting all this time without punishing you, to give you time to turn from your sin? His kindness is meant to lead you to repentance.

Romans 2:4

Make the most of your chances to tell others the Good News. Be wise in all your contacts with them.

Let your conversation be gracious as well as sensible, for then you will have the right answer for everyone.

Colossians 4:5,6

Quietly trust yourself to Christ your Lord, and if anybody asks why you believe as you do, be ready to tell him, and do it in a gentle and respectful way.

Do what is right; then if men speak against you, calling you evil names, they will become ashamed of themselves for falsely accusing you when you have only done what is good.

1 Peter 3:15,16

Dear brothers, if anyone has slipped away from God and no longer trusts the Lord, and someone helps him understand the Truth again, that person who brings him back to God will have saved a wandering soul from death, bringing about the forgiveness of his many sins.

James 5:19,20

When There Is Family Strife

Happy are those who strive for peace — they shall be called the sons of God.

Matthew 5:9

Dear brothers, don't ever forget that it is best to listen much, speak little, and not become angry; for anger doesn't make us good, as God demands that we must be.

James 1:19,20

If you are angry, don't sin by nursing your grudge. Don't let the sun go down with you still angry — get over it quickly; for when you are angry, you give a mighty foothold to the devil.

If anyone is stealing he must stop it and begin using those hands of his for honest work so he can give to others in need.

Don't use bad language. Say only what is good and helpful to those you are talking to, and what will give them a blessing.

Don't cause the Holy Spirit sorrow by the way you live. Remember, he is the one who marks you to be present on that day when salvation from sin will be complete.

Stop being mean, bad-tempered, and angry. Quarreling, harsh words, and dislike of others should have no place in your lives.

Instead, be kind to each other, tenderhearted, forgiving one another, just as God has forgiven you because you belong to Christ.

Ephesians 4:26-32

And by all means don't brag about being wise and good if you are bitter and jealous and selfish; that is the worst sort of lie.

For jealousy and selfishness are not God's kind of wisdom. Such things are earthly, unspiritual, inspired by the devil.

For wherever there is jealousy or selfish ambition, there will be disorder and every other kind of evil.

But the wisdom that comes from heaven is first of all pure and full of quiet gentleness. Then it is peace-loving and courteous. It allows discussion and is willing to yield to others; it is full of mercy and good deeds. It is wholehearted and straightforward and sincere.

And those who are peacemakers will plant seeds of peace and reap a harvest of goodness.

James 3:14-18

A soft answer turns away wrath, but harsh words cause quarrels.

A wise teacher makes learning a joy; a rebellious teacher spouts foolishness.

The Lord is watching everywhere and keeps his eye on both the evil and the good.

Gentle words cause life and health; griping brings discouragement.

Proverbs 15:1-4

Never criticize or condemn — or it will all come back on you. Go easy on others; then they will do the same for you.

Luke 6:37

Since you have been chosen by God who has given you this new kind of life, and because of his deep love and concern for you, you should practice tenderhearted mercy and kindness to others. Don't worry about making a good impression on them, but be ready to suffer quietly and patiently.

Be gentle and ready to forgive; never hold grudges. Remember, the Lord forgave you, so you must forgive others.

Most of all, let love guide your life, for then the whole church will stay together in perfect harmony.

Colossians 3:12-14

Hatred stirs old quarrels, but love overlooks insults.

Proverbs 10:12

When You Live in a Broken Home

For if my father and mother should abandon me, you would welcome and comfort me.

Psalm 27:10

Yes, the Lord hears the good man when he calls to him for help and saves him out of all his troubles.

The Lord is close to those whose hearts are breaking; he rescues those who are humbly sorry for their sins.

Psalm 34:17,18

I have been young and now I am old. And in all my years I have never seen the Lord forsake a man who loves him; nor have I seen the children of the godly go hungry.

Instead, the godly are able to be generous with their gifts and loans to others, and their children are a blessing.

Psalm 37:25,26

Lord, you see what they are doing. You have noted each evil act. You know what trouble and grief they have caused. Now punish them. O Lord, the poor man trusts himself to you; you are known as the helper of the helpless.

Psalm 10:14

He is a father to the fatherless; he gives justice to the widows, for he is holy.

He gives families to the lonely, and releases prisoners from jail, singing with joy! But for rebels there is famine and distress.

Psalm 68:5,6

He protects the immigrants and cares for the orphans and widows. But he turns topsy-turvy the plans of the wicked.

Psalm 146:9

And it is he who will supply all your needs from his riches in glory because of what Christ Jesus has done for us.

Philippians 4:19

God is able to make it up to you by giving you everything you need and more so that there will not only be enough for your own needs but plenty left over to give joyfully to others.

2 Corinthians 9:8

For the Lord your God is merciful — he will not abandon you nor destroy you nor forget the promises he has made to your ancestors.

Deuteronomy 4:31

And he who sent me is with me — he has not deserted me — for I always do those things that are pleasing to him.

John 8:29

He heals the brokenhearted, binding up their wounds.

Psalm 147:3

III. Relationship With Friends

Choosing the Right Friends

For how can we walk together with your sins between us?

Amos 3:3

You are like an unfaithful wife who loves her husband's enemies. Don't you realize that making friends with God's enemies — the evil pleasures of this world — makes you an enemy of God? I say it again, that if your aim is to enjoy the evil pleasure of the unsaved world, you cannot also be a friend of God.

James 4:4

Stop loving this evil world and all that it offers you, for when you love these things you show that you do not really love God; for all these worldly things, these evil desires — the craze for sex, the ambition to buy everything that appeals to you, and the pride that comes from wealth and importance — these are not from God. They are from this evil world itself.

And this world is fading away, and these evil, forbidden things will go with it, but whoever keeps doing the will of God will live forever.

1 John 2:15-17

Don't be fooled by those who say such things. If you listen to them you will start acting like them.

Get some sense and quit your sinning. For to your shame I say it; some of you are not even Christians at all and have never really known God.

1 Corinthians 15:33,34

Be with wise men and become wise. Be with evil men and become evil.

Proverbs 13:20

If young toughs tell you, "Come and join us" — turn your back on them!

"We'll hide and rob and kill," they say.

"Good or bad, we'll treat them all alike.

And the loot we'll get! All kinds of stuff!

Come on, throw in your lot with us; we'll split with you in equal shares."

Don't do it, son! Stay far from men like that, for crime is their way of life, and murder is their specialty.

When a bird sees a trap being set, it stays away, but not these men; they trap themselves! They lay a booby trap for their own lives.

Such is the fate of all who live by violence and murder. They will die a violent death.

Proverbs 1:10-19

Young men who are wise obey the law; a son who is a member of a lawless gang is a shame to his father.

Proverbs 28:7

A man who robs his parents and says, "What's wrong with that?" is no better than a murderer.
Proverbs 28:24

If you are looking for advice, stay away from fools.
Proverbs 14:7

Keep away from angry, short-tempered men, lest you learn to be like them and endanger your soul.
Proverbs 22:24,25

Sometimes you were laughed at and beaten, and sometimes you watched and sympathized with others suffering the same things.
Hebrews 10:33

A true friend is always loyal, and a brother is born to help in time of need.
Proverbs 17:17

There are "friends" who pretend to be friends, but there is a friend who sticks closer than a brother.
Proverbs 18:24

Friendly suggestions are as pleasant as perfume.
Proverbs 27:9

Run from anything that gives you the evil thoughts that young men often have, but stay close to anything that makes you want to do right. Have faith and love, and enjoy the companionship of those who love the Lord and have pure hearts.

2 Timothy 2:22

I was glad for the suggestion of going to Jerusalem, to the Temple of the Lord.

Psalm 122:1

Oh, the joys of those who do not follow evil men's advice, who do not hang around with sinners, scoffing at the things of God.

But they delight in doing everything God wants them to, and day and night are always meditating on his laws and thinking about ways to follow him more closely.

They are like trees along a riverbank bearing luscious fruit each season without fail. Their leaves shall never wither, and all they do shall prosper.

Psalm 1:1-3

Anyone is my brother who fears and trusts the Lord and obeys him.

Psalm 119:63

Follow the steps of the godly instead, and stay on the right path.

Proverbs 2:20

What fellowship we had, what wonderful discussions as we walked together to the Temple of the Lord on holy days.

Psalm 55:14

Choosing the Right Entertainment

Take no part in the worthless pleasures of evil and darkness, but instead, rebuke and expose them. It would be shameful even to mention here those pleasures of darkness that the ungodly do.

Ephesians 5:11,12

And now, brothers, as I close this letter, let me say this one more thing: Fix your thoughts on what is true and good and right. Think about things that are pure and lovely, and dwell on the fine, good things in others. Think about all you can praise God for and be glad about.

Keep putting into practice all you learned from me and saw me doing, and the God of peace will be with you.

Philippians 4:8,9

And be sure to put into practice what you hear. The more you do this, the more you will understand what I tell you.

Mark 4:24

Turn me away from wanting any other plan than yours. Revive my heart toward you.

Psalm 119:37

Help me to refuse the low and vulgar things; help me to abhor all crooked deals of every kind, to have no part in them.

Psalm 101:3

If you let Christ be Lord in these affairs, God will be glad; and so will others.

In this way aim for harmony in the church, and try to build each other up.

Romans 14:18,19

When They Pressure You To Do Wrong

Don't join mobs intent on evil. When on the witness stand, don't be swayed in your testimony by the mood of the majority present, and do not slant your testimony in favor of a man just because he is poor.

Exodus 23:2,3

Don't do as the wicked do.

Avoid their haunts — turn away, go somewhere else, for evil men can't sleep until they've done their evil deed for the day. They can't rest unless they cause someone to stumble and fall.

They eat and drink wickedness and violence!

But the good man walks along in the ever-brightening light of God's favor; the dawn gives way to morning splendor, while the evil man gropes and stumbles in the dark.

Proverbs 4:14-19

Don't envy evil men but continue to reverence the Lord all the time, for surely you have a wonderful future ahead of you. There is hope for you yet!

O my son, be wise and stay in God's paths; don't carouse with drunkards and gluttons, for they are on their way to poverty.

And remember that too much sleep clothes a man with rags.

Proverbs 23:17-21

"Watch out! Don't let my sudden coming catch you unawares; don't let me find you living in careless ease, carousing and drinking, and occupied with the problems of this life, like all the rest of the world.

Keep a constant watch. And pray that if possible you may arrive in my presence without having to experience these horrors."

Every day Jesus went to the Temple to teach, and the crowds began gathering early in the morning to hear him.

And each evening he returned to spend the night on the Mount of Olives.

Luke 21:34-38

Don't follow their example in worshiping their gods. Do not ask, ''How do these nations worship their gods?'' and then go and worship as they do!

Deuteronomy 12:30

They rejected his laws and the covenant he had made with their ancestors, and despised all his warnings. In their foolishness they worshiped heathen idols despite the Lord's stern warnings.

2 Kings 17:15

''Quick!'' he told the people, ''get away from the tents of these wicked men, and don't touch anything that belongs to them, lest you be included in their sins [and be destroyed with them].''

Numbers 16:26

If young toughs tell you, ''Come and join us'' — turn your back on them!

Don't do it, son! Stay far from men like that, for crime is their way of life, and murder is their specialty.

Proverbs 1:10,15,16

Let there be no sex sin, impurity or greed among you. Let no one be able to accuse you of any such things.

Dirty stories, foul talk, and coarse jokes — these are not for you. Instead, remind each other of God's goodness, and be thankful.

You can be sure of this: The Kingdom of Christ and of God will never belong to anyone who is impure or greedy, for a greedy person is really an idol worshiper — he loves and worships the good things of this life more than God.

Don't be fooled by those who try to excuse these sins, for the terrible wrath of God is upon all those who do them.

Don't even associate with such people.

For though once your heart was full of darkness, now it is full of light from the Lord, and your behavior should show it!

Ephesians 5:3-8

And so, dear brothers, I plead with you to give your bodies to God. Let them be a living sacrifice, holy — the kind he can accept. When you think of what he has done for you, is this too much to ask?

Romans 12:1

If a godly man compromises with the wicked, it is like polluting a fountain or muddying a spring.

Proverbs 25:26

Keep away from every kind of evil.

May the God of peace himself make you entirely pure and devoted to God; and may your spirit and soul and body be kept strong and blameless until that day when our Lord Jesus Christ comes back again.

1 Thessalonians 5:22,23

Fear of man is a dangerous trap, but to trust in God means safety.

Proverbs 29:25

Begone, you evil-minded men! Don't try to stop me from obeying God's commands.

Psalm 119:115

When They Drink or Take Drugs

Be very, very careful never to compromise with the people there in the land where you are going, for if you do, you will soon be following their evil ways.

Exodus 34:12

Even though the Lord had clearly instructed his people not to marry into those nations, because the women they married would get them started worshiping their gods. Yet Solomon did it anyway.

1 Kings 11:2

You have had enough in the past of the evil things the godless enjoy — sex, sin, lust, getting drunk, wild parties, drinking bouts, and the worship of idols, and other terrible sins.

Of course, your former friends will be very surprised when you don't eagerly join them anymore in the wicked things they do, and they will laugh at you in contempt and scorn.

But just remember that they must face the Judge of all, living and dead; they will be punished for the way they have lived.

1 Peter 4:3-5

Once you were under God's curse, doomed forever for your sins.

You went along with the crowd and were just like all the others, full of sin, obeying Satan, the mighty prince of the power of the air, who is at work right now in the hearts of those who are against the Lord.

All of us used to be just as they are, our lives expressing the evil within us, doing every wicked thing that our passions or our evil thoughts might lead us into. We started out bad, being born with evil natures, and were under God's anger just like everyone else.

Ephesians 2:1-3

The night is far gone, the day of his return will soon be here. So quit the evil deeds of darkness and put on the armor of right living, as we who live in the daylight should!

Be decent and true in everything you do so that all can approve your behavior. Don't spend your time in wild parties and getting drunk or in adultery and lust or fighting or jealousy.

But ask the Lord Jesus Christ to help you live as you should, and don't make plans to enjoy evil.

Romans 13:12-14

O my son, be wise and stay in God's paths; don't carouse with drunkards and gluttons, for they are on their way to poverty.

Proverbs 23:19,20

What I meant was that you are not to keep company with anyone who claims to be a brother Christian but indulges in sexual sins, or is greedy, or is a swindler, or worships idols, or is a drunkard, or abusive. Don't even eat lunch with such a person.

1 Corinthians 5:11

Woe to you for making your neighboring lands reel and stagger like drunkards beneath your blows, and then gloating over their nakedness and shame.

Habakkuk 2:15

Don't drink too much wine, for many evils lie along that path; be filled instead with the Holy Spirit and controlled by him.

Ephesians 5:18

You can be sure of this: The kingdom of Christ and of God will never belong to anyone who is impure or greedy, for a greedy person is really an idol worshiper — he loves and worships the good things of this life more than God.

Don't be fooled by those who try to excuse these sins, for the terrible wrath of God is upon all those who do them.

Don't even associate with such people.

Ephesians 5:5-7

Take no part in the worthless pleasures of evil
and darkness, but instead, rebuke and expose them.
Ephesians 5:11

Wine gives false courage; hard liquor leads to
brawls; what fools men are to let it master them,
making them reel drunkenly down the street!
Proverbs 20:1

And it is not for kings, O Lemuel, to drink wine
and whiskey.

Proverbs 31:4

Be with wise men and become wise. Be with
evil men and become evil.

Proverbs 13:20

Young men who are wise obey the law; a son
who is a member of a lawless gang is a shame to
his father.

Proverbs 28:7

Hard work brings prosperity; playing around
brings poverty.

Proverbs 28:19

Never be in a hurry about choosing a pastor;
you may overlook his sins, and it will look as if
you approve of them. Be sure that you yourself
stay away from all sin.

1 Timothy 5:22

They will betray their friends; they will be hotheaded, puffed up with pride, and prefer good times to worshiping God.

They will go to church, yes, but they won't really believe anything they hear. Don't be taken in by people like that.

2 Timothy 3:4,5

Worldliness

For how can we walk together with your sins between us?

Amos 3:3

You are like an unfaithful wife who loves her husband's enemies. Don't you realize that making friends with God's enemies — the evil pleasures of this world — makes you an enemy of God? I say it again, that if your aim is to enjoy the evil pleasure of the unsaved world, you cannot also be a friend of God.

James 4:4

Stop loving this evil world and all that it offers you, for when you love these things you show that you do not really love God; for all these worldly things, these evil desires — the craze for sex, the ambition to buy everything that appeals to you, and the pride that comes from wealth and importance — these are not from God. They are from this evil world itself.

And this world is fading away, and these evil, forbidden things will go with it, but whoever keeps doing the will of God will live forever.

1 John 2:15-17

Don't copy the behavior and customs of this world, but be a new and different person with a fresh newness in all you do and think. Then you will learn from your own experience how his ways will really satisfy you.

Romans 12:2

As for me, God forbid that I should boast about anything except the cross of our Lord Jesus Christ. Because of that cross, my interest in all the attractive things of the world was killed long ago, and the world's interest in me is also long dead.

Galatians 6:14

I'm not asking you to take them out of the world, but to keep them safe from Satan's power.

They are not part of this world any more than I am.

John 17:15,16

So now you can look forward soberly and intelligently to more of God's kindness to you when Jesus Christ returns.

Obey God because you are his children; don't slip back into your old ways — doing evil because you knew no better.

But be holy now in everything you do, just as the Lord is holy, who invited you to be his child.

He himself has said, "You must be holy, for I am holy."

1 Peter 1:13-16

Dear brothers, you are only visitors here. Since your real home is in heaven, I beg you to keep away from the evil pleasures of this world; they are not for you, for they fight against your very souls.

1 Peter 2:11

Before every man there lies a wide and pleasant road that seems right but ends in death.

Proverbs 14:12

It is by faith that Moses, when he grew up, refused to be treated as the grandson of the king, but chose to share ill-treatment with God's people instead of enjoying the fleeting pleasures of sin.

Hebrews 11:24,25

Don't let others spoil your faith and joy with their philosophies, their wrong and shallow answers built on men's thoughts and ideas, instead of on what Christ has said.

Colossians 2:8

Dear brothers, pattern your lives after mine, and notice who else lives up to my example.

For I have told you often before, and I say it again now with tears in my eyes, there are many who walk along the Christian road who are really enemies of the cross of Christ.

Their future is eternal loss, for their god is their appetite: they are proud of what they should be ashamed of; and all they think about is this life here on earth.

But our homeland is in heaven, where our Savior, the Lord Jesus Christ, is; and we are looking forward to his return from there.

Philippians 3:17-20

IV. Dating Relationship

What Kind of Person Should You Date?

Run from anything that gives you the evil thoughts that young men often have, but stay close to anything that makes you want to do right. Have faith and love, and enjoy the companionship of those who love the Lord and have pure hearts.

2 Timothy 2:22

May God who gives patience, steadiness, and encouragement help you to live in complete harmony with each other — each with the attitude of Christ toward the other.

And then all of us can praise the Lord together with one voice, giving glory to God, the Father of our Lord Jesus Christ.

Romans 15:5,6

Be beautiful inside, in your hearts, with the lasting charm of a gentle and quiet spirit that is so precious to God.

1 Peter 3:4

Is there any such thing as Christians cheering each other up? Do you love me enough to want to help me? Does it mean anything to you that we are brothers in the Lord, sharing the same Spirit? Are your hearts tender and sympathetic at all?

Then make me truly happy by loving each other and agreeing wholeheartedly with each other, working together with one heart and mind and purpose.

Don't be selfish; don't live to make a good impression on others. Be humble, thinking of others as better than yourself.

Don't just think about your own affairs, but be interested in others, too, and in what they are doing.

Philippians 2:1-4

Since you have been chosen by God who has given you this new kind of life, and because of his deep love and concern for you, you should practice tenderhearted mercy and kindness to others. Don't worry about making a good impression on them, but be ready to suffer quietly and patiently.

Be gentle and ready to forgive; never hold grudges. Remember, the Lord forgave you, so you must forgive others.

Most of all, let love guide your life, for then the whole church will stay together in perfect harmony.

Colossians 3:12-14

Don't be teamed with those who do not love the Lord, for what do the people of God have in common with the people of sin? How can light live with darkness?

And what harmony can there be between Christ and the devil? How can a Christian be a partner with one who doesn't believe?

And what union can there be between God's temple and idols? For you are God's temple, the home of the living God, and God has said of you, "I will live in them and walk among them, and I will be their God and they shall be my people."

That is why the Lord has said, "Leave them; separate yourselves from them; don't touch their filthy things, and I will welcome you,

"And be a Father to you, and you will be my sons and daughters."

2 Corinthians 6:14-18

Having such great promises as these, dear friends, let us turn away from everything wrong, whether of body or spirit, and purify ourselves, living in the wholesome fear of God, giving ourselves to him alone.

2 Corinthians 7:1

When I wrote to you before I said not to mix with evil people.

1 Corinthians 5:9

What I meant was that you are not to keep company with anyone who claims to be a brother Christian but indulges in sexual sins, or is greedy, or is a swindler, or worships idols, or is a drunkard, or abusive. Don't even eat lunch with such a person.

1 Corinthians 5:11

Anyone is my brother who fears and trusts the Lord and obeys him.

Psalm 119:63

Keep away from angry, short-tempered men, lest you learn to be like them and endanger your soul.

Proverbs 22:24

Don't use bad language. Say only what is good and helpful to those you are talking to, and what will give them a blessing.

Ephesians 4:29

Let your conversation be gracious as well as sensible, for then you will have the right answer for everyone.

Colossians 4:6

When she speaks, her words are wise, and kindness is the rule for everything she says.

Proverbs 31:26

If you can find a truly good wife, she is worth more than precious gems!

Proverbs 31:10

Next, learn to put aside your own desires so that you will become patient and godly, gladly letting God have his way with you.

This will make possible the next step, which is for you to enjoy other people and to like them, and finally you will grow to love them deeply.

2 Peter 1:6,7

If you want a happy, good life, keep control of your tongue, and guard your lips from telling lies.

Turn away from evil and do good. Try to live in peace even if you must run after it to catch and hold it!

1 Peter 3:10,11

"Quick!" he told the people, "get away from the tents of these wicked men, and don't touch anything that belongs to them, lest you be included in their sins [and be destroyed with them]."

Numbers 16:26

I will reject all selfishness and stay away from every evil.

Psalm 101:4

But I will not allow those who deceive and lie to stay in my house.

Psalm 101:7

Don't tell your secrets to a gossip unless you want them broadcast to the world.

Proverbs 20:19

Now here is a command, dear brothers, given in the name of our Lord Jesus Christ by his authority: Stay away from any Christian who spends his days in laziness and does not follow the ideal of hard work we set up for you.

2 Thessalonians 3:6

How Far Should You Go?

Don't you realize that all of you together are the house of God, and that the Spirit of God lives among you in his house?

If anyone defiles and spoils God's home, God will destroy him. For God's home is holy and clean, and you are that home.

1 Corinthians 3:16,17

For instance, take the matter of eating. God has given us an appetite for food and stomachs to digest it. But that doesn't mean we should eat more than we need. Don't think of eating as important because some day God will do away with both stomachs and food. But sexual sin is never right: our bodies were not made for that, but for the Lord, and the Lord wants to fill our bodies with himself.

And God is going to raise our bodies from the dead by his power just as he raised up the Lord Jesus Christ.

Don't you realize that your bodies are actually parts and members of Christ? So should I take part of Christ and join him to a prostitute? Never!

And don't you know that if a man joins himself to a prostitute she becomes a part of him and he becomes a part of her? For God tells us in the Scripture that in his sight the two become one person.

But if you give yourself to the Lord, you and Christ are joined together as one person.

That is why I say to run from sex sin. No other sin affects the body as this one does. When you sin this sin it is against your own body.

Haven't you yet learned that your body is the home of the Holy Spirit God gave you, and that he lives within you? Your own body does not belong to you.

For God has bought you with a great price. So use every part of your body to give glory back to God because he owns it.

1 Corinthians 6:13-20

Now about those questions you asked in your last letter: my answer is that if you do not marry, it is good.

1 Corinthians 7:1

Now you can have real love for everyone because your souls have been cleansed from selfishness and hatred when you trusted Christ to save you; so see to it that you really do love each other warmly, with all your hearts.

1 Peter 1:22

And everyone who really believes this will try to stay pure because Christ is pure.

1 John 3:3

Don't let anyone think little of you because you are young. Be their ideal; let them follow the way you teach and live; be a pattern for them in your love, your faith, and your clean thoughts.

1 Timothy 4:12

Above all else, guard your affections. For they influence everything else in your life.

Spurn the careless kiss of a prostitute. Stay far from her.

Look straight ahead; don't even turn your head to look.

Watch your step. Stick to the path and be safe.

Don't sidetrack; pull back your foot from danger.

Proverbs 4:23-27

Treat the older women as mothers, and the girls as your sisters, thinking only pure thoughts about them.

1 Timothy 5:2

When Things Have Already Gone Too Far

Oh, wash me, cleanse me from this guilt. Let me be pure again.

For I admit my shameful deed — it haunts me day and night.

It is against you and you alone I sinned, and did this terrible thing. You saw it all, and your sentence against me is just.

Psalm 51:2-4

Sprinkle me with the cleansing blood and I shall be clean again. Wash me and I shall be whiter than snow.

And after you have punished me, give me back my joy again.

Don't keep looking at my sins — erase them from your sight.

Create in me a new, clean heart, O God, filled with clean thoughts and right desires.

Don't toss me aside, banished forever from your presence. Don't take your Holy Spirit from me.

Restore to me again the joy of your salvation, and make me willing to obey you.

Psalm 51:7-12

What happiness for those whose guilt has been forgiven! What joys when sins are covered over!

What relief for those who have confessed their sins and God has cleared their record.

There was a time when I wouldn't admit what a sinner I was. But my dishonesty made me miserable and filled my days with frustration.

All day and all night your hand was heavy on me. My strength evaporated like water on a sunny day until I finally admitted all my sins to you and stopped trying to hide them. I said to myself, "I will confess them to the Lord." And you forgave me! All my guilt is gone.

Now I say that each believer should confess his sins to God when he is aware of them, while there is time to be forgiven. Judgment will not touch him if he does.

You are my hiding place from every storm of life; you even keep me from getting into trouble! You surround me with songs of victory.

Psalm 32:1-6

But if we confess our sins to him, he can be depended on to forgive us and to cleanse us from every wrong. [And it is perfectly proper for God to do this for us because Christ died to wash away our sins.]

1 John 1:9

"No, sir," she said. And Jesus said, "Neither do I. Go and sin no more."

John 8:11

Attitude in Dating

And he will give them to you if you give him first place in your life and live as he wants you to.

Matthew 6:33

Let me say this, then, speaking for the Lord: Live no longer as the unsaved do, for they are blinded and confused. Their closed hearts are full of darkness; they are far away from the life of God because they have shut their minds against him, and they cannot understand his ways.

They don't care anymore about right and wrong and have given themselves over to impure ways. They stop at nothing, being driven by their evil minds and reckless lusts.

Ephesians 4:17,18

Treat the older women as mothers, and the girls as your sisters, thinking only pure thoughts about them.

1 Timothy 5:2

Happy are those whose hearts are pure, for they shall see God.

Matthew 5:8

Never be in a hurry about choosing a pastor; you may overlook his sins and it will look as if you approve of them. Be sure that you yourself stay away from all sin.

1 Timothy 5:22

Now you can have real love for everyone because your souls have been cleansed from selfishness and hatred when you trusted Christ to save you; so see to it that you really do love each other warmly, with all your hearts.

1 Peter 1:22

Love each other with brotherly affection and take delight in honoring each other.

Romans 12:10

I pray that you will live good lives, not because that will be a feather in our caps, proving that what we teach is right; no, for we want you to do right even if we ourselves are despised.

2 Corinthians 13:7

Be careful how you behave among your unsaved neighbors; for then, even if they are suspicious of you and talk against you, they will end up praising God for your good works when Christ returns.

1 Peter 2:12

Pray for us, for our conscience is clear and we want to keep it that way.

Hebrews 13:18

Be decent and true in everything you do so that all can approve your behavior. Don't spend your time in wild parties and getting drunk or in adultery and lust, or fighting, or jealousy.

Romans 13:13

How To Trust God for a Mate

The man who finds a wife finds a good thing; she is a blessing to him from the Lord.

Proverbs 18:22

And the Lord will guide you continually, and satisfy you with all good things, and keep you healthy too; and you will be like a well-watered garden, like an ever-flowing spring.

Isaiah 58:11

And the Lord God said, "It isn't good for man to be alone; I will make a companion for him, a helper suited to his needs."

Genesis 2:18

Remember, your Father knows exactly what you need even before you ask him!

Matthew 6:8

Then, knowing what lies ahead for you, you won't become bored with being a Christian, nor become spiritually dull and indifferent, but you will be anxious to follow the example of those who receive all that God has promised them because of their strong faith and patience.

Hebrews 6:12

A father can give his sons homes and riches, but only the Lord can give them understanding wives.

Proverbs 19:14

Be delighted with the Lord. Then he will give you all your heart's desires.

Psalm 37:4

He is close to all who call on him sincerely.
He fulfills the desires of those who reverence and trust him; he hears their cries for help and rescues them.

Psalm 145:18,19

So let it grow, and don't try to squirm out of your problems. For when your patience is finally in full bloom, then you will be ready for anything, strong in character, full and complete.

James 1:4

Never again shall you be called "The God-forsaken Land" or the "Land That God Forgot." Your new name will be "The Land of God's Delight" and "The Bride," for the Lord delights in you and will claim you as his own.

Your children will care for you, O Jerusalem, with joy like that of a young man who marries a virgin; and God will rejoice over you as a bridegroom with his bride.

Isaiah 62:4,5

For Jehovah God is our Light and our Protector. He gives us grace and glory. No good thing will he withhold from those who walk along his paths.

Psalm 84:11

May he grant you your heart's desire and fulfill all your plans.

Psalm 20:4

And in the same way — by our faith — the Holy Spirit helps us with our daily problems and in our praying. For we don't even know what we should pray for, nor how to pray as we should; but the Holy Spirit prays for us with such feeling that it cannot be expressed in words.

And the Father who knows all hearts knows, of course, what the Spirit is saying as he pleads for us in harmony with God's own will.

And we know that all that happens to us is working for our good if we love God and are fitting into his plans.

Romans 8:26-28

V. What To Do When:

What To Do When You Are Anxious

Don't worry about anything; instead, pray about everything; tell God your needs and don't forget to thank him for his answers.

If you do this you will experience God's peace, which is far more wonderful than the human mind can understand. His peace will keep your thoughts and your hearts quiet and at rest as you trust in Christ Jesus.

Philippians 4:6,7

"And besides, what's the use of worrying? What good does it do? Will it add a single day to your life? Of course not!

"And if worry can't even do such little things as that, what's the use of worrying over bigger things?"

Luke 12:25,26

Let him have all your worries and cares, for he is always thinking about you and watching everything that concerns you.

1 Peter 5:7

"Come to me and I will give you rest — all of you who work so hard beneath a heavy yoke.

"Wear my yoke — for it fits perfectly — and let me teach you; for I am gentle and humble, and you shall find rest for your souls;

"For I give you only light burdens."

Matthew 11:28-30

"So don't worry at all about having enough food and clothing. Why be like the heathen? For they take pride in all these things and are deeply concerned about them. But your heavenly Father already knows perfectly well that you need them,

"And he will give them to you if you give him first place in your life and live as he wants you to."

Matthew 6:31,32

The ground covered with thistles represents a man who hears the message, but the cares of this life and his longing for money choke out God's Word, and he does less and less for God.

Matthew 13:22

I want you to trust me in your times of trouble, so I can rescue you, and you can give me glory.

Psalm 50:15

Give your burdens to the Lord. He will carry them. He will not permit the godly to slip or fall.

Psalm 55:22

I will call to you whenever trouble strikes, and you will help me.

Psalm 86:7

I am holding you by your right hand — I, the Lord your God — and I say to you, Don't be afraid; I am here to help you.

Isaiah 41:13

Then trust the Lord completely; don't ever trust yourself.

In everything you do, put God first, and he will direct you and crown your efforts with success.

Proverbs 3:5,6

What a glorious Lord! He who daily bears our burdens also gives us our salvation.

Psalm 68:19

"I have told you all this so that you will have peace of heart and mind. Here on earth you will have many trials and sorrows; but cheer up, for I have overcome the world."

John 16:33

Some nations boast of armies and of weaponry, but our boast is in the Lord our God.

Psalm 20:7

"I am leaving you with a gift — peace of mind and heart! And the peace I give isn't fragile like the peace the world gives. So don't be troubled or afraid."

John 14:27

Listen in silence before me, O lands beyond the sea. Bring your strongest arguments. Come now and speak. The court is ready for your case.

Who has stirred up this one from the east, whom victory meets at every step? Who, indeed, but the Lord? God has given him victory over many nations and permitted him to trample kings underfoot and to put entire armies to the sword.

He chases them away and goes on safely, though the paths he treads are new.

Isaiah 41:1-3

What To Do When You Are Angry

If you are angry, don't sin by nursing your grudge. Don't let the sun go down with you still angry — get over it quickly;

For when you are angry you give a mighty foothold to the devil.

Ephesians 4:26,27

Stop your anger! Turn off your wrath. Don't fret and worry — it only leads to harm.

Psalm 37:8

A short-tempered man is a fool. He hates the man who is patient.

Proverbs 14:17

It is better to be slow-tempered than famous; it is better to have self-control than to control an army.

Proverbs 16:32

A wise man restrains his anger and overlooks insults. This is to his credit.

Proverbs 19:11

Don't be quick-tempered — that is being a fool.

Ecclesiastes 7:9

Dear brothers, don't ever forget that it is best to listen much, speak little, and not become angry.

James 1:19

Don't say, "Now I can pay him back for all his meanness to me!"

Proverbs 24:29

If your enemy is hungry, give him food! If he is thirsty, give him something to drink!

Proverbs 25:21

Happy are the kind and merciful, for they shall be shown mercy.

Matthew 5:7

But I say: Love your enemies! Pray for those who persecute you!

Matthew 5:44

And forgive us our sins, just as we have forgiven those who have sinned against us.

Matthew 6:12

Your heavenly Father will forgive you if you forgive those who sin against you;
But if you refuse to forgive them, he will not forgive you.

Matthew 6:14,15

Even if he wrongs you seven times a day and each time turns again and asks forgiveness, forgive him.

Luke 17:4

Don't let evil get the upper hand but conquer evil by doing good.

Romans 12:21

Instead, be kind to each other, tenderhearted, forgiving one another, just as God has forgiven you because you belong to Christ.

Ephesians 4:32

Be gentle and ready to forgive; never hold grudges. Remember, the Lord forgave you, so you must forgive others.

Colossians 3:13

Don't repay evil for evil. Don't snap back at those who say unkind things about you. Instead, pray for God's help for them, for we are to be kind to others, and God will bless us for it.

1 Peter 3:9

What To Do When You Are Confused

Then trust the Lord completely; don't ever trust yourself.

In everything you do, put God first, and he will direct you and crown your efforts with success.

Don't be conceited, sure of your own wisdom.
Instead, trust and reverence the Lord, and turn your
back on evil;

When you do that, then you will be given
renewed health and vitality.

Proverbs 3:5-8

Ask me and I will tell you some remarkable
secrets about what is going to happen here.

Jeremiah 33:3

Every young man who listens to me and obeys
my instructions will be given wisdom and good
sense.

Yes, if you want better insight and dis-
cernment,

And are searching for them as you would for
lost money or hidden treasure,

Then wisdom will be given you and knowledge
of God himself; you will soon learn the importance
of reverence for the Lord and of trusting him.

For the Lord grants wisdom! His every word
is a treasure of knowledge and understanding.

He grants good sense to the godly — his saints. He is their shield,
Protecting them and guarding their pathway.
Proverbs 2:1-8

Show me the path where I should go, O Lord; point out the right road for me to walk.
Lead me; teach me; for you are the God who gives me salvation. I have no hope except in you.
Psalms 25:4,5

If you want to know what God wants you to do, ask him, and he will gladly tell you, for he is always ready to give a bountiful supply of wisdom to all who ask him; he will not resent it.
But when you ask him, be sure that you really expect him to tell you, for a doubtful mind will be as unsettled as a wave of the sea that is driven and tossed by the wind;
And every decision you then make will be uncertain, as you turn first this way and then that.
If you don't ask with faith, don't expect the Lord to give you any solid answer.
James 1:5-8

So ever since we first heard about you we have kept on praying and asking God to help you understand what he wants you to do; asking him to make you wise about spiritual things.
Colossians 1:9

Later, in one of his talks, Jesus said to the people, "I am the Light of the world. So if you follow me, you won't be stumbling through the darkness, for living light will flood your path."

John 8:12

Tell me where you want me to go and I will go there. May every fiber of my being unite in reverence to your name.

Psalm 86:11

Tears of joy shall stream down their faces, and I will lead them home with great care. They shall walk beside the quiet streams and not stumble. For I am a Father to Israel, and Ephraim is my oldest child.

Jeremiah 31:9

I will instruct you (says the Lord) and guide you along the best pathway for your life; I will advise you and watch your progress.

Psalm 32:8

I will bless the Lord who counsels me; he gives me wisdom in the night. He tells me what to do.

Psalm 16:7

As your plan unfolds, even the simple can understand it.

Psalm 119:130

Open my eyes to see wonderful things in your Word.

Psalm 119:18

God is not one who likes things to be disorderly and upset. He likes harmony, and he finds it in all the other churches.

1 Corinthians 14:33

Think over these three illustrations, and may the Lord help you to understand how they apply to you.

2 Timothy 2:7

What To Do When You Are Disappointed

O my people, trust him all the time. Pour out your longings before him, for he can help!

Psalm 62:8

And we know that all that happens to us is working for our good if we love God and are fitting into his plans.

Romans 8:28

And I am sure that God who began the good work within you will keep right on helping you grow in his grace until his task within you is finally finished on that day when Jesus Christ returns.

Philippians 1:6

I pray that your hearts will be flooded with light so that you can see something of the future he has called you to share. I want you to realize that God has been made rich because we who are Christ's have been given to him!

Ephesians 1:18

I am always thinking of the Lord; and because he is so near, I never need to stumble or to fall. Heart, body, and soul are filled with joy.

Psalm 16:8,9

God, who called you to become his child, will do all this for you, just as he promised.

1 Thessalonians 5:24

You believed that God would do what he said; that is why he has given you this wonderful blessing.

Luke 1:45

"What's more, I am with you, and will protect you wherever you go, and will bring you back safely to this land; I will be with you constantly until I have finished giving you all I am promising."

Genesis 28:15

We depend upon the Lord alone to save us. Only he can help us; he protects us like a shield.

No wonder we are happy in the Lord! For we are trusting him. We trust his holy name.

Yes, Lord, let your constant love surround us, for our hopes are in you alone.

Psalm 33:20-22

Now glory be to God who by his mighty power at work within us is able to do far more than we would ever dare to ask or even dream of — infinitely beyond our highest prayers, desires, thoughts, or hopes.

Ephesians 3:20

He is my strength, my shield from every danger. I trusted in him, and he helped me. Joy rises in my heart until I burst out in songs of praise to him.

Psalm 28:7

That is why I am suffering here in jail and I am certainly not ashamed of it, for I know the one in whom I trust, and I am sure that he is able to safely guard all that I have given him until the day of his return.

2 Timothy 1:12

God is not a man, that he should lie; he doesn't change his mind like humans do. Has he ever promised, without doing what he said?

Numbers 23:19

For Jehovah God is our Light and our Protector. He gives us grace and glory. No good thing will he withhold from those who walk along his paths.

Psalm 84:11

Be delighted with the Lord. Then he will give you all your heart's desires.

Psalm 37:4

What To Do When You Are Frustrated

Then he said, "This is God's message to Zerubbabel: 'Not by might, nor by power, but by my Spirit, says the Lord Almighty — you will succeed because of my Spirit, though you are few and weak.' "

Zechariah 4:6

"I am leaving you with a gift — peace of mind and heart! And the peace I give isn't fragile like the peace the world gives. So don't be troubled or afraid."

John 14:27

So there is a full complete rest still waiting for the people of God.

Christ has already entered there. He is resting from his work, just as God did after the creation.

Let us do our best to go into that place of rest, too, being careful not to disobey God as the children of Israel did, thus failing to get in.

For whatever God says to us is full of living power: it is sharper than the sharpest dagger, cutting swift and deep into our innermost thoughts and desires with all their parts, exposing us for what we really are.

Hebrews 4:9-12

So let us come boldly to the very throne of God and stay there to receive his mercy and to find grace to help us in our times of need.

Hebrews 4:16

Now I say that each believer should confess his sins to God when he is aware of them, while there is time to be forgiven. Judgment will not touch him if he does.

You are my hiding place from every storm of life; you even keep me from getting into trouble! You surround me with songs of victory.

I will instruct you (says the Lord) and guide you along the best pathway for your life; I will advise you and watch your progress.

Don't be like a senseless horse or mule that has to have a bit in its mouth to keep it in line!

Many sorrows come to the wicked, but abiding love surrounds those who trust in the Lord.

So rejoice in him, all those who are his, and shout for joy, all those who try to obey him.

Psalm 32:6-11

But the good man walks along in the ever-brightening light of God's favor; the dawn gives way to morning splendor.

Proverbs 4:18

Commit your work to the Lord, then it will succeed.

Proverbs 16:3

I am expecting the Lord to rescue me again, so that once again I will see his goodness to me here in the land of the living.

Don't be impatient. Wait for the Lord, and he will come and save you! Be brave, stouthearted and courageous. Yes, wait and he will help you.

Psalm 27:13,14

My health fails; my spirits droop, yet God remains! He is the strength of my heart; he is mine forever!

But those refusing to worship God will perish, for he destroys those serving other gods.

But as for me, I get as close to him as I can! I have chosen him, and I will tell everyone about the wonderful ways he rescues me.

Psalm 73:26-28

He will keep in perfect peace all those who trust in him, whose thoughts turn often to the Lord!

Trust in the Lord God always, for in the Lord Jehovah is your everlasting strength.

Isaiah 26:3,4

In this way aim for harmony in the church and try to build each other up.

Romans 14:19

Let the peace of heart that comes from Christ be always present in your hearts and lives, for this is your responsibility and privilege as members of his body. And always be thankful.

Colossians 3:15

Jesus said to them, "You are truly my disciples if you live as I tell you to.

"And you will know the truth, and the truth will set you free."

John 8:31,32

What To Do When You Have Failed

How we thank God for all of this! It is he who makes us victorious through Jesus Christ our Lord!

1 Corinthians 15:57

"Yes, be bold and strong! Banish fear and doubt! For remember, the Lord your God is with you wherever you go."

Joshua 1:9

For I can do everything God asks me to with the help of Christ who gives me the strength and power.

Philippians 4:13

The good man does not escape all troubles — he has them too. But the Lord helps him in each and every one.

Psalm 34:19

The steps of good men are directed by the Lord. He delights in each step they take.
If they fall it isn't fatal, for the Lord holds them with his hand.

Psalm 37:23,24

For every child of God can obey him, defeating sin and evil pleasure by trusting Christ to help him.

1 John 5:4

With God's help we shall do mighty things, for he will trample down our foes.

Psalm 60:12

But with the help of God we shall do mighty acts of valor. For he treads down our foes.

Psalm 108:13

You have done so much for me, O Lord. No wonder I am glad! I sing for joy.

Psalm 92:4

But thanks be to God! For through what Christ has done, he has triumphed over us so that now wherever we go he uses us to tell others about the Lord and to spread the Gospel like a sweet perfume.

2 Corinthians 2:14

But Caleb reassured the people as they stood before Moses. "Let us go up at once and possess it," he said, "for we are well able to conquer it!"

Numbers 13:30

What can we ever say to such wonderful things as these? If God is on our side, who can ever be against us?

Since he did not spare even his own Son for us but gave him up for us all, won't he also surely give us everything else?

Romans 8:31,32

I am saying these things to you older men because you really know Christ, the one who has been alive from the beginning. And you young men, I am talking to you because you have won your battle with Satan. And I am writing to you younger boys and girls because you, too, have learned to know God our Father.

And so I say to you fathers who know the eternal God, and to you young men who are strong, with God's Word in your hearts, and have won your struggle against Satan.

1 John 2:13,14

"Because of your little faith," Jesus told them. "For if you had faith even as small as a tiny mustard seed you could say to this mountain, 'Move!' and it would go far away. Nothing would be impossible."

Matthew 17:20

Jesus looked at them intently and said, "Humanly speaking, no one. But with God, everything is possible."

Matthew 19:26

Jesus looked at them intently, then said, "Without God, it is utterly impossible. But with God everything is possible."

Mark 10:27

"For every promise from God shall surely come true."

Luke 1:37

He replied, "God can do what men can't!"
Luke 18:27

What To Do When You Are Insecure

For I can do everything God asks me to with the help of Christ who gives me the strength and power.

Philippians 4:13

You need not be afraid of disaster or the plots of wicked men, for the Lord is with you; he protects you.

Proverbs 3:26

Reverence for God gives a man deep strength; his children have a place of refuge and security.
Proverbs 14:26

For the Lord God, the Holy One of Israel, says: Only in returning to me and waiting for me will you be saved; in quietness and confidence is your strength; but you'll have none of this.

Isaiah 30:15

I am holding you by your right hand — I, the Lord your God — and I say to you, Don't be afraid; I am here to help you.

Isaiah 41:13

How happy this makes me, now that I am sure all is well between us again. Once again I can have perfect confidence in you.

2 Corinthians 7:16

I am trusting the Lord to bring you back to believing as I do about these things. God will deal with that person, whoever he is, who has been troubling and confusing you.

Galatians 5:10

For it isn't the cutting of our bodies that makes us children of God; it is worshiping him with our spirits. That is the only true "circumcision." We Christians glory in what Christ Jesus has done for us and realize that we are helpless to save ourselves.

Philippians 3:3

And we are sure of this, that he will listen to us whenever we ask him for anything in line with his will.

1 John 5:14

What can we ever say to such wonderful things as these? If God is on our side, who can ever be against us?

Romans 8:31

But despite all this, overwhelming victory is ours through Christ who loved us enough to die for us.

Romans 8:37

And in the same way — by our faith — the Holy Spirit helps us with our daily problems and in our praying. For we don't even know what we should pray for, nor how to pray as we should; but the

Holy Spirit prays for us with such feeling that it cannot be expressed in words.

Romans 8:26

For every child of God can obey him, defeating sin and evil pleasure by trusting Christ to help him.

1 John 5:4

For God took the sinless Christ and poured into him our sins. Then, in exchange, he poured God's goodness into us!

2 Corinthians 5:21

Asking God, the glorious Father of our Lord Jesus Christ, to give you wisdom to see clearly and really understand who Christ is and all that he has done for you. I pray that your hearts will be flooded with light so that you can see something of the future he has called you to share. I want you to realize that God has been made rich because we who are Christ's have been given to him!

I pray that you will begin to understand how incredibly great his power is to help those who believe him. It is that same mighty power

That raised Christ from the dead and seated him in the place of honor at God's right hand in heaven.

Ephesians 1:17-20

The wicked flee when no one is chasing them! But the godly are bold as lions!

Proverbs 28:1

So let us come boldly to the very throne of God and stay there to receive his mercy and to find grace to help us in our times of need.

Hebrews 4:16

That is why we can say without any doubt or fear, "The Lord is my Helper and I am not afraid of anything that mere man can do to me."

Hebrews 13:6

What To Do When You Are Jealous

Never envy the wicked!

Psalm 37:1

Rest in the Lord; wait patiently for him to act. Don't be envious of evil men who prosper.

Psalm 37:7

Jealousy is more dangerous and cruel than anger.

Proverbs 27:4

Then I observed that the basic motive for success is the driving force of envy and jealousy! But this, too, is foolishness, chasing the wind.

Ecclesiastes 4:4

Be decent and true in everything you do so that all can approve your behavior. Don't spend your time in wild parties and getting drunk or in adultery and lust, or fighting, or jealousy.

Romans 13:13

For you are still only baby Christians, controlled by your own desires, not God's. When you are jealous of one another and divide up into quarreling groups, doesn't that prove you are still babies, wanting your own way? In fact, you are acting like people who don't belong to the Lord at all.

1 Corinthians 3:3

Love is very patient and kind, never jealous or envious, never boastful or proud.

1 Corinthians 13:4

But when you follow your own wrong inclinations your lives will produce these evil results: impure thoughts, eagerness for lustful pleasure,

Idolatry, spiritism (that is, encouraging the activity of demons), hatred and fighting, jealousy and anger, constant effort to get the best for yourself, complaints and criticisms, the feeling that everyone else is wrong except those in your own little group — and there will be wrong doctrine,

Envy, murder, drunkenness, wild parties, and all that sort of thing. Let me tell you again as I have before, that anyone living that sort of life will not inherit the kingdom of God.

Galatians 5:19-21

Then we won't need to look for honors and popularity, which lead to jealousy and hard feelings.

Galatians 5:26

And by all means don't brag about being wise and good if you are bitter and jealous and selfish; that is the worst sort of lie.

James 3:14

Don't grumble about each other, brothers. Are you yourselves above criticism? For see! The great Judge is coming. He is almost here. [Let him do whatever criticizing must be done.]

James 5:9

So get rid of your feelings of hatred. Don't just pretend to be good! Be done with dishonesty and jealousy and talking about others behind their backs.

1 Peter 2:1

For the woman's husband will be furious in his jealousy, and he will have no mercy on you in his day of vengeance.

Proverbs 6:34

What To Do When You Are Lonely

The eternal God is your Refuge, and underneath are the everlasting arms. He thrusts out your enemies before you; it is he who cries, "Destroy them!"

Deuteronomy 33:27

All those who know your mercy, Lord, will count on you for help. For you have never yet forsaken those who trust in you.

Psalm 9:10

Even when walking through the dark valley of death I will not be afraid, for you are close beside me, guarding, guiding all the way.

Psalm 23:4

I have been young and now I am old. And in all my years I have never seen the Lord forsake a man who loves him; nor have I seen the children of the godly go hungry.

Psalm 37:25

For the Lord loves justice and fairness; he will never abandon his people. They will be kept safe forever; but all who love wickedness shall perish.

Psalm 37:28

Stay away from the love of money; be satisfied with what you have. For God has said, "I will never, never fail you nor forsake you."

That is why we can say without any doubt or fear, "The Lord is my Helper, and I am not afraid of anything that mere man can do to me."

Hebrews 13:5,6

O God, defend me from the charges of these merciless, deceitful men.

For you are God, my only place of refuge. Why have you tossed me aside? Why must I mourn at the oppression of my enemies?

Psalm 43:1,2

What can we ever say to such wonderful things as these? If God is on our side, who can ever be against us?

Romans 8:31

Who then can ever keep Christ's love from us? When we have trouble or calamity, when we are hunted down or destroyed, is it because he doesn't love us anymore? And if we are hungry, or penniless, or in danger, or threatened with death, has God deserted us?

Romans 8:35

But despite all this, overwhelming victory is ours through Christ who loved us enough to die for us.

For I am convinced that nothing can ever separate us from his love. Death can't, and life can't. The angels won't, and all the powers of hell itself cannot keep God's love away. Our fears for today, our worries about tomorrow,

Or where we are — high above the sky, or in the deepest ocean — nothing will ever be able to separate us from the love of God demonstrated by our Lord Jesus Christ when he died for us.

Romans 8:37-39

What To Do When You Have Lied

But if we confess our sins to him, he can be depended on to forgive us and to cleanse us from every wrong. [And it is perfectly proper for God to do this for us because Christ died to wash away our sins.]

1 John 1:9

Someone may say, "I am a Christian; I am on my way to heaven; I belong to Christ." But if he doesn't do what Christ tells him to, he is a liar.

1 John 2:4

Yes, you must be a new and different person, holy and good. Clothe yourself with this new nature.

Stop lying to each other; tell the truth, for we are parts of each other and when we lie to each other we are hurting ourselves.

Ephesians 4:24,25

Instead, we will lovingly follow the truth at all times — speaking truly, dealing truly, living truly — and so become more and more in every way like Christ who is the Head of his body, the Church.

Ephesians 4:15

But to do this, you will need the strong belt of truth and the breastplate of God's approval.

Ephesians 6:14

And now, brothers, as I close this letter let me say this one more thing: Fix your thoughts on what is true and good and right. Think about things that are pure and lovely, and dwell on the fine, good things in others. Think about all you can praise God for and be glad about.

Philippians 4:8

Lead me; teach me; for you are the God who gives me salvation. I have no hope except in you.

Psalm 25:5

You deserve honesty from the heart; yes, utter sincerity and truthfulness. Oh, give me this wisdom.

Psalm 51:6

For I have chosen to do right.

Psalm 119:30

Everything I say is right and true, for I hate lies and every kind of deception.

Proverbs 8:7

"And you will know the truth, and the truth will set you free."

John 8:32

And by all means don't brag about being wise and good if you are bitter and jealous and selfish; that is the worst sort of lie.

James 3:14

What To Do When You Are Persecuted

But you know from watching me that I am not that kind of person. You know what I believe and the way I live and what I want. You know my faith in Christ and how I have suffered. You know my love for you, and my patience.

You know how many troubles I have had as a result of my preaching the Good News. You know about all that was done to me while I was visiting in Antioch, Iconium and Lystra, but the Lord delivered me.

Yes, and those who decide to please Christ Jesus by living godly lives will suffer at the hands of those who hate him.

In fact, evil men and false teachers will become worse and worse, deceiving many, they themselves having been deceived by Satan.

But you must keep on believing the things you have been taught. You know they are true for you know that you can trust those of us who have taught you.

2 Timothy 3:10-14

Happy are those who are persecuted because they are good, for the Kingdom of Heaven is theirs.

When you are reviled and persecuted and lied about because you are my followers — wonderful!

Be happy about it! Be very glad! for a tremendous reward awaits you up in heaven. And remember, the ancient prophets were persecuted too.

Matthew 5:10-12

The good man does not escape all troubles — he has them too. But the Lord helps him in each and every one.

Psalm 34:19

They left the Council chamber rejoicing that God had counted them worthy to suffer dishonor for his name.

Acts 5:41

For I am not ashamed of this Good News about Christ. It is God's powerful method of bringing all who believe it to heaven. This message was preached first to the Jews alone, but now everyone is invited to come to God in this same way.

This Good News tells us that God makes us ready for heaven — makes us right in God's sight — when we put our faith and trust in Christ to save us. This is accomplished from start to finish by faith. As the Scripture says it, "The man who finds life will find it through trusting God."

Romans 1:16,17

But chose to share ill-treatment with God's people instead of enjoying the fleeting pleasures of sin.

Hebrews 11:25

Of course, you get no credit for being patient if you are beaten for doing wrong; but if you do right and suffer for it, and are patient beneath the blows, God is well pleased.

1 Peter 2:20

After you have suffered a little while, our God, who is full of kindness through Christ, will give you his eternal glory. He personally will come and pick you up, and set you firmly in place, and make you stronger than ever.

1 Peter 5:10

And anyone who gives up his home, brothers, sisters, father, mother, wife, children, or property, to follow me, shall receive a hundred times as much in return, and shall have eternal life.

Matthew 19:29

And to the rest of you I say, dear brothers, never be tired of doing right.

2 Thessalonians 3:13

We work hard and suffer much in order that people will believe it, for our hope is in the living God who died for all, and particularly for those who have accepted his salvation.

1 Timothy 4:10

"Anyone who is not for me is against me; if he isn't helping me, he is hurting my cause.

"When a demon is cast out of a man, it goes to the deserts, searching there for rest; but finding none, it returns to the person it left,

"And finds that its former home is all swept and clean.

"Then it goes and gets seven other demons more evil than itself, and they all enter the man. And so the poor fellow is seven times worse off than he was before."

Luke 11:23-26

So don't be surprised, dear friends, if the world hates you.

1 John 3:13

Dear young friends, you belong to God and have already won your fight with those who are against Christ, because there is someone in your hearts who is stronger than any evil teacher in this wicked world.

These men belong to this world, so, quite naturally, they are concerned about worldly affairs and the world pays attention to them.

But we are children of God; that is why only those who have walked and talked with God will listen to us. Others won't. That is another way to know whether a message is really from God; for if it is, the world won't listen to it.

1 John 4:4-6

And as we live with Christ, our love grows more perfect and complete; so we will not be ashamed and embarrassed at the day of judgment, but can face him with confidence and joy, because he loves us and we love him too.

We need have no fear of someone who loves us perfectly; his perfect love for us eliminates all dread of what he might do to us. If we are afraid, it is for fear of what he might do to us, and shows that we are not fully convinced that he really loves us.

1 John 4:17,18

This is only one example of the fair, just way God does things, for he is using your sufferings to make you ready for his Kingdom,

While at the same time he is preparing judgment and punishment for those who are hurting you.

2 Thessalonians 1:5,6

Fear of man is a dangerous trap, but to trust in God means safety.

Proverbs 29:25

What To Do When You Feel Rejected

Long ago, even before he made the world, God chose us to be his very own, through what Christ would do for us; he decided then to make us holy in his eyes, without a single fault — we who stand before him covered with his love.

His unchanging plan has always been to adopt us into his own family by sending Jesus Christ to die for us. And he did this because he wanted to!

- 114 -

Now all praise to God for his wonderful kindness to us and his favor that he has poured out upon us, because we belong to his dearly loved Son.

Ephesians 1:4-6

See how very much our heavenly Father loves us, for he allows us to be called his children — think of it — and we really are! But since most people don't know God, naturally they don't understand that we are his children.

1 John 3:1

So he has made many parts, but still there is only one body.

The eye can never say to the hand, "I don't need you." The head can't say to the feet, "I don't need you."

And some of the parts that seem weakest and least important are really the most necessary.

Yes, we are especially glad to have some parts that seem rather odd! And we carefully protect from the eyes of others those parts that should not be seen,

While of course the parts that may be seen do not require this special care. So God has put the body together in such a way that extra honor and care are given to those parts that might otherwise seem less important.

This makes for happiness among the parts, so that the parts have the same care for each other that they do for themselves.

1 Corinthians 12:20-25

This High Priest of ours understands our weaknesses, since he had the same temptations we do, though he never once gave way to them and sinned.

So let us come boldly to the very throne of God and stay there to receive his mercy and to find grace to help us in our times of need.

Hebrews 4:15,16

And in the same way — by our faith — the Holy Spirit helps us with our daily problems and in our praying. For we don't even know what we should pray for, nor how to pray as we should; but the Holy Spirit prays for us with such feeling that it cannot be expressed in words.

And the Father who knows all hearts knows, of course, what the Spirit is saying as he pleads for us in harmony with God's own will.

Romans 8:26,27

And when you draw close to God, God will draw close to you. Wash your hands, you sinners, and let your hearts be filled with God alone to make them pure and true to him.

James 4:8

He subdues the nations before us.

Psalm 47:3

And let us not get tired of doing what is right, for after a while we will reap a harvest of blessing if we don't get discouraged and give up.

Galatians 6:9

There are "friends" who pretend to be friends, but there is a friend who sticks closer than a brother.

Proverbs 18:24

The Lord is close to those whose hearts are breaking; he rescues those who are humbly sorry for their sins.

Psalm 34:18

The Lord will not forsake his people, for they are his prize.

Psalm 94:14

When the poor and needy seek water and there is none and their tongues are parched from thirst, then I will answer when they cry to me. I, Israel's God, will not ever forsake them.

Isaiah 41:17

But some will come to me — those the Father has given me — and I will never, never reject them.
For I have come here from heaven to do the will of God who sent me, not to have my own way.
And this is the will of God, that I should not lose even onc of all those he has given me, but that I should raise them to eternal life at the Last Day.

John 6:37-39

What To Do When You Sin

But if we confess our sins to him, he can be depended on to forgive us and to cleanse us from every wrong. [And it is perfectly proper for God to do this for us because Christ died to wash away our sins.]

1 John 1:9

O loving and kind God, have mercy. Have pity upon me and take away the awful stain of my transgressions.

Oh, wash me, cleanse me from this guilt. Let me be pure again.

For I admit my shameful deed — it haunts me day and night. It is against you and you alone I sinned and did this terrible thing. You saw it all, and your sentence against me is just.

Psalm 51:1-4

Sprinkle me with the cleansing blood and I shall be clean again. Wash me and I shall be whiter than snow.

Psalm 51:7

Don't keep looking at my sins — erase them from your sight.

Create in me a new, clean heart, O God, filled with clean thoughts and right desires.

Don't toss me aside, banished forever from your presence. Don't take your Holy Spirit from me.

Psalm 51:9-11

What happiness for those whose guilt has been forgiven! What joys when sins are covered over!

What relief for those who have confessed their sins and God has cleared their record.

There was a time when I wouldn't admit what a sinner I was. But my dishonesty made me miserable and filled my days with frustration.

All day and all night your hand was heavy on me. My strength evaporated like water on a sunny day until I finally admitted all my sins to you and stopped trying to hide them. I said to myself, "I will confess them to the Lord." And you forgave me! All my guilt is gone.

Now I say that each believer should confess his sins to God when he is aware of them, while there is time to be forgiven. Judgment will not touch him if he does.

You are my hiding place from every storm of life; you even keep me from getting into trouble! You surround me with songs of victory.

Psalm 32:1-6

A man who refuses to admit his mistakes can never be successful. But if he confesses and forsakes them, he gets another chance.

Proverbs 28:13

O Lord, from the depths of despair I cry for your help:

"Hear me! Answer! Help me!"

Lord, if you keep in mind our sins then who can ever get an answer to his prayers?

But you forgive! What an awesome thing this is!

Psalm 130:1-4

I bless the holy name of God with all my heart.
Yes, I will bless the Lord and not forget the glorious things he does for me.
He forgives all my sins. He heals me.

Psalm 103:1-3

He is merciful and tender toward those who don't deserve it; he is slow to get angry and full of kindness and love.

Psalm 103:8

For his mercy toward those who fear and honor him is as great as the height of the heavens above the earth.
He has removed our sins as far away from us as the east is from the west.
He is like a father to us, tender and sympathetic to those who reverence him.

Psalm 103:11-13

This High Priest of ours understands our weaknesses, since he had the same temptations we do, though he never once gave way to them and sinned.
So let us come boldly to the very throne of God and stay there to receive his mercy and to find grace to help us in our times of need.

Hebrews 4:15,16

''This is the agreement I will make with the people of Israel, though they broke their first

agreement: I will write my laws into their minds
so that they will always know my will, and I will
put my laws into their hearts so that they will want
to obey them.''

And then he adds, ''I will never again
remember their sins and lawless deeds.''

Now, when sins have once been forever
forgiven and forgotten, there is no need to offer
more sacrifices to get rid of them.

And so, dear brothers, now may we walk right
into the very Holy of Holies where God is, because
of the blood of Jesus.

This is the fresh, new, life-giving way which
Christ has opened up for us by tearing the curtain
— his human body — to let us into the holy
presence of God.

And since this great High Priest of ours rules
over God's household,

Let us go right in, to God himself, with true
hearts fully trusting him to receive us, because we
have been sprinkled with Christ's blood to make
us clean, and because our bodies have been washed
with pure water.

Now we can look forward to the salvation God
has promised us. There is no longer any room for
doubt, and we can tell others that salvation is ours,
for there is no question that he will do what he says.

Hebrews 10:16-23

I will see that they are well treated and I will
bring them back here again. I will help them and

not hurt them; I will plant them and not pull them up.

I will give them hearts that respond to me. They shall be my people and I will be their God, for they shall return to me with great joy.

Jeremiah 24:6,7

But Lord, my sins! How many they are. Oh, pardon them for the honor of your name.

Psalm 25:11

What To Do When You Have Questions About the End of the World

For since we believe that Jesus died and then came back to life again, we can also believe that when Jesus returns, God will bring back with him all the Christians who have died.

I can tell you this directly from the Lord: that we who are still living when the Lord returns will not rise to meet him ahead of those who are in their graves.

For the Lord himself will come down from heaven with a mighty shout and with the soul-stirring cry of the archangel and the great trumpet-call of God. And the believers who are dead will be the first to rise to meet the Lord.

Then we who are still alive and remain on the earth will be caught up with them in the clouds to meet the Lord in the air and remain with him forever.

So comfort and encourage each other with this news.

1 Thessalonians 4:14-18

You may as well know this too, Timothy, that in the last days it is going to be very difficult to be a Christian.

For people will love only themselves and their money; they will be proud and boastful, sneering at God, disobedient to their parents, ungrateful to them, and thoroughly bad.

They will be hardheaded and never give in to others; they will be constant liars and troublemakers and will think nothing of immorality. They will be rough and cruel, and sneer at those who try to be good.

They will betray their friends; they will be hotheaded, puffed up with pride, and prefer good times to worshiping God.

They will go to church, yes, but they won't really believe anything they hear. Don't be taken in by people like that.

2 Timothy 3:1-5

And we know that all that happens to us is working for our good if we love God and are fitting into his plans.

Romans 8:28

First, I want to remind you that in the last days there will come scoffers who will do every wrong they can think of, and laugh at the truth.

This will be their line of argument: "So Jesus promised to come back, did he? Then where is he? He'll never come back! Why, as far back as anyone can remember everything has remained exactly as it was since the first day of creation."

They deliberately forget this fact: that God did destroy the world with a mighty flood, long after he made the heavens by the word of his command, and had used the waters to form the earth and surround it.

And God has commanded that the earth and the heavens be stored away for a great bonfire at the judgment day, when all ungodly men will perish.

But don't forget this, dear friends, that a day or a thousand years from now is like tomorrow to the Lord.

He isn't really being slow about his promised return, even though it sometimes seems that way. But he is waiting, for the good reason that he is not willing that any should perish, and he is giving more time for sinners to repent.

The day of the Lord is surely coming, as unexpectedly as a thief, and then the heavens will pass away with a terrible noise and the heavenly bodies will disappear in fire, and the earth and everything on it will be burned up.

And so since everything around us is going to melt away, what holy, godly lives we should be living!

You should look forward to that day and hurry it along — the day when God will set the heavens on fire, and the heavenly bodies will melt and disappear in flames.

But we are looking forward to God's promise of new heavens and a new earth afterwards, where there will be only goodness.

Dear friends, while you are waiting for these things to happen and for him to come, try hard to live without sinning; and be at peace with everyone so that he will be pleased with you when he returns.

2 Peter 3:3-14

Yes, dear friends, we are already God's children, right now, and we can't even imagine what it is going to be like later on. But we do know this, that when he comes we will be like him, as a result of seeing him as he really is.

And everyone who really believes this will try to stay pure because Christ is pure.

1 John 3:2,3

"But as for me, I know that my Redeemer lives, and that he will stand upon the earth at last.

"And I know that after this body has decayed, this body shall see God!

"Then he will be on my side! Yes, I shall see him, not as a stranger, but as a friend! What a glorious hope!"

Job 19:25-27

Yet we have this assurance: Those who belong to God shall live again. Their bodies shall rise again! Those who dwell in the dust shall awake and sing for joy! For God's light of life will fall like dew upon them!

Isaiah 26:19

But I am telling you this strange and wonderful secret: we shall not all die, but we shall all be given new bodies!

It will all happen in a moment, in the twinkling of an eye, when the last trumpet is blown. For there will be a trumpet blast from the sky and all the Christians who have died will suddenly become alive, with new bodies that will never, never die; and then we who are still alive shall suddenly have new bodies too.

1 Corinthians 15:51,52

For you have become a part of him, and so you died with him, so to speak, when he died; and now you share his new life, and shall rise as he did.

Romans 6:5

And when Christ who is our real life comes back again, you will shine with him and share in all his glories.

Colossians 3:4

His coming will not be delayed much longer.

Hebrews 10:37

"There are many homes up there where my Father lives, and I am going to prepare them for your coming.

"When everything is ready, then I will come and get you, so that you can always be with me where I am. If this weren't so, I would tell you plainly. And you know where I am going and how to get there."

John 14:2,3

And said, "Men of Galilee, why are you standing here staring at the sky? Jesus has gone away to heaven, and some day, just as he went, he will return!"

Acts 1:11

See! He is arriving, surrounded by clouds; and every eye shall see him — yes, and those who pierced him. And the nations will weep in sorrow and in terror when he comes. Yes! Amen! Let it be so!

Revelation 1:7

The steps of good men are directed by the Lord. He delights in each step they take.

Psalm 37:23

What To Do When You Are Uncertain

I am expecting the Lord to rescue me again, so that once again I will see his goodness to me here in the land of the living.

Don't be impatient. Wait for the Lord, and he will come and save you! Be brave, stouthearted and courageous. Yes, wait and he will help you.

Psalm 27:13-14

Now we can look forward to the salvation God has promised us. There is no longer any room for doubt, and we can tell others that salvation is ours, for there is no question that he will do what he says.

Hebrews 10:23

But when you ask him, be sure that you really expect him to tell you, for a doubtful mind will be as unsettled as a wave of the sea that is driven and tossed by the wind.

James 1:6

All green things along the river bank will wither and blow away. All crops will perish; everything will die.

Isaiah 19:7

Your royal decrees cannot be changed. Holiness is forever the keynote of your reign.

Psalm 93:5

All he does is just and good, and all his laws are right.

Psalm 111:7

But God's truth stands firm like a great rock, and nothing can shake it. It is a foundation stone with these words written on it: "The Lord knows those who are really his," and "A person who calls himself a Christian should not be doing things that are wrong."

2 Timothy 2:19

Then believe what I am telling you now, and share it with others.

Proverbs 22:21

VI. When You Need:

When You Need Ability

For I can do everything God asks me to with the help of Christ who gives me the strength and power.

Philippians 4:13

They can see that you are a letter from Christ, written by us. It is not a letter written with pen and ink, but by the Spirit of the living God; not one carved on stone, but in human hearts.

We dare to say these good things about ourselves only because of our great trust in God through Christ, that he will help us to be true to what we say.

2 Corinthians 3:3,4

I can never stop thanking God for all the wonderful gifts he has given you, now that you are Christ's:

He has enriched your whole life. He has helped you speak out for him and has given you a full understanding of the truth;

What I told you Christ could do for you has happened!

Now you have every grace and blessing; every spiritual gift and power for doing his will are yours during this time of waiting for the return of our Lord Jesus Christ.

1 Corinthians 1:4-7

God has given each of you some special abilities; be sure to use them to help each other, passing on to others God's many kinds of blessings.

Are you called to preach? Then preach as though God himself were speaking through you. Are you called to help others? Do it with all the strength and energy that God supplies so that God will be glorified through Jesus Christ — to him be glory and power forever and ever. Amen.

1 Peter 4:10,11

And have filled him with the Spirit of God, giving him great wisdom, ability, and skill in constructing the Tabernacle and everything it contains.

Exodus 31:3

And I have appointed Oholiab (son of Ahisamach of the tribe of Dan) to be his assistant; moreover, I have given special skill to all who are known as experts, so that they can make all the things I have instructed you to make.

Exodus 31:6

Do you want more and more of God's kindness and peace? Then learn to know him better and better.

For as you know him better, he will give you, through his great power, everything you need for living a truly good life: he even shares his own glory and his own goodness with us!

2 Peter 1:2,3

Bless the Lord who is my immovable Rock. He gives me strength and skill in battle.

Psalm 144:1

Take care to live in me, and let me live in you. For a branch can't produce fruit when severed from the vine. Nor can you be fruitful apart from me.

Yes, I am the Vine; you are the branches. Whoever lives in me and I in him shall produce a large crop of fruit. For apart from me you can't do a thing.

John 15:4,5

But if you stay in me and obey my commands, you may ask any request you like, and it will be granted!

John 15:7

Now in your strength I can scale any wall, attack any troop.

Psalm 18:29

But despite all this, overwhelming victory is ours through Christ who loved us enough to die for us.

Romans 8:37

And it is he who will supply all your needs from his riches in glory, because of what Christ Jesus has done for us.

Philippians 4:19

When You Need a Friend

You are my hiding place from every storm of life; you even keep me from getting into trouble! You surround me with songs of victory.

Psalm 32:7

When he calls on me I will answer; I will be with him in trouble, and rescue him and honor him.

Psalm 91:15

There are "friends" who pretend to be friends, but there is a friend who sticks closer than a brother.

Proverbs 18:24

A true friend is always loyal, and a brother is born to help in time of need.

Proverbs 17:17

Be with wise men and become wise. Be with evil men and become evil.

Proverbs 13:20

Don't be selfish; don't live to make a good impression on others. Be humble, thinking of others as better than yourself.

Don't just think about your own affairs, but be interested in others, too, and in what they are doing.

Philippians 2:3,4

For Jehovah God is our Light and our Protector. He gives us grace and glory. No good thing will he withhold from those who walk along his paths.

Psalm 84:11

Be delighted with the Lord. Then he will give you all your heart's desires.

Psalm 37:4

I can never be lost to your Spirit! I can never get away from my God!

Psalm 139:7

Even there your hand will guide me, your strength will support me.

Psalm 139:10

When You Need Comfort

And I will ask the Father and he will give you another Comforter, and he will never leave you.

He is the Holy Spirit, the Spirit who leads into all truth. The world at large cannot receive him, for it isn't looking for him and doesn't recognize him. But you do, for he lives with you now and some day shall be in you.

No, I will not abandon you or leave you as orphans in the storm — I will come to you.

John 14:16-18

But when the Father sends the Comforter instead of me — and by the Comforter I mean the Holy Spirit — he will teach you much, as well as remind you of everything I myself have told you.

John 14:26

But the fact of the matter is that it is best for you that I go away, for if I don't, the Comforter won't come. If I do, he will— for I will send him to you.

John 16:7

What a wonderful God we have — he is the Father of our Lord Jesus Christ, the source of every mercy,

And the one who so wonderfully comforts and strengthens us in our hardships and trials. And why does he do this? So that when others are troubled, needing our sympathy and encouragement, we can pass on to them this same help and comfort God has given us.

You can be sure that the more we undergo sufferings for Christ, the more he will shower us with his comfort and encouragement.

2 Corinthians 1:3-5

But if your gift is that of being able to "speak in tongues," that is, to speak in languages you haven't learned, you will be talking to God but not to others, since they won't be able to understand you. You will be speaking by the power of the Spirit, but it will all be a secret.

But one who prophesies, preaching the messages of God, is helping others grow in the Lord, encouraging and comforting them.

1 Corinthians 14:2,3

So encourage each other to build each other up, just as you are already doing.

1 Thessalonians 5:11

But you, dear friends, must build up your lives ever more strongly upon the foundation of our holy faith, learning to pray in the power and strength of the Holy Spirit.

Jude 20

David was seriously worried, for in their bitter grief for their children, his men began talking of killing him. But David took strength from the Lord.

1 Samuel 30:6

The eternal God is your Refuge, and underneath are the everlasting arms. He thrusts out your enemies before you; it is he who cries, "Destroy them!"

Deuteronomy 33:27

Even when walking through the dark valley of death I will not be afraid, for you are close beside me, guarding, guiding all the way.

Psalm 23:4

There I'll be when troubles come. He will hide me. He will set me on a high rock out of reach of all my enemies. Then I will bring him sacrifices and sing his praises with much joy.

Psalm 27:5,6

His anger lasts a moment; his favor lasts for life! Weeping may go on all night, but in the morning there is joy.

Psalm 30:5

I am radiant with joy because of your mercy, for you have listened to my troubles and have seen the crisis in my soul.

Psalm 31:7

Give your burdens to the Lord. He will carry them. He will not permit the godly to slip or fall.

Psalm 55:22

You have seen me tossing and turning through the night. You have collected all my tears and preserved them in your bottle! You have recorded every one in your book.

The very day I call for help, the tide of battle turns. My enemies flee! This one thing I know: God is for me!

I am trusting God — oh, praise his promises!

Psalm 56:8-10

They give me strength in all my troubles; how they refresh and revive me!

Psalm 119:50

From my earliest youth I have tried to obey you; your Word has been my comfort.

Psalm 119:52

For these laws of yours have been my source of joy and singing through all these years of my earthly pilgrimage.

Psalm 119:54

When You Need Encouragement

When I pray, you answer me, and encourage me by giving me the strength I need.

Psalm 138:3

Though I am surrounded by troubles, you will bring me safely through them. You will clench your fist against my angry enemies! Your power will save me.

The Lord will work out his plans for my life
— for your lovingkindness, Lord, continues
forever. Don't abandon me — for you made me.

Psalm 138:7,8

Lord, don't you desert me! Be gracious, Lord,
and make me well again so I can pay them back!

Psalm 41:10

When you go through deep waters and great
trouble, I will be with you. When you go through
rivers of difficulty, you will not drown! When you
walk through the fire of oppression, you will not
be burned up — the flames will not consume you.

Isaiah 43:2

And the Lord will bless Israel again, and make
her deserts blossom; her barren wilderness will
become as beautiful as the Garden of Eden. Joy
and gladness will be found there, thanksgiving and
lovely songs.

Isaiah 51:3

I, even I, am he who comforts you and gives
you all this joy. So what right have you to fear mere
mortal men, who wither like the grass and
disappear?

Isaiah 51:12

For I know the plans I have for you, says the Lord. They are plans for good and not for evil, to give you a future and a hope.

Jeremiah 29:11

May our Lord Jesus Christ himself and God our Father, who has loved us and given us everlasting comfort and hope which we don't deserve,

Comfort your hearts with all comfort, and help you in every good thing you say and do.

2 Thessalonians 2:16,17

For God is not unfair. How can he forget your hard work for him, or forget the way you used to show your love for him — and still do — by helping his children?

And we are anxious that you keep right on loving others as long as life lasts, so that you will get your full reward.

Then, knowing what lies ahead for you, you won't become bored with being a Christian, nor become spiritually dull and indifferent, but you will be anxious to follow the example of those who receive all that God has promised them because of their strong faith and patience.

Hebrews 6:10-12

But the lovingkindness of the Lord is from everlasting to everlasting, to those who reverence him; his salvation is to children's children.

Psalm 103:17

Be strong! Be courageous! Do not be afraid of them! For the Lord your God will be with you. He will neither fail you nor forsake you.

Deuteronomy 31:6

But even so, you love me! You are holding my right hand!

Psalm 73:23

Yes, be bold and strong! Banish fear and doubt! For remember, the Lord your God is with you wherever you go.

Joshua 1:9

Then he said, "This is God's message to Zerubbabel: 'Not by might, nor by power, but by my Spirit, says the Lord of Hosts — you will succeed because of my Spirit, though you are few and weak.' "

Zechariah 4:6

Trust in the Lord instead. Be kind and good to others; then you will live safely here in the land and prosper, feeding in safety.

Be delighted with the Lord. Then he will give you all your heart's desires.

Commit everything you do to the Lord. Trust him to help you do it and he will.

Psalm 37:3-5

Let everyone bless God and sing his praises;
For he holds our lives in his hands. And he
holds our feet to the path.

Psalm 66:8,9

But thanks be to God! For through what Christ
has done, he has triumphed over us so that now
wherever we go he uses us to tell others about the
Lord and to spread the Gospel like a sweet
perfume.

2 Corinthians 2:14

Then I will praise God with my singing! My
thanks will be his praise.

Psalm 69:30

The humble shall see their God at work for
them. No wonder they will be so glad! All who
seek for God shall live in joy.

Psalm 69:32

And I am sure that God who began the good
work within you will keep right on helping you
grow in his grace until his task within you is finally
finished on that day when Jesus Christ returns.

Philippians 1:6

But the good man walks along in the ever-
brightening light of God's favor; the dawn gives
way to morning splendor.

Proverbs 4:18

When You Need Faith

For salvation that comes from trusting Christ
— which is what we preach — is already within

easy reach of each of us; in fact, it is as near as our own hearts and mouths.

Romans 10:8

Yet faith comes from listening to this Good News — the Good News about Christ.

Romans 10:17

As for God, his way is perfect; The word of the Lord is true. He shields all who hide behind him.

2 Samuel 22:31

All who are oppressed may come to him. He is a refuge for them in their times of trouble.

All those who know your mercy, Lord, will count on you for help. For you have never yet forsaken those who trust in you.

Psalm 9:9,10

It is better to trust the Lord than to put confidence in men.

It is better to take refuge in him than in the mightiest king!

Psalm 118:8,9

Those who trust in the Lord are steady as Mount Zion, unmoved by any circumstance.

Psalm 125:1

No! My help is from Jehovah who made the mountains! And the heavens too!

He will never let me stumble, slip or fall.

For he is always watching, never sleeping.
Psalm 121:2-4

But make everyone rejoice who puts his trust in you. Keep them shouting for joy because you are defending them. Fill all who love you with your happiness.
Psalm 5:11

So I pray for you Gentiles that God who gives you hope will keep you happy and full of peace as you believe in him. I pray that God will help you overflow with hope in him through the Holy Spirit's power within you.
Romans 15:13

And we will never stop thanking God for this: that when we preached to you, you didn't think of the words we spoke as being just our own, but you accepted what we said as the very Word of God — which, of course, it was — and it changed your lives when you believed it.
1 Thessalonians 2:13

But just the opposite happened: those yearly sacrifices reminded them of their disobedience and guilt instead of relieving their minds.
Hebrews 10:3

And those whose faith has made them good in God's sight must live by faith, trusting him in everything. Otherwise, if they shrink back, God will have no pleasure in them.

But we have never turned our backs on God and sealed our fate. No, our faith in him assures our souls' salvation.

Hebrews 10:38,39

For every child of God can obey him, defeating sin and evil pleasure by trusting Christ to help him.

1 John 5:4

Don't be afraid, for the Lord will go before you and will be with you; he will not fail nor forsake you.

Deuteronomy 31:8

Early the next morning the army of Judah went out into the wilderness of Tekoa. On the way Jehoshaphat stopped and called them to attention. "Listen to me, O people of Judah and Jerusalem," he said. "Believe in the Lord your God, and you shall have success! Believe his prophets, and everything will be all right!"

2 Chronicles 20:20

"Be strong, be brave, and do not be afraid of the king of Assyria or his mighty army, for there is someone with us who is far greater than he is!

He has a great army, but they are all mere men, while we have the Lord our God to fight our battles for us!" This greatly encouraged them.

2 Chronicles 32:7,8

Fear not, my people; be glad now and rejoice, for he has done amazing things for you.

Joel 2:21

Note this: Wicked men trust themselves alone [as these Chaldeans do], and fail; but the righteous man trusts in me, and lives!

Habakkuk 2:4

Then he continued, "Be strong and courageous and get to work. Don't be frightened by the size of the task, for the Lord my God is with you; he will not forsake you. He will see to it that everything is finished correctly."

1 Chronicles 28:20

Because the Lord is my Shepherd, I have everything I need!

Psalm 23:1

When You Need Finances

And it is he who will supply all your needs from his riches in glory, because of what Christ Jesus has done for us.

Philippians 4:19

But I replied, "The God of heaven will help us, and we, his servants, will rebuild this wall; but you may have no part in this affair."

Nehemiah 2:20

You know how full of love and kindness our Lord Jesus was: though he was so very rich, yet to help you he became so very poor, so that by being poor he could make you rich.

2 Corinthians 8:9

Do you remember what the Scriptures say about this? "He that gathered much had nothing left over, and he that gathered little had enough." So you also should share with those in need.

2 Corinthians 8:15

But remember this — if you give little, you will get little. A farmer who plants just a few seeds will get only a small crop, but if he plants much, he will reap much.

Every one must make up his own mind as to how much he should give. Don't force anyone to give more than he really wants to, for cheerful givers are the ones God prizes.

God is able to make it up to you by giving you everything you need and more, so that there will not only be enough for your own needs, but plenty left over to give joyfully to others.

It is as the Scriptures say: "The godly man gives generously to the poor. His good deeds will be an honor to him forever."

For God, who gives seed to the farmer to plant, and later on, good crops to harvest and eat, will give you more and more seed to plant and will make it grow so that you can give away more and more fruit from your harvest.

2 Corinthians 9:6-10

So my counsel is: Don't worry about things — food, drink, and clothes. For you already have life and a body — and they are far more important than what to eat and wear.

Look at the birds! They don't worry about what to eat — they don't need to sow or reap or store up food — for your heavenly Father feeds them. And you are far more valuable to him than they are.

Will all your worries add a single moment to your life?

And why worry about your clothes? Look at the field lilies! They don't worry about theirs.

Yet King Solomon in all his glory was not clothed as beautifully as they.

And if God cares so wonderfully for flowers that are here today and gone tomorrow, won't he more surely care for you, O men of little faith?

So don't worry at all about having enough food and clothing.

Why be like the heathen? For they take pride in all these things and are deeply concerned about them. But your heavenly Father already knows perfectly well that you need them,

And he will give them to you if you give him first place in your life and live as he wants you to. So don't be anxious about tomorrow. God will take care of you tomorrow too. Live one day at a time.

Matthew 6:25-34

If anyone is stealing he must stop it and begin using those hands of his for honest work so he can give to others in need.

Ephesians 4:28

For if you give, you will get! Your gift will return to you in full and overflowing measure, pressed down, shaken together to make room for more, and running over. Whatever measure you use to give — large or small — will be used to measure what is given back to you.

Luke 6:38

Don't be misled; remember that you can't ignore God and get away with it: a man will always reap just the kind of crop he sows!

Galatians 6:7

I have been young and now I am old. And in all my years I have never seen the Lord forsake a man who loves him; nor have I seen the children of the godly go hungry.

Instead, the godly are able to be generous with their gifts and loans to others, and their children are a blessing.

Psalm 37:25,26

Bring all the tithes into the storehouse so that there will be food enough in my Temple; if you do, I will open up the windows of heaven for you and pour out a blessing so great you won't have room enough to take it in! "Try it! Let me prove it to you!

"Your crops will be large, for I will guard them from insects and plagues. Your grapes won't shrivel away before they ripen," says the Lord of Hosts.

"And all nations will call you blessed, for you will be a land sparkling with happiness. These are the promises of the Lord of Hosts."

Malachi 3:10-12

Honor the Lord by giving him the first part of all your income,

And he will fill your barns with wheat and barley and overflow your wine vats with the finest wines.

Proverbs 3:9,10

"If I can?" Jesus asked. "Anything is possible if you have faith."

Mark 9:23

Give generously, for your gifts will return to you later.

Ecclesiastes 11:1

The Lord will not let a good man starve to death, nor will he let the wicked man's riches continue forever.

Proverbs 10:3

The Lord, your Redeemer, the Holy One of Israel, says, "I am the Lord your God, who punishes you for your own good and leads you along the paths that you should follow.

Isaiah 48:17

When You Need To Forgive

And always be thankful to the Father who has made us fit to share all the wonderful things that belong to those who live in the kingdom of light.

For he has rescued us out of the darkness and gloom of Satan's kingdom and brought us into the kingdom of his dear Son,

Who bought our freedom with his blood and forgave us all our sins.

Christ is the exact likeness of the unseen God. He existed before God made anything at all, and, in fact,

Christ himself is the Creator who made everything in heaven and earth, the things we can see and the things we can't; the spirit world with its kings and kingdoms, its rulers and authorities; all were made by Christ for his own use and glory.

He was before all else began and it is his power that holds everything together.

Colossians 1:12-17

Try to stay out of all quarrels and seek to live a clean and holy life, for one who is not holy will not see the Lord.

Look after each other so that not one of you will fail to find God's best blessings. Watch out that no bitterness takes root among you, for as it springs up it causes deep trouble, hurting many in their spiritual lives.

Hebrews 12:14,15

If you are angry, don't sin by nursing your grudge. Don't let the sun go down with you still angry — get over it quickly;

For when you are angry you give a mighty foothold to the devil.

Ephesians 4:26,27

Follow God's example in everything you do just as a much loved child imitates his father.

Be full of love for others, following the example of Christ who loved you and gave himself to God as a sacrifice to take away your sins. And God was pleased, for Christ's love for you was like sweet perfume to him.

Ephesians 5:1,2

Love is very patient and kind, never jealous or envious, never boastful or proud,

Never haughty or selfish or rude. Love does not demand its own way. It is not irritable or touchy. It does not hold grudges and will hardly even notice when others do it wrong.

It is never glad about injustice, but rejoices whenever truth wins out.

If you love someone you will be loyal to him no matter what the cost! You will always believe in him, always expect the best of him, and always stand your ground in defending him.

All the special gifts and powers from God will someday come to an end, but love goes on forever. Someday prophecy, and speaking in unknown languages, and special knowledge — these gifts will disappear.

1 Corinthians 13:4-8

A wise man restrains his anger and overlooks insults. This is to his credit.

Proverbs 19:11

If you come upon an enemy's ox or donkey that has strayed away, you must take it back to its owner.

If you see your enemy trying to get his donkey onto its feet beneath a heavy load, you must not go on by, but must help him.

Exodus 23:4,5

Happy are the kind and merciful, for they shall be shown mercy.

Matthew 5:7

But I say: Don't resist violence! If you are slapped on one cheek, turn the other too.

If you are ordered to court, and your shirt is taken from you, give your coat too.

If the military demand that you carry their gear for a mile, carry it two.

Give to those who ask, and don't turn away from those who want to borrow.

There is a saying, "Love your friends and hate your enemies." But I say: Love your enemies! Pray for those who persecute you!

In that way you will be acting as true sons of your Father in heaven. For he gives his sunlight to both the evil and the good, and sends rain on the just and on the unjust too.

If you love only those who love you, what good is that? Even scoundrels do that much.
Matthew 5:39-46

And forgive us our sins, just as we have forgiven those who have sinned against us.
Matthew 6:12

Your heavenly Father will forgive you if you forgive those who sin against you;
But if you refuse to forgive them, he will not forgive you.
Matthew 6:14,15

But when you are praying, first forgive anyone you are holding a grudge against, so that your Father in heaven will forgive you your sins too.
Mark 11:25

Love your enemies! Do good to them! Lend to them! And don't be concerned about the fact that they won't repay. Then your reward from heaven will be very great, and you will truly be acting as sons of God: for he is kind to the unthankful and to those who are very wicked.
Try to show as much compassion as your Father does.
Never criticize or condemn — or it will all come back on you. Go easy on others; then they will do the same for you.
Luke 6:35-37

Rebuke your brother if he sins, and forgive him if he is sorry.

Even if he wrongs you seven times a day and each time turns again and asks forgiveness, forgive him.

Luke 17:3,4

If someone mistreats you because you are a Christian, don't curse him; pray that God will bless him.

Romans 12:14

Never pay back evil for evil. Do things in such a way that everyone can see you are honest clear through.

Romans 12:17

Dear friends, never avenge yourselves. Leave that to God, for he has said that he will repay those who deserve it. [Don't take the law into your own hands.]

Romans 12:19

Don't let evil get the upper hand but conquer evil by doing good.

Romans 12:21

Instead, be kind to each other, tenderhearted, forgiving one another, just as God has forgiven you because you belong to Christ.

Ephesians 4:32

y evil for evil. Don't snap back at
y unkind things about you. Instead,
d's help for them, for we are to be kind
, and God will bless us for it.

1 Peter 3:9

When You Need Healing

Yet it was our grief he bore, our sorrows that weighed him down. And we thought his troubles were a punishment from God, for his own sins!

But he was wounded and bruised for our sins. He was chastised that we might have peace; he was lashed — and we were healed!

Isaiah 53:4,5

That evening several demon-possessed people were brought to Jesus; and when he spoke a single word, all the demons fled; and all the sick were healed.

This fulfilled the prophecy of Isaiah, "He took our sicknesses and bore our diseases."

Matthew 8:16,17

He personally carried the load of our sins in his own body when he died on the cross, so that we can be finished with sin and live a good life from now on. For his wounds have healed ours!

1 Peter 2:24

But Christ has bought us out from under the doom of that impossible system by taking the curse for our wrongdoing upon himself. For it is written in the Scripture, ''Anyone who is hanged on a tree is cursed'' [as Jesus was hung upon a wooden cross].

Galatians 3:13

''If you will listen to the voice of the Lord your God, and obey it, and do what is right, then I will not make you suffer the diseases I send on the Egyptians, for I am the Lord who heals you.''

Exodus 15:26

You shall serve the Lord your God only; then I will bless you with food and with water, and I will take away sickness from among you.

There will be no miscarriages nor barrenness throughout your land, and you will live out the full quota of the days of your life.

Exodus 23:25,26

For the eyes of the Lord search back and forth across the whole earth, looking for people whose hearts are perfect toward him, so that he can show his great power in helping them. What a fool you have been! From now on you shall have wars.

2 Chronicles 16:9

How then can evil overtake me or any plague come near?

Psalm 91:10

I will satisfy him with a full life and give him my salvation.

Psalm 91:16

Yes, I will bless the Lord and not forget the glorious things he does for me.
He forgives all my sins. He heals me.

Psalm 103:2,3

He spoke, and they were healed — snatched from the door of death.

Psalm 107:20

So also is my Word. I send it out and it always produces fruit. It shall accomplish all I want it to, and prosper everywhere I send it.

Isaiah 55:11

But whatever is good and perfect comes to us from God, the Creator of all light, and he shines forever without change or shadow.

James 1:17

Look! A leper is approaching. He kneels before him, worshiping. "Sir," the leper pleads, "if you want to, you can heal me."
Jesus touches the man. "I want to," he says. "Be healed." And instantly the leprosy disappears.

Matthew 8:2,3

And you no doubt know that Jesus of Nazareth was anointed by God with the Holy Spirit and with power, and he went around doing good and healing all who were possessed by demons, for God was with him.

Acts 10:38

The thief's purpose is to steal, kill and destroy. My purpose is to give life in all its fullness.

John 10:10

When Jesus heard what had happened, he found the man and said, "Do you believe in the Messiah?"

John 9:35

Jesus Christ is the same yesterday, today, and forever.

Hebrews 13:8

In solemn truth I tell you, anyone believing in me shall do the same miracles I have done, and even greater ones, because I am going to be with the Father.

John 14:12

Is anyone sick? He should call for the elders of the church and they should pray over him and pour a little oil upon him, calling on the Lord to heal him.

And their prayer, if offered in faith, will heal him, for the Lord will make him well; and if his sickness was caused by some sin, the Lord will forgive him.

James 5:14,15

Dear friend, I am praying that all is well with you and that your body is as healthy as I know your soul is.

3 John 2

Dear young friends, you belong to God and have already won your fight with those who are against Christ, because there is someone in your hearts who is stronger than any evil teacher in this wicked world.

1 John 4:4

This is the absolute truth — you can say to this Mount of Olives, "Rise up and fall into the Mediterranean," and your command will be obeyed. All that's required is that you really believe and have no doubt!

Listen to me! You can pray for anything, and if you believe, you have it; it's yours!

Mark 11:23,24

When You Need Joy

You have let me experience the joys of life and the exquisite pleasures of your own eternal presence.

Psalm 16:11

Majesty and honor march before him, strength and gladness walk beside him.

1 Chronicles 16:27

Many sacrifices were offered on that joyous day, for God had given us cause for great joy. The women and children rejoiced too, and the joy of the people of Jerusalem was heard far away!

Nehemiah 12:43

Yes, the gladness you have given me is far greater than their joys at harvest time as they gaze at their bountiful crops.

Psalm 4:7

I will be glad, yes, filled with joy because of you. I will sing your praises, O Lord God above all gods.

Psalm 9:2

They [God's laws] protect us, make us wise, and give us joy and light.

Psalm 19:8

He is my strength, my shield from every danger. I trusted in him, and he helped me. Joy rises in my heart until I burst out in songs of praise to him.

Psalm 28:7

But I will rejoice in the Lord. He shall rescue me!

Psalm 35:9

Oh, revive us! Then your people can rejoice in you again.

Psalm 85:6

Blessed are those who hear the joyful blast of the trumpet, for they shall walk in the light of your presence.

They rejoice all day long in your wonderful reputation and in your perfect righteousness.

Psalm 89:15,16

Shout with joy before the Lord, O earth!

Obey him gladly; come before him, singing with joy.

Psalm 100:1,2

When Jehovah brought back his exiles to Jerusalem, it was like a dream!

How we laughed and sang for joy. And the other nations said, "What amazing things the Lord has done for them."

Psalm 126:1,2

Your words are what sustain me; they are food to my hungry soul. They bring joy to my sorrowing heart and delight me. How proud I am to bear your name, O Lord.

Jeremiah 15:16

However, the important thing is not that demons obey you, but that your names are registered as citizens of heaven.

Luke 10:20

I have told you this so that you will be filled with my joy. Yes, your cup of joy will overflow!
John 15:11

You will give me back my life, and give me wonderful joy in your presence.
Acts 2:28

And their converts were filled with joy and with the Holy Spirit.
Acts 13:52

For, after all, the important thing for us as Christians is not what we eat or drink but stirring up goodness and peace and joy from the Holy Spirit.
Romans 14:17

For though once your heart was full of darkness, now it is full of light from the Lord, and your behavior should show it!
Ephesians 5:8

Keep putting into practice all you learned from me and saw me doing, and the God of peace will be with you.
Philippians 4:9

You love him even though you have never seen him; though not seeing him, you trust him; and even now you are happy with the inexpressible joy that comes from heaven itself.
1 Peter 1:8

When You Need Love

Then, when that happens, we are able to hold our heads high no matter what happens and know that all is well, for we know how dearly God loves us, and we feel this warm love everywhere within us because God has given us the Holy Spirit to fill our hearts with his love.

Romans 5:5

My prayer for you is that you will overflow more and more with love for others, and at the same time keep on growing in spiritual knowledge and insight,

For I want you always to see clearly the difference between right and wrong, and to be inwardly clean, no one being able to criticize you from now until our Lord returns.

May you always be doing those good, kind things that show you are a child of God, for this will bring much praise and glory to the Lord.

Philippians 1:9-11

And may the Lord make your love to grow and overflow to each other and to everyone else, just as our love does toward you.

This will result in your hearts being made strong, sinless and holy by God our Father, so that you may stand before him guiltless on that day when our Lord Jesus Christ returns with all those who belong to him.

1 Thessalonians 3:12,13

But concerning the pure brotherly love that there should be among God's people, I don't need to say very much, I'm sure! For God himself is teaching you to love one another.

Indeed, your love is already strong toward all the Christian brothers throughout your whole nation. Even so, dear friends, we beg you to love them more and more.

1 Thessalonians 4:9,10

May the Lord bring you into an ever deeper understanding of the love of God and of the patience that comes from Christ.

2 Thessalonians 3:5

In this act we see what real love is: it is not our love for God, but his love for us when he sent his Son to satisfy God's anger against our sins.

Dear friends, since God loved us as much as that, we surely ought to love each other too.

For though we have never yet seen God, when we love each other God lives in us and his love within us grows ever stronger.

1 John 4:10-12

We know how much God loves us because we have felt his love and because we believe him when he tells us that he loves us dearly. God is love, and anyone who lives in love is living with God and God is living in him.

And as we live with Christ, our love grows more perfect and complete; so we will not be ashamed and embarrassed at the day of judgment, but can face him with confidence and joy, because he loves us and we love him too.

We need have no fear of someone who loves us perfectly; his perfect love for us eliminates all dread of what he might do to us. If we are afraid, it is for fear of what he might do to us and shows that we are not fully convinced that he really loves us.

1 John 4:16-18

Hatred stirs old quarrels, but love overlooks insults.

Proverbs 10:12

Seal me in your heart with permanent betrothal, for love is strong as death and jealousy is as cruel as Sheol. It flashes fire, the very flame of Jehovah.

Many waters cannot quench the flame of love, neither can the floods drown it. If a man tried to buy it with everything he owned, he couldn't do it.

Song of Solomon 8:6,7

Love forgets mistakes; nagging about them parts the best of friends.

Proverbs 17:9

A true friend is always loyal, and a brother is born to help in time of need.

Proverbs 17:17

Honor your father and mother, and love your neighbor as yourself!

Matthew 19:19

You must love him with all your heart, soul, and might.

Deuteronomy 6:5

And now, Israel, what does the Lord your God require of you except to listen carefully to all he says to you, and to obey for your own good the commandments I am giving you today, and to love him, and to worship him with all your hearts and souls?

Deuteronomy 10:12,13

Be sure to continue to obey all of the commandments Moses gave you. Love the Lord and follow his plan for your lives. Cling to him and serve him enthusiastically.

Joshua 22:5

I love the Lord because he hears my prayers and answers them.

Psalm 116:1

And so I am giving a new commandment to you now — love each other just as much as I love you.

Your strong love for each other will prove to the world that you are my disciples.

John 13:34,35

Next is your question about eating food that has been sacrificed to idols. On this question everyone feels that only his answer is the right one! But although being a "know-it-all" makes us feel important, what is really needed to build the church is love.

1 Corinthians 8:1

What I am eager for is that all the Christians there will be filled with love that comes from pure hearts, and that their minds will be clean and their faith strong.

1 Timothy 1:5

Most important of all, continue to show deep love for each other, for love makes up for many of your faults.

1 Peter 4:8

But whoever loves his fellow man is "walking in the light" and can see his way without stumbling around in darkness and sin.

1 John 2:10

When You Need Motivation

You slaves must always obey your earthly masters, not only trying to please them when they are watching you but all the time; obey them willingly because of your love for the Lord and because you want to please him.

Work hard and cheerfully at all you do, just as though you were working for the Lord and not merely for your masters.

Colossians 3:22,23

When you enter a village, don't shift around from home to home, but stay in one place, eating and drinking without question whatever is set before you. And don't hesitate to accept hospitality, for the workman is worthy of his wages!

Luke 10:7

This being so, I want to remind you to stir into flame the strength and boldness that is in you, that entered into you when I laid my hands upon your head and blessed you.

For the Holy Spirit, God's gift, does not want you to be afraid of people, but to be wise and strong, and to love them and enjoy being with them.

2 Timothy 1:6,7

Then the Israeli army wept before the Lord until evening and asked him, "Shall we fight further against our brother Benjamin?" And the Lord said, "Yes." So the men of Israel took courage and went out again the next day to fight at the same place.

Judges 20:22-24

Lazy men are soon poor; hard workers get rich.
Proverbs 10:4

Work hard and become a leader; be lazy and never succeed.
Proverbs 12:24

Do you know a hard-working man? He shall be successful and stand before kings!
Proverbs 22:29

My paths are those of justice and right.
Those who love and follow me are indeed wealthy. I fill their treasuries.
Proverbs 8:20,21

Never be lazy in your work but serve the Lord enthusiastically.
Romans 12:11

A lazy man sleeps soundly — and goes hungry!
Proverbs 19:15

A wise youth makes hay while the sun shines, but what a shame to see a lad who sleeps away his hour of opportunity.
Proverbs 10:5

Hard work means prosperity; only a fool idles away his time.
Proverbs 12:11

Wealth from gambling quickly disappears; wealth from hard work grows.

Proverbs 13:11

If you love sleep, you will end in poverty. Stay awake, work hard, and there will be plenty to eat!

Proverbs 20:13

This should be your ambition: to live a quiet life, minding your own business and doing your own work, just as we told you before.

As a result, people who are not Christians will trust and respect you, and you will not need to depend on others for enough money to pay your bills.

1 Thessalonians 4:11,12

Even while we were still there with you we gave you this rule: "He who does not work shall not eat."

2 Thessalonians 3:10

Then, knowing what lies ahead for you, you won't become bored with being a Christian, nor become spiritually dull and indifferent, but you will be anxious to follow the example of those who receive all that God has promised them because of their strong faith and patience.

Hebrews 6:12

Laziness lets the roof leak, and soon the rafters begin to rot.

Ecclesiastes 10:18

But despite all this, overwhelming victory is ours through Christ who loved us enough to die for us.

Romans 8:37

When You Need Patience

Rest in the Lord; wait patiently for him to act. Don't be envious of evil men who prosper.

Stop your anger! Turn off your wrath. Don't fret and worry — it only leads to harm.

For the wicked shall be destroyed, but those who trust the Lord shall be given every blessing.

Psalm 37:7-9

Finishing is better than starting! Patience is better than pride! Don't be quick-tempered — that is being a fool.

Ecclesiastes 7:8,9

For if you stand firm, you will win your souls.

Luke 21:19

We can rejoice, too, when we run into problems and trials for we know that they are good for us — they help us learn to be patient.

Romans 5:3

And let us not get tired of doing what is right, for after a while we will reap a harvest of blessing if we don't get discouraged and give up.

Galatians 6:9

I beg you — I, a prisoner here in jail for serving the Lord — to live and act in a way worthy of those who have been chosen for such wonderful blessings as these.

Ephesians 4:1

Be humble and gentle. Be patient with each other, making allowance for each other's faults because of your love.

Ephesians 4:2

And asking that the way you live will always please the Lord and honor him, so that you will always be doing good, kind things for others, while all the time you are learning to know God better and better.

We are praying, too, that you will be filled with his mighty, glorious strength so that you can keep going no matter what happens — always full of the joy of the Lord.

Colossians 1:10,11

Dear brothers, warn those who are lazy; comfort those who are frightened; take tender care of those who are weak; and be patient with everyone.

1 Thessalonians 5:14

May the Lord bring you into an ever deeper understanding of the love of God and of the patience that comes from Christ.

2 Thessalonians 3:5

O Timothy, you are God's man. Run from all these evil things and work instead at what is right and good, learning to trust him and love others and to be patient and gentle.

1 Timothy 6:11

Then, knowing what lies ahead for you, you won't become bored with being a Christian, nor become spiritually dull and indifferent, but you will be anxious to follow the example of those who receive all that God has promised them because of their strong faith and patience.

Hebrews 6:12

Then Abraham waited patiently until finally God gave him a son, Isaac, just as he had promised.

Hebrews 6:15

You need to keep on patiently doing God's will if you want him to do for you all that he has promised.

Hebrews 10:36

Since we have such a huge crowd of men of faith watching us from the grandstands, let us strip off anything that slows us down or holds us back, and especially those sins that wrap themselves so tightly around our feet and trip us up; and let us run with patience the particular race that God has set before us.

Hebrews 12:1

For when the way is rough, your patience has a chance to grow.

So let it grow, and don't try to squirm out of your problems. For when your patience is finally in full bloom, then you will be ready for anything, strong in character, full and complete.

James 1:3,4

Dear brothers, don't ever forget that it is best to listen much, speak little, and not become angry.

James 1:19

Now as for you, dear brothers who are waiting for the Lord's return, be patient, like a farmer who waits until the autumn for his precious harvest to ripen.

Yes, be patient. And take courage, for the coming of the Lord is near.

James 5:7,8

But to obtain these gifts, you need more than faith; you must also work hard to be good, and even that is not enough. For then you must learn to know God better and discover what he wants you to do.

Next, learn to put aside your own desires so that you will become patient and godly, gladly letting God have his way with you.

2 Peter 1:5,6

Let this encourage God's people to endure patiently every trial and persecution, for they are his saints who remain firm to the end in obedience to his commands and trust in Jesus.

Revelation 14:12

He isn't really being slow about his promised return, even though it sometimes seems that way. But he is waiting, for the good reason that he is not willing that any should perish, and he is giving more time for sinners to repent.

2 Peter 3:9

When You Need Peace

When a man is trying to please God, God makes even his worst enemies to be at peace with him.

Proverbs 16:7

It is an honor for a man to stay out of a fight. Only fools insist on quarreling.

Proverbs 20:3

And work for the peace and prosperity of Babylon. Pray for her, for if Babylon has peace, so will you.

Jeremiah 29:7

Happy are those who strive for peace — they shall be called the sons of God.

Matthew 5:9

Quit quarreling with God! Agree with him and you will have peace at last! His favor will surround you if you will only admit that you were wrong.

Job 22:21

Yet when he chooses not to speak, who can criticize?

Job 34:29

He will keep in perfect peace all those who trust in him, whose thoughts turn often to the Lord!
Trust in the Lord God always, for in the Lord Jehovah is your everlasting strength.

Isaiah 26:3,4

Lord, grant us peace; for all we have and are has come from you.

Isaiah 26:12

Where is the man who fears the Lord? God will teach him how to choose the best.

He shall live within God's circle of blessing, and his children shall inherit the earth.

Psalm 25:12,13

But the good man — what a different story! For the good man — the blameless, the upright, the man of peace — he has a wonderful future ahead of him. For him there is a happy ending.

Psalm 37:37

I am listening carefully to all the Lord is saying – for he speaks peace to his people, his saints, if they will only stop their sinning.

Psalm 85:8

Those who love your laws have great peace of heart and mind and do not stumble.

Psalm 119:165

Those who trust in the Lord are steady as Mount Zion, unmoved by any circumstance.

Psalm 125:1

They could have rest in their own land if they would obey him, if they were kind and good. He told them that, but they wouldn't listen to him.

Isaiah 28:12

"The future splendor of this Temple will be greater than the splendor of the first one! For I have plenty of silver and gold to do it! And here I will give peace," says the Lord.

Haggai 2:8,9

The purpose of these laws was to give him life and peace, to be a means of showing his respect and awe for me, by keeping them.

Malachi 2:5

To give light to those who sit in darkness and death's shadow, and to guide us to the path of peace.

Luke 1:79

I am leaving you with a gift — peace of mind and heart! And the peace I give isn't fragile like the peace the world gives. So don't be troubled or afraid.

John 14:27

So now, since we have been made right in God's sight by faith in his promises, we can have real peace with him because of what Jesus Christ our Lord has done for us.

Romans 5:1

For, after all, the important thing for us as Christians is not what we eat or drink but stirring up goodness and peace and joy from the Holy Spirit.

Romans 14:17

Don't worry about anything; instead, pray about everything; tell God your needs and don't forget to thank him for his answers.

If you do this you will experience God's peace, which is far more wonderful than the human mind can understand. His peace will keep your thoughts and your hearts quiet and at rest as you trust in Christ Jesus.

Philippians 4:6,7

Let the peace of heart that comes from Christ be always present in your hearts and lives, for this is your responsibility and privilege as members of his body. And always be thankful.

Colossians 3:15

May the Lord of peace himself give you his peace no matter what happens. The Lord be with you all.

2 Thessalonians 3:16

Though the tide of battle runs strongly against me, for so many are fighting me, yet he will rescue me.

Psalm 55:18

When You Need Protection

We live within the shadow of the Almighty, sheltered by the God who is above all gods.

This I declare, that he alone is my refuge, my place of safety; he is my God, and I am trusting him.

For he rescues you from every trap, and protects you from the fatal plague.

He will shield you with his wings! They will shelter you. His faithful promises are your armor.

Now you don't need to be afraid of the dark any more, nor fear the dangers of the day;

Nor dread the plagues of darkness, nor disasters in the morning.

Though a thousand fall at my side, though ten thousand are dying around me, the evil will not touch me.

I will see how the wicked are punished but I will not share it.

For Jehovah is my refuge! I choose the God above all gods to shelter me.

How then can evil overtake me or any plague come near?

For he orders his angels to protect you wherever you go.

They will steady you with their hands to keep you from stumbling against the rocks on the trail.

You can safely meet a lion or step on poisonous snakes, yes, even trample them beneath your feet!

For the Lord says, "Because he loves me, I will rescue him; I will make him great because he trusts in my name.

"When he calls on me I will answer; I will be with him in trouble, and rescue him and honor him.

"I will satisfy him with a full life and give him my salvation."

Psalm 91:1-16

Now I say that each believer should confess his sins to God when he is aware of them, while there is time to be forgiven. Judgment will not touch him if he does.

You are my hiding place from every storm of life; you even keep me from getting into trouble! You surround me with songs of victory.

Psalm 32:6,7

For the Lord himself will be a wall of fire protecting them and all Jerusalem; he will be the glory of the city.

Zechariah 2:5

God is our refuge and strength, a tested help in times of trouble.

And so we need not fear even if the world blows up, and the mountains crumble into the sea.

Psalm 46:1,2

God himself is living in that City; therefore it stands unmoved despite the turmoil everywhere. He will not delay his help.

Psalm 46:5

But when I am afraid, I will put my confidence in you.

Yes, I will trust the promises of God. And since I am trusting him, what can mere man do to me?

Psalm 56:3,4

Yes, Lord, help us against our enemies, for man's help is useless.

With God's help we shall do mighty things, for he will trample down our foes.

Psalm 60:11,12

O God, listen to me! Hear my prayer!

For wherever I am, though far away at the ends of the earth, I will cry to you for help. When my heart is faint and overwhelmed, lead me to the mighty, towering Rock of safety.

For you are my refuge, a high tower where my enemies can never reach me.

I shall live forever in your tabernacle; oh, to safe beneath the shelter of your wings!

Psalm 61:1-4

Reverence for God gives a man deep strength; his children have a place of refuge and security.

Reverence for the Lord is a fountain of life; its waters keep a man from death.

Proverbs 14:26,27

As for God, his way is perfect; the word of the Lord is true. He shields all who hide behind him.

2 Samuel 22:31

That is why I am suffering here in jail and I am certainly not ashamed of it, for I know the one in whom I trust, and I am sure that he is able to safely guard all that I have given him until the day of his return.

2 Timothy 1:12

And now — all glory to him who alone is God, who saves us through Jesus Christ our Lord.

Jude 24

When You Need Self-Control

But ask the Lord Jesus Christ to help you live as you should, and don't make plans to enjoy evil.

Romans 13:14

Your old evil desires were nailed to the cross with him; that part of you that loves to sin was crushed and fatally wounded, so that your sin-loving body is no longer under sin's control, no longer needs to be a slave to sin.

Romans 6:6

And don't stuff yourself, though it all tastes so good.

Proverbs 23:2

It is better to be slow-tempered than famous; it is better to have self-control than to control an army.

Proverbs 16:32

I can do anything I want to if Christ has not said no, but some of these things aren't good for me. Even if I am allowed to do them, I'll refuse to if I think they might get such a grip on me that I can't easily stop when I want to.

1 Corinthians 6:12

I have been crucified with Christ: and I myself no longer live, but Christ lives in me. And the real life I now have within this body is a result of my trusting in the Son of God, who loved me and gave himself for me.

Galatians 2:20

I advise you to obey only the Holy Spirit's instructions. He will tell you where to go and what to do, and then you won't always be doing the wrong things your evil nature wants you to.

Galatians 5:16

Those who belong to Christ have nailed their natural evil desires to his cross and crucified them there.

Galatians 5:24

And as Christ's soldier do not let yourself become tied up in worldly affairs, for then you cannot satisfy the one who has enlisted you in his army.

2 Timothy 2:4

Dear brothers, you are only visitors here. Since your real home is in heaven I beg you to keep away from the evil pleasures of this world; they are not for you, for they fight against your very souls.

1 Peter 2:11

Since Christ suffered and underwent pain, you must have the same attitude he did; you must be ready to suffer, too. For remember, when your body suffers, sin loses its power,

And you won't be spending the rest of your life chasing after evil desires, but will be anxious to do the will of God.

1 Peter 4:1,2

Do you like honey? Don't eat too much of it, or it will make you sick!

Proverbs 25:16

To win the contest you must deny yourselves many things that would keep you from doing your best. An athlete goes to all this trouble just to win a blue ribbon or a silver cup, but we do it for a heavenly reward that never disappears.

So I run straight to the goal with purpose in every step. I fight to win. I'm not just shadow-boxing or playing around.

Like an athlete I punish my body, treating it roughly, training it to do what it should, not what it wants to. Otherwise I fear that after enlisting others for the race, I myself might be declared unfit and ordered to stand aside.

1 Corinthians 9:25-27

Let everyone see that you are unselfish and considerate in all you do. Remember that the Lord is coming soon.

Philippians 4:5

When You Need Strength

The Lord is my strength, my song, and my salvation. He is my God, and I will praise him.

He is my father's God — I will exalt him.

Exodus 15:2

God is my strong fortress; he has made me safe.

2 Samuel 22:33

He is my strength and song in the heat of battle, and now he has given me the victory.

Psalm 118:14

See, God has come to save me! I will trust and not be afraid, for the Lord is my strength and song; he is my salvation.

Isaiah 12:2

For you have given me strength for the battle and have caused me to subdue all those who rose against me.

2 Samuel 22:40

He fills me with strength and protects me wherever I go.

Psalm 18:32

For you have armed me with strong armor for the battle. My enemies quail before me and fall defeated at my feet.

Psalm 18:39

May my spoken words and unspoken thoughts be pleasing even to you, O Lord my Rock and my Redeemer.

Psalm 19:14

He will give his people strength. He will bless them with peace.

Psalm 29:11

The Lord makes us strong! Sing praises! Sing to Israel's God!

Psalm 81:1

My health fails; my spirits droop, yet God remains! He is the strength of my heart; he is mine forever!

Psalm 73:26

A wise man is mightier than a strong man. Wisdom is mightier than strength.

Proverbs 24:5

Trust in the Lord God always, for in the Lord Jehovah is your everlasting strength.

Isaiah 26:4

He gives power to the tired and worn out, and strength to the weak.

Isaiah 40:29

Each time he said, "No. But I am with you; that is all you need. My power shows up best in weak people." Now I am glad to boast about how weak I am; I am glad to be a living demonstration of Christ's power, instead of showing off my own power and abilities.

2 Corinthians 12:9

Summon your might; display your strength, O God, for you have done such mighty things for us.

Psalm 68:28

Last of all I want to remind you that your strength must come from the Lord's mighty power within you.

Ephesians 6:10

When You Need Wisdom

Asking God, the glorious Father of our Lord Jesus Christ, to give you wisdom to see clearly and really understand who Christ is and all that he has done for you.

I pray that your hearts will be flooded with light so that you can see something of the future he has called you to share. I want you to realize that God has been made rich because we who are Christ's have been given to him!

I pray that you will begin to understand how incredibly great his power is to help those who believe him. It is that same mighty power

That raised Christ from the dead and seated him in the place of honor at God's right hand in heaven.

Ephesians 1:17-20

So ever since we first heard about you we have kept on praying and asking God to help you understand what he wants you to do asking him to make you wise about spiritual things.

Colossians 1:9

If you want to know what God wants you to do, ask him, and he will gladly tell you, for he is always ready to give a bountiful supply of wisdom to all who ask him; he will not resent it.

But when you ask him, be sure that you really expect him to tell you, for a doubtful mind will be as unsettled as a wave of the sea that is driven and tossed by the wind;

And every decision you then make will be uncertain, as you turn first this way, and then that. If you don't ask with faith, don't expect the Lord to give you any solid answer.

James 1:5-8

For jealousy and selfishness are not God's kind of wisdom. Such things are earthly, unspiritual, inspired by the devil.

For wherever there is jealousy or selfish ambition, there will be disorder and every other kind of evil.

But the wisdom that comes from heaven is first of all pure and full of quiet gentleness. Then it is peace-loving and courteous. It allows discussion and is willing to yield to others; it is full of mercy and good deeds. It is wholehearted and straightforward and sincere.

And those who are peacemakers will plant seeds of peace and reap a harvest of goodness.

James 3:15-18

But whoever loves his fellow man is "walking in the light" and can see his way without stumbling around in darkness and sin.

For he who dislikes his brother is wandering in spiritual darkness and doesn't know where he is going, for the darkness has made him blind so that he cannot see the way.

1 John 2:10,11

Ask me and I will tell you some remarkable secrets about what is going to happen here.

Jeremiah 33:3

But you are not like that, for the Holy Spirit has come upon you, and you know the truth.

1 John 2:20

But you have received the Holy Spirit and he lives within you, in your hearts, so that you don't need anyone to teach you what is right. For he teaches you all things, and he is the Truth, and no liar; and so, just as he has said, you must live in Christ, never to depart from him.

1 John 2:27

And if you leave God's paths and go astray, you will hear a Voice behind you say, "No, this is the way; walk here."

Isaiah 30:21

Don't be hot-headed and rush to court! You may start something you can't finish and go down before your neighbor in shameful defeat.

So discuss the matter with him privately. Don't tell anyone else.

Proverbs 25:8,9

It is a badge of honor to accept valid criticism.

Proverbs 25:12

I will instruct you (says the Lord) and guide you along the best pathway for your life; I will advise you and watch your progress.

Psalm 32:8

For you are the Fountain of life; our light is from your Light.

Psalm 36:9

As your plan unfolds, even the simple can understand it.

Psalm 119:130

Come here and listen to me! I'll pour out the spirit of wisdom upon you, and make you wise.

Proverbs 1:23

For the Lord grants wisdom! His every word is a treasure of knowledge and understanding.
He grants good sense to the godly — his saints. He is their shield.

Proverbs 2:6,7

Oh, send out your light and your truth — let them lead me. Let them lead me to your Temple on your holy mountain, Zion.

Psalm 43:3

Think over these three illustrations, and may the Lord help you to understand how they apply to you.

2 Timothy 2:7

When You Need Deliverance

I stand silently before the Lord, waiting for him to rescue me. For salvation comes from him alone.

Yes, he alone is my Rock, my rescuer, defense and fortress. Why then should I be tense with fear when troubles come?

Psalm 62:1,2

But I stand silently before the Lord, waiting for him to rescue me. For salvation comes from him alone.

Yes, he alone is my Rock, my rescuer, defense, and fortress — why then should I be tense with fear when troubles come?

My protection and success come from God alone. He is my refuge, a Rock where no enemy can reach me.

O my people, trust him all the time. Pour out your longings before him, for he can help!

Psalm 62:5-8

He is loving and kind and rewards each one of us according to the work we do for him.

Psalm 62:12

So also the Lord can rescue you and me from the temptations that surround us, and continue to punish the ungodly until the day of final judgment comes.

2 Peter 2:9

He reached down from heaven and took me and drew me out of my great trials. He rescued me from deep waters.

He delivered me from my strong enemy, from those who hated me — I who was helpless in their hands.

On the day when I was weakest, they attacked. But the Lord held me steady.

He led me to a place of safety, for he delights in me.

Psalm 18:16-19

Hide your loved ones in the shelter of your presence, safe beneath your hand, safe from all conspiring men.

Psalm 31:20

For I cried to him and he answered me! He freed me from all my fears.

Psalm 34:4

The good man does not escape all troubles — he has them too. But the Lord helps him in each and every one.

Psalm 34:19

Jesus said to them, "You are truly my disciples if you live as I tell you to,

"You will know the truth, and the truth will set you free."

John 8:31,32

One day Jesus called together his twelve apostles and gave them authority over all demons — power to cast them out — and to heal all diseases.

Luke 9:1

Jesus called his twelve disciples to him, and gave them authority to cast out evil spirits and to heal every kind of sickness and disease.

Matthew 10:1

And I have given you authority over all the power of the Enemy, and to walk among serpents and scorpions and to crush them. Nothing shall injure you!

Luke 10:19

That evening several demon-possessed people were brought to Jesus; and when he spoke a single word, all the demons fled; and all the sick were healed.

This fulfilled the prophecy of Isaiah, "He took our sicknesses and bore our diseases."

Matthew 8:16,17

Yes, and the Lord will always deliver me from all evil and will bring me into his heavenly kingdom. To God be the glory forever and ever. Amen.

2 Timothy 4:18

When You Need Guidance

For all who are led by the Spirit of God are sons of God.

Romans 8:14

A man's conscience is the Lord's searchlight exposing his hidden motives.

Proverbs 20:27

The gatekeeper opens the gate for him, and the sheep hear his voice and come to him; and he calls his own sheep by name and leads them out.
He walks ahead of them; and they follow him, for they recognize his voice.
They won't follow a stranger but will run from him, for they don't recognize his voice.

John 10:3-5

You have led the people you redeemed. But in your lovingkindness you have guided them wonderfully to your holy land.

Exodus 15:13

God protected them in the howling wilderness as though they were the apple of his eye.

Deuteronomy 32:10

O Lord, you are my light! You make my darkness bright.

2 Samuel 22:29

But in your great mercy you didn't abandon them to die in the wilderness! The pillar of cloud led them forward day by day, and the pillar of fire showed them the way through the night.

You sent your good Spirit to instruct them, and you did not stop giving them bread from heaven or water for their thirst.

Nehemiah 9:19,20

Lord, lead me as you promised me you would; otherwise my enemies will conquer me. Tell me clearly what to do, which way to turn.

Psalm 5:8

He lets me rest in the meadow grass and leads me beside the quiet streams. He restores my failing health. He helps me do what honors him the most.

Psalm 23:2,3

Lead me; teach me; for you are the God who gives me salvation. I have no hope except in you.

Psalm 25:5

He will teach the ways that are right and best to those who humbly turn to him.

Psalm 25:9

Tell me what to do, O Lord, and make it plain because I am surrounded by waiting enemies.

Psalm 27:11

Yes, you are my Rock and my fortress; honor your name by leading me out of this peril.

Psalm 31:3

I will instruct you (says the Lord) and guide you along the best pathway for your life; I will advise you and watch your progress.

Psalm 32:8

For this great God is our God forever and ever. He will be our guide until we die.

Psalm 48:14

For wherever I am, though far away at the ends of the earth, I will cry to you for help. When my heart is faint and overwhelmed, lead me to the mighty, towering Rock of safety.

Psalm 61:2

You will keep on guiding me all my life with your wisdom and counsel; and afterwards receive me into the glories of heaven!

Psalm 73:24

If I ride the morning winds to the farthest oceans,
Even there your hand will guide me, your strength will support me.

Psalm 139:9,10

Point out anything you find in me that makes you sad, and lead me along the path of everlasting life.

Psalm 139:24

He will bring blind Israel along a path they have not seen before. He will make the darkness bright before them and smooth and straighten out the road ahead. He will not forsake them.

Isaiah 42:16

The Lord, your Redeemer, the Holy One of Israel, says, I am the Lord your God, who punishes you for your own good and leads you along the paths that you should follow.

Isaiah 48:17

And the Lord will guide you continually, and satisfy you with all good things, and keep you healthy too; and you will be like a well-watered garden, like an ever-flowing spring.

Isaiah 58:11

To give light to those who sit in darkness and death's shadow, and to guide us to the path of peace.

Luke 1:79

When the Holy Spirit, who is truth, comes, he shall guide you into all truth, for he will not be presenting his own ideas, but will be passing on to you what he has heard. He will tell you about the future.

John 16:13

For when the way is rough, your patience has a chance to grow.

James 1:3

Ask me and I will tell you some remarkable secrets about what is going to happen here.

Jeremiah 33:3

VII. How To Be An Overcomer

Knowing Christ's Victorious Position

The sin of this one man, Adam, caused death to be king over all, but all who will take God's gift of forgiveness and acquittal are kings of life because of this one man, Jesus Christ.

Yes, Adam's sin brought punishment to all, but Christ's righteousness makes men right with God, so that they can live.

Adam caused many to be sinners because he disobeyed God, and Christ caused many to be made acceptable to God because he obeyed.

The Ten Commandments were given so that all could see the extent of their failure to obey God's laws. But the more we see our sinfulness, the more we see God's abounding grace forgiving us.

Before, sin ruled over all men and brought them to death, but now God's kindness rules instead, giving us right standing with God and resulting in eternal life through Jesus Christ our Lord.

Romans 5:17-21

And many people can build houses, but only God made everything.

Hebrews 3:4

And now Barnabas and I are here to bring you this Good News — that God's promise to our ancestors has come true in our own time, in that God brought Jesus back to life again. This is what the second Psalm is talking about when it says concerning Jesus, "Today I have honored you as my son."

Acts 13:32,33

I pray that you will begin to understand how incredibly great his power is to help those who believe him. It is that same mighty power that raised Christ from the dead and seated him in the place of honor at God's right hand in heaven, far, far above any other king or ruler or dictator or leader. Yes, his honor is far more glorious than that of anyone else either in this world or in the world to come.

And God has put all things under his feet and made him the supreme Head of the Church — which is his body, filled with himself, the Author and Giver of everything everywhere.

Ephesians 1:19-23

And he humbled himself even further, going so far as actually to die a criminal's death on a cross.

Yet it was because of this that God raised him up to the heights of heaven and gave him a name which is above every other name, that at the name of Jesus every knee shall bow in heaven and on earth and under the earth, and every tongue shall confess that Jesus Christ is Lord, to the glory of God the Father.

Philippians 2:8-11

But if you keep on sinning, it shows that you belong to Satan, who since he first began to sin has kept steadily at it. But the Son of God came to destroy these works of the devil.

1 John 3:8

In this way God took away Satan's power to accuse you of sin, and God openly displayed to the whole world Christ's triumph at the cross where your sins were all taken away.

Colossians 2:15

He was before all else began and it is his power that holds everything together.
He is the Head of the body made up of his people — that is, his Church — which he began; and he is the Leader of all those who arise from the dead, so that he is first in everything; for God wanted all of himself to be in his Son.

Colossians 1:17-19

You no doubt know that Jesus of Nazareth was anointed by God with the Holy Spirit and with power, and he went around doing good and healing all who were possessed by demons, for God was with him.

Acts 10:38

Don't be afraid! Though I am the First and Last, the Living One who died, who is now alive forevermore, who has the keys of hell and death — don't be afraid!

Revelation 1:18

Knowing Satan's Defeated Position

In this way God took away Satan's power to accuse you of sin, and God openly displayed to the whole world Christ's triumph at the cross where your sins were all taken away.

Colossians 2:15

This great Dragon — the ancient serpent called the devil, or Satan, the one deceiving the whole world — was thrown down onto the earth with all his army.

Revelation 12:9

The thief's purpose is to steal, kill and destroy. My purpose is to give life in all its fullness.

John 10:10

Your might and power are gone; they are buried with you. All the pleasant music in your palace has ceased; now maggots are your sheet, worms your blanket!

How you are fallen from heaven, O Lucifer, son of the morning! How you are cut down to the ground — mighty though you were against the nations of the world.

For you said to yourself, "I will ascend to heaven and rule the angels. I will take the highest throne. I will preside on the Mount of Assembly far away in the north.

I will climb to the highest heavens and be like the Most High."

But instead, you will be brought down to the pit of hell, down to its lowest depths.

Everyone there will stare at you and ask, "Can this be the one who shook the earth and the kingdoms of the world?"

Isaiah 14:11-16

Then the devil who had betrayed them will again be thrown into the Lake of Fire burning with sulphur where the Creature and False Prophet are, and they will be tormented day and night forever and ever.

Revelation 20:10

Knowing Your Risen Position of Authority

When someone becomes a Christian, he becomes a brand new person inside. He is not the same anymore. A new life has begun!

2 Corinthians 5:17

Like an athlete I punish my body, treating it roughly, training it to do what it should, not what it wants to. Otherwise I fear that after enlisting others for the race, I myself might be declared unfit and ordered to stand aside.

1 Corinthians 9:27

Admit your faults to one another and pray for each other so that you may be healed. The earnest prayer of a righteous man has great power and wonderful results.

Elijah was as completely human as we are, and yet when he prayed earnestly that no rain would fall, none fell for the next three and a half years!

James 5:16,17

Now here is what I am trying to say: All of you together are the one body of Christ, and each one of you is a separate and necessary part of it.

Here is a list of some of the parts he has placed in his Church, which is his body:

Apostles,

Prophets — those who preach God's Word,

Teachers,

Those who do miracles,

Those who have the gift of healing;

Those who can help others,

Those who can get others to work together,

Those who speak in languages they have never learned.

1 Corinthians 12:27,28

At that time you won't need to ask me for anything, for you can go directly to the Father and ask him, and he will give you what you ask for because you use my name.

You haven't tried this before, [but begin now]. Ask, using my name, and you will receive, and your cup of joy will overflow.

John 16:23,24

In solemn truth I tell you, anyone believing in me shall do the same miracles I have done, and even greater ones, because I am going to be with the Father.

You can ask him for anything, using my name, and I will do it, for this will bring praise to the Father because of what I, the Son, will do for you.

Yes, ask anything, using my name, and I will do it!

If you love me, obey me; and I will ask the Father and he will give you another Comforter, and he will never leave you.

John 14:12-14

But Peter said, "We don't have any money for you! But I'll give you something else! I command you in the name of Jesus Christ of Nazareth, walk!"

Acts 3:6

But God is so rich in mercy; he loved us so much that even though we were spiritually dead and doomed by our sins, he gave us back our lives again when he raised Christ from the dead — only by his undeserved favor have we ever been saved — and lifted us up from the grave into glory along with Christ, where we sit with him in the heavenly realms — all because of what Christ Jesus did.

Ephesians 2:4-6

Dear young friends, you belong to God and have already won your fight with those who are against Christ because there is someone in your hearts who is stronger than any evil teacher in this wicked world.

1 John 4:4

He has kept this secret for centuries and generations past, but now at last it has pleased him to tell it to those who love him and live for him, and the riches and glory of his plan are for you Gentiles too.

And this is the secret: that Christ in your hearts is your only hope of glory.

Colossians 1:26,27

But despite all this, overwhelming victory is ours through Christ who loved us enough to die for us.

Romans 8:37

Christ is the exact likeness of the unseen God. He existed before God made anything at all.

Colossians 1:15

For in baptism you see how your old, evil nature died with him and was buried with him; and then you came up out of death with him into a new life because you trusted the Word of the mighty God who raised Christ from the dead.

Colossians 2:12

One day Jesus called together his twelve apostles and gave them authority over all demons — power to cast them out — and to heal all diseases.

Then he sent them away to tell everyone about the coming of the Kingdom of God and to heal the sick.

Luke 9:1,2

And I have given you authority over all the power of the Enemy, and to walk among serpents and scorpions and to crush them. Nothing shall injure you!

However, the important thing is not that demons obey you, but that your names are registered as citizens of heaven.

Luke 10:19,20

Jesus called his twelve disciples to him and gave them authority to cast out evil spirits and to heal every kind of sickness and disease.

Matthew 10:1

And he called his twelve disciples together and sent them out two by two, with power to cast out demons.

Mark 6:7

For when you are angry, you give a mighty foothold to the devil.

Ephesians 4:27

In every battle you will need faith as your shield to stop the fiery arrows aimed at you by Satan.

Ephesians 6:16

I use God's mighty weapons, not those made by men, to knock down the devil's strongholds.

2 Corinthians 10:4

So give yourselves humbly to God. Resist the devil and he will flee from you.

James 4:7

Be careful — watch out for attacks from Satan, your great enemy. He prowls around like a hungry, roaring lion, looking for some victim to tear apart.

Stand firm when he attacks. Trust the Lord; and remember that other Christians all around the world are going through these sufferings too.

After you have suffered a little while, our God, who is full of kindness through Christ, will give you his eternal glory. He personally will come and pick you up, and set you firmly in place, and make you stronger than ever.

1 Peter 5:8-10

And now I will send the Holy Spirit upon you, just as my Father promised. Don't begin telling others yet — stay here in the city until the Holy Spirit comes and fills you with power from heaven.

Luke 24:49

Knowing Who You Are in Christ

But despite all this, overwhelming victory is ours through Christ who loved us enough to die for us.

Romans 8:37

Dear young friends, you belong to God and have already won your fight with those who are against Christ because there is someone in your hearts who is stronger than any evil teacher in this wicked world.

1 John 4:4

For every child of God can obey him, defeating sin and evil pleasure by trusting Christ to help him.

1 John 5:4

But thanks be to God! For through what Christ has done, he has triumphed over us so that now wherever we go he uses us to tell others about the Lord and to spread the Gospel like a sweet perfume.

2 Corinthians 2:14

How we thank God for all of this! It is he who makes us victorious through Jesus Christ our Lord!
1 Corinthians 15:57

For I can do everything God asks me to with the help of Christ who gives me the strength and power.

Philippians 4:13

How To Resist the Devil

They defeated him by the blood of the Lamb and by their testimony; for they did not love their lives but laid them down for him.

Revelation 12:11

Fight on for God. Hold tightly to the eternal life that God has given you and that you have confessed with such a ringing confession before many witnesses.

1 Timothy 6:12

For it is by believing in his heart that a man becomes right with God; and with his mouth he tells others of his faith, confirming his salvation.
Romans 10:10

For whatever God says to us is full of living power: it is sharper than the sharpest dagger, cutting swift and deep into our innermost thoughts and desires with all their parts, exposing us for what we really are.

Hebrews 4:12

Last of all I want to remind you that your strength must come from the Lord's mighty power within you.

Put on all of God's armor so that you will be able to stand safe against all strategies and tricks of Satan.

For we are not fighting against people made of flesh and blood, but against persons without bodies — the evil rulers of the unseen world, those mighty satanic beings and great evil princes of darkness who rule this world; and against huge numbers of wicked spirits in the spirit world.

So use every piece of God's armor to resist the enemy whenever he attacks, and when it is all over, you will still be standing up.

But to do this, you will need the strong belt of truth and the breastplate of God's approval.

Wear shoes that are able to speed you on as you preach the Good News of peace with God.

In every battle you will need faith as your shield to stop the fiery arrows aimed at you by Satan.

And you will need the helmet of salvation and the sword of the Spirit — which is the Word of God.

Pray all the time. Ask God for anything in line with the Holy Spirit's wishes. Plead with him, reminding him of your needs, and keep praying earnestly for all Christians everywhere.

Ephesians 6:10-18

But let us who live in the light keep sober, protected by the armor of faith and love, and wearing as our helmet the happy hope of salvation.

1 Thessalonians 5:8

It is true that I am an ordinary, weak human being, but I don't use human plans and methods to win my battles.

I use God's mighty weapons, not those made by men, to knock down the devil's strongholds.

These weapons can break down every proud argument against God and every wall that can be built to keep men from finding him. With these weapons I can capture rebels and bring them back to God and change them into men whose hearts' desire is obedience to Christ.

2 Corinthians 10:3-5

In reply Jesus said to the disciples, "If you only have faith in God — this is the absolute truth — you can say to this Mount of Olives, 'Rise up and fall into the Mediterranean,' and your command will be obeyed. All that's required is that you really believe and have no doubt!

Listen to me! You can pray for anything, and if you believe, you have it; it's yours!"

Mark 11:22-24

"Does not my word burn like fire?" asks the Lord. "Is it not like a mighty hammer that smashed the rock to pieces?"

Jeremiah 23:29

Stand firm when he attacks. Trust the Lord; and remember that other Christians all around the world are going through these sufferings too.

1 Peter 5:9

So give yourselves humbly to God. Resist the devil and he will flee from you.

James 4:7

But God shows his anger from heaven against all sinful, evil men who push away the truth from them.

Romans 1:18

VIII. How To Overcome:

How To Overcome Bitterness

And mark out a straight, smooth path or your feet so that those who follow you, though weak and lame, will not fall and hurt themselves, but become strong.

Try to stay out of all quarrels and seek to live a clean and holy life, for one who is not holy will not see the Lord.

Look after each other so that not one of you will fail to find God's best blessings. Watch out that no bitterness takes root among you, for as it springs up it causes deep trouble, hurting many in their spiritual lives.

Hebrews 12:13-15

If you are angry, don't sin by nursing your grudge. Don't let the sun go down with you still angry — get over it quickly;

For when you are angry you give a mighty foothold to the devil.

Ephesians 4:26,27

Stop being mean, bad-tempered and angry. Quarreling, harsh words, and dislike of others should have no place in your lives.

Instead, be kind to each other, tenderhearted, forgiving one another, just as God has forgiven you because you belong to Christ.

Ephesians 4:31,32

There is a saying, "Love your friends and hate your enemies." But I say: Love your enemies! Pray for those who persecute you!

In that way you will be acting as true sons of your Father in heaven. For he gives his sunlight to both the evil and the good, and sends rain on the just and on the unjust too.

If you love only those who love you, what good is that? Even scoundrels do that much.

If you are friendly only to your friends, how are you different from anyone else? Even the heathen do that.

But you are to be perfect, even as your Father in heaven is perfect.

Matthew 5:43-48

Since you have been chosen by God who has given you this new kind of life, and because of his deep love and concern for you, you should practice tenderhearted mercy and kindness to others. Don't worry about making a good impression on them but be ready to suffer quietly and patiently.

Be gentle and ready to forgive; never hold grudges. Remember, the Lord forgave you, so you must forgive others.

Most of all, let love guide your life, for then the whole church will stay together in perfect harmony.

Let the peace of heart which comes from Christ be always present in your hearts and lives, for this is your responsibility and privilege as members of his body. And always be thankful.

Remember what Christ taught and let his words enrich your lives and make you wise; teach them to each other and sing them out in psalms and hymns and spiritual songs, singing to the Lord with thankful hearts.

And whatever you do or say, let it be as a representative of the Lord Jesus, and come with him into the presence of God the Father to give him your thanks.

Colossians 3:12-17

Happy are the kind and merciful, for they shall be shown mercy.

Matthew 5:7

Those who love your laws have great peace of heart and mind and do not stumble.

Psalm 119:165

He will keep in perfect peace all those who trust in him, whose thoughts turn often to the Lord!

Trust in the Lord God always, for in the Lord Jehovah is your everlasting strength.

Isaiah 26:3,4

But when you are praying, first forgive anyone you are holding a grudge against, so that your Father in heaven will forgive you your sins too.

Mark 11:25

I am warning you! Rebuke your brother if he sins, and forgive him if he is sorry.

Even if he wrongs you seven times a day and each time turns again and asks forgiveness, forgive him.

Luke 17:3,4

If someone mistreats you because you are a Christian, don't curse him; pray that God will bless him.

Romans 12:14

Never pay back evil for evil. Do things in such a way that everyone can see you are honest clear through.

Romans 12:17

Dear friends, never avenge yourselves. Leave that to God, for he has said that he will repay those who deserve it. [Don't take the law into your own hands.]

Romans 12:19

Don't let evil get the upper hand but conquer evil by doing good.

Romans 12:21

We have worked wearily with our hands to earn our living. We have blessed those who cursed us. We have been patient with those who injured us.

1 Corinthians 4:12

How To Overcome Depression

You have let me experience the joys of life and the exquisite pleasures of your own eternal presence.

Psalm 16:11

- 216 -

His anger lasts a moment; his favor lasts for life! Weeping may go on all night, but in the morning there is joy.

Psalm 30:5

Then he turned my sorrow into joy! He took away my clothes of mourning and gave me gay and festive garments to rejoice in.

Psalms 30:11

I will be glad, yes, filled with joy because of you. I will sing your praises, O Lord God above all gods.

Psalm 9:2

He is for me! How can I be afraid? What can mere man do to me?
The Lord is on my side, he will help me. Let those who hate me beware.

Psalm 118:6,7

Quit quarreling with God! Agree with him and you will have peace at last! His favor will surround you if you will only admit that you were wrong.

Job 22:21

God's laws are perfect. They protect us, make us wise, and give us joy and light.

Psalm 19:7,8

He is my strength, my shield from every danger. I trusted in him, and he helped me. Joy rises in my heart until I burst out in songs of praise to him.

Psalm 28:7

So rejoice in him, all those who are his, and shout for joy, all those who try to obey him.

Psalm 32:11

But may the joy of the Lord be given to everyone who loves him and his salvation. May they constantly exclaim, ''How great God is!''

Psalm 40:16

And after you have punished me, give me back my joy again.

Psalm 51:8

Restore to me again the joy of your salvation, and make me willing to obey you.

Psalm 51:12

Oh, revive us! Then your people can rejoice in you again.

Psalm 85:6

Blessed are those who hear the joyful blast of the trumpet, for they shall walk in the light of your presence.

Psalm 89:15

Glory in the Lord; O worshipers of God, rejoice.

Psalm 105:3

So he brought his chosen ones singing into the Promised Land.

Psalm 105:43

Those who sow tears shall reap joy.

Yes, they go out weeping, carrying seed for sowing, and return singing, carrying their sheaves.

Psalm 126:5,6

Yes, they shall sing about Jehovah's glorious ways, for his glory is very great.

Psalm 138:5

O Israel, rejoice in your Maker. O people of Jerusalem, exult in your King.

Psalm 149:2

Let his people rejoice in this honor. Let them sing for joy as they lie upon their beds.

Psalm 149:5

In that day the people will proclaim, "This is our God, in whom we trust, for whom we waited. Now at last he is here." What a day of rejoicing!

Isaiah 25:9

The time will come when God's redeemed will all come home again. They shall come with singing to Jerusalem, filled with joy and everlasting gladness; sorrow and mourning will all disappear.

I, even I, am he who comforts you and gives you all this joy. So what right have you to fear mere mortal men, who wither like the grass and disappear?

Isaiah 51:11,12

Your words are what sustain me; they are food to my hungry soul. They bring joy to my sorrowing heart and delight me. How proud I am to bear your name, O Lord.

Jeremiah 15:16

I have heard Ephraim's groans: "You have punished me greatly; but I needed it all, as a calf must be trained for the yoke. Turn me again to you and restore me, for you alone are the Lord, my God."

Jeremiah 31:18

For I have given rest to the weary and joy to all the sorrowing.

(Then Jeremiah wakened. "Such sleep is very sweet!" he said.)

Jeremiah 31:25,26

You will give me back my life, and give me wonderful joy in your presence.

Acts 2:28

If you do as I say in this letter, then you, too, will be full of joy, and so will we.

1 John 1:4

How To Overcome Doubt

As for God, his way is perfect; the word of the Lord is true. He shields all who hide behind him.

2 Samuel 22:31

Then Jesus told them, "Truly, if you have faith, and don't doubt, you can do things like this and much more. You can even say to this Mount of Olives, 'Move over into the ocean,' and it will.

"You can get anything — anything you ask for in prayer — if you believe."

Matthew 21:21,22

"If I can?" Jesus asked. "Anything is possible if you have faith."

Mark 9:23

This is the absolute truth — you can say to this Mount of Olives, "Rise up and fall into the Mediterranean," and your command will be obeyed. All that's required is that you really believe and have no doubt!

Listen to me! You can pray for anything, and if you believe, you have it; it's yours!

Mark 11:23,24

Yet faith comes from listening to this Good News — the Good News about Christ.

Romans 10:17

And because his faith was strong, he didn't worry about the fact that he was too old to be a father, at the age of one hundred, and that Sarah his wife, at ninety, was also much too old to have a baby.

But Abraham never doubted. He believed God, for his faith and trust grew ever stronger, and he praised God for this blessing even before it happened.

He was completely sure that God was well able to do anything he promised.

And because of Abraham's faith God forgave his sins and declared him "not guilty."

Romans 4:19-22

In every battle you will need faith as your shield to stop the fiery arrows aimed at you by Satan.

Ephesians 6:16

Do not let this happy trust in the Lord die away, no matter what happens. Remember your reward!

Hebrews 10:35

And those whose faith has made them good in God's sight must live by faith, trusting him in everything. Otherwise, if they shrink back, God will have no pleasure in them.

But we have never turned our backs on God and sealed our fate. No, our faith in him assures our souls' salvation.

Hebrews 10:38,39

For every child of God can obey him, defeating sin and evil pleasure by trusting Christ to help him.

1 John 5:4

God is not a man, that he should lie; he doesn't change his mind like humans do. Has he ever promised, without doing what he said?

Numbers 23:19

God, who called you to become his child, will do all this for you, just as he promised.

1 Thessalonians 5:24

Early the next morning the army of Judah went out into the wilderness of Tekoa. On the way Jehoshaphat stopped and called them to attention. "Listen to me, O people of Judah and Jerusalem," he said. "Believe in the Lord your God and you shall have success! Believe his prophets, and everything will be all right!"

2 Chronicles 20:20

Be strong, be brave, and do not be afraid of the king of Assyria or his mighty army, for there is someone with us who is far greater than he is!

2 Chronicles 32:7

Don't be impatient. Wait for the Lord, and he will come and save you! Be brave, stouthearted and courageous. Yes, wait and he will help you.

Psalm 27:14

O my people, trust him all the time. Pour out your longings before him, for he can help!

Psalm 62:8

I want the company of the godly men and women in the land; they are the true nobility.
Psalm 16:3

Trust in the Lord God always, for in the Lord Jehovah is your everlasting strength.
Isaiah 26:4

Fear not, for I am with you. Do not be dismayed. I am your God. I will strengthen you; I will help you; I will uphold you with my victorious right hand.
Isaiah 41:10

But now the Lord who created you, O Israel, says, "Don't be afraid, for I have ransomed you; I have called you by name; you are mine.

When you go through deep waters and great trouble, I will be with you. When you go through rivers of difficulty, you will not drown! When you walk through the fire of oppression, you will not be burned up — the flames will not consume you."
Isaiah 43:1,2

So don't be afraid, little flock. For it gives your Father great happiness to give you the Kingdom.
Luke 12:32

"If your faith were only the size of a mustard seed," Jesus answered, "it would be large enough to uproot that mulberry tree over there and send it hurtling into the sea! Your command would bring immediate results!"
Luke 17:6

Then he continued, "Be strong and courageous and get to work. Don't be frightened by the size of the task, for the Lord my God is with you; he will not forsake you. He will see to it that everything is finished correctly."

1 Chronicles 28:20

How To Overcome Guilt

Give your burdens to the Lord. He will carry them. He will not permit the godly to slip or fall.
Psalm 55:22

But if we confess our sins to him, he can be depended on to forgive us and to cleanse us from every wrong. [And it is perfectly proper for God to do this for us because Christ died to wash away our sins.]

1 John 1:9

This High Priest of ours understands our weaknesses, since he had the same temptations we do, though he never once gave way to them and sinned.

So let us come boldly to the very throne of God and stay there to receive his mercy and to find grace to help us in our times of need.

Hebrews 4:15,16

When someone becomes a Christian he becomes a brand new person inside. He is not the same any more. A new life has begun!

2 Corinthians 5:17

For God took the sinless Christ and poured into him our sins. Then, in exchange, he poured God's goodness into us!

2 Corinthians 5:21

But now you belong to Christ Jesus, and though you once were far away from God, now you have been brought very near to him because of what Jesus Christ has done for you with his blood.

Ephesians 2:13

Now all of us, whether Jews or Gentiles, may come to God the Father with the Holy Spirit's help because of what Christ has done for us.

Ephesians 2:18

Now we can come fearlessly right into God's presence, assured of his glad welcome when we come with Christ and trust in him.

Ephesians 3:12

Just think how much more surely the blood of Christ will transform our lives and hearts. His sacrifice frees us from the worry of having to obey the old rules, and makes us want to serve the living God. For by the help of the eternal Holy Spirit, Christ willingly gave himself to God to die for our sins — he being perfect, without a single sin or fault.

Hebrews 9:14

"This is the agreement I will make with the people of Israel, though they broke their first agreement: I will write my laws into their minds so that they will always know my will, and I will put my laws in their hearts so that they will want to obey them."

And then he adds, "I will never again remember their sins and lawless deeds."

Now, when sins have once been forever forgiven and forgotten, there is no need to offer more sacrifices to get rid of them.

And so, dear brothers, now we may walk right into the very Holy of Holies where God is, because of the blood of Jesus.

This is the fresh, new, life-giving way which Christ has opened up for us by tearing the curtain — his human body — to let us into the holy presence of God.

And since this great High Priest of ours rules over God's household,

Let us go right in, to God himself, with true hearts fully trusting him to receive us, because we have been sprinkled with Christ's blood to make us clean, and because our bodies have been washed with pure water.

Now we can look forward to the salvation God has promised us. There is no longer any room for doubt, and we can tell others that salvation is ours, for there is no question that he will do what he says.

Hebrews 10:16-23

Since we have such a huge crowd of men of faith watching us from the grandstands, let us strip off anything that slows us down or holds us back, and especially those sins that wrap themselves so tightly around our feet and trip us up; and let us run with patience the particular race that God has set before us.

Keep your eye on Jesus, our leader and instructor. He was willing to die a shameful death on the cross because of the joy he knew would be his afterwards; and now he sits in the place of honor by the throne of God.

Hebrews 12:1,2

What can we ever say to such wonderful things as these? If God is on our side, who can ever be against us?

Since he did not spare even his own Son for us but gave him up for us all, won't he also surely give us everything else?

Who dares accuse us whom God has chosen for his own? Will God? No! He is the one who has forgiven us and given us right standing with himself.

Who then will condemn us? Will Christ? No! For he is the one who died for us and came back to life again for us and is sitting at the place of highest honor next to God, pleading for us there in heaven.

Who then can ever keep Christ's love from us? When we have trouble or calamity, when we are hunted down or destroyed, is it because he doesn't love us anymore? And if we are hungry, or penniless, or in danger, or threatened with death, has God deserted us?

No, for the Scriptures tell us that for his sake we must be ready to face death at every moment of the day — we are like sheep awaiting slaughter; but despite all this, overwhelming victory is ours through Christ who loved us enough to die for us.

For I am convinced that nothing can ever separate us from his love. Death can't, and life can't. The angels won't, and all the powers of hell itself cannot keep God's love away. Our fears for today, our worries about tomorrow,

Or where we are — high above the sky, or in the deepest ocean — nothing will ever be able to separate us from the love of God demonstrated by our Lord Jesus Christ when he died for us.

Romans 8:31-39

So we should not be like cringing, fearful slaves, but we should behave like God's very own children, adopted into the bosom of his family, and calling to him, "Father, Father."

Romans 8:15

God's grace be with you all. Good-bye.

Hebrews 13:25

And when you draw close to God, God will draw close to you. Wash your hands, you sinners, and let your hearts be filled with God alone to make them pure and true to him.

James 4:8

Yes, I will bless the Lord and not forget the glorious things he does for me.

He forgives all my sins. He heals me.

Psalm 103:2,3

How To Overcome Enemies

Do not rejoice when your enemy meets trouble. Let there be no gladness when he falls —

For the Lord may be displeased with you and stop punishing him!

Proverbs 24:17,18

If your enemy is hungry, give him food! If he is thirsty, give him something to drink!

This will make him feel ashamed of himself, and God will reward you.

Proverbs 25:21,22

If someone mistreats you because you are a Christian, don't curse him; pray that God will bless him.

Romans 12:14

Instead, feed your enemy if he is hungry. If he is thirsty give him something to drink and you will be "heaping coals of fire on his head." In other words, he will feel ashamed of himself for what he has done to you.

Romans 12:20

Listen, all of you. Love your enemies. Do good to those who hate you.

Pray for the happiness of those who curse you; implore God's blessing on those who hurt you.

If someone slaps you on one cheek, let him slap the other too! If someone demands your coat, give him your shirt besides.

Give what you have to anyone who asks you for it; and when things are taken away from you, don't worry about getting them back.

Treat others as you want them to treat you.

Do you think you deserve credit for merely loving those who love you? Even the godless do that!

And if you do good only to those who do you good — is that so wonderful? Even sinners do that much!

And if you lend money only to those who can repay you, what good is that? Even the most wicked will lend to their own kind for full return!

Love your enemies! Do good to them! Lend to them! And don't be concerned about the fact that they won't repay. Then your reward from heaven will be very great, and you will truly be acting as sons of God: for he is kind to the unthankful and to those who are very wicked.

Try to show as much compassion as your Father does.

Luke 6:27-36

He rescues me from my enemies; he holds me safely out of their reach and saves me from these powerful opponents.

Psalm 18:48

We broke camp at the Ahava River at the end of March and started off to Jerusalem; and God protected us and saved us from enemies and bandits along the way.

Ezra 8:31

They make me wiser than my enemies, because they are my constant guide.

Psalm 119:98

How To Overcome Fear

We need have no fear of someone who loves us perfectly; his perfect love for us eliminates all dread of what he might do to us. If we are afraid, it is for fear of what he might do to us, and shows that we are not fully convinced that he really loves us.

1 John 4:18

For I cried to him and he answered me! He freed me from all my fears.

Psalm 34:4

God is our refuge and strength, a tested help in times of trouble.

And so we need not fear even if the world blows up, and the mountains crumble into the sea.

Let the oceans roar and foam; let the mountains tremble!

Psalm 46:1-3

You will live under a government that is just and fair. Your enemies will stay far away; you will live in peace. Terror shall not come near.

Isaiah 54:14

That is why we can say without any doubt or fear, "The Lord is my Helper and I am not afraid of anything that mere man can do to me."

Hebrews 13:6

No, do not be afraid of those nations, for the Lord your God is among you, and he is a great and awesome God.

Deuteronomy 7:21

For the Lord is great, and should be highly praised; He is to be held in awe above all gods.

The other so-called gods are demons, but the Lord made the heavens.

1 Chronicles 16:25,26

Fear not, for I am with you. Do not be dismayed. I am your God. I will strengthen you; I will help you; I will uphold you with my victorious right hand.

Isaiah 41:10

Encourage those who are afraid. Tell them, "Be strong, fear not, for your God is coming to destroy your enemies. He is coming to save you."

Isaiah 35:4

Then as I looked over the situation, I called together the leaders and the people and said to them, "Don't be afraid! Remember the Lord who is great and glorious; fight for your friends, your families, and your homes!"

Nehemiah 4:14

But you have seen these mighty miracles!

Deuteronomy 11:7

The Lord shouts from his Temple in Jerusalem and the earth and sky begin to shake. But to his people Israel, the Lord will be very gentle. He is their Refuge and Strength.

Joel 3:16

But when I am afraid, I will put my confidence in you.

Psalm 56:3

You are my hiding place from every storm of life; you even keep me from getting into trouble! You surround me with songs of victory.

Psalm 32:7

He does not fear bad news, nor live in dread of what may happen. For he is settled in his mind that Jehovah will take care of him.

That is why he is not afraid but can calmly face his foes.

Psalm 112:7,8

How To Overcome Impure Thoughts

Commit your work to the Lord, then it will succeed.

Proverbs 16:3

Don't worry about anything; instead, pray about everything; tell God your needs and don't forget to thank him for his answers.

If you do this you will experience God's peace, which is far more wonderful than the human mind can understand. His peace will keep your thoughts and your hearts quiet and at rest as you trust in Christ Jesus.

And now, brothers, as I close this letter let me say this one more thing: Fix your thoughts on what is true and good and right. Think about things that are pure and lovely, and dwell on the fine, good things in others. Think about all you can praise God for and be glad about.

Keep putting into practice all you learned from me and saw me doing, and the God of peace will be with you.

Philippians 4:6-9

I hate those who are undecided whether or not to obey you; but my choice is clear — I love your law.

Psalm 119:113

I made a covenant with my eyes not to look with lust upon a girl.

Job 31:1

The laws of Moses said, "You shall not commit adultery."

But I say: Anyone who even looks at a woman with lust in his eye has already committed adultery with her in his heart.

Matthew 5:27,28

Happy are those whose hearts are pure, for they shall see God.

Matthew 5:8

It is true that I am an ordinary, weak human being, but I don't use human plans and methods to win my battles.

I use God's mighty weapons, not those made by men, to knock down the devil's strongholds.

These weapons can break down every proud argument against God and every wall that can be built to keep men from finding him. With these weapons I can capture rebels and bring them back to God and change them into men whose hearts' desire is obedience to Christ.

2 Corinthians 10:3-5

How can a young man stay pure? By reading your Word and following its rules.

Psalm 119:9

Don't copy the behavior and customs of this world, but be a new and different person with a fresh newness in all you do and think. Then you will learn from your own experience how his ways will really satisfy you.

Romans 12:2

So get rid of all that is wrong in your life, both inside and outside, and humbly be glad for the wonderful message we have received, for it is able to save our souls as it takes hold of our hearts.

And remember, it is a message to obey, not just to listen to. So don't fool yourselves.

James 1:21,22

For when you are angry you give a mighty foothold to the devil.

Ephesians 4:27

Make them pure and holy through teaching them your words of truth.

John 17:17

He has already tended you by pruning you back for greater strength and usefulness by means of the commands I gave you.

John 15:3

Now you can have real love for everyone because your souls have been cleansed from selfishness and hatred when you trusted Christ to save you; so see to it that you really do love each other warmly, with all your hearts.

1 Peter 1:22

A man is known by his actions. An evil man lives an evil life; a good man lives a godly life.
Proverbs 21:8

How To Overcome Lust

I advise you to obey only the Holy Spirit's instructions. He will tell you where to go and what to do, and then you won't always be doing the wrong things your evil nature wants you to.

For we naturally love to do evil things that are just the opposite from the things that the Holy Spirit tells us to do; and the good things we want to do when the Spirit has his way with us are just the opposite of our natural desires. These two forces within us are constantly fighting each other to win control over us, and our wishes are never free from their pressures.

When you are guided by the Holy Spirit you need no longer force yourself to obey Jewish laws.
Galatians 5:16-18

Temptation is the pull of man's own evil thoughts and wishes.

These evil thoughts lead to evil actions and afterwards to the death penalty from God.
James 1:14,15

Stop loving this evil world and all that it offers you, for when you love these things you show that you do not really love God;

For all these worldly things, these evil desires — the craze for sex, the ambition to buy everything that appeals to you, and the pride that comes from wealth and importance — these are not from God. They are from this evil world itself.

And this world is fading away, and these evil, forbidden things will go with it, but whoever keeps doing the will of God will live forever.

1 John 2:15-17

Dear brothers, you are only visitors here. Since your real home is in heaven I beg you to keep away from the evil pleasures of this world; they are not for you, for they fight against your very souls.

1 Peter 2:11

Like an athlete I punish my body, treating it roughly, training it to do what it should, not what it wants to. Otherwise I fear that after enlisting others for the race, I myself might be declared unfit and ordered to stand aside.

1 Corinthians 9:27

I have been crucified with Christ: and I myself no longer live, but Christ lives in me. And the real life I now have within this body is a result of my trusting in the Son of God, who loved me and gave himself for me.

Galatians 2:20

And you won't be spending the rest of your life chasing after evil desires, but will be anxious to do the will of God.

1 Peter 4:2

They proudly boast about their sins and conquests, and, using lust as their bait, they lure back into sin those who have just escaped from such wicked living.

"You aren't saved by being good," they say, "so you might as well be bad. Do what you like; be free." But these very teachers who offer this "freedom" from law are themselves slaves to sin and destruction. For a man is a slave to whatever controls him.

2 Peter 2:18,19

Your old evil desires were nailed to the cross with him; that part of you that loves to sin was crushed and fatally wounded, so that your sin-loving body is no longer under sin's control, no longer needs to be a slave to sin;

For when you are deadened to sin you are freed from all its allure and its power over you.

And since your old sin-loving nature "died" with Christ, we know that you will share his new life.

Christ rose from the dead and will never die again. Death no longer has any power over him.

He died once for all to end sin's power, but now he lives forever in unbroken fellowship with God.

So look upon your old sin nature as dead and unresponsive to sin, and instead be alive to God, alert to him, through Jesus Christ our Lord.

Do not let sin control your puny body any longer; do not give in to its sinful desires.

Romans 6:6-12

Yes, dear friends, we are already God's children, right now, and we can't even imagine what it is going to be like later on. But we do know this, that when he comes we will be like him, as a result of seeing him as he really is.

And everyone who really believes this will try to stay pure because Christ is pure.

1 John 3:2,3

Those who let themselves be controlled by their lower natures live only to please themselves, but those who follow after the Holy Spirit find themselves doing those things that please God.

Following after the Holy Spirit leads to life and peace, but following after the old nature leads to death.

Romans 8:5,6

Your attitude should be the kind that was shown us by Jesus Christ.

Philippians 2:5

Remember what Christ taught and let his words enrich your lives and make you wise; teach them to each other and sing them out in psalms and hymns and spiritual songs, singing to the Lord with thankful hearts.

Colossians 3:16

How To Overcome Masturbation/Fornication

And so, dear brothers, I plead with you to give your bodies to God. Let them be a living sacrifice, holy — the kind he can accept. When you think of what he has done for you, is this too much to ask?

Romans 12:1

And the men, instead of having a normal sex relationship with women, burned with lust for each other, men doing shameful things with other men and, as a result, getting paid within their own souls with the penalty they so richly deserved.

Romans 1:27

Do not let sin control your puny body any longer; do not give in to its sinful desires.

Do not let any part of your bodies become tools of wickedness, to be used for sinning; but give yourselves completely to God — every part of you — for you are back from death and you want to be tools in the hands of God, to be used for his good purposes.

Sin need never again be your master, for now you are no longer tied to the law where sin enslaves you, but you are free under God's favor and mercy.

Does this mean that now we can go ahead and sin and not worry about it? (For our salvation does not depend on keeping the law but on receiving God's grace!) Of course not!

Don't you realize that you can choose your own master? You can choose sin (with death) or else obedience (with acquittal). The one to whom you offer yourself — he will take you and be your master and you will be his slave.

Thank God that though you once chose to be slaves of sin, now you have obeyed with all your heart the teaching to which God has committed you.

And now you are free from your old master, sin; and you have become slaves to your new master, righteousness.

I speak this way, using the illustration of slaves and masters, because it is easy to understand: just as you used to be slaves to all kinds of sin, so now you must let yourselves be slaves to all that is right and holy.

Romans 6:12-19

Don't you realize that all of you together are the house of God, and that the Spirit of God lives among you in his house?

If anyone defiles and spoils God's home, God will destroy him. For God's home is holy and clean, and you are that home.

1 Corinthians 3:16,17

For instance, take the matter of eating. God has given us an appetite for food and stomachs to digest it. But that doesn't mean we should eat more than we need. Don't think of eating as important, because some day God will do away with both stomachs and food. But sexual sin is never right: our bodies were not made for that but for the Lord, and the Lord wants to fill our bodies with himself.

And God is going to raise our bodies from the dead by his power just as he raised up the Lord Jesus Christ.

Don't you realize that your bodies are actually parts and members of Christ? So should I take part of Christ and join him to a prostitute? Never!

And don't you know that if a man joins himself to a prostitute she becomes a part of him and he becomes a part of her? For God tells us in the Scripture that in his sight the two become one person.

But if you give yourself to the Lord, you and Christ are joined together as one person.

That is why I say to run from sex sin. No other sin affects the body as this one does. When you sin this sin it is against your own body.

Haven't you yet learned that your body is the home of the Holy Spirit God gave you, and that he lives within you? Your own body does not belong to you.

For God has bought you with a great price. So use every part of your body to give glory back to God, because he owns it.

Now about those questions you asked in your last letter: my answer is that if you do not marry, it is good.

1 Corinthians 6:13-7:1

Don't be teamed with those who do not love the Lord, for what do the people of God have in common with the people of sin? How can light live with darkness?

And what harmony can there be between Christ and the devil? How can a Christian be a partner with one who doesn't believe?

And what union can there be between God's temple and idols? For you are God's temple, the home of the living God, and God has said of you, "I will live in them and walk among them, and I will be their God and they shall be my people."

That is why the Lord has said, "Leave them; separate yourselves from them; don't touch their filthy things, and I will welcome you,

"And be a Father to you, and you will be my sons and daughters."

Having such great promises as these, dear friends, let us turn away from everything wrong, whether of body or spirit, and purify ourselves, living in the wholesome fear of God, giving ourselves to him alone.

2 Corinthians 6:14-7:1

So she seduced him with her pretty speech, her coaxing and her wheedling, until he yielded to her. He couldn't resist her flattery.

He followed her as an ox going to the butcher, or as a stag that is trapped,

Waiting to be killed with an arrow through its heart. He was as a bird flying into a snare, not knowing the fate awaiting it there.

Listen to me, young men, and not only listen but obey;

Don't let your desires get out of hand; don't let yourself think about her. Don't go near her; stay away from where she walks, lest she tempt you and seduce you.

For she has been the ruin of multitudes — a vast host of men have been her victims.

If you want to find the road to hell, look for her house.

Proverbs 7:21-27

Only wisdom from the Lord can save a man from the flattery of prostitutes;
These girls have abandoned their husbands and flouted the laws of God.
Their houses lie along the road to death and hell.
The men who enter them are doomed. None of these men will ever be the same again.
Follow the steps of the godly instead, and stay on the right path.

Proverbs 2:16-20

• A wise son makes his father happy, but a lad who hangs around with prostitutes disgraces him.
Proverbs 29:3

Away then with sinful, earthly things; deaden the evil desires lurking within you; have nothing to do with sexual sin, impurity, lust, and shameful desires; don't worship the good things of life, for that is idolatry.

Colossians 3:5

For God wants you to be holy and pure, and to keep clear of all sexual sin so that each of you will marry in holiness and honor —
Not in lustful passion as the heathen do, in their ignorance of God and his ways.
1 Thessalonians 4:3-5

For God has not called us to be dirty-minded and full of lust, but to be holy and clean.
1 Thessalonians 4:7

Then Jesus stood up again and said to her, "Where are your accusers? Didn't even one of them condemn you?"

"No, sir," she said. And Jesus said, "Neither do I. Go and sin no more."

John 8:10,11

Those who belong to Christ have nailed their natural evil desires to his cross and crucified them there.

Galatians 5:24

A good man is guided by his honesty; the evil man is destroyed by his dishonesty.

Proverbs 11:3

How To Overcome Homosexuality

Don't you know that those doing such things have no share in the Kingdom of God? Don't fool yourselves. Those who live immoral lives, who are idol worshipers, adulterers or homosexuals — will have no share in his kingdom.

1 Corinthians 6:9

So God let them go ahead into every sort of sex sin, and do whatever they wanted to — yes, vile and sinful things with each other's bodies.

Romans 1:24

That is why God let go of them and let them do all these evil things, so that even their women turned against God's natural plan for them and indulged in sex sin with each other.

Romans 1:26

So it was that when they gave God up and would not even acknowledge him, God gave them up to doing everything their evil minds could think of.

Romans 1:28

But they were not made for us, whom God has saved; they are for sinners who hate God, have rebellious hearts, curse and swear, attack their fathers and mothers, and murder.

Yes, these laws are made to identify as sinners all who are immoral and impure: homosexuals, kidnappers, liars, and all others who do things that contradict the glorious Good News of our blessed God, whose messenger I am.

1 Timothy 1:9-11

But when you follow your own wrong inclinations your lives will produce these evil results: impure thoughts, eagerness for lustful pleasure,

Idolatry, spiritism (that is, encouraging the activity of demons), hatred and fighting, jealousy and anger, constant effort to get the best for yourself, complaints and criticisms, the feeling that everyone else is wrong except those in your own little group — and there will be wrong doctrine,

Envy, murder, drunkenness, wild parties, and all that sort of thing. Let me tell you again, as I have before, that anyone living that sort of life will not inherit the kingdom of God.

Galatians 5:19-21

But remember this — the wrong desires that come into your life aren't anything new and different. Many others have faced exactly the same problems before you. And no temptation is irresistible. You can trust God to keep the temptation from becoming so strong that you can't stand up against it, for he has promised this and will do what he says. He will show you how to escape temptation's power so that you can bear up patiently against it.

1 Corinthians 10:13

Homosexuality is absolutely forbidden, for it is an enormous sin.

Leviticus 18:22

How To Overcome the Past

Don't copy the behavior and customs of this world, but be a new and different person with a fresh newness in all you do and think. Then you will learn from your own experience how his ways will really satisfy you.

Romans 12:2

No, dear brothers, I am still not all I should be, but I am bringing all my energies to bear on this one thing: Forgetting the past and looking forward to what lies ahead.

Philippians 3:13

For I'm going to do a brand new thing. See, I have already begun! Don't you see it? I will make a road through the wilderness of the world for my people to go home, and create rivers for them in the desert!

Isaiah 43:19

Everything I prophesied came true, and now I will prophesy again. I will tell you the future before it happens.

Isaiah 42:9

For the winter is past, the rain is over and gone.

Song of Solomon 2:11

For God sent Christ Jesus to take the punishment for our sins and to end all God's anger against us. He used Christ's blood and our faith as the means of saving us from his wrath. In this way he was being entirely fair, even though he did not punish those who sinned in former times. For he was looking forward to the time when Christ would come and take away those sins.

Romans 3:25

For his mercy toward those who fear and honor him is as great as the height of the heavens above the earth.

He has removed our sins as far away from us as the east is from the west.

Psalm 103:11,12

How To Overcome a Negative Self-Image

When someone becomes a Christian, he becomes a brand new person inside. He is not the same anymore. A new life has begun!

2 Corinthians 5:17

For God took the sinless Christ and poured into him our sins. Then, in exchange, he poured God's goodness into us!

2 Corinthians 5:21

And since we are his children, we will share his treasures — for all God gives to his Son Jesus is now ours too. But if we are to share his glory, we must also share his suffering.

Romans 8:17

For every child of God can obey him, defeating sin and evil pleasure by trusting Christ to help him.

1 John 5:4

For I can do everything God asks me to with the help of Christ who gives me the strength and power.

Philippians 4:13

And now you have become living building-stones for God's use in building his house. What's more, you are his holy priests; so come to him — [you who are acceptable to him because of Jesus Christ] — and offer to God those things that please him.

1 Peter 2:5

But you are not like that, for you have been chosen by God himself — you are priests of the King, you are holy and pure, you are God's very own — all this so that you may show to others how God called you out of the darkness into his wonderful light.

1 Peter 2:9

You should have as little desire for this world as a dead person does. Your real life is in heaven with Christ and God.

Colossians 3:3

For though once your heart was full of darkness, now it is full of light from the Lord, and your behavior should show it!

Ephesians 5:8

Dear young friends, you belong to God and have already won your fight with those who are against Christ because there is someone in your hearts who is stronger than any evil teacher in this wicked world.

1 John 4:4

So God made man like his Maker. Like God did God make man. Man and maid did he make them.

Genesis 1:27

As God's messenger I give each of you God's warning: Be honest in your estimate of yourselves, measuring your value by how much faith God has given you.

Just as there are many parts to our bodies, so it is with Christ's body.

We are all parts of it, and it takes every one of us to make it complete, for we each have different work to do. So we belong to each other, and each needs all the others.

Romans 12:3-5

And not because we think we can do anything of lasting value by ourselves. Our only power and success comes from God.

2 Corinthians 3:5

Stop fooling yourselves. If you count yourself above average in intelligence, as judged by this world's standards, you had better put this all aside and be a fool rather than let it hold you back from the true wisdom from above.

1 Corinthians 3:18

And so, dear brothers, I plead with you to give your bodies to God. Let them be a living sacrifice, holy — the kind he can accept. When you think of what he has done for you, is this too much to ask?

Don't copy the behavior and customs of this world, but be a new and different person with a fresh newness in all you do and think. Then you will learn from your own experience how his ways will really satisfy you.

Romans 12:1,2

How To Overcome Grief

I heard a loud shout from the throne saying, "Look, the home of God is now among men, and he will live with them and they will be his people; yes, God himself will be among them.

He will wipe away all tears from their eyes, and there shall be no more death, nor sorrow, nor crying, nor pain. All of that has gone forever.''

Revelation 21:3,4

These, the ransomed of the Lord, will go home along that road to Zion, singing the songs of everlasting joy. For them all sorrow and all sighing will be gone forever; only joy and gladness will be there.

Isaiah 35:10

The eternal God is your Refuge, And underneath are the everlasting arms. He thrusts out your enemies before you; It is he who cries, ''Destroy them!''

Deuteronomy 33:27

But no! I would speak in such a way that it would help you. I would try to take away your grief.

Job 16:5

Even when walking through the dark valley of death I will not be afraid, for you are close beside me, guarding, guiding all the way.

Psalm 23:4

His anger lasts a moment; his favor lasts for life! Weeping may go on all night, but in the morning there is joy.

Psalm 30:5

He gives families to the lonely, and releases prisoners from jail, singing with joy! But for rebels there is famine and distress.

Psalm 68:6

He heals the brokenhearted, binding up their wounds.

Psalm 147:3

Arise, my people! Let your light shine for all the nations to see! For the glory of the Lord is streaming from you.

Darkness as black as night shall cover all the peoples of the earth, but the glory of the Lord will shine from you.

All nations will come to your light; mighty kings will come to see the glory of the Lord upon you.

Isaiah 60:1-3

But to the poor, O Lord, you are a refuge from the storm, a shadow from the heat, a shelter from merciless men who are like a driving rain that melts down an earthen wall.

Isaiah 25:4

"Comfort, yes, comfort my people," says your God.

Isaiah 40:1

He gives power to the tired and worn out, and strength to the weak.

Isaiah 40:29

When you go through deep waters and great trouble, I will be with you. When you go through rivers of difficulty, you will not drown! When you walk through the fire of oppression, you will not be burned up — the flames will not consume you.

Isaiah 43:2

And the Lord will bless Israel again, and make her deserts blossom; her barren wilderness will become as beautiful as the Garden of Eden. Joy and gladness will be found there, thanksgiving and lovely songs.

Isaiah 51:3

The young girls will dance for joy, and men folk — old and young — will take their part in all the fun; for I will turn their mourning into joy, and I will comfort them and make them rejoice, for their captivity with all its sorrows will be behind them.

Jeremiah 31:13

For I have given rest to the weary and joy to all the sorrowing.

Jeremiah 31:25

Those who mourn are fortunate! for they shall be comforted.

Matthew 5:4

Come to me and I will give you rest — all of you who work so hard beneath a heavy yoke.

Matthew 11:28

When the Lord saw her, his heart overflowed with sympathy. "Don't cry!" he said.

Luke 7:13

Let not your heart be troubled. You are trusting God, now trust in me.

John 14:1

If you love me, obey me; and I will ask the Father and he will give you another Comforter, and he will never leave you.

John 14:16

No, I will not abandon you or leave you as orphans in the storm — I will come to you.

John 14:18

I am leaving you with a gift — peace of mind and heart! And the peace I give isn't fragile like the peace the world gives. So don't be troubled or afraid.

John 14:27

You have sorrow now, but I will see you again and then you will rejoice; and no one can rob you of that joy.

John 16:22

I have told you all this so that you will have peace of heart and mind. Here on earth you will have many trials and sorrows; but cheer up, for I have overcome the world.

John 16:33

For I am convinced that nothing can ever separate us from his love. Death can't, and life can't. The angels won't, and all the powers of hell itself cannot keep God's love away. Our fears for today, our worries about tomorrow, or where we are — high above the sky, or in the deepest ocean — nothing will ever be able to separate us from the love of God demonstrated by our Lord Jesus Christ when he died for us.

Romans 8:38,39

Are we beginning to be like those false teachers of yours who must tell you all about themselves and bring long letters of recommendation with them? I think you hardly need someone's letter to tell you about us, do you? And we don't need a recommendation from you, either!

The only letter I need is you yourselves! By looking at the good change in your hearts, everyone can see that we have done a good work among you.

They can see that you are a letter from Christ, written by us. It is not a letter written with pen and ink, but by the Spirit of the living God; not one carved on stone, but in human hearts.

We dare to say these good things about ourselves only because of our great trust in God through Christ, that he will help us to be true to what we say, and not because we think we can do anything of lasting value by ourselves. Our only power and success comes from God.

2 Corinthians 3:1-5

Each time he said, "No. But I am with you; that is all you need. My power shows up best in weak people." Now I am glad to boast about how weak I am; I am glad to be a living demonstration of Christ's power, instead of showing off my own power and abilities.

2 Corinthians 12:9

And now, dear brothers, I want you to know what happens to a Christian when he dies so that when it happens, you will not be full of sorrow, as those are who have no hope.

For since we believe that Jesus died and then came back to life again, we can also believe that when Jesus returns, God will bring back with him all the Christians who have died.

I can tell you this directly from the Lord: that we who are still living when the Lord returns will not rise to meet him ahead of those who are in their graves.

For the Lord himself will come down from heaven with a mighty shout and with the soul-stirring cry of the archangel and the great trumpet-call of God. And the believers who are dead will be the first to rise to meet the Lord.

Then we who are still alive and remain on the earth will be caught up with them in the clouds to meet the Lord in the air and remain with him forever.

So comfort and encourage each other with this news.

1 Thessalonians 4:13-18

This High Priest of ours understands our weaknesses, since he had the same temptations we do, though he never once gave way to them and sinned.
So let us come boldly to the very throne of God and stay there to receive his mercy and to find grace to help us in our times of need.

Hebrews 4:15,16

His loved ones are very precious to him, and he does not lightly let them die.

Psalm 116:15

The godly have a refuge when they die, but the wicked are crushed by their sins.

Proverbs 14:32

Living or dying we follow the Lord. Either way we are his.

Romans 14:8

For to me, living means opportunities for Christ, and dying — well, that's better yet!
Philippians 1:21

This tremendous choir — 144,000 strong — sang a wonderful new song in front of the throne of God and before the four Living Beings and the twenty-four Elders; and no one could sing this song except those 144,000 who had been redeemed from the earth.

Revelation 14:3

Don't be afraid! Though I am the First and Last, the Living One who died, who is now alive forevermore, who has the keys of hell and death — don't be afraid!

Revelation 1:18

Don't be so surprised! Indeed the time is coming when all the dead in their graves shall hear the voice of God's Son, and shall rise again — those who have done good, to eternal life; and those who have continued in evil, to judgment.

John 5:28,29

For Christ will be King until he has defeated all his enemies, including the last enemy — death. This too must be defeated and ended.

1 Corinthians 15:25,26

I weep with grief; my heart is heavy with sorrow; encourage and cheer me with your words.

Psalm 119:28

How To Overcome Complacency

Where there is ignorance of God, crime runs wild; but what a wonderful thing it is for a nation to know and keep his laws.

Proverbs 29:18

I will climb my watch tower now and wait to see what answer God will give to my complaint.

And the Lord said to me, "Write my answer on a billboard, large and clear, so that anyone can read it at a glance and rush to tell the others.

But these things I plan won't happen right away. Slowly, steadily, surely, the time approaches when the vision will be fulfilled. If it seems slow, do not despair, for these things will surely come to pass. Just be patient! They will not be overdue a single day!

Habakkuk 2:1-3

But these teachers have missed this whole idea and spend their time arguing and talking foolishness.

They want to become famous as teachers of the laws of Moses when they haven't the slightest idea what those laws really show us.

1 Timothy 1:6,7

But the Lord Jesus Christ has showed me that my days here on earth are numbered, and I am soon to die.

2 Peter 1:13

Never be lazy in your work, but serve the Lord enthusiastically.

Romans 12:11

Dearest friends, when I was there with you, you were always so careful to follow my instructions. And now that I am away you must be even more careful to do the good things that result from being saved, obeying God with deep reverence, shrinking back from all that might displease him.

For God is at work within you, helping you want to obey him, and then helping you do what he wants.

In everything you do, stay away from complaining and arguing.

Philippians 2:12-14

That is why God says in the Scriptures, "Awake, O sleeper, and rise up from the dead; and Christ shall give you light."

Ephesians 5:14

Then, knowing what lies ahead for you, you won't become bored with being a Christian nor become spiritually dull and indifferent, but you will be anxious to follow the example of those who receive all that God has promised them because of their strong faith and patience.

Hebrews 6:12

Another reason for right living is this: you know how late it is; time is running out. Wake up, for the coming of the Lord is nearer now than when we first believed.

Romans 13:11

Watch out! Don't let my sudden coming catch you unawares; don't let me find you living in careless ease, carousing and drinking, and occupied with the problems of this life, like all the rest of the world.

Luke 21:34,35

But anyone who won't care for his own relatives when they need help, especially those living in his own family, has no right to say he is a Christian. Such a person is worse than the heathen.

1 Timothy 5:8

I walked by the field of a certain lazy fellow and saw that it was overgrown with thorns; it was covered with weeds, and its walls were broken down.

Then, as I looked, I learned this lesson: "A little extra sleep, A little more slumber, A little folding of the hands to rest" means that poverty will break in upon you suddenly like a robber and violently like a bandit.

Proverbs 24:30-34

Laziness lets the roof leak, and soon the rafters begin to rot.

Ecclesiastes 10:18

Work hard and become a leader; be lazy and never succeed.

Proverbs 12:24

A lazy man won't even dress the game he gets while hunting, but the diligent man makes good use of everything he finds.

The path of the godly leads to life. So why fear death?

Proverbs 12:27,28

Wealth from gambling quickly disappears; wealth from hard work grows.

Proverbs 13:11

If you love sleep, you will end in poverty. Stay awake, work hard, and there will be plenty to eat!

Proverbs 20:13

How To Overcome Temptation

Don't bring us into temptation, but deliver us from the Evil One. Amen.

Matthew 6:13

So be careful. If you are thinking, ''Oh, I would never behave like that'' — let this be a warning to you. For you too may fall into sin.

But remember this — the wrong desires that come into your life aren't anything new and different. Many others have faced exactly the same problems before you. And no temptation is irresistible. You can trust God to keep the temptation from becoming so strong that you can't stand up against it, for he has promised this and will do what he says. He will show you how to escape temptation's power so that you can bear up patiently against it.

1 Corinthians 10:12,13

Happy is the man who doesn't give in and do wrong when he is tempted, for afterwards he will get as his reward the crown of life that God has promised those who love him.

And remember, when someone wants to do wrong it is never God who is tempting him, for God never wants to do wrong and never tempts anyone else to do it.

Temptation is the pull of man's own evil thoughts and wishes.

These evil thoughts lead to evil actions and afterwards to the death penalty from God.

So don't be misled, dear brothers.

But whatever is good and perfect comes to us from God, the Creator of all light, and he shines forever without change or shadow.

James 1:12-17

So also the Lord can rescue you and me from the temptations that surround us, and continue to punish the ungodly until the day of final judgment comes.

He is especially hard on those who follow their own evil, lustful thoughts, and those who are proud and willful, daring even to scoff at the Glorious Ones without so much as trembling.

2 Peter 2:9,10

No woman can escape their sinful stare, and of adultery they never have enough. They make a game of luring unstable women. They train themselves to be greedy; and are doomed and cursed.

2 Peter 2:14

So be prepared, for you don't know what day your Lord is coming.

Just as a man can prevent trouble from thieves by keeping watch for them, so you can avoid trouble by always being ready for my unannounced return.

Matthew 24:42-44

Watch with me and pray lest the Tempter overpower you. For though the spirit is willing enough, the body is weak.

Mark 14:38

"And though all heaven and earth shall pass away, yet my words remain forever true.

Watch out! Don't let my sudden coming catch you unawares; don't let me find you living in careless ease, carousing and drinking, and occupied with the problems of this life, like all the rest of the world.

Keep a constant watch. And pray that if possible you may arrive in my presence without having to experience these horrors."

Every day Jesus went to the Temple to teach, and the crowds began gathering early in the morning to hear him. And each evening he returned to spend the night on the Mount of Olives.

Luke 21:33-36

Dear brothers, is your life full of difficulties and temptations? Then be happy, for when the way is rough, your patience has a chance to grow.

James 1:2,3

Happy is the man who doesn't give in and do wrong when he is tempted, for afterwards he will get as his reward the crown of life that God has promised those who love him.

James 1:12

So be truly glad! There is wonderful joy ahead, even though the going is rough for a while down here.

These trials are only to test your faith, to see whether or not it is strong and pure. It is being tested as fire tests gold and purifies it — and your faith is far more precious to God than mere gold; so if your faith remains strong after being tried in the test tube of fiery trials, it will bring you much praise and glory and honor on the day of his return.

1 Peter 1:6,7

For since he himself has now been through suffering and temptation, he knows what it is like when we suffer and are tempted, and he is wonderfully able to help us.

Hebrews 2:18

Dear friends, don't be bewildered or surprised when you go through the fiery trials ahead, for this is no strange, unusual thing that is going to happen to you.

1 Peter 4:12

Don't let evil get the upper hand but conquer evil by doing good.

Romans 12:21

For when you are angry you give a mighty foothold to the devil.

Ephesians 4:27

If you want to keep from becoming fainthearted and weary, think about his patience as sinful men did such terrible things to him.

After all, you have never yet struggled against sin and temptation until you sweat great drops of blood.

Hebrews 12:3,4

I am warning you ahead of time, dear brothers, so that you can watch out and not be carried away by the mistakes of these wicked men, lest you yourselves become mixed up too.

2 Peter 3:17

Dear young friends, you belong to God and have already won your fight with those who are against Christ, because there is someone in your hearts who is stronger than any evil teacher in this wicked world.

1 John 4:4

How To Overcome the Occult

Don't be afraid of those who can kill only your bodies — but can't touch your souls! Fear only God who can destroy both soul and body in hell.

Matthew 10:28

Dear young friends, you belong to God and have already won your fight with those who are against Christ, because there is someone in your hearts who is stronger than any evil teacher in this wicked world.

1 John 4:4

For every child of God can obey him, defeating sin and evil pleasure by trusting Christ to help him.

1 John 5:4

Dear children, this world's last hour has come. You have heard about the Antichrist who is coming — the one who is against Christ — and already many such persons have appeared. This makes us all the more certain that the end of the world is near.

These "against-Christ" people used to be members of our churches, but they never really belonged with us or else they would have stayed. When they left us it proved that they were not of us at all.

1 John 2:18,19

Oh, dear children, don't let anyone deceive you about this: if you are constantly doing what is good, it is because you are good, even as he is.

But if you keep on sinning, it shows that you belong to Satan, who since he first began to sin has kept steadily at it. But the Son of God came to destroy these works of the devil.

The person who has been born into God's family does not make a practice of sinning, because now God's life is in him; so he can't keep on sinning, for this new life has been born into him and controls him — he has been born again.

So now we can tell who is a child of God and who belongs to Satan. Whoever is living a life of sin and doesn't love his brother shows that he is not in God's family.

1 John 3:7-10

In this way God took away Satan's power to accuse you of sin, and God openly displayed to the whole world Christ's triumph at the cross where your sins were all taken away.

Colossians 2:15

Yet it was because of this that God raised him up to the heights of heaven and gave him a name which is above every other name, that at the name of Jesus every knee shall bow in heaven and on earth and under the earth, and every tongue shall confess that Jesus Christ is Lord, to the glory of God the Father.

Philippians 2:9-11

That raised Christ from the dead and seated him in the place of honor at God's right hand in heaven, far, far above any other king or ruler or dictator or leader. Yes, his honor is far more glorious than that of anyone else either in this world or in the world to come.

And God has put all things under his feet and made him the supreme Head of the Church.

Ephesians 1:20-22

Jesus called his twelve disciples to him and gave them authority to cast out evil spirits and to heal every kind of sickness and disease.

Matthew 10:1

[A Psalm of David when he fled from his son Absalom].

O Lord, so many are against me. So many seek to harm me. I have so many enemies.

So many say that God will never help me.

But Lord, you are my shield, my glory, and my only hope. You alone can lift my head, now bowed in shame.

I cried out to the Lord, and he heard me from his Temple in Jerusalem.

Then I lay down and slept in peace and woke up safely, for the Lord was watching over me.

And now, although ten thousand enemies surround me on every side, I am not afraid.

I will cry to him, "Arise, O Lord! Save me, O my God!" And he will slap them in the face, insulting them and breaking off their teeth.

For salvation comes from God. What joys he gives to all his people.

Psalm 3:1-8

Put your trust in the Lord, and offer him pleasing sacrifices.

Psalm 4:5

I am Jehovah your God! You must not eat meat with undrained blood nor use fortune telling or witchcraft.

Leviticus 19:26

Do not defile yourselves by consulting mediums and wizards, for I am Jehovah your God.

Leviticus 19:31

So why are you trying to find out the future by consulting witches and mediums? Don't listen to their whisperings and mutterings. Can the living find out the future from the dead? Why not ask your God?

Isaiah 8:19

How To Overcome Suicide

They defeated him by the blood of the Lamb, and by their testimony; for they did not love their lives but laid them down for him.

Revelation 12:11

Dear friends, don't be bewildered or surprised when you go through the fiery trials ahead, for this is no strange, unusual thing that is going to happen to you.

1 Peter 4:12

The thief's purpose is to steal, kill and destroy. My purpose is to give life in all its fullness.

John 10:10

Let him have all your worries and cares, for he is always thinking about you and watching everything that concerns you.

Be careful — watch out for attacks from Satan, your great enemy. He prowls around like a hungry, roaring lion, looking for some victim to tear apart.

Stand firm when he attacks. Trust the Lord; and remember that other Christians all around the world are going through these sufferings too.

1 Peter 5:7-9

So give yourselves humbly to God. Resist the devil and he will flee from you.

And when you draw close to God, God will draw close to you. Wash your hands, you sinners, and let your hearts be filled with God alone to make them pure and true to him.

James 4:7,8

How we thank God for all of this! It is he who makes us victorious through Jesus Christ our Lord!

1 Corinthians 15:57

But thanks be to God! For through what Christ has done, he has triumphed over us so that now wherever we go he uses us to tell others about the Lord and to spread the Gospel like a sweet perfume.

2 Corinthians 2:14

"For I know the plans I have for you," says the Lord. "They are plans for good and not for evil, to give you a future and a hope."

Jeremiah 29:11

The steps of good men are directed by the Lord. He delights in each step they take.

If they fall it isn't fatal, for the Lord holds them with his hand.

Psalm 37:23,24

I, yes, I alone am he who blots away your sins for my own sake and will never think of them again.

Oh, remind me of this promise of forgiveness, for we must talk about your sins. Plead your case for my forgiving you.

Isaiah 43:25,26

Not one sparrow (What do they cost? Two for a penny?) can fall to the ground without your Father knowing it.

And the very hairs of your head are all numbered.

So don't worry! You are more valuable to him than many sparrows.

Matthew 10:29-31

Arise, my people! Let your light shine for all the nations to see! For the glory of the Lord is streaming from you.

Darkness as black as night shall cover all the peoples of the earth, but the glory of the Lord will shine from you.

Isaiah 60:1,2

And I am sure that God who began the good work within you will keep right on helping you grow in his grace until his task within you is finally finished on that day when Jesus Christ returns.

Philippians 1:6

For his mercy toward those who fear and honor him is as great as the height of the heavens above the earth.

He has removed our sins as far away from us as the east is from the west.

He is like a father to us, tender and sympathetic to those who reverence him.

For he knows we are but dust.

Psalm 103:11-14

I have told you all this so that you will have peace of heart and mind. Here on earth you will have many trials and sorrows; but cheer up, for I have overcome the world.

John 16:33

Now we rejoice in our wonderful new relationship with God — all because of what our Lord Jesus Christ has done in dying for our sins — making us friends of God.

When Adam sinned, sin entered the entire human race. His sin spread death throughout all the world, so everything began to grow old and die, for all sinned.

Romans 5:11,12

Last of all I want to remind you that your strength must come from the Lord's mighty power within you.

Put on all of God's armor so that you will be able to stand safe against all strategies and tricks of Satan.

Ephesians 6:10,11

So cheer up! Take courage if you are depending on the Lord.

Psalm 31:24

Since I know it is all for Christ's good, I am quite happy about "the thorn," and about insults and hardships, persecutions and difficulties; for when I am weak, then I am strong — the less I have, the more I depend on him.

2 Corinthians 12:10

My soul claims the Lord as my inheritance; therefore I will hope in him.

Lamentations 3:24

I am leaving you with a gift — peace of mind and heart! And the peace I give isn't fragile like the peace the world gives. So don't be troubled or afraid.

John 14:27

So I pray for you Gentiles that God who gives you hope will keep you happy and full of peace as you believe in him. I pray that God will help you overflow with hope in him through the Holy Spirit's power within you.

Romans 15:13

Don't worry about anything; instead, pray about everything; tell God your needs and don't forget to thank him for his answers.

Philippians 4:6

For I am waiting for you, O Lord my God. Come and protect me.
Put an end to their arrogance, these who gloat when I am cast down!

Psalm 38:15,16

How To Overcome Pride

Pride goes before destruction and haughtiness before a fall.

Proverbs 16:18

The Lord loathes all cheating and dishonesty.
Proverbs 20:23

The pastor must not be a new Christian, because he might be proud of being chosen so soon, and pride comes before a fall. (Satan's downfall is an example.)

1 Timothy 3:6

Anyone who says he is a Christian should live as Christ did.

1 John 2:6

But if you don't follow me, if you refuse the laws I have given you and worship idols.

2 Chronicles 7:19

Because you are sorry and have humbled yourself before God when you heard my words against this city and its people, and have ripped your clothing in despair and wept before me — I have heard you, says the Lord.

2 Chronicles 34:27

It is harder to win back the friendship of an offended brother than to capture a fortified city. His anger shuts you out like iron bars.

Proverbs 18:19

Therefore anyone who humbles himself as this little child is the greatest in the Kingdom of Heaven.

Matthew 18:4

But those who think themselves great shall be disappointed and humbled; and those who humble themselves shall be exalted.

Matthew 23:12

He replied, "If you only knew what a wonderful gift God has for you, and who I am, you would ask me for some living water!"

John 4:10

You younger men, follow the leadership of those who are older. And all of you serve each other with humble spirits, for God gives special blessings to those who are humble, but sets himself against those who are proud.

If you will humble yourselves under the mighty hand of God, in his good time he will lift you up.

1 Peter 5:5,6

Then when you realize your worthlessness before the Lord, he will lift you up, encourage and help you.

James 4:10

Pride ends in a fall, while humility brings honor.

Proverbs 29:23

How To Overcome Abuse

We live within the shadow of the Almighty, sheltered by the God who is above all gods.

This I declare, that he alone is my refuge, my place of safety; he is my God, and I am trusting him.

For he rescues you from every trap and protects you from the fatal plague.

He will shield you with his wings! They will shelter you. His faithful promises are your armor.

Now you don't need to be afraid of the dark any more, nor fear the dangers of the day; nor dread the plagues of darkness, nor disasters in the morning.

Though a thousand fall at my side, though ten thousand are dying around me, the evil will not touch me.

I will see how the wicked are punished but I will not share it.

For Jehovah is my refuge! I choose the God above all gods to shelter me. How then can evil overtake me or any plague come near? For he orders his angels to protect you wherever you go.

They will steady you with their hands to keep you from stumbling against the rocks on the trail.

You can safely meet a lion or step on poisonous snakes, yes, even trample them beneath your feet!

For the Lord says, "Because he loves me, I will rescue him; I will make him great because he trusts in my name.

When he calls on me I will answer; I will be with him in trouble, and rescue him and honor him.

I will satisfy him with a full life and give him my salvation."

Psalm 91:1-16

Have two goals: wisdom — that is, knowing and doing right — and common sense. Don't let them slip away, for they fill you with living energy and are a feather in your cap.

They keep you safe from defeat and disaster and from stumbling off the trail.

With them on guard you can sleep without fear; you need not be afraid of disaster or the plots of wicked men, for the Lord is with you; he protects you.

Don't withhold repayment of your debts. Don't say "some other time," if you can pay now. Don't plot against your neighbor; he is trusting you.

Proverbs 3:21-26

Now I say that each believer should confess his sins to God when he is aware of them, while there is time to be forgiven. Judgment will not touch him if he does.

You are my hiding place from every storm of life; you even keep me from getting into trouble! You surround me with songs of victory.

Psalm 32:6,7

But when I am afraid, I will put my confidence in you. Yes, I will trust the promises of God. And since I am trusting him, what can mere man do to me?

Psalm 56:3,4

Yes, Lord, help us against our enemies, for man's help is useless.

With God's help we shall do mighty things, for he will trample down our foes.

Psalm 60:11,12

If someone mistreats you because you are a Christian, don't curse him; pray that God will bless him.

Romans 12:14

Never pay back evil for evil. Do things in such a way that everyone can see you are honest clear through.

Romans 12:17

Dear friends, never avenge yourselves. Leave that to God, for he has said that he will repay those who deserve it. [Don't take the law into your own hands.]

Romans 12:19

Don't let evil get the upper hand, but conquer evil by doing good.

Romans 12:21

Stay away from the love of money; be satisfied with what you have. For God has said, "I will never, never fail you nor forsake you."

That is why we can say without any doubt or fear, "The Lord is my Helper and I am not afraid of anything that mere man can do to me."

Hebrews 13:5,6

Those who trust in the Lord are steady as Mount Zion, unmoved by any circumstance.

Psalm 125:1

Fear not, for I am with you. Do not be dismayed. I am your God. I will strengthen you; I will help you; I will uphold you with my victorious right hand.

Isaiah 41:10

Don't you yet understand? Don't you know by now that the everlasting God, the Creator of the farthest parts of the earth, never grows faint or weary? No one can fathom the depths of his understanding.

He gives power to the tired and worn out, and strength to the weak.

Even the youths shall be exhausted, and the young men will all give up.

But they that wait upon the Lord shall renew their strength. They shall mount up with wings like eagles; they shall run and not be weary; they shall walk and not faint.

Isaiah 40:28-31

I will instruct you (says the Lord) and guide you along the best pathway for your life; I will advise you and watch your progress.

Psalm 32:8

Then, when that happens, we are able to hold our heads high no matter what happens and know that all is well, for we know how dearly God loves us, and we feel this warm love everywhere within us because God has given us the Holy Spirit to fill our hearts with his love.

Romans 5:5

But God showed his great love for us by sending Christ to die for us while we were still sinners.

Romans 5:8

Who then can ever keep Christ's love from us? When we have trouble or calamity, when we are hunted down or destroyed, is it because he doesn't love us anymore? And if we are hungry or penniless or in danger or threatened with death, has God deserted us?

No, for the Scriptures tell us that for his sake we must be ready to face death at every moment of the day — we are like sheep awaiting slaughter;

but despite all this, overwhelming victory is ours through Christ who loved us enough to die for us.

For I am convinced that nothing can ever separate us from his love. Death can't, and life can't. The angels won't, and all the powers of hell itself cannot keep God's love away. Our fears for today, our worries about tomorrow, or where we are — high above the sky, or in the deepest ocean — nothing will ever be able to separate us from the love of God demonstrated by our Lord Jesus Christ when he died for us.

Romans 8:35-39

IX. God's Purpose for Your Life

To Witness and To Advance God's Kingdom

You are the world's light — a city on a hill, glowing in the night for all to see.

Don't hide your light! Let it shine for all; let your good deeds glow for all to see, so that they will praise your heavenly Father.

Matthew 5:14-16

For Christ didn't send me to baptize, but to preach the Gospel; and even my preaching sounds poor, for I do not fill my sermons with profound words and high sounding ideas, for fear of diluting the mighty power there is in the simple message of the cross of Christ.

I know very well how foolish it sounds to those who are lost, when they hear that Jesus died to save them. But we who are saved recognize this message as the very power of God.

For God says, "I will destroy all human plans of salvation no matter how wise they seem to be, and ignore the best ideas of men, even the most brilliant of them."

So what about these wise men, these scholars, these brilliant debaters of this world's great affairs? God has made them all look foolish and shown their wisdom to be useless nonsense.

For God in his wisdom saw to it that the world would never find God through human brilliance, and then he stepped in and saved all those who believed his message, which the world calls foolish and silly.

It seems foolish to the Jews because they want a sign from heaven as proof that what is preached is true; and it is foolish to the Gentiles because they believe only what agrees with their philosophy and seems wise to them.

So when we preach about Christ dying to save them, the Jews are offended and the Gentiles say it's all nonsense.

But God has opened the eyes of those called to salvation, both Jews and Gentiles, to see that Christ is the mighty power of God to save them; Christ himself is the center of God's wise plan for their salvation.

This so-called "foolish" plan of God is far wiser than the wisest plan of the wisest man, and God in his weakness — Christ dying on the cross — is far stronger than any man.

Notice among yourselves, dear brothers, that few of you who follow Christ have big names or power or wealth.

Instead, God has deliberately chosen to use ideas the world considers foolish and of little worth in order to shame those people considered by the world as wise and great.

He has chosen a plan despised by the world, counted as nothing at all, and used it to bring own to nothing those the world considers great, so that no one anywhere can ever brag in the presence of God.

1 Corinthians 1:17-29

Dear brothers, even when I first came to you I didn't use lofty words and brilliant ideas to tell you God's message.

For I decided that I would speak only of Jesus Christ and his death on the cross.

I came to you in weakness — timid and trembling.

And my preaching was very plain, not with a lot of oratory and human wisdom, but the Holy Spirit's power was in my words, proving to those who heard them that the message was from God.

I did this because I wanted your faith to stand firmly upon God, not on man's great ideas.

1 Corinthians 2:1-5

But thanks be to God! For through what Christ has done, he has triumphed over us so that now wherever we go he uses us to tell others about the Lord and to spread the Gospel like a sweet perfume.

2 Corinthians 2:14

To those who are not being saved, we seem a fearful smell of death and doom, while to those who know Christ we are a life-giving perfume. But who is adequate for such a task as this?

2 Corinthians 2:16

He has kept this secret for centuries and generations past, but now at last it has pleased him to tell it to those who love him and live for him, and the riches and glory of his plan are for you Gentiles too. And this is the secret: that Christ in your hearts is your only hope of glory.

So everywhere we go we talk about Christ to all who will listen, warning them and teaching them as well as we know how. We want to be able to present each one to God, perfect because of what Christ has done for each of them.

This is my work, and I can do it only because Christ's mighty energy is at work within me.

Colossians 1:26-29

Work hard so God can say to you, "Well done." Be a good workman, one who does not need to be ashamed when God examines your work. Know what his Word says and means.

2 Timothy 2:15

So that no one can speak a word of blame against you. You are to live clean, innocent lives as children of God in a dark world full of people who are crooked and stubborn. Shine out among them like beacon lights.

Philippians 2:15

And then teach these new disciples to obey all the commands I have given you; and be sure of this — that I am with you always, even to the end of the world.

Matthew 28:20

And then he told them, "You are to go into all the world and preach the Good News to everyone, everywhere."

Mark 16:15

Your strong love for each other will prove to the world that you are my disciples.

John 13:35

All these new things are from God who brought us back to himself through what Christ Jesus did. And God has given us the privilege of urging everyone to come into his favor and be reconciled to him.

2 Corinthians 5:18

We are Christ's ambassadors. God is using us to speak to you: we beg you, as though Christ himself were here pleading with you, receive the love he offers you — be reconciled to God.

2 Corinthians 5:20

But you are not like that, for you have been chosen by God himself — you are priests of the King, you are holy and pure, you are God's very own — all this so that you may show to others how God called you out of the darkness into his wonderful light.

1 Peter 2:9

And the Good News about the Kingdom will be preached throughout the whole world, so that all nations will hear it, and then, finally, the end will come.

Matthew 24:14

The Spirit of the Lord God is upon me, because the Lord has anointed me to bring good news to the suffering and afflicted. He has sent me to comfort the brokenhearted, to announce liberty to captives, and to open the eyes of the blind.

Isaiah 61:1

Pray for me, too, and ask God to give me the right words as I boldly tell others about the Lord and as I explain to them that his salvation is for the Gentiles too.

Ephesians 6:19

For I am not ashamed of this Good News about Christ. It is God's powerful method of bringing all who believe it to heaven. This message was preached first to the Jews alone, but now everyone is invited to come to God in this same way.

This Good News tells us that God makes us ready for heaven — makes us right in God's sight — when we put our faith and trust in Christ to save us. This is accomplished from start to finish by faith. As the Scripture says it, "The man who finds life will find it through trusting God."

Romans 1:16,17

You Are Destined To Win

Because of his kindness you have been saved through trusting Christ. And even trusting is not of yourselves; it too is a gift from God.

Salvation is not a reward for the good we have done, so none of us can take any credit for it.

It is God himself who has made us what we are and given us new lives from Christ Jesus; and long ages ago he planned that we should spend these lives in helping others.

Ephesians 2:8-10

Moreover, because of what Christ has done we have become gifts to God that he delights in, for as part of God's sovereign plan we were chosen from the beginning to be his, and all things happen just as he decided long ago.

God's purpose in this was that we should praise God and give glory to him for doing these mighty things for us, who were the first to trust in Christ.
Ephesians 1:11,12

Don't let anyone think little of you because you are young. Be their ideal; let them follow the way you teach and live; be a pattern for them in your love, your faith, and your clean thoughts.

Until I get there, read and explain the Scriptures to the church; preach God's Word.

Be sure to use the abilities God has given you through his prophets when the elders of the church laid their hands upon your head.

Put these abilities to work; throw yourself into your tasks so that everyone may notice your improvement and progress.

Keep a close watch on all you do and think. Stay true to what is right and God will bless you and use you to help others.
1 Timothy 4:12-16

After I have poured out my rains again, I will pour out my Spirit upon all of you! Your sons and daughters will prophesy; your old men will dream dreams, and your young men see visions.

And I will pour out my Spirit even on your slaves, men and women alike.
Joel 2:28,29

No! What you see this morning was predicted centuries ago by the prophet Joel — ''In the last days,'' God said, ''I will pour out my Holy Spirit upon all mankind, and your sons and daughters shall prophesy, and your young men shall see visions, and your old men dream dreams.

Yes, the Holy Spirit shall come upon all my servants, men and women alike, and they shall prophesy."

Acts 2:16-18

I will climb my watchtower now and wait to see what answer God will give to my complaint.

And the Lord said to me, "Write my answer on a billboard, large and clear, so that anyone can read it at a glance and rush to tell the others.

But these things I plan won't happen right away. Slowly, steadily, surely, the time approaches when the vision will be fulfilled. If it seems slow, do not despair, for these things will surely come to pass. Just be patient! They will not be overdue a single day!"

Habakkuk 2:1-3

The time will come when all the earth is filled, as the waters fill the sea, with an awareness of the glory of the Lord.

Habakkuk 2:14

Young men and maidens, old men and children — all praise the Lord together. For he alone is worthy. His glory is far greater than all of earth and heaven.

Psalm 148:12,13

I am saying these things to you older men because you really know Christ, the one who has been alive from the beginning. And you young men, I am talking to you because you have won your battle with Satan. And I am writing to you younger boys and girls because you, too, have learned to know God our Father.

And so I say to you fathers who know the eternal God, and to you young men who are strong with God's Word in your hearts, and have won your struggle against Satan: Stop loving this evil world and all that it offers you, for when you love these things you show that you do not really love God; for all these worldly things, these evil desires — the craze for sex, the ambition to buy everything that appeals to you, and the pride that comes from wealth and importance — these are not from God. They are from this evil world itself.

And this world is fading away, and these evil, forbidden things will go with it, but whoever keeps doing the will of God will live forever.

1 John 2:13-17

When You Are Graduating

I will instruct you (says the Lord) and guide you along the best pathway for your life; I will advise you and watch your progress.

Psalm 32:8

Give your burdens to the Lord. He will carry them. He will not permit the godly to slip or fall.

Psalm 55:22

The Lord will work out his plans for my life — for your loving kindness, Lord, continues forever. Don't abandon me — for you made me.

Psalm 138:8

Commit your work to the Lord, then it will succeed.

Proverbs 16:3

Only a simpleton believes what he is told! A prudent man checks to see where he is going.

Proverbs 14:15

The intelligent man is always open to new ideas. In fact, he looks for them.

Proverbs 18:15

Don't go to war without wise guidance; there is safety in many counselors.

Proverbs 24:6

Everything I prophesied came true, and now I will prophesy again. I will tell you the future before it happens.

Isaiah 42:9

He will bring blind Israel along a path they have not seen before. He will make the darkness bright before them and smooth and straighten out the road ahead. He will not forsake them.

Isaiah 42:16

For I'm going to do a brand new thing. See, I have already begun! Don't you see it? I will make a road through the wilderness of the world for my people to go home, and create rivers for them in the desert!

Isaiah 43:19

When You Are Deciding on a College

I will bless the Lord who counsels me; he gives me wisdom in the night. He tells me what to do.
Psalm 16:7

As your plan unfolds, even the simple can understand it.
Psalm 119:130

For the Lord grants wisdom! His every word is a treasure of knowledge and understanding.
Proverbs 2:6

If you want favor with both God and man, and a reputation for good judgement and common sense, then trust the Lord completely; don't ever trust yourself.

In everything you do, put God first, and he will direct you and crown your efforts with success.
Proverbs 3:4-6

I have never stopped thanking God for you. I pray for you constantly, asking God, the glorious Father of our Lord Jesus Christ, to give you wisdom to see clearly and really understand who Christ is and all that he has done for you.

I pray that your hearts will be flooded with light so that you can see something of the future he has called you to share. I want you to realize that God has been made rich because we who are Christ's have been given to him!
Ephesians 1:16-18

So ever since we first heard about you we have kept on praying and asking God to help you understand what he wants you to do; asking him to make you wise about spiritual things.

Colossians 1:9

If you want to know what God wants you to do, ask him, and he will gladly tell you, for he is always ready to give a bountiful supply of wisdom to all who ask him; he will not resent it.

James 1:5

But the wisdom that comes from heaven is first of all pure and full of quiet gentleness. Then it is peace-loving and courteous. It allows discussion and is willing to yield to others; it is full of mercy and good deeds. It is wholehearted and straightforward and sincere.

James 3:17

When You Are Choosing a Career

Be strong! Be courageous! Do not be afraid of them! For the Lord your God will be with you. He will neither fail you nor forsake you.

Deuteronomy 31:6

O Lord, you are my light! You make my darkness bright.

2 Samuel 22:29

I will instruct you (says the Lord) and guide you along the best pathway for your life; I will advise you and watch your progress.

Psalm 32:8

Teach us to number our days and recognize how few they are; help us to spend them as we should.

Psalm 90:12

Plans go wrong with too few counselors; many counselors bring success.

Proverbs 15:22

Though good advice lies deep within a counselor's heart, the wise man will draw it out.

Proverbs 20:5

Don't refuse to accept criticism; get all the help you can.

Proverbs 23:12

He will bring blind Israel along a path they have not seen before. He will make the darkness bright before them and smooth and straighten out the road ahead. He will not forsake them.

Isaiah 42:16

But don't begin until you count the cost. For who would begin construction of a building without first getting estimates and then checking to see if he has enough money to pay the bills?

Otherwise he might complete only the foundation before running out of funds. And then how everyone would laugh!

"See that fellow there?" they would mock. "He started that building and ran out of money before it was finished!"

Luke 14:28-30

When You Are Afraid of the Future

Constantly remind the people about these laws, and you yourself must think about them every day and every night so that you will be sure to obey all of them. For only then will you succeed.

Joshua 1:8

"Listen to me, all you people of Judah and Jerusalem, and you, O king Jehoshaphat!" he exclaimed. "The Lord says, 'Don't be afraid! Don't be paralyzed by this mighty army! For the battle is not yours, but God's!'"

2 Chronicles 20:15

Commit your work to the Lord, then it will succeed.

Proverbs 16:3

In reply Jesus said to the disciples, "If you only have faith in God — this is the absolute truth — you can say to this Mount of Olives, 'Rise up and fall into the Mediterranean,' and your command will be obeyed. All that's required is that you really believe and have no doubt!

Mark 11:22,23

I am leaving you with a gift — peace of mind and heart! And the peace I give isn't fragile like the peace the world gives. So don't be troubled or afraid.

John 14:27

Don't worry about anything; instead, pray about everything; tell God your needs and don't forget to thank him for his answers.

Philippians 4:6

So let us come boldly to the very throne of God and stay there to receive his mercy and to find grace to help us in our times of need.

Hebrews 4:16

Do not let this happy trust in the Lord die away, no matter what happens. Remember your reward!
Hebrews 10:35

Let him have all your worries and cares, for he is always thinking about you and watching everything that concerns you.
1 Peter 5:7

When You Begin Looking for a Job

Don't be afraid, for the Lord will go before you and will be with you; he will not fail nor forsake you.
Deuteronomy 31:8

Fear of man is a dangerous trap, but to trust in God means safety.
Proverbs 29:25

And if you leave God's paths and go astray, you will hear a Voice behind you say, "No, this is the way; walk here."
Isaiah 30:21

The Lord, your Redeemer, the Holy One of Israel, says, "I am the Lord your God, who punishes you for your own good and leads you along the paths that you should follow."
Isaiah 48:17

But blessed is the man who trusts in the Lord and has made the Lord his hope and confidence.
Jeremiah 17:7

Remember, your Father knows exactly what you need even before you ask him!

Matthew 6:8

Look at the birds! They don't worry about what to eat — they don't need to sow or reap or store up food — for your heavenly Father feeds them. And you are far more valuable to him than they are.

Matthew 6:26

"If I can?" Jesus asked. "Anything is possible if you have faith."

Mark 9:23

God is able to make it up to you by giving you everything you need and more so that there will not only be enough for your own needs but plenty left over to give joyfully to others.

2 Corinthians 9:8

X. Scriptural Prayers

How To Pray for Yourself

I pray for you constantly, asking God, the glorious Father of our Lord Jesus Christ, to give you wisdom to see clearly and really understand who Christ is and all that he has done for you.

I pray that your hearts will be flooded with light so that you can see something of the future he has called you to share. I want you to realize that God has been made rich because we who are Christ's have been given to him!

I pray that you will begin to understand how incredibly great his power is to help those who believe him. It is that same mighty power that raised Christ from the dead and seated him in the place of honor at God's right hand in heaven, far, far above any other king or ruler or dictator or leader. Yes, his honor is far more glorious than that of anyone else either in this world or in the world to come.

And God has put all things under his feet and made him the supreme Head of the Church — which is his body, filled with himself, the Author and Giver of everything everywhere.

Ephesians 1:17-23

When I think of the wisdom and scope of his plan I fall down on my knees and pray to the Father of all the great family of God — some of them already in heaven and some down here on earth — that out of his glorious, unlimited resources he will give you the mighty inner strengthening of his Holy Spirit.

And I pray that Christ will be more and more at home in your hearts, living within you as you trust in him. May your roots go down deep into the soil of God's marvelous love; and may you be able to feel and understand, as all God's children should, how long, how wide, how deep, and how high his love really is; and to experience this love for yourselves, though it is so great that you will never see the end of it or fully know or understand it. And so at last you will be filled up with God himself.

Now glory be to God who by his mighty power at work within us is able to do far more than we would ever dare to ask or even dream of — infinitely beyond our highest prayers, desires, thoughts, or hopes.

May he be given glory forever and ever through endless ages because of his master plan of salvation for the Church through Jesus Christ.
Ephesians 3:14-21

My prayer for you is that you will overflow more and more with love for others, and at the same time keep on growing in spiritual knowledge and insight, for I want you always to see clearly the difference between right and wrong, and to be inwardly clean, no one being able to criticize you from now until our Lord returns.

May you always be doing those good, kind things that show you are a child of God, for this will bring much praise and glory to the Lord.
Philippians 1:9-11

So ever since we first heard about you we have kept on praying and asking God to help you understand what he wants you to do; asking him to make you wise about spiritual things; and asking that the way you live will always please the Lord and honor him, so that you will always be doing good, kind things for others, while all the time you are learning to know God better and better.

We are praying, too, that you will be filled with his mighty, glorious strength so that you can keep going no matter what happens— always full of the joy of the Lord, and always thankful to the Father who has made us fit to share all the wonderful things that belong to those who live in the Kingdom of light.

For he has rescued us out of the darkness and gloom of Satan's kingdom and brought us into the Kingdom of his dear Son, who bought our freedom with his blood and forgave us all our sins.
Colossians 1:9-14

And so we keep on praying for you that our God will make you the kind of children he wants to have — will make you as good as you wish you could be! — rewarding your faith with his power.

Then everyone will be praising the name of the Lord Jesus Christ because of the results they see in you; and your greatest glory will be that you belong to him. The tender mercy of our God and of the Lord Jesus Christ has made all this possible for you.

2 Thessalonians 1:11,12

Timothy, you are like a son to me in the things of the Lord. May God our Father and Jesus Christ our Lord show you his kindness and mercy and give you great peace of heart and mind.

As I said when I left for Macedonia, please stay there in Ephesus and try to stop the men who are teaching such wrong doctrine.

Put an end to their myths and fables, and their idea of being saved by finding favor with an endless chain of angels leading up to God — wild ideas that stir up questions and arguments instead of helping people accept God's plan of faith.

What I am eager for is that all the Christians there will be filled with love that comes from pure hearts, and that their minds will be clean and their faith strong. But these teachers have missed this whole idea and spend their time arguing and talking foolishness. They want to become famous as teachers of the laws of Moses when they haven't the slightest idea what those laws really show us.

1 Timothy 1:2-6

Pray all the time. Ask God for anything in line with the Holy Spirit's wishes. Plead with him, reminding him of your needs, and keep praying earnestly for all Christians everywhere.

Pray for me, too, and ask God to give me the right words as I boldly tell others about the Lord and as I explain to them that his salvation is for the Gentiles too.

I am in chains now for preaching this message from God. But pray that I will keep on speaking out boldly for him even here in prison, as I should.
Ephesians 6:18-20

The Priority of God's Word in Your Life

Constantly remind the people about these laws, and you yourself must think about them every day and every night so that you will be sure to obey all of them. For only then will you succeed.
Joshua 1:8

The whole Bible was given to us by inspiration from God and is useful to teach us what is true and to make us realize what is wrong in our lives; it straightens us out and helps us do what is right.
2 Timothy 3:16

Heaven and earth shall disappear, but my words stand sure forever.
Mark 13:31

But Jesus told him, "No! For the Scriptures tell us that bread won't feed men's souls: obedience to every word of God is what we need."
Matthew 4:4

For whatever God says to us is full of living power: it is sharper than the sharpest dagger, cutting swift and deep into our innermost thoughts and desires with all their parts, exposing us for what we really are.

Hebrews 4:12

For no prophecy recorded in Scripture was ever thought up by the prophet himself. It was the Holy Spirit within these godly men who gave them true messages from God.

2 Peter 1:21

But they delight in doing everything God wants them to, and day and night are always meditating on his laws and thinking about ways to follow him more closely.

Psalm 1:2

Your words are a flashlight to light the path ahead of me, and keep me from stumbling.

Psalm 119:105

I have sent him on this special trip just to see how you are, and to comfort and encourage you.

Colossians 4:8

He spoke, and they were healed — snatched from the door of death.

Psalm 107:20

Now that you realize how kind the Lord has been to you, put away all evil, deception, envy, and fraud. Long to grow up into the fullness of your salvation; cry for this as a baby cries for his milk.

1 Peter 2:2

And remember, it is a message to obey, not just to listen to. So don't fool yourselves.

James 1:22

Jesus said to them, "You are truly my disciples if you live as I tell you to, and you will know the truth, and the truth will set you free."

John 8:31,32

Yet faith comes from listening to this Good News — the Good News about Christ.

Romans 10:17

But the Word of the Lord will last forever. And his message is the Good News that was preached to you.

1 Peter 1:25

Remember his covenant forever — The words he commanded to a thousand generations.

1 Chronicles 16:15

But when I am afraid, I will put my confidence in you. Yes, I will trust the promises of God. And since I am trusting him, what can mere man do to me?

Psalm 56:3,4

These things that were written in the Scriptures so long ago are to teach us patience and to encourage, us so that we will look forward expectantly to the time when God will conquer sin and death.

Romans 15:4

The Priority of Prayer in Your Life

Then if my people will humble themselves and pray, and search for me, and turn from their wicked ways, I will hear them from heaven and forgive their sins and heal their land.

2 Chronicles 7:14

My heart has heard you say, "Come and talk with me, O my people." And my heart responds, "Lord, I am coming."

Psalm 27:8

Ask, and you will be given what you ask for. Seek, and you will find. Knock, and the door will be opened.

For everyone who asks, receives. Anyone who seeks, finds. If only you will knock, the door will open.

Matthew 7:7,8

In reply Jesus said to the disciples, "If you only have faith in God — this is the absolute truth — you can say to this Mount of Olives, 'Rise up and fall into the Mediterranean,' and your command will be obeyed. All that's required is that you really believe and have no doubt!

Listen to me! You can pray for anything, and if you believe, you have it; it's yours!''

Mark 11:22-24

Don't worry about anything; instead, pray about everything; tell God your needs and don't forget to thank him for his answers.

Philippians 4:6

But if you stay in me and obey my commands, you may ask any request you like, and it will be granted!

John 15:7

You can ask him [the Father] for anything, using my name, and I will do it, for this will bring praise to the Father because of what I, the Son, will do for you.

Yes, ask anything, using my name, and I will do it!

John 14:13,14

At that time you won't need to ask me for anything, for you can go directly to the Father and ask him, and he will give you what you ask for because you use my name.

You haven't tried this before, [but begin now]. Ask, using my name, and you will receive, and your cup of joy will overflow.

John 16:23,24

But you, dear friends, must build up your lives ever more strongly upon the foundation of our holy faith, learning to pray in the power and strength of the Holy Spirit.

Jude 20

And we are sure of this, that he will listen to us whenever we ask him for anything in line with his will.

And if we really know he is listening when we talk to him and make our requests, then we can be sure that he will answer us.

1 John 5:14,15

So let us come boldly to the very throne of God and stay there to receive his mercy and to find grace to help us in our times of need.

Hebrews 4:16

Admit your faults to one another and pray for each other so that you may be healed. The earnest prayer of a righteous man has great power and wonderful results.

James 5:16

For the eyes of the Lord are intently watching all who live good lives, and he gives attention when they cry to him.

Psalm 34:15

Ask me and I will tell you some remarkable secrets about what is going to happen here.

Jeremiah 33:3

I also tell you this — if two of you agree down here on earth concerning anything you ask for, my Father in heaven will do it for you.

Matthew 18:19

You can get anything — anything you ask for in prayer — if you believe.

Matthew 21:22

XI. The Salvation Experience

There are three basic reasons to believe the Bible is the infallible and pure Word of God.

1. **No human would have written a standard this high.** Think of the best person you know. You must admit he would have left certain Scriptures out had he written the Bible. So the Bible projects an inhuman standard and way of life. It has to be God because no man you know would have ever written a standard this high.

2. **There is an aura, a climate, a charisma, a presence the Bible generates which no other book in the world creates.** Lay an encyclopedia on your table at the restaurant — nobody will look at you twice. But when you lay your Bible on the table, they will stare at you, watch you chew your food, and even read your license plate when you get in your car! Why? The Bible creates the presence of God and forces a reaction in the hearts of men.

3. **The nature of man is changed when he reads the Bible.** Men change. *Peace* enters into their spirits. Joy wells up within their lives. Men like what they become when they read this book. Men accept Christ, because this Bible says Jesus Christ is the Son of God and that all have sinned

and the wages of sin bring death; and the only forgiveness that they can find is through Jesus, the Son of God.

Three Basic Reasons for Accepting Christ

1. **You needed forgiveness.** At some point in your life, you will want to be clean. You will hate guilt; you will crave purity. It's a built-in desire toward God, and you will have to address that appetite at some point in your life.

2. **You needed a friend.** You may be sitting there saying, "But, don't I have friends?" Yes, but you have never had a friend like Jesus. Nobody can handle the information about your life as well as He can. He is the most consistent relationship you will ever know. Human friends vacillate in their reaction, depending on your mood or theirs. Jesus Christ never changes His opinion of you. Nobody can tell Him anything which will change His mind about you. You cannot enjoy His world without His companionship.

3. **You needed a future.** All men have a built-in need for immortality, a craving for an eternity. God placed it within us. D.L. Moody once made a statement, "One of these days you are going to hear that I'm dead and gone. When you do, don't

believe a word of it. I'll be more alive then, than at any other time in my life.'' Each of us wonders about eternity. What is death like? What happens when I die? Is there a hell? a heaven? a God? a devil? What happens? Every man wants to be around tomorrow. The only guarantee you will have a future is to have the Eternal One on the inside of you. *He is Jesus Christ, the Son of God.*

The Gospel means Good News, you can change; your sins can be forgiven; your guilt can be dissolved; God loves *You*. He wants to be the difference in your life. ''All have sinned and come short of the glory of God,'' Romans 3:23. ''The wages of sin is death,'' Romans 6:23. You might say, what does that mean? It means that all unconfessed sin will be judged and penalized, but that is not the end of the story. The second part of verse 23 says, ''but the gift of God is eternal life through Jesus Christ our Lord.'' What does that mean? It means that between the wrath and judgment of God upon your sin, Jesus Christ the Son of God stepped in and absorbed your judgment and your penalty for you. God says if you recognize and respect Him and His worth as the Son of God, judgment will be withheld, and you will receive a pardon, forgiveness of all your mistakes.

What do you have to do? "If you believe in your heart that Jesus is the Son of God and that God raised Him from the dead on the third day, and confess with your mouth, confession is made unto salvation, then you will be saved," Romans 10:9,10. What does the word "saved" mean? *Removed from danger!* It simply means if you respect and recognize the worth of Jesus Christ, God will take you out of the danger zone and receive you as a child of the Most High God. What is His gift that you are to receive? His Son. "For God so loved the world that He gave His only begotten Son, that whosoever believeth in Him should not perish but have everlasting life," John 3:16. How do you accept His Son? Accept His mercy. How do you reject your sins? Confess them and turn away from them. "If I confess my sins He is faithful and just to forgive me my sins and to cleanse me from all unrighteousness," 1 John 1:9. That is the Gospel.

Additional copies of
The Teen's Topical Bible
are available from your local bookstore
or by writing:

Honor Books
P. O. Box 55388 • Tulsa, OK 74155

INSPIRATIONAL LEATHER GIFT SERIES

The Mother's Topical Bible

The Father's Topical Bible

The Teen's Topical Bible

The Businessman's Topical Bible

Our Life Together

Dare To Succeed

Image of Excellence

Student's Gold

Available from your local bookstore

WORLD MUSIC

THE BASICS

"*World Music: The Basics* is a one-of-a-kind book . . . that fills a void in this evolving genre, a book that may be used both as a reference and to explore new musical vistas. It is a book that I will consult for years to come" —Branford Marsalis

- A complete introduction to world music styles
- Includes a complete list of key recordings, videos, websites, and books

World Music: The Basics gives a brief introduction to popular musical styles found around the world. Organized in chapters by continent/region, and then A to Z by country, the book features both background information on the cultural and musical history of each area, along with succinct reviews of key recordings. The reader can quickly find out enough about each musical style to appreciate its subtleties, and is also directed to the best available CDs for further listening.

World Music: The Basics is an excellent introduction to the players, the music, and the styles that make world music one of the most exciting new musical genres.

Richard Nidel is a world-music enthusiast who booked leading acts into his New York-based club for many years. A lawyer by day, Nidel has written extensively on world music, as well as his other passion, wine.

You may also be interested in the following Routledge Student Reference titles:

BLUES: THE BASICS

Dick Weissman

FOLK MUSIC: THE BASICS

Ronald Cohen

JAZZ: THE BASICS

Christopher Meeder

OPERA: THE BASICS

Denise Gallo

WORLD MUSIC: THE BASICS

Richard Nidel

WORLD MUSIC
THE BASICS

richard o. nidel

Routledge
Taylor & Francis Group

NEW YORK AND LONDON

Published in 2005 by
Routledge
Taylor & Francis Group
270 Madison Avenue
New York, NY 10016
www.routledge-ny.com

Published in Great Britain by
Routledge
Taylor & Francis Group
2 Park Square
Milton Park, Abingdon
Oxon OX14 4RN
www.routledge.co.uk

10 9 8 7 6 5 4 3 2 1

Library of Congress Cataloging-in-Publication Data

Nidel, Richard.
  World music : the basics / Richard Nidel.
    p. cm.
  Includes bibliographical references and index.
  ISBN 0-415-96800-3 (hb : alk. paper)—ISBN 0-415-96801-1 (pb : alk. paper)
  1. World music—History and criticism. I. Title.
  ML3545.N54 2005
  780'.9–dc22   2004019817

In Memory of Lenore Hill

CONTENTS

FOREWORD

The late Avant Garde tenor saxophonist Albert Ayler was on the mark when he proclaimed some thirty-five years ago that "Music is the healing force in the universe." As we move forward in the new millennium, mankind indeed needs some healing.

I believe that music is an undervalued commodity, one that can be an important force in the quest for greater understanding among cultures around the world. The future of the media will involve the dynamic mixing of cultures as people grow closer through all forms of communication. Music is the one form of communication that is devoid of prejudice, a language without borders that speaks to us all as equals in the most profound way.

Throughout my career I have taken great care to accept musical challenges and expand the scope of my musical horizons and awareness. While my training and love of music is based in America's greatest art form, the one known as jazz, I have always studied and revered other disciplines. I have had the good fortune to be able to practice my art in a wide variety of settings and venues across the globe with many truly remarkable artists who are fluent and erudite in their chosen genres, which has broadened my perspective on life and increased my musical vocabulary exponentially over the years. I have always made it a practice to listen to music of all persuasions, including that which is commercially defined as world music, especially the wonderful music from Brazil, West Africa and the Caribbean.

Several years ago, while touring with the Orpheus Chamber Orchestra I became friendly with Orpheus's wonderful flutist, Susan Palma Nidel, who introduced me to her husband Richard. He is a true music devotee, well versed in the history of jazz and classical music, and is currently focusing on and passionate about world music. Over the past several years, we have discussed his idea for this book, engaged in friendly arguments about our favorite artists and their best recordings and I have wholeheartedly supported him in this most worthy endeavor.

World Music: The Basics is a one-of-a-kind book, one I would have bought, sight unseen, even if I did not know Richard and Susan. It is an important work that fills a void in this evolving genre, a book that may be used both as a reference and to explore new musical vistas. *World Music* is also a well reasoned argument that advocates the power and value of music in the modern world and how music is relevant and vital when considering the issues of the day that confront us all.

World Music: The Basics is a book that I will consult for years to come.

Branford Marsalis, August 2004

ACKNOWLEDGEMENTS

Undying thanks to my wife Susan for her encouragement, patience, love, and support and to my sons Danny, Brett, and Sam for always checking and mocking my musical taste.

The book could not have been written without the inspiration from my friends, colleagues, and New York City based World Musicians including: Howard Alden, Pablo Aslan, Ronnie Bauch, Dunandanie Bhehespat, Richard Bona, Elizabeth Brown, Café, Richard Carlin, Tony Cedras, Vanessa Fallabella, Chris Finckel, Jose Gherardi, Philip Hamilton, Aaron Heick, David Krakauer, Bakhiti Kumalo, Mark Lambert, Branford Marsalis, Hector Martignon, Joan Ma Ramirez Mestre, Paul Meyers, Chauncey Northern, Susan Davis Pereira, Vanderlai Pereira, Kimson Plaut, Neil Portnow, Ethel Raim, Ira Rosenbloom, Sasha at Tower Records, Maciek Scheijbal, Yousef Sheronick, Jon Sholle, Etienne Stadjwiik, Ettore Stratta, Cecilia Tenconi, Michael Tosi, Leo Traversa, Keith Underwood, Murray Wall, Jon Waxman, and Pablo Ziegler.

INTRODUCTION

Despite the growing interest in world music, especially in the United States, there are remarkably few books available that give an overview on the entire subject under one cover. The ten volume *Garland Encyclopedia of World Music* (retail price $2,500) is the leading work in the field, but it is an ethnomusicological treatise, not a popular survey. The incomparable *Rough Guide to World Music* from England is the most recognized popular work, but it is not designed as a quick reference to be carried around.

This *Basics* survey is organized by continent, with each country on a particular continent listed in alphabetical order. We have endeavored to include as many countries as possible (a total of 130), omitting only those where the available music is either wholly derivative of a neighboring country or *de minimis*. Virtually every entry in the survey includes a brief statement about the history of the country, a discussion of the major genres and styles, a list and description of instruments found in that country, and references to the most important artists and innovators.

We have included recommended recordings for each country so that the reader can explore the music in conjunction with the survey. All recommendations are for the most important works of an artist or group. The list of recordings is by no means comprehensive or complete, rather, it is an informed starting point, directing the reader to compact discs we know are representative, significant, and, in our humble opinion, the artist's best.

Our reverence for the music should be apparent to all who read this work. We have endeavored to present a balanced view of the music of the world, highlighting countries, artists, and genres that have made the most significant contributions to world music. We have accordingly allotted more space to certain countries (e.g., India, Brazil, France, Egypt, and Spain, to name a few) without regard to any political or economic importance the country may otherwise possess, but because the music from that country has had a proportionately far-reaching effect on the music of the world.

WHAT IS *WORLD MUSIC*?

Any term that attempts to reduce an art form to a single phrase is of course suspect, but world music works better than most as an accurate, descriptive label. It is easy to generally agree on a few things; namely, that the term refers most often to traditional, folk, or roots music: (a) created and played by indigenous musicians; (b) naturally incorporating other musical forms; and (c) part of virtually every culture and society on the planet. A more succinct definition is that world music includes the many forms of music of various cultures that remain closely informed or guided by indigenous music of the regions of their origin.

In some respects it is easier to state what is not world music. It is widely agreed in the world music press and among the international entities selling music that rock & roll, R&B, soul, jazz, Broadway, classical, heavy metal, new age, fusion, country, alternative rock, blues, disco, hip hop (with some exceptions), techno, karaoke, trip hop, and pure pop are *not* World Music.

Having set forth a definition and listed genres that fall outside the purview of world music, we must assert that world music can *be* popular music. Once any folk music is uprooted from the medium that produced it, once it is transferred to an artistic production and performance (rather than used in its original form), it is automatically altered, adjusting to a new stage, function, and setting. Most of what even the staunchest purists call traditional or folk music really is, in the context of an individual country, popular music.

Ideally, *all* music is world music and, admittedly, there is no way to comprehensively define or even agree on the parameters of the term. Clearly jazz and Western classical music (both vague terms) are the basis of and incorporated into much world music, just as a great deal of world music, as defined here, is an essential element of Western classical and jazz. Nevertheless, our working definition conforms to generally accepted definitions of world music in the trade and serves as a helpful common frame of reference for the *Basics* Survey.

AFRICA

North Africa   East Africa
West and Central Africa   South Africa

NORTH AFRICA

Algeria   Mauritania   Tunisia
Libya   Morocco   Western Sahara

For the purposes of this book, North Africa is defined as including the countries commonly referred to as the Maghreb—Algeria, Morocco, and Tunisia—as well as Libya, and, due to a musical kinship with the region, Mauritania and Western Sahara. Although Egypt is geographically part of Northern Africa, it is the musical epicenter for all Arabs and not conceptually part of the musical culture of North Africa. The largest recording industry for Arab music is in Cairo—the musical *lingua franca* of the Arab world—and we have therefore included Egypt under the Middle East section, which also includes virtually every other Arab country. North African music caters to a more European-based market and historically includes major influences from southern Europe and West Africa.

The oft-used term *"Sub-Saharan Africa,"* a euphemism for Black Africa, has in modern times come to connote an internationally accepted geographic demarcation, a default term conveniently applied in many fields, including world music, to discuss related traditions, musical styles, and genres. In fact, musical forms below the amorphous Saharan line in the sand are mostly unrelated to the music from North Africa. There are notable exceptions, including music of the nomadic Tuareg people who inhabit portions of Mali and Libya. The European and Moorish influence so prevalent in *al Andalous* music (discussed in the Moroccan section) is almost completely absent in black African music but is an integral part of the music of virtually all of North Africa.

THE MOORS, JUDEO-CHRISTIAN CULTURE, AND THE RECONQUISTA

The Moors ruled much of southern Europe for many centuries prior to their expulsion during the Inquisition circa 1492. The ubiquitous musical form *al Andalous* traveled across the Mediterranean to North Africa along with the Moors and the Jewish Ladino culture and has been the most revered musical form in the region for more than 500 years.

Many Moors and Jews from parallel diasporas settled in Morocco, Algeria, and Tunisia, the area commonly referred to as the *Maghreb*. Muslims, Christians, and Jews continued to coexist in relative harmony for many centuries in essentially Muslim-governed countries much as they did in Iberia before the Inquisition. While this harmony was disrupted in the middle of the twentieth century, the tradition carries on in different guises across the Maghreb with each country enhancing the music with its own cultural flavors.

Local North Africans who shared a love of ancient poetry and a reverence for the prestigious role that music held in society assimilated their collective music with the transplanted Europeans. From this mosaic a series of related forms arose including *hawzi, gnawa,* and eventually *rai*. These musical forms borrowed from many sources, including Judeo-Christian liturgy, synthesizing and combining different musical cultures to create a new, cohesive genre of North African music.

ALGERIA

Home to *rai*, classical *al-Andalous*, and *kabyle*, Algeria is the most important voice in North African world music today. Algeria's exposure to Ottoman, Sub-Saharan, and West African culture has been more extensive over the past millennium than its Moroccan, Tunisian, and Libyan neighbors, and its folk and traditional music has evolved accordingly. It is a country of vast musical treasures, but the Algeria of today is paradoxical. It is an epicenter for part of the fundamentalist horror plaguing our planet in the new millennium, with a draconian government whose view of life seems guided by chauvinism and disregard for human rights. Another segment of society, however, craves today's modern culture and is in the vanguard of the world music movement. Despite the political situation that plagues the country, Algerians (most living as expatriates in France and across Europe) continue to produce the richest, most diverse music in all of the Maghreb.

ORAN

Known as the "Little Paris of North Africa" prior to Algeria's independence in 1962, Oran has a rich musical history dating back many centuries. *Al Andalous* has evolved over the centuries into several modern styles, all of which retain their classical, melodic tonal center and tight structural form, richly enhanced by Arabic poetry. The music was furthered enhanced by the Jewish population who lived harmoniously with the Moors both in Spain and North Africa. Today, as in centuries past, *al Andalous* is a subtly structured music, performed by highly trained musicians with lyrics sung mostly by women.

After World War I, Oran served as a cultural center and playground for a multitude of ethnic groups from Europe and the Middle East. During the period between the two World Wars, the cafés and cabarets in Oran became famous for exotic forms of entertainment. The city was divided into French, Jewish, Spanish, and Arab quarters, all with distinct sets of rules and settings. Spanish Civil War fighters and refugees, Muslims from all parts of North Africa, and the ruling French frequented Oran's musical venues, mostly in the Jewish quarter where alcohol could be sold and the rigid Islamic morality and French colonial rule were conveniently not enforced. A diverse mixture of cultures coexisted peacefully in Oran during this period and for a short time after World War II music served as the common denominator and healing force. These exotic haunts produced some of the most soulful music of the day, sounds that have lasting integrity and a modern appeal.

In contrast to the formal, highly structured *al Andalous*, a Bedouin folk music emerged during this same period, a music spawned by an oppressive street life and its characteristically raunchy vernacular. *Bedoui*, a vocal genre that incorporated Egyptian popular music and Cuban rhythms, gained popularity in the bars, bordellos, and hash dens of Oran, much to the consternation of the Islamic rebels who would eventually overthrow their French Colonizers. The music was performed by *Cheikhas*—a term of respect referring to the *Bedoui* singers—women from peasant backgrounds, often abused and cast out by the vain morality of the fundamentalists, the singers became a unique part of the local street culture. They were known for their extraordinary ability to improvise and their scandalous behavior. They performed in the grungiest clubs, singing of the poverty and harshness of their difficult lives. This music was the forerunner of Algeria's most popular musical export, *rai*.

The Cheikhas reign was short-lived. After independence in 1962 Algeria quickly fell into the hands of a ruthless military dictatorship. The new government's intolerant, anti-Semitic policies forced many citizens into exile in Paris, Marseilles, and Western Europe. The diaspora, comprising a great deal of progressive, artistic, and educated members of Algerian society, were forced to perpetuate their culture and distinct musical forms as expatriates in the New World.

THE MUSIC

Rai. The children of the Algerian diaspora have developed the genre now collectively referred to as *rai*, which spiritually, if not musically, derives from the Bedouin folk music of the Cheikhas. *Rai* has a disco-style dance rhythm and a pop sound that combine with provocative lyrics that exhort the listener to party at all costs. It is sung in Arabic (or Tamazight dialect) laced with French, and possesses a street sensibility and message that parallels and rivals

American hip-hop. The essence of *rai* is the direct expression of heartfelt opinion with a high value placed on improvisation. Like hip-hop, ample borrowing and sampling from other musical genres is a regular component of the music, which has become a staple of the international dance floor

Kabylie and the Berbers. The most traditional and arguably greatest musical tradition of Algeria resides within the unique Berber culture. The Berbers (more accurately Tamazghas; "*Berber*" is an Arabic term meaning stranger) are a nation within a nation in Algeria. Their region is known as Kabylia, the music *kabyle*, the culture Amazigh, and the language Tamazight—the poetic soul of Algeria's indigenous people. The Berbers are fiercely independent, far more progressive than their fundamentalist brethren and the rest of Algeria, a mountain-dwelling people whose presence across North Africa predates Arab culture by at least a millennium.

Prior to independence in 1962, the Berbers were staunch supporters of the national movement to overthrow their French oppressors. However, since the revolution the various governments have turned on Algeria's indigenous people. In the late 1960s the military dictators became obsessed with curtailing the very freedoms the Berbers thought they had achieved as supporters of the revolution. Since the 1970s Berber poets, politicians, artists, journalists, and musicians have been blatantly murdered for their views and way of life. Many Berbers are now naturalized French citizens. The Berbers' plight is analogous to that of the Kurds in Iraq and in Turkey; they enjoy virtually no freedom of the press or speech, suffering under harsh laws obsessively enforced against speaking or writing their language, performing their music, and expressing their culture, a policy reminiscent of Fascist Spain's approach to Catalan, Galician, and Basque culture during Franco's rule.

Despite this ongoing persecution, a strong musical culture continues to flourish both in Kabylia and among expatriates in France. Since the 1980s, a soulful, more commercially viable form of *kabyle* has evolved, deriving its initial inspiration from the worldwide civil rights movement of the 1960s and sharing a textual context with the South American *Nueva Cancion* movement of the 1970s. (See *Argentina, Chile, Cuba, and Portugal Sections.*)

Reinette l'Oranaise (1910–1998) is considered the "First Lady" of North African music, renowned for classic interpretations of the *al Andalous* based classical song form, *hawzi*. She gained her fame between the two World Wars singing in the cafes in the Jewish quarter of Oran. Blind from the age of two, Reinette (born Sultana Daoud), was the voice of Moorish North African music in her day, a voice that was bluesy and bittersweet, sexy and seductive. Although Jewish, she was a student of Arab literature, respected by Muslims and Jews throughout the Maghreb and an early proponent of the musical form now known as *rai*. She was forced to flee the anti-Semitic Algerian regime that took over in 1962, settling into obscurity in France. On the heels of the world music revival before her death in 1998, she recorded three CDs accompanying herself masterfully on the oud.

RECOMMENDED CDs

ABDELLI. Berber composer/singer with a Celtic flare. *Among Brothers* (Real World, 2003).

DJURA ABOUDA. Parisian based singer/songwriter. *Songs of Silence* (Luaka Bop, 1998).

AL-DJAZARIA. Traditional string orchestra playing *al Andalous* instrumental music. *Classical Music of Algeria* (Harrnonia Mundi, 1999).

SLIMANE AZEM. Father figure of *kabyle* music, achieved popularity at home and in France just after Wolrd War II. *Le Fabuliste*; *Le Grands Maitres de la Chanson kabyle Vol. 3*, (Club dudisque Arabe, 1979).

HASNA EL BECHARIA. Female Berber vocalist, guitarist, and gimbri player forced to perform only in private for 30 years. *Djazair Johara, Gnawa tradition* (Blue Indigo, 2001).

LILI BONICHE. Legendary singer-guitarist, integral part of the Jewish-Algerian diaspora. *Alger, Alger* (Sachem, 1998) with Maurice el Medioni, produced by Bill Laswell.

CHERIFA. The diva of Berber music in the 1950s and 1960s. *Chants Berbers*, (1964) with colleague *Hanifa*.

DAHMANE EL HARRACHI. Composer and the Algerian Charles Aznavour, el Harrachi was an early advocate for women's rights and a tragic figure who died in a car crash in 1980. *Le Chaabi, Vol. III* (Club du disque Arabe, 1977).

FAUDEL. The current Prince of *rai*, a star in the United States and France, long touted as Cheb Mami and Khaled's successor; he sings *rai* from the Parisian ghetto. *Baida* (Mercury, 1999).

FERHAT. With Idir and Ait Menguelett, Ferhat changed the face of *kabyle* music. He ceased performing in 1989 after numerous arrests for his outspoken lyrics. *Tuyac n ddkir* is a compilation from 1972 to 1992 (Blue Silver, 1994).

IDIR. Idir's *A Vava Inouva/My little father* (Blue Silver, 1973) is widely credited as the first recording of *kabyle* music to gain popularity outside of North Africa; also, *Chaussiers des Lumieres.*

KHALED. King of *rai*, responsible for the worldwide popularity of the genre. *N'ssi N'ssi* (Barclay, 1998) is the best. *Khaled* (Barclay); *1,2,3 Soliel*, live w/Rachid Taha and Faudel (World Village, 2000).

CHEB MAMI. Heir apparent to Khaled. *Meli Meli* (Mondo Melodia, 1996) made him a star. *Saida* (Mondo Melodia, 1994).

SAOUD MASSI. Composer/guitarist/vocalist; *Raoui* (Island, 2001) is a masterful recording of modern *kabyle*, French chanteuse, and American pop. *Deb* (Universal, 2003).

LOUNES MATOUB. The conscience of modern *kabyle* music was murdered in 1998 by the forces of Arabization. *Lettre Ouverte Aux,* (Blue Silver, 1997) was Matoub's last recording; *Se trouver dans l'ombre* is folksier (Disky, 1986); *Kenza* (Blue Silver, 1997) is strident & political; *Ironie du Sort* (Blue Silver, 1996).

MAURICE EL MEDIONI. (b.1928) Clever pianist who draws on jazz, Cuban rhythms, klezmer, and Middle Eastern classical music with a reverence for Art Tatum and Fats Waller. *Café Oran* (Piranha, 1994) with Klezmatics stars David Krakauer and Frank London.

LOUNES AIT MENGUELETT. Dean of living Kabylie artists and a leading poet. *Inasen* (Melodie, 2000); *Inagen* (1999); *Chants & Poesie de Kabylie* is a good Compilation (Blue Silver, 1995); *Aftis, Awel,* from the early 1990s.

REINETTE L' ORANAISE. See Profile. *Memoires* (Blue Silver, 1991*); Tresors de la Musique; Chanson Judeo Arabe; Reinette l'Oranaise* (Blue Silver).

ORCHESTRE NATIONAL DE BARBES. ONB is a pan-cultural, postcolonial ensemble living in Paris. *En concert* (Tinder, 1996) is a breathtaking tour de force, combining *rai, gnawa,* and a Rolling Stones attitude; close to the final word for hip world music.

CHEIKHA REMITTI. The scamp of Oran, café singer, performer, and octogenarian, whose voice can sand wood. *rai Roots* (Buda, 1998).

TAYFA. Celtic Berber group. *Assif* (Sony, 2000).

VARIOUS ARTISTS. *La Kabylie au Coeur,* (2001), is a good place to start. Includes Menguelett, Idir, Lounes Matoub, Takfarinas, ONB, hip-hop group 113 and more.

LIBYA

Qaddafi's repressive regime has stifled music and art in Libya as nowhere else on the planet in the past 30 years. Idi Amin died in Saudi Arabia in 2003, Saddam Hussein is in custody, Pinochet is declawed and dying in Chile, Marcos, Somosa, and Suharto no longer rule and plunder, but the Colonel is alive and well. Only George W. Bush's brain trust could conceive of orchestrating his comeback.

The dearth of music from this ancient and historically important country is but one of the selfish legacies Qadaffi will leave the world. A few artists have made headway in the Arab market playing a type of *chaabi* with Tunisian *malouf* clearly an influence, but Libya has no presence to speak of on the world music scene. Nasser al Mizdawi and Mustafa Taalib are the leading singers. Tuareg group Tinariwen were born in refugee camps in Libya, but are Malian and their remarkable music is included in the Mali section.

MAURITANIA

Taking its name from the Moors who dominated the region centuries ago, Mauritania lies between Morocco and Senegal where the Maghreb meets the Sahara and is musically and culturally related to North Africa. This mostly desert land is inhabited by Berbers and Bedouin Arabs, but women are far freer here than in any Arab country. Class distinctions are precise in Mauritanian society with musicians, called *Iggiws*, in the lowest class by heredity. They are the only members of society permitted to be professional musicians. Traditionally the Iggiws (also Iggi) function at the behest of other classes. Their music extols the bravery of warriors and praises ancestors. Their role is similar to *griots* in Mali and Guinea. Iggiws are also often poets or jesters.

The primary instruments in Mauritania are the *tidinit*, a small 4-stringed lute played by men that is similar to the Mande *ngoni*, and the *ardin*, a small *kora*-type instrument. In southern Mauritania, the population lives with Senegalese Wolofs and the Mbara of Mali.

For a nation clearly out of the mainstream of modern life, Mauritania has produced several significant musicians and singers, including Dimi Mint Abba and her husband Khalifa Ould Eide, who accompanies her on tidinit and guitar.

RECOMMENDED CDs

MALOUMA. Malouma has been outspoken against her government and thus forced to perform and record abroad. *Dunya* (Marabi, 2003) is a moving work, North African blues with traditional sounds and some electric guitar.

DIMI MINT ABBA. Mauritania's leading singer, one of the great female vocalists of the Muslim world. *Moorish Music from Mauritania* (World Circuit, 1992), accompanied by husband Kahlifa Ould Eide on tidinit and guitar, replete with *palmas* and an Iberian Moorish feeling.

MOROCCO

With many ancient, historical cities (Rabat, Fez, Casablanca, Tangier, and Marrakech), a strong tourist trade, and a rich multicultural history and identity, Morocco is the geopolitical center of North Africa. The powers-that-be have recently begun efforts to modernize the government in an attempt to catch up with the global economy. The Parliament, while only partially empowered—Morocco is still a monarchy—has embarked on a campaign to increase female representation and expand human rights. Morocco's unequivocal denouncement of terrorism after 9/11 has opened many Western doors. This was a bold and significant stance for a country that is 98 percent Islamic and where the predominant musical sound heard everywhere is the call to prayer of the muezzin.

Historically, along with Egypt and West Africa, Morocco is one of the three points of a cultural triangle where various ethnic groups have traded in the region throughout the past millennium. Goods and ideas have always flowed through this triangle from Guinea and Timboctou (Mali) to Fez and Cairo and back. Eventually the trade route expanded to parts of southern Europe and its Moorish enclaves. The exchange always included music. For centuries, Morocco has been fertile soil for many diverse cultures including the Berbers, Arabs, and the Moors. As recently as 1940, Jews constituted 20 percent of the population in Morocco.

THE MUSIC

The classic *al Andalous* form, inextricably tied to the Moors and the period of their rule in Iberia, remains an integral part of Moroccan musical life both in the conservatories and throughout the popular and world music scene. Morocco's connection to Cordoba and the rest of southern Spain is essential to understanding the music. Today music is an especially fundamental form of communication in Moroccan society. Due to the high illiteracy rate, much history and folklore exists only in song form and the oral tradition.

Al Andalous. The classical music of the Maghreb was brought from Cordoba, Granada, and Sevilla more than 1,000 years ago—called *gharnata* in Morocco, *malouf* in Tunisia, and *Ala* in Algeria—allegedly by Ziryab, the legendary Iraqi who is also credited as a seminal figure in the development of flamenco. *Al Andalous* from Morocco centers on the *nuba* (also called *nawbat*), the name for a classical suite which originally was composed of 24 parts, one for each hour of the day, reminiscent of North Indian music. In its modern incarnation, only four parts have survived intact, but the form remains rigidly adhered to in performance and composition.

Trance and the Gnawa Brotherhood. Trance music is most closely associated with the gnawas in North Africa. Prevalent in Sufi sects of Islam elsewhere, it is the one form of music encouraged by the Orthodox branch of Islam, who view the trance state as a way to communicate with Allah.

The gnawa are a fraternity of musicians who combine their abilities in healing the sick with performance of music. They are of black African origin with roots in Mali and the Sudan. The founding of the gnawa order is reputed to date back to the time of Bilal, Mohammed's Abyssinian slave who later became his companion. Oral history suggests that Bilal was the first muezzin—the first man to call followers to prayer. Legend has it that he also invented the *qarqabat*, small iron-vessel clappers heard as accompaniment to chant that allegedly have healing powers and are only played by the gnawa. The main therapeutic musical tool of the gnawa is the *hajouj*, a canoe-shaped lute that is played only by esteemed musicians called *maalem*. Gnawa chant is also accompanied by the *tbel*, a bass drum slung across the shoulder and played with two sticks.

Other approved musical associations are permitted to function in Moroccan Islamic society in conjunction with Friday-night ceremonies. This concept is reminiscent of the haute music of Western Europe during the Renaissance and Middle Ages. It can be heard when preapproved groups process to the tombs of saints playing the *ghaita* (a shawm-type, end-blown flute) and *bendir* (frame drum).

Sephardic Music. The current international revival of Sephardic music is strongly connected to Morocco. Israeli artists such as Emil Zrihan and the Orchestre al Andalous have perpetuated the cultural links between Jews and Muslims by collaborating with many North African, Arab, and Spanish musicians in numerous recordings and concerts since the late 1980s.

Chaabi. Morocco, like Egypt, is rife with the pop-folk music craze known as Chaabi. Studio pyrotechnics, dance beats, and modern sounds abound. Najat Aatabou, a Berber woman who now sings in Arabic (not Tamazight) and French, is a leading proponent who enjoys a large following with expatriated Moroccans in Paris. Chaabi is commercial music with a strong allegiance to regional North African roots.

Amina Alaoui is Morocco's most prominent female world-music personality. Born in Fez, Amina began her musical education at the conservatory in Rabat at the age of 6, where she studied classical piano, traditional Arabo-Andalusian music, and Moroccan dance. When she was 10 years old, she published a collection of poems and was already well versed in philosophy and linguistics in Arabic, Spanish, and French.

Alaoui has recently had major impact on the evolution of Middle Eastern classical music, both through a series of recordings as a vocalist with cohort and oud master/arranger Henri Agnel and through her ongoing commitment to modernizing the genre and exposing its beauty to the world. Alaoui has performed with fellow Moroccan artists as well as with world musicians such as Iranian Djamichid Chemirani, Pedro Soler from Spain, Hameed Khan, Greek Vocalist Angelique Ionatas, and Catalan Star Lluis Llach, and she has collaborated with classical orchestras frequently. She is an outspoken champion for democracy in North Africa, as radical a female voice as one could imagine in a region that is slow to acknowledge many human rights. She opposes oppression of women and is an advocate of tolerance and the sharing of the culture of the Maghreb.

RECOMMENDED CDs

NAJAT AATABOU. Feminist with a bold message that rocked Maroc; the Moroccan Madonna. *Shouffi Rhiroua* (1987) was a smash; *The Voice of the Atlas* (Globestyle,1991).

AMINA ALAOUI. *Alcantara,* ("the bridge") (Auvidis, 1998), an acoustic chamber work with arrangements by Henri Agnel and Amina singing in Arabic, Portuguese, French, Spanish, and Hebrew. *Gharnati,* (Auvidis, 1995) a collaboration with a top Arabo-Andalous Orchestra.

SI MOHAMED CHAOUQI. Master of gnawa chant and the gimbri, descendant of the Tuareg from Timbouctu. *Les Gnawa du Maroc, Ouled el Abidi* (Auvidis, 1995) is raw, soulful, and mesmerizing.

CHERIFA. Cherifa is an Amazight singer, not to be confused with the Algerian diva of the same name. *Berbere Blues* (Label Bleu, 1993) is an apt title for this recording.

NASS EL GHIWANE. Gnawa, traditional music. *Chants du Muroc* (Buda, 1995).

HASSAN HAKMOUN. Based in New York City, Hakmoun performs gnawa with Western instruments and a rock persona. *Gift of the Gnawa* (Flying Fish, 1991) with Adam Rudolph, Don Cherry, and Richard Horowitz is world beat.

EDUARDO PANIAGUA. Master of *al Andalous* and leader of numerous historical projects, all played and produced at the highest level. Paniagua is a Spaniard whose musical roots are in North Africa. His recordings are all important for anyone interested in classical al Andalous. *The Alhambra* (Pneuma/AECI, 2000); Jardin de al Andalous (Pneuma, 1998).

SIDI SEDDIKI. Popular singer-songwriter form Rabat. *Shourf* (Globestyle, 1995). Flute and Chaabi.

OMAR METIOUI. *Al Andalous* vocalist and cohort of Eduardo Paniagua *Omar Metiou* (Pneuma, 2000); *Ibn'Arabi* (Pneuma, 2002).

CHIEK SALAH. Classical orchestra leader. *Arabo-Andalusian Music* (Buda, 1998).

ALBERT BOUHADAENA. Renowned, Jewish, al Andalous vocalist.

MUSTAPHA BAQBOU. Renowned gimbri player and vocalist. *Gnawa Trance Music* (Sounds of the World, 1999).

TUNISIA

Dwarfed by its contiguous neighbors and geographically situated closer to Sicily than Egypt, Tunisia has served as a vital crossroads linking the Middle East with North Africa, Sub-Saharan Africa, and Europe.

Prior to 814 BCE and the founding of Carthage by Phoenician settlers, the population of the area now referred to as Tunisia consisted solely of Berber tribes and was an extension of Libyan culture. Today less than 1 percent of all Tunisians speak Berber, though demographically most are descended from them. This initial mingling of cultures established a pattern marking Tunisia as a meeting place of east and west.

Carthage's main rival was Rome, with whom they fought a series of wars for the domination of the Mediterranean, ending with Carthage's destruction, the loss of colonies (parts of the Iberian Peninsula, Sardinia, and Sicily), and the incorporation of the region into the Roman Empire.

The takeover of Carthage by the Arabs and the dominance of Islam began in 670 CE. In the thirteenth century Tunisia became part of a unified empire that linked the Maghreb and Muslim Andalusia. In the twentieth century, French domination (which began in 1881) predominated until WWII. When German forces withdrew from North Africa in 1943, control of Tunisia was handed over to the Free French. Opposition to the French authorities resulted in open violence until 1956, when Tunisia gained independence and was recognized as a constitutional monarchy. A republic was proclaimed with Habib Bourguiba serving as President. Bourguiba is responsible for establishing Tunisia as the most educated, peaceful, and modern country in North Africa, a nation where 75–80 percent of its denizens are truly middle class. In 1995, Tunisia became the first country south of the Mediterranean to sign a free-trade agreement with the European Union. Tunisia's unique position in the Muslim world is evident in its policy to actively contribute to the search for peace between Israel and the Palestinians. The bombing of Jewish Synagogues in Tunisia in 2002 is clear evidence that the fundamentalists do not care for Tunisia's progressive outlook.

THE MUSIC

Hadra. Hadra is a part of a Sufi ceremony similar to the *gnawa* of Morocco. It is trance music based on exorcism and a healing ritual. Improvised vocals, accompanied by *bendirs* (frame drums), the *tarija*, (a small drum), and the *ghaita* (reed flute) encourage the trance, the therapeutic function of the performance.

Jeel and Mouachah. Jeel is similar to modern Egyptian pop of the Arab east. Latifa (Arfaoui) is perhaps the most prominent artist associated with the style. *Mouachah* is based on the classical *wasla* of the orient rather than pop, typified by Sonia M'Barek, Leila Hejaïej, and Chakri Hannachi.

Malouf. In Tunisia as in Libya, *al Andalous* is referred to as *malouf.* The term has generally come to comprise all forms of

Tunisian classical singing. At the center is the *nuba* (suite), and the *maqam* (mode). *Malouf* survives today in weddings and circumcision ceremonies, guarded by devotees and supported by the Tunisian government.

Anaour Brahem is a classical oud master and composer, an ECM recording star, and the most renowned Tunisian artist in the West. The oud has traditionally been an instrument used to back vocalists, but Brahem has brought it to prominence as a solo instrument through his eclectic style and virtuosity reaching world audiences far from North Africa. Brahem has the persona and approach of an American jazz musician, but his roots are clearly North African. He studied in the National Conservatory and with influential oud player Ali Sitri, emerging as a world artist after living in Paris in the early 1980s where he won the National Award of Excellence in Music for a collaboration with choreographer Maurice Béjart for "A Return to Carthage."

Following a return to Tunis in 1987 where he performed regularly and was director of various ensembles, Brahem began to focus on his career as a soloist. In 1991 *Barzakh*, recorded for ECM with fellow countrymen Bechir Selmi and Lassad Hosni, garnered rave reviews. His recording career at ECM has continued into the new millennium, and he is constantly exploring new combinations with musicians from Norway, Turkey, France, Pakistan, and the United Kingdom. As with all artists recorded by Manfred Eicher, Brahem has become an ECM-style recording artist much as have Dino Saluzzi from Argentina, Jan Garbarek from Norway, and jazz pianist Keith Jarrett. Today he is in demand as an international performer and film composer.

RECOMMENDED CDs

ANOUAR BRAHEM. *Barzakh* (ECM, 1991) his masterpiece; *Conte de L'incroyable* (ECM, 1997) with clarinetist Barbaros Erkose; *Astrakan Café*, (ECM, 2001) pensive, French influenced compositions.

GHALIA BENALI & TIMNAA. *Wild Harissa* (World Network, 2001).

YAACOV BICHIRI. *Recollection of the Jews of Djerba* (2002).

LOUTFI BOUCHNAK. *Live in Berlin* (Wergo, 2002), *Allemni Ya Sidi* (1996), *With Latifa* (Inedit, 1996), *Malouf Tunisien* (Inedit, 1994).

SONIA M'BAREK. *Twicht*, Malouf with standard Egyptian-style orchestra (Disque du Monde Arabe, 1995).

WESTERN SAHARA

The former Spanish colony has endured more than 20 years of war with Morocco, with many of its people—known as Saharawis—living in refugee camps in Algeria. Musically, Western Sahara shares a strong Moorish influence with its neighbor Mauritania, although the griot system is not in place and the electric guitar is favored over the native tidinit.

RECOMMENDED CDs

MARIEM HASSAN. A leading female vocalist, *Con Leeyoad* (NubaNegra, 2002).

SAHARAUIS. (NubaNegra, 1998) 3 CD set of various artists.

WEST AND CENTRAL AFRICA

Benin	Gabon	Niger
Burkina Faso	Gambia	Nigeria
Cameroon	Ghana	Senegal
Cape Verde	Guinea Bissau	Sierra Leone
Congo	Guinea Conakry	
Cote d'Ivoire	Mali	

The very notion of "world music" began in the late 1940s with the sounds of *High Life* from Ghana. Strongly influenced by Afro-Cuban Son, High Life was the beginning of the recapturing of a vast musical culture and tradition that had been hijacked to the Western Hemisphere via slavery centuries earlier. The slave trade was responsible for the initial presence of Africans throughout all regions of the Western Hemisphere. The great majority of these slaves came from West Africa, including the countries discussed in this section.

In the twentieth century, a different type of indentured servitude was imposed on Africans. It was subtler, modern, and perhaps even subconscious. This time the exploitation targeted their music, prima-rily by the American recording industry. Blues, Jazz, Calypso, Ska, Samba, Tango, Son, Bolero, Guajira, Danzon, Habanera, and other genres were styles created by Africans who did not live in Africa. During the first half of the twentieth century, the record conglomer-ates marketed this music as a Western product and had little if any interest in exploring the music from the mother continent.

High Life and its leading proponent, E.T. Mensah, began to change this in the 1950s. Mensah was one of the first Africans on the continent to turn the tables on the Western Music monopoly by incorporating popular Western sounds (albeit sounds of the African Diaspora) into his own music. Numerous styles followed High Life, virtually all of which are covered below.

East-West-South-North Africa classifications can be arbitrary and we acknowledge that our divisions are to a degree based on convenience for the reader. To the extent possible, in Africa and else-where in this survey, we have created groupings based on general geographic location and logic, historically accepted references, and musical affiliations.

BENIN

Benin (fomerly Dahomey) is a strip of land between Togo and Nigeria divided into a savannah in the north, where the population is Muslim, and a green forested region in the south populated by Christians. Benin is historically part of the powerful Yoruban Empire and has a strong drumming tradition. As with most of West Africa, Benin was an impor-tant location for the European-operated slave trade. Much of Brazil's Yoruban culture comes from slaves brought over from Benin. In the late 1800s, the French established the colony of Dahomey, but exercised little influence in the northern part of the country because of the paucity of natural resources. Independence came in 1960 after which Dahomey suffered at the hands of a series of military dictators, including Major Mathieu Kerekou who ruled from 1973–1991 and who renamed the country Benin. After years of disastrous economic policy, Benin appears to be experiencing improved conditions and political stability as the twenty-first century begins, for the first time in its brief history.

In addition to being well know for voodoo and drumming, Benin is home to one of the true divas of world music, Angelique Kidjo, a superstar by any definition of the word.

There can be no argument that Angelique Kidjo (b.1960) has been the leading female voice of African music since the early 1990s. More than any female artist since Miriam Makeba, Kidjo has succeeded in presenting African music to a worldwide audience in an artistic, original, and provocative way. Her charismatic style allows her to communicate subtle political messages in a commercially viable format. She is a brilliant singer and a dynamo in live performance. Her records are powerful, sexy, tuneful, funky, and thought provoking. It doesn't matter that you may not understand the lyrics; if you are breathing, her message, should be clear.

Angelique's concerts sell out all over the world and are truly happenings. It was both memorable and a privilege to watch a burgeoning Kidjo perform at Summer Stage in Central Park in 1993 to an enraptured, enthusiastic crowd of New Yorkers of every ethnic background. She sang and danced the crowd into a frenzy. Kidjo's recording career has been extremely successful, recently featuring pop stars from all over the world. Angelique has become the prototype, modern-day international music star, and an ambassador extraordinaire for world music and world causes.

RECOMMENDED CDs

WALLY BADAROU. *Echoes* (Island, 1995).

GANGBE BRASS BAND. *Gangbe* (1998); *Togbe* (2001) Voodoo rhythms.

ANGELIQUE KIDJO. (see profile) *Logozo* (Mango, 1991), with Branford Marsalis and a host of African stars is still her best; *Black Ivory Soul* (Sony, 2002) a nod to Brazil with help from Carlinhos Brown and Vinicius Cantuaria; Oyaya (Sony, 2004) Caribbean sounds—merenjue, salsa, rumba—her best in many years.

BURKINA FASO

Until the nineteenth century, Burkina Faso ("Land of Upright/ Honorable People") was dominated by the Mossi people, believed to have come from eastern Africa during the eleventh century. For centuries thereafter the Mossi were able to defend and maintain their religious beliefs and social structure against forcible attempts to convert to Islam. Located in the interior of West Africa, Burkina Faso is rich in culture (Mande, Mossi, Fulani, Bobo, Lobi) but poor in natural resources with little or no arable land. This made it a low priority for the French and British in the scramble to annex African territories during the nineteenth century.

France did take control of the region, but made little effort to develop, control, or challenge existing traditions and the political structure, choosing to use the population primarily as a source of labor. Unlike many of its neighboring countries, Burkina Faso (whose name was changed from Upper Volta in 1983) has recently experienced economic growth, peace, and a modicum of political stability. It is becoming a cultural center of the region, and now hosts the African Film Festival in its capital, Ouagadougou. Musically, although not a major name on the world music map, Burkina Faso is known for its strong drumming tradition and balafon music.

RECOMMENDED CDS

BADENYA LES FRERES COULIBALY. A family of Griots who have performed with Baaba Maal, Youssou N'Dour, and Peter Gabriel. *Anka Dia* (Auvidis, 1993); *Badenya* (Trace, 2001).

FARAFINA. One of the great rhythm bands of West Africa. Tuned percussion with balafons is their trademark. They backed the Rolling Stones on *Steel Wheels* tour in 1989.

Faso Denu (Real World, 1993) is their best; *Bolomokote* (Intuition, 1988); *Kanou* (L'Empreinte, 2002).

SAABA. *Koudougou* (Dacqui, Harmonia Mundi, 1999). Fine percussion group.

CAMEROON

The first European colonizers arrived in Cameroon in1472 from Portugal. As with much of West Africa, Cameroon suffered as a target of the slave trade, especially in the south. By 1884 the Germans, Brits, and French were dividing up the country, with the French eventually dominating, improving the infrastructure, building railroads, and developing cocoa and palm oil plantations.

Cameroon achieved independence from France in 1960 with the Northern portion of the country joining Nigeria. The brutal dictator Ahmadou Ahidjo ruled through the 1980s, but he did build many schools, improved health care, and developed a sound agricultural base. His handpicked successor Paul Biya has ruled with an iron fist into the twenty-first century, maintaining strong ties with France. Despite improved conditions Cameroon continues to experience political turmoil with a reputation as one of the most corrupt countries on the planet.

Cameroon is a multilingual nation with two major cities, Douala and Yaounde. It is famous for its rainforests, Pygmy culture in the southeast, an impressive football tradition, and is home to the popular music known as *makossa*.

THE MUSIC

The seminal figure in Cameroonian music history is Frances Bebey, who left his native land for Paris in 1956 with an arsenal of Banu songs, a knowledge of Pygmy polyphony, and a great deal of ambition and pride. Trained in the baroque music of Handel and Bach, Bebey was nevertheless a staunch advocate of traditional African music. His mission in moving to Europe was to make all Black people conscious of their own culture and for non-Africans to become aware of its existence and importance. In addition to his work as a poet, novelist, journalist, guitarist, and singer, Bebey was an advocate of the concept of *Negritude* (Blackness) a movement dedicated to artistic, literary, and political promotion of the common values of black civilization, supported at the time by such luminaries as Richard Wright, Rene Depestre, Jean-Paul Sartre, Andre Gide, and Albert Camus. His death in 2001 was a great loss to the world of music and West African culture.

The most popular genre in Cameroon is *makossa*, associated with the language, people, and the city of Douala. The rhythm of the music is said to derive from a children's handclapping game. *Bikoutsi*, from the Yaounde Region, is the music of the Beti people. The most famous world music to come out of Cameroon is that of the Pygmies who reside in the southeastern forests of Cameroon. Their music has been the subject of numerous field recordings and world artists, including Belgian a cappella group Zap Mama and outback guitarist Martin Craddick, who have visited the forests to digest the unique yodeling style of singing, fusing the Pygmy sounds into their modern music.

Richard Bona is one of the brightest stars on the international scene, a brilliant songwriter with a sensual and mesmerizing voice. He is a multitalented musician, arguably the best bass player on the planet. Born in Minta in East Cameroon in 1967, Richard was a prodigy who began performing publicly at the age of 5. He was obsessed with all musical instruments and soon built his own balafon. He moved to Douala at age 11 where he soon began to perform with local musicians. His musical vision changed when he first heard a Jaco Pastorious record. He moved to Paris in 1989 and was quickly sought out by the best musicians in the city, including Didier Lockwood, fellow countryman Manu Dibango, and Malian superstar Salif Keita. On the advice of his friend, jazz guitarist Mike Stern, he moved to New York in 1995 and immediately connected with Joe Zawinul. He eventually signed a major recording contract (first with Sony, now with Verve) and has become a fixture on the world and jazz circuits.

Bona possesses an enormous musicality, rarely experienced in any field of music. Despite his utter virtuosity on a number of instruments (bass, guitar, percussion, piano, flute), his aesthetic sensibility never allows his awesome technique to overwhelm his creativity. It is not an exaggeration to compare him (musically) to the late Charlie Parker; his talent and vision is that remarkable.

RECOMMENDED CDs

FRANCIS BEBEY. *Dibye* (Pee Wee Music, 1998), *Akwaaba* (Ceddia, 1985).

RICHARD BONA. *Scenes from my Life* (1999, Sony); *Reverence* (2001, Sony); *Munia: The Tale* (2003, Verve) is his best to date.

MANU DIBANGO. Africa's most famous jazz saxophonist is the one who put makossa on the map, although he really doesn't play the style. *Soul Makossa* (Accord, 1972); *Gone Clear* (1980), with Charlotte M'Bango and English rapper MC Mello; *Mboa' Su* (Mango, 2000).

HENRI DIKONGUE. Acoustic Cameroon folk music. *Wa* (Tinder, 1995); *C'est La Vie* (1998) is dedicated to Fela Kuti and Robert Mitchum.

GUY LOBE. *Dikalo* (Blue Silver 1998).

EBOA LOTIN. Lotin was a forerunner of makossa beginning in the 1960s. *Best of Eboa Lotin* (Sonodisc, 1995).

LAPIRO DE MBANGA. Outspoken singer/songwriter, political activist. *Ndinga Man - Contre Attaque; Na Wou Go Pay* (Indigo, 1991).

COCO MBASSI. Pop singer. *Sepia* (Tinder, 2003) made a big splash in America.

SALLY NYOLO. Former Zap Mama member, Sally is a leading vocalist. *Tribu* (Tinder, 1995), sung in her native Eton, is folksy with yodeling; *Beti* (Lusafrica, 2001); *Zaione* (2003, Lusafrica).

LES TETES BRULEES. *Bikoutsi Rock* (Bleu Caraibes, 1992) is gold coast funk, with Mory Kante's band and Charlotte M'Bango on vocals; *Ma Musique a Moie* (Melodie, 1993).

SAM FAN THOMAS. *Makassi* (1984) is a lighter style of makossa, big in the 1980s.

COMPILATION. *Baka Beyond - Heart of the Forest* is a field recording made by Outback guitarist Martin Craddick that includes pygmy polyphony, yodeling, birds, and crickets; *Spirit of the Forest* is his follow up.

CAPE VERDE

Equidistant from the coasts of Senegal and Brazil, Cape Verde is an archipelago that has been inhabited by the Portuguese since 1460. Legend has it that the Portuguese were the first people on the islands. Due to its unfortunate location, Cape Verde was home to the cruelest aspect of the slave trade, the site of Portuguese fortresses where imprisoned West Africans were kept before being sent across the Atlantic to the horrors that awaited them. The harsh physical realities of the island and sparse vegetation made it the ideal prison. The island population currently consists of the ancestors of those who were forced to intermarry with the Portuguese,

Africans who remained in Cape Verde to build roads, homes, and to work on plantations despite the hostile, dry climate. The callous rule of the Portuguese caused nearly 40 percent of the population to die during the droughts of the eighteenth and nineteenth centuries. Today more Cape Verdeans live abroad than on the island, many in New England, especially in Rhode Island, where ties are kept with the homeland and its culture.

THE MUSIC

To most world music fans, Cape Verde is synonymous with Cesaria Evora from the island of Sao Vicente. Her music is *Morna*, a combination of Portuguese *fado* that came out of the brothels of Lisbon and Coimbra in Portugal during the middle of the nineteenth century, Brazilian *modinha*, and West African percussion with a strong influence from the innumerable sailors who frequented Cap-Vert. It is a languid, sensual, slow-paced song form, melancholy music that is instantly recognizable and lovable. *Coladeira* is the Cape's upbeat, festive form, and *funana* is a jazz-tinged dance music, both lesser known than morna but more popular among the Cape Verdean diaspora.

Since Cesaria's breakthrough on the international scene and due to the seductive appeal of morna, many fine musicians and groups from Cape Verde have released recordings.

Since the United States release of *Miss Perfumado* in 1993, Cesaria Evora (b.1941) has taken the world music community by storm. Cesaria is living proof that the impossible can happen i.e., a true artist plying her trade in obscurity for decades can achieve critical acclaim and popularity at an age when most singers contemplate retirement. She has done this without compromising her musical integrity. She not only has become one of the leading voices of world music, but also is an international pop star who sells millions of CDs.

Cesaria is relishing her fame, singing the music she has sung her entire life, the *Saudade*-laced Portuguese *morna* from her island home of Cape Verde. *Morna* is an ambling, relaxed, soothing music style, cousin to a slow Samba or Modinha and the blues, related to *fado* but with an unmistakable "Island" rhythm that hints at Cuban *Son*. Cesaria has not forgotten her roots and performs barefoot as a show of solidarity with the poor women of the world.

RECOMMENDED CDs

BANA. Bana is a male morna singer and former producer for Cesaria. *Chant La Magie du Cap-Vert* (Lusafrica, 1996).

AMANDIO CABRAL. Composer of the famous *Sodade* which opens Cesaria's classic *Miss Perfumado CD*. *Tristalegria* (Lusafrica, 1996).

TEOFILO CHANTRE. A fine guitarist and composer. *Di Alma* (Lusafrica, 1998).

CESARIA EVORA. *Miss Perfumado* (Melodie, 1992) is one of the great world music recordings, the one to get; *Mar Azul* (Melodie, 1988).

FANTCHA. Protégé of Cesaria. *Criolinha* (Tinder, 1998).

SIMENTERA. A ten-musician ensemble from the island of Santiago, Cape Verde's leading roots group, popular before Cesaria. *Raiz* (Melodie, 1995).

CONGO

The very concept of "*Afropop*" has its roots in the Congolese music of the early 1950s at a time when the continent was beginning to emerge from colonial rule. Nowhere was the change more visible and vibrant than in the former Belgian colony. The head-on collision of African tradition with the brute force of imposed "modern" European culture and religion created a whirlpool of economic, social, political, and cultural upheaval that has wreaked havoc on the region ever since. The duplicitous King Leopold was *de jure* owner of the Congo in the 1950s and along with his henchmen played the role of villain with impunity. Despite the confusion, exploitation, and hypocrisy, it was a time of hope embodied most clearly in the martyred Patrice Lumumba, a time that would set the tone for much of the decolonization of the rest of the continent in the decades that followed.

Beginning in the 1950s, two Congos emerged on either side of the great river. The stubborn, frugal, determined Belgians established their capital in Leopoldville (now Kinshasa) on the southeast bank of the Congo. Leopoldville mirrored the Belgian character: industry and efficiency were the priority; adherence to rigidly enforced rules and laws; compulsory art and leisure activities came in a distant third. The French Congo (part of French Equatorial Africa) established its capital in Brazzaville on the northwest side of the river. Brazzaville reflected the French way, loosely organized, more colorful and relaxed, outwardly tolerant, an African city albeit one with *chic* shops and a touch of Paris. Both colonial rulers, however, were out for the same thing: absolute exploitation and control of the incomparable natural riches of the Congo.

THE MUSIC

With decolonization of the Congo, Africans flocked to the cities with the hope of achieving a better life, bringing their language, tribal customs, and music with them. The turmoil of the times was reflected in the emergence of new musical forms that retained traditional flavor and nuance while absorbing and modifying what the European culture flaunted. In a short time, the identity of individual tribal music became difficult to discern as the new wave of performers began to experiment with the glut of Western instruments suddenly available, especially the almighty electric guitar. The African sound remained in the music, but a new form developed, originally called simply *Congo*, now known as *soukous* in the West.

The story of modern Congolese music begins with Henry Bowane, a talented guitarist and entrepreneur whose band was the first to perform outside the Congo, in Angola in 1955. The emergence of Congolese music, with its unmistakable rumba influence and a kinship with the Ghanian High Life of E.T. Mensah that had already begun to explode, was the beginning of Afropop. Bowane discovered the Congo's most famous star, Francois Lubambo Makiadi, known simply as "Franco," giving him his first gigs in Kinshasa in 1955. Bowane started the craze that swept the continent and to this day the music has great influence in virtually all forms of upbeat Afropop music. Joseph Kabasele, a peer of Bowane, pioneered African jazz and discovered the great Tabu Ley Rochereau, Manu Dibango, and many other stars.

Tabu Ley and Franco are the giants of Congolese music. Franco died in 1989, but Tabu Ley is going strong today (2004). He combines his trademark high voice with a high octane mix of soukous, Zairean folk, Soul, R&B, Latin, synthesizers, and a silken guitar style.

THE DIASPORA RETURNS

The Cuban influence in Congolese music is a noteworthy phenomenon that evidences the strength, power, and durability of African culture over time under the most dire of circumstances. Cuban music, especially what is loosely referred to as rumba, has always been characterized by the world music cognoscenti as the most African of all Caribbean and South American musical forms. Cuban music is in reality African music deposited and sustained in the Western Hemisphere from the time of the slave trade. It made its first excursion back to the motherland in the form of Congolese music. Yes, it was modified, modernized, and popularized, even Europeanized, but Congolese music is a concrete affirmation of the power of African culture.

One of the most naturally beautiful voices on the world music scene belongs to the gifted Lokua Kanza. He has apprenticed as arranger, sideman, and vocalist with Ray Lema, Papa Wemba, and Youssou N'Dour, and is now emerging as a different kind of African pop star. Pyrotechnics and dazzling percussion is not his bag. Lokua is a folksy troubadour with universal appeal, an effortless, suave, sexy delivery that recalls the great Brazilian artist Djavan. He is also a fine guitar player and composer. His 2002 *Toyebi Te* was one of the most important releases of that year, in a class with Salif Keita's *Moffu*, Youssou N'Dour's *Nothing's in Vain*, and Orchestra Baobab's *Specialist* in *All Styles*. His use of (his) children's voices, references to '1950s American R&B, and knack for arranging will make you smile.

RECOMMENDED CDs

M'BILIA BEL. The Congo's greatest female singer was popular in the late 1980s. *Bameli Soy* (1984, Shanachie) is her best; *Phenomene* (IMA, 1988).

HENRY BOWANE. The Father figure of Zairean music has only one recorded album: *Double Take-Tala Kaki* (Retro Africa, 1974).

FRANCO & OK JAZZ. *Franco and his All Powerful TPOK Jazz* (Makossa, 1984); *Originalite* (RetroAfric, 1999) contains his best from 1955–1956; *Franco & Sam Mangwana* (Sonodisc 1994) top material from 1980–1982; *Francophonic: The Essential Recordings 1953–85* (Sterns) 4 CD Box set.

KANDA BONGA MAN. Paris-based singer with a high tenor voice plays rippling, upbeat, dance groove music. Diblo Dibala and Rigo Starr have held down the guitar chair with distinction. *Amour Fou* (Hannibal, 1988), *Sai-Liza* (Melodie, 1988).

LOKUA KANZA. *Toyebe Ti* (Yewo, 2001) is luscious and essential; *Wapi Yo* (Catalyst, 1996); *Lokua Kanza* (RCA, 1994).

KEKELE. *Congo Life* (Stern's, 2003). Popular '1970s group returns with a winner on the coattails of the Orchestra Baobab phenomenon.

RAY LEMA. Euro Congo. *Safi* (Tinder, 2001), Gaia (Mango, 1991).

M'PONGO LOVE. The earliest female star. *Partager* (Syllart, 1985)

SAM MANGWANA. The last of the great Zairean Rumba stars presents the lighter side of the music. *Sings Dinu Vangu* (Sterns, 2000), *Aladji* (Shanachie, 1977), *Maria Tebbo* (Sterns, 1995).

TSHALA MUANA. Queen of *Mutashi*, the Afro-Cuban music from the Democratic Republic of Congo, Tshala is a sensuous performer; *Nasi Nabili* (Sonodisc 1987); *Soukous Siren* (Shanachie, 1985).

KOFFI OLOMIDE. Papa Wemba alumni went solo in the 1980s moving to Paris, known for the *Tcha Tcho* beat. *Force de Frappe* (Sonodisc, 2000), *Tcha Tcho* (Sterns, 1994).

TABU LEY ROCHEREAU. *Babeti Soukous* (Plan, 1989) is a live set; *Omana Wapi* (Shanachie, 1976) is one of his best; *Africa Worldwide: 35th Anniversary Album* (1996, Shanachie) is a great recap; *Tabu Ley* (Shanachie, 1967) is an important early CD.

PAPA WEMBA. Wemba is the flamboyant, snazzy dressing one who fused Afro with pop and rock, the most modern of the big stars. *L'Esclave* (Gitta, 1986), *Le Voyageur* (Earthbeat, 1992), *Papa Wemba* (Sterns, 1994), *Emotion* (Caroline, 1995).

ZAIKO LANGA LANGA. New Wave collective plays electrified Soukous. *Zaire-Ghana* (RetroAfrique, 1993), *Avis de Recherche* (Sterns 1995).

COTE D' IVOIRE

One of the most economically advanced countries in West Africa, the Ivory Coast (formerly part of French West Africa) has maintained a political philosophy of non-interference with other African nations implemented by its long-time President Felix Houphouet-Boigny who died in 1993. Despite questionable handling of the national treasury, he was a revered figure in French West African politics.

THE MUSIC

Abidjan. Cote d'Ivoire's greatest contribution to world music has long been its stature as the center for the African recording industry. Abidjan maintains numerous top-flight studios that have drawn the greatest stars from all over Africa, including Salif Keita, Manu Dibango, Mory Kante, Sam Mangwana, and home-grown artist Alpha Blondy.

Ziglibithy. Cote d'Ivoire had not developed a distinctive national music style until Ernesto Djedje (1948–1983) combined the local tradition of the Bete people with Congolese rhythms to make a new Ivoirian music known as *ziglibithy*. It is slightly slower than the Cameroon *makossa*, characterized by a jerky, almost frenzied rhythm. Ziglibithy became the national music in the 1970s.

Cote d'Ivoire boasts one true international star, the African Rasta known as Alpha Blondy. He has been a force on the scene since the early 1980s when he got the reggae bug at a Burning Spear concert. He made pilgrimages to Jamaica thereafter and recorded with the Wailers at Tuff Gong studios. Almost single-handedly, he has made reggae a popular music in his country. He sings in Duoala, English, French, Arabic, and Hebrew with a top international band. His music is easily appealing, politically sophisticated, and has evolved with less of an edge than Jamaican reggae. He is the most famous musical artist from Cote d'Ivoire, revered throughout West Africa.

RECOMMENDED CDS

ALPHA BLONDY. *Yitzhak Rabin* (Lightyear, 1998), *Apartheid is Nazism* (1987, Shanachie), *The Best of Alpha Blondy* (1990, Shanachie).

ERNESTO DJEDJE. *Roi du ziglibithy* (P.A.M, 2001 reissue). Popular singer who died in 1983 as a national idol and inventor of ziglibithy.

AICHA KONE. The grande dame of Ivoirian pop combines soukous and zouglou, the youth music of the '1990s, and the closest thing Cote d'Ivoire has to a national music. *Adouma* (Bolibana).

ZAGAZOUGOU. Traditional, acoustic, breakneck speed sounds reviving an early twentieth century tradition. *Zagazougou Coup: Accordions from Abidjan* (Piranha).

GABON

Part of Equatorial Africa from 1912–1957, Gabon has shared the experience of colonial rule and French influence along with its West African neighbors, including being ravaged by the slave trade until the 1880s. Gabon's history in the twentieth century includes greater independence and home rule than other West African French territories. During World War II, the Free French seized control from Vichy and by 1960 independence was achieved. During the Nigerian civil war in the late 1960s, Gabon was one of the few African countries to give aid to Biafra. Gabon's oil industry accounts for the highest per capita income of any Sub-Saharan country.

THE MUSIC

Pierre Akendengue is the leading name from Gabon, a giant of world music before the term was ever used. He was both partner and counterpart to Cameroonian Frances Bebey as an advocate for the wider exposure of African music as a means of transmitting culture. He collaborated with Hugues de Courson (of Bretagne folk group Malicorne fame) to produce the prodigious *Lambarena* oratorio in homage to Albert Schweitzer, who established a hospital at Lambarene on the Ogooue River in 1913. More than 150 musicians and singers took part in the project, which took 6 months to prepare and 3 months to record.

RECOMMENDED CDs

PIERRE AKENDENGUE. *Lambarena: Bach to Africa* (Celluloid); *Piroguier* (Melodie, 1986); *Maladalite* (Celluloid, 1996); *Nandipo* (1974) was his first.

FIELD RECORDING: *Musique d Pygmees Bibayak: Chantres de l'epope* (Ocora, 1988). Ethnomusicological recording with the usual high standards of Ocora.

GAMBIA

The Gambia is surrounded by Senegal on three sides with a shore-line on the Atlantic Ocean. It was the smallest of the West African nations in the Mandinka Empire and the most popular West African tourist destination at the turn of the new millennium. Its music and economy are dominated by Senegal. Gambia was colonized by the British, gaining independence in 1965. Gambian music is performed by Fula, Suso, and Wolof griots who are the keepers of the oral history. Its neighbors dominate its musical culture.

RECOMMENDED CDs

PAPA SUSSO. Kora master. *Sotuma Sere* (2003, Traditional Crossroads). Susso's solo outing is a beautiful recording, showing his stark playing with subtle vocal undertones.

IFANG BONDI "Be Yourself" (formerly the Super Eagles). Popular Beatles-influenced band from the early 1970s that has become more traditional since their Western pop beginnings. *Saraba* (1978), *Senegambian Sensation* (Retro Afrique, 2001).

GHANA

Ghana is arguably the most stable and economically successful country in Africa midway through the first decade of twenty-first century. It boasts a constitutional government with separation of powers (i.e., a democratically elected president who has succeeded a democratically elected president, and a Parliament and an independent judiciary modeled after Western democracies). It is the home of United Nations Secretary General Kofi Annan and *High Life*, the seminal Afro Beat music genre of the twentieth century.

Prior to the fifteenth century, oral history refers to migrations from the ancient kingdoms of Western Sudan, Mauritania, and Mali. The first white colonists were Portuguese, who arrived in the region circa 1470. The Europeans named the region the Gold Coast (because of its rich mineral reserves). By 1553 the English, Danes, Dutch, and Germans had followed, setting up trading forts along the coast and in Togo. By 1821 the British had taken control of all the trading and in 1841 the Fanti chiefs signed an agreement that led to the formation of colonial states. From 1826–1900, the inland Ashanti people fought prolonged battles with the British, who thereafter consolidated the Ashanti territory with Togoland.

In 1957, the Gold Coast became the first Sub-Saharan nation to achieve independence under Kwame Nkrumah, with Togoland being absorbed as part of the newly named Ghana (the name came from an ancient African kingdom, whose people supposedly emigrated to the area from the south). Nkrumah formed modern, semi-industrial Ghana as a unitary socialist state. He was one of the great Pan African activists who used music as a tool to affirm the culture of his people, regularly supporting artists and musicians in their careers, and establishing an undying allegiance from the people as a result. By 1979, a constitution was adopted and separation of powers in place. Despite periods of military rule, especially under Flight Lt. Rawlings in the 1980s, Ghana has emerged to be the unquestioned leader of the region in the twenty-first century.

THE MUSIC

High life music is in part indebted to the instruments brought by the sailors, soldiers, and missionaries of colonization in West Africa. When fortresses were set up along the Gold Coast, they included military bands that featured flugelhorns, bugles, guitars, accordions, banjos, saxophones, and the like. Soon local bars, cafés, and clubs began presenting musical groups who incorporated the new instruments into their repertoire, eventually developing into a style known as *High Life,* a fusion of American jazz rhythms with the local *osib* music, a percussion-based dance music of the Akan people whose existence was inextricably linked to the gold trade.

Ghana is where the first Afropop music was born. *High life* developed its name because the music—originally played by big bands with large horn sections—was performed in swank dance clubs along the coast. Those who could afford to get in were said to be living the "high life" by everyone else who congregated outside the clubs to catch the sounds. The outsiders were the ones who dubbed the music *High Life.*

The music of Ghana is inextricably tied to the vision and genius of one man, E.T. Mensah (1919–1996), who is widely recognized as the King of *High Life* and a founding father of African popular music. A pharmacist by trade, Mensah cut his musical teeth with the orchestra of legendary musician/teacher Joe Lamptey in Accra in the early 1930s, first on the piccolo but later as an accomplished saxophone and trumpet player. During World War II, Accra was a center where Allied forces mobilized for the campaign in North Africa and the Middle East. Along with the soldiers came musicians who introduced jazz, swing, and Caribbean sounds to the local rhythms and music. Mensah absorbed everything, eventually teaming up with renowned drummer Guy Warren (b. Kofi Ghanaba) in the famous Tempos band, which toured Europe in 1947, playing mostly Afro-Cuban rhythms. E.T. was a humble man who never claimed to have invented *High Life,* stating: "No one can lay claim to its creation. It had always been there, entrenched in West African Culture. What I did was give it world acceptance."

High Life is sung in many local dialects including Ga, Ganti, Twi, Ewe, Ibo, Hausa, and Efik, as well as in English and Spanish. E.T.'s popularity and acclaim was so great that in 1956 Louis Armstrong sat in and jammed with his band in a series of live concerts before enormous crowds. E.T. brought the music to Nigeria, Cote d'Ivoire; Guinea, Liberia, and Sierra Leone, playing for heads of state everywhere. He was responsible for elevating the level of professionalism of African dance music and was the first to truly popularize it throughout the rest of West Africa.

RECOMMENDED CDs

GEORGE WILLIAMS AINGO. *The Roots of Highlife* (Sterns, 1992).

AK BANNERMAN. Top studio guitarist formerly with *Osibisa* performs modern High Life with his band Boombaya. *Ghana Gone Jazz* (1998).

AB CRENTSIL. The hot name in High Life in the 1970s with his band Sweet Talks, Crentsil is active in the recording studio scene in Accra. *Reminiscin' in Tempo* (African Music, 1991); *Kafo Mpo Dzidzi* (Dymtex, 1983); *Hollywood Highlife Party* (World Circuit 1999), a 1978 reissue.

ALEX KONADU. Carrying the torch for High Life and avoiding Afro Beat, Konadu is a purist, a guitarist who sings in Ashanti. *One Man Thousand* (Akuboat, 1998) is his nickname, and also the name of his best, most available recording.

E.T. MENSAH (see Profile). *All for You* (Retro Africa, 1986), *Day by Day* (Retro Africa, 1987).

OSIBISA. One of the first African bands to achieve worldwide recognition. *Mystic Energy* (Terrapin Music, 1980), *Woyaya* (Aim, 1971).

GUINEA-BISSAU

The former Portuguese colony is landlocked in West Africa between Senegal and Guinea. After independence in 1974, a new nation led by popular President Luis Cabral enjoyed a cultural revolution and a period of freedom and rejoicing. *Kriolu*, the local language, is a combination of Portuguese and Creole tongues, as well as the name of the music identified with liberation in Guinea-Bissau. The music played a mobilizing and unifying part in the struggle for independence. The group Cobiana Djazz, led by poet/composer Ze Carlos (Jose Carlos Schwartz), was at the forefront of the movement. Ze Carlos died in a "mysterious" plane crash in 1977. Sadly, after a decade of relative tranquility, war has ravaged the country since the mid-1990s and the people have experienced virtually nothing but civil strife and economic hardship.

The one upbeat note has been Guinea-Bissau's *gumbe* music, a genre related to the Brazilian samba, the *morna* of Cape Verde, and the *semba* of Angola. Gumbe borrows from many local folk styles and contains unique West African polyrhythms, non-Portuguese forms that date back to the 1850s. Although the future of this small country is currently in doubt as of this writing, several remarkable artists continue to record and make important music.

RECOMMENDED CDs

BIDINTE. The leading light of *gumbe* music. *Kumura* (NubaNegra, 1998) is a soothing recording combining gumbe with the Flamenco guitar of Paco Cruz and the backup vocals of Sudanese Star Rasha.

MANECAS COSTA. Costa is a great singer/guitarist/composer. *Paraiso de Gumbe* (BBC Music, 2003) was engineered by Jerry Boys of Buena Vista Social Club fame, notable as the first recording to be made in Guinea Bissau; a great CD.

KABA MANE. *The Best of Kaba Mane* (Melodie).

ZE MANEL. A national figure after independence, Ze's composition *Tustumunhol di Aonti* ("yesterday's testimony") became a National anthem. *Maron di Mar* (Cobiana, 2001) contains one of the hippest Afropop tracks ever, *Tchico Te*.

GUINEA

Due to its proximity to Europe and the Americas, Guinea was a prime source for the lucrative slave trade. Colonial powers— Portugal, England, and France—traded with local chiefs, obtaining cheap, hard labor workers. The boundaries of the country were established under French rule in 1890 when the country became known as French Guinea.

Sekou Tour was the leader of the independence movement in Guinea after World Word II. When confronted with the choice of autonomy or independence, he chose the latter, mistakenly thinking he would be supported by Cote d'Ivoire and Senegal. Independence came in 1958, but it was the beginning of economic and political decline. Tour turned to the Soviet Union for help and promptly started a communist regime, which in the long run caused the fall of the country and its ruin. In 1967, a Chinese-style Cultural Revolution was implemented, which led to an exodus of around 2 million Guineans, including most of the educated population, and further impoverished the country. As recently as 1994 Guinea was considered the poorest country in the world, despite vast natural resources of gold, diamonds, iron, and other minerals.

THE MUSIC

Guinea is part of the great Mande culture whose music is inextricably tied to Mali. A great kora and balafon tradition and caste system of griots exists in Guinea much as in Mali. Stars such as More Kante, Bembeya Jazz, and Kante Manfila are among the great names in African music/superstars of world music.

RECOMMENDED CDs

BEMBEYA JAZZ. Once the official band of the government, Bembeya have been in business since the late 1960s and are back on the scene with *Bembeya Jazz* (World Village, 2002). They play big-band style Congolese music with trademark four guitars, touches of Cuban son, Islamic gnawa influences, and swing like crazy. *Montagne: Yekeke: Regard Sur Le Passe* (Bolibana, 1968) was a tribute to Samory Toure, founder of the Mande Kingdom in 1870.

FULA FLUTE ENSEMBLE. Traditional music performed on the *Tambin* flute, led by Bailo Bah and Sylvan Leroux from Montreal. *Fula Flute* (Blue Monster, 2003) cooks with more than a smidgen of Roland Kirk, an intense, trance-like recording.

EL-HADJ DJELI SORY KOUYATE. The Legendary Kora master. *Anthologie du Balafon Mandingue* (Buda, 1991).

MORY KANTE. Kante is a griot who at the age of 7 was sent to Mali to learn to play the kora. He permanently relocated in Bamako a decade later and joined the famous Rail Band. He stayed with the band for 7 years, eventually developing a rivalry with Salif Keita. In 1981 he recorded *Courougnegne*, the beginning of crossover projects incorporating Mandinkan music, which brought him fame in Africa and Europe. *Akwaba Beach* (Barclay, 1987); *Touma* (Mango, 1990); *10 Cola Nuts* (Barclay, 1986).

KANTE MANFILA. Former member of the Ambassadeurs, Manfila is one of Africa's great guitarists. *Kankan Blues* (World Circuit, 1991).

MALI

Mali is a landlocked nation comprised mostly of desert with a rich culture dating back to its thirteenth century kingdoms. Situated between the Arab world and "Black Africa," Mali is at the cultural crossroads of West Africa. Moors and the nomadic *Tuareg* and *Sahel* people populate the north, with the Manding culture inhabiting the south. Mali is a poor country whose Islamic influence remains pervasive in the twenty-first century. It once was a cliché in the West to refer to Timbuktu as the quintessential, mythical far away place. Today, despite Mali's traditional lifestyle and customs, Timbuktu is no longer an unknown location, in great part due to Mali's rich musical tradition, perhaps the greatest in all of West Africa. Bamako is the country's musical and cultural center, and Mali is quite simply a major world music powerhouse.

JELIS AND PRAISE MUSIC

In the Mande tradition of Northern Mali, professional musicians are born into a caste separated from the rest of society. Only these *jelis (griots* in other regions of West Africa*)*, or female *jelimusolus*, are allowed to become professional musicians or singers. Malian superstars Toumani Diabate, Kasse Mady, Kandia Kouyate, and Guinean Mory Kante are all jelis/jelimsolus, born into castes where praise music—which pays homage to great deeds and exalted figures in Malian history—dominates, and the lyrics display little regard for the common man. Salif Keita, Mali's greatest singer and musician, is an exception to the ancient caste system. He was born into a regal family, allegedly descended from the ancient Malian warrior-king Sunjata Keita, who united many small kingdoms and who remains an important figure in modern Mali. Salif's regal background forbade him from becoming a musician, but he broke the mold and tradition by becoming a performer as a non-jeli and in the process helped bring Malian music to the world stage.

Ancient tradition is revered by the Mande people and the culture of the old kingdoms continues to be part of modern society, a polygamous one that has been slow to address the rights of women and modern technology due both to its poor economic state and religious orthodoxy. The rigid structure of Mande society is such that virtually every surname has a specific connotation relating to class, occupation, or profession. The limited number of names—Kouyate, Keita, Diabate, Sissiko, Toure, and Traore (approximately twelve in total with spelling variations)—are familiar to world-music fans, but create considerable confusion for the uninitiated.

The Wassoulou culture south of Bamako does not adhere to the class restrictions of the Northern Mande people, and permits anyone to be a musician. This region possesses a strong musical heritage that came into world prominence in the early 1990s and dates back only to the late 1960s as a distinct form. Many current West African stars come from this area, including the incomparable diva Oumou Sangare (see profile).

WEST AFRICAN MUSICAL INSTRUMENTS

There are four musical instruments that are inextricably part of traditional Malian music (and prominent throughout the West African Mandinkan culture) invariably featured on most recordings. The *kora* is a cross between a harp and a lute, usually constructed with 21–25 strings and played sitting down with the instrument in a vertical position, much as the classical western harp. It is the melodic center of Malian music, widely heard throughout West Africa. The *balafon*, (a wooden xylophone) and its rich percussive sound is the other signature voice of Malian music. The *ngoni*, a long, lute-like instrument, is not as prevalent as the kora or balafon, but is an integral part of most Malian recordings. A wide range of drums are also part of the tradition especially the *djembe* (pronounced "'jem-bay"), which is played throughout the world in a multitude of musical settings and genres because of its adaptability, mellifluous sound, and wide sonic range.

BAMAKO, ABIDJAN, AND PARIS

West African music exploded onto the international scene in the early 1970s with Bamako and Abidjan as the fertile musical centers of the region for live performance and recording. The styles that emerged at the time ostensibly combined Cuban and Latin rhythms with traditional Malian forms. Many of these Latin rhythms had of course been brought from West Africa to the Caribbean and the Americas centuries ago.

Since the mid-1980s, much of the West African recording scene has maintained its center in Paris. Leading musicians from Mali, Senegal, Cameroon, Guinea, and Ghana, upon achieving economic success and therefore freedom, have expatriated from their native lands (mostly former French colonies) and moved to Paris where opportunity to be heard on the world stage far exceeds that available at home.

Afropop, while undeniably *popular* music, has become a calling card from the region, popular for sure, but always maintaining its unique cultural identity. Although not "traditional" in the purest sense of the word, Afropop has evolved into a legitimately indigenous music of many countries of West Africa having shed the initial Latin influence in favor of a more contemporary focus. It has also evolved into West Africa's most significant cultural export.

The great Wassoulou singer/songwriter Oumou Sangare (b.1968) burst onto the world music scene in the late 1980s on the strength of her incredible voice and advocacy for the common people and women's issues. Sangare's 1989 release *Moussolou (Women)*, a gorgeous acoustic set, catapulted her to fame in the region even though her outspoken views against polygamy and arranged marriage were expressed clearly on the recording. This did not endear her to the older male population in Mali, who cling to the culture's history of oppressing women. The women of Mali and West Africa heard her call, though, and immediately related to her message, as did the younger generation of men. *Moussolou sold* over 200,000 copies in West Africa, an incredible number for any world music recording, but an unheard of number for the continent where retail shops barely exist and disposable income is a foreign concept to most. The subsequent World Circuit Label release of the recording elevated Sangare to major diva status. She has continued to prosper and get her message out, with a series of great recordings, songs for international film soundtracks, and a demanding touring schedule.

RECOMMENDED CDs

TOUMANI DIABATE. Toumani is a leading instrumentalist in Malian music. *Kaira* (Hannibal, 1988) is the first solo kora recording released in the west; *Djelika* (Hannibal, 1995) with balafon wiz Keletigui Diabate is a more realized work; *Songhai* (Hannibal, 1989) is early fusion with Flamenco group Katema hetama.

NAHAWA DOUMBIA. The new Malian Diva *Dibi* (Cobatt, 2004).

SALIF KEITA. Salif is a master of praise music and Mali's greatest musical ambassador. *Soro* (Mango, 1987) is a breathtaking masterpiece, the standard against which all Afropop is judged; *Folon* (Mango, 1998); *Moffu* (World Circuit, 2002) is Salif's best since *Soro*, a mature work by a true genius.

HABIB KOITE. Guitarist/Vocalist Habib Koite combines virtuosity and taste. *Baro* (Putumayo, 2001) is a gem; *Maya* (Putumayo, 1998).

KANDIA KOUYATE. The most powerful and revered female jelismusolu singer in Mali. She is Arethaesque. *Kity Kan* (Mango, 1993), *Biriko* (Mango, 2002).

KASSE MADY. Praise singer with a Mandinkan griot voice that rivals Salif Keita. *Kelu Tradition* (Sterns, 1994).

OUMOU SANGARE. (See profile). *Moussolou (Women)* (World Circuit, 1991) is a gorgeous acoustic set that catapulted her to fame. *Worotan* (World Circuit, 1996) is popish.

MAMA SISSIKO. Sissiko is a guitarist/composer who has been revered at home for decades, but whose haunting, lyrical work has only recently hit the American market. *Soleil du Minuit* (Tinder, 2001).

SUPER RAIL BAND. The Rail Band began in Bamako at the Hotel de la Gare train station circa 1970 as part of a government-sponsored program promoting traditional music. Salif Keita, Mory Kante, and many other stars served their apprenticeships in the band under the tutelage of visionary guitarist and leader Djelimady Tounkara. *Mansa*, (Mango, 1996).

TAMA. Tama is an Afropop collaboration including Malian Kora player Toumani Diakite, percussionist Djanuno Dabo from Guinea-Bissau, and English guitarist Sam Mills. *Espace* (Real World, 2002) is a gentle, soulful outing.

TINARIWEN. Malian Tuareg group born in refuge camps in Libya are in the forefront of Sub-Saharan rock; Jimi Hendrix in the desert with robes, a lot of attitude, eclectic and haunting. *The Radio Tisdas Sessions* (World Village, 2001); Amassahoul (World Village, 2004).

DJELIMADY TOUNKARA. Tounkara released his first solo recording in 2002—*Sigui* (Indigo, 2001), which highlights his Western influenced folk guitar style in an "unplugged" set.

ALI FARKA TOURE. Toure is a major world music star, an African counterpart to Son House, John Lee Hooker, and the acoustic guitar tradition of Afro-American blues from the mid-twentieth century. His roots are from the Songhai and Tuareg cultures near Timbuktu. *Talkin' Timbuktu* (World Circuit, 1994); *Niafunke* (Hannibal, 1999) is pure Malian Blues; *Radio Mali* (Elektra, 1996/1977) is a fascinating look at the beginning of Toure's career.

BOUBACAR TRAORE. Kar Kar is the dean of the folk branch of Malian music. *Mariama* (Sterns, 1991) is his best side; *Je Chanterai pour Toi* (Melodie, 2002), with Rokia Traore, Ali Farka Toure, Madieye Niang, and Keletigui Diabate sitting in.

ROKIA TRAORE. Rokia has discarded the conceptual confines of chauvinistic Malian society for stardom in the real world. *Bowmboi* (Label Bleu, 2003) is a breakout recording by an exciting artist. *Wanita* (Label Bleu, 1998).

NIGER

In 1993, 35 years after independence from France, Niger held its first free and open elections. A five-year Tuareg insurgency in the north ended in 1995 and true civilian rule took hold in 1999. Musically overshadowed by its neighbors in West Africa, Niger has a close historical and cultural affinity with Mali and Senegal. Niger is essentially a desert land that is still reeling from the devastating drought in the Sahel region in the 1970s, a country where it doesn't rain for 9 months of the year! It is home to the nomadic Tuareg tribes who are of Berber descent and live in the north and central west. Unlike virtually every other culture in West Africa (and in Africa as a whole), women in Tuareg society hold positions of power and have property rights. They are also singers and musicians whose role in nomadic culture is highly regarded.

RECOMMENDED CDs

HAROUNA GOGE. *Dendi Music* (Ocora, 2000). This is a stark recording from the ever-reliable Ocora label. The Goge is the traditional single stringed spiked fiddle of Niger.

MAMAR KASSY. A group with a true vision that combines old and new, Niger's most adventuresome band performs with flute, bass, molo and komsa (two-and three-stringed lutes), calabash, chorus, kalangou (hand drum), and guitar. *Denke, Denke* (Dacqui, 1999) is an essential West African roots CD. *Alatoumi* (World Village, 2001).

COMPILATION. *Traditional Tuareg Music of Niger* (Ocora, 1990).

NIGERIA

The earliest Nigerians were Nok people who virtually disappeared at the beginning of the first millennium CE when the state of Kanem northeast of Lake Chad flourished. By the thirteenth century, much of Kanem was Islamic, as were the kingdoms of Kano and Katsina, whose wealth came from control of the trans-Saharan trade route from West Africa to the Mediterranean. These northern Islamic states remained untouched by Europeans until well into the nineteenth century. The southern states were dominated in the fourteenth and fifteenth centuries by Yoruba empires with traditional kings (Obas) who cultivated European contact through the Portuguese spice trade and retained power through the nineteenth century.

By the end of the eighteenth century, Fulani religious zealots in the north, resenting the dominance of the region by the Hausa states, created the largest unified caliphate in Africa, centered in Sokoto under the jihad of Usman dan Fodio. Fodio's dominance spread Islam throughout West Africa from Senegal to the Red Sea. The original conflict between the Islamic government in the north and the Yoruba tribes in the south has never truly subsided. Over the years intertribal fighting and civil wars have repeatedly exacerbated old wounds.

After the spice trade lost its force, the Portuguese and then the British began to deal in slavery. By 1807, when slavery was banned, the British took control of the Jos mines, destroying the livelihood of independent tin producers. The reliance on the mining trade was achieved at the expense of Nigeria's food crops, which led to the first-ever food shortage. In 1851 the British annexed Lagos and seized control of the rest of the region by 1886. In 1914 the region became the Protectorate of Nigeria.

In 1960 Nigeria declared independence and became a member of the United Nations, organized into a loose federation of states with the daunting task of unifying 250 ethnic and linguistic groups. However, by 1966, after a series of massacres, hostilities, and a military coup, the dream of a unified Nigeria was floundering. The Ibo seceded from the federation and declared the independent republic of Biafra, which started a full civil war. One million were left dead and the name "Biafra" has since come to be synonymous with mass destruction and famine.

A reversal of fortunes occurred in the 1970s due to the increase in oil prices, providing oil rich Nigeria with a chance to go on a spending spree of reckless proportions. Corruption became de rigueur, crime increased, and chaos became the rule of the day. The world recession of the 1980s sent oil prices plummeting and Nigeria sunk into massive debt, with inflation and unemployment rampant. In 1993, Nigeria succumbed to the rule of dictator General Abacha, who promised a United States type of democracy, but who ruled as a despot showed his despotic nature by executing well-known playwright Ken Saro-Wiwa and eight others for expressing their antigovernment views. Abacha died in 1998, replaced by Major General Abubakar, who brought modest civilian rule to the country. Olusegun Obasanjo, a former military ruler and political prisoner, was elected in 1999. It seemed for a moment that Nigeria would be free of military rule, but things reverted to disharmony soon, as rival religious and tribal groups, no longer threatened by army intervention, entered into a protracted conflict. The Sharia riots over full implementation of Islamic law thrust Igbo Christians and Hausa Muslims in Kaduna into a spiraling conflict.

Despite its unstable political history, Nigeria remains the superpower of West Africa, a position enhanced by its military interventions in civil wars in Liberia and Sierra Leone. As the twenty-first century proceeds, Nigeria must be a major player in determining the plight of West Africa if stability in the region is to be achieved.

FELA, KING SUNNY, AND NIGERIAN MUSIC

Two stars rise above all others in a country with a wealth of musical talent. *Fela* Anikulapo Kuti was the father of Afro Beat, a powerful singer and saxophonist and Nigeria's most famous musician, whose music is best described as Yoruban jazz. His career went from controversy to dilemma due to his immense talent, larger ego, and his attcks on the oppressive Nigerian government. Fela was truly a militant activist who chose song over the gun, embraced the Black Power movement in the United States in the '1960s and transported the attitude to West Africa. He was an arrogant egotist, an obsessive marijuana user, a notorious womanizer, and an international figure who lived by the proverbial sword and died of AIDS in 1997. His absence has left a void that cannot be filled.

Nigeria's other megastar is King Sunny Ade, champion of Juju, and an institution in West Africa. His live performances command several hundred thousand dollars each and his records sell in the millions. If Fela was the brash outspoken Mingus type, a foil and thorn in the side of the government because of his vocal opposition to the military juntas and his advocacy of human rights (including his right to have 100 wives and for marijuana to be legalized), King Sunny has reamained above the fray. Born to a wealthy family, and himself a business tycoon (oil wells and night clubs), Sunny is not exactly in concert with the powers that be, but simply above reproach in the manner of Duke Ellington—a regal being as his moniker suggests.

JUJU

Juju is one of Africa's great musical genres, a derivative of palm wine music from Sierra Leone, with beginnings in the early 1940s. I.K. Dairo, known as the "Father of Juju Music," introduced the talking drum, accordion, and steel guitar to the music and pioneered the short refrain that characterizes the vocal style and format of juju. His Morning Star Orchestra, later called the Blue Spots, was the most popular band in Nigeria just before and after independence in 1960. Following the successful recordings of Ebenezer Obey in the 1960s, juju became the prime popular music of the Yoruban people, with King Sunny presiding as its Chairman of the Board from the late 1970s to the present. Despite its popularity, juju retains a distinctive roots quality. It is laconic dance music, which draws on its Yoruban roots. Yoruban culture has sustained its strength and primacy, spreading throughout South America and the Caribbean, surviving the slave trade, especially in Cuba and in the Brazilian province of Bahia.

NIGERIAN MUSIC AT A CROSSROADS

Globalization has hit the Nigerian music scene with a resounding blow. Even before the death of Fela in 1997, Nigeria had begun to lose its musical identity. Following the reggae mania in the 1980s, the music scene and younger generation have become obsessed with hip-hop and/or rap, pulling the scene further away from its roots, even mocking and deriding I.K. Dairo in popular lyrics, an ignorant attitude akin to making fun of Louis Armstrong.

RECOMMENDED CDs

KING SUNNY ADE. *Juju Music* (Mango, 1982) helped put world music on the map in the United States; *Vintage King Sunny Ade* (Nigeria, 1985); *E Dide/Get Up* (Mesa, 1995) is his best from the 1990s.

AYINDE BARRISTER. Juju composer/bandleader who performs a stripped down version of the music. *More Fuji Garbage* (Globestyle, 1991).

I.K. DAIRO. The seminal figure in popular Nigerian music, father of juju, and the only African to be made a MBE (Member of the British Empire) by Queen Elizabeth in 1963. *Juju Master* (Original Music, 1993); *Ashika* (Green Linnet, Xenophile, 1994); *Definitive Dairo* (Green Linnet, 1996).

MAJEK FASHEK. Reggae star and Rasta figure. *Spirit of Love* (Interscope, 1991) is a great reggae recording.

FELA KUTI. Kuti released more than 50 CDs of varying quality. *Gentlemen* (Creole, 1973); *Confusion* (Polydor, 1975); *The '69 LA Sessions* (Universal, 1970; reissue 2000); *Expensive Shit* (Polygram, 1975); *Underground System* (Sterns, 1992).

PRINCE NICO MBARGA. Guitarist-vocalist. *Aki Special* (Rounder, 1987) contains *Sweet Mother*, which sold 13 million copies.

CHIEF COMMANDER EBENEZER OBEY. Early juju star, fore-runner and competitor of King Sunny Ade. *Je Ka Jo* (Shanachie, 1985); *Juju Jubilee* (Shanachie, 1985) is an early compilation; *Juju Jubilation* (Hemisphere, 1998) is excellent.

SONNY OKUSUNS. Pop star from the 1960s, switched to gospel in the '1990s. *Liberation* (Shanachie, 1984).

BABA OLATUNJI. The late percussion legend was one of the first international stars from Africa, a peer of Hugh Masekela and Miriam Makeba, and an influence on John Coltrane. *Drums of Passion* (Sony reissue, 1959).

SENEGAL

Senegal is a powerhouse of West African music rivaled only by Mali, Nigeria, and the Congo. The vibrant music scene in Dakar, Senegal's largest city, is arguably the most important on the continent, and along with the legendary Abidjan studio scene in neighboring Côte d'Ivoire, Senegal is the center of Afropop in the twenty-first century. Senegal shares Mali's musical caste system of griots, hereditary musicians born to sing and play praise music in the Wolof dialect. However, Senegal is a far more progressive and sophisticated nation than Mali, leading the region in literature, cinema, and the visual arts. Many Senegalese think of themselves as French and in fact have dual citizenship dating back to the time they achieved independence in 1959. Senegal in many ways is a paradox, a nation that is 95 percent Muslim, but with a modern view toward the world that reveres music. After successive democratic elections, the government is quite stable and the future is bright.

THE MUSIC

Senegal boasts two of world music's greatest artists—Baaba Maal and Youssou N'Dour—and West Africa's most renowned band, Orchestra Baobab. Along with other Senegalese stars such as Ismael Lo and Amadou and Mariam, they are now based in Paris. At home, followers of the charismatic Cheikh Ahmadou Bamba and the Mouride sect of Muslims that follow him control virtually all of the music business. Bamba is a revered religious icon who brought modern Islam to Senegal, a more contemporary and tolerant brand than that found in Mali, North Africa, and the Middle East. Most Senegalese musicians sing in the Wolof dialect and are griots, including N'Dour and the mystical Cheikh Lo.

MBALAX

Senegal's most important musical import is *mbalax* (em-bah-lakh), an infectious, syncopated dance music that originated in the early 1960s. It is played by a series of drums known as the *sabar*, which include the *mbung mbung* (lead drum), *jembe, tama* (talking drum), *ngorum, bougarabu, tungune, ndende, nder, tiol,* and *talmbeut,* collectively called "tam tams," each with a slightly different pitch and role in the rhythm. As with much West African music, mbalax has roots in Cuban music. Beginning with his tenure in the group Etoile de Dakar in the late 1970s, Youssou N'dour has been the artist most responsible for popularizing the music. He was the first to combine traditional music with sabar drums, saxophones, and electric guitars. N'dour and members of Etoile de Dakar contributed the mbalax beat on "Diamonds on the Souls of Her Shoes," from Paul Simon's 1986 *Graceland* album, the first truly global exposure for the music and the rhythm. Since its explosion on the world music scene in the early '1980s, the music has continued to evolve, incorporating global sounds and hip-hop.

RECOMMENDED CDs

AMADOU AND MARIAM. The blind vocalists have been performing since the late 1960s and now incorporate American blues, Cuban son, Indian rhythms, and French folk songs into their music. The duo gained worldwide exposure as featured performers on the Putumayo collection, *Mali to Memphis* (2000); *Sou Ni Tile* (Universal, 1999); *Tje Ni Mousso* (Circular Moves, 2000).

ORCHESTRA BAOBAB. Leader and guitar virtuoso Thione Seck recycled Afro-Cuban sounds back to the motherland and established the orchestra as the most popular West African Group of the 1970s and '1980's. *Pirate's Choice* (World Circuit 2000/1982) is the classic; *Specialists in all Styles* (World Circuit, 2002), their first recording in 18 years, produced by Jerry Boys of Buena Vista fame, may even be better.

BAABA MAAL. Singer, composer, dancer, and world music giant Baaba Maal is one of the most exciting performers in the world. *Djam Leeli* (Mango, 1985), a recording with mentor and partner Mansour Seck, is arguably *the* classic acoustic West African recording of all time; *Baayo* (Mango, 1991) is mostly acoustic and less somber, also excellent; *Firin n Fouta* (Mango, 1994) moves to a large ensemble backing an upbeat Baaba; *Mi Yeewnii/missing you* (Nonesuch, 2002) gets back to the roots.

DAARA J. Exciting Paris based hip-hop group. *Boomerang* (Wrasse, 2003) features a guest spot by Malian diva Rokia Traore.

EL HADJ N'DIAYE. Composer, Wolof vocalist, and political activist, El Hadj N'Diaye is a new voice on the scene; *Xel* (2001).

YOUSSOU N'DOUR. The biggest star from Senegal, if not all of Africa, N'Dour virtually created *mbalax*. Most of his recordings do not accurately display his true genius. *Set*, from 1990, is perhaps the most traditional; *Nothing's in Vain* (World Circuit, 2002); Egypt (Nonesuch, 2004) a reflective turn to Islam and his most realized recording.

AFRICANDO. Afro-Cuban group with a formula, mostly Salsa Africano; *Africando 1 & 2; Sabador* (Melodie, 1997).

WASIS DIOP. Wolof singer with a smooth voice; *Toxu* (Triloka, 1998).

ISMAEL LO. Former lead singer from seminal group Super Diamano is a great stylist and a major star. *Iso* (Mango, 1994), *Diawar* (Stern's, 1994), *Natt* (Melodie, 1996).

CHEIKH LO. Born in Burkina Faso, but lives in Senegal, Lo is a mystic and follower of Muslim leader Cheikh Ahmadou Bamba. *Ne la Thiass* (World Circuit, 1998) is superb.

MANSOUR SECK. Blind guitarist, griot, and mentor of Baaba Maal. *Nider Fouta Toro Vol. 1* (Stern's, 1994), with vocalists Ousmane Hamady Diop and Baaba Maal.

SUPER DIAMANO. The seminal mbalax group, there before Youssou N'Dour, broke up in 1991 after 20 years as the political conscience of the otherwise conservative Senegalese praise music scene. Old sides hard to find; grab anything pre-1991.

TOURA KUNDA. *Toure Kunda 1983–84* (Celluloid).

DOUDOU N'DIAYE ROSE. The Senegalese Wolof percussionist supreme, the "Jimi Hendrix of the skins" who plays the sabar drum, native to Senegal. *Djabote* (Real World, 1994).

SIERRA LEONE

A country of mineral riches, Sierra Leone is surrounded by Guinea, Cote d'Ivoire, and Liberia, with a border on the Atlantic Coast. In the late eighteenth century, it was established as a colony for freed slaves who wanted to safely return to their home continent, and when the British abolitionists colonized Sierra Leone their intent was to create a free state for slaves throughout the New World. Freetown was the site of this plan in 1792, evolving as an economic center and home to the *Krio* people, a new culture. In the early part of the twentieth century, diamond and gold mining supported the economy handsomely. Despite periods of prosperity in the 1980s, in 1991 Liberia's Charles Taylor brought his civil war to Sierra Leone and chaos has ruled ever since. Taylor's resignation coupled with interim support from Nigeria and the United States in 2003 temporarily quelled atrocities, but the jury is still out on whether or not peace and stability will come any time soon.

THE MUSIC

Portuguese sailors brought the first guitars to Sierra Leone and the locals took to it with a passion, creating *palm wine* music, or *maringa* as it is known locally. Palm wine music is characterized by a light, easy, lilting song style that hints at calypso. Its origins are in the Krio culture, the seagoing, guitar-playing people of Sierra Leone and Liberia.

Few artists in the world are as closely associated with a genre as Sooliman Ernest Rogie is with plum wine music. Rogie used Western pop, folk music, American country star Jimmie Rodgers' records, and High Life to create his unique sound. Palm wine music expresses the everyday trials and tribulations of life; as Rogie has said, "Emotions are the same all over the world . . . the difference is in the way you express them."

RECOMMENDED CDs

ABDUL TEE-JAY. Leader of dance band Rkoto and heir to S.E. Rogie. *Palm Wine A Go Go* (Farside, 2003).

ROKOTO. *Kanka Kura* (Rogue, 1989), *E'Go Lef Pan You* (1997).

S.E. ROGIE. *The Sixties Sounds of S.E. Rogie* (Cooking Vinyl, 1986), *Dead Men Don't Smoke Marijuana* (Real World, 1994).

SEYDU. Percussionist, poet, and vocalist combines local folk with Jazz and R&B. *Freetown* (NubaNegra, 1999).

EAST AFRICA

Burundi	Kenya	Sudan
Comoros Islands	La Reunion	Tanzania
Eritrea	Madagascar	Uganda
Ethiopia	Somalia	

East Africa possesses majestic beauty, some of the most magnificent animals on the planet, beautiful lakes, towering mountain ranges, vast savannahs, but it has also experienced famine, civil war, murderous dictators, and been a geographic pawn played both by the Islamic militarists and Western powers alike. The influence of Islam is especially profound in the Sudan, Somalia, and Tanzania. Kenya's alliance with the West, especially its trading relationship with Israel, made it a target for Islamic terrorism. The Indian Ocean coast has long been a gateway for trade with the Arab world, crucial to OPEC and the international oil cartels.

The music of East Africa is the least known, internationally, of all the music from the continent. However, there are some incredibly unique sounds from the region, including a booming scene in Ethiopia that has reemerged since the end of the war with Eritrea; the vibrant musical cauldron of Madagascar; and the unique sounds of Maloya from Reunion Island in the Indian Ocean.

BURUNDI

The Central African nation of Burundi is the size of Maryland in the United States, with a population of approximately 6 million,

85 percent of whom are Christians and Hutus. Burundi gained independence from Belgium in 1962. It is a landlocked country with few natural resources. Poverty is endemic. At the time of this writing, Burundi had not recovered from the horrific "ethnic" violence sustained during the widespread war in the region from 1993–2000, which spilled over to the neighboring Democratic Republic of Congo. The stability of Burundi is extremely fragile. The problems of the region in general have been greatly exacerbated by the AIDS epidemic, which continues to plague Central and South Africa despite promises from the United States to give financial aid to combat the crisis.

While there is little recorded music available from Burundi, Khadja Nin is a major vocalist, one of Africa's most popular and talented singers. Khadja, who is based in Europe, fled Burundi in the early 1980s when she lost her husband and other relatives to the wars. She continues to record her brand of acoustic Afropop that speaks of the tragedy of her homeland, the politics and poverty, always with an optimistic attitude that communicates her love of life. Miriam Makeba has been her idol since childhood.

RECOMMENDED CDs

KHADJA NIN. Her first eponymous recording, *Khadja Nin* (1991), preceded the world music boom. *Ya Pili* (1994) shows her Sade-Cassandra Wilson influence with Khadja singing in Kishwahili and French. *Sombolera*, (2000) is beautifully produced and put her on the map, selling more than 400,000 copies worldwide.

ERITREA

After 30 years of brutal war, Eritrea broke away from Ethiopia in 1993. Eritrea is the youngest country in Africa, with a long border on the Red Sea, a land full of hope and spirit. The music coming out of Eritrea is also promising, especially female vocalist Faytinga who is a burgeoning world music diva. She is the daughter of a well-known soldier and as a teenager was a combatant during the struggle for independence. Her music features ballads, love songs, and compositions praising the soldiers and mourning those who died in the war. The music has a decidedly oriental feeling, evidencing Eritrea's proximity to the Arab world and Asia.

RECOMMENDED CDs

FAYTINGA. One of the first international releases to come out of Eritrea was *Muney* (Cobalt, 2000), backed by percussion, the *wata*, a one stringed violin, and the *krar*, a six-stringed lyre that is prominent in the highlands of Ethiopia and Eritrea; *Eritrea* (Cobalt/ Melodie, 2003) is a breakout recording on a major label that showcases her immense vocal talent, promising great things to come.

ETHIOPIA

The only African nation never to have been colonized—Mussolini only occupied it, and a brief bout with Portuguese colonialism was repelled in the nineteenth century—Ethiopia has known a great deal of isolation since its rise from the Axum kingdom in 500 BCE. It is one of the most unique and fascinating cultures on the planet. It was a Christian nation long before Islam swept through North Africa and even today retains a minority Afro-Jewish community, although many of Ethiopia's Jews moved to Israel in the latter part of the twentieth century.

Ethiopia's history in the twentieth century is inextricably tied to the Emperor Haile Selassie. He came to power in 1930 and modernized the country before losing the confidence of his people after almost 40 years as a mostly revered ruler. Selassie also played an indirect role in the development of reggae. The Emperor became a quasi-deity in the eyes of Jamaican Rastafarians in the 1950s, who revere Ethiopia as the promised land and Selassie as a divine Rasta.

Following Selassie's demise in the early 1970s, the repressive, Marxist Mengistu regime capitalized on the Emperor's failures, sending the country into isolation from the west until 1991. Mengistu's inhumane policies led to the horrific famine that gained international attention and spawned the "We are the World" benefit recording. Due to the lack of sophisticated farming technique, periodic horrific droughts and a deterioration of Ethiopia's infrastructure, at the time of this writing the country was facing yet another catastrophic famine that threatened to be as severe and devastating as 1984, when more than a million Ethiopians starved to death.

Ethiopia has more than 75 ethnic groups, but the Amharic-speaking people from the central highlands near Addis Ababa dominate the music scene. Amharic musicians have recited their oral history through song for centuries, usually accompanied by the *krar*, a 6-stringd lyre that dates back 4,000 years and is said to be one of the ancestors of the banjo, the *masenqo*, a one string fiddle, and *washint*, an end-blown flute. In the 1920s, a young Haile Selassie brought Armenian refugees from Jerusalem to Ethiopia to form a military brass band, and the style served as the backdrop for the country's early recording artists including Tilahoun Gessesse, the Hindi-styled Neway Debebe, and Ethiopia's most famous musical artist, Mahmoud Ahmed. These stars sang both traditional and popular repertoires playing the large halls of Addis where the *iskista* dance was performed, replete with shaking shoulders, heaving chests, and heads snapping back. The music is characterized by a fast triplet beat with quivering voices and a call-and-response exchange between brass and reeds that brings the music to a rock and roll volume level.

The unique character of Ethiopian music comes from the use of the five-note, pentatonic scale and a penchant for large intervals between the notes that creates an eerily incomplete, lingering, unresolved feeling. The music is also asymmetrical and has an uncanny similarity to American soul music. *Eskeusta*, or ecstasy, is the term used to describe the shaking motion that is produced by the very best singers, an orgasmic state that is communicated to the listener during performance, analogous to the concept of *duende* in flamenco, although there is no musical relationship between these two styles. The history of the suffering that is part of life in Ethiopia finds its way into the traditional music as *achinoy*, a melancholy and treasured quality in Ethiopian music, somewhat analogous to the Brazilian *saudade*.

Since the lifting of the infamous curfews that were prevalent during the Mengistu regime, the established stars of Ethiopia can now travel to many isolated communities long out of touch with their favorite artists. Addis has become a hotbed for new stars, who incorporate Kenyan pop, American hip-hop, and reggae into their sound. The long dominant Amharic music currently has competition from the neo-traditional styles from regions such as Tigray, Gonder, and Oromo, led by Kiross Alemayehu who spent 4 years in Mengistu's jails for his songs about freedom and democracy.

RECOMMENDED CDs

ALEMU AGA. Tender vocals from rural Ethiopia accompanied by *beganna*, an Ethiopian harp. *The Harp of King David – Ethiopiques Vol. 11* (Buda, 1995).

MAHMOUD AHMED. His best material is from 1975–1978 including his masterpiece *Ere Mela Mela* (Hannibal, 1975), also known as *Ethiopiques Vol. 7* (Buda); *Soul of Addis* (Earthworks, 1997)

ASTER AWEKE. Ethiopia's most famous singer lives in Washington, D.C. East African Motown sung in Amharic; *Aster* (Sony, 1989); *Kabu* (1990, Triple Earth); *Live in London* (Bamboo, 1995).

TLAHOUN CESSESSE. From the golden age of Ethiopian music in the 1950s, a husky voiced microtonal rock and roll crooner. *Tlahoun Cessesse/Ethiopiques Vol. 17* (Buda, 2003).

SELESHE DEMESSAE. Master of the *kirar*, Demessae is a poet, dancer, singer, composer, teacher, and ethnomusicologist. *Songs from Ethiopia* (Wergo, 1993).

ALEMAYU ESHETE. Eshete is credited with disseminating Ethiopian music abroad; he started his own record label in 1948. *Ethiopiques Vol. 9* (Buda, 2001).

EJIGAYEHU SHIBABAW "GIGI." Gigi is the brightest female vocal star of East Africa. *Zion Roots/Abyssinia Infante* (Network, 2003) with Hubby Bill Laswell producing and New York-based South African multi-instrumentalist Tony Cedras in support, is a great recording, sung in Amharic; *Gigi* (Palm, 2001) was her debut.

ASNAQETCH WERQU. Legendary actress, dancer, singer, and krar player. *Ethiopiques 16/the lady with the Krar* (Buda, 2003).

KENYA

The very mention of Kenya conjures images of fantastic wildlife, savannas, Lake Victoria, safaris, incredible landscapes, and total domination in the field of marathon running and long distance track and field. The name itself comes from the Kikuyu people who live near present day Mt. Kenya. They called the mountain Kirinyaga ("White Capped Mountain"); the English Colonizers' inability to pronounce the name led to "Kenya." Kenya's history is one of ancient African civilization and early Arab settlement. As is the case with much of East Africa, Kenya's past is inextricably associated with the Arab slave trade; Zanzibar was used as the shipping point for sending slaves to India and China.

The ubiquitous Vasco da Gama and Portugal were the first white invaders to reach Kenya circa 1480. Late in the nineteenth century, the Portuguese and British reasserted their interest in Kenya by instituting apartheid-type controls and land regulation. Britain ruled Kenya as a protectorate for more than 70 years and modern Kenya still shows the influence of colonial rule. Following Britain's brutal repression of the Mau Mau in the mid-1950s, the country gained independence in 1963, initially ruled by pro-western Jomo Kenyatta, who instituted harsh yet sound economic policies, which have served Kenya well to the present. Kenyan political leader Daniel Arap Moi's dream of a nonethnic democracy hasn't quite happened, but Kenya remains the most stable country in the region, neutral on political issues and a force for peace. The embassy bombings in 1998 in Nairobi marked the city as a target for fundamentalist Islamic militarism and exploitation because of its stature as the largest and most important city in East Africa.

THE MUSIC

Nairobi sustains a vibrant nightlife that features music from all over the continent. Benga is the genre most associated with Kenya, originating in the lake region near Lake Victoria in the 1960s and combining local rhythms with Cuban rumba and Congolese styles. Daniel O. Misiani was the leading proponent of this style, who sang in his native *Luo* (he is still active), and the term itself is commonly used to refer to any kind of Kenyan popular music. Much of Kenya's music is derivative of other Afropop forms, most obviously Congolese, but the singing, high-pitched guitar work, use of the national instrument the *nyatiti* (a seven-stringed harp), and bottle percussion give it a unique, identifiable sound.

RECOMMENDED CDs

AYUB OGADA. Ogada is a wonderful folksinger and songwriter who also plays the Nyatiti. His gentle voice and warm persona have made him an international star, leading to roles in the films *Out of Africa* with Robert Redford and in *The Color Purple. En Mana Kouyo* (Real World, 1993).

SAM MAPANGALA AND ORCHESTRA VIRUNGA. Born in the Congo, Sam Mapangala is a long-time Kenyan resident, one of the most popular musicians in the country. *Virunga Volcano* (Earthworks, 1990); *Feet on Fire* (Sterns, 1991).

JABALI AFRIKA. *Rootsganza* (Converge, 2003).

THE MIGHTY KINGS OF BENGA. High-pitched guitar Dance music; Congolese time to the third power. *The Victoria Kings* (Globestyle, 1993).

DANIEL KAMAU. *Kenyafrica* (PlayaSound). Love songs in the Kikuyu style.

DANIEL O. MISIANI AND SHIRATI JAZZ. Benga pioneer. *Piny Ose Mer: The World Upside Down* (Globestyle, 1995); *Benga Blast* (Earthworks, 1993).

LA REUNION

Prior to 1693, La Reunion, an island in the Indian Ocean east of Madagascar, was uninhabited by humans. The first colonizers were French who brought Malagasy slaves to the island to establish the spice trade. Eventually sugarcane became the main industry and more slaves were brought from Mozambique and India. Slavery theoretically ended in 1848, but indentured labor took its place, although the people were allowed to practice their religion and keep their names and culture. In 1946, the island became part of the Departement of France, at which time many ruling class administrators arrived accounting for the white population still present on the island.

MALOYA

Ile de la Reunion is home to an extraordinary music called *maloya*, also known as the *Reunion blues*. The music consists predominantly of vocals, sung in Creole backed only by percussion, a music that dates back to the chants of the slaves who sang on the sugar cane plantations. As recently as the 1960s, the French authorities in Reunion banned the music because of its strong identification with Creole culture and to the descendants of slaves brought to Reunion. Maloya has an affinity to West African folk, the Malagasy of southeastern Africa, and most obviously the blues, but is truly a unique Creole genre combining the music of many varied cultures. The racial mix of La Reunion is a true melting pot with Creole terms that identify (not classify) the denizens as *yaf* (black), *malbar* (Indian), *yab* (white), *zoreille* (French), and *zarab* (Indian Muslims). The leading modern proponent of maloya is Danyel Waro, known as the "Black Soul of Reunion," even though he is yab. He is reknowned for his commitment to maintaining the purity of the music and the Creole culture and staunchly resists the integration of electronics and nontraditional instruments. Waro has performed throughout West Africa and Europe. He differs from other Reunion artists in that he writes original compositions, using his poetry to relate the daily trials and tribulations of Reunion life to his audience. He is a gifted singer and charismatic performer. Waro's mentor is Firmin Viry, widely credited as having saved maloya from extinction. Viry plays the *kayamb*, a shaker that is a wooden box filled with seeds. Traditional maloya is usually accompanied by berimbau-type bowed instruments, triangles, chants, and a panoply of primitive wooden percussion vessels.

RECOMMENDED CDs

FIRMIN VIRY. *Ti Marde* (Indigo, France).

GRANMOUN LELE. Lele's music has strong connections to West Africa. His rough voice is soulful and communicates quite clearly even without understanding the lyrics. *Namouniman* (Indigo, Label Bleu, 1999).

DANYEL WARO. *Sega La Pente* (1996) is a collaboration with fellow Reunionite Françoise Guimbert; *Fouton Fonnker* (1999) won prestigious French music awards in 2000; *Bwarouz* (Indigo, 2002) is his best with his working group performing traditional maloya, as bluesy a recording as anything Ali Farka Toure or John Lee Hooker ever did.

MADAGASCAR

Madagascar floats just off the southeastern corner of Africa in the Indian Ocean where it broke off from the continent many million years ago. It is widely thought that settlers first arrived there by traveling in canoes from Indonesia around 500 CE. Arabic, African, and European influences were eventually mixed into this Southeast Asian base, giving the island its unique and culturally complex composition.

Formerly known as the Malagasy Republic, Madagascar is the fourth largest island on the planet (considerably larger than California) with its own peculiar flora and fauna, variegated terrain, and distinctive culture. Virtually everything on the island has evolved in isolation. The people appear as a combination of Indonesian, East Asian, West African, and South American. The cities and villages reflect the cultures of these regions as well as parts of Europe.

While Madagascar's music clearly has an island sensibility and its own unique style, the African influence predominates, with European and Arabic tinges (due to settlers from Comoros) in the background. There is no one genre that can rightfully be called Madagascaran. "*Malagasy*" is a term used to describe many forms throughout the island with a common style and rhythm, but the music varies greatly from region to region, defying convenient categorization.

MERINA, BETSILEO, AND SAKALAVA

Three kingdoms developed on the island in the eighteenth century— Merina, Betsileo, and Sakalava—with a wide range of secular music and art proliferating. Women's choirs, minstrels, and haiku-like poetry thrived throughout the nineteenth century. With the French conquest in 1896 came Christianity. The art forms of the three kingdoms eventually melted into a variety of folk traditions and styles, spreading and dispersing across the island. The music of the

Merina and Antaimoro has been influenced by Europe and is based on diatonic modes. The *valiha,* a 16-string tubed zither that sounds like a Western harp, is the main voice of Merina and Antaimoro, the instrument most associated with the music of Madagascar. The harmonic structure from these regions is based on parallel thirds with an independent bass line and complex rhythms. The melodies are long and beautiful, with other instruments such as the accordion, clarinet, flute, and trumpet incorporated from European settlers.

Arabic music arrived with the Comorian settlers and Islam. Double reed oboes, tambourine, viol, ud, and drums found in Madagascar are similar to those used in traditional Arabic music.

RECOMMENDED CDs

MILY CLEMENT. Reggae-influenced singer. *Madagascar Banja Malalaka* (Playasound, 1994).

D'GARY. Since his emergence on the world music scene with his debut album *Malagasy Guitar/Music from Madagascar* (Shanachie, 1991), D'Gary has garnered fans all over Europe and America, particularly among electric guitar freaks. Son of a Bara shepherd from the southwest, he has transcended the music of his homeland to join a small coterie of guitarists who enjoy an avid worldwide following. *Horombe* (Shanachie, 1995); *Akata Meso* (Label Bleu, 2002) demonstrates D'Gary's astounding technique.

JEAN EMILIEN. Betsileo Folk singer/harmonica/*kabosy* (small guitar) player. *Miandraza* (Cobalt, 1998).

FENOAMBY. *Ravo* (Cobalt, 1998).

JAOJOBY. Saleg and rock vocalist who has helped internationalize the music. *Saleyg: Hot Dance Music from Madagascar* (Xenophile, 1996); *E Tiako: Madagascar* (Indigo, 1998); Malagassy (Discorama, 2004).

RAJERY. Valiha wiz. *Fanamby* (Indigo, 2000).

RAKOTO FRAH. Master of the indigenous *sodina* flute. *Flute Master of Madagascar* (Globestyle, 1999).

SOLO RAZAFINDRAKOTO. Guitar legend who combines Madagascaran folk with French Chanteuse and appears on many of the CDs listed in this section.

ROSSY. The first Malagasy star to go international in the early 1980s, accordionist, composer, producer, and proponent of the raunchy streetcorner style, *soava*. *Island of Ghosts* (Caroline, 1991); *One Eye on the Future* (Shanachie 1992).

TARIKA SAMMY. Formed by Samoela in 1983, Sammy, as they are now called, is the leading Malagasy band. *Balance* (Green Linnet, 1994); *Fanafody* (Green Linnet, 1992).

JUSTIN VALI. The number-one valiha master has recorded extensively in many contexts. He has several recordings with many Galician artists, most notably with Basque *trikitrixa* virtuoso Kepa Junkera on the classic *Bilbao 00:00* (Resistancia, 1998). Solo outings include *Truth* (Real World, 1995) and *Genius of Valiha* (Real World, 1997).

VARIOUS ARTISTS. *The Moon and the Banana Tree* (Shanachie, 1996) D'Gary, Johnny, Sol Razaf, Etienne Ramboatiana, and many more; the place to start and learn the music.

SOMALIA

As we begin the twenty-first century, the former Italian colony and British protectorate known as Somalia is a war-torn society run by clan-based militias. The country exists with no central government and is a veritable hotbed for mercenary activity. Due to its strategic value as a coastal stop on the Horn of Africa near Arab strongholds in the Middle East, Somalia has become a political football in the war on Militant Islam. In 1994, following joint efforts with the United Nations (UN) called "Operation Restore Hope" designed to aid Somalia in fighting the dual horrors of starvation and AIDS, the United States pulled its troops out and the country has been a free zone ever since, with various Saudi-backed Islamic groups the dominant force for chaos. With this backdrop of virtual anarchy, it is remarkable that a music scene has survived in Somalia.

THE MUSIC

The language and music of Somalia is a mixture of African and Arabic. The instruments prevalent in Somali music include West Indian lutes and frame drums from Egypt that predate Islam. After the arrival of Islam in the Horn of Africa during the fourteenth century, the oud and Egyptian-style orchestras began to permeate Somali music. Pentatonic and Arabic microtonal scales can be heard in Somali song. Somalia's most famous and revered artist is Maryam Mursal, who fled the country during the civil war in the early 1990s by walking for 6 months with her five children, eventually reaching Djibouti where she was airlifted by the UN to Denmark where she now makes her home. She is a soulful singer who has clearly listened to Ray Charles, and her recordings are virtually the only ones from Somalia available in the West.

RECOMMENDED CDs

MAYRAM MURSAL. *The Journey* (Real World 1998). Backed by singers Kadra Dahir and Abdi Nuur Allale and the roots group Waaberi.

WAABERI. The ethereal quality of the oud and the rhythm of African percussion combine here for a unique blend of Arabo-African sound. *New Dawn* (Real World, 1998).

SUDAN

The largest country in Africa—one-quarter the size of the United States—Sudan has been controlled by military dictatorships since its independence from the United Kingdom circa 1956. Since 1989, censorship and oppression have become state policy under the Islamic Fundamentalist Arabs who live in the north and control the country. They have systematically persecuted and enslaved the Black Christian and Animist population in the south, banned virtually all music, and forced the majority of Sudanese artists and musicians into exile. Despite the oppressive rule, Sudan has experienced economic growth since the mid '1990s due to increased oil exports, which has unfortunately enhanced the fundamentalist's ability to rule with an iron fist. Needless to say, the despots have all but shut down the music business.

Despite the current dearth of artistic expression in the Sudan, the mix of Arabic, Nubian, and Black African cultures has a rich musical past based on a convergence of cultures unlike any other on the continent. The Sufis brought the whirling dervishes, the

Arab influence is strong, and the Nubian tradition has survived the tyranny, albeit outside of the country. Expatriated Sudanese artists living in Egypt and Europe continue to contribute to the world music library. The indigenous Nubian population continues to combat Arab fundamentalists, keeping tradition alive in the south. The Nubian culture is not Arabic and shares a plight and struggle similar to the Berbers in Algeria and the Tuareg people in Mali and Libya.

THE MUSIC

Hamza El Din is the father of modern Nubian music, an oud virtuoso, vocalist, ethnomusicologist, and international star. Exiled from his native land (southern Egypt/northern Sudan) when it was destroyed by the runoff from the Aswan Dam in the early 1960s, El Din has traveled all over the world teaching the oud, spreading his music, and studying everywhere he goes. He is one of the first world musicians recognized as such, having established an international career in the 1960s. He spent 15 years in Japan and China studying the biwan (Japanese lute), and the pipa (Chinese lute), lived in Rome and Vienna, and has made Oakland, California, his home for more than 20 years.

Bandleaders Abdel Aziz el Mubarak and Abdel Gadir Salim have kept their careers going, despite censorship due the innocuous content of the lyrics in their music. Similarly, Sudan's traditional folk music *haqibah* (a harmonic, essentially a cappella music based on the pentatonic scale) has survived because it is derived from Islamic gospel. Sudan's music tends to be melancholy and introspective and not as rhythmically vibrant as other African music.

RECOMMENDED CDs

HAMZA EL DIN. His most famous recording is *Escalay-Waterwheel* (Nonesuch, 1968) from 1968, which contains three Zen-like improvisations, including a song by Egyptian composer Mohamed Abdel Wahab originally written for Umm Kulthum. *Muwashshah* (the veil before the voice) is a tribute piece to the legendary African slave musician from Baghdad, Ziryab, with Hamza's Japanese students using synthesizer to mimic an Egyptian string orchestra.

ABDEL AZIZ EL MUBARAK. The Sudan's most popular musician. *Straight from the Heart* (World Circuit, 1991) is replete with accordions, saxophones, and a ten-piece band—live, Afro-Arab pop.

RASHA. The Sudan's most renowned female vocalist and an international star, Rasha is an expatriate living in Spain who has collaborated with Galicia's Uxia. *Sudaniyat* (NubaNegra, 1997).

ABDEL GADIR SALIM. *Le Blues de Khartoum* (Harmonia Mundi, 1999); *The Merdoum Kings play Songs of Love* (Shanachie, 1992); *Stars of the Night* (Globestyle, 1989).

MOHAMMED WARDI. Political activist, poet, and singer who fled to Egypt in 1990. *Live in Addis Ababa* (Rags, 1994).

TANZANIA

Prior to the eighteenth century there was no central political authority in what is now called Tanzania, although the Arabian/ Swahili island of Zanzibar has long been a center of trade and political power in East Africa. A Sultanate was established in Zanzibar by 1800. The first Europeans to try to colonize the region were Germans, who slaughtered countless numbers of people, but they were eventually repelled, unable to establish a foothold in the region. After World War I, the British took over, instituting a plantation system. Colonial rule helped establish a working infrastructure in the country, which continues to function today. Tanzania was the first East African Nation to achieve independence in the 1950s under its visionary prime minister, Julius Nyerere. While hardly thriving today, Tanzania is a true democracy, remarkably free of corruption with credible institutions. It is a stable nation in a region despite having experienced war, poverty, and the worst of the AIDS epidemic since the early 1990s.

THE MUSIC

The traditional music of the more than 120 ethnic groups united by Nyerere found expression in the urban dance music of the 1930s in Tanzania's capital and main city, Dar Es Salaam. Popular Tanzanian music is a hybrid of other African musical forms. Cuban rumba led the way, followed by the Congo influence. During

Nyerere's administration, he wisely used the state radio to dissemi-
nate music and keep a cohesive feeling in the country.

Taarab is Tanzania's most famous musical genre, originally simply
wedding music sung in Swahili. It is a blend of African, Indian,and
Arabic sonorities based primarily on the island of Zanzibar. Female
vocalist Siti Bint Saad was the most famous singer, recording as
early as 1928. Bi Kidude is the doyen of Taarab. The music at times
sounds Egyptian with its classical orchestral style, but also has a
clear affinity to Indian film music. Taarab is above all based on
poetry, most often performed by female singers in the high register.
Bands always include at least three percussionists, ouds, zithers,
banjos, guitar, and bass.

RECOMMENDED CDs

ZEIN L' ABDIN. Oud master and vocalist. *The Swahili Songbook*
(Dizim, 1995).

REMMY ONGALA. Zaire-born Remmy Ongala is the Fela Kuti of
Tanzania, the voice of social conscience since 1978, who heads the
Orchestra Super Matimila. *Songs for the Poor Man* (1990, Real
World); *Mambo* (1991, Real World); *Sema* (1996).

HUKWE ZAWOSE. Thumb piano specialist, vocalist, and popular
Zanzibar artist sings in Swahili. *Chibite* (1996, Real World);
Tanzania Yetu (1994, Triple Earth Terra).

UGANDA

The land Winston Churchill dubbed "The Pearl of Africa" has experienced a period of relative peace and prosperity in the new
millennium and is one of the fastest growing economies on the
continent. Recent good times have come at a price however; for the
past 50 years Uganda has endured a series of despotic rulers and
some of the most horrific regimes anywhere in Africa.

Prior to 1600, Uganda was inhabited primarily by bushmen and
had no central governing body or unified kingdom. When European
explorers arrived in the early 1800s, the largest groups were the
Bantus from the West followed by the Nilotics from the North. A
search for the source of the Nile brought the first European explorers,

and the opening of the Suez Canal in 1869 opened trade. After a period where Egypt governed the region (then known as Equatoria), the British took control, opening the door for the ubiquitous Protestant and Catholic missionaries in the late 1800s. The clash between Islam and Christianity began a pattern of murder that was to terrify Ugandans for a century.

By the early 1900s, Uganda was a locally administered British protectorate. Independence came in 1961. After becoming a republic, Idi Amin Dada took over as ruler in a military coup in 1971, giving himself absolute power. Amin's systematic massacre of the Acholi and Langi people removed any hope for the reform that his new leadership had promised and the country plunged into perpetual nightmare. Amin soon expelled more than 50,000 people. His meglomaniacal murder and plunder continued until the Israeli raid at Entebbe airport in 1976, which marked the beginning of the end for Amin as leader.

As the twenty-first century begins, Uganda is a small beacon of hope in the region, reclaiming its once thriving coffee industry and notably instituting a successful campaign against AIDS. Freedoms have expanded and, after a quarter of a century, businesses have slowly returned.

THE MUSIC

Ugandan folk music houses the country's oral history and survives today in sporadic form among the numerous rural tribes. The *ndigindi* (lyre), *entongoli* (harp), *amandinda* (xylophone), and *lukeme* (thumb piano) are the commonly played instruments, which have been incorporated into a national Afropop style that is reminiscent of Caribbean zouk and music from Martinique.

Geoffrey Oreyma is a talented singer-songwriter who grew up under the Amin regime. He fled to Kenya after his father was assassinated and has enjoyed a successful career since the late 1980s. New York based multi-instrumentalist Samite is a musician of exceptional sensitivity and gentleness.

ABAYUDAYA

One of the more interesting developments in African folk music in recent years is that of Uganda's Abayudaya, African Jews who have survived a century of persecution to emerge as a new voice in an increasingly tolerant country. The Abayudaya currently comprise only 600 or so individuals living in villages surrounding Mbale in eastern Uganda. In the early part of the twentieth century, there were thousands of Ugandan Jews, enough to sustain more than 30 synagogues. Throughout most of the twentieth century, however, the Abayudaya were forced to convert or worship and practice their religion in secrecy due to pressure from both the Christian missionaries and Islamic militants. Recent contact with and economic aid from Israel has bolstered the entire region near Mbale.

RECOMMENDED CDs

THE ABAYUDAYA. *Abayudaya: Music from the Jewish People of Uganda* (Smithsonian Folkways, 2003). A truly unique and uplifting collection of African Jewish music. Vocal harmonies are backed by simple guitar, and the voices are moving.

GEOFFREY ORYEMA. His music incorporates European melodies, African harmonies, and Uganda's traditions. *Exile* (Real World, 1990); *Night to Night* (Real World 1997), produced by the talented Lokua Kanza and sung mostly in English.

SAMITE. Born in Kampala, Samite is a master of the *kalimba* (a thumb piano), marimba, *litungu* (a cross between a kora and a lyre), as well as a variety of flutes. He left Uganda in the early 1980s and has become a fixture on the world music scene in New York. His gentle voice is perfect on *Dance My Children, Dance* (Shanachie, 1988); *Tulunu Eno* (Triloka, 2003) is a soothing gem.

SOUTH AFRICA

Angola	Namibia	Zimbabwe
Botswana	Republic ofSouth Africa	Zambia
Mozambique		

The region of South Africa is truly a separate part of the great continent, the richest and in many ways most important region as Africa emerges in the age of globalization. Since Nelson Mandela's election and the end of apartheid, much progress has been made in the Republic of South Africa (RSA), but progress in this region of the world is slow and difficult. The horror of Robert Mugabe's regime in Zimbabwe has indeed been a setback that was unforeseeable when Ian Smith's government was disbanded, and it will take many decades before the country gains stability.

The music from the Southern Africa is quite distinct from the rest of the continent, influenced by centuries of colonial rule, but notably uninfluenced by Islam and in many ways older and more purely traditional. Botswana (formerly Beuchanland), Lesotho, Namibia, and Zambia (formerly Northern Rhodesia) have fledgling music scenes and mostly stable governments, but remarkably few available recordings and prominent artists. Conversely, the RSA and Zimbabwe have been at the forefront of the Afropop/Afro Beat explosion for decades. Angola and Mozambique are important to Lusaphone culture with ties to the motherland and Brazil, but with rich individual musical traditions of their own.

ANGOLA

It has often been postulated that millions of years ago, before the world's land mass split apart to form five continents, Angola and Brazil had been fused together. Examining the current coastlines of each country seems to support this possibility. What is undeniably true is that both countries were colonized by the Portuguese, and were major cogs in the slave trade, countries that continue to share cultural and musical ties with each other and their colonizers.

The Portuguese landed in what is now northern Angola circa 1482, encountering the kingdom of the Congo and to the south the Ngona people and their King Ngola, from whence the modern name of the country is derived. The Portuguese slaving system began in the sixteenth century, and by the nineteenth century Angola was one of the largest sources of slaves for Brazil and the Americas. Incredibly, slavery, redefined after the 1880s as the euphemistic "forced labor," continued until 1961.

After the fall of the Salazar dictatorship in Portugal in 1974, a coalition of three separate movements that had been fighting the Portuguese in Angola came to power. The coalition soon broke down and civil war erupted into an international conflict. Despite periodic attempts at peace accords, guerilla forces have kept the conflict going into the twenty-first century, keeping Angola and its incredible mineral wealth in a state of turmoil.

THE MUSIC

Semba is Angola's traditional music, believed by many scholars to lie at the heart of the more famous Brazilian samba. The two styles sound quite different but share similar names and dance forms. *Semba* is an ancient dance rhythm accompanied by smooth undulation of the hips, originally played to celebrate good harvests, marriages, and other happy occasions. It developed in the coastal centers of Luanda and Benguela in the seventeenth century and to this day is regarded as the music of the sea.

Liceu Vierira Dias is credited as the modern pioneer of Angolan music. He was greatly influenced by American jazz and Portuguese fado and fronted Angola's most famous band, Ngola Ritmos, in the 1940s. The colonial authorities arrested him in the late 1950s, and his removal from the scene was a setback to the music and established a trend whereby a seemingly never-ending series of oppressive governments persecuted musicians. There have been periodic flurries of a recording industry over the last few decades, but freedom of musical expression, which inevitably includes speaking out against tyrants, has met with censorship and in some instances murder, as in the case of David Zee and Urbano de Castro. As a result, the leading musicians of the current generation have been forced to record abroad.

Barcelo de Carvalho, also known as Bonga, is Angola's most famous musical artist. The former African 400 meter track champion and staunch anticolonialist was forced into exile in the Netherlands in 1972, eventually going totally underground when Holland cooperated with Portugal in returning political activists. After forming his band Kissueia in the early 1970s, he was coaxed into singing. The band likened his mournful, raspy voice to those of Louis Armstrong, Ray Charles, and James Brown. While in exile he recorded *Angola 72*, one of the most popular and powerful African records ever. At first, the authorities didn't understand the revolutionary message of the record since Bonga did not sing in Portuguese. Eventually it was banned in Angola and anyone caught with it was arrested on the spot.

Waldemar Bastos was born in Zaire and raised in Angola. He was something of a child prodigy, comfortable playing the accordion, organ, and piano by the time he was 7. His parents were both nurses and Waldemar absorbed a variety of musical styles while traveling with them as a child. Following Angola's independence in 1974, Bastos was disillusioned by the new government's continued oppression of artists and musicians. He was imprisoned for his part in several protests and eventually defected to Brazil in 1982 where he recorded his first album. After a short stint in Paris, he moved to Portugal where he currently resides in the new, open Lusaphone culture that has exploded in Lisbon and Coimbra. His music has a Brazilian tinge to it, showcasing the Angolan version of the beautiful Portuguese language and rhythms in an ethereal, seamless way. His voice and compositions have a relaxed sensibility. Bastos is a clever arranger as well as an enchanting singer and instrumentalist who has captured a delightful version of the Afro-Portuguese persona.

RECOMMENDED CDs

BONGA. *Angola 72* (Lusafrica, reissue 1997) an important document; *Angola 74* (Lusafrica, reissue, 1997) contains the classic Cape Verdean *Sodade* 20 years before Cesaria Evora made it a hit; *Mulemba Xangola* (Lusafrica, 2000); *Kaxexe* (Lusafrica, 2004).

WALDEMAR BASTOS. *Angola Minha Namorada/My Sweetheart Angola* (EMI, 1990) put him on the World Music map; *Pretaluz* (Luaka Bop, 2000).

PAULO FLORES. Semba/zouk guitarist/bassist, popular throughout the the Lusaphone world, especially in Lisbon. *Inocenti* (Discosette, 1996) with Guinean Manecas Costa on guitar; *Perto de Fim* (Energy, 1999).

VICTOR GAMA. Gama, who makes his own percussion instruments and thumb pianos, is a one-of-a-kind Afro Ambient musician incorporating subtle violin and guitar with suggestions of koras and voices. *Pangeia Instrumentos* (2003).

KAFALA BROTHERS. Acoustic-guitar based band. *Ngola* (A.A., 1994).

CARLOS LAMARTINE. *Memorias* (RMS, 1997).

RUY MINGAS. Temas Angolanas (Nuba Negia, 1973/95) an early peer of Bonga with a delightful voice.

FILIPE MUKENGA. Noted composer of the classics *Nvula ie,za Kia* and *Humbiumbi*, and featured as a duet with Gilberto Gil on Brazilian star Djavan's *Seduzir*, Mukenga is also a fine guitarist and vocalist. *Kianda Ki Anda* (Lusafrica, 1995); Le Chant du Siren (Lusafrica, 1996).

EDUARDO PAIM. Another star vocalist who has yet to gain exposure outside Angola and Lisbon due to Portugal's inexplicable reluctance to allow international recording companies access to artists unless they sing fado. *Mujimbos* (Vidisco, 1998).

RUKA VANDUNEN. *Sem Kigila* (Ze Orlando, 1991). Dance music and great vocals, with Eduardo Paim and Paulo Flores.

MOZAMBIQUE

Difficult terrain, ethnic diversity, and dense vegetation have made Mozambique hard to unify throughout its history. When Vasco da Gama arrived in 1497, the Portuguese found more than 10 ethnic groups, many trading with Arabs along the Zambezi River. Portugal's ruthless colonial crusade began with the *pazos* system whereby settlers were encouraged to lay claims on land, protected by armies of slaves. Despite a long, brutal struggle, Portugal prevailed in this southeastern African land, which was a primary supplier for the slave trade to Brazil.

As was the case in much of Portuguese-dominated Africa, after centuries of domination, rebellion erupted in the late 1960s. The FRELIMO faction took control, fighting both Portugal and troops from Apartheid South Africa. Despite decades of turmoil, Mozambique began to emerge as an economic miracle in the 1990s, with free, multi-party elections in 1994, until the disastrous flood of 1999 halted progress. Today, Mozambique is on the road to recovery, a glimmer of hope in the South African region amidst an ocean of turmoil.

THE MUSIC

Current world music sensation Mariza was born in Mozambique as were many other Portuguese singers, including the eclectic Amelia

Muge. Mozambique's urban dance music is *marrabenta*, with its own distinctive, catchy beat that includes calypso, salsa, and merengue rhythms marrabenta has made waves on the world scene since the founding of Orchestra Marrabenta Star de Mozambique in 1979 by leader and singer Wazimbo. The *timbla* music of the Chopa people of the northeast is based on the indigenous *mbila*, a type of xylophone said to derive from Indonesia. It is Mozambique's strongest surviving roots music, although recordings of the genre are virtually nonexistent.

RECOMMENDED CDs

DILON DJINDI. At 75, Djindi made his first recording, *Dilon* (Riverboat 2002), an acoustic, roots CD with female choral support and an old master at the helm.

EDUARDO DURAO. Master of the Mbila, a small xylophone. *Timbila* (Globestyle, 1991); Venacio Mbande/Timbila ensemble (Naxos, 2002).

FANI PFUMO. Marrabenta vocalist and star. *Nyoxanine* (Visodisc).

EYUPHURO. Fine *marrabenta* band. *Mama Mosambiki* (Real World, 1986); *Yellela* (World Network, 2001).

MABULU. This intergenerational groove band is driven by guitars, saxophones, and incorporates all forms of Afropop, hip-hop, and dance-hall. *Karimbo* (Riverboat, 2000); *Soul Marrabenta* (Riverboat, 2002).

ORCHESTRA MARABENTA: Urban dance music replete with electric Congolese guitars, horns, and a full rhythm section, originally featuring Wazimbo and female singer Mingas. *Independence* (Piranha, 1994).

WAZIMBO. *Nwahulwana* (Riverboat, 1999).

REPUBLIC OF SOUTH AFRICA

The Republic of South Africa (RSA) is the most important and influential nation on the African continent, especially since the late twentieth century. RSA has the best geographical resume on the planet: an abundance of rare nuclear elements, minerals, diamonds, and gold; thousands of kilometers of scenic coastline with incomparable panoramas; an immensely attractive and diverse climate; gorgeous mountains; vast tracts of arable land and national parks chock-full of unique wildlife; world-class wineries; a sporting tradition second to none (especially in rugby); and a rich culture that is only now beginning to express itself fully. RSA will be the first African Nation to host the Soccer World Cup in 2010. However, the fledgling democracy is undergoing growing pains and trouble abounds as of this writing. The legacy of Nelson Mandela is more analogous to the achievements of Gandhi than Martin Luther King; his international significance and his accomplishments are emblematic of the future of the entire continent.

THE MUSIC

South Africa possesses the most diverse culture in Africa, including the most vibrant recording scene. While much of South African music borrows from American jazz, hip-hop, and gospel, a rich folk tradition still exists based on the native Bantu languages including Sotho, Xhosa, and Zulu, and features one of the oldest "call and response" repertoires in the world. RSA's most popular musical genre is a rural dance music known as *mbaqanga*, popularized by Simon Mahlathini and the Mahotella Queens. Ladysmith Black Mambazo brought the Zulu a cappella tradition to international attention, and the Manhattan Brothers and the Skylarks, with whom the great Miriam Makeba made her debut, pioneered *Township* music in the 1950s and '1960s.

The changing political scene has paradoxically led to the stagnation of its modern musical evolution. The music is wallowing in derivative jazz, hip-hop, and soul much like the United States. South Africa is no longer the musical powerhouse on the continent, a title that clearly belongs to West Africa at the start of the twenty-first century.

Actress, singer, and activist Miriam Makeba (b.1932) has been an international household name since the early 1960s. A protégé of Harry Belafonte and born a Xosa tribeswoman, Makeba made her singing debut in 1954 with the '1950s vocal group The Manhattan Brothers, a South African version of the Mills Brothers. She appeared in the film *Come Back Africa* in 1957 and reached the peak of her popularity in her homeland in 1959. Due to the apartheid policies of the South African government, however, she was forced into exile and moved to the United States in 1960 with her then-husband and musical partner, trumpeter Hugh Masekela.

Megahits *The Click Song* and *Pata Pata* made Makeba the first true worldwide celebrity from her country and arguably the first true world music Diva. Makeba also used her gorgeous voice, strength, and charisma to expose a naïve world to the atrocities being perpetrated by the South African government against its people. Her courage and outspokenness made her a target for the powers that be both in South Africa and the United States. She married Stokely Carmichael and was again forced into exile because of the United States government's obsession with persecuting Carmichael for his then-radical political views. She became a citizen of Guinea and testified against apartheid before the United Nations as a delegate from that West African nation. Since the 1970s, still as an expatriate, she has immersed herself in the traditional music of her people. Happily, the end of apartheid in the 1990s finally allowed her to return to her homeland. Makeba is much more than a world music diva; she is an important figure in the history of the twentieth century.

Busi Mholongo was born in Kwa Zulu, Natal, and got her start as a performer by winning a talent contest in Johannesburg in 1963 singing the Millie Small hit "My Boy Lollipop." She worked in the theater through the 1960s while also playing with South Africa's jazz and mbaqanga bands at festivals. She then toured the Portuguese music circuit, where she worked for 5 years, with detours in Angola and Mozambique. She recorded with South African jazz saxophonist Dudu Pukwana and worked with the seminal Afropop Band Osibisa (from Ghana) as lead singer in the early 1970s.

Busi moved to the United States briefly due to a bout with cancer and settled in Toronto to sing Billy Holiday and Bessie Smith tunes in a show. Her music took her back to South Africa in 1979, but she returned to Europe when the Apartheid security forces tried to arrest her. By 1989, Busi was sharing the bill with Salif Keita and Manu Dibango as the highlight of the African Music Festival in Delft, Holland. During this period, she met renowned Cameroonian percussionist Brice Wassy, which led to *Urban Zulu*, her best known work.

Busi draws on many styles including *mbaqanga* and *maskanda* (a traditional Zulu music sung by working-class Zulu men), and her lyrics deliver poignant, controversial messages, which concern the empowerment of women. Busi is a powerful, charismatic singer with a stage presence that has made her one of the leading South African female vocalists.

RECOMMENDED CDs

AMADUDUZO. In the tradition of Solomon Linda's "Whimaway," a Christian group paying tribute to mbube (Lion) music from the early twentieth Century. *The Sound of African Mbube* (ARC, 2002).

BOYOYO BOYS. Upbeat guitar riffs, funky bass/drum, saxophone interplay, and fine vocal harmonies; Township music for the masses. *Back in Town* (Rounder, 1987).

TONY CEDRAS. Multi-instrumentalist Cedras is from Capetown but now resides in New York City. A fixture in Paul Simon's band for decades, he also plays with Ladysmith, Harry Belafonte, and is in demand as an accordionist, keyboard, and guitar player around the globe. He is a talented singer/songwriter in his own right.

(*See* Ethiopia *Zion Roots*, under Gigi.)

JOHNNY CLEGG. Clegg formed South Africa's first multiracial band, Juluka, which recorded two platinum and five gold albums. A native of Lancashire, England, Clegg moved to South Africa at an early age and became obsessed with Zulu music and Inhlangwini dancing. *Ubuhle Bemvelo* (Rhythm Safari, 1982); *Third World Child* (Alliance, 1987) includes an anthem for Mandela; *Scatterlings* (Priority, 1982) is one of Juluka's best with cohort Sipho Mchunu.

DARK CITY SISTERS. Township soul group from the 1960s that presaged *mbaqanga*. *Dark City Sisters and the Flying Jazz Queens* (Earthworks, 1993/1966).

LUCKY DUBE. Mbaqanga singer who moved to reggae in 1984; one of South Africa's biggest selling artists. *Prisoner* (Shanachie, 1991); *House of Exile* (Shanachie, 1992).

BRENDA FASSIE. Township Jive singer with a tremendous following. *Brenda Fassie* (Capitol, 1990).

SIBONGILE KHUMALO. Classically trained with chops to die for; like Virginia Rodrigues from Brazil, there can be no question as to Sibongile's awesome vocal gifts. However, also like Rodrigues, her recordings are unfortunately mediocre. *Live at the Market Theatre* (Sony, 2000).

BAKITHI KUMALO. Legendary bassist from Soweto who came to prominence on Simon's *Graceland*, Kumalo is an in-demand New York player, composer, and vocalist who has been a fixture in Simon's band for almost 20 years. *San Bonan* (Siam, 1998).

LADYSMITH BLACK MAMBAZO. Leader and founder Joseph Shabalala put it best: "In Zulu singing there are three major sounds, a high keening ululation; a grunting, puffing sound that we make when we stomp our feet and a certain way of singing melody. Before Black Mambazo you didn't hear these three sounds in the same songs. So it is new to combine them, although it is still done in a traditional style." Ladysmith is the signature South African group. *Shaka Zulu* (Warner, 1987); *Induku Kethu* (Shanachie, 1984); *Ulwadle Oluncgwele* (Shanachie, 1985) early and uninhibited by later international sales pressure.

SIPHO MABUSE. Known for the mbaqanga hit of the late 1980s, "Jive Soweto." *The Indestructible Beat of Soweto* (1986) precursor to *Graceland; Sipho Mabuse* (Mango, 1987).

MFILISENI MAGUBANE. Mbaqanga Zulu vocalist. *Woza Sihambe* (Celluloid, 1994).

VUSI MAHLASELA. Major vocalist with an international following, starred in the film *Amandla! Silang Mabele* (Indigo, 1997); *When You Come Back* (Indigo, 1994).

SIMON MAHLATHINI. The late Mahlathini specialized in a deep bass style of singing in South African township forms. *The Lion of Soweto* (Caroline, 1987) is a compilation of growling Mbaqanga, South African blues; *King of the Groaners* (Caroline, 1993); *Rhythm and Art* (Shanachie, 1990) with the Mahotella Queens in support.

MAHOTELLA QUEENS. Established in 1964 as a session harmony group, they came to prominence in the 1970s with their tough vocal style and rock-solid mbaqanga backing band. *Izibani Zomgqashiyo* (Shanachie, 1986).

MIRIAM MAKEBA AND THE SKYLARKS. (See Profile). *Makeba & the Skylarks* (Teal-Polygram/Gallo Reissue 1997) is from the 1950s, demonstrating her early talents; *The Voice of Africa* (RCA, 1964); *Welela* (Phillips, 1989) is Makeba's last great album.

MANHATTAN BROTHERS. The Manhattan Brothers recorded their first hit in 1948 and are one of the most influential vocal groups in South Africa's musical history. The group influenced succeeding generations with their style of dress, speech, attitude, and lifestyle, and were the first South African group to have a Top 100 hit in *Billboard* ("Lovely Lies") in 1956. They gave Miriam Makeba and Hugh Masekela their start. *The Very Best of the Manhattan Brothers* (Sterns, 2000).

DOROTHY MASUKA. Zimbabwean-born singer and peer of Makeba, forced to leave South Africa, but has performed for more than 40 years. *Pata Pata* (Mango, 1991) is a reprise of her 1950s hits: *Hamba Notsokolo and Other Hits from the '50s* (Gallo, 1997 reissue).

MZWAKHE MBULI. Dub poet and political activist who has been shot, imprisoned, and falsely accused to the point of absurdity. Mbuli fused his politically hard-edged message with *marabi* (South African jazz), *kwela* (pennywhistle music), and *mbaqanga*, and is a cult figure. Mbuli spoke at Nelson Mandela's inauguration in 1994. *Unbroken Spirit* (Shifty, 1989); *Resistance is Defiance* (Earthworks, 1992).

BUSI MHLONGO. (See Profile). *Babemu* (Munich, 1993); *Urban Zulu* (Melt, 1998) is her classic with Brice Wassy on percussion and Lokua Kanza on guitar and vocals.

WEST NKOSI. Arranger, composer, and pennywhistle player from Pretoria who began performing in the late 1950s and is a pioneer of *mbaqanga*. He went on to produce and manage groups like Ladysmith Black Mambazo and Mahlathini and the Mahotella Queens.

DUDU PUKWANA. The late alto sax great expatriated to London in the late 1960s and joined the avant-garde scene in Europe, playing with Eric Dolphy alumni, drummer Han Bennik, and pianist Mish Mengelberg. *In the Townships* (Caroline, 1973).

PAUL SIMON. There is no question that *Graceland* (Warner, 1986) is an important world music recording, the one that expanded American listeners' interest in African music, showcased *mbaqanga*, and gave international exposure to Ladysmith Black Mambazo, Ray Phiri, Bakithi Kumalo, and South African music in general. Controversial because of a perceived exploitation of Apartheid at the time, the recording remains a classic, Simon's most important work since *Sounds of Silence* in 1965.

SOUL BROTHERS. Township jive group who have kept their sound close to the pulse of township rhythms and folk melodies. *Rough Guide to the Soul Brothers* (Rough Guide, 2001) is the place to start, a great intro.

ZULU CHORAL MUSIC FROM SOUTH AFRICA: *1930s–1960s* (Rounder, 1990) is a compilation including Solomon Linda's stolen treasure, "Whimaway" (a.k.a. "The Lion Sleeps Tonight").

ZIMBABWE

The history of Western, white exploitation of the land and people is nowhere more scandalous, obscene, inhumane, and outrageous than in Zimbabwe. The first contact that the *Shona* people of the plains of Zimbabwe had with white men was Cecil Rhodes and his henchmen, who tricked the people into believing he was looking for minerals and that he had no intention of interfering with their culture or control of the land. The fight with the Shona was short-lived, as Rhodes's forces overwhelmed them and eventually their *Ndebele* neighbors, who had only recently settled in the region having fled South Africa after a brutal war with the Zulu nation. It wasn't enough for Rhodes to murder, pilfer, and rape the environment and land of the Shona; he also was obsessed with obliterating their culture. Fortunately, he was unsuccessful in this regard, although his tyranny has left long-lasting scars throughout the region.

A bitter war fought guerilla style finally erupted in the 1970s and Southern Rhodesia became Zimbabwe in 1979. As Rhodes knew, Zimbabwe is awash in nuclear elements and precious stones and metals. The horrors of Rhodesian apartheid have sadly been replaced by corruption perhaps more openly brazen and widespread than in any other nation on the continent in the twenty-first century. The violent taking back of white farmer's land has back-fired on Herr Mugabe. Many of these farmers have been welcomed by neighboring Zambia to the north and are beginning to prosper. The utter failure of democracy and the rapid regression in the areas of civil rights, economic productivity, health care, and international relations is in direct contrast to its closest neighbor South Africa. The tremendous hope and promise that emerged after Ian Smith stepped down as ruler of Rhodesia has vanished in a sea of greed, abuse, and exploitation. Rampant AIDS, starvation, and the use of terror by Mugabe's henchmen on black and white Zimbabweans alike permeate the landscape in a country whose wealth has been looted and squandered and its people abandoned.

THE MUSIC

The *mbira dzavadzimu* is a thumb piano with 22–46 metal keys (formerly iron, now steel), played with the thumb and right fore-finger. It is played inside a *zeze* (a hollowed gourd), which serves as a resonator. Beads and bottle caps are often attached to the zeze for additional sound color. The mbira is inextricably associated with Zimbabwean traditional music, and is truly the national instru-ment. Two major names stand out in the recent history of the instrument. Ephat Mujuru, who died in 2001, was an outspoken opponent of White Rhodesian rule and a mentor and teacher of many of today's greatest players. He appeared on the Kronos Quartet's *Pieces of Africa* (Nonesuch, 1992). Dumisani Maraire was a marimba and mbira virtuoso who fled to the United States in the early 1970s, where he taught Shona culture and music at the University of Washington until his death in 1999.

Despite century-long attempts by the colonizers to repress and censor music and virtually all expression of culture by the Shona and Ndebele people, Zimbabwe's music has survived and produced several major world music artists. The main music genre is known as *chimurenga*, a guitar-driven, mbira-based, Afropop style, pioneered by the irrepressible Thomas Mapfumo, forced to live in exile in the northwest United States due his outspoken opposition to the oppressive Mugabe regime. Along with Oliver "Tuku" Mtukudzi, Mapfumo propelled chimurenga and South African *mbaqanga* to the international stage. The other great star is Stella Chiwshe, who resides in Germany, a spiritual being, fabulous singer, and one of the true female instrumental and vocal stars of African world music. Stella is the diva of Zimbabwe, queen of the mbira, an instrument women are not traditionally allowed to play. Zimbabwe's pop scene takes much from the southern part of the continent with its own harare beat called *jit*; it is all the rage and the Bhundu Boys are the name band in this style.

RECOMMENDED CDs

BHUNDU BOYS. Proponents of jit, a disco/High Life take on chimurenga. *The Shed Sessions* (1998); Shabini (Disque Afrique, 1986).

BLACK UMFOLOSI. Ndebele a cappella group who followed in Ladysmith's footsteps, sometimes singing with a huge choir. *Unity* (World Circuit, 1990).

STELLA CHIWESHE. *Talking Mbira: Spirits of Liberation* (2001, Piranha) is a spiritual gem that will calm and lift the soul, her first recording of new material in 8 years; *Shingu* (1994), a live set.

FOUR BROTHERS. *Makorokoto* (Cooking Vinyl, 1994).

THOMAS MAPFUMO. Now expatriated and living in Oregon, Mapfumo is the political conscience of the troubled country, an activist since the 1980s, and now an outspoken critic of the oppressive dictatorship of Robert Mugabe. *Thomas Mapfumo and the Blacks Unlimited, Chamunorwa* (Mango, 1991); *Spirit of the Eagle* (Virgin, 1991); *Chimurenga Explosion* (Anonym, 2000).

DUMISAMI MARAIRE. Modern mbira master. *African Mbira: Music of the Shona People of Rhodesia* (Nonesuch, 1971) is a pure, simple classic and a must for any African music collection; *Shona Spirit* (Music of the World, 1996) with Ephat Mujuru.

OLIVER "TUKU" MTUKUDZI. Tuku is a major artist whose music unites the bush with the city. He mixes the mystical Shona with mbaqanga, the South African style made up of township jive, jit, and other traditional elements, and utilizes the Bantu African structure of interlocking patterns, to create a mesmerizing sound. *Vhunze Moto* (Putumayo, 2002); *Tuku Music* (Putumayo, 1999).

VIRGINIA MUKWESHA. Chiweshe's daughter and new Princess of the mbira, Mukwesha is a chronicler of Zimbabwean folk music and new star on the South African roots horizon. *Tsika* (Shava, 2000).

EPHAT MUJURU. *Journey of the Spirit* (Alula, 2002); *Rhythms of Life* (Lyrichord, 1989). The late Mbira master and teacher's best recordings.

VARIOUS ARTISTS. *The Rough Guide to Zimbabwe* (1996) is an excellent and representative compilation.

EUROPE

Until the advent of Mr. Edison's invention at the beginning of the twentieth century, the exchange of musical traditions among European countries was limited to the repertoire of touring classical ensembles and orchestras. The innumerable forms of folk music in Europe rarely traveled far from their local origins. Even as radio and phonograph records became part of everyday life for many Europeans, the musical diet was quite restricted, with only the best-selling (usually American) records gaining widespread exposure.

When the term *world music* began to receive widespread use in the early 1980s most people associated it with another imperfect label, the euphemistic "Third World." Once the compact disc began replacing vinyl (1984), roots and traditional music from Europe began to attract the attention of record companies as a new genre for a growing worldwide, middle-class market. As computer technology besieged Western homes in the early 1990s, world music became established and the definition expanded to "First World" European culture. Today European world music is an essential part of an evolving musical phenomenon, broadening the concept of world music while giving synergy and contrast to music from other continents.

WESTERN EUROPE

Austria	Germany	Portugal
Belgium	Greece	Scotland
Denmark	Holland	Spain
England	Ireland	Sweden
Finland	Italy	Switzerland
France	Norway	Wales

AUSTRIA

The land of Haydn, Mozart, and Strauss waltzes has a classical music tradition second to none. This legacy has made it difficult for other local forms to emerge, but Austria has produced its own urban folk music known as *Schrammelmusik*, created by the brothers Josef and Johann Schrammel in Vienna in 1878. The music traditionally includes clarinet, accordion, violin, and contra guitar, and is steeped in Alpine tradition that can be found in neighboring countries. The leading modern proponent of *schrammelmusik* is Roland Neuwirth, one of the few Austrian musicians to establish himself in world-music circles. Austrian-born jazz luminary Joe Zawinul has been involved in many world-music projects since leaving Weather Report, but he has focused on Africa, not Western Europe, and is not truly an Austrian musician in the context of world music.

RECOMMENDED CDS

ROLAND NEUWIRTH. *Herzton-Schrammein* (Ariola, 1997). Old time Viennese folk.

DIE EXTREMSCHAMMEIN. *Essig and Oi* (WEA, 1994).

BELGIUM

Belgium is an integral part of the European Union and an economic epicenter for much of the world diamond and banking trade, a financial powerhouse second only to Switzerland. As with Switzerland, language varies region by region. The north is Flemish and speaks Dutch; the southern Walloons speak French; and German is spoken in the east. Belgians are closely tied to their Dutch cousins both culturally and politically.

As the brutal colonizers of the Congo during the reign of King Ferdinand, Belgium has inevitably become home to many expatriated Africans, including many of its most successful musicians. It boasts a growing world and folk music scene because of the diversity of business people and families who have settled in Brussels, Brugge and Antwerp from all over the continent and Africa. In fact, Belgium's two most famous world music artists are of African descent—Zap Mama and Natasha Atlas—however, many interesting roots groups have come to the fore in the past decade contributing to a fresh, pan-Euro style now pervasive throughout the continent. The music borrows heavily from Romani, Balkan, Klezmer, and Celtic cultures. The ongoing influx of the African Diaspora is transforming Belgium into a poor man's France when it comes to world music, including one of the strongest festival scenes in Europe.

Jacques Brel was an immensely talented songwriter and singer whose work was literate, geared to the theatre, and contained true pathos and wit. His lush melodies and sensitive lyrics, which were usually based on engaging stories, garnered him fame and a devoted following in Paris in the late 1950s. He became an international cause celebre in the 1960s, which led to his tunes being recorded by such diverse artists as Damita Jo ("If you go away"), The Kingston Trio ("Seasons in the Sun"), Frank Sinatra, Leonard Cohen, and David Bowie. After retiring from the hectic performing scene in 1967, his absence spawned the United States play *Jacques Brel is Alive and Well in Paris*. The off-Broadway show ran for more than 2,000 performances, still one of the longest runs ever, and solidified his legendary status. Ironically the public and producers of the play had no knowledge of his bout with lung cancer (from which he died in 1978) when the play was conceived. As a result of the success of the show, Brel appeared in several French films, and his last recording reputedly sold over 600,000 copies on the first day of its release.

RECOMMENDED CDs

AMBROZIJN. Avant-garde folk/roots group led by vocalist Sylvie Berger. *Kabouka* (Wild Boar, 2003); *Naradie* (Virgin, 2000); *Ambrozijn* (Wild Boar, 1999).

JAQUES BREL. Yes, he was a pop composer and singer, but how can we not recommend a couple of his recordings? *Volume 6* (Barclay, 1964) is his most widely acclaimed; *Jacques Brel 3* (Philips, 1958); *Brel* (Barclay, 1977) was his last.

JAUNE TOUJOURS. Accordions, brass, Flemish singing, jazz, musette, and folk. *Brusk* (Wildboar, 2000).

KADRIL. Belgian's most famous roots group from Flanders also operates the successful Wild Boar label, the brainchild of Erwin Libbrecht, Kadril's leader and founder. *All the Best* (Wild Boar, 2001), a compilation of the last 25 years; *Eva* (Wild Boar, 1999).

LAIS. Celtic-sounding female song trio backed by Kadril. *Lais* (Wild Boar, 1998); *Dorothea* (Virgin, 2000); Douce Victime (Virgin, 2004).

THINK OF ONE. Hot new ensemble making waves in North Africa and Europe. *Naft 2* (Zonk, 2003); *Marrakech Emballages* (De Beek, 2000).

TRIO TRAD. Pan-Euro music from Sweden, Hungary, Serbia, Shetland, and Italy; Accordions and hyper violins. *Musique d' Europe* (Wild Boar, 2003); *Trio Viool* (Wild boar, 2000).

ZAP MAMA. Zaire native Marie Daulne was born in the Congo to a Belgian father (killed during the revolution in 1960) and a Zairian mother, who fled to the forests to escape the horror, sheltered by a tribe of Pygmies. Marie was raised in Europe, but at 20 she returned to the rainforests where she was trained in vocal techniques by the Pygmies. She returned to Europe to form *Zap Mama*, an a cappella group that uses little or no instrumental backup or percussion other than what the singers do with their remarkable voices. *Adventures in Afropea I* (1993, Luaka Bop); *A Ma Zone* (2000, Luaka Bop).

DENMARK

Denmark is Scandinavia's link to the European continent, a progressive nation whose national character is synonymous with liberalism and a staunch advocacy for human rights. The Danes would not succumb to the Nazi's during World War II, courageously protecting its Jewish population while much of the rest of Western Europe (except the United Kingdom) acquiesced to or otherwise collaborated with the fascists. Denmark has long been a welcome home to expatriated American jazz legends who took up residence there after World War II. The famous *Café Monmartre* in Copenhagen (Kobenhaven) has been home to the likes of Dexter Gordon, Kenny Drew, Kenny Clarke, and Scandinavia's own Neils Henning Orsted-Pederesen. Not surprisingly, Denmark has recently emerged as a vibrant locale for innovative intercultural music making.

Denmark has been influenced by many political, architectural, theatrical, culinary, and musical trends from the continent. As a result, Danish music is distinct form other Scandinavian folk traditions, more influenced by the British Isles and northern Europe than Sweden or Norway.

Because it is virtually surrounded by water, Denmark has many harbors that receive traffic from all over the region, including musical traffic. The Western island of Fano is home to arguably the greatest traditional music, a folk style called *sonderhoning*. The Carl Nielsen Academy in Odense, named after the great classical composer, is currently a center for folk music education.

RECOMMENDED CDS

BALTINGET. Progressive swing-folk band. *Classic* (2002).

HARALD HAUGAARD AND MORTEN ALFRED HOIRUP. Haugaard plays fiddle, viola, and hurdy-gurdy, and Hoirup, the guitar. Together they form Denmark's leading traditional musical voices, both as a duo and in combination with numerous other folk bands. *Om Sommeren* (Folk Music, 2003); *Duo for Violin and Guitar* (2002); *Lets Dansk-Live in Germany* (2001); *Lys Ligh Ljus Licht Val Luce Lumiere, Luz* (1998).

INSTINKT. Folk group with a rock sensibility. *Hur* (Folkmusic, 2001).

KAREN MOSE AND HELENE BLUM. Exciting folk duo Solen (Go, 2004).

PHONIX. Nordic Roots group produced by Morten Hoirup. *Pigen & Drengen* (*The Girl and the Boy*, 2002) is their best and first with vocals; *Live* (Folk Music, 2000).

SERRAS. Leading folk group featuring fiddler Harald Haugaard and saxophonist Hans Mydskov. *Serras (*1998); *Second Hand* (2002), a laidback Danish folk jazz.

SORTEN MULD. Popular roots group who play techno renditions of Danish folk tunes with guitar, bagpipe, sound loops, electronics, and vocals by Ulla Bendixen. *Mark II* (NorthSide, 1999); *III* (NorthSide 2002) is a mature recording.

ENGLAND

Somehow the notion of "roots" does not readily spill off the tongue in the same phrase as "White Anglo Saxon Protestant." More often than not the folk music heard in England since the middle of the twentieth century has been music from other folks, victims of colonization who regularly settle and repatriate in England. Nevertheless, classical composers Ralph Vaughan-Williams, Frederick Delivs, and Benjamin Britten, among others, often based their works on English folk themes to great effect. Vaughan-Williams collected traditional music and today there is a tremendous revival afoot and a growing body of work that must be considered in any review of world music.

REGIONAL ENGLAND: SUSSEX, YORKSHIRE, AND NORTHUMBRIA

The Copper Family from rural Sussex, and the Watersons of Yorkshire have been the most prominent English folk roots names during the past 40 years, families of musicians and song interpreters of the highest caliber. Their commitment to traditional material and local styles has greatly contributed to the worldwide folk movement since the late 1950s.

The Coppers are the first family of English roots music, vital to its history and a frame of reference for the new generation that is reviving a tradition of earthy, hard edged, story based music. Martin Carthy, wife Norma Waterson, brother Mike and the late Lal Waterson from Yorkshire have also been major world music personalities for decades. Their progeny, including Eliza Carthy and Oliver Knight (Lal's son), are current hot names on the folk music circuit, artists who truly respect the history of the music.

The Northumbrian region south of Scotland is home to a little-known piping tradition championed by the incomparable Kathryn Tickell who has single-handedly kept Northumbria on the world music map with her virtuoso work on the small pipes and violin.

HEADQUARTERS OF THE WORLD MUSIC PRESS

Although England has not produced a wealth of world music stars, it is clearly and undeniably the leader and most important contributor to the world music press. London and the outlying areas are second only to Paris as presenters of live world music and England is the information center for our genre. It is fair to say that the entire world music phenomenon over the past 25 years would not have been possible had England not taken the lead in reporting, discovering, and promoting the work of previously unexposed and unheralded artists from all over the planet. The dedication, scholarship, and integrity of English world music journalists is astounding and refreshing, especially when one considers the otherwise chauvinistic, payola infected reputation of the rest of the music business.

The Monthly Magazine *fRoots* (formerly *FolkRoots*) is the leader in coverage of the world music scene, headed by Editor-in-Chief Ian Anderson. It features in-depth profiles of artists, up-to-the-minute news, reviews of CDs and books from every region of the world, as well as detailed lists of performances everywhere. *fRoots*'s historical retrospectives, coverage of live concerts, and an outspoken political commentary keep the edge sharp and make it compulsory reading for anyone truly interested in the music. *fRoots* does not produce its own line of recordings, is not beholden to any artist or label, and focuses on its role as an objective chronicler of an important musical phenomenon.

The *Rough Guide* conglomerate, which publishes travel guides for every inch of the planet, is the leading source of encyclopedic world-music information, led by the indomitable Simon Broughton. The second edition (two volumes) of *The Rough Guide to World Music*, released in 2000, is an essential work of great scope that has had a significant impact on defining the genre. The *Rough Guide*'s bimonthly world music magazine, *Songlines*, returned to the newsstands in the summer of 2002 in an enlarged version after a year off for retooling. It is an informative publication, beautifully produced, and a worthy rival to *fRoots*. The one minor quibble with *Songlines* is its close relationship to the Rough Guides. They promote and publish a seemingly endless number of these releases in every issue. Songlines is, nevertheless, an up-to-the-minute publication that is essential reading for all world music fans..

Charlie Gillette and Andy Kershaw are the Radio equivalents to *fRoots* and *Songlines*; their BBC 3 radio shows are required listening, available online on the BBC and *fRoots* sites. They also frequently contribute as print journalists to the world music press.

THE BEATLES AND THE BRITISH INVASION

Surprised we even mentioned the Fab Four? It is difficult to justify inclusion of the Beatles in a book on world music. However, it would be negligent to omit them from the introduction to the English section of this survey. The influence the Beatles have had on the careers of world musicians all over the globe has been profound. The list of those who credit the Beatles with "turning them on" to music is endless and knows no geographic boundary. Luminaries such as Milton Nascimento from Brazil, the late Fela Kuti from Nigeria, and George Dalaras in Greece have proudly credited the Beatles as their main inspiration. Certainly the late George Harrison's association with Ravi Shankar expanded the minds of the Western record industry. Stars such as Peter Gabriel, David Byrne, and Bill Laswell would undoubtedly acknowledge the influence the Beatles have had on their careers.

In retrospect, the British Invasion was not about world music. The Liverpool sound was derivative of early rock 'n roll and R&B—Chuck Berry, Little Richard, and Co.—not based on traditional or roots music as we view it. Nevertheless, the phenomenon of the Beatles was the tipping point that began to internationalize popular music. The Beatles' influence (with help from their friends) is analogous to that of impressionist painters and their effect on visual art, that is to say, pervasive and eternal.

THE OTHER UNITED KINGDOM

The ever-expanding ethnic landscape of music in the United Kingdom has quite naturally developed its own pop musical culture including the world beat, disco-infested Banghra (see India).

RECOMMENDED CDs

ALBION BAND. Folk-rock band led by the eclectic Ashley Hutchings, with many different lineups over the decades. *The BBC Sessions* (Strange Fruit, 1998).

BILLY BRAGG. Bragg's sarcastic, digging style and knowing delivery qualify him as England's #1 new song representative and political singer. *Mermaid Avenue* (Rhino, 1998) is a set of Woody Guthrie lyrics put to music. *English, Half English,* (Elektra, 2002) while barely a world music recording, is a fine outing; *Reaching to the Converted* (Rhino, 2000) is a compilation of "B sides," from 1986–1996, a great place to start.

ELIZA CARTHY. The former "folk Brat" has burgeoned into a major artist. Her powerfully expressive voice, virtuoso fiddle playing, and original compositions incorporate English roots music from bygone centuries as well as the mid-twentieth century roots revival. Her records don't reveal her real talent. *Anglicana* (Topic, 2002) is her best.

MARTIN CARTHY. Carthy is the icon of roots music in England, father of Eliza, and husband of Norma Waterson. Knighted by Queen Elizabeth, Carthy has been performing since the mid-1960s, first in a duo with fiddler Dave Swarbrick, then as a member of the second lineup of Steeleye Span, and finally as a solo guitarist and vocalist of great power. *Byker Hill* (Topic, 1967); *Skin and Bone,* with fiddler David Swarbrick (Topic, 1991).

SHIRLEY COLLINS. Important folk singer from the 1960s, virtually unknown outside of England, a specialist in traditional music. *Anthems in Eden* (Amaranth, 1999/1970); *Love, Death and the Lady* (Harvest, 1970).

THE COPPERS. *Coppersongs* (EFDSS, 1988); *Come Write Me Down* (Topic, 2002 reissue).

FLOOK. One of England's hottest bands in the Celtic mold. *Rubai* (World Village, 2002) is a gem that cooks with an urgency and spirit reminiscent of an early 1960s hard-bop jazz ensemble.

NIC JONES. Folk icon and songwriter whose career was halted by an injury in the 1980s. *Penguin Eggs* (Shanachie, 1982) is his classic.

JOHN KIRKPATRICK. Accordion master, Morris fan, and folk purist. *Plain Capers: Morris Tunes from the Cotswolds* (Topic, 1976) with oboist (then wife) Sue Harris and Martin Carthy.

JIM MORAY. The new kid on the block brings an experimental edge to British folk, a talent for turning a song and a reverence for the past. *Sweet England* (Niblick, 2003).

OYSTER BAND. British folk rock. *Holy Bandits* (Rykosisc, 1993); *Wide Blue Yonder* (Cooking Vinyl, 1987).

MADDY PRIOR. Former singer with Steeleye Span, one of England's folk rock divas. *Silly Sisters* (BGO, 1976) with June Tabor. (Compass, 1999).

KATE RUSBY. Kate is England's young female standard-bearer for the traditional song, perhaps heir to June Tabor. *Hourglass* (Compass, 1998) is austere; *Sleepless* (Compass, 1999) is a more mature work; *10* contains new versions of previously recorded tunes and re-mastered old ones (Compass, 2000).

MARTIN SIMPSON. Fine fingerpicking guitarist. *Righteousness and Humidity* (Topic, 2003) is a tasteful interpretation of the blues from New Orleans and the American South.

SPIERS & BODEN. Move over Eliza Carthy. Fiddle/accordion duo making waves. *Bellow* (Topic, 2002).

JUNE TABOR. After more than 30 years on the scene, Tabor's *An Echo of Hooves* (Topic, 2003) confirms her lofty status as England's most daring folk artist. *Aqaba* (Shanachee, 1982) is our favorite older side; *Airs & Graces* (Topic, 1976) is highly recommended, as is *Angel Tiger* (Cooking Vinyl, 1992) and *Against the Streams* (Cooking Vinyl, 1994).

KATHERYN TICKELL. *Northumbrian Collection* (1998) contains vocals by Carolyn Robson and Terry Conway; *Debatable Lands* (Park, 2001) is an instrumental record.

LAL WATERSON. The loss of Lal in 1998 was a permanent blow to the very fiber of the Watersons. *Once in a Blue Moon* (Topic, 1996) is an important folk music document. Her own gorgeous tunes showcase her deep, laconic, wizened voice. *Bed of Roses* (Topic, 1999), the posthumously released follow-up, is even better.

WATERSON-CARTHY. Common Tongue (Topic, 1997) Broken Ground (Topic, 1997).

FINLAND

The language and genetic history of the Finns is closer to Hungarian than to their fellow Scandinavians, and it has taken some time for Finland to find its niche in the European community. The Finns were aligned with the Axis powers during World War II, have had a long history of conflict with their closest neighbor Russia, and until recently were never particularly cordial to their Scandinavian neighbors (or the rest of the world for that matter). All that has changed in recent decades. No longer the outcasts of Scandinavia, Finland has emerged as a society of stability, a country with real economic power (the home of cell phone giant Nokia), and an independent voice of rationality in an ever changing, dangerous world. In many ways Finland is the role model of a healthy nation in the new millennium, one whose people are thriving, a nation that is passionate about its culture, obsessed with music, and not afraid to look to the future.

A CENTER FOR CLASSICAL MUSIC AND TANGO

During the 1990s Finland evolved greatly as an economic entity, expanding from a country whose main resource was its timber and paper products to a center for cutting edge electronics and computer science. As Finnish stature and self-image grew in the economic world, so did its cultural life and influence on the region, especially in the field of classical music. Finland today is arguably the hottest spot on the globe for classical music, producing a disproportionate number (in relation to its population of 5.2 million) of talented conductors and composers whose works are now performed in the most prestigious venues around the world.

Finnish world music has also exploded since the early 1990s. Oddly enough, the Argentine tango has become a national musical obsession. In addition to a proliferation of accordion players, the folk tradition is based around the violin as elsewhere in Scandinavia. The Finns have another national instrument as well, the *kantele*, which is a kind of zither-harp that is a staple in Finnish traditional music.

RECOMMENDED CDs

MARIA KALANIEMI. Kalaniemi is a professor at the Sibelius Conservatory in Helsinki, a musicologist and virtuoso on the standard and free bass accordions. Her recordings range from traditional folk to tango and eclectic modern. *Iho* (Hannibal, 1996) with renowned Finnish ensemble Aldargaz. *Ahmo* (NorthSide, 2001).

SANNA KURKI SUONIO. Former vocalist with Gjallarhorn, Suonio is now a solo artist whose electrocentric recordings are an open window into the modern music boom flourishing in Finland. *Musta* (NorthSide, 1998).

MARKKU LEPISTO: Lepisto plays with the super group Varttina and is considered by many to be the finest accordionist on the Finnish scene today. *Silta* (Aito, 2002) with cittern, violins, pandeiro, and guitar shows his virtuosity and versatility.

PAULIINA LERCHE. Accordionist-singer with a modern slant and contemporary attitude. *Katrilli* (2002).

KIMMO POHJONI. One of the truly great accordion players anywhere. *Pielo* (Rockadillo Zen, 1999).

HANNU SAHA. Kantele player. *Mahla* (2000) was produced by Andy Cronshaw and quite exhilarating.

TALLARI. The #1 folk group in Finland. *Virtaa* (1999) with Anita Lehtola from Henningarna on vocals; *Komiammasti* (Kansanmusikki, 1996).

VARTTINA. The #1 Finnish supergroup (whose name means "spindle") focuses on Finno-Ugric poems and songs presented in a modern context. The group began with five female lead singers and is down to three, but sounding better than ever. *Oi Dai* (1991) sparked international interest. *Seleniko* (1992, Green Linnet); *Kokko* (1997, NorthSide); *Iki,* (NorthSide, 2003) is their best.

LIISA MAVEINENT & TELLU VIRKKALA. Kanteles, beautiful singing, and stylized vocalese. *Matelii (*2002); *Suden Aika/*"Time of the Wolf" (1996).

FRANCE

France's influence on twentieth century world culture cannot be overestimated. French food, wine, art, fashion, and even soccer stars are the standards against which the world continues to judge all competition. Without question, Paris is also the leading world music city on the planet. When it comes to music and art, France possesses a style that has universal appeal and stamina. Impressionism reigns supreme in the art world and the genius of composers Saint-Saens, Fauré, Ravel, Debussy, and Milhaud continues to be the model for modern film and world music arrangements. It is worth noting that the French language spoken abroad retains a bond with the homeland unlike that of any other language (OK, maybe not Quebec). Whenever music is sung in the French language throughout the world, it retains an unmistakable reverence for the motherland.

In many ways France is two distinct countries consisting of (a) Paris and (b) the rest of France. No other European city represents an entire country to the rest of the world to the degree that Paris does as the essence of France. Lyon, Marseilles, Bordeaux, Toulouse, Strasbourg, and Nantes are of course important cities with individual attributes. Other than Bordeaux's position as the center of the international wine trade however, the influence of France's other major cities is dwarfed by the might of Paris.

Due to this Parisian omnipresence, the breadth and wealth of the musical traditions of regional France remains unknown to most of the outside world. Nonetheless, Bretagne, Angers, Auvergne, and French Catalonia are centers of folk and roots music where a host of remarkable styles have reemerged and flourished since the early 1990s.

REGIONAL FRANCE

The Loire Valley lays claim to the super eclectic roots band Lo'Jo, who hail from Angers and have made international waves with their brand of cabaret-cum-North African pop, led by vocalist Dennis Pean, the quintessential twenty-first century hipster. Le Chavannes from central France is a fine instrumental roots group, and the island of Corsica, replete with its radical politics, boasts a strong polyphonic a cappella tradition and many folk artists. The *cobles* piping tradition is alive and well in the central regions, with many double reed led roots bands taking painstaking care to maintain the tradition. Bal musette, the accordion-based dance music from the early part of the twentieth century originates from the Auvergne, and is perhaps the most well-known French roots music internationally. The musette is at the core of most French folk music and is a staple of much of the great Chanteuse repertoire. Toulouse remains a center for North African and Middle Eastern expatriates from Algeria, Morocco, and Syria who produce their own music in this southern city, just north of the Pyrenees.

Bretagne: Approximately 1,500 years ago British Celts, who spoke a Brythonic dialect now called Breton, invaded Brittany, that northwestern portion of France that sticks out from the rest of the country. From the time of the French Revolution until the 1970s, the French government tried to eradicate the Breton language, which perpetuated a militant regionalism that faded only after a strong national patriotism set in following World War II. Nonetheless, the language, a vibrant folk tradition, and a unique call and response singing style—*kan ha diskan*—have flourished in Bretagne. The *veuze* (played through one double reed and a single reed drone); the high-pitched *binou* (single drone), and *bombarde* (a type of double-reed recorder) create a distinctive reed and piping combination, far softer and more fluid than the Irish and Scottish counterparts. The Celtic influence permeates Brittany's roots music scene, but the Bretagne sensibility has its own voice, having evolved outside the purview of Western erudite music. It is a music that uses intervals foreign to the Western diatonic scale, monadic and even microtonal in many instances, akin to Eastern modal music, Taqsim, and nonmeasured forms.

French Catalonia. Near the Pyrenees and the Spanish border, French Catalonia possesses a wealth of wonderful traditional music. As in Spain, the *sardana* is the popular dance form and the instruments of choice are double reeds, notably the lower register *tenora*. In addition to the cobles piping tradition prevalent in the southwest, the region is home to most of France's gypsy population, including the great guitarists Thierry Robin and Angelo Debarre, the latter a torch carrier for the legendary Django Reinhardt.

PARIS AND THE LIGHTS

World musicians from Africa, South America, the Caribbean, and Europe can find no better place to ply their trade than Paris. The City of Lights accepts and encourages a musical melting pot other cities can only dream of cultivating. World Artists sell out arenas in

Paris as rock stars do elsewhere: Kabyle star Ait Menguelett, Malian guitarist Habib Koite, Klezmer clarinetist David Krakauer, and Cameroonian virtuoso singer/bassist Richard Bona are all big stars in Paris who can fill concert halls with ease. Paris is also the place to find the greatest variety of world music in retail stores. FNAC, the retail department store, and fnac.com not only have the widest selection of French language world music anywhere, but their selection of European, Middle Eastern, African, Asian, and South American music is extraordinary, often including many items listed as out of print by other megastores.

African, Middle Eastern, and Caribbean musicians who reside in France for a plethora of political and artistic reasons dominate the local scene. The music of these countries—Algeria, Morocco, Lebanon, Senegal, Mali, Cameroon, Haiti, and Trinidad—thrives in Paris Because the musical genres of these countries are so culturally specific, we will discuss their work under the separate country entries.

FRENCH POP

At the risk of inspiring criticism from the traditionalists, we have included a smattering of French pop artists in this section. The truth is that the French pop scene is so ingrained in the fabric of the French culture that it has become an indigenous part of the national persona. Call us infidels if you wish, but we would be remiss in ignoring artists such as Bernard Lavilliers, although he is undeniably a pop singer. We have also included the immortal Edith Piaf, Charles Trenet, and George Brassens, three giants who transcend categorization and are the aural property of the music world.

Marilis Orionaa (b.1959) is a new name on the world music scene presently known only to true aficionados but making waves on the French roots music scene. She is from the Bearn region near the Pyrenees in French Catalonia. Marilis sings in the enchanting, ethereal Bearnais language and is a compelling, charismatic performer. She has created a unique world minimally influenced by conventional music (with perhaps some hints of flamenco, Catalan rumba, and Romani) yet her work is familiar and accessible. Her voice seems to arrive in a floating mist propelled by a strong wind, painting a picture of her mountain culture. Her vocal skill, phrasing, and soul are astounding, powerful, self-assured, and filled with a sense of urgency and yearning. She sings traditional (not to be confused with familiar) tunes and original compositions with strong "green" leanings and a studied aesthetic sense; she recites poetry that is beautiful, even if the listener does not understand the meaning of her dialect. Orionaa is that rare artist who combines vocal virtuosity with an impeccable natural artistry, taste, and originality. She is a star in the making, a remarkable talent.

Bernard Lavilliers (b.1946) started as a left-wing political singer, and rose to stardom in France in the mid-1970s as the quintessential freethinking singer/songwriter, the conscience of the French bourgeoisie. Lavilliers has harvested songs from his many travels in South America and Africa and was one of the first French singers to make truly world music.

Lavilliers possesses movie star looks and a genuine tough guy persona. He picked up boxing at age 13 and after spending a year in reformatory, worked in the steel mills with his father, at which time he began to sing and write songs. Three years later he left for Brazil, working as a jungle truck driver, only to be jailed for skipping his military service upon his return to France in 1967. When released, he began to perform on the Paris cabaret circuit. Bernard's break came in 1976 when he signed with Barclay and recorded *Les Barbares*, which made him a star. His songs were anarchic and highly critical of the government and society, an approach that chilled both media and public in the early 1980s. He eventually began to include more South American and African rhythms and tunes in his repertoire as he investigated the political realities of Nicaragua and Cuba. Thirty years on, his recording career is as vital as ever.

RECOMMENDED CDs

BAGAD KEMPER. Perennial national bagpipe champs; for purists only. *Liparmaout* (Keltia, 1994).

JEAN BARON. Breton pipe virtuoso performs traditional music on *bombarde* and *binou. The Land of King Morvan* (Keltia, 1996) contains a series of songs and wedding marches dating back 1,500 years. *Jean Baron & Georges Epinette* (Keltia, 1993); *Danses De Bretagne* (Keltia, 1988).

JANE BIRKIN. There are dozens of Birkin and Serge Gainsbourg records to explore, but Jane's recent *Arabesque* (Narada, 2003) is a great addition to the couple's recorded legacy with Birkin singing the late wild man's tunes.

GEORGES BRASSENS. The late singer, poet, and composer influenced everyone to follow after his debut in 1952. He is still France's all-time popular vocalist, revered throughout Europe and the French-speaking world. *Les Copains de Abord* (PolyGram, 1998 reissue); *Vol. I* (Philips, 1952–1955); *Vol. III* (Philips) up-tempo songs from 1954–1956. Caveat emptor the innumerable exploitative compilations.

BRATSCH. Parisian-based, gypsy-style roots group on the scene since 1980. *Rien Dans Les Poches* (World Network, 1998) features Angelo Debarre and Hungarian gypsy band Ando Drom, with dirge-like accordéon instrumentals and Django-style swing; *Sans Domicile Fixe* (1990 Azimuth-Niglo); *Live in Bochum* (Correspondence, 1994).

DAN AR BRAZ. Guitarist who began with Bretagne harpist Alan Stivell, a Celtic new age artist. *La Memoire des Volets Blancs* (Columbia, 2001).

FRANCOIZ BREUT. Downbeat, bohemian pop singer straight out of the 1950s jazz scene of Chet Baker and Serge Gainsbourg. *Vingt a Trente Mille Jours* (Virgin, 2001) recalls the *Cowboy Junkies* and Arthur Lee's mid-1960s group *Love*.

MANU CHAO. The #1 French/Catalan artist today, with an ear for what is *au currant* and beyond. *Clandestino* (Virgin, 1999) is an important alternative recording.

DONNILUSANNA. A cappella Corsican female vocal group. *Per Ahate* (Auvidis, 1996) is a dazzling tour de force.

RICHARD GALLIANO. Galliano has kept the accordéon tradition alive and well; influences include Piazzolla, Hermeto Pascoal, Lucio Dalla, bal musette, and jazz. *French Touch* (Koch, 1998).

FRANCOISE HARDY. The 1960s model and Ye Ye Girl transformed into a chanteuse with style in the 1990s, releasing a string of sexy CDs. *Clair Obscur* (Virgin, 1997); *Love Songs* (1973–1974) was arranged by Michele Jarre and Serge Gainsbourg; *Le Danger* (Virgin, 1988).

KORNOG. Instrumental Celtic group. The group has disbanded, but is an important name in Bretagne music. *Premiere* (Green Linnet, 1992) recorded live in Minneapolis; *Ar Seizh Avel - Seven Winds* (1985).

KOUN. Modern Bretagne group. *Cest en Souhai taut Bonsor* (Keltia, 2000); *An Dro: Danses Bretonnes* (Keltia, 1995).

BERNARD LAVILLIERS. More Dylan than Aznavour. *Arret sur Image* (Barclay, 2001) showcases his understated, sexy delivery with Samba, Cuban son, hip-hop, and folk; *Les Barbares* (Barclay, 1976) made him a star; *Histories* (PolyGram, 1999) is his "best of" from 1976–1997.

GILLES LE BIGOT. Bretagne Lite. *Empreintes* (Heltia, 2002) is mellow with beautiful vocals.

LE PRIMITIFS DU FUTUR. *World Musette* (2000) is a look at 1930s accordion music with a bit of ragtime and scat vocals with cover art by R. Crumb of *Zap Comix* fame.

LES NUBIANS. *Princesses Nubiennes* (CBS, 1999) is Afropean-Pop—Wyclef Jean meets Zap Mama, hip-hop, soul, French chanteuse, reggae, you name it. *One Step Forward* (Virgin, 2003), with a cameo from rapper Talip Kweli is twenty-first century music for the young at heart.

LO'JO. The hippest roots band in France. *Boheme de Cristal* (World Village, 2001) an *avant*-bohemian excursion through French, North, and West Africa with a reverence for 1950s French cabaret; Dennis Pean's gravelly Tom Waits meets Paolo Conte voice leads the way.

ERIK MARCHAND. Singer/clarinetist Marchand is a master of the *kan ha diskan* form of Bretagne response singing. *Chants du Centre-Bretagne* (Auvidis, 1991) with Thierry Robin and Moroccan Hameed Khan on Tabla; with Les Balkanitis (Le Chant du Monde, 2004).

JACKY MICAELLI. Former member of Donnilusanna (see above), Micaelli is a formidable folk singer and composer. *Amor'Esca* (Auvidis, 2000); *Corsica Sacra* (Naïve, 1998).

I MUVRINI. Corsican duo who use world fusion rhythms as a backdrop to their polyphonic singing in dialect. *Pulifunie* (High Octave, 2003).

MARIILIS ORIONAA. *Cai-!*, (1996) is a stunner, well supported by an acoustic trio of guitar, bass, and percussion. *FemeLis* (2001).

PARIS CAFÉ MUSIC. *Paris Café Music* (Rough Guide, 2002) is an essential collection featuring 25 bal musette musicians and groups Emile Vacher, Gus Viseur, contemporary roots groups Bell OEil, and Les Hurlements D'Leo, and chanteuses Frehel and Michele Bernard are all here.

PARIS COMBO. A little jazz, a bit of chanson, some cabaret, a hint of bal musette, a wink at Piaf, and a taste of Django and Erik Satie. *Attraction* (ark, 2001).

MARC PERRONE. Modern musette accordionist. *Voyages* (Le Chant du Monde, 2001).

EDITH PIAF. There are hundreds of compilations, but *The Voice of the Sparrow* (Capitol, 1991 reissue) is essential and has it all. *Live at the Paris Olympia* (EMI 1982) includes performances over a span of 8 years and is excellent. Proceed with caution thereafter.

THIERRY ROBIN. Gypsy guitarist extraordinaire runs the gamut from Catalan rumba to Indian ghazal with traditional Bretagne-style double reeds, accordions, and flamenco vocals always in the mix. *Gitans* (Silex, 1993) is his best; the live recording, also called *Gitans* (Auvidis, 1998), is almost as good. *Thierry Robin with Gulab Superi* (Naïve, 2002).

HENRI SALVADOR. French Guinean born, Parisian entertainer, a prescient artist and charismatic performer, à la Cab Calloway. *Maladie d'Amour* (Milan, 1999) is a compilation from the 1940s with big band; *Chambre Avec Vue* (Virgin, 2000).

TRIO SOLEDONNA. Hi-tech Corsican polyphony with modern support. *Isulanima* (Philips, 2001).

ALAN STIVELL. Stivell brought modern Bretagne music to the international stage in the early 1970s and is one of the earliest world musicians. *Renaissance of the Breton Harp* (Philips, 1971) is an essential recording; *Chemins de Terre* (1973) introduced rock to the genre; *Au Dela des Monts* (Keltia, 2002) is his best recording in decades.

CHARLES TRENET. Songwriter-singer from the 1930s, the last of the Chevalier era. There are hundreds of compilations, so beware. *Les plus Grands Succes de Charles Trenet* (Replay, 1995 reissue) is a budget CD that contains all the essentials (i.e., *La Mer, Minilmontant, Que Reste T Il de nos Amours,* and more).

EMILE VACHER. Bal musette pioneer. *Accordéon* (Fremeaux), snippets from 1913–1941.

GUY VISEUR. Viseur helped to create the accordion-jazz style called manouche and backed Edith Piaf. *Les As du Musette: Guy Viseur Live in Brussels* (Paris Jazz, 2002/1941); *Compositions 1934–42* (Fremeaux).

GABRIEL YACOUB. Vocalist-guitarist with now defunct Bretagne rock group Malicorne, Yacoub was a moving force in the resurgence of Bretagne music. *Babel* (Chants Suis Truie, 1997); *Elementary Level of Faith* (Chants Suis Truie, 1987); *Bel* (Chants Suis Truie, 1990); with Malicorne: *Balancorre en deu* (Acousteah, 1997); *La Beastiaire* (Balon, 1977); *Marlicorne I, II* (Antigone, 1974).

GERMANY

The oral tradition of folk music in Germany, called *volksmusik,* was superseded by literary culture as elsewhere in much of Europe. Early in the nineteenth century, spontaneous music making gave way to organized musical activity and folk music became "folk like," bound by notation and the diatonic major scale. Ethnic music survived in the regions of Swabia, Bavaria, the Alps, and Westphalia, but barely made it into the era of recorded music before it was usurped by politics.

In the twentieth century *volksmusik* was co-opted by the Nazis, who controlled and manipulated it for propaganda purposes. After World War II, West Germans found it difficult to retrieve their folk roots and instead became obsessed with American music. At the same time, communist East Germany again appropriated *volksmusik* for its own purposes in a failed attempt to make it the music of the proletariat. The net result was devastating, virtually eliminating all traces of tradition for more than 40 years.

Despite one of the most progressive youth cultures in Europe today, Germany has produced precious little world music, preferring until very recently to embrace jazz, rock, Turkish, Iranian, or almost any other roots music rather than explore its own troubling past. In the late 1970s, the *stadtfestes* (festivals) began to feature a smattering of folk artists, the first glimmer of hope for a return to traditional music. Recently a dance-hall circuit similar to the tanchez phenomenon in Hungary has begun to emerge, providing new venues for the music. Since the wall came down in 1989, Germany has increasingly tried to recapture its folk music in earnest without the constraints of political pressure, but has yet to make a splash in the big pool.

To date, Germany's most notable contribution to world music remains the invention of the *bandoneon*, a button-accordion that is the signature voice of Argentine tango, invented in the city of Essen in the Ruhr Valley in the late nineteenth century. Variations of the instrument—including diatonic concertinas and melodians—are heard in various world music cultures, including Cajun, Tex Mex, French Canadian, and other styles.

RECOMMENDED CDs

FRANZ JOSEF DEGENHARDT. Renowned singer with dozens of records to his credit. *Junge Paare Auf Banken* (Polygram, 1999 reissue) with French icon, Georges Brassens; *Stationen* (Polygram, 1999) is a compilation.

DISSIDENTEN. Pop trio who play anything but German music. *The Jungle Book* (Triloka, 1993), Coltrane meets Rudyard Kipling.

THOMAS FELDER. Avant-garde voice and hurdy gurdy player from Swabia. *Schwaebisch Vesper* (Musik & Wort, 1995) commemorating the fiftiethth anniversary of the firebombing of Dresden.

LIEDERJAN. Eclectic, pop-oriented World Beat. *Klammheimliche Hits der Fruhen Achtziger* (Plane, 1990).

WOLFGANG MEYERING. Multi-instrumentalist and composer who explores "low" German and Scandinavian language and music with hurdy-gurdies, bagpipes, harps, voices, and flutes. *Malbrook* (Westpark, 2003).

SCHAL SICK BRASS BAND. Big band with Persian lead vocalist. *Majnoun* (Network, 1998).

ROBERT ZOLLITSCH. Eclectic composer, painter, zither player, and ethnomusicologist who performs his native Bavarian yodeling as well as Tibetan chant and Tuvan throat Singing. *Zwiefach* (Oriente, 2000).

GREECE

Musically speaking, Greece is where East-meets-West most profoundly and clearly, ground zero for cultural cross-pollination. Modern Greek folk music (*dhimotika tragoudhia*) can be traced to the days of the Ottoman Empire, and has been influenced by a broad range of musical traditions from as far away as India and as nearby as Anatolia. Whatever the style—and there are a plethora of Greek musical styles—the music instantly evokes palpable nostalgia and conjures stereotypical images of the Greek persona that continue to be reinforced in contemporary literature and cinema in the twenty-first century.

Much of Greek music is based on ritual dances from the region, including the many Greek isles, Turkey, Israel, and the Balkans. The current music has amalgamated into forms that at once hearken to the past and look forward to a new world. Music remains a vital part of daily Greek life, especially with the collective Greek Diaspora in Europe, North America, and South America. Industry studies indicate that Greeks buy more recordings of their own music than any other European nation.

RECENT HISTORY AND POLITICS

A mass migration to Greece in 1923 following the horrors of the Grecian-Turkish war inundated the major port cities of Athens and Thessaloniki with huge numbers of refugees. The people who fled Smyrna (Anatolia) and Constantinople (Istanbul) were more educated and sophisticated than the inner-city Greek denizens with whom they were forced to coexist. These dispossessed souls were Greeks living away from their native land, Jews, Armenians, and Gypsies, all of whom had owned and/or worked in coffeehouses and hashish dens throughout Anatolia, Asia Minor, and Thrace. Because Islamic Turks were not permitted to own, operate, or frequent such establishments, these groups dominated the operation of the music venues.

THE MUSIC

Over time the music of the dispossessed acquired the label *café aman*, an improvised, sophisticated folk music, which took its name from the Turkish word meaning "alas," often shouted out during musical performance. When the refugees arrived in Greece, they lived on the edge of society with few tangible possessions, but they were free to perform their music.

Rembetika emerged from the café aman tradition to become the most celebrated music of the Greek ports. It spoke of illicit love affairs, poverty, hardship, and persecution much in the same way as tango, flamenco, fado, samba, son, and jazz did in Buenos Aires, Seville, Lisbon, Rio de Janeiro, Havana, and New Orleans. The musical relationship between rembetika and other musical genres from port cities around the world is remote, but the shared message and social foundations are remarkably similar. These groups all lived in defiance of local authorities and were persecuted (or enslaved) but they never conformed to imposed societal customs. They resorted to crime, drug trafficking, and con games to survive, but always maintained a pride in their own culture and approached their music with dignity and as an art form. Music was often their only means of free expression and the sole manifestation of their identity, self-respect, and hope.

Rembetika was forbidden under the brutal Metaxas dictatorship of the mid-1930s and virtually disappeared from the musical radar until well after World War II. Coinciding with the end of the military rule in the early 1970s, a major rembetika revival spawned renewed interest in many forms of traditional Greek music. *Laiko* (popular music), *antiphon* (art music), and traditional folk music from the Greek Islands also experienced a renaissance. This led to the emergence of a new wave of artists most prominently George

Dalaras, Haris Alexiou, Apostolis Kaldharis, and Maria Farantouri. Inspired by the international success of composer Mikos Theodorakis, Dalaras and Co. emerged to spearhead a vibrant, modern musical industry. These artists were careful to incorporate roots music into newly developing forms while borrowing heavily from the 1960s American folk revival.

The recent economic and political stability in Greece was palpable upon visiting the country as it prepared to host the 2004 Summer Olympics. In addition to becoming a member of the European Union (EU), Greece is enjoying unprecedented and vastly improved relations with Turkey following two earthquakes that have brought the siblings together on a humanitarian basis. These developments have enhanced the music business at home and abroad. As with fine wine or jazz, effort is required to appreciate the nuances and beauty of the Greek musical charm, but once one invests the time, vast treasures can be discovered.

There are many Rembetika singers whose credentials qualify them for diva status, including Rita Abatzi and Sotiria Bellou, but it is the Jewish singer, Roza Eskenazi (1890–1980), who stands out as *the* great Greek voice of her time. Eskenazi began singing in the bars and cabarets of Istanbul that were owned by Jews, Armenians, Greeks, and Gypsies and collectively referred to as *café aman*. She moved to Greece with her family after World War I and continued her career in the small clubs and hashish dens in the depths of the worst areas of Athens and Thessaloniki. She was discovered in the late 1920s singing in a taverna in Piraeus and began her recording career for Columbia in 1929. Shortly thereafter she rose to stardom, recording more than 500 songs in Greek, Turkish, Arabic, Italian, Ladino, and Armenian, including her own composition *"To Kanarini"* (The Canary) in 1934, for which she is most famous.

While operating a restaurant in Athens during the Nazi occupation, Roza became a valuable member of the resistance, tirelessly working for the cause and risking her life on numerous occasions. She visited the United States after World War II where she recorded extensively during the 1950s. In the

1970s, Roza regained prominence with the rembetika revival, appearing as late as 1975 on a TV show with Haris Alexiou.

A leading proponent of the rembetika revival of the late 1970s was current international superstar Eleftheria Arvanitaki (b.1954), clearly the major female voice in Greek music today. She has numerous recordings with a wide-ranging repertoire incorporating rembetika, folk, laiko, and entakhno. Her collaborations with new-wave composer Nikos Xydhakis are mesmerizing, and her recordings of the music of American-based Armenian composer Ari Dinkjian transcend ethnic stereotyping. She is a charismatic stage performer who communicates viscerally, eliminating the need for her listeners to understand the lyrics. Eleftheria has eclectic taste and recently has begun to collaborate with other world musicians. Her most recent recording includes duets with Senegalese star Ismael Lo and nova fado singer Dulce Pontes. She is the one Greek star who regularly performs around the globe.

RECOMMENDED CDs

HRONIS AIDONIDIS. Aidonidis is the great name in Greek-Thracian music. *Ta Aidonia tis Anatolis* (Minos, 1992) is a classic, featuring George Dalaras and a small ensemble led by the eclectic Ross Daly; an essential recording for any lover of Greek music.

HARIS ALEXIOU. The first great female voice in the new rembetika era is going strong after 30 years. *The Giddiness of Love* (Minos, 1978) with composer Thanos Mikroutsikos and Alexiou's deep, throaty voice in top form; *Laiko Tragoudia-12 Folk Songs* (Minos, 1988); *Kratai Hronia Aeti I Kolonia*, (Minos, 1990) with Lina Nikolakopoulou; *The Best of Haris Alexiou* (Minos, 1998) is the compilation to get.

ELEFTHERIA ARVANITAKI. (See Profile). *Extos Programmatos* (Mercury, 1998), live CD with compositions by Tsitsanis, Vamvakaris, and Hiotis that will make you dance; *Bodies and Knives* (Polydor, 1994) with New York-based Armenian Composer Ara Dinkjian; *Menos Extos* (Polydor, 1991) is a classic.

SOTIRIA BELLOU. A bluesy, troubled soul, addicted gambler, and one of Greece's great voices from the 1940s and again in the rembetika revival of the 1970s who died in 1997. *Sotiria Bellou* (Margo, 1995).

GEORGE DALARAS. The leading singer, simpatico with the nueva trova of Silvio Rodriguez, often called the Bob Dylan of Greece. *Thessaloniki Gannena Me Dio* (EMI, Minos, 2000) driven by Serb Goran Bregovic's brass arrangements; *50 years of Rembetika Songs* (Minos, 1975); *Mikra Asia* (Minos, 1975) is a showcase for Apostolis Kaldharis's compositions, which kicked off the new rembetika craze on vinyl; *A Portrait* (EMI Hemisphere, 1997) is a tasteful compilation produced by the always astute Gerald Seligman.

ROSS DALY. A long-time resident of Crete, Daly is a string virtuoso who was born in Ireland, one of the most eclectic purists on the planet. *Mitos* (World Network, 1995); *At the Café Aman* (World Network, 1999) with Niki Tramba; *Iris* (Protasis, 2003).

ANDONIOS "Dalgas" DHIAMANTHIDIS. Early rembetika star. *Dalgas* (Heritage, 1999), recorded 1928–1933.

ROSA ESKENAZI. (See Profile). *Rembetissa 1933–36* (Heritage, 1996); *Rebetiko of Rosa Eskenazi* (Orata).

MARIA FARANTOURI. Renowned for her early interpretations of Theodorakis, Maria was a symbol for the resistance against the junta of military rulers in the 1960s and early 1970s. *Avec Zulfu Livaneli Ensemble* (Kalan, 1983) is a very special recording, her best. *Sings Theodorakis* (Minos, 1970).

GLYKERIA. Female laiko singer, who is also popular in Israel. *Maska* (Columbia, 1998).

MANOLIS HIOTIS. The great bouzouki master/composer is credited with adding two sets of strings to the instrument, and was the first major artist to go electric. *30 Xponi* (Minos) a compilation from the 1950s–1960s.

ANGELIQUE IONATAS. Theatrical, dark, deliberate vocals with a reverence for Kurt Weill. *Di un Bleu Tres Noir* (Siviana, 2000); *Mia Thalassa I* (Auvidis, 1994); *O Erotas I,* (Auvidis, 1992).

XANTIIIPPE KARATHANASSI. Female folk singer and leading proponent of traditional music from Greek Macedonia. *Tunes and Songs of Macedonia* (1990) is a vocal documentary.

YANNIS MARKOPOULOS. Significant composer, singer, and Entekhno pioneer. *Brightness Reverberations* (Orata, 1995); *30 Chrises Epitihes* (Minos, 1999).

MARIKA NINOU. Post-World War II star, popular in New York. See Tsitsanis.

MARIA PAPANIKALAOU. From the modern Arvanitaki school *7 Zoes* (Virgin, 1999) is a moving ballad recording; *San Petalouda* (Virgin, 1996).

YANNIS PARIOS. Second only to Dalaras in popularity, Yannis hails from the Cylclades Islands. *Ta Nissiotika/The Islanders* (Minos, 1982) is treasured by all Greeks; *Otan Bradasa* (Minos, 1983); *Ego Ki Esi/You and I* (Minos).

KRISTI STASSINOPOULOU. Modern vocalist with a Western rock sensibility and Manu Chao vision. *Echotropia* (Tinder, 2000) is techno; *Secret of the Rocks* (Tinder, 2002) is mesmerizing.

MIKOS THEODORAKIS. Composer, known for film work (*Zorba the Greek, Z*, et al.), considered the father figure of modern Greek music. The unfortunate anti-Semitic remarks that he made in 2003 are only the latest in a career littered with faux pas after faux pas. *Axion Esti* (two CDs) *Epitafios* (EMI, Minos, 1987). Avoid his singing.

VASSILIS TSITSANIS. Composer, singer, and bouzouki virtuoso, perhaps the greatest name in twentieth century Greek music. He modernized rembetika, and defied German occupiers and Communist opportunists by playing the music in his cafe during World War II. *Greek Music Tradition with Sotiria Bellou & Marika Ninou* (Lyra, 1995 reissue) features Ninou from 1951–1954 and Bellou from 1969–1977, an exhilarating work; *Vassilis Tsitsanis 1936–1946* (Minos).

MARKOS VAMVAKARIS. Grandfather of rembetika emerged on the Piraeus music scene from the *tekhedes* tradition (clubs where musicians met to improvise, dance, and smoke hashish) of the early 1930s. Vamvakaris's raspy, hash-influenced voice became the prototype for the Male rembetika singing style. *Bouzouki Pioneer* (Rounder, 1988); *Rembetica in Piraeus* (British Heritage).

NIKOS XYDHAKIS. New wave laiko composer whose work contains Brazilian, jazz, and new age components, yet is traditional in feel and scope. *To Medi Ton Okpemon* (Lyra, 1992); *Konda sti Dhxa mia Stigmi* (Lyra, 1987) with Eleftheria and Ross Daly.

SAVINA YANNATOU. Savina has explored music from dozens of countries in the eastern Mediterranean, the Middle East, and the Balkans. *Ii Primavera en Salonika* (Misurgia Graeca, 1994); *Mediterranea* (Sounds True, 2000).

IRELAND

Celtic music has enjoyed a renaissance in Scotland, Brittany, Galicia, and in Cape Breton, Canada, but its heart remains in Ireland. The folk tradition that began with the Clancy Brothers, Tommy Makem, the Dubliners, and the pre-Chieftains roots groups led by harpist Sean O' Riada was the precursor to the current international popularity of Celtic music. The Celtic phenomenon has its roots in local protest music passed down by oral tradition over centuries and the folk movement of the 1960s in the United States and the United Kingdom.

HISTORY

After centuries of fighting for sovereignty, the Irish began to make headway in 1914 just as the British took a leading role in the fight against Germany. Prior to the war, the British Parliament passed the long-awaited Home Rule Bill. The bill was annulled, however, as war took center stage and engulfed the European continent and the British Isles. The annulment led to the Easter Uprising in 1916. Although the revolt failed, the imprisonment and execution of the uprising's leaders resulted in outrage throughout Ireland and lent credence and support to the struggle and movement for an independent Irish State.

In 1919, Irish Republican leaders again declared their independence. The Irish Republican Army (IRA) began a series of guerrilla attacks against the British forces stationed in Ireland. Due to pressure from the United States, the British passed the Government of Ireland Act in 1920, followed by the Anglo-Irish Treaty in December 1921. The former divided Ireland into two areas with limited powers of self-government within the United Kingdom, giving Ireland the same status as Canada, Australia, New Zealand, and South Africa

Many Republicans rejected the Treaty, as it did not give Ireland complete sovereignty and separated the six northernmost counties from the rest of the main body of Ireland, a split that would cause later generations much strife. Eventually the Republicans capitulated and Eamon De Valera became Prime Minister in 1932. Britain did not recognize the free status of Ireland until 1937, and even then it declared that the six northern counties would not be ceded without the agreement of the Northern Ireland Parliament.

Since independence, the possibility of reunification of the entire Isle of Eire has constantly been on the agenda of the Republic of Ireland. The partition has become a long-standing dilemma with guerrilla tactics by both the IRA and the Unionists of Northern Ireland regularly receiving international attention. After the 1998 Good Friday Pact and the formation of the new Northern Ireland Assembly in 1999, the peace process has faced stumbling blocks, but there was real hope for continued progress as of 2004.

THE MUSIC

The worldwide interest in Celtic music since the late 1970's has coincided with the rise of the term "world music." Celtic music is in reality its own genre, but has been made a part of the world-music oeuvre, which loosely includes indigenous, traditional, and folk music from all cultures.

Sean-nos. In Irish music the most famous traditional style of singing is known as *sean-nos,* translated as "old style," which developed over the course of several centuries in Gaelic-speaking communities. It is the cornerstone of Irish oral tradition. Historically, *sean-nos* songs were performed at intimate social gatherings: dances or ceilis, weddings or wakes. Recently, *sean-nos* has moved into the festival and competition arena with a proliferation of recordings available.

The folk-song revival of the late 1950s and early 60s brought the ballad form to the forefront of Irish music, led by the Clancy

Brothers and the Dubliners. Folk music is thriving today, led by the incomparable Karan Casey (see Profile) who is once again bringing the music to audiences all over the world.

Fiddle Tradition. Ireland possesses a strong fiddling tradition with styles varying throughout the country. There was a time when those in the know could tell a fiddler from Sligo, Sliabh Luachra, Donegal, or Clare in a heartbeat, but the homogenizing effect of globalization, the ease of travel, radio, and recordings has begun to make former distinctions evaporate into an overall "Irish" style. Nevertheless, the names are still used and discernable to connoisseurs, and local legends such as Tommy People, Frankie Gavin, Sean Keane, and Kevin Burke are as popular as ever.

First Wave of Irish Bands. Following Sean O'Riada's Ceoltoiri Chualann, the Chieftains emerged in the early 1960s leading the first wave of instrumental traditional music. Riding the crest of the worldwide explosion of Celtic music, they parlayed their concept into a viable commercial art form, in no small part because of the masterful marketing wizardry of uillean piper and band leader Paddy Moloney. In the 1970s groups such as Planxty, The Bothy Band, Da Danaan, Altan, Clannad, and others followed in Ireland, setting the stage for a movement that expanded throughout Scotland, Wales, Galicia, and Brittany.

There is one star on the scene today whose incredible voice and style set her apart from all the rest, singer Karan Casey (b.1969). The former lead singer with the group Solas is one of the most talented and exciting female vocalists anywhere, a leading light on the Celtic music scene. Casey's voice is captivating and unique, not an easy trick in a genre filled with talented singers who often perform from the same pool of material in a very standardized format. Casey sings without inhibition, reaching into her inner voice in a way few singers in any genre are able to do.

Karan started her career in her native Ballyduff Lower, Ireland, and studied voice and piano at University College Dublin and at the Royal Irish Academy of Music in the late 1980s. She moved to New York in the early 1990s to study jazz at Long Island University. During this period she thrived in the American-based Celtic band Solas, also working with the

Chieftains and Donal Lunny, but soon outgrew the limitations of being part of an ensemble and struck out on her own. At the risk of blasphemy, her voice recalls the talent of all-time greats in other genres such as Joni Mitchell and Elis Regina. One can hear the jazz influence in her phrasing. Karan's debut solo recording, *Songlines*, is a masterpiece that has established her career and made her a name performer on the world-music concert circuit.

RECOMMENDED CDs

ALTAN and MAIREAD NI MHAONAIGH. Fiddler/vocalist Mairead Ni Mhaonaigh is a true world music star. *Altan* (Green Linnet, 1986) the band's debut, highlighted by the late Frankie Kennedy's virtuosic wooden flute. *Horse with a Heart* (Green Linnet, 1988); *Island Angel* (Green Linnet, 1989), Kennedy's last; *Blue Idol* (Green Linnet, 2002).

MARY BLACK. Her early work is her best, recent recordings show the effects of wear and tear on her voice. *Babes in the Woods* (Gifthorse, 1991).

BOTHY BAND. Along with Planxty, the Bothy Band broke the ice for the new Celtic day with Matt Molloy, Paddy Keenan, Kevin Burke, Triona and Micheal O' Domhnaill, and of course Donal Lunny. *Old Hag You Have Killed Me* (Green Linnet, 1979), contender for greatest title ever; *Bothy Band* (Mulligan, 1974); *Out of the Wind into the Sun* (Mulligan 1976)

KEVIN BURKE. *If the Cap Fits* (Mulligan, 1978) is a classic Irish fiddling record.

LIZ CARROLL. Virtuoso Chicago-born fiddler. *Lost in the Loop* (Green Linnet, 2000).

KARAN CASEY. (See Profile). *Songlines* (Green Linnet, 1997), sung in English, will appeal to children of all ages; *Distant Shore* (Green Linnet, 2003) is introspective, restrained and moving.

CHIEFTAINS. Going strong 35 years on, the Chieftains are ambassadors to the world for Celtic music. *Chieftains 3* (Green Linnet, 1971) put them on the World map; *Chieftains 4* (Green Linnet, 1972) is the Standard for all instrumental Celtic recordings;

Chieftains 5 (Green Linnet, 1973); *Bonaparte's Retreat* (1976) features a young Dolores Keane.

CHERISH THE LADIES. The New York based band has included at one time or another Eileen Ivers, Aoife Clancy, and Liz Carroll. *The Back Door* (Green Linnet, 1992).

THE CLANCY BROTHERS AND TOMMY MAKEM. Tommy Makem formed the group in Greenwich Village, New York, in the 1950s. They initially covered Irish standards but later played original songs. *Come Fill Your Glass with Us* (Tradition, 1957); *In Person at Carnegie Hall* (1964, Columbia).

CLANNAD. Irish revival band focused on the Brennan family (vocalist/harpist Marie, vocalist/guitarist/keyboard player Ciaran, guitarist/flute player Pol), who began its life playing traditional music, but then veered into more new-age flavored work. One time-band member, sister Enya, had success as a solo artist with her new agey single "Orinoco Flow," (a.k.a. "Sail Away") in 1988. *Dulaman* (1976, Shanachie) more traditional than their later, new-age work. *Macalla* (Shanachie).

DANU. Talented, traditional septet. *The Road Less Traveled* (Shanachie, 2003).

DE DANNAN. Led by fiddler Frankie Gavin from Galway. *Song for Ireland,* (Sugar Hill, 1990).

MAIGHREAD NI DHOMHNAILL. Maighread is from one of Ireland's first families of music. *No Dowry* (Shanachie, 1989).

JOHNNY DORAN. Legendary piper from the 1930–1940s. *Bunch of Keys* (Irish Folklore, 1999 reissue) from 1947.

SEAMUS ENNIS. Renowned radio host, musicologist, and piper. *Feidlim Tonn Ri's Castle* (Claddagh, 1977).

ANDY IRVINE. *see Parallel Lines,* with Dick Gaughan (Green Linnet, 1983).

DOLORES KEANE. Often called the voice of Ireland. *Sail Og Rua* (1984, Green Linnet); *Farewell to Eirinn* (1981).

PADDY KEENAN. Former Bothy Band uillean piper and one of the best. *Poirt an Phiobaire* (Gael-Linn, 1982).

LUNASA. Current instrumental super group pushing the Celtic envelope. *Merry Sisters of Fate* (Green Linnet, 1999); *Redwood* (Green Linnet, 2003).

DONAL LUNNY. As member of Bothy Band and Planxty, Lunny helped set the standard that Irish groups have used as a model of excellence. Since the mid-1980s, he has focused on producing and TV.
(See Planxty, Bothy Band, and Moving Hearts for CD reviews.)

MATT MOLLOY. The leading flutist of Irish music. *Matt Molloy* (Green Linnet, 1976) with Donal Lunny on Bouzouki; *Stoney Steps* (Green Linnet, 1987); *Shadows on Stone* (Caroline, 1996).

CHRISTY MOORE. The greatest Irish troubadour of the last quarter of the twentieth century, Moore is a storyteller without peer, great singer-songwriter, and political commentator. *Live at the Point* (Grapevine, 1994) is his masterpiece. *Prosperous* (Tara, 1972) presaged Planxty; the *Iron Behind The Velvet* (Tara, 1978); *Ordinary Man* (WEA, 1985); *The Time has Come* (WEA, 1983)

NOMOS. Iconoclastic band with a take-no-prisoners attitude. Niall Vallely (now with Karan Casey) was the force. *I Won't Be Afraid Anymore* (1985).

LIAM O'FLYNN. Uillean piper formerly with Planxty. *Fine Art of Piping* (Celtic Music, 1991).

TOMMY PEOPLES. Master fiddler, a nationalist from eastern County Donegal, near Northern Ireland. *The High Part of the Road* (1976, Shanachie); *Tommy Peoples* (1978, Green Linnet), like a pub session; *The Iron Man* (1985, Shanachie).

PLANXTY. Planxty paralleled the impact of the Bothy Band with Christy Moore, Donal Lunny, Andy Irvine, Liam O'Flynn, and Matt Molloy forming the all-star cast. *Planxty* (Tara, 1976), known as the "Black Album" revolutionized Celtic ensemble playing; *Well Below the Valley* (Polydor, 1978); *After the Break* (Tara, 1979).

SHARON SHANNON. Ireland's current star on the "squeezebox." *Each Little Thing* (Green Linnet, 1997).

SOLAS. The New York-based Irish quintet has regrouped after vocalist Karan Casey's departure. *Solas* (Shanachie, 1996), produced by the late, ex-Silly Wizard fiddler Johnny Cunningham; *Sunny Spells and Scattered Showers* (Shanachie, 1997).

ITALY

It was not until the mid-1800s that the concept of *Italia* as one nation became a geopolitical fact, and the country today remains a fractious association of independent cultures. Nevertheless, Italy has undeniably achieved world status as a nation whose lifestyle, cuisine, eye for fashion and design, and rich culture are the envy of the rest of the world. Italy is a self-contained, self-sufficient, self-conscious patchwork of people who have become increasingly insular in their relations with the outside world, content to drink their own wine, eat their own food, wear their own fashion, and rely on their own industry and resources. Italy is resolute in holding on to its precious possessions and does so by steadfastly restricting virtually all immigration lest any outsider spoil the party. As the rest of the world explodes with conflict, the amiable arrogance of twenty-first century Italia is palpable to anyone who visits. Internationally, The Vatican augments Italy's role as an international force whose profound impact on virtually every society on earth cannot be underestimated.

REGIONAL DIVERSITY

Despite its outward appearance of coherence, every region in Italy functions within its own orbit to the virtual exclusion of all other areas of the country. Northern Italians—roughly defined as anything north of Rome—frown upon the South as an unsophisticated, lesser race. Milano, Torino, Genova, Firenze, Parma, Verona, and Bologna are more rivals than partners, especially when it comes to cuisine and *calcio* (soccer). Southern Italians detest the elitist northerners who wield power throughout the country with their great wealth. Disdain for anything other than one's own cloistered region is epidemic in Italy. The denizens of Naples have recently begun to refer to the growing North African population—mostly from Tunisia and allowed in for cheap labor—as *Talibani*. Casual racism in Italian society is more open and matter of fact than elsewhere in Western Europe. It is pervasive in athletics, both in the stands and on the field. 2001 saw the first Black Italian play in Serie A, and anti-Semitic posters have been fixtures at Lazio (Mussolini's team) games in Rome for decades.

POLITICS

The country has seen a marked shift to the right in the past decade, particularly in the industrial north. Italian President Silvio Berlusconi, based in Milan, controls a substantial portion of the national media through his newspapers and owns all but one private TV station. He also owns one of Italy's premiere Serie A Soccer Clubs (AC Milan) and numerous other powerful businesses. Imagine New York Yankee Baseball owner George Steinbrenner being President of the United States and also owning the Daily News, Newsday, Fox, ESPN, and ABC. Berlusconi is the Western European leader whose politics and philosophy most closely resemble that of the George W. Bush administration. Sizeable left-wing pockets exist in Bologna, Urbina, Naples, and the south among the working class, but the state of Italian political consciousness seems at an all-time low since the end of World War II.

Counterbalancing Italian xenophobia and hedonism is a wonderfully idealistic segment of Italian society that is humanitarian, color-blind, politically progressive (Italy has the largest Communist Party in Europe), internationally aware, and in the vanguard of the global struggle for human rights. This small minority captures the famous Italian *spiritus* and is cognizant of the importance of folk and traditional music.

BAROQUE MUSIC AND OPERA

The music of Italy is first and foremost associated with the Opera of Verdi, Puccini, Bellini, and Rossini. *La Scala* in Milan remains one of the most prestigious Opera Houses (and concert halls) in the World. Opera is the national musical treasure, an international commodity of unlimited appeal. Critics of World music who argue that not being able to understand the language is a barrier to gaining mass appeal should consider the popularity of Opera, the other music where virtually no one understands or needs to understand the lyrics *verbatim*.

Baroque music continues to go through cyclical revival periods, appealing to each new generation as its musical taste matures. The Early Music and Baroque masterpieces of Monteverdi, Corelli, Boccherini, Vivaldi, Scarlatti and their progeny are Italy's other eternal musical contribution.

ROOTS MUSIC

Roots music is where progressive modernism is most clearly and artistically expressed in Italian society today and where Italy's regional divisions are absolute. Italy's center of progressive music is Napoli (Naples). Trailblazers such as Daniele Sepe and the roots ensembles Port' Alba, Spaccinapoli, and Calicanto have enjoyed long, successful careers performing and recording their unique brand of traditional music steeped in Neapolitan folk tradition. The tarantella dance form is ubiquitous and the music is seasoned with flutes, lutes, organetto (accordion), zampogna (bagpipes), and brass.

The regions of Piemonte, Calabria, Puglia, Sicily, Sardinia, and Lazio all boast their own styles, also rarely heard outside the particular province. Italy has its own bagpipe tradition—the *zampogna*—prominent in the south, especially in Naples and Calabria. The organetto (accordion) tradition is strong throughout Tuscany, and polyphonic a cappella groups are found in Genoa, Sardinia, and Sicily.

Don't try to find this music in Italy however, unless you have the patience to dig deep in Naples or the city from which a particular artist or group hails. Even the salespeople in the world music sections of Fnac, Messagiore, or Virgin Megastores don't know the greatest roots musicians.

ITALIAN POP

Italy is uncharacteristically united when it comes to Pop, perhaps because it is music that is mostly devoid of roots implications from any one region. As in France, the music can be cheesy, but there are several important Italian Pop artists recommended in this section. These International stars—including Pino Daniele and Lucio Dalla—possess a sophistication and World appeal that separates them from the endless onslaught of Eros and Mina clones. The best Italian pop has an authentic World sensibility. In many ways, Italian Pop is now the indigenous music of the country.

Umbrian singer Lucilla Galeazzi is known for her work in the theatre, opera, and most significantly for reviving local Italian folk music and performing it in a modern context. She began performing in 1977 in theatres throughout Europe, moving to opera tchoral productions in the 1980s, including parts in *Stabat Mater* and *Requiem per Pier Paolo Pasolini* She sang with the Neapolitan roots group Nuova Compagnia di Canto Popolare (NCCP) in the early 1980s and has recorded several solo albums since 1992. Lucilla is virtually unknown in her own country despite her incredibly expressive voice, a passion for her work, and an allegiance and reverence for the folk history of her native Umbria. Her relative obscurity is due in part to Italian region-alism and Italy's preference for cheesy, American style pop. Lucilla is a singer whose work must be heard, a true diva on the Italian roots scene.

RECOMMENDED CDs

AGRICANTUS. Ethnic Mediterranean rhythms mixed with ambient and trance. *Agave: Maavro* (1989); *Gnazu!* (CNI, 1993); *Tuareg* (Ludos, CNI, 1996).

BANDA IONICA. Brass and reeds, Sicilian drama, traditional versus avant-garde, mysterious narratives. *Matri Mia* (2002, Felmay); *Passione* (1999) is a series of traditional funeral marches.

CARLO BUTI. From the 1920s–1930s; Caruso meets Bing Crosby. *Firenze* (DV More, 2003 reissue); *Carlo Buti* (Replay, 1999).

CALICANTO. One of the most talented and original roots groups anywhere, Calicanto remain barely mentioned by the world music press. They play zamponas, lutes, and hurdy gurdy as a backdrop to delicately detailed harmonies. *Venezia* (Annagrumba/CNI, 1997).

LA CIAPA RUSA. Roots band from Torino led by hurdy gurdy specialist Maurizio Martinotti. *Retanavota* (Robi Droli, 2000); *Agi and Safran* (Robi Droli, 2000).

LUCIO DALLA. Singer Songwriter Dalla is a national treasure, raconteur, TV personality, and radical thinker who has been performing and recording since the 1960s. *Liberi* (BMG, 1994); *Canzoni* (BMG, 1996).

PINO DANIELE. The most respected Italian pop star on the scene today. His raspy tenor is expressive and soulful. *Sotto 'o Sole* (CDG, 1991) is his best; *Dimmi Cosa Succede Sulla Terra* (WEA, 1997); *Medina* (EMI, 2001), the duet with Salif Keita is classic; *Amore Senza Fine* (CDG, 2002) is a ballad compilation.

LUCILLA GALEAZZI (see Profile). *Lunario*, (CNI, 2001) runs the gamut of colloquial Italian atmosphere and style. *Cuore di Terra* (1997).

FRATELLI MANCUSO. The roots duo is a leading light on the Italian scene, in demand as film composers. They play Italian chamber music with a Sicilian core. *Cantu* (Amiata, 2003) is nearly perfect.

PIETRA MONTECORVINO. Smoky voiced singer and filmstar from Napoli not to be missed. *Napoli Mediterrano* (Discmed, Blau, 2004).

NOVALIA. Archaeologists of Italian roots music. *Canti & Briganti* (Campagnia, 1996) includes bagpipes, Balkan pipes, ouds, saz, and sequencers.

NCCP (Nuova Compagnia di Canto Popolare). Neapolitan group who combine roots music with modern sounds, in the biz since 1967. *Collezione* (EMI, 2001).

ENRICO RAVA. Italy's leading jazz trumpeter from Trieste is an eclectic musician whose work is always challenging and fresh. *Italian Ballads* (Music Makers, 1996) includes Fellini film scores, classical music, and famous arias with accordionist Richard Galliano in support.

PORT' ALBA. The Naples roots octet combine traditional instruments and bohemian poetry with a dramatic political presentation. *Violando; Il Manifesto* (1998); *A Capa e na sfoglia; Ciento pais.*

ZIZI POSSI. Zizi is Brazilian by way of Naples. *Per Amore* (WEA, 1998) contains Neapolitan Love songs (attention all Romantics).

DANIELE SEPE. Sepe combines opera buffo, southern Italian Banda, Baroque, avant-garde jazz, classical, and chamber music. *Senza Filtro*, (Felmay, 2002); Jurnateri (Felmay, 2001); *Truffe & other Sturiellett* (2000); *Spiritus Mundi* (Polusud, 1995); *Conosci Victor Jara?* (CIAE, 2000), a tribute to the martyred Chilean poet.

SPACCANAPOLI. Tarantella band named after a part of Naples once famous for thieves and prostitutes and now an upscale shopping haven loathed by the band. *Lost Souls* (Real World, 2000).

RICARDO TESI. Italy's melodeon virtuoso. *Thapsos*, (Felmay, 2001) with *Banditaliana*, is a mélange of accordion, clarinet, saxophone, guitar, vibraphone, and hurdy gurdy, mixed on a modern palate with delicious spices; *Acqua Focoe Vento* (Felmay, 2003) music from his native Tuscany with vocalist Maurici Geri.

ORNELLA VANONI. Pop vocalist who embraced the sounds of Brazil. *La Voglia La Pazzia L' Incoccienzus L' Allegria* (Warner, 1976/1990) is a gem with Vinicius de Moraes and Toquinho.

VARIOUS ARTISTS. Putamayo's compilation of Italian roots music *Italian Musical Odyssey* (2000) is the label's finest contribution to the Western European musical lexicon, an absolutely essential CD that recognizes the talent of La Ciapa Rusa, Lucilla Galeazzi, Rua Port' Alba, Ricardo Tesi, Calicanto, Fratelli Mancuso, and other artists seperate CD. Harmonia Mundi's *Sicilia Canto Nuovo* (2003) is a welcome survey of the best roots artists performing in Sicily today including Maria Cecilia Pitino, Giancarlo Parisi, Massimo Laguardia, Alfredo Anelli, Sara Cappello, and Alfio Antico, singing and performing on tammorra (frame drum), zampogna (bagpipes), friscalettu (cane flute), organetto, and guitar.

NORWAY

Home to classical composer Edvard Grieg, Vikings, fjords, and most of Scandinavia's indigenous Samis, Norway is one of the most homogeneous societies on the planet with its own brand of old-world world music.

THE MUSIC

When Norwegian folk music is discussed, you often hear the term *slattemusikk*. The music is tied to certain instruments, most prominently the Hardanger fiddle, the violin, Jews harp, and *langeleik* (a dulcimer relative). Other instruments associated with older folk music include the willow flute, *neverlur* (a deer horn covered with birch bark), and ram's horn. Norway's traditional vocal music is called *kveding*. The Stetesdal region in the east is the center of Norwegian traditional music. Norwegian and Swedish folk music are unusual in European culture because they developed among small farmers, outside urban areas, and have remained independent of influences from most current European musical trends. The old tonality with variable intervals and natural scales gives Norwegian folk its unique, identifiable sound.

Hardingfele. The Hardanger fiddle (*hardingfele*) is regarded as Norway's national instrument, taking its name from the region of its origin. The modern Hardanger is smaller than the standard violin, richly decorated with engraved, mother-of-pearl inlays on the body, and usually has 4 or 5 resonating understrings. It is an exclusively Norwegian phenomenon and dates back to 1651. The music that developed on the instrument is extremely complex, microtonal, and not easy to play or understand upon first hearing; an acquired taste for sure.

Joik. *Sámiland* (formerly Lapland) is an ancient Arctic region whose people are the indigenous Scandinavians. The Sámi—formerly known by the pejorative moniker "Laplanders"—live throughout northern Scandinavia (in Norway, Sweden, and Finland). Sámi culture is inextricably tied to the reindeer, although today they are herded with snowmobiles. The *joiking* of the Sámi people forms the basis of a popular, electrified fusion music whose leading proponent is vocalist Mari Boine. Most often linked to shamanism, *joiking* is a kind of phonetic poetry consisting mainly of untranslatable vocables and yodeling sounds, sung in a chanting fashion reminiscent of certain Native American music. The tradition has a minimalist sensibility to it—not quite avant-garde or new age—with plenty of sensuality, panting panpipes, throbbing synth beats, and expectant percussion.

RECOMMENDED CDs

KIRSTEN BRATEN BERG. Kirsten Braten Berg is known for her unique, richly resonant *kveding*. *Juletid* (Norsk, 1991); *Sagn*, with Arild Andersen, Nana Vasconceles, Bugge Wesseltoft (Kirkelig, 1992); *Suède et Norvège*, with Lena Willemark & Ale Møller. (Ocora, 1993); *From Senegal to Setesdal* (6 Degrees, 1999) with Solo Sissiko (Grappa Musikkforlag, 1997).

HALLVARD T. BJORGUM. Hallvard is a powerful fiddler and master storyteller, regarded as one of Norway's most gifted Hardanger Fiddle players. *Kunkaren* (Norway Music, 1996) *Toneflaum* (Sylvartun SYLVCD 6, 1998); *Runarstreng*, with Kirsten Braten Berg (Grappa Musikkforlag, 1999).

MARI BOINE. Boine is the most famous Sámi in the world, the leading female joik singer. Her music is dominated by her urgent voice and African drum, a combination that goes back to ancient Sámi culture and pre-Christian shamanism. *Radiant Warmth* (PolyGram, 1996); *Remixed* (NorthSide, 2001); *Eight Seasons* (NorthSide, 2003).

BUKKENE BRUSE. One of the top Norwegian groups, appointed as official Olympic musicians for the 1994 Winter Games at Lillehammer in 1994. *Bukkene Bruse* (Norway Music, 1993) with Annbjørg Lien and Steiner Ofsdal on Flute; *Steinstolen Heilo* (Grappa Musikkforlag, 1998); *The Stone Chair* (NorthSide, 2001).

KNUT BUEN. Solo Hardanger. *As Quick as Fire: The Art of the Norwegian Hardanger Fiddle* (Henry Street, 1996).

JAN GARBAREK. Saxophonist who is Norway's greatest jazz musician, one of the first to bring a global sensibility to America's greatest art form. He has recorded with Mari Boine on *12 Moons* (ECM, 1992) and Agnes Buen Garnas on *Rosenfole* (ECM, 1988), but his best is still *Witchi Tai To* (ECM, 1973).

HAKON HOGEMO. The Crown Prince of the Hardanger fiddle. His unique sound and technique have lifted the art to a higher level. *Juv* (Norway Music, 1993); *Dans* (Norway Music, 1999).

ANNBJORG LIEN. Norway's best known world musician and Hardanger fiddler. *Annbjørg* (Kirkelig Kulturverksted, 1989); *Prisme* (Shanachie, 1996) is her best International release; *Aliens alive* (NorthSide, 2002).

KNUT REIERSRUD. Renowned guitarist and composer. *Footwork* (Shanachie, 1994) includes the Five Blind Boys from Alabama and a hip rendition of "Baby Please Don't Go"; *Soul of a man* (Kirkelig Kulturverksted, 1998).

UTLA. Trio from western Norway with Hakon Hogemo (Hardanger Fiddle), Terje Isungset (percussion, Jew's Harp), and Karl Seglem

(Tenor Sax, Norwegian Ram's horns). *Song* (Nor CD, 2003) with Berit Opheim on vocals; *Utla* (Norway Music, 1992); *Brodd* (Norway Music, 1995).

NILS-ASLAK VALKEPAA. One of the first artists to present traditional Sámi *Joik* on stage. He opened the 1994 Winter Olympics in Lillehammer. *Magic of Sami Yoik* (Phantom, 2003).

PORTUGAL

The last Western European country to rid itself of authoritarian rule, Portugal is reemerging on the global scene politically, economically, and culturally. It has become a focal point for trade with Africa and a hot spot for tourism. Its ancient architecture, gorgeous Atlantic ambience, and rich history provide visitors with a unique look back at an old world elegance that is rapidly vanishing elsewhere on the continent.

During the latter half of the twentieth Century, the motherland was musically outperformed by her former colonies (Brazil, Angola, Cape Verde, and Guinea), however Portugal is in the midst of a musical renaissance that began with the 1976 downfall of the Salazar dictatorship, and is exploding in the twenty-first century. The music scene in Lisbon, Coimbra, and Oporto is vibrant. Recordings are being released at a lightning pace and new Portuguese stars abound on the world music scene. While the mother tongue does not flow in song as beautifully as its Brazilian cousin, it remains incredibly expressive, especially as sung in Portugal's main musical tradition, fado.

FADO

The roots of fado reach back to Africa and the Moorish culture that once dominated Iberia. Its modern form can be traced to the early 1800s when the interaction with Portuguese colonies (and slave trade) changed the face of the port cities. Unlike other colonial powers, the Portuguese socialized and intermarried with the people they conquered. Shortly after its independence, Brazil was a more influential nation globally than Portugal and by the 1820s Lisbon and Coimbra reflected a multiracial population that has had a permanent effect on Portuguese culture. It is believed that the earliest fado was an offshoot of the Brazilian *modinha*, and that the music took a different shape only when transported from Brazil.

Maria Severa is credited as the first Portuguese fadista (circa 1840) whose persona—a troubled life (including a scandalous affair with a count), mysterious beauty, and a habit of always appearing with a black shawl—defined the classic fadista image that survives today. Fado eventually crystallized in the backstreet brothels, flophouses, cafes, and clubs of Lisbon and Coimbra in the early 1900s. It is an art song form with lyrics full of regret, mourning, and a mood that is forlorn. Its tones are dark, bluesy, and most of all eternally fatalistic, some might say depressing. Fado singers are traditionally accompanied by *Guitarra Portuguesa*, a 12-stringed guitar with a small body and long neck, *violao*, a smaller guitar used to play chords, and occasionally violin, flute, and accordion.

Many wonderful fadistas gained fame during the middle part of the last century, including Argentina Santos, Beth Cardozo, Marcia Condessa, and Adelina Ramos. No one could compete with the late Amalia Rodrigues (see Profile) however, and she is still the greatest musical star of Portugal, Edith Piaf and Carlos Gardel rolled into one. It is virtually impossible to sing traditional fado and not sound like Amalia.

As a result of Amalia's omnipotence, a *nova fado* movement has developed in Portugal, producing a number of rising stars who have added a modern twist to the music while remaining true to the art form. Cristina Blanco is receiving well-deserved acclaim with her folk-oriented slant on the music. Dulce Pontes has begun to branch out from the restrictive discipline of traditional fado to become a major voice on the world music scene. Misia, the mystical muse raised in Oporto, not traditionally a center of fado, has succeeded in defying the Amalia mold by bringing a degree of gaiety and mischief to the music. Her performances are quite theatrical, incorporating elements of the Japanese Noh tradition. Perhaps the best of all is Mozambique-born Mariza who, at a mere 26 years of age (in 2004), sounds remarkably like the young Amalia, but in a modern context that bodes well for the future of the genre.

NOVA CANCAO

Portugal has a diverse folk tradition, a strong classical guitar repertoire, and its own version of nueva cancion: *nova cancao*. The giant of nova cancao is the late Jose Afonso, the revolutionary folk singer/songwriter whose music was suppressed during Salazar's regime. Unlike his colleagues, Afonso never left his native land and emerged as a national hero in the late 1970s as Portugal finally entered the modern world. His legend lives today in rural artists such as roots group Brigada Victor Jara, whose name is taken from the martyred Chilean poet/songwriter, an Afonso colleague. Brigada are the foremost proponents of the *Tras-os-Montes* (behind the Mountains) style from a region in the Northeast of Portugal near the Spanish border. Former Brigada member Ne Ladeiras is the leading female folk artist. The Celtic influence dominant in neighboring Galicia can be heard in Tras-os-Montes, as well as other Portuguese roots music from Beira Baixas and Altenejo.

Born into poverty in the Alfama district of Lisbon, Amalia Rodrigues (1920–1999) is the unchallenged Queen of Fado who single-handedly transformed the genre into a virtually female discipline. Like Gardel before her in Argentina, Amalia was always bigger than life, a star singer, actress, and personality who transcended politics and was dear to her people. Her death in 1999 left a void that cannot be filled.

Amalia's career extended from the early 1940s through 1999, during which time her reign was never challenged. In 1944, she traveled to Brazil, drawing huge crowds at the Copacabana Casino in Rio de Janeiro, where she soon returned to make her first recordings. Amalia not only popularized fado throughout South America, she successfully combined the urban and rural styles of Lisbon and Coimbra, performing compositions that went far beyond the traditional scope of the music. She incorporated tales of failed romance that explored the depths of the soul and spirit. Her performances were unmatched for their fatalistic power and haunting beauty.

Amalia's voice, persona, and life became synonymous with the art form itself during her lifetime. Although Maria Severa is credited as the first fadista whose forlorn personality, sad life, and mysterious beauty defined the classic fadista traits, it is Amalia who will be forever associated with the music. Her stature is on a par with that of France's Edith Piaf and Egypt's Umm Kulthum as a national icon and goddess who is eternally loved and revered by the entire population of her country.

RECOMMENDED CDs

JOAO AFONSO. Joao's voice recalls a young Chico Buarque. *Zanzibar* (Resistancia, 2002) is sensitive and well crafted; *Missangas* (1997); *Barco Voador* (CBS, 1998).

JOSE AFONSO. Afonso was the leader of the nova cancao movement in Europe, a colleague of Silvio Rodriguez and Victor Jara, a troubadour and political activist who used the folk song to help sabotage Salazar. *Baladas y Cancoes* with Rui Pato on guitarra (Emi-Valentim, 1967/1996) contains classic Coimbran Fado and Folk tunes; *Cantigas do Maio* (Valentim, 1971).

AT-TAMBUR. Modern Folk music with hurdy gurdy, fiddles, and pipes; *At Tambur* (Tradisom Music, 2003).

CRISTINA BRANCO. Christina is not afraid to venture out from the safe haven of fado. *Corpo Illuminado* (Universal, 2000) features folk music and Fado; *Sensus* (Universal, 2003), is comprised of ballads set to classic Iberian poetry; her best recording to date.

BRIGADA VICTOR JARA. The roots ensemble performs traditional music from the Tras-os-Montes, Beira-Alta, and des Acores regions. *15 Years of Traditional Portuguese Music,* (Auvidis, 1992) is a treasure, a compilation from 1975–1989.

LUZ DESTINO. Maria Ana Bobone (vocals), Ricardo Rocha (guitarra portuguesa), and Joao Paulo (harpsichord) present an intriguing baroque spin on nova fado with *Luz Destino* (MA, 1996). Rocha and Paulo are former members of Brigada Victor Jara.

FAUSTO. Fausto Bordalo Dias is one of the most important songwriters in Portugal. *A Preto e Branco,* (CBS Portugal, 1988) rivals the best work of MPB giants from the same period; *Por Este Rio Acima* (Columbia Portugal, 1984) is about Fernao Mendes Pinto (1509–1583), who traveled the Far East for 21 years, was shipwrecked, imprisoned, and enslaved and then established the first Western settlement in Japan at Yokohama in 1548.

JOSE FERNANDO. Former violao accompanist for Amalia Rodrigues, Fernando sings in a sweet tenor voice, a rare fadisto.

Velho Fado (Times Square, 2001). He also arranged Mariza's *Fado em Mim*, reviewed below.

GAITEROS DE LISBOA. Roots group that plays strident folk on original instruments; for the purists. *Macareu* (Aduf Edicios, 2002); *Danca Chamas* (Farol, 2002).

NE LADEIRAS. Former vocalist with Brigada Victor Jara and Trovante, Ladeiras is a major talent, overlooked due to the omnipotence of fado. *Tras-os-Montes* (EMI-Valentim, 1994) focuses on the rural sounds from this northeast. *Todo este Ceu* (Sony Portugal, 1997) is a recording of Fausto compositions with a stellar acoustic ensemble.

MADREDEUS. From the Madre de Deus section of Lisbon, Madredeus has been at the forefront of new music from Lisbon since appearing in Wim Wenders's 1993 *Lisbon Story*, in which the band portrays themselves. *Ainda* (Blue Note, 1995); *Movimento* (Blue Note, 2001).

MARIZA. The brightest star on the scene. *Fado em Mim* (Times Square, 2001); *Fado Curvo* (Times Square, 2003).

MISIA. Guiding light of the nova fado movement since *Garras dos Sentidos* (Detour, 1996). *Paixoes Diagonais* (Detour, 1999) features world renowned classical Pianist Maria Joao Pires on the title track.

AMELIA MUGE. Born in Mozambique, Muge frequently collaborates with musicians from Galicia and is comfortable in folk and fado settings. *A Monte* (Vacier & Associates, 2002) is ambitious, albeit disjointed.

CARLOS PAREDES. The leading virtuoso of the *guitarra* possesses a sound that is one of the extraordinary pleasures in all of world music. *Guitarra Portuguese* (1970); *O Melhor de Carlos Paredes* is a compilation spanning 1962–1975.

JULIO PEREIRA. A major figure in Portuguese roots music, master of the braguesa violao (small guitar). He accompanied Jose Afonso in the 1970s. *Braguesa* (Sony Portugal, 1983); *Cavaquinho* (Sony Portugal, 1981); *Lau Eskutara* with Kepa Junkera (Sony, 1992).

DULCE PONTES. *O Primeiro Canto* (MCA, 2001) is an eclectic blend of folk, fado, jazz, and pop arranged by Brazilian Cellist

Jaques Morelenbaum with Angolan Waldemar Bastos, Indian percussionist Trilok Gurtu, and jazz Luminary Wayne Shorter.

AMALIA RODRIGUES (see Profile). *The Art of Amalia* (EMI, 1998), a compilation from 1952–1970, is a good starting point. *The First Recordings* (EPM, France); *Raizes* (Planet, Switzerland); *Coimbra* (World Of Fado, 1992 reissue) is a classic. Beware the plethora of reissued compilations.

SCOTLAND

Kilts and Clans, Bagpipes and Castles, Whisky and Haggis, and Mythical Lake Monsters are only a part of the northernmost part of the United Kingdom. Scotland is a land of great beauty and history, quite distinct culturally, politically, and musically from England. The famous Highlands and the Isle of Skye in the north are among the most breathtaking natural landscapes to be found anywhere on the planet, straight out of a fairytale book.

Despite its long history, Scotland did not win the right to self-governance via its own Parliament until 1998. While Scots revere their Royalty and have the famous Holyrood Palace (The Queen's residence in Scotland) at the end of the Royal Mile in Edinburgh to prove it, deep inside their collective psyche they despise the English for the abuse they have foisted upon the Scots through the ages. It is no secret that the fiercely independent, freedom conscious Scots crave total independence now more than ever. The message of William Wallace lives on.

THE MUSIC

Although the bagpipes are universally identified as Scottish, the truth is that the instrument has been prominent for centuries throughout the Celtic lands of Ireland, Wales, Northumbria (England), Bretagne (France), and Galicia (Spain) as well as in Italy, North Africa, and Eastern Europe. Scotland's brand of Celtic music is truly unique, however, centering on a great fiddling tradition, its own piping style, a female a cappella tradition, popularly known as "mouth music," and a pub scene of jam sessions second to none. The Shetland and Orkney Islands north of the mainland are a hotbed for fiddlers, as is Cape Breton in Canada. The community there, mostly of Scottish heritage, has had a profound effect on the music from the motherland since the early part of the twentieth century and the current relationship is thriving.

The folk revival in Scotland began with Ewan MaColl and Peggy Seeger in the 1950s and has experienced a much-needed resuscitation during the recent world music boom, led by the incomparable singer/guitarist Dick Gaughan. Numerous folk singers and groups have proliferated since the 1990s, recapturing an old tradition from the 1700s that was near extinction a half century ago. The new Scottish roots music combines Celtic tradition and unparalleled instrumental discipline and virtuosity with an international mentality to form one of the most vital world music genres on the planet.

Scotland is a place to catch live world music with venues such as Queens Hall, Usher Hall, Mambo, and the legendary pub Sandy Bell's in Edinburgh that rivals any club on the planet for genuine dedication to music.

RECOMMENDED CDs

ALY BAIN. Bain is from the Shetland Islands and is the standard-bearer for Scottish Fiddling. *Aly Bain & Friends* (Greentrax, 1989) is a soundtrack from a TV series; *Fully Rigged* (NorthSide, 2002).

BATTLEFIELD BAND. Battlefield began in 1969 and is still going strong. *Happy Daze* (Temple, 2001) with Karine Polwart is our favorite; *Rain, Hail or Shine* (Temple, 2000); *Home is Where the Van is,* (Temple, 1980) with Duncan MacGillivray; *Opening Moves* (Temple, 1993) is a nice compilation.

BOYS OF THE LOUGH. Supergroup with Irish, English and Welch mates aboard. Members have included piper/Temple Records owner Robin Morton, Dick Gaughan, Irish flute virtuoso Cathal McConnell, and Aly Bain. The Boys are a seminal band that parallels the achievements of Irish outfits Planxty and the Bothy Band. *Boys of the Lough* (Shanachie, 1973).

CAPERCAILLE. The leading popular Scottish band. *Sidewaulk* (Green Linnet, 1989) put them on the map; *Beautiful Wasteland* (1998) successfully incorporates Afro beats. *Live* (Valley, 2002) is solid. *Choice Language* (Sanctuary, 2003) is their best, more folk-rock than World.

PHIL CUNNINGHAM. Scotland's finest accordionist. His best work is with the group *Silly Wizard*. *Palomino Waltz* (Green Linnet, 1989) is Phil's best solo outing; *Fire in the Glen* with Wizard alumni Manus Lunny and Stewart is a classic. (see Andy M. Stewart)

DICK GAUGHAN. Scotland's leading folksinger is still making waves through his pointed lyrics and political approach. *Handful of Earth* (Green Linnet, 1981) is hard to top; *Parallel Lines* (Appleseed, 1983); *Redwood Cathedral* (Appleseed, 1998).

ALISON KINNAIRD. Traditional harp player. *The Harp Key*, (Temple, 1978) is reputed to be the first recording of (strictly) Scottish Harp music. *The Quiet Tradition*, (Temple, 1990) a duet with singer Christine Primrose.

ISHBEL MACASKILL. From the Hebrides Island of Lewis, Ishbel is a TV personality in Scotland and fervent advocate of the Gaelic language. *Essentially Ishbel* (Both are on private no name labels, 1999) is a classic recording of its kind, reminiscent of the best of early Judy Collins; *Sioda* (1994).

EWAN MACCOLL. MacColl led the international folk revival in the 1950s and is a legend who influenced every folksinger from Bob Dylan to Karan Casey. His passing in 1988 has not diminished his stature. *Classic Scottish Ballads* (Tradition, 1960) with wife Peggy Seeger; *Black and White* (Cooking Vinyl, 1998) a compilation from 1972–1986; *Scottish Popular Ballads* (Riverside, 1956).

CATRIONA MACDONALD. From the Shetland Islands; standard-bearer for the new generation of Scottish fiddlers. *Bold* (Compass, 2000).

IAIN MACINNES. Session man, piper extraordinaire. *Tryst* (Greentrax, 2000) is a gem.

MAIRI MACINNES. One of the most versatile of the current crop of Scotch Gaelic vocalists. *Orosay* (Greentrax, 2001).

CATHERINE ANN MACPHEE. The Barra born, Hebrides native began her recording career after appearing as an actress and singer with the 7:84 Theatre in Edinburgh in 1981 and has been a star ever since. *Language of the Gael/Canan Nan Gaidhead*; (Greentrax, 1987).

MALINKY. The current hot group in Edinburgh focuses on the tunes, not the solos. *Last Leaves* (Greentrax, 1999) was *fRoots* magazine's runner-up for album of the year in 2000. *3 Ravens* (Greentrax, 2002) with singers Karine Polwart and Steve Byrne is even better.

JOHN MCCUSKER. *Goodnight Ginger* (Compass, 2002) a soulful instrumental side from former Battlefield fiddler.

HAMISH MOORE. Great piper and pipe maker. *Bees Knees* (Green Linnet, 1995) with saxophonist Dickie Lee.

OSSIAN. Seminal 1970s group with harpist William Jackson. *Borders* (Iona, 1984).

PEATBOG FAERIES. Funk, trad, reggae, and Gaelic. *Mellowosity* (Greentrax, 1997).

CRISTINE PRIMROSE. Scottish Gaelic soprano with a delicate elegance and subtle power. *Without Seeking, Without Asking* (Temple, 2001); *S' Tu Nam Chuimhne* (Temple, 1987).

EDDI READER. Glasgow songstress who sings mostly in English *Sings the Songs of Robert Burns* (Compass, 2003).

JEAN REDPATH. Ethnomusicologist and teacher (New School for Social Research and Harvard) Redpath is a folk institution in the United States. *Robert Burns Series, Volumes 1 & 2* (Philo, 1995).

RUNRIG. Rock and soul Gaelic style. *Once in a Lifetime* (1988, Chrysalis).

SHOOGLENIFTY. The #1 Celtic rock band. *Whiskey Kiss* (Greentrax, 1997) one of the all-time best selling Scottish sides; *The Arms Dealer's Daughter* (Compass, 2003).

SILLY WIZARD. The early supergroup broke barriers with their modernized version of authentic Scottish Gaelic music, led by the late fiddler Johnny Cunningham, brother Phil, and the incomparable vocals of Andy M. Stewart. *Live Wizardry* (Green Linnet, 1988); *Wild and Beautiful* (Shanachie, 1981).

SKYEDANCE & ALISDAIR FRASER. *Live in Spain* (Culburnie, 2000) is a collaboration with Basque Trikitixa virtuoso Kepa Junkera, Galician Gaita specialist Xose Manuel Budino, Mercedes Peon, and Basque legend Mikel Laboa.

EMILY SMITH. Enchanting vocalist/accordionist, a new artist to watch. *A Day Like Today* (Foot Stompin', 2003).

SAVOURNA STEVENSON. In-demand harpist and June Tabor collaborator. *Touch Me Like the Sun* (1998); *Cutting the Chord* (Eclectic, 1993).

ANDY M. STEWART. The most recognizable Scottish male voice of them all. *Dublin Lady* (Green Linnet 1987) is a splendid affair; *Fire in the Glen* (Green Linnet, 1986).

TANNAHILL WEAVERS. The acoustic Weavers sing traditional songs in English. *Capernaum* (Green Linnet; 1994) *Tannahill Weavers 4* (Green Linnet, 1982).

WOLFSTONE. Rock and Scot. *Unleashed* (Green Linnet, 1991).

SPAIN

Spain's historical propensity to plant its genetic seed wherever it conquered and exploited indigenous cultures continues to mold the global ethnic profile 500 years later. The Inquisition and laws of conversion, which devastated and expelled the Moors, Gypsies, and Jews from Iberia in the fifteenth Century, is a dark period in the country's history. Fortunately the music produced by these cultures while part of Spain has survived and blossomed throughout the Mediterranean. As we enter the new millennium, the music of the Motherland's progeny is prominent throughout the Western Hemisphere, Africa, the Middle East, and Asia.

MOORS, GYPSIES, AND JEWS

The architecture of the Moors, who ruled much of Spain prior to the Inquisition, is a vital part of Spain's southern landscape, perhaps more significant in today's political climate than at any time in the past 500 years. African influence on Spain's southern region, especially its music, also remains profound. Gypsies migrated to Spain many centuries ago from their native Hindustan, making their way through Eastern Europe, detouring in North Africa, and finally landing in Iberia. They were persecuted before and after the Inquisition, but have maintained a permanent social presence throughout Andalusia, somehow surviving constant oppression to create and perpetuate Spain's greatest musical gift to the world, flamenco.

The history of the Sephardic Jews and their Ladino culture also continues to resonate in twenty-first century Spain. Permanent memorials are displayed and preserved in Andalusia, Toledo, and the Catalan city of Gerona. Ancient Sefardi music has survived as a vital genre both in Spain and North Africa with Jewish influence intact.

REGIONAL SPAIN

Since Franco's death in 1975, Spain's numerous ethnic regions have embraced democracy and agreed to nationhood as an acceptable compromise in exchange for economic security and geopolitical stability. Don't be fooled, however; each region fancies itself a separate nation and as a result Spain possesses a rich, localized musical diversity where traditional forms are confined to individual regions and rarely exported, even within Spain.

Galicia. In 810 CE, claims that the remains of one of Christ's apostles (Saint James's) were found in Galicia created a rallying point for Christianity in its war against the Islamic infidels. At the time the Moors ruled all of south and central Spain but never the northern corridor from Galicia and Asturias east to the Pyrenees. Despite the fact that the Moors greatly enhanced and advanced Spanish (and Portuguese) culture, science, technology, and diet, the Christians considered them infidels. The site of the apostle's remains, Santiago de Compostela, attracted pilgrims from throughout Europe and Scandinavia, and to this day the northwestern regions of Spain retain a distinct culture, each with its own language, devoid of the Arabic influence still prevalent elsewhere in the country.

Along with the pilgrims came the music. The piping tradition prevalent in Galicia and Asturias, where bagpipes are called *gaitas*, is unmistakably Celtic and shares tradition with the Traz-as-Montes region in northeastern Portugal. Galician instrumentation—pipes, flute, accordion, tamboril (tambourin played with a stick), and pandeiro (tambourine) —is similar to that found in Ireland and Scotland. Paradoxically, conservative Galicia has a contemporary music scene that is the most progressive and internationally recognized in all of Spain.

Catalonia. Catalonia is Spain's leading province economically, intellectually, and artistically. Catalans view themselves as an autonomous nation and boast one of the most modern, sophisticated, cohesive societies in the Western world. Their culture bears only a surface resemblance to Spain and their language is quite different. Musically, Catalonia is home to *rumba gitano*, many top flamenco artists, international rock and pop stars, and a rich folk tradition shared with their sister island of Mallorca.

Euskadi. The physically breathtaking, naturally rich region in the northeast known as the Basque Country has a well-documented history of political terrorism, but possesses an otherwise progressive, artistic tradition, its own ancient language, and a fierce independence quite foreign to Castilian Spain. Donostia (San Sebastian) is one of the most sophisticated cities in Europe, decidedly not Spanish. Basque a cappella vocal music and Trikitixa (accordion-based music) are unique genres indigenous to Euskadi that survived Franco's rule and are popular today.

FLAMENCO

The legendary ninth century musician Ziryab, who settled in Cordoba from his native Baghdad, is credited as the seminal figure in the history of flamenco. Over the centuries the music was influenced by Arab song and codified by oral tradition as the Gypsies migrated west performing and living in Bohemian troupes. The word *flamenco* is thought to derive from the Arabic *felamengu* meaning fugitive peasant, or *fel lah mangu*, songs of laborers. Most musicologists feel the Gypsies brought *cante flamenco* from India with detours and modifications interjected into the music as they moved west.

When the Gypsies settled in Seville, Cadiz, Jerez, Malaga, and Utrera, Andalusia became the center of the music, with Jewish and Muslim influences part of the mix. As the Gypsies, Jews, and Muslims were forced into hiding to avoid the laws of conversion, the music underwent an expansion and hibernation. During the next three centuries flamenco was kept alive through the oral tradition of the Gypsies and became forever linked to and characterized by the generosity, boisterousness, and recklessness associated with the Gypsy lifestyle. The historical message of the music expresses an obsessive need for self-esteem, something that Gypsy culture has rarely been granted by the outside world.

The flamenco we know today came to full prominence in the mid-eighteenth century, first in Triana, the gypsy quarter of Seville, and then in Jerez de la Frontera, Cadiz, and other port cities in southern Spain. Cultivated society initially rejected the music. Flamenco was confined to taverns and performed exclusively by gypsies until 1850 when *cante jugo* (deep song) became popular in Spanish society and was sung in cabarets throughout Andalusia by Gypsies and Payos (non-gypsies) alike. The professional flamenco performer was born.

The popularity of flamenco declined in the early twentieth century as commercialization took over. The great Spanish poet Federico Garcia Lorca attempted to rejuvenate the form at a famous *Cante Jondo* competition in 1923 attended by Segovia, Manuel de Falla, and other major artists of the day. An 11-year old Manolo Caracol, the first flamenco star, won the competition, and an old *cantaor*, Diego Bermudez, allegedly walked 80 miles from Puente Genil to Granada for the event. Lorca, who was murdered by the Fascists at the onset of the Civil War in 1936, remained a staunch supporter of the music throughout his life, but it was not until 1957, when a Chair of Flamencology was created at the University in Jerez, that a flamenco revival was spawned. Today the music is experiencing an unprecedented renaissance and Lorca's poems are inextricably associated with the music.

In order to appreciate flamenco, it is essential to understand the concept of *duende*. As a singer performs, the voice bursts with an intense, furious, emotionally charged urgency that reaches a catharsis. Heartfelt sobbing and a risky vulnerability are exhibited during performance, which lead to a deep connection between the singer and the audience, so there is nothing else in either's mind or body but the sheer emotion, sorrow, and pain expressed through the music. According to Lorca, *duende* could only be found "in the depths of abandonment, in the final blood filled room of the soul."

Despite the numerous and talented female singers of flamenco, including Fernanda and Bernarda Utrera, Carmen Linares and the current young star Estrella Morente, there is one singer from Spain whose international stature and accomplishments outstrip that of any flamenco star, the Mallorcan folk singer Maria del mar Bonet (b.1948). Maria is a charismatic performer respected throughout the world; a folk diva in the Joni Mitchell vein; a bohemian artist whose advocacy for the rights of her people and language (Catalan) has not diminished since the late 1960s.

Maria began her career with the 1960s Barcelona folk group Els Setze Jutges, fighting to preserve the Catalan language forbidden by Franco. Spiritually and politically she is an ally of the nueva cancion movement (see South American reviews) and the 1960s folk and Civil Rights movements. She is that rare artist whose work has retained its political and artistic integrity while evolving over a long and distinguished career. Her recordings are similar only in their extraordinarily high quality, originality, and taste. Maria can silence an audience with her startling beauty and voice. Her musical philosophy embodies Turkish Composer Zulfu Livaneli's theory that the Balearic Islands (Mallorca, Ibiza, Formentera) are part of a 6th Continent in the Mediterranean region also including Corsica, Sardinia, Sicily, Crete, The Maghreb, Cypress, and parts of Spain and France

RECOMMENDED CDs

LUIS EDUARDO AUTE. Philippine-born, folk/pop icon, nueva cancion artist; the Silvio Rodriguez of Spain. *Alevosia* (EMI, 1995); *Mano e Mano* (RCA, 1994) is live with Rodriguez.

ANA BELEN. Ana can enthrall a packed stadium and enchant in a cabaret setting. *Mucho Mas que Dos* (BMG, 1994); *Lorquiana* (Ariola, 1998) is set to the poems of Lorca; *Calle del Oso* (Philips, 1975).

BERROGUETTO. Galician (mostly instrumental) Celtic band respected throughout the United Kingdom. *Viaxe por Urticaria* (Dofol, 1999).

MARIA DEL MAR BONET (see Profile). *Primeres Cancons* (Discmedi, 1967–1969) a precious period piece; *Jardi Tancat/Walled*

Garden (Ariola, 1984); *Salmaia* (Picap, 1995) an excursion through Greece and Turkey; *Cavall de Foc/Horse on Fire* (Picap, 2000); *Raixa* (World Muxxic, 2001) is a live set.

XOSE MANUEL BUDINO. Innovative piper specializing in the Galician gaita. *Paralaia* (Resistancia, 1999).

CAMARON DE ISLA (JOSE MONJE CRUZ). The legendary flamenco singer is the bridge from old to new. He died young (42) from lung cancer, alcohol, and heroin abuse, but achieved pop star status during his life. His collaborations with Paco de Lucia are central to the history of flamenco in the last quarter of the twentieth century. *El Camaron Colaboracion* (Alex, 1993) with de Lucia; *Canastera* (PolyGram, 1982; 1993); *Una Leyenda Flamenco* (Philips, 1993) is a good retrospective.

FALTRIQUIERA. Leaders of the Galician *pandeiretera* (female singing-tambourine groups) revival. *Faltriqueira* (Resistancia, 2003).

ANTONIO FERNANDEZ DIAZ "FOSFORITO." A missionary for the cause of flamenco as well as a great singer who died in 1982. *Figuras del Cante Jondo* (Planet, 1999 reissue).

KEPA JUNKERA. Basque trikitixa (diatonic accordian) virtuoso; a unifying force on the Celtic music scene. *Bilbao 00:00h* (Resistancia, 1998) with Carlos Nunez, Xose Manuel Budino, Justin Vali, Oskorri, La Bottine Souriante, Mercedes Peon, Dulce Pontes, Hedningarna, and others is a masterpiece; *Maren* (EMI Spain, 2002) defies the sophomore jinx; *K* (EMI, Spain, 2003).

MIKEL LABOA. Legendary composer, arranger, and singer/ guitarist; a National Treasure in Euskadi. *Gernika-Zuzenean 2* (Elkar, 1999).

LEILIA. *Pandeiretera* group, a cappella. *Madama* (Discmedi Blau, 2003).

L'HAM DE FOC. Roots group from Valencia incorporates North African, Greek, and Indian music into their local style. *U* (Sonifolk 1999); *Canco de Dona I Home* (Sonifolk, 2001).

CARMEN LINARES. Leading female flamenco singer, intense and soulful. *La Luna en el Rio* (Auvidis, 1991); *Cantaora* (Riverboat, 1994).

LLUIS LLACH. Singer/songwriter, political activist, dedicated antifascist, and Catalan, the Art Blakey of Catalan song— a musical messenger who showcases new artists. *Temps de Revoltes,* (Picap, 2000); *Live in Camp Nou* (Caja Madrid,1987); *Lluis Llach* (1977).

LUAR NA LUBRE. Galician group from La Coruna in the nineteenth century tradition. *O Cabo do Mundo* (Warner, 1999).

PACO DE LUCIA. Flamenco guitarist without peer. *Sirocco* (Polydor, 1987) and *Luzia* (PolyGram, 1998) are his finest; *12 Cancions of Lorca* (PolyGram, 1992); *Cositas Buenas* (Blue Thumb, 2004).

MACACO. Modern Catalan ensemble on the cutting edge of world music. *Rumbo Sumbmarino* (Edel, 2002) is hip-hop, electro, world, and infectious.

JOSE MERCE. The most compelling male flamenco vocalist on the scene today in the style of the late El Camaron. *Aire* (Virgin Espana, 2000) is unbeatable; *Del Amanecer* (Virgin, 1999).

MILLADOIRO. The first Galician Celtic supergroup. *Augu de Maio* (Green Linnet, 2000) is a blend of traditional and original pieces skillfully played on gaita, clarinet, oboe, flute, whistle, guitar, percussion, bouzouki, and Uillean pipes.

FERNANDO FERNANDEZ MONJE ("TERREMOTO DE JEREZ"). "The Earthquake from Jerez" (1936–1981) was one of the most soulful flamenco performers ever. *Figuras del Cante Jongo* (Planet, 1993).

ENRIQUE MORENTE. The dean of living male flamenco singers (b.1942). *Cante Flamenco* (Hispavox, 1967) is an early, slow, pensive take on the tradition pointing to Morente's bright future. *Morente sings Lorca* (Narada, 1999) is eclectic and ventures out of the mold with success.

ESTRELLA MORENTE. Daughter of Enrique, the newest flamenco diva, a future star. *My Songs and a Poem* (Real World, 2002).

OJOS DE BRUJOS ("Eyes of the Wizard"). Flamenco, rumba, scratching, Indian subtleties, a Catalan band that has it all in the Manu Chao style. *Bari.* (Colores, 2002).

CARLOS NUNEZ. A leading star from Galicia, piper extraordinaire, one of Spain's most famous artists. *Brotherhood of the Stars* (RCA, 1997).

LA NINA DE LOS PEINES. The first great female cante jongo singer from the 1920s favored the hard style over the milder Chacon style that had been in vogue. *La Vol. I* (Planet).

MERCEDES PEON. Galicia's female vocal sensation has a powerful, eerie voice and an avant-garde approach. *Isue* (2000, Resistancia) is startling and abrasive; *Ajru* (Dicmedi Blau, 2003) is a major recording, a breakthrough CD.

MIGUEL POVEDA. Young flamenco star from Barcelona. *Zaguan* (Harmonia Mundi, 2001).

RADIO TARIFA. The quintessential world music recording group; enchanting vocals, middle-eastern double reeds, Moroccan gimbris, electric guitars, and flamenco style. *Cruzando El Rio* (World Circuit, 2002) is their best; *Rumba Argelina* (World Circuit, 1996) put them on the map.

MARINA ROSSELL. With the release of *Cap al Cel* (World Village, 2003), a collection of Catalan folk tunes from the early twentieth century, Marina is no longer the best-kept secret in Catalan music; *Barca del Temps* won the 1985 award for Record of the Year in Spain; *Y Rodara el Mundo* (Movie Play, 2000); *Marina* (PDI, 1993).

SABICAS. The flamenco guitarist was the first to take the music out of Spain. *Flamenco Fiesta* (Legacy, 1999 reissue).

PEIO SERBEILLE. Disciple of Mikel Laboa, Serbeille brings the Euskadi feeling into the twenty-first century with apocalyptic compositions wrought with the Basque nationality. *Euskadi Kanta Lur* (Declic, 2000).

JOAN MANUEL SERRAT. Catalan idol, one of Spain's greatest folk and pop singer/songwriters, going strong since 1965. *Mediterraneo* (BMG Latino, 1971) made him a star; *La Paloma* (RCA Int'l, 1975/98); *1978* (RCA Int'l, 1978/2000).

SUSANA SEIVANE. twenty-first century Galician gaita (pipe) star. *Alma de Buxo* (Green Linnet, 2002); Mares de Tempo (Dofol, 2004) is finevocals by Susana too.

TOMATITO. Flamenco guitarist discovered by Paco de Lucia. *Rosas del Amor* (EMI 1987/2001) important, groundbreaking CD.

FERNANDA AND BERNARDA UTRERA. In flamenco, dynasty counts, and the Gypsy sisters Utrera, granddaughters of the legendary Pinini, are repositories of the music. *Ritmo en Le Sangre, Cante Flamenco* (Hispavox, 1969/98).

UXIA. Female vocalist from Galicia. *La Sal de la Vida* (NubaNegra 1998) collaboration with Rasha (Sudan) and Maria Salgado; *Estou Vivindo No Ceo* (NubaNegra, 1995). Uxia sings in Gallego, Portuguese, and Spanish.

AMAIA ZUBIRIA. Eclectic Basque Vocalist. *Haatik* (Elkar, 2002).

SWEDEN

As with Sweden's film industry, government, and social structure, their approach to traditional music is modern and progressive. In the early 1980s the Swedes began to retrieve much of their ancient Nordic music from a long period of dormancy. A vibrant new roots music movement, which began strictly as an instrumental genre, has blossomed into a crusade to unearth treasures of a rich musical past.

Despite its mostly homogeneous society, unlike many other European countries, Sweden does not possess a dominant national folk music genre identified as Swedish. Instead Sweden's musical tradition is a regional affair manifesting itself in various configurations of dance and performance music. *Polska* is the dominant folk dance form in many regions. Dalarna in the North is home to the most famous fiddling tradition and has become a focal center for the new Swedish folk scene.

SWEDISH SONG

Regional music throughout the country, whether for dancing, celebratory ceremonies, working, drinking, or helping to survive the long, solitary winters, has always centered on song. Two styles predominate. The most unique and indigenous is the penetrating high-pitched singing called *kulning,* originally used as a cow-calling cry. It has become a trademark of contemporary Swedish vocalists, with world renowned Lena Willemark the most prominent proponent.

The other traditional form is the *ballad,* a song form that is always based on a story mostly consisting of tales dating back to the Middle Ages with references from all parts of Europe and strong roots in ancient Nordic folklore.

INSTRUMENTS

Nyckelharpa (a keyed fiddle; c. 1350). The fiddle is at the center of most Scandinavian roots music. The Swedish version is called *nyckelharpa,* with a body shaped like a guitar, much larger and more boat-like than a classical violin. Sympathetic strings were added to the instrument in the eighteenth century, which gives it a distinctive sound far more resonant and coarse than its classical cousin. *Bagpipes (sackpipa)* are found in Dalarna, used more frequently following the death of the main proponent, the legendary Gudmunds Nils Larsson who died in 1949. Due to the efforts of popular artists Per Gudmundson and Leif Eriksson, the sackpipa is now an integral part of the roots music scene. Dalarna pipes are small with a sweet, reedy tone, mouth blown, with a single drone; similar in size to the Irish uillean pipes

The *spelpipa* is a small wooden whistle, also from Dalarna, played much as the tin whistle in the Celtic tradition, with Ale Moller the leading player and expert.

RECOMMENDED CDs

FRIFOT. Frifot is comprised of Lena Willemark (vocals, fiddles); Ale Moller (mandolas, flutes, cow's horn, pipes, vocals) and Per Gudmundson (Dalarna fiddle, viola and bagpipes), the most prominent Swedish group on the world music stage. *Sluring* (NorthSide, 2003) is a balanced, exciting excursion into polyphony, microtonal playing and *kulning. Jarven* (Caprice, 1996); *Frifot* (ECM, 1999).

GARMARNA. A modern folk band that reveres the tradition and the dark side. *Vengence* (NorthSide, 1999); *God's Musicians* (Omnium, 1996).

GJALLARHORN. From Finland but of Swedish heritage, Gjallarhorn plays completely acoustic Swedish music. The band fuses folk music from the Bothnian region of Finland with didgeridoo, wooden whistles, traditional fiddles, and mandolas. *Ranarop: Call of the Sea-Witch* (Elektra, 1998) put them on the map; *Sjofn* (NorthSide, 2000); *Grim Borg* (NorthSide, 2002) is their best.

PETER "PUMA" HEDLUND. Renowned nyckelharpa player. *Another Way* (RPM, 2003) includes support on guitar, uillean pipes, cello, and even dobro, *Vagen* (RPM, 2001).

HEDNINGARNA. Experimental, amplified rock band, heavy on the sampling. Finnish vocalists Sanna Kurki-Suonio and Anita Lehtola joined to record *Tra* (NorthSide, 1994) and *Kaksi* (NorthSide, 1992).

VASEN. *Nyckelharpa*-powered band led by Olov Johansson that combines jazz, classical, dance, and Swedish folk. *Whirled* (NorthSide, 1997); *Gront* (NorthSide, 1999).

LENA WILLEMARK. The first lady of Swedish roots music, a warm vocalist prone to wild forays into controlled microtonal soaring (called *kulning*) and an innovative fiddler. *Nordan* (1994, ECM); *Agram* (1997, ECM); *Windogur* (1999, Amigo).

SWITZERLAND

Switzerland is the most idyllic of countries, picturesque beyond imagination, with a conservative, sophisticated, homogeneous population who reside at the epicenter of Europe and the magnificent Alps. The Swiss are the world's leading bankers, renowned makers of fine timepieces, cheese, and chocolate, a people who steadfastly profess neutrality in all political situations.

In reality, Switzerland is anything but neutral. It has been the safe haven for Sadaam Hussein, Manuel Noriega, Imelda Marcos, Baby Doc Duvallier, Fidel Castro, August Pinochet, Yasser Arafat, Robert Mugabe, Silvio Berlusconi, Vladimir Putin, Osama bin Laden, the House of Saud, Hezbollah, the IRA and a host of other notorious and ignominious characters and organizations — their money that is — who have plundered the world through the ages.

There are pockets of ethnic music within the Swiss borders that center around the unique and enormous Alpine horn and a long yodeling tradition, but Switzerland is neither an important stop on the world music circuit nor a significant musical force on the continent.

RECOMMENDED CDs

STIMMHORN. A popular outfit that make their own horns and instruments and experiment with Mongolian overtone singing and yodeling. *Menken* (EMI, 1997).

COMPILATION. *Air Mail Music: Traditional Instruments of Switzerland*. A sampling of instruments and not too much yodeling.

WALES

Dwarfed by Scotland, Ireland, Galicia, and Bretagne, the Celtic-based music from Wales (along with that of Cornwall and the Isle of Man) is one of the best kept secrets in the United Kingdom, if not all of world music. The Welsh have traditionally been more separated from the English by their language than the Scots or Irish. Also, unlike the oral traditions of Scotland and Ireland, Welsh music has been perpetuated through old manuscripts and books, although the current revival is now incorporating music from older musicians to form a new modern idiom and oral tradition.

The folk music from Wales—*gwerin*—is quite unique with an ancient history rejuvenated during the worldwide folk revival in the 1960s. The stereotype of the all-male choir comprised of downtrodden miners as the sum and substance of Welsh music—a notion acceptable to the Church and reinforced by Hollywood—is disappearing as a proliferation of Welsh artists make their mark on the world music scene, especially across the United Kingdom. The Welsh language is also enjoying revitalization. Tom Jones and Shirley Bassey now have to share the stage!

THE EISTEDDFOD

Derived from festive competitions from the twelfth Century, *Eisteddfods* (festivals) are currently going strong throughout Wales and Cornwall. The competitive aspect of these festivals has dwindled in recent years as the music has expanded in scope. The Eisteddfod now more closely resembles the Irish fleadh, the Edinburgh Festival, or the Biannale in Italy as showcases for artistic talent and recognized masters. The middle of the summer is the time to hear this music live if you are in the United Kingdom.

INSTRUMENTS

The voice has always been and still is the center of Welsh music, followed closely by the harp. The *triple harp* is everywhere, consisting of 2 parallel rows of strings that sound the same note, and a third row of "accidentals" in between. Nansi Richards, one of the greatest Welsh harpists of the twentieth century, helped reintroduce this instrument, which dates back to the eighteenth century tradition. The *pibgorn* is also prevalent, a reed instrument with a cow's horn for a bell at the end, a relative of the *veuve* or *binou* in Bretagne music. Also traditional and long part of the music is the bagpipes, called *pibe cwd*. Since the 1960s, the fiddle, guitar, and accordion have come to the forefront greatly expanding the sonic and emotional scope of the music.

RECOMMENDED CDS

AR LOG. A groundbreaking group that widened the appeal of Welsh music in the 1970s. *Ar Log IV* (Sain, 1996).

ROBIN HUW BOWEN. Along with Nansi Richards, Bowen is responsible for the modern revival of the triple harp. *Old Hearth* (Sain, 1999) is tranquil, pensive, and ethereal.

CALLENIG. Quartet including concertina that plays and sings seafaring songs. *Trade Winds* (Sain, 1997).

CRASDENT. Popular ensemble that features Robin Huw Bowen. *Welsh Traditional Music* (Marquis, 2000).

FERNHILL. The most famous and commercially successful group from Wales led by Ceri Rys Matthews and vocalist Julie Murphy. *Whilia* (Beautiful Jo, 2000) was their breakthrough recording; *Ca Nos* (Beautiful Jo, 1996); *Hynt,* (Beautiful Jo, 2003) may be their best yet.

FYNNON. Voice/piano/harp trio. *Celtic Music from Wales* (Green Linnet, 2002).

DAFYDD IWAN. The leading name on the Welsh folk scene, Iwan began in the mid-1960s in the early Bob Dylan mold. *Can Celt* (Sain, 1995); *Caneunon Gwerin* (Sain, 1997).

SIAN JAMES. Important female vocalist and harpist. *Distaw/ Silent* (Sain, 1993); *Di-gwsg/Sleepless* (Sain, 1997).

THE KILBRIDES. Bernard and Gerard are the fiddlers, Daniel the guitarist in this Cardiff-based band. *Kilbride* (Fflach Tradd, 1997).

MABSANT. An important modern Welsh ensemble. *Trwy'r Weiar* (Sain, 1987).

CERI RHYS MATTHEWS. Matthews is a leading figure on the scene, a piper and founder of the Fflach Tradd record label. *Pibau*, (Fflach Tradd, 1999).

LLIO RHYDDERCH. The current triple harp star and the virtuoso of today. *Enlli* (Fflach Tradd, 2003); *Telyn* (Fflach Tradd, 1997).

DYLAN THOMAS. *A Child's Christmas in Wales*. The one and only. Of course it's not world music, but oh, Mrs. Prothero.

VARIOUS ARTISTS. *Gorau Gwerin: The Best of Welsh Folk Music* (Sain, 1992); *The Rough Guide to the Music of Wales* is a perfect collection to survey the Welsh scene (Rough Guide, 2001).

EASTERN EUROPE, THE BALTIC STATES, AND THE BALKANS

Albania	Estonia	Russia
Armenia	Georgia	Slovakia
Bosnia	Hungary	Turkey
Bulgaria	Latvia	Ukraine
Croatia	Poland	Yugoslavia (Serbia &
Czech Republic	Romania	Montenegro)

As the new millennium unfolds, Eastern Europe, the Baltic States, and the Balkans are emerging from nearly a century of Soviet hegemony, during which time the individual history and identity of virtually every country was hidden from the rest of the world. Since the fall of the Soviet Empire and the Berlin Wall, conflicts in the Balkans and the ongoing war on Islamic militantism continue to resonate throughout these regions, threatening the economies, culture, and very existence of the component nations. Life-and-death struggles are being fought on many fronts to reclaim the treasures and glories of the past and to retain long suppressed ethnic identity. Music is playing its customary role as a healing force and repository of oral tradition, more important now than at any time since the Bolshevik Revolution. This survey covers virtually every musical form from the region, vibrant sounds that are part of the growing international world music library.

ALBANIA

Albania is a Balkan nation that was ruled by Enver Hoxha's socialist government for the latter part of the twentieth century. Throughout its history, Albania has been dominated by the cultures that surround it, most notably the Ottoman Empire and the former Yugoslavian provinces. Albania is Europe's least developed country and its music is the least known, heard, or discussed folk music in Europe.

Albanians are commonly divided into three groups: the northern Ghegs, the southern Labs, and the Tosks. During Hoxha's rule, music was restricted to patriotic themes and used as a propaganda tool to extol the virtues of the state. Since the arrival of democracy in 1991 lyrics have become less restricted and have focused on previously taboo subjects such as *kurbet* (seeking work outside of Albania), politics, and even new ideas about modern life.

The Ghegs are known for a distinctive variety of epic poetry called *Rapsodi Kreshnike* sung by elderly men. The city of Shkodër is the cultural capital of Albania, and its music is the most sophisticated in the country. Bosnian *sevdalina* is a major influence in Shkodër. Albania's capital, Tirana, is dominated by Gypsy music that has a decidedly Turkish influence. Southern Albanian music is softer, gentler, and polyphonic in nature. Albania has yet to make its mark on world music and the recorded lexicon is indeed limited.

RECOMMENDED CDS

TIRANA FOLK ENSEMBLE. *Songs and Dances from Albania* (Arc, 2000)

EDA ZARI. Female polyphonic singer with a jazz influence. *Statement* (Intuition, 2003) is available in English and Albanian.

VARIOUS ARTISTS. *Albanian Village Music* (Heritage UK, 1998); *Polyphonic Chants of Albania* (Iris, 1999).

ARMENIA

Home to the famous Mount Ararat and classical composers Aram Khachaturian and Alan Hovhaness, the story of modern Armenia is one of tragedy and suffering. Armenians and Turks lived in harmony under the Ottoman Empire for centuries, until the 1880s when the rise of nationalism began to change the political face of the region. Despite admonishment from European powers, the Turkish government began to openly persecute the Armenians, the only Christian minority between Turkey and Central Asia, and by the 1890s hundreds of thousands of Armenians died in pogroms ordered by Sultan Abdul Hamid II. Turkish nationalists took dictatorial control in 1908 and began implementing a plan to eradicate the Armenian race in a step towards fulfilling their pan-Turkic dreams.

With the distraction of World War I as a backdrop, on April 24, 1915, hundreds of Armenian leaders were murdered in Istanbul, beginning a program of mass murder that methodically moved from village to village and province to province. The modern history of Armenia is inextricably related to this holocaust that remains a scar on the conscience of humanity. Today, the residual effect of Soviet control permeates the landscape, as the country is barely reawakening, and new conflicts are brewing with Azerbaijan.

THE MUSIC

Despite its history, music has been kept alive by the Armenian diaspora in America and by a growing number of musicians in the capital of Yerevan. Armenia is known for classical choral music and medieval sacred lyric songs that have been preserved over centuries. Much of the music called "folk" is analogous to the classical music of neighboring cultures. Armenian music is characterized by a generally modal style, which fits in the niche between the music of Iran and Turkey, albeit in a specifically Christian, more Occidental way. The instruments of Armenian music are similar to that of its neighbors—*tar* (long neck lute), *kamencha* (fiddle), *kanun* (zither)—with one exception: The Armenian *duduk*.

The duduk, an end-blown, double-reed, recorder-type instrument made from apricot wood, is the national musical symbol of Armenia. Its sad, mournful, reedy sound is emblematic of the history and plight of the Armenian people. Classical Composer

Aram Khachaturian said of the duduk: "It is the only instrument whose sound makes me cry." Djivan Gasparyan is the instrument's most renowned player, the artist who has brought it international recognition. Most of Gasparyan's repertoire features traditional Armenian folk songs. He is also a composer and singer of considerable talent who has won numerous worldwide competitions organized by UNESCO (1959, 1962, 1973, and 1980) and is the only musician to be given the honorary title of People's Artist of Armenia from the Armenian government.

Following the horrors of 1915, many Armenians settled in Fresno, California, where a thriving community continues to grow. Musicians such as ud master Richard Hagopian and his son Harold, who runs the Traditional Crossroads record label, have worked tirelessly to keep Armenian music alive.

RECOMMENDED CDS

GEVORG DABAGHYAN. Gevorg is a duduk master who toured with Yo Yo Ma's *Silk Road Project*. *Masterworks for Armenian Duduk* (Traditional Crossroads, 2002), features liturgical and folk music.

ARI DINKJIAN. Talented New York based composer/oudist. *Bodies and Knives* (Polydor, 1994); with Greek star Eleftheria Arvanitaki; with *Night Ark: Moments* (1988).

DJIVAN GASPARYAN. *I Will Not Be Sad in This World* (All Saints Opa, 1989) is the classic, dedicated to the victims of the Armenian earthquake; *Apricots from Eden* (Traditional Crossroads, 1996).

RICHARD HAGOPIAN. The ud master's interpretations add modernity to the tradition while keeping it alive. *Armenian Music through the Ages* (Smithsonian, 1993); *Gypsy Fire* (Traditional Crossroads, 1995) is belly dancing music with Omar Faruk Tekbilek on Ney and Yuri Yunakov on Saxophone.

UDI HRANT KENKULIAN. Born in Armenia in 1901 (he lived most of his life in Istanbul) and blind at birth, Hrant is a legendary figure, a modern stylist, bluesy player and singer who was way ahead of his time technically and conceptually. *The Early Recordings Volume 1 and Volume 2* (Traditional Crossroads, 1995).

SHOGHAKEN ENSEMBLE. *Armenian Anthology* (Traditional Crossroads, 2002) contains 19 varied selections of Armenian folk music—lullabies, funeral songs, harvest melodies, love songs, tales of immigration and exile—a deeply haunting recording.

ARTO TUNCBOYACIYAN. Arto is an in-demand international percussionist who has recorded with Gerardo Núñez, Joe Zawinul, Dino Saluzzi, Omar Faruk Tekbilek, Eleftheria Arvanitaki, Ara Dinkjian, and Turkish star Sezen Aksu. *Tears Of Dignity* (Libra, 1996); *Every Day is a New Life* (Living Music, 2000) with Paul Winter; *Serart* (Serjical Strike/Columbia, 2003).

BOSNIA AND HERZEGOVINA

The war in southeastern Europe in the early 1990s hit Bosnia-Herzegovina hard, devastating the center of the former Yugoslavia and all but annihilating a passive population that mistakenly felt the atrocities would not extend to their region. Prior to the war, especially in the sophisticated capital of Sarajevo that was home to a veritable melting pot of Muslims, Catholics, Orthodox Christians, and Jews, Bosnians were widely recognized as the most tolerant population in Yugoslavia. Bosnians failed to understand the depth of hatred felt by the Serbs due to the Muslims' complicity with the Fascists during World War II. Long memories prevail in the region. Since the Balkan war, Bosnia remains a shambles. It will take a long time for Bosnia to recover economically and spiritually.

SEVDALINKA

The most famous music from Bosnia is *sevdalinka*, which roughly translates as "love song." The name derives from the Turkish word *sevda*, a kind of amorous yearning or passion, an unrequited love akin to the Brazilian concept of *saudade*. Bosnia has always had a strong Turkish influence dating back to the days when it was part of the Ottoman Empire, and its music reflects this influence. Beginning in the early twentieth century, professional musicians performed in the aristocratic courts of Bosnian Muslims and in the urban *kafana* (cafes). Singers of epic songs accompanied themselves on the *gusle* (a bowed lute with one or two strings) or on the *tambura* (a smaller long-necked lute with two or four strings). *Sevdalinka* is performed at secular occasions, used to foster a mood of intimacy and reflection.

Accordions are also frequently played in *sevdalinka* ensembles along with a violin, *zurna* (a kind of oboe), and the *sargija* (a lute akin to the Turkish *saz*). During the twentieth century, the Turkish modal system yielded to the European major-minor system. Free rhythm and melismatic melodies were replaced by metrical and melodic rhythm. Modernization of the genre and the introduction of new instruments have not diminished the value and significance of the *sevdalinka* in Bosnia; it continues to enjoy popularity as a traditional, evolving musical genre

Bosnia remains a predominantly a Muslim culture. Rural Muslims were less exposed to Ottoman culture and their music has remained closer to that of Croats and Serbs, characterized by a limited tonal range with narrow intervals, limited melodic movement, and singing at extremely low dynamic levels.

RECOMMENDED CDs

GORAN BREGOVIC. Bosnian-born film composer Bregovic is one of Yugoslavia's most successful and influential world music artists. He has collaborated with the acclaimed Serbian film director Emir Kusturica since 1978, for whom he scored the 1995 Cannes Film Festival winner *Underground* (Mercury France, 1995). He has also worked with Turkish Diva Sezen Aksu on *Weddings and Funerals* (See Aksu, Turkey), and Greek legend George Dalaras. His own *Ederlezi* (Mercury, 1998) is another fine Kusturica film score.

VARIOUS ARTISTS. *Echoes from an Endangered World* (Smithsonian, 1993) is a good cross section of the music and the place to start.

BULGARIA

The Greek hero Orpheus, son of the muse Calliope, was born in Rhodopes in the southern part of Bulgaria historically known as Thrace. It is said that Orpheus's musical power was such that he could charm wild beasts and coax rocks into movement. Mythology tells us that while Orpheus was traveling with Jason and the Argonauts, his music prevented the Argo from being lured by the Sirens into destruction. Keeping women from controlling you by playing music? That's power (or was it rock n' roll?). Bulgarian music is powerful. Bulgaria is one of the richest and most exciting musical sites on the world music map.

Bulgarian society has always been fiercely independent, moreso than other Eastern European nations, unafraid to take and hold difficult stands on issues, regardless of the political fallout. Bulgaria's care and respect for gypsies and Jews during World War II was an act of singular daring in a region where many neighbors were willing and proud Nazi supporters. The attempts by Todor Zhivkov—Bulgaria's former dictator who ruled from 1954–1998 and repressed any music not approved by the state and not specifically "Bulgarian" in origin—to cleanse the region of Roma (Gypsy in the pejorative sense) failed. Unlike other Eastern European countries, Bulgaria refused to allow its traditional music to die. For decades under Communist rule, state-funded choirs presented rearrangements of folk melodies.

The former Soviet Republic has jettisoned itself directly into the global village, overtly separating from its Eastern European neighbors economically and politically in the first decade of the twenty-first century. Since the fall of the Berlin wall and the demise of Zhivkov, the underground music movement that had been building for decades has exploded. Bulgaria's mostly harmonious, contemporary relationship with its Gypsy population evidences a far more progressive and humane society than is found in most other parts of Eastern Europe and the Balkans. The obsession with freedom is exploding in the capitol of Sofia in every walk of Bulgarian life, nowhere more than in the musical arena.

"Wedding music," a unique genre that goes well beyond the concept of the traditional music that accompanies the wedding ceremony, combines Bulgarian, Turkish, and Rom (Gypsy) folk tunes with jazz, always prioritizing improvisation. Wedding music is all the rage in the Balkans, played by ensembles that include clarinet, saxophone, *kaval* (end-blown shepherd's flute), duduk, accordion, guitar, santur, and drums. The leading proponent of the music is the indomitable clarinetist Ivo Papasov, one of the most amazing musicians in the world. Wedding Music is invariably played at a breakneck pace and its traditional, intricate Bulgarian rhythms are navigated in famously difficult meters (5/16, 11/16).

Many of Bulgaria's finest musicians have today turned an eye toward western music, especially jazz, which relates to their obsession with freedom, a commodity that was in short supply until the past decade.

RECOMMENDED CDS

YASKO ARGIROV. Wedding music by a great clarinetist. *Hot Blood* (Dunya, 2002); *Yasko* (Dunya, 2000).

ROZA BRANCSEVA. Traditional Bulgarian folk music, accompanied by tambura, tupan, duda (bagpipe), gadulka, violin, accordion, cimbalom, and kaval. *Jana-Janika* (2002).

GALINA DURMUSHLIYSKA. Galina is from the northeast region of Dobrudzha and possesses a gorgeous Mezzo Soprano voice. *The Enchanting Voice of Bulgaria* (Arc, 2002) evidences the power and control of the closed throat technique employed in Bulgaria and throughout Thrace; Theodosii Spassov arranged several pieces.

JONY ILIEV. Iliev is the new vocal sensation from the Gypsy town of Kjustendil on the road to Macedonia. *Ma Maren Mu*, (Gema, Piranha, 2003) includes great ballads and hip Balkan Swing recalling legendary Serbian Gypsy Saban Bajramovic.

LES MYSTERE DES VOIX BULGARES. The singers use the constricted throat technique, a trait said to be genetically particular to Bulgarians. *Le Mystere des Voix Bulgares* (Elektra/Nonesuch 1987).

IVO PAPASOV. A Bulgarian Turk from Thrace, Ivo is one of today's most talented clarinet players, recalling Charlie Parker. *Balkanology* (Hannibal, 1991) is a startling record for its sheer virtuosity, inventive improvisation, and ensemble tightness. *Orpheus Ascending* (Hannibal, 1989) has more Thracian singing and ballads; *Fairground* (Kuker, 2003) is Ivo's first in 10 years.

PETAR RALCHEV. Accordion works from Bulgaria, Serbia, Romania, and France with small ensemble. *Bulgaria* (Gega, 2003).

THEODOSII SPASSOV. Virtuoso Kaval player and composer, at home in Western classical, American jazz, or Balkan roots styles, sounding like a modern day Eric Dolphy. *Titla* (Traditional Crossroads, 1998); *Na Trapeza* (Gega, 2000).

YURI YUNAKOV. The New York-based saxophone virtuoso got his start with Ivo Papasov in the early 1980s and was an important part of the wedding music boom. *Balada* (Traditional Crossroads, 1998); *New Colors in Balkan Wedding Music* (Traditional Crossroads, 2000).

CROATIA

Part of the former Yugoslavia, Croatia possesses a diverse landscape consisting of large tracts of barren land and mountains with dramatic views of the Adriatic, fertile farmland with rolling hills, deep rivers, and dense forests. The Croatian language uses the Latin alphabet, and Croatia reflects a more western European culture than the other former Yugoslav republics. Croatia is about half the size of Louisiana, lying directly across the Adriatic Sea from Italy. Its beautiful capital city Zagreb and numerous "undiscovered" islands made Croatia a tourist mecca before the Balkan war, and Croatia is rapidly recapturing that trade as a twenty-first century tourist bargain.

TAMBURICA

The *tamburica* is an Eastern European lute used in most folk and dance music from Croatia and the surrounding regions. It has a sound that is a cross between a bouzouki and a mandolin with a high-pitched timbre that gives Croatian folk music its uplifting feeling, quite different from the more brooding, introspective traditional music found to the east. As with most stringed instruments, there are various sizes of *tamburicas*: *Samicas* are small and generally play the lead with the *bas tamburica* handling rhythm and bottom lines. The *diple*, a double-chanter bagpipe with no drone, is prominent in folk music throughout the former Yugoslavia.

RECOMMENDED CDs

LIDIJA BAJUK. Bajuk is one of Croatia's leading folk singers, dedicated to preserving Slavic mythology. *Zora Djevojka/The Dawn Maiden* (CBS Zagreb, 1997); *Tira les/Springing Trees* (CBS Zagreb, 2001).

LEGEN. Croatia's leading world beat group featuring folksingers Lidija Bajuk and Dunja Knebl. The artists perform traditional

Croatian songs in a folk style. *Ethno Ambient Live: Archaic Songs from Croatia* (Kopito, 1995). Live recording; soulful and moving, even for listeners who can't understand the language; loneliness, fear, sadness, and longing are communicated through simple melodies.

TAMARA OBROVAC. Singer, flutist. *Transhistria* (Cantus, 2001).

PATRIA. Six-piece tamburica ensemble that also performs Hungarian *csardas*, Romanian *horas*, and Gypsy ballads, with a nod to Mozart, Bach, and Brahms. *Sviraj* (Orfej, 2000); *Kad mi padneš na pamet* (Orfej, 2003).

VERITAS. *Tamburica* band led by singer Marica Perinic. *Folk Music from Croatia* (Arc, 1997) sounds similar to a lively Greek folk ensemble.

ZAGREB FOLK DANCE ENSEMBLE. Croatia's leading roots ensemble has strived to conserve Croatia's traditional musical and dance-oriented customs for almost 60 years. *Misnices, gajdes,* and *dudes* (types of bagpipes), tamburas (a bowl lyre), accordions, and polyphonic vocals keep it real on *Folk Music of Croatia* (Arc, 1994).

VARIOUS ARTISTS. *Croatia: Music from Long Ago* (Ocora, 1997) another excellent entry from the French label.

CZECH REPUBLIC

Czechoslovakia was created in 1918 out of the former Habsburg territories of Bohemia, Moravia, and Slovakia. After World War II and liberation from Nazi control, Czechoslovakia fell under Soviet rule. The grip loosened during the Prague Spring of 1968, but Soviet domination continued for another 20 years, although the Czechs were never compliant subjects. Artists such as author Milan Kundera and National hero Vaclav Havel kept the fire burning until the fall of the Berlin Wall in 1989. Shortly thereafter the Czech Republic and Slovakia reformed as separate countries.

FOLK MUSIC AND THE CLASSICS

The Czech Republic is home to a host of major classical music composers, all of whom borrowed heavily from their national folk music in creating numerous masterpieces. The works of Antonin

Dvořák, Bedřich Smetana, Bohuslav Martinů, and Leoš Janáček explored Slavic folk rhythms and traditions in virtually every one of their compostions. Janáček, like his colleague Béla Bartók in Hungary, produced important field recordings as early as the 1880s and is credited with reviving a folk tradition previously threatened with extinction.

Czech traditional music is steeped in folk and dance tunes from Bohemia and Moravia. The music has a decidedly Western European influence due to the regions' border with Austria and Germany. Czech folk music features regular melodic construction, definite tonality, well-defined rhythm, and symmetrical form. Bohemian music is characterized by triads and a monophonic sound, and contains few modulations. By contrast, the music of eastern Moravia and Silesia near Slovakia contains a freer structure—melodically, harmonically, and rhythmically—and utilizes nondiatonic, chromatic scales.

INSTRUMENTS

The most important instrument associated with Czech song is the bagpipe called *dudy* or *gajdy* in Moravia. Clarinets, violins, and accordions are also commonly played. Folk music from Slovakia is a bridge between Eastern and Western Europe, greatly influenced by Hungarian music. Slovakian music clearly borrows from the traditional music of the Ukraine, Bulgaria, Serbia, Croatia, and Slovenia. There are 28 different forms of fipple flutes (a fipple flute is an end-blown instrument, featuring a notched mouthpiece), making it the most popular Slovakian instrument. The *koncovka* has no finger holes; the pitch is controlled by closing and opening the end. The *fujara* is a three-foot long vertical flute with several holes. The *dvojanka* is a smaller double fipple that is ubiquitous in traditional music circles throughout the region.

RECOMMENDED CDs

VERA BILA & KALE. Powerful singer from a small town in Bohemia who has been called the Ella Fitzgerald of Gypsy music. Physically she is closer to Jimmy Rushing, "Mr. 5 × 5." All but 600 Gypsies from Czechoslovakia were exterminated during World War II (over 100,000 were murdered) and Vera is a survivor. *Kale Kalore* (Tindar, 1998), with working band *Kale* is jazzy with a tinge of South America; *Queen of Romany* (BMG, 1999) is a "best of" compilation.

IVA BITTOVA. Iva is one of the few Czech Republic artists to enjoy an international career. Her original voice and fondness for the avant garde and minimalism has made her popular throughout Eastern Europe. She is also an accomplished violinist and composer. *White Inferno/Bile Inferno* (Orchard, 1997); *Cikori* (Indies, 2001); *Iva Bittová* (Nonesuch, 1998).

CZECHMOR. An eclectic band (violin, cello, bagpipe, accordion, electric guitar) that has explored Czech wedding music and folk songs, Bretagne music, Nordic music, and the avant-garde. They have become ambassadors of Moravian music in Prague, one of former President Vaclav Havel's favorite groups. *Dovecnosti* (Globus 1991); *Céskomor* (Universal, 2000).

GOTHART. Their repertoire originally focused on Czech Gothic and European medieval music, until the release of *Adio Querida* (Blackpoint, 1999), which contains Sephardic romances, Gypsy songs, and Balkan ethnic dance tunes; a hot recording.

MARTIN HRBAC. Traditional northern Moravian string band ensemble with cimbalom and bagpipes. Hrbac is a legend of Moravian folk music. *Hornacky hudec Marttin* (Gnosis, Brno, 1996).

MUZIGA. Founded by Jiri Vedral (vocals, guitar, mandolin, etc.) and Helena Vedralova (vocals, violin, viola), the group uses acoustic, folk instruments to play Moravian folk songs with classical and jazz elements. *Hello From the Forest* (Tritón, 1998); *About Love* (Indies Records, 2002).

ESTONIA

Estonia boasts a substantial jazz scene, a booming rock underground, and numerous classical composers who were prominent in Western music in the latter part of the twentieth century. Since the end of Soviet rule, which confined Estonia's vibrant musical history to Romantic composition and politically correct themes, Estonia has blossomed as a center for classical composers. Historically, Estonians are related to the Finns and their music shares some similarities to Finnish music, including a penchant for progressive, northern European sound.

RUNIC SONG

Runo-song dates back more than 3,000 years and is the distinctive national folk music of Estonia. It has been extensively recorded, primarily sung by women, and includes work songs, ballads, and epic legends. Traditional wind instruments used by shepherds were once widespread, but are now more rarely played. Other instruments, including the fiddle, kannel (dulcimer), concertina, and accordion are used to play polka or other dance music. The kannel is a native instrument now more popular among Estonian-Americans than in its homeland. Kannel astists include Igor Tõnurist and Tuule Kann. The zither is also a prominent Estonian folk music.

Traditional music from Estonia features *tintinnabulation*, a bell-ringing ornamentation and style. It has been adopted most notably in the compositions of Estonia's best-known composer, Arvo Pärt (pronounced "pairt"). Pärt adopted this technique in 1976 and is one of the most revered composers of the late twentieth century in the classical field. His style is rooted in tonic melodies, whereby the piece does not stray from or modulate the key note, but proceeds in small intervals, enveloped by the notes of the tonic chord that decorate the melodies. In Pärt's music, the tonic function remains static for long periods throughout a piece, creating a truly mesmerizing feeling. Although Pärt began his career as an avant-garde composer, he was influenced by the modal music of the middle ages. The medieval feeling is palpable in virtually all of his compositions. The ancient folk music promoted by Estonian composer Veljo Tormis also influenced the "single tonality" that characterizes a lot of Pärt's work. Urmas Sisask is another contemporary Estonian composer whose work is related to tonic chords.

The one artist who has made a direct impact on the world music Scene is Kirile Loo, whose enchantingly beautiful vocals and dedication to the aboriginal Runic songs are truly moving. Her music is readily accessible without understanding the lyrics. Her recordings alternate between otherworldly and new age, but she is an original voice whose music has immense spiritual appeal.

RECOMMENDED CDs

KIRIKLE LOO. *Saatus* (Alula, 1997) is her best, with support from the kannel, roopill (small reed pipes), and Jews harp; *Lullabies for Husbands* (ErdenKlang, 1999).

AARVO PÄRT. Estonia's most renowned composer and leading proponent of tintinnabulation. *Te Deum* (ECM, 1994); *Tabula Rasa* (ECM, 1991) with Gidon Kremer and Keith Jarrett.

GEORGIA

Georgia's history dates back more than 2,500 years and its language is one of the oldest in the world. From the seventhth to the eighteenth centuries, Georgia was invaded and controlled by Mongols and Arabs, and eventually was annexed by Russia in 1801. The first Republic of Georgia was established after the collapse of Tsarist Russia in 1918. Nevertheless, Georgia became part of the Soviet Union in 1921. After 70 years of rule, Georgia declared independence in 1991.

With the Black Sea to the west, Russia to the northeast, and Turkey to the south, Georgia occupies politically essential turf in the international struggle facing the world today. Eighty percent of Georgia is covered by the Caucasus Mountains. The fertile lowlands that lie between the mountains and the landlocked sea constitute important east-west and north-south routes between Europe and Asia. Because of its location, Georgia has always been an important link on the Silk Road. Recently, however, access to the vast oil reserves in the Caspian area has made Georgia a vital passageway for building a pipeline. Georgia is also a pivotal country in the region for the west because it is predominantly Christian.

Prior to the breakup of the Soviet Union, Georgia was the main supplier of wine for more than 250 million Soviets. When the Russians cut Georgia off, Georgia's economy collapsed and, as is the case everywhere in such circumstances, corruption and a black market economy prevailed. Georgian leader Edward Shevardnadze took the fall, resigning in 2003. Peace in the separatist regions of Abkhazia and South Ossetia remains fragile, and pressure on Georgia (from Russia) to withdraw all support for Chechnya remains a volatile situation. The work and money the pipeline will bring seems to be the only immediate glimmer of hope for the extremely educated, sophisticated Georgian society.

THE MUSIC

Georgians consider themselves among the most cultured people on earth. As far back as the sixth century BCE, Greek writers portrayed Georgia as a fabulously wealthy land with an advanced civilization. The golden age of the eleventh and twelfth centuries saw advances in architecture, art, philosophy, music, and science that predated the Italian Renaissance by over two hundred years. Sacred music exists in all societies, but in Georgia chant enjoys enormous popularity and is the center of its musical culture. Folk and church songs are an inseparable component of the Georgian musical treasury and a vital part of the national identity.

The renowned Georgian polyphonic vocal tradition is characterized by special vocal techniques and the use of tones that are very close in pitch to each other. By oral tradition, the songs and the music have been passed on from generation to generation. A typical Georgian song is sung a cappella by men, in three voices. While Georgia is not a major presence on the world music map, there are a few artists whose works have been recorded and are available.

RECOMMEND CDs

LELA TATARAIDZE. Lela is an accordionist, panduri player (3-stringed lute, a balalaika-type instrument), and vocalist who sings folk songs of the Caucasus Mountains. *Janghi—Morning Fog* (Pan Records, 1999).

HAMLET GONASHVILI. An outstanding singer, influential teacher, and brilliant performer of traditional Georgian music, Gonashvili played an important role in the world-famous Rustavi choir. He died in a tragic accident in 1985. *Hamlet* (JARO, 1985) is a collection of his most impressive songs.

HUNGARY

Long before the term *world music* came into vogue, Hungary's greatest composer—Béla Bartók and his colleague Zoltán Kodály—

awakened the world to the wealth of folk music in the rural areas of their native land. Along with the prescient work of American Alan Lomax in numerous other regions of the world, Bartók's field recordings of traditional Hungarian, Romanian, and Slavic village music were the most significant early efforts to document ethnic traditional music. Both Bartók and Kodály incorporated their findings and songs into their compositions.

HISTORY, POLITITCS, AND CULTURE

The Magyar culture is a variegated one, an island unto itself in a sea of Eastern Europe. Hungary's linguistic ties are to Finland, not to neighboring Slavic languages. Hungary's historical plight of domination by forces from both the east and the west has created a unique society unlike anything in the region. Following more than 150 years as subjects of the Sultan and Turkish rule, Hungary aligned with the Austrian Habsburg Empire and became a westernized society during the eighteenth century, evolving and modernizing well into the twentieth century.

Much of Eastern Europe underwent a series of dramatic political and geographic changes following World War II, and the after effects of Communist rule have only recently begun to fade into the past in an ethnically complicated region. The town where Bartók was born, Nagyszentmilkos, is now part of Romania; Transylvania is alternately claimed as part of Hungary or Romania. Many Hungarians live in Romania and Transylvania. The Gypsy culture of the three regions, especially the folk tradition, has always been mixed and the musical styles shared.

Perhaps more than any other Eastern Bloc country, the staunchly independent and industrious Hungarians suffered terrible repression under Communist rule beginning in 1956. Well before 1989 however, Hungary's insuperable industriousness broke through and the country has grown economically to become the leader in the region. Over the past decade, Budapest has recaptured the grandeur of past ages and blossomed into the renaissance city of the new Europe. It has surpassed Prague as a destination for young travelers of the twenty-first century, boasting a rich culture and artistic sensibility and creativity unrivalled anywhere in Eastern Europe. It is one of the best places anywhere to catch authentic, live roots music all year round.

TANCHEZ

The *tanchez* (dance house) phenomenon in Budapest is one of the most exciting folk scenes anywhere. The movement began in the early 1970s as a reaction to the strict and boring Communist regimented music forced on the people. The idea was to bring the music from the countryside into the urban setting without changing the character of the music. The tanchez are huge barn-like establishments for dancing that also exude a folk-music café feeling. The music embodies centuries of local aesthetic values that have not been eroded by time. The scene is dominated by Transylvanian music. As in much of Europe, Gypsies have kept the folk tradition alive and have provided continuity with the past for their own culture as well as for non-Gypsy cultures of the region. Whatever the nationality, the number of virtuoso fiddlers, guitarists, and cimbalom players on the musical horizon of Budapest is astonishing. Most of the musicians come from Transylvania (Romania), where many transplanted Hungarians lived during the Communist era.

INSTRUMENTS

Hungary favors Western classical and folk instruments including violins, flutes, clarinets, darbukas (goblet drums), and the local cimbalom. The cimbalom is a hammered dulcimer, related to the Indian santur, and thought to have been brought to Europe by Gypsies from their Rajasthani homeland.

Most music buffs know Marta Sebestyen (b.1952) as the eerie voice on the soundtrack to the motion picture *The English Patient*, (particularly on the song *Szerelem, Szerelem (Love, Love)*, but her musical career began long before that film. Her considerable body of recorded work is steeped in Hungarian and Eastern European traditional music. As a frequent collaborator with the Hungarian Gypsy/Folk Instrumental group Muzsikas, Marta has performed all over the world to rave reviews and is a vocalist of exceptional talent.

Marta comes from a family of professional musicians who were immersed in local Transylvanian music and her musical indoctrination began at a very early age. Her mother was an ethnomusicologist of note who studied at the prestigious Liszt Academy and with the great Hungarian composer/folklorist

Zoltan Kodály. Marta was the first folk musician to win her country's coveted Liszt Award.

Sebestyen's distinct, versatile soprano voice is comfortable in several languages. She has recorded in Hungarian, Bulgarian, Bosnian, Hindi, and Yiddish. Her knowledge of and dedication to all forms of Eastern European folk music is extensive, and her ability to improvise (jazz vernacular would call it *scat*) is extraordinary for a folk artist. She is an ardent spokesperson for human rights in a part of the world that has experienced horror both before and after the fall of the Berlin Wall. Marta is a staunch world music advocate who understands the interrelationships of world culture and politics and is dedicated to using her art to help her fellow human beings. Since the recording of the *English Patient* soundtrack, her international star has descended somewhat, but her musical talents have not. Marta is a treasured advocate for the survival of world music.

RECOMMENDED CDs

ANDO DROM. Andro Drom, "On the Road" in Romani, is a leading proponent of modern Gypsy music. Lead Singer Mistou's piercing, soulful voice is their trademark. *Phari Mamo* (Network, 1995) with French Roots group Bratsch; *Gypsy Life on the Road* (North Pacific, 1997).

KALMON BALOGH. Hungary's leading cimbalom player. *The Art of the Gypsy Cimbalom* (ARC, 1998); *Gipsy Jazz* (Rounder, 1999).

BESH O DROM. The hot Hungarian Gypsy group is in the forefront of modern Romani music. *Nekemtenemmutogatol! (Can't Make Me!)* (asphalt Tango, 2003) is a potpourri of Hungarian, Romanian, Bulgarian, Jewish, Greek, and Afghani themes masterfully woven into a cohesive whole.

SANDOR NETI FODOR. Hungary's elder statesman and leading traditional fiddler. *Folk Music from Kalotoszeg* (Hungaraton, 1995).

BELA HALMOS. One of the great fiddlers. *Hungarian Folk Music from Transylvania* (Hungaraton, 1996).

AGNES HERCZKU. Up-and-coming folk singer. *With Gold and Blue Words* (Fono Deluxe, 2002) with Kalmon Balogh.

KALYI JAG. "Black Fire" is a Gypsy ensemble from Szatmar County who follow in the Bartók tradition of collecting folk songs. *Gypsy Folk Songs from Hungary* (Hungaraton, 1995) contains beautiful Balkan, Russian, and eastern Hungarian Gypsy-style dances and ballads with fine guitar work, water cans, spoons, and "oral bass."

MUZSIKAS. Folk string band that worked to keep Hungarian musical traditions alive under Soviet occupation when any expression of cultural identity risked imprisonment. *Morning Star* (Hannibal, 1997) with Marta Sebestyn, is their most realized work; *Bartok Album* (Hannibal, 1999); *Prisoner's Song* (Hannibal, 1988) is music from the end of the Cold War.

OKROSE ENSEMBLE. Violinist Csaba Okros and ethnomusicologist Laszlo Kelemen have created a masterful recording, *I Left My Sweet Homeland* (Rounder, 2001), that comprises Transylvanian Gypsy folk tunes, including the title cut discovered by Bartók in the middle of the twentieth century. *Transylvania Village Music* (Rounder, 1999).

MARTA SEBESTYEN. *Muzsikas* (Hannibal, 1987); *Apocrypha* (Hannibal 1992) is a soft, pensive compilation; *Dudoltam* (Hungaraton, 2000).

SZASZCSAVAS. A traditional band that plays Hungarian Gypsy, folk, and Transylvanian music on stringed instruments only. *Muzica populara maghiara din valea Tîrnavelor* (Electrorecord, 1989); *Live in Chicago* (Thermal Comfort, 2000).

LATVIA

The resurgence of the folklore movement in the small Baltic state of Latvia began in the early 1980s, a political phenomenon linked to the independence movement. In 1981, Ilga Reizniece formed Latvia's most renowned folk ensemble, ILGI, in Riga. The members of the group made their own traditional instruments and nationalist costumes, and began touring the country, teaching and helping to revive Latvian national pride through the ancient traditions. ILGI eventually transformed from a traditional folk ensemble into a band with its own contemporary music identity and are the only Latvian group with any presence in world music.

RECOMMENDED CDs

ILGI. *Speleju Dancoju/I Played and Danced* (Upe, 2003); *Latvju Danci/Latvian Folk Dances*. (Upe, 1999); *Seju Veju* Sow the Wind (Upe, 2000) is postmodern folklore.

LAIKSNE. Female folk band. *Kyukova Dzagyuze/The Cukoo Called Out* (1999).

JAUNS MENESS. Latvian rock. *Dzivotajs* (Upe, 1998).

VALDIS MUKTUPAVELS. Latvia's leading ethnomusicologist, composer and zither (kokle) master. *Muktukokles* (Upe, 2000).

BIRUTA OZOLINA. Ethereal female vocalist; the Latvian Enya. *Sirdsgriezi/Hear Solstice* (Upe, 2002).

POLAND

Poland is a western Slavic country that has been historically ravaged by its neighbors, Russia and Germany. Germany's invasion of Poland in 1939 marked the official beginning of mankind's most horrific conflagration and Poland suffered total devastation. Six million Poles were exterminated during the war including three million Jews—97 percent of Poland's Jewish population. After almost 40 years of domination by the Soviet Union following World War II, the Solidarity movement led by Gdansk dockworker Lech Walesa brought Poland to international prominence in a positive light in 1980. In many ways, Solidarity's demand for the right to form labor unions was a clarion call signaling the beginning of the end of Communism in Eastern Europe, aided in no small part by the influence of Pope John Paul II, the first ever Polish Pope. Since the early 1990s Poland has become a liberal democracy and is today an economic force in Eastern Europe.

THE MUSIC

Music has always been a significant part of Polish culture, especially in the classical realm. The great works of Frederic Chopin in the eighteenth century and the modern day symphonic work of Krzysztof Penderecki are major contributions to the classical music lexicon. Any list of the greatest virtuosi of classical music must include violinist Henryk Szeryng, harpsichordist Wanda Landowska, and pianists Ignacy Paderewski, Leopold Godowsky, and Artur Rubinstein, all of whom are Poles.

Quite ironically, the folk and traditional music scene in Poland in the early part of the twenty-first century focuses on klezmer, the music of Eastern European Jews, who were so callously abandoned and virtually offered as sacrificial lambs by Poland during World War II. Throughout the Cold War, klezmer and Jewish music in Poland were virtually nonexistent, but today, it is thriving. Poland's most important world music Band Kroke plays Jewish klezmer and hails from Krakow. Since the late 1990s, the folk and traditional music scenes have begun to explode in Warsaw, Krakow, Wroclaw, and other Polish cities. The success of the Warsaw Village Band, Poland's hottest roots group, bodes well for a musical hotbed that has been dormant far too long.

RECOMMENDED CDs

CHUDOBA. Traditional, all-acoustic band from Wroclaw. *Nasza Polka/Folk Time* (1996); *Masza Muzyka* (Pomaton, EMI, 1999).

KRAKOW KLEZMER BAND. Virtuoso klezmer musicians with a strong Gypsy influence. De Profundis (Tzadik, 2000); *Bereshit* (Tzadik, 2003).

KROKE. Klezmer band from Krakow comprising violist/flutist Tmasz Kukurba, accordion player Jerzy Bawol, and bass player Tomasz Lato. *The Sound of the Vanishing World* (Oriente, 1999), old European Jewish dreams meet new global, secular dreams; *East Meets West* (EMI, 2003), with classical maverick and violin virtuoso Nigel Kennedy; a dramatic, soothing, emotionally tormented and romantically yearning CD that features Natasha Atlas on "Ajde Jano."

MUZYKANCI. Fiddle and accordion based folk quartet with a soulful, rootsy focus. *Muzykanci* (Mediastat, 1999).

TREBUNIA FAMILY BAND. *Music of the Tatra Mountains* (Nimbus, 1995).

WARSAW VILLAGE BAND (KAPELA ZE WSI WARSZAWA). Minimalist Polish folk tunes accompanied by drums, strings, trumpets, dulcimer, and voice; hardcore folk and bio techno, *bio* as in "living" and *techno* referring to the Greek translation "skill" or "art." The music is heavy on rhythm and drone and has a likeness to the Swedish music of *Gjallarhorn*. *People's Spring* (Jaro, 2001).

ROMANIA

Romania is the seventh largest country in Europe both in area and population. Although thought of as Eastern European, geographically Romania is located in the south-central portion of the continent. Romanians are of Roman descent, inhabiting the area between the Carpathian Mountains, the Danube, and the Black Sea. More than half of the population comprises rural peasants whose life is based on producing what is needed for their family to survive day to day, reliant on a community existence. The Communist collectivization of agriculture that forced the peasants to be laborers on their own land nearly destroyed the country. To a great degree, Romanians withstood social and economic annihilation through cultural resistance, including their rich musical heritage. The country that many outsiders think of as the home of Dracula and Transylvania is still reeling from the reign of the most brutal dictator in the Soviet Bloc, the illiterate Nicolae Ceaucescu, but there are signs of progress.

GYPSY MUSICIANS

The earliest record of gypsies working as musicians is a Persian reference to a caste of musicians and dancers who had come from India around 420 BCE. Many stories and theories exist, but it is clear that thereafter Gypsies wandered for centuries from the Middle East through Turkey and into Europe. It is equally clear that they have had a far-reaching cultural impact across a range of European societies. The Roma, as many tribes called themselves, had dispersed throughout Europe by the fifteenth century, living on the fringes of society as tinkers, craftsmen, or horse traders. Wherever they moved, certain families among them always had an extraordinary aptitude for music and as entertainers.

In the nineteenth century, Gypsy musicians began to enjoy the patronage of the aristocracy, who viewed their music as emblematic of a Romantic freedom. In the southern Balkan regions of Macedonia, Serbia, Albania, Epiros, Thrace, and Greece, Gypsies preserved traditional music. Without their oral tradition and improvisatory skills, much regional folk music would have been lost. Professional Gypsy musicians were highly socialized into the fabric of the host cultures, and being "Gypsy" was not the pejorative stereotype of the itinerant beggar that the word connotes to most Europeans today.

Roma musicians eventually became known as *lautarii* (from Romanian for "the fiddlers"). Today, lautarii are often treated with contempt for their way of life and are not accepted by the majority of Romanians. Paradoxically, when engaged as professional musicians for weddings or other ceremonies, they suddenly become everybody's beloved friends and are rewarded lavishly. Part and parcel to the racist attitudes the world continues to foist upon Gypsies is the debate (in Romania and elsewhere) as to whether all music interpreted by Gypsies is "Gypsy." Gypsies everywhere adopt the music of the host people or ethnic group among whom they live and in a sense are the greatest chroniclers of traditional music throughout Eastern Europe, the Balkans, and in Iberia.

WESTERN CLASSICAL TRADITION

Romania's greatest classical composer George Enescu was one of the most prodigiously gifted musicians of the twentieth century. A great violinist, distinguished conductor, accomplished pianist, able cellist, and a violin teacher who numbered Arthur Grumiaux and Yehudi Menuhin among his pupils, Enescu was trained at the Vienna Conservatory and studied with Massenet and Fauré in Paris.

Damian Draghici is one of Romania's most versatile and renowned musical personalities. Draghici is a Gypsy who fled the brutal Ceaucescu regime in the 1980s for Athens. After Ceaucescu's ouster, Draghici had no desire to move back to Romania and remained in Athens, where he played the piano in Greek nightclubs. While living in Athens he applied to Boston's Berklee College of Music and was accepted as a pianist. After playing Charlie Parker's "Yardbird Suite" on pan flute for Berklee faculty members, he was awarded a fully paid, four-year scholarship. He is comfortable in virtually all genres imaginable, including classical, jazz, salsa, flamenco, Andean, and world music.

He is a master of the pan-flute and has performed on the instrument with the London Philharmonic Orchestra, London Festival Orchestra, Slovak Chamber Orchestra, Bucharest Symphony Orchestra, and Camerata Chamber Orchestra. He has also performed with Paul Winter, Omar Faruk Tekbilek, and the Sabri Brothers.

RECOMMENDED CDS

DAMIAN DRAGHICI. (See Profile.) *Romanian Gypsy Pan Flute Virtuoso* (Lyrichord, 2001) was his first United States release. *Damian in Concert from Bucharest* (Naimad Records, 2002).

FANFARE CIOCARLIA. Gypsy brass band whose music has origins in Turkish military music. They emerged at the beginning of the nineteenth century. *Wild Sounds from Transylvania, Wallachia & Moldavia* (Network, 1997); *Radio Pascani* (Piranha, 1998); *Baro Biao* (Piranha, 1999); *Iag Bari—The Gypsy Horns from the Mountains Beyond* (Piranha, 2001).

PANSELUTA FERARU. Popular "restaurant singes, a Roma Diva with great style + range" *Lautar Songs from Bucharest* (Long Distance, 2000).

MARIA TANASE. Tanase (1913–1963) was the authentic voice of Romanian folk music in the middle of the twentieth Century. Romanian's think of her as their Edith Piaf. Her style contains Arab and Gypsy influences, usually sung in French. *Malediction d'Amour* (Oriente); *Ciuleandra* is a collection of remastered songs from 1955–1957; *Maria Tanase* (Electrecord, 1994).

TARAF DE HAIDOUKS. The "Band of Brigands" introduced westerners to the rich world of the Gypsy music of Romania, the Turkish style of Balkan dances, and the characteristic vocals reminiscent of their Gypsy roots from India. They have recorded with Yehudi Menhuin and appeared in the acclaimed documentary *Latcho Drom*, by French Gypsy director Tony Gatlif. *Honourable Brigands, Magic Horses and Evil Eye* (Crammed World, 1994); *Dumbala Dumba* (Crammed World, 1998); *Taraf de Haidouks, Compilation* (Nonesuch, 1999).

RUSSIA

Since the fall of the Soviet Union, ethnic music from Eastern Europe and across Central Asia has exploded onto the world music scene, a cathartic release of pent-up cultural energy that has been dormant for decades. Any overt expression of cultural identity in Russia was strictly forbidden and controlled behind the Iron Curtain, but the spirit of the people subjected to totalitarian rule never died. Oral tradition, a reverence for the past, and the hope of freedom in the future kept the music alive.

FOLK AND TRADITIONAL MUSIC

Russian folk and roots music has been hidden from Western ears for nearly a century. The genre known as *Blatny Pesny* (delinquent song) regularly depicted the hard life in the Soviet Union in graphic detail, blatantly glorifying sexual prowess, drinking, and street fighting. As with fundamentalists anywhere, these topics were officially outlawed by the Russian authorities and the perpetrators were subjected to a strictly enforced censorship that often included prison. Many of Russia's most talented composers and folksingers were unable to publish any of their music until Mikhail Gorbachev came to power circa 1980, and even then it was a slow and arduous process. Recordings of important songwriters and singers have become widely available in the West only since the mid-1990s.

INSTRUMENTS

Perhaps the best way to get a feel for Russian world music is by becoming acquainted with the instruments used in performance over the centuries. Although individual ethnic diversity was frowned upon in the days of the Soviet Union, the Soviets permitted the exhibition of national instruments and nationalist music (as defined by the state) at approved functions as an expression of Soviet culture. The complexity and range of the music is vast, incorporating regional dance, folklore, and ceremonies of all kinds. Although ethnic music differs from region to region, in most cases the instruments are similar.

The *balalaika* has its origins in the Oriental *dombra*, a two-stringed, oval-faced, lute-type instrument brought to Russia by the

Mongols in the thirteenth century. Over the years, the design evolved to a triangular shape. For centuries the balalaika was an instrument of the peasant class, also used by minstrels and court musicians to accompany singing. The *zhaleika* (zhal-YAY-ka) is the most commonly used Russian folk wind instrument, a single-reed clarinet with a wooden barrel, finger holes, and a flared bell. The *volynka* (val-In-ka) or Belarusian *duda* is the basic Slavic bagpipe, consisting of a chanter and 1–2 drones. The *brelka* (briOl-ka) is a double-reeded zhaleika; a diatonic oboe. The *rozhok* (ra-zhOk) is a wooden horn with trumpet-style mouthpiece and finger holes, and is most common in the northeast-central parts of European Russia near Vladimir. The *svirel'* (svir-YEl']) is a Russian pennywhistle. The *sopil'ka* (common in the Ukraine) is a classic recorder. The *dvadyensivka* is a diatonic, double-barreled *sopil'ka*. *Kugikly* are panpipes, most often played by groups of women in the East. *Gusli* is a table zither of the psaltery family, used as the kanun or cimbalom in other parts of Europe. The traditional Russian accordion is the *bayan*, with rows of buttons under the right hand rather than the Western-style piano keyboard.

CLASSICAL MUSIC

In contrast to folk and roots music, which was uniformly suppressed, the Soviet Union was proud of its classical tradition, including the works of Glinka, Tchaikovsky, Mussorgsky, Stravinsky, Rachmaninoff, and Rimsky-Korsakov. In the case of Shostakovich in particular, the state regularly edited or censored his compositions not deemed nationalistic, but his music did reach a world audience with cryptic messages intact, even during the Cold War. In the case of Prokofiev and Stravinsky, their greatest works were written as expatriates in France and the United States, but their work retained a strong Russian identity.

JAZZ AND ROCK

Prior to the break-up of the Soviet Union, American jazz and rock n' roll became available through underground tapes, and for a time served as the only line of communication to the west for young Russians. The message of American jazz, the Beatles, and the folk movement in the United States and the United Kingdom was quite clear, and it is widely accepted today that western music played an important role in the eventual downfall of the Soviet system by providing an uncensored vision of freedom.

RECOMMENDED CDs

THE KARELIAN FOLK MUSIC ENSEMBLE. KFME is the only touring group playing traditional folk songs from Karelia, a large region that is partially in Russia and partially in Finland. They sing in Finnish, Karelian, and Russian. *The Karelian Folk Music Ensemble* (Gadfly Records, 1995); *From the Land of the Kalevala* (Gadfly Records, 2001).

VLADIMIR DENISSENKOV. Master of the Russian *bajan* (accordion). *Bajan* (Robi, 2000) is a collection of traditional and classical tunes and songs of Eastern Europe.

DREVA. Dreva specializes in Russian urban folk songs. The repertoire is based on material from the Belgorod, Voronezh, and Briansk regions. *Russian Traditional Music of Western and Southern Regions of Russia* (1994); *Jolly Talking* (2001).

FARLANDERS. Bagpipes, dual clarinets, and saxophones playing klezmer, Russian folk, and Oriental melodies distinguish this modern Russian Band. Inna Zhelannaya's powerful voice sets them apart from other bands from Russia. *Dream of Endless Nights* (Shanachie, 1999).

BORIS GREBENSHIKOV. One of Russia's greatest living songwriters and singers. *Russian Songwriter* (Naxos, 2002).

LOYKO. The most internationally famous Russian Gypsy ensemble. *Road of the Gypsies* (Network, 1995); *Gypsies Time for Nunia* (Network, 2001).

MOSCOW ART TRIO. Pianist Mikhail Alperin's trio plays Russian and Balkan folk songs in a modern jazz idiom. The Armenian *duduk, balalaika,* and *melodica* are heard in these haunting modal songs. *Live in Karlsruhe* (Boheme, 1998).

VALENTINA PONOMAREVA. Diva with a 4-octave range. *Russian Gypsy Queen* (Arc, 2001).

RUSSIAN FOLK ENSEMBLE BALALAIKA. *Kamarinskaya* (Arc/Melodiya, 2001).

TEREM QUARTET. Founded by students in St. Petersburg, the Terem Quartet was well known only in Russia until Peter Gabriel brought them into the recording studio in 1991. *No, Russia Cannot Be Perceived by Wit* (Intuition Music, 1998)—with alto-domra, soprano-domra, bayan-accordion, and bass-balalaika—is a quirky, nontraditional folk album.

VLADIMIR VYSOTSKY. Vystotsky began performing in the 1960s, criticizing the government in his many songs from the *blatny pesny* tradition. He was never formally published during his life, although he had written 100s of songs known to virtually every Russian. After his death in 1980, Gorbachev permitted a 20-album retrospective to be released. *Tatuirovka* (Russian Enterprise, 2000); *Criminal Law* (Musicrama, 2001); *Legendi Ruskogo Shansona* (Russian Enterprise, 2003).

INNA ZHELANNAYA. One of Russia's finest female vocalists. *Vodrosli/Water Fronds* (1997).

VARIOUS ARTISTS. *Russian Gypsy Soul.* (Network, 1998). The first recorded anthology to present Russian Gypsy music. Siberian Gypsies perform nomad music; choirs sing Roma hymns, performances by the famous group *Loyko*, and fiddler Sergeij Erdenko pays homage to his friend Yehudi Menuhin.

SLOVENIA

Slovenia was the first of the Yugoslav republics to break away, declaring independence in June 1991 following a 10-day war. Power transferred with remarkable continuity.

Since the mid-1960s, a generation of Slovenian modernist composers has established themselves, avoiding American minimalism and the avant-garde, preferring instead to work with popular and folk-derived idioms prominent in central and southeastern Europe. Aldo Kumar in particular has received widespread acclaim for his compositions utilizing a classical discipline with local folk motifs. Folk music includes *velike golsarije*, a type of big band music with bowed zither, panpipes,and harmonic vocals. Slovenian music is related to German and Austrian music due to a common history and shared Alpine culture; polka is especially popular.

RECOMMENDED CDs

AMALA. Leading Gypsy group that has accompanied Esma Redzepova. *Gypsy Music* (1997).

SLAVKO AVSENIK. One of the most influential and popular polka and waltz musicians, Avsenik's ensemble plays Slovenian pop called *oberkainer* music, a country folk style with a mix of accordion, clarinet, and oompah. *Freude an Musik mit* (Koch).

BEGNAGRAD. Avant-garde Slovenian rock, a trendsetting band in the Balkans. *Begnagrad* (Mio, 1982/2003).

BRATKO BIBIC. Bratko is an accordion star in the region, a composer, filmmaker, and early world-music advocate from Slovenia's capital, Ljubljana. *Na Domacem Vrtu/In the Family Garden* (Slovenska, 2002).

MATIJA TERLEP. Flutist and vocalist for folk group Tutamora Slovenica, Terlep has played an essential role in the preservation of traditional, pre-polka music since the 1970s. Slovene Folk Songs and Instruments (CDG, 1998).

TURKEY

The Ottoman Empire and its 38 generations of successive rulers is a major part of world history; the last Islamic dynasty to wield great power and influence throughout the world. Beginning with the Empire's collapse in Europe, Turkish dominance deteriorated, and over several centuries Turkey became a backward, stagnant, ineffectual state. At the end of World War I the Turks were all but conquered and the country was about to be divided up by the victors (England, France, Russia), when Mustafa Kemal Ataturk miraculously turned the tide. His rise to power and subsequent deification transformed Turkey, virtually overnight, into a secular state.

Ataturk implemented an immediate and total separation of state and religion, reestablished the national language as Turkish (from Arabic), had all the laws and the Koran translated into Turkish, banned the symbolic Fez and Burkha in public, gave women the right to vote and participate as equals in government and society, instituted sweeping educational reforms to bring the country's minions out of the darkness of illiteracy, allowed personal freedoms, including the consumption of alcohol, and permitted the practice of religions other than Islam. His use of excessive force, at times atrocious, wiped out all opposition. When it became clear that his intent was to actually create a freer, more modern Turkey with a higher standard of living, however, he won the undying support of the entire nation and became a living God to them.

Following Ataturk's death in 1938, a succession of Kemalist military leaders have run the country along with an elected parliament as a quasi-democracy, steadfastly insisting on secularism at every turn in the road, guided by "What Ataturk would do" during every crisis.

Most of the Muslim world's leaders vehemently opposed a secular Turkey because its population is 90 percent Muslim. The truth is that Turkey has never turned its back on Islam; to the contrary, it has taken the position that Islam can exist and thrive in the modern world provided the government for the people is a secular one. The National victory by a moderate Islamic party in the fall of 2002 will be watched closely by the entire world. Today Turkey faces its toughest challenge since Kemalism took hold: how to finally join the European Economic Community and adhere to a truly democratic form of government while respecting its overwhelmingly Islamic population.

Despite its distinction as the most modern Islamic society in the world, respect for human rights by the Turkish government has been slow to catch up with most Western standards. The country has yet to deal with its genocide of the Armenians in 1915. The civil war with the Kurds is a disturbing reminder of the Turks propensity for brutality and obsession for secrecy. Nevertheless, relations with Greece are the best they have been in 50 years, following the tragic earthquakes that occurred in the two countries in 1999, and Turkey is clearly a country on the rise, rapidly improving its image as a valuable citizen of the World community.

THE MUSIC

Turkey is a major stop on the world music map with a broad variety of styles, an incomparable ancient tradition, and a thriving folk and pop scene.

The first music to be associated independently with Turkey can be traced to the whirling dervishes and the Mevlevi order founded in the thirteenth century by the mystic Celaleddin Rumi. Folk bards or *Asik* historically sing with the three-stringed Turkish *saz* and have an affiliation with protest music and the left. Asik Veysel, a blind singer from the province of Sivas is perhaps the most famous of all. The saz, the long-necked Turkish lute, can be traced back to that time and remains one of the most prominent instruments in modern Turkish music.

Classical music has much in common with the music of the Arab world. Compositions focus on modes or *makams* with improvisation (*takism*) an important component of live performances and recordings. The voice is the central instrument in Turkish classical music, beginning with Munir Nurettin Selcuk (1900–1981), the most revered of all Turkish classical male singers.

As is the case throughout Eastern Europe and western Asia, Gypsies are prominent in the current Turkish musical scene. Clarinetist Mustafa Kandirali rivals Bulgarian Ivo Papasov for sheer virtuosity and is an icon of the Gypsy music genre known as *fasil*. The Istanbul Oriental Ensemble is a talented Roma group whose recordings are extraordinary examples of intuitive ensemble playing.

Until the late 1990s, traditional, folk, and classical Turkish music was not widely heard outside the country and the outlying Kurdish territories. Turkey has recently taken bold steps to participate in all arenas of Western life, especially in music and sport. The classical tradition, folk music, and art songs of the former Anatolia are currently enjoying resurging interest from music scholars worldwide even as cheesy pop music rules the Turkish airwaves.

Sezen Aksu is the most renowned singer in Turkey today, a quintessential diva and national personality. Although her recordings are geared for the pop audience, she is a true world music artist whose work shows a reverence for classical and folk forms. She has cleverly used her recordings and fame to speak out for secular movements in her homeland, a delicate matter indeed in Turkey. Sezen has been vocal about discrimination against women and the persecution of ethnic groups, particularly the large Kurdish population in Turkey, and has challenged the government's propensity to "disappear" young men (à la Argentina) who actively protest government policy.

Sezen's recordings are provocative, varied, soulful, sexy, and jazz-influenced. Recently, American pop stars have covered her work. Her recent collaboration *Dugun ve Cenaze*, with noted Bosnian film composer Goran Bregovic, shows her interest in connecting with other cultures and folk traditions in the region, particularly the Balkans. Aksu is a staunchly independent soul, with a powerful, husky contralto voice that packs an emotional wallop and a visceral message. She is an international star of the highest magnitude.

RECOMMENDED CDs

SEZEN AKSU. (See Profile above). *Dugun ve Cenaze/Wedding and Funeral* (Polygram Raks, 1997) arranged by Serbian Goran Bregovic; *Deliveren* (Post Musik, 2000) features Ara Djinkian, nd master Erkan Ugur, and Greek diva Haris Alexiou; *Isik dogudan Yukselir/Ex Oriente Lux* (Foneks, 1993).

MAZRAHAN ALANSON. There are pop stars in Europe who are an intrinsic part of a country's musical identity and culture; Alanson is in that category, a Turkish Aznavour. *Turk Lokumuyla Tatli Ruyalar* (Universal, 2002).

BENJI BAGLAMA. Modern acoustic instrumental folk group on the cutting edge of Anatolian sound. *Sel Gider...Kum Kalir* (Kalan, 2001); *Gunes bahcesinden Ezgiler/Songs from the Garden of Sun* (Kalan, 1999).

SERTAB ERENER. Student and disciple of Sezen Aksu, one of the bright lights on the Turkish music scene. *La'l* (Foneks, 1994) is a cover of Aksu compositions deftly arranged by Levent Yuksel.

KUDSI ERGUNER ENSEMBLE. Ney virtuoso Erguner's historical recordings pay homage to a series of classical Turkish composers. *Vocal Masterpieces of Kemani Tatyos Efendi* (Traditional Crossroads, 1996) is an important recording for anyone interested in classical Turkish music; *Islam Blues* (Times Square, 2001) incorporates jazz and features Vietnamese guitar wonder Nguyen Le.

UDI HRANT. The late blind Armenian ud virtuoso from Istanbul is a soulful player and singer, a Turkish Lightning Hopkins. *Udi Hrant Vol. 1* (Traditional Crossroads, 1995/1950).

ISTANBUL ORIENTAL EXPRESS. The Gypsy sextet (darbuka, tar, clarinet, violin, oud, kanun) led by percussionist Burcan Ocal is a skilled instrumental Roma ensemble. *Caravanserai* (Network, 2000) is our favorite, the last recording of clarinetist Ferdi Nadaz; *Gypsy Rum* (Network, 1995).

KAMKARS. Kurdish family ensemble. *Nightingale with a Broken Wing* (Womad, 1997); *Chant of Drums* (Quartertone, 1999).

KARDES TURKULER. One of Turkey's most diverse folk-roots ensembles explores Greek, Armenian, Gypsy, Kurdish, and Alevi songs, performed in Turkish and Kurdish. *Hemavaz/To Be Singing Together* (Kalan, 2002); *Kardes Turkuler* (1997); *Dogu* (1999).

KAYAHAN ACAR. The leading popular male vocalist. *Ne Oldu Can* (Universal, 2002).

ZULFU LIVANELI. Livaneli has had an illustrious and controversial career that has included outspoken advocacy for Leftist/ Communist causes, historic collaborations with Greek counterpart Mikos Theodorakis, and a recent attempt to become Mayor of Istanbul. He has been credited with helping to keep peace in the Aegean and is a Turkish institution. *Maria Farantouri avec Zulfu Livaneli* (Raks, 1982) is a gorgeous outing. *Merhaba* (ADA, 1977/02) is a solo CD with Zulfu singing and accompanying himself on saz, à la Leonard Cohen.

ERKAN OGUR. Saz virtuoso, guitarist, and vocalist Ogur is a master of the Anatolian folk tradition. *Anadolu Besik Anatolia: The Cradle* (Kalan, 1998) is a collaboration with Ismail H. Demircioglu, a moody, dark mesmerizing work; *Hic-Nothing but Infinite* (Kalan, 1997).

TALIP OZKAN. One of Turkey's greatest traditional artists. *The Dark Fire* (Axiom, 1988) Vocals and saz; *Lard Vivant de Talip Ozkan* (Ocora, 1995 reissue).

SIVAN PERWER. The vocal star of Kurdish music. *Songs of Kurdistan* (Ethnic, 1995).

IBRAHAM TATLISES. "Ibo" is one of Turkey's most popular Arabesk singers and a famous film actor. *Haydo Soyle* (Atoll, 1999); *Selam Olsun* (Universal, 1999)

UKRAINE

Largest of the former Soviet Republics, with a population of more than 45 million, the Ukraine achieved independence in 1991 and is slowly reemerging after 70 years of Soviet domination and the horrors experienced in the middle of the twentieth century. When the Nazis invaded the Soviet Union in 1941, many Ukrainians in the west saw it as liberation from communist rule, but this fantasy was short-lived. German brutality was primarily directed at Ukraine's Jews, of whom an estimated 1 million were killed, but also against many other Ukrainians. Babyn Yar in Kiev was the site of one of the most horrific Nazi massacres of the war. Thereafter Ukrainians began to resist the Nazis as well as the Soviets.

The Old European city of Kyiv (Kiev) was once the major urban center of Eastern Europe. It is now slowly beginning to return to its former glory. A vibrant music scene, fashionable denizens, and the presence of perennial soccer giant Dinamo Kyiv are helping revive the city.

THE MUSIC

The Ukraine has a rich cultural history, but sadly much of its folk and traditional music has been neglected, lost, or repressed over the past century. A musical revival of sorts is in the works however, led by a vocal Ukrainian diaspora that fled to Canada and the United States during Soviet repression. The irrepressible vocalist and musicologist Alexis Kochan (who resides in Edmonton) and New York-based bandura player Julian Kytasty have spearheaded the revival, which is beginning to establish a presence in the world music arena.

THE BANDURA. The *bandura* is a unique Ukrainian instrument that dates back to the seventh century. It was originally used to accompany folk ballads and dances and became popular between the fifteenth and eighteenth centuries with traveling musicians called Kobzars, who sang about the exploits of the Kozaks (Ukrainian warriors). The bandura is actually a type of zither with 21 to 55 strings, played upright and plucked. It is a cross between a large lute and a Celtic harp and its sound resembles that of a harpsichord. Most Ukrainian traditional music includes the bandura, but during the Soviet occupation of the Ukraine it fell into disfavor as the symbol of Ukrainian national culture and was rarely played in public. Julian Kytasty is one of a handful of musicians who dedicate themselves to reconstituting the lost tradition of the bandura and to reestablishing its stature as the Ukraine's primary musical instrument.

RECOMMENDED CDs

ALEXIS KOCHAN. *Paris to Kyiv; Prairie Nights and Peacock Feathers* (Olesia, 2001) with Julian Kytasty; *Czarivna* (Olesia, 1982); *Paris to Kyiv Variances* (Olesia, 1996). In addition to folksongs, Kochan searches out ritual songs: pre-Christian koliadky and shchedrivky (winter cycle), hahilky and vesnianky (spring cycle), Kupalo songs (Midsummer's Night), obzhynky songs (harvest), wedding songs, lullabies, and laments. Kochan's lush voice and passion drive the music.

JULIAN KYTASTY. Julian Kytasty is a third-generation bandura player. He plays Kobzar songs that have a strong Eastern European (Armenia, Uzbekistan, and Turkmenistan) flavor. Kytasty's is mainly a bandura player, but his voice is sincere, emotive, and charged by the experience of his life. *Black Sea Wind; Kobzario of Ukraine* (November Music, 2001). In addition to the bandura, this album includes two short pieces on the sopilka, a traditional flute, providing a touch of variety to this truly remarkable recording.

YUGOSLAVIA (SERBIA AND MONTENEGRO)

Yugoslavia was formed after World War I in an attempt to unite south-central Europe with the Slavic and west Balkan regions. It included Slovenia, Croatia, Vojrodina (North Serbia), Bosnia and Herzegovina, Montenegro, and Macedonia. After World War II it became a socialist state under its war hero and partisan leader (backed by the Allies), Josip Braz, better known by his nom de guerre, Marshal Tito. Tito held the country together despite the fact that no region actually felt "Yugoslavian" per se. Rather, each ethnic group identified with its own culture, many harboring hatred against those who sided with the Nazis and the Axis powers during World War II. Many atrocities occurred following the war in the early days of Tito's rule, rationalized and tolerated as justifiable retribution for participation in genocide during the war. Nevertheless, Tito emerged as the most beloved and respected leader the Balkan region has ever known. Before his death in 1980, he opposed the Soviet invasion of Afghanistan; proof positive that he was not (or ever was) a Soviet puppet. Until Tito's death, Yugoslavia functioned together in a peaceful union, enjoying relative freedom and little interference with artistic endeavors, including music. After his death, ethnic hatred erupted into ethnic cleansing and devastation. After the war, Yugoslavia was reduced to the territories of Serbia, Montenegro, and Macedonia.

The music of Serbia and Montenegro bears great similarity to that of Croatia, with the notable exception being the language. Serb-Croat is based on the Cyrillic alphabet. Tamburica music, accordions, clarinets, wedding music, bagpipes, flutes, and other folk instruments relating to ceremonial life provide the basis for most of Serbian traditional music. As in other neighboring Balkan countries, the Romani culture has been revitalized in recent decades. Virtually the entire Gypsy population was exterminated during World War II, but the Romani culture is strong in Serbia, providing some rich and very attractive music.

As with every Gypsy, fantastic stories and legends abound about the great Gypsy singer Saban Bajramovic. It is believed he was born in April 1936 in Nis, Yugoslavia, and that he picked up his musical education on the street and in prison. At 19, he ran away from the army (for a girl) and was sentenced to prison for desertion. He survived as star goalkeeper of the prison football team and as a member of the prison orchestra that played Armstrong, Sinatra, and Coltrane. He was incorrigible, though, and ended up serving over 5 years on a 3-year sentence.

After prison, Bajramovic led his own group called (for 20 years) "Black Mamba" that toured much of the world. Indira Ghandi invited him to India where he was proclaimed as the world king of Gypsy music. Legend has it that Gypsies respect and love Tito the most, Saban second, and that no one else occupies the next 10 positions! Hidden behind his dark, scarred face and deep gravelly voice lays an uncanny ear for music and a true Gypsy soul. Saban has also appeared in several Kusturica films—his persona is straight out of central casting—and his compositions have been adapted by Goran Bregovic among others.

RECOMMENDED CDs

SABAN BAJRAMOVIC. (See Profile). *A Gypsy Legend, with Mostar Sevdah Reunion* (Times Square, 2000).

GORAN IVANOVIC. A native of Yugoslavia, Ivanovic fled the conflagration with his family and resides in the United States. He is a classically trained guitarist. *Macedonian Blues: Laments and Dances,* with Fareed Haque (Proteus, 2001).

BORIS KOVAC AND THE LADAABA ORCHEST. Boris is from Novi Sad, the capital of the Pannonian part of Serbia. He is a leader of the new chamber music ensemble Ritual Nova and LaDaABa Orchest. *Ballads at the End of Time* (Piranha, 2003) is music after the apocalypse, for the end of time; *Last Balkan Tango* (Piranha, 2001).

MOSTAR SEVDAH REUNION. Talented roots ensemble. *A Secret Gate* (Snail, 2003).

EZMA REDZEPOVA. Called the "Queen of Gypsy Singers," Ezma is the product of a Rom Muslim and Jewish family—a Serbian father and Turkish mother. With husband Stevo Teodosievski, Ezma has helped Rom children escape impoverishment, providing a home for more than 40 musically gifted boys. *Songs of a Macedonian Gypsy* (Montior, 1994); *Chaje Shukarije* (Times Square, 2001).

MIDDLE EAST

Egypt	Israel	Palestine
Iran	Kurdistan	Syria
Iraq	Lebanon	Yemen

EGYPT

Although geographically in North Africa, Egypt is the epicenter for all Arab and Middle Eastern music. Cairo is home to the largest recording industry in the Middle East, the musical hub of the region. Cairo has always been the focus of the Arab music world, a very insular world remarkably unaffected by Western culture and outside musical trends.

The Arab music industry has no apparent interest in marketing its considerable product to the rest of the world and clearly dances to the beat of its own drums, of which there are many. From the Arab point of view, there is no reason to seek other cultural influence, because the broad spectrum of the Middle East (including Egypt, the Sudan, the Levant [Syria, Jordan, Lebanon, Yemen, Palestine], The United Arab Emirates, Saudi Arabia, Iraq, and parts of Georgia) provides a large audience who follow and appreciate a vast array of musical styles and genres. To illustrate just how isolated the Middle Eastern music industry is, it is instructive to note that it has taken almost 20 years for the Arab street to make the transformation from the thriving cassette-based musical culture (which is still quite alive) to Compact Disc. The music is obsessively consumed locally and there is no major move afoot to expand the audience. This is unfortunate, because the music is a healing force that could have a profoundly positive effect on the rest of the world, if only it were more broadly known.

ANCIENT EGYPT

Documented Egyptian music predates Arab culture and Islam by more than a millennium. The deities Isis, Osiris, Amun, and Hathor all had specific musical associations in ancient times. Osiris was dubbed "The Sistrum Player" by Virgil. Depictions of musicians playing end-blown flutes have been discovered on rock drawings and pottery from Egypt circa 3000 BCE. Depictions of harp (with women playing), pipe, and clarinet-type instruments have been found in Tombs circa 2686 BCE. No one knows what this music "sounded" like or indeed how extensive the musical literature was.

ART MUSIC

Eastern art music from Egypt, Syria, Lebanon, and Iraq—the historical, cultural and musical centers of the Arab world—is derived from court music of the Umayyad and early Abbaid periods (seventh to ninth centuries CE). Prior to the emergence of Islam, art music consisted of Caravan songs and folk songs related to mundane life events. Middle Eastern art music is related to a wide set of traditions. Reciprocal influences and similarities in nomenclature, theory, modal structure, and instrumentation are apparent in many Arabic Middle Eastern countries as well as in Turkey and Iran.

EARLY ISLAM AND MUSIC

In the early days of Islam, entertainment music was permitted, initially dominated by effeminates renowned for immoral behavior. *Qaynas*—singing slave girls—were the first singers, usually non-Arabs and of low-class status. Eventually the Muslim Legists condemned art music and entertainment, a view that continues today in the twenty-first century.

INNOVATORS OF ISLAMIC MUSIC

Ibn-Misjah and Ibn Muhriz began the tradition of accompanying themselves on the ud/oud (lute) and worked in the modal system comprising eight modes, also playing diatonic flutes, circa 715. When the Umayyads (of Syria) were ousted by the Abbasids, the musical center of the Arab world moved from Damascus to Baghdad. Ishaq al Mawsili was the most important musician of the time, a composer and singer of great renown. The first rival of Ishaq al-Mawsili was the famous Ziryab (850 CE). The legendary udist eventually moved to Spain from Baghdad and is widely considered to be the seminal figure in the creation of flamenco (see Spain). He is credited with adding a fifth string to the ud, and was a virtuoso performer and renowned teacher. This period is considered the Golden Age of Arabic music, a time just prior to the prohibition (soon to become edict) against all music except the rigid call to prayer and (eventually) the trance-ecstasy music of the Sufis.

Al-Ghazali (1111) is famous for having broken through the legal restrictions on music imposed by the Orthodox Islamic leaders. He initiated the concept of music as mystical literature that "does not produce in the heart that which is not already there." This concept is the basis of the musical philosophy behind Sufism. The language of profane love became a recognized vehicle to express religious yearning and experience. Al-Ghazali pioneered the concept of acceptability of erotic music as an aid to the progress of the Sufi path.

In the early 20th century, Lebanese theorist Mikha Mashaqa devised a new system of Arabic modal music whereby an octave was divided into 24 intervals (one for each hour of the day), each a quarter-tone, making it possible to transpose modes containing a neutral third to any scale degree.

In 1932 the Egyptian congress attempted to codify and classify melodic modes (maqamat, the plural of maqam). The structure of Arabic music became uniform (i.e., a piece opened with a taqism, an improvised solo instrumental prelude for virtuosi, which prepares and defines the written mode). The principal form of Arab-Near

East Music became the nawba or wasla, a piece of music consisting of eight movements centered around a mode.

MUSIC TODAY

Despite the historical reverence for music, virtually all Middle Eastern cultures now suffer from the tensions resulting from the hostile attitude of Islam to musical practitioners and independent artists in general. This was not always as true or extreme as it is in the twenty-first century, when much of Middle Eastern Islam maintains a backward, narrow perspective that is anathema to creativity, progress, and freedom of expression.

As already noted, Sufism slipped through the loophole and escaped the overall Islamic ban on music. Mulids—festivals that celebrate the Saint of a particular Mosque—are convened by Muslims to defy the authorities. The zikr is a ritual whereby song and dance is used to open a path to divine ecstasy. The Sufis believe that music is the food of the spirit, and when it receives food it turns away from the authority of the body. This exception appeals to fundamentalist philosophy and continues to be the only true musical genre tolerated by the reactionaries.

MUSIC ON THE ARAB STREET

Shaabi is working class pop music from Cairo light and removed from the classical focus of classical Arabic music and rooted in folk. Al jil is also a popular form, analogous to Algerian rai, and is a music that allows the youth in Egypt to break from authority. Al jil stars are "face men" (i.e., known for their good looks rather than their singing talents); they are fed their tunes by producers and are purely entertainers. Hamid el Shaeri and Ehab Tawfik are big name al-Jil singers. Shaabi and al-Jil have replaced the obsession with Umm Kulthum (see profile below) on the arab street.

INSTRUMENTS

The ud (oud, lute), rahab (bowed, single stringed), qanon (zither), violin, nay (end blown flute), darabukka (goblet drum), and daff (frame drum) all became prevalent after 1900.

Over the past 50 years, there has been only one topic that the entire Arab world has agreed upon with unquestioned unanimity: Umm Kulthum (1904–1975) was the greatest singer of music in the Arabic language. A diva of the highest order, Kulthum represented the essence of Arab culture with every note she sang. She was a major force and personality in Egypt and the Middle East a veritable goddess. Virginia Danielson, author of *The Voice of Egypt: Umm Kulthum, Arabic Song and Egyptian Society in the Twentieth Century*, wrote, "Imagine a singer with the virtuosity of Joan Sutherland or Ella Fitzgerald, the public persona of Eleanor Roosevelt and the audience of Elvis and you have Umm Kulthum, the most accomplished singer of her century in the Arab world."

Kulthum supported Nasser's pan-Arab vision in the 1950s, and Nasser adjusted the time of his national radio addresses so as to never interfere with Umm Kulthum's weekly Thursday night radio broadcasts. Virtually every Egyptian in Cairo listened to these programs in public places or at street kiosks, because few owned their own radio. No patriotic Egyptian would countenance any interruption when their goddess was singing. Her concerts were legendary improvisational excursions of emotion and sonic beauty.

Kulthum was a perfectionist who was reputed to prepare for her rare performances by smoking hashish just before going onstage. She would dramatically appear only after an ominous 5–7 minute introduction by the orchestra, handkerchief in hand like Louis Armstrong, at which point the crowd would go crazy. At the end of her performance, Kulthum was carried off stage, fully spent and unable to move, à la James Brown. Her power and fame were so great that the Israeli army still broadcasts her music in public areas to divert their enemies. More than 3 million people crowded Cairo for her funeral.

RECOMMENDED CDs

AHMED ALAWEYAH. *Shaabi* singer who pioneered the use of synths and drum machines. Al Tarik (Soutelphan, 1994)

NATASHA ATLAS. Daughter of an English mother and a Sephardic Jewish father, Atlas grew up in a Moroccan suburb of

Brussels, but is of Egyptian ancestry. She was heavily influenced by Arabic culture and has become a world music pop star. *Ayeshteni* (Mantra, 2001).

FARID AL ATRACHE. (1914–1974). Born in Syria, al Atrache settled in Cairo and became a fine composer, virtuoso oud player, actor, and singer. *Addi Arabi* (Voice of, 1973) is a live concert; *Farid el Atrache* (Voice of, 1973) is done with a female chorus.

SAMUEL BALBY. Extraordinary trumpeter who collaborates with Nubian and world musicians. *Love Letter from King Tut-An* (Piranha, 2000).

AMR DIAB. The biggest young name in Egyptian pop music. His *al-Jil* style is derived from the raw street pop shaabi without the rough edges. *Allem Albi* (Mondo Melodia, 2003).

HAMZA EL DIN. Father of modern Nubian music, oud virtuoso, vocalist, ethnomusicologist, and international star. Exiled from southern Egypt/northern Sudan in the 1960s, he is one of the first world musicians recognized as such. *Escalay-Waterwheel* (Nonesuch, 1968) contains three Zen-like improvisations, including a song by Egyptian composer Mohamed Abdel Wahab written for Umm Kulthum; *Muwashshah* (JVC, 1996) is a tribute to the legendary African slave musician from Baghdad.

MAHMOUD FADL. Egyptian Nubian drummer dedicated to exploring the old Nubian rhythms, even pairing them with more modern drum'n'bass beats. *Love Letter from King Tut-An* (Piranha, 2000); *Drummers of the Nile Go South* (Piranha, 1997).

ABDEL EL HALIM HAFEZ. The "Nightingale of the Nile" was the golden boy of the Nationalist revolution in 1952 when pan-Arabism arose, the darling of Nasser and the street, eventually collaborating with the well-known composer Mohammed Abdel Wahab and returning to the classical form. *Ala Hasb Weddad* (Soutelpan, 2000 reissue) is live with full string orchestra.

HAKIM. King of shaabi street-pop known as al-Jil. Hakim sells millions at home and was the first Egyptian singer to make any kind of breakthrough internationally. *Yaho* (Mondo Melodia, 2000) is his American debut.

ALI HASSAN KUBAN. In the mid 1950s, Kuban added electric guitars, keyboards, a horn section, and percussion to Nubian music, fusing traditional with up-tempo pop in a Western-influenced mix. *From Nubia to Cairo* (Piranha, 1980); *Walk Like a Nubian* (Piranha, 1994).

UMM KULTHUM. (See Profile). *Al Ataal* (Sidi); *Ana fi Intizarak* (Sony Cairo); *Sahran Lewahdi* (Sony Cairo) is a gorgeous song written by Riad el Soumbati; *Rubayeat el Khayyam* (Sony Cairo) is an early piece with chamber back up; *Hakam Alena al-Hawa* (Sony Cairo) is her last recording.

MOHAMED MOUNIR. One of the great Egyptian pop singers. *Earth . . . Peace* (Ark 21, 2002) is Nubian funk mixed with Prince; slickly produced and hip.

LAYLA MURAD. Born in Cairo in 1918 to a Moroccan Jewish family, Murad converted to Islam in 1946 and became a popular film star and singer. *Best of Leila Mourad* (Cairophon, reissue, 1999).

MOHKTAR AL SAID. Accordion player. *Amar 14* (Piranha, 1994) is great belly dance music with fine tabla solos and that irresistible ambience. *Raks Sharki: Classic Egyptian Dance Music* (Pirahna, 1998) is more belly dance and great ensemble playing.

SALAMAT. Salamat is a Nubian roots band who also plays North African and Middle Eastern roots music. *Mambo El Soundani: Nubian Al Jeel Music from Cairo* (Piranha, 1993). *Ezzayukoum* (Piranha, 1999).

RIAD EL SOUMBATI. The great oud master was Umm Kulthum's accompanist and orchestra leader. *Roubaiyat El Khayam* (EMI, 1975/2000) is a breathtaking, 49-minute solo piece with El Soumbati's singing and playing—simply superb.

MOHAMMED ABDEL WAHAB. Originally a singer, Abdel Wahab became Egypt's greatest composer who popularized the Arab classical form and added a western influence to the hitherto Oriental discipline. *Cleopatra* (EMI Arabia, 1991); *Vol 1, 4 & 10*, compilations (Aristes, 1971).

WARDA. Not Egyptian, but if there is an heir to Umm Kulthum, Warda is it. She is actually part Lebanese and part Algerian, but a star in Arab popular music. *Warda* (Capitol, 1997); *Tabaan Ahbab* (EMI, 1989).

IRAN

Since the Islamic Revolution of the late 1970s, many aspects of Iranian life have been greatly restricted by the fundamentalist government, including music. Nevertheless, the Oriental music from Persia is among the most ancient and sophisticated of all the world music styles. Many musical forms and poetry predate Islam, and Iran possesses a strong classical tradition—*Musiqi-e assil* ("pure, noble" in Farsi)—that can be traced back two millennia.

CLASSICAL MUSIC

Classical Iranian music is intense, bluesy, refined, contemplative, and almost always involves poetry. Medieval poets Hafez and Jalal-e are still extremely popular. Ancient Persian poetry gives the music a respectability that appeals to the revolutionary Islamists who have encouraged a return to the classical while banning everything popular. The singing is characteristically nasal and the melodic line ornate. The greatest examples of classical Iranian singing, known as *tahrir*, are virtuosic and executed at a rapid speed, usually in the high vocal range, often likened to the voice of a nightingale. The classical form centers on prescribed modes (*radifs*) and has a kinship with Sufi mysticism and philosophy. Classical Persian music was confined to the homes of monarchs and royalty until the early 1920s, but since that time has been taught in the conservatories

Unlike Western classical forms, Iranian musicians rely on memorization, never performing from notated music. Theoretically, Iranian musicians never repeat themselves in performance, much like the revered nightingale, as they are creating spontaneously, albeit from a memorized piece. The music is linear—with no harmony—and often has no regular pulse or beat. Iranian classical music traditionally proceeds with the pitch gradually getting higher throughout the piece until reaching a climax at which point there is a descent back to the opening pitch mode.

REGIONAL FOLK MUSIC

Iranian folk music centers on the life cycle, agriculture, and religious ceremony. Zurnas (double reed, recorder type wind instruments) and bagpipes are found in rural music where styles vary geographically. Iran's diverse ethnic mix includes Kurds, Baluchis, Azerbaijanis, and peasants from the musically fertile Khorasan region in the North. Virtually half of all Iranians still live in rural areas and colloquial music forms are an important part of each region's culture.

Common musical instruments include:

- *Barbat*: an oud/ud.
- *Dotar*: Long-necked, two-stringed lute.
- *Kamencheh/violin*: Spiked fiddle played in front of the musician on the lap or kneeling on the floor; it has a taut nasal sound that goes with the singing in Iranian classical music.
- *Ney*: End-blown flute with breathy sound, originally a shepherd's instrument. "Listen to the ney as it speaks to us, for it cries out against separation"—the poet Rumi.
- *Santur*: Dulcimer played on a small table in from of the musician, who uses two felt hammers.
- *Tar and Setar*: Long-necked lutes whose strings are plucked and strummed. The tar is larger, louder, more resonant, and twangy; the belly is skin, not wood, and a metal plectrum is used; Setar is softer and refined. It is said to embody the spirit of Iranian music, but is hard to hear in a large theatre without amplification.
- *Tombek (zarb)*: Goblet drum played with fingers and palms of both hands; an accompanying instrument, that provides the rhythmic pulse.

Mohammad Shajarian is the greatest singer of Iranian Classical music. He possesses flawless technical skill and voice control, a knowledge of Iranian poetry second to none, and a voice that is the closest thing on record to the revered nightingale.

Born in the northeastern region of Khorasan in 1940, Shajarian was inspired by the late master, Gholam Hossein Banan, and studied with Abdollah Davami, from whom he learned the most ancient songs and radif (modes). He appeared on Iranian TV in the 1970s and became a star. Shajarian is devoted to teaching and research as well as international performance. Despite the restrictions imposed by the revolution, Shajarian has continued to expand his audience and was a leader in the musical branch of the Cultural Revolution, even though he is not a fundamentalist. All of his recordings are worth owning. Perhaps the most remarkable is *The Abu-Ata Concert*, a live recording made during the turmoil of repression imposed by the Khomeini fascism. On the night of the recording, the fundamentalists clashed with the students at the German Cultural Center in Tehran. Many students were arrested and detained, including Mohammad Reza Lotfi, who was the head of the Music School at the time. The intensity of Shajarian's singing and Lotfi's playing, made just hours later on this recording, is palpable.

RECOMMENDED CDs

HOSSEIN ALIZADEH. Tar and setar genius, contemporary musician, and composer involved in Western as well as traditional Iranian music. *Ney Nava* (Kereshmeh 1993).

SIMA BINA. One of the most respected and famous folk singers, Sima is an internationally recognized icon. Her recordings are intense and stark, centered on her unique interpretation of rural music. *Songs from the Plains; the Music of Khorasan* (Caltex, 1999); *Persian Classical Music* (Nimbus, 1995).

KAYHAN KALHOR. Born in Tehran in 1963, Kalhor is well known in the West as the leading proponent of the kamencheh, the spiked fiddle indigenous to Iran. He studied classical music with masters in Tehran as well as Kurdish folk in Kermanshah. In 2002 he was an integral part to Yo Yo Ma's *Silk Road* project, with whom he recorded. *Moon Rises over the Silk Road* (Traditional Crossroads, 2000) is a collaboration with the popular group Ghazal; *Masters of Persian Music* (Traditional Crossroads, 2002) is an aesthetically beautiful recording; *Scattering Stars Like Dust* (Trad Crossroads, 1998) his debut.

MOHAMMAD REZA LOTFI. Tar and setar player. *Mystery of Love, Live in Copenhagen* (Chereshmesh, 1994); see Abu-Ata Concert under Shajarian.

PARVIZ MESHKATIAN. Santur virtuoso with dazzling speed, member of the Aref Ensemble. *Dawn* (Kereshmeh, 1996).

SHARAM NAZERI. Kurdish sufi singer and, after Shajarian, the most respected and revered male singer of Persian music. *Shahram Nazeri & the Dastan Ensemble* (Wagram, 2001) is a live performance of great beauty, sensitivity, and taste; *Masters of World Music, Vol. 3* (Ocora, 1995); *Nowruz* (World Network, 1997).

PARISA. The most respected female vocalist from Iran, an international star whose performances sell out throughout Europe and the United States, with a large following among the Iranian diaspora in New York City, Los Angeles, and London. *Parisa with the Dastan Ensemble* (World Network, 2003) is extraordinary; *Parisa 1* (Caltex, 1996) is a live concert; *Baz Amadam* (Playasound, 1996).

MOHAMMAD SHAJARIAN. (See Profile). All of his recordings are worth owning, but perhaps the most remarkable is *The Abu-Ata Concert* (Kereshmeh, 1981); *Night Silence Desert* (Traditional Crossroads, 2000), Kayhan Kalhor's Khorason Suite; *Masters of Persian Music* with Kalhor and Hossein Alizadeh; *Iran: Mohammad Reza Shajarian and the Ensemble Aref* (World Network, 1987) is gorgeous, with Meshkatian (santur) and Jamshid Andalibi (ney) outstanding.

DARIUSH TALAI. One of the great Tar virtuosi, also fluent in Indian disciplines. *Masters of Traditional Music, Vol. 1* (Ocora, 1979); *Radif Vol. 1* (Al Sur, 1995).

I R A Q

The current state of affairs in Mesopotamia is hardly conducive to music making, and the scene under the deposed Hussein was barely a remnant of the rich musical tradition of Iraq, literally the cradle of Middle Eastern music. Some believe that the purist form of Arabic music originated here. Without question, the most important Arabic musician of all time is the legendary Ziryab (850 CE), a virtuoso oudist, composer, and seminal figure of Flamenco.

RECOMMENDED CDs

MUNIR BACHIR. The late oud master is the Ravi Shankar of the Arab world, (i.e., the most renowned oud player in modern times, although not necessarily the greatest). *En Concert in Paris* (Inedit, 1988); *Maqamat* (Inedit, 1994).

SADDOOUN AL BAYATI. *Songs of Iraq* (Samar, 1973).

FARIDA ALI. Renowned female vocalist whose work is true to the ancient, pure Eastern form. She performs with the Iraqi Maqam Ensemble, which includes Mohammed Gomar on the *joze* (Iraqi spike fiddle). *The Voice of Mesopotamia* with the Iraqi Maqam Ensemble (Long Distance, 2003) is a work of art; *Classical Music from Iraq* (Pan, 1999); *Departure* (New Samarkand Records, 2001).

NAZEM AL GHAZALI. Modern Iraqi Singer in the Arabic tradition. *Nazem al Ghazali* (Duniaphon).

FILFEL GOURGY. Iraqi legend, singer, and oudist who died in 1983, a major artist in Baghdad, who fled to Israel when exposed as a Jew, and became a star. *The World is Happy* (Magda, 1979).

HAKKI OBADIA. Iraqi fiddler who fled to the United States and taught music on Long Island. *Iraqi Jewish and Iraqi Music* (Global Village, 1995); an amateur recording from a technical standpoint, but fascinating.

YUSEF OMAR. For serious world music lovers familiar with maqam tradition. *Irak: Les Maqams de Baghdad* (Ocora, 1996/1972).

KAZEM EL SAHER. He is well known for singing the beautiful love poems of the Syrian poet Nizar Qabbani. Born in Mosul, he is perhaps the most popular singer in the Middle East. *The Impossible Love* (Ark 21, 2000); *Habibati Wal Matar* (EMI, 2003 reissue).

ISRAEL

The Jewish diaspora has been mass migrating back to Israel for centuries, especially since Theodor Herzl's proclamation of Zionism. Since 1882 Eastern European immigrants, Yemenis, and Jews from across the Maghreb who had been expelled from Portugal and Spain during the inquisition 400 years earlier have returned to Israel. After World War II, the entire Jewish populations of several countries (Bulgaria, Iraq, Yemen) made their way to the "Promised Land" and most recently émigrés have come from Russia and Ethiopia. In many ways, Israel is the melting pot of the Middle East and a natural home for world music.

The Israeli music scene is a large one and, for the most part, the roots and popular factions are staunch supporters of the peace process and actively opposed to the Sharon government. The horrors that have occurred since the aborted Oslo Accords have widened the gap, but the musicians continue to represent the voice of reason, much as was the case in South America in the 1970s and the United States in the 1960s. Artists such as Yair Dalal and roots group Bustan Abraham continue to champion the cause of peaceful Arab-Israeli relations, performing and singing the music of the region in Hebrew, Arabic, and on Classic Arab, Turkish, Greek, and Middle Eastern instruments.

Israel is more westernized than any other nation in the Middle East, and the record purchasing demographics of its citizens reflect a correspondingly Western influence. Arabo-Andalous from Morocco and the rest of North Africa and the Ladino song tradition from Sephardic Jews from Iberia, Turkey, and Greece was initially not accepted by the mostly western population. During the past 25 years, however, traditional music from the various ethnic cultures of the Jewish diaspora now living in Israel—Yemeni, Iraqi, Eastern European, Ethiopian, and North African—has experienced a dramatic renaissance and become part of the national culture.

Born in Poland in 1946, Chava Alberstein came to Israel in 1950. Impoverished from the ravages of war, her family participated in the early building of the Israeli nation. She scored her first hit record in 1964, the year after she was drafted into the Israeli army. For more than 35 years she has been the most popular and talented Israeli folksinger in the world, with an extensive recording legacy. She is a champion of liberal causes, always working for the peace process, human rights for all people, and unity between Israel and its Arab neighbors. Chava is a child of the 1960s, a peer of Joan Baez and a disciple of Pete Seeger. She has used her podium and gorgeous voice to protest injustice and fight oppression and violence much in the same way as Victor Jara, Silvio Rodriguez, Daniel Viglietti, and Violeta Parra did as part of the nueva cancion movement in South America. In fact, Chava has toured in South America with Mercedes Sosa, pleading the causes of human rights and ecology, using her guitar and voice as her weapons. Chava sings in Hebrew, Polish, English, and Yiddish with equal facility. She is a talented composer, guitarist, storyteller, and TV personality, perhaps the most internationally recognized artist from Israel.

RECOMMENDED CDs

CHAVA ALBERSTEIN. (See Profile) Israel's greatest folk artist and singer. *At Home* (1983; 1994; 2001 Reissue) is folksy and near her peak; *For Children* (MMC, 1982) is a wonder, a perfect album for all children; *Be Right Back* is pure folk; *The Well*, with the Klezmatics (Xenophile, 1998); *Yiddish Songs* (Blue Note, 2000); *London* (1989).

JOE AMAR. The great Cantor and Andalous singer. *Orchestre Andalous D'Israel with Joe Amar* (Madga, 2001).

BUSTAN ABRAHAM. World music, multicultural virtuoso acoustic group at the forefront of the peace movement. *Bustan Abraham* (Narada, 1992); *Abadai with Ross Daly* (Nada Records, 1996); *Hamsa* (Nada Records, 2000).

SCHLOMO CARLEBACH. The Master of Hebrew and Jewish folk songs was a rabbi who fiddled way above the roof. *Live at the Village Gate* (1963); *A Melava Malka* (Noam, 1995); *In Jerusalem; Holy Brothers and Sisters* (1997 reissue); *In the Palace of the King; With Neshama Carlebach* (Sameach, 1997), Daughter and Schlomo make like Nat and Natalie.

YAIR DALAL. Eclectic violinist/oudist/composer, Iraqi-Jew, and staunch supporter of the peace process who collaborates with Palestinean Arabs and Iraqi Muslims. His ensemble Al Ol performed at the Oslo Accords in 1994. *Azazame with the Tarab Ensemble* (Amiata, 2002); *Asmal; Silan* (Amiata, 1998).

ESSEV BAR. Contemporary Israeli acoustic folk-rock. *Darashia* (Adama, 2000); *Prayer for the Way* (Magda 2001); *Song through the Meadow* (Adama, 2001).

YEHORAM GAON. The Israeli Sinatra? *Ladino Masterpieces Vol. 1 & 2.* (NMC, 1988).

FILFEL GOURGY. (See IRAQ).

HABREIRA HATIV'IT. *Wandering* (1990); *Waiting for Samson* (1980); *Barefoot* (Hed Azri,1996); *David and Salomon* (Hed Arzi, 1995); *Black Beats* (Magda, 1993).

OFRA HAZA. The late Yemeni singer and world beat artist. *Yemenite Songs* (Shanachie, 1985); *Shaday* (War, 1988) sold over a million copies.

GUY KARK. Kark is an oud/guitar player and vocalist who performs music from Yemen to Eastern Europe in Hebrew and Arabic. *Canaan* (Personal World, 1999); *Mayim* (Personal World, 2003).

NOA. Born in Israel of Yemenite descent as Achinoam Nini, Noa grew up in the United States and is an international pop singer who has collaborated with Pino Daniele and Sting. *Noa* (Geffen, 1994) with Pat Metheny and Co. is hardly World but a pretty side.

ORCHESTRE ANDALOU D' ISRAEL. Al Andalous outfit performing traditional North African music with soloists in Hebrew, Arabic, and French. *Maghreb I & II* (Magda, 2000, 2001).

ZIRYAB TRIO. Arab-Israeli group with oud, violin, and Zohar Fesco, a world class percussionist. *Mashreq Classics* (Crammworld, 1997).

EMIL ZRIHAN. Cantor and Moroccan Jew, a star on the world music scene and living proponent of al Andalous music from his native Maghreb roots. *Ashkelon* (Piranha, 1999). See his many recordings with Orchestre Andalous D'Israel.

KURDISTAN

There is currently no nation of Kurdistan, and there hasn't been one since the early part of the twentieth century. Nevertheless, the Kurds are a nation of peoples scattered about the Middle East, living in exile in Turkey, Iraq, Iran, Armenia, and Syria. The Arab world does not advocate the reformation of Kurdistan. Although they have endured as much or more hardship and persecution than their fellow Muslims in Palestine, the Kurds are not Arabs and their plight is not a *cause celebre* in the Islamic world.

Like their Berber counterparts in the Maghreb, the Kurds predate the Arabs. Kurds are more progressive and more uniformly educated than other Muslims in the region and have embraced democratic principles more than any society in the Middle East save Israel. Despite the unconscionable abandonment of the Kurds by the Senior Bush administration in the early 1990s, which resulted in the Iraqi Kurds Loyal to the Untied States being gassed, during the past 10 years Kurdish culture and society has flourished, making tremendous economic gains that have helped establish a society that is the most stable, prosperous, and open in Iraq as 2004 comes to a close, the Kurds hold an important key in the resolution of the Iraqi debacle.

THE MUSIC

Kurdish music is quite distinct from the neighboring Arabic and Iranian traditions. Both borrow and utilize the Kurdish dorian mode, however, which is named *Kurd* in both Arabic and Iranian music. Because they have been repressed for so long, Kurdish music is memorized and has been the primary means of communicating cultural traditions.

There are two types of Kurdish music. The first is modal, based on the traditional maqam or mode, which is called *Kurdi*. The maqams are based on microtonal tuning. The second form of Kurdish music is based on melodies known as *gourani*, which have distinct and structured rhythms. The word *gourani* literally means "one who worships fire" and is related to the ancient rituals of the Zoroastrians. Musical instruments used in *gourani* include the bloor (flute), ghol (drum), duduk (oboe), tenbur (saz, lute), kamanche (spike fiddle), and zurna (a wooden shawm).

RECOMMENDED CDs

AYNUR. Leading female Kurdish singer in Turkey with folk leanings, influenced by Sezen Aksu; *Kece Kurdan* (Kalan, 2004)

KAMKARS. Nine-member family ensemble that fuses Kurdish folk compositions with Persian classical music. *Nightingale with a Broken Wing* (Womad, 1997); *Kani Sepi* (Kereshmeh, 1999).

SHARAM NAZERI. (See IRAQ.)

SIVAN PERWER. The moral conscience of Kurdistan *Songs of Kurdistan* (Ethnic, 1995).

ALI MARDAN. (See IRAQ.)

IRBRAHIM TATLISES. TV star and popular vocalist living in Turkeys revered by the diaspora in Germany Selam Olsun (Universal, 1999); Ayaginda kandura (Kalan, 1978)

LEBANON

In the early part of the twentieth century, Beirut was justly known as the "Paris of the Middle East," a Mediterranean port where the rich and famous expatriates fled tyrannical governments in their homeland for sanctuary. It was an open city with Christians and Muslims coexisting in harmony. Lebanon of the mid-1900s boasted a nightlife second to none in the region and was an arts and cultural center of significance. Chateau Musar, which miraculously continues to make fine wine into the twenty-first century, was renowned worldwide as a worthy competitor to the great Chateaux of Bordeaux and Negociants of Burgundy that dominated the world wine scene at the time, before the American explosion circa 1974.

Prior to the 17 years of civil war and the current dominance by Syria and Islamic fundamentalists, Beirut was a center for Arab music that rivaled Cairo. Since the war, the scene has moved to Paris, but there has been a resurgence in recent years, with the French influence on the music unmistakable.

Born in Beirut in 1934, Fairouz began her musical career as a chorus member at the Lebanese Radio Station. Her early songs expressed romantic love and a nostalgia for village life. By the early 1960s Fairouz was a celebrity throughout the Arab world, including Arabs living in Europe and the Americas.

Today, Fairouz is the Arab world's greatest living diva, second only to the late Umm Kulthum in popularity and stature in the Middle East. She worked for three decades with her husband, composer/arranger Asi Rahbani and his brother, lyricist Mansour Rahbani, expanding the Arabic repertoire by incorporating western compositions, new key signatures, and western instruments into Arabic music. Her recordings from the 1970s are her best, remarkable and groundbreaking for her sheer vocal prowess and expansion of the scope of Middle Eastern vocal music. Fairouz is also renowned for her ventures in musical theatre in Beirut in the 1970s, which were innovative, provocative, and revolutionary. Her refusal to leave Lebanon during the civil war has forever endeared her to her public as a courageous patriot.

Since the death of Asi several years ago, Fairouz has performed and recorded with her son Ziad Rahbani, who has taken over as her musical director. She continues to have an active career and touring schedule, and has recently begun to move away from the purely Middle Eastern mold, expanding her style and repertoire by incorporating Brazilian and other global sounds into her recordings.

RECOMMENDED CDs

RAGHEB ALAMA. Award-winning pop singer. *Albi Achikha* (Relax-In, 1990); *Allamtini* (Relax-In, 1996); Tab Ley (Mondo Musica, 2002); *Saharouny Elleil* (Mondo Melodia/Ark 2001); Al Mahatta (Voix de Lebanon, 1974).

WADI' AL-SAFI. One of Lebanon's most influential vocalists, best-known for his interpretations of Mawals of Arabic poets. Luciano Pavoratti has said of Al-Safi "This man does not sing alone, it feels like somebody sings with him." *Lebanon Live* (Monitor, 1994).

CLAUDE CHALHOUB. Fusionist violinist trained at London Royal College of Music. *Claude Chalhoub* (Elektra Asylum, 2001), with Nusrat's brother Forroukh on vocals.

FAIROUZ. Her best recordings are from the 1970s, especially the classic *Shat Eskandaria/The Shores of Alexandria* (Virgin, Relax-in, reissue, 1995); *Ya Rayeh* (1994/1971 reissue); *Dabke, Folk Songs and Dances from Lebanon*, with Sabeh (Voix de, 1971); *Mechwar* (DPH, 1996) is a compilation of romantic ballads and a good place to start.

RABIH ABOU KHALIL. Jazz-influenced oud player, Khalil is Lebanon's musical goodwill ambassador and international spokeperson. He resides in the United States and is highly sought by cable TV music stations and festivals both as a musician and personality. *Morton's Foot* (Enja, 2003) is his most realized recording to date. *Il Sospiro* (Enja, 2002) is solo oud; *The Sultan's Picnic* (Enja, 1996).

CHARBEL ROUHANA. One of the finest young ud players in Lebanon. *Salamat-Greetings* (Le Chant du Monde, 1997).

SABEH. Female vocalist, lighter in style than Fairouz or Warda, a musical comedy specialist. *Zay el Assal* (Voix de, 1975).

GEORGE WASOOF. *Zaman Ajayeb* (EMI, 2001).

SYRIA

The name Syria comes from the Greek, referring to the land at the eastern end of the Mediterranean between Egypt and Arabia, stretching inland to Mesopotamia. Syria once encompassed Palestine, Judea, Phoenicia, and Damascena. It is said that Damascus is the oldest city in the world, and during the eighth century rule of the Umayyads, Damascus was the main center of music in the Arab world.

Shortly after World War II, Syria achieved independence from French rule and has constantly been in conflict with Israel and other neighbors in the region since. In the twenty-first century, Syria is trying to shake its modern image as a training ground for terrorists, an image cultivated by its late dictator Hafez al-Assad, who ruled from 1970–2000. His son Bashar was "elected" in 2000 and has attempted to distance his own Baathist regime from its counterpart in Iraq.

THE MUSIC

The northern city of Aleppo is the cultural center of modern day Syrian music, a city that is well known for its rich musical heritage where the ancient tradition of Arabic music is most alive and well in Syria.

As in other Islamic countries, *Sufism*, replete with the famed whirling dervishes, is the only Islamic sect permitted to perform spiritual music. Islam bans all other forms of music except the daily broadcast of the call to prayer. Musicians often accompany Sufi chants although musical instruments are not allowed in mosques. Sufi songs are meditative, spiritual, and deeply mystical. The music of the intense *dhikr* rituals, the spiraling dances of the whirling dervishes known as *mawlawiyya*, produces a state of mind where the spirit is said to leave the body, creating a trance from which true ecstasy is said to derive.

Syria is no longer the center of classical Arab music that it was a millennium ago and is mostly on the sidelines in the world music scene, but there are a number of artists and recordings to explore for those with a true interest in Arabic music.

RECOMMENDED CDs

ENSEMBLE AL-KINDI. One of the most respected musical groups in the Middle East. Sheikh Habboush's voice is divine and earthy. *Aleppian Sufi Trance* (Le Chant du Monde, 2003) is a double CD; *Crusades: Seen through the Eyes of the Orient* (Le Chant du Monde, 2003).

FARID AL-ATRASH. (See Egypt.)

ABED AZRIE. Born in Aleppo in 1945, Azrie traveled to Beirut as a teenager, and moved to Paris in 1967 to study Western classical music, translating Arab poetry to French, including the Sumerian Epic of *Gilgamesh*. He sings almost in a whisper, and is a sophisticated composer and stylist. *Aromates* (Elektra/Nonesuch, 1990); *Suerte* (L'Empriente, 1994); *Lapis Lazuli* (Columbia, 1996).

ABDULLAH CHHADEH. Innovative qanun player who plays a wide variety of Middle Eastern classical music, also trained in western classical music. *Ya mal al-Sham'* (2000); *Abdullah Chhadeh and Nara* (ABYC, 2002).

SULEYMAN DAWUD. Sufi singer. *Chants d'Extase en Syrie* (Al Sur, 1996).

SABAH FAKHRI. Syria's leading contemporary interpreter of Andalusian song, with a Byzantine slant. *Mouwachah Iksi Al Itash* (Duniaphon).

YEMEN

Historically, Yemen has been the most populous region of Arabia and an important seat of Arab culture. Geographically, it is the highest and broadest end of the Hijaz, facing Ethiopia across the Red Sea. Prior to the creation of the state of Israel, the Jewish population figured prominently in the musical culture of Yemen. Since the middle of the twentieth century, however, both the Jewish Yemeni population and its rich cultural heritage have moved to Israel, where the music survives. Today Yemen remains both a culturally rich and diverse society as well as a hotbed of Islamic militantism.

THE MUSIC

The most significant individual style of art music in Yemen is based on classical Arabic poetry as well as that of Yemeni poets over the past several centuries. Performance style most often consists of a solo singer with ud and hand percussion accompaniment and can be heard in the high plateau region around the Yemeni capital of Sana'a. The Yemeni style of Arabic music is especially fluid in rhythm, with a wide variety of metrical patterns derived from poetic language, and articulated without strong rhythmic accents.

RECOMMENDED CDs

HAMUD AL JUNAYD. *Traditional Yemen Songs* (Nimbus, 1996).

MOHAMMAD AL-HARITHI. *Yémen - L'Heure de Salomon* (Institut du Monde Arabe).

VARIOUS ARTISTS. *The Music of Islam, Volume 11, Music of Yemen - Sana'a Yemen* (Celestial Harmonies); *Yémen - Le chant de Sanaa Hasan al Ajami/Ahmed Ushaysh* (Institut du Monde Arabe); *Songs from Hadramawt* (Auvidis, Musicians of the World).

4

ASIA

Afghanistan	Kyrgyzstan	Tibet
Azerbaijan	Malaysia	Turkmenistan
China	Mongolia	Tuva/Mongolia
India	Pakistan	Uzbekistan
Indonesia	Philippines	Viet Nam
Japan	Tadjikistan	
Korea	Thailand	

Asia is the largest continent on the planet and contains a vast and varied number of musical styles, instruments, and traditions. To a remarkable degree, all of Asia is truly musically interrelated. The status of music, where it is played, and for what purpose or ceremony, how it is used as a means of communication, the content of folk songs and work songs, the type and range of instruments used, and how music has been treated over time are just some of the facets of Asian world music that share a common base, from Azerbaijan to Korea. All of these shared features of Asian world music, coupled with how the music has been accepted, used, or banned by the ruling powers, gives strong substance to the argument that music is part of the human genome.

This survey has listed the countries whose contribution to world music is the most significant on the continent from India—arguably the most important contributor to world music on the entire planet—to the former Soviet Republics in Central Asia where the musical heritage has not had widespread exposure either through recording or the media. The music from Laos, Bangladesh, Cambodia, East Timor, and Sri Lanka is encompassed in the Thai, Indian, and Indonesian sections.

AFGHANISTAN

Afghanistan has always been at the crossroads of a myriad of Asian civilizations, a physically striking land with harsh, mountainous terrain and a varied climate. During the past 25 years, it has been besieged and exploited by communists, fundamentalists, drug lords, fascists, and capitalists.

Music has not flourished in an environment where the basic needs of daily life are barely attainable and human rights is a four-letter word, often punishable by rape or death. Music in general has been suppressed by the fascist fundamentalists who ran the country under the Taliban, and recordings from outsiders and expatriates have been sparse. The Taliban banned instrumental music and public music-making throughout the country and destroyed musical instruments on the spot whenever and wherever they found them.

Despite the horrors of the last three decades, a cadre of expatriate musicians has kept the musical tradition alive to a degree. Although Kabul is the cultural captial of Afghanistan, most of the music centers around the southern city of Herat and has a decidedly Persian character due to its proximity to Iran, with its rich musical heritage. Most of the vocal music in the country is sung in Farsi or Pashto, languages common to both countries. Afghani classical music (klasik) includes both instrumental (ragas and naghmehs) and vocal forms (ghazals, love poetry). Much Afghani music is related to Indian music and uses Hindi terminology, although Afghani ragas focus more on the rhythm and are played mostly with percussion instruments.

INSTRUMENTS

The most important Afghani instrument is the *rebab (rabab, rubab)*, a short-necked lute related to the Indian *sarod*. The rebab has three main strings and a number of sympathetic strings over a hollow neck, with a goat skin resonator and a very deep body, making it somewhat awkward to hold. It is the national instrument. Other instruments include *dutar* (14-string lute); *sitar; dilruba* (bowed lute); *tulak* (transverse bamboo flute); *tanbur* (long neck lute); *dhol* (small drum played with sticks), and *zirbaghali* (claypot drum with large top covered with animal skin and long, narrow base).

RECOMMENDED CDs

KHALED ARMAN. Leading rebab player and a force behind Radio Kaboul. *Radio Kaboul* (Accords, 2003). In the early 1950s, Afghanistan's first radio station began broadcasting and the title is in reference to that moment.

BALUCHI ENSEMBLE OF KARACHI. From the stateless area near Pakistan, Iran, and Afghanistan where al Qaeda allegedly is headquartered, the Baluchi Ensemble incorporates Indian and Arab influences into their Middle Eastern trance style. The sarud (a wooden lap fiddle with a goat skin sounding board) is the dominant sound. *Love Songs and Trance Hymns* (Shanachie, 1997).

ENSEMBLE KABUL. Expatirates living in Switzerland recreating the sound of Radio Afghanistan from the 1960s, sung in Pashto and Dari. *Nastaran* (Arion, 2001).

AZIZ HERAWI. Herawi is a dutar and rubab virtuoso from Herat, but plays ragas in the Indian style, with tabla. *Master of the Afghani Lutes* (Arhoolie, 1992); *Memories of Heart: Music of Afghanistan* (Music of the World, 1996) is a hypnotic collection of instrumentals and folk songs.

KABUL WORKSHOP. Collective led by Khaled Arman and Francesco Russo, who reside in France and play traditional music in a Western contemporary electronic setting. *Trigana* (Tinder, 2002).

ESSA KASSIMI. Vocalist and lutist. *The Art of Rabab Of Afghanistan* (Arion, 1999). Two Afghani Ragas.

MOHAMMAD RAHIM KHUSHNAWAZ. One of the masters of the rubab. *Rubab of Heart* (Gallo, 1995) is traditional.

USTAD FARIDA MAWASH. Leading female vocalist who rose to fame in the 1970s, but fled to California in 1991; the voice on the *Radio Kaboul* recording (see Khaled Arman).

USTAD MOHAMMED OMAR. Rebab virtuoso who brought the rebab to classical music from its folk origins. *Virtuoso from Afghanistan* (Simithsonian, 2002) is from a concert in the United States in 1974 with Zakir Hussein on Tabla the recording requires attention but will reward listening for Omar'a improvisational ability.

CENTRAL ASIA

TRANSOXANIA

Uzbekistan	Turkmenistan
Tadjikistan	Kyrgyzstan

The classical music of the former Soviet Republics in Central Asia— collectively known as *Transoxania* (across the Oxus River)—possess a unique and compelling variety of traditional styles. Music from the region is strongly influenced by Turkish and Iranian disciplines.

The Soviets carved out convenient boundaries from what was once Russian Turkestan, formerly comprising the feudal city-states of Bukhara and Khiva. Prior to the 1920s, the region knew no true political demarcations and was comprised of a series of clans and tribes who hadn't especially considered the notion of nation or country. The region was an important center of Muslim civilization after the Arabic conquest and today retains a rich Islamic character despite the remnants of Soviet domination.

Despite recent ethnic and political divisions that are a result of decades of Soviet domination, the music, especially the Uzbek and Tajik classical repertory, is relatively uniform across national boundaries. Central to the music of Transoxania is *shash maqam* (6 modes). It is a compendium of instrumental and vocal music that embodies Central Asian poetry and music, linked to the *maqam* tradition of other Islamic countries by a common language of musical terminology and theory. This ancient music tradition survives today in Transoxania along with a growing popular music scene influenced by Europe.

During Soviet rule there were attempts to fuse Western, European classical traditions with Central Asian Eastern disciplines, most notably by Alexei Federovich Kozlovsky, a Russian classical composer of Polish heritage who was banished by Stalin to Tashkent in 1936. He absorbed the music of the region and wrote many pieces, most notably the opera *Ulugbek*, reputedly the first polyphonic piece to reach a wide Uzbek audience. His counterpart, Mutavaqqil Burxanov, is an Uzbek composer who understands the value of incorporating Western music into his own tradition. They believed that the traditional arts must develop in relation to the rest of the world.

Because of the limited availability of recordings from Central Asia, we have combined recordings from the region in a single section with the artist's native land indicated in the short review.

RECOMMENDED CDs

TURGUN ALIMATOV. Alimatov is an unparalleled master of the *tanbur, dutar,* and *sato*, Central Asian lutes. *Turgen Alimatov: Ouzbekistan* (Ocora, 1996).

BUHARA: MUSICAL CROSSROADS OF ASIA (Smithsonian Folkways, 1990), Wedding music, chant, and art songs performed by Jewish and Muslim musicians including Tohfaxan Pinkhasova and Mahdi Ibadov.

ILYAS MALAYEV MAQAM ENSEMBLE. *Buzruk* (Shanachie, 1996) recording in the proper cyclic sequence of a single maqam from Uzbekistan, recorded in New York.

MATLUBEH. From a Tajik village near Samarkand, she sings classical and folk music in Tajik (related to Farsi) and Uzbek (closer to Turkish). *Turquoise of Samarkand* (Long Distance, 1996); *Yar Kelour* (Iris, 2000).

SEVARA NAZARKHAN. Along with Yulduz Usmanova, Sevara is the most famous world music star from the region. She is a vocalist and dutar player (2-stringed lute) with western sensibilities and production values. *Yol Bosin* (Real World, 2003) is sexy and provocative; a hit in the West [Uzbekistan].

GOLTCHEREH SADIKOVA. Tadjik folksinger. *Tadjikistan Falak* (Fonti Musicali, 1992).

SALAMAT SADIKOVA. The best-known singer in Kyrgyzstan accompanies herself on the *komaz*, a 3-stringed lute. On several tunes she is supported by the ultra traditional Kambarkan Folk Ensemble. *Voice of Kyrgyzstan* (Frequency, 2002).

YULDUZ USMANOVA. A former Silk Road worker, Usmanova began as a traditional wedding singer. Her songs were once subject to official state scrutiny, but today she represents a new spirit of freedom, independence, and innovation, the voice of the future in her native Uzbekistan. In Europe she is an icon of authenticity who connects the old to the new, the East to the West. *Alma, Alma* (Blue Flame, 1993) is her western debut; *Yulduz* (Sony, 1999) is pop/dance music; *Binafscha* (Blue Flame, 1996) is more traditional.

MONAJAT YULCHIVA. Disciplined mezzo-soprano, perhaps the top female classical singer of Uzbekistan. *Monajat Yulciva* (World Circuit 1996) with Shaqat Mirzaev, rabab master, and his ensemble.

VARIOUS ARTISTS

Asie centrale: Traditions classiques (Ocora, 1991) 2 CD anthology concentrating on the classical court styles.

Maqam d'Asie Centrale Ouzbekistan: Ferghâna Qalimattov, Monâjât Yultchieva (Ocora, 1996). Singer Monâjât Yultchieva accompanied by Shawqat Mirzâev (rabâb) and his ensemble.

Maqam d'Asie Centrale: Tadjikistan: Tradition of Bukhara (Ocora, 1996). The Bukhara style is built of extended cycles on single modes, the Shash Maqam.

Uzbekistan Instrumental Art Music (Gallo, 1999) with Alimov, Sawqat Mirzaev, Ikram Matanov and other virtuosi.

From Samarkand to Bukhara: A Musical Journey through Uzbekistan (Ocora, 1996). A vital collection (as folk and as classical) with lutes, flutes, reeds, fiddle, and hand drums; accessible and beautiful.

AZERBAIJAN

The former Soviet republic of Azerbaijan is a Caucasus country, geographically grouped with Armenia, Georgia, and Chechnya. It is, however, closely linked musically and religiously to the Turkic Central Asisan States and Persian Islamic culture.

Classical Azeri music is referred to as *mugam*, which is traditionally in the form of a suite and includes Sufi-influenced poetry praising Allah, with instrumental interludes interspersed during the performance or piece. A kind of throat singing, more akin to yodeling, is not the exclusive province of Tuva, and is practiced in Azeri classical music.

Azeri instruments are similar to those found elsewhere in Central Asia and include the *tar*, a small, fretted lute with three sets of double strings, also prominent in Iran; the *balaban*, a double reed duduk (like an oboe); the *def* (frame drum); and the *kamancha* (spike fiddle). Travelling musicians known as Ashiqs are common in Azerbaijan. They are bards who sing poetry and play the Turkish *saz*, a long necked lute.

RECOMMENDED CDs

RAHMAN ASADOLLAHI. Garmon (Accordion) player who has performed around the world. *Ana* (7/8 Music Production, 2000) was recorded with the Azerbaijani National Orchestra in the capital city of Baku with conductor Nariman Azimoff.

SAKINE ISMAILOVA. Azerbaijan's leading female singer. *Anthology of the Mugam Vol. 5* (Inedit, 1993).

JABBAAR KARYAGDI ENSEMBLE. Iranian-style ensemble playing folk songs and mugam with tar, kamanch, and def. *Land of Flames* (Pan, 1994).

LOK BATAN FOLKLORE GROUP. *Music of Azerbaijan* (Digital Sound, 2001) Not for the uninitiated; soaring rocals, raw and piercing.

ALIM QASIMOV. Azerbaijan's greatest singer and most renowned musician, a master of the maqam with an incredible voice of searing power. *Love's Deep Ocean* (World Network, 2000) showcases his amazing falsetto voice with balaban, lute, kemenche (spike fiddle), clarinet backing; *Legendary Art of the Mugam* (World Network, 1998) is with his full ensemble.

CHINGIZ SADYAKHOV. *Piano Music of Azerbaijan* (Panda Music, 2003). Folk and original tunes by a classical pianist.

ALIHAN SAMEDOV. Clarinet, balaban, zurna and sax player now residing in Turkey. *Balaban: The Land of Fire, Music of Azerbaijan* (Mega Muzic, 2001).

YAGHOB ZOROOFCHI. Singer trained in Iran who performs with the Azerbaijan National Ochestra. *Best of Zoroofchi* (X Dot 25, 1995).

CHINA

As the most populous nation on the planet immerses itself in the global economy, Chinese culture is gradually becoming more open, progressive, and westernized. Due to the size of its workforce and the immense wealth of knowledge, ingenuity, and resolve, the twenty-first century is well on its way to being the Chinese century.

It is hoped that the oppressive regimes that have ruled China in the past will become more attentive to the human rights of its own people as China interacts with the world. To date, China has been extremely slow in improving its human rights record. The West must bear some responsibility for the continued abuse; when it opened the floodgates to trade with China in the 1990s, the sole item on the agenda seemed to be profit. By demanding no standards or guidelines regarding human rights in exchange for doing business, the United States and its allies implicitly sanctioned China's widespread abuses. Hopefully, as China prepares to host the 2008 Summer Olympics and becomes more transparent, the practices of the past will change.

CONFUCIUS AND MAO

Confucius taught that music is not meant to amuse but that its sole purpose was to purify one's thoughts. He also taught that the single tone was more significant than melody. These concepts are crucial in understanding the history of Chinese music through the ages. Until quite recently, music in China was controlled by these precepts.

Historically, musicians have been relegated to an extremely low social status in China. During the revolution and until Mao's death in

1976, the very idea of new music or music as a career was anathema. Mao didn't like traditional music either. He took his lead from Confucius and understood that music must be controlled lest individuality and free thought—the arch enemies of all autocrats—threaten his control. He banned music for ten years during which time artists and intellectuals were shot or put to work in the fields. Mao's philosophy regarding music was that it must espouse state purposes and promote the cause, remarkably in line with the fundamentalist Islamic view on the same subject.

THE MUSIC REVIVAL

Under the backdrop of Confucius, Mao Ze Dong and the dynasties that ruled between them, China is emerging with a music scene that is beginning to record the traditions of the past while also creating new music for the World. Composers such as Tan Dun and Qu Xiaosong are part of an iconoclastic generation who are becoming recognized for their compositions and film scores world wide.

THE PIPA

Perhaps the most important instrument in the Chinese arsenal is the *pipa*, a four-stringed lute used predominantly in classical music. Pipa music has been confined to the conservatory since the 1950s and has retained its traditional style more than most Chinese music taught at the conservatories. The pipa is at the core of Chinese chamber music, which is often called silk and bamboo (*sizhu*), played by ensembles of plucked and bowed lutes and bamboo wind instruments such as the transverse (*dizi*) and end blown (*xiao*) flutes and the free-reed mouth organ (*sheng*). Chinese chamber music is remarkably parallel in approach to Irish Celtic music's heterophony whereby each musician plays a version of the same melody with individual variations appropriate for his or her instrument.

THE PROVINCES

Although most of China can be characterized as *Han*, there are numerous ethnic groups throughout the country who have always revered and used music in their daily lives, remarkably retaining their traditions even during the revolution. The *Uighurs* in the northwest share an Islamic culture and musical tradition with much of Central Asia. The *Manchu* in the Northeast still conduct shamanistic music rituals and share a history with Koreans in the region. The *Mongols* live in Inner Mongolia, within China and share a horse culture and throat singing tradition (*xoomei*) with Tuva and Outer Mongolia.

INSTRUMENTS

Musical instruments in China have ancient heritages and are played throughout the country:

- *Pipa:* The major concert instrument in modern China, a large lute; earliest versions appeared in the Qin dynasty with a long neck, leather surface, circular sound box, and was played upright. Today it has a semi-pear-shaped sound box, a wood top board, the fretted neck curves backward with four strings and four or five octave intervals.
- *Ruan:* Long-necked lute once know as the qin pipa, dating back to 220 BCE. Ruan's are constructed in a family of soprano, alto tenor, and bass and used in modern Chinese orchestras—alto and tenor most commonly—and are played with a plectrum;
- *Liuqin:* Smaller pipa, with two open holes on the face of the body; pear shaped;
- *Sheng:* China's oldest free-reed instrument. It comes in various sizes (13, 14, 17, 19, or 36 reeds). There is a round wooden bowl at the bottom into which bamboo pipes are inserted and arranged in a cluster. On the right side are finger holes. At the base of each pipe is a copper ring to hold the reed and adjust the note. The *sheng* is widely used in folk and opera orchestras;
- *Zheng:* zither (half-tube), with a sound box of wood; strings can be of silk or steel wire, usually plucked with both hands using fingernails;
- *Suona:* Trumpet with 8 holes, body of wood with a thin brass tube that bells at the end and a reed attachment at the other;
- *Yanqin:* Adaptation of the santur from the Middle East and therefore a "foreign" instrument;

- *Sanxan:* Three-string, skin-headed lute with a long neck;
- *Erhu (huqin):* Two-stringed instrument with hexagonal or octagonal sound box, snake skin covering one end, and an open carved vent on the other with a long neck; played upright like a cello;
- *Dizi:* Transverse bamboo flute; blowing hole, stop hole, 6 finger holes; 2 1/2 octave range;
- *Jinghu:* Two-Stringed instrument played with a vine bow, five octave range, sound box at bottom;
- *Gongs, Kettle drums, tympanis:* As in the West.

POP

When Mao died and the revolution abruptly ended, his successor, Deng Xiao Ping, eased many restrictions on musical performances. Unfortunately, a cloyingly sweet Westernized ballad style became all the rage, copying the form popular in Taiwan and Hong Kong. These vapid songs can still be heard today China.

RECOMMENDED CDs

JIE-BING CHEN. Erhu virtuoso who resides in California. She has performed with V.M. Bhatt, Max Roach, and other jazz artists. *Two Flowers on a Stem* (Soul Note, 1999); *Chinese Erhu: The art of Chen Jiebing* (Wing, 1991); *Tabula Rasa* (Water Lily Acoustics, 1996) with Bela Fleck ; winner of a World Music Grammy.

LIN SHI CHENG. Pipa master, Wu Mans' teacher. *Overall Ambush Flourishing Spring Moon* (Chinese Dragon, 2003).

XIAO FEN-MIN. Pipa virtuoso who has premiered works for Tan Dun. *Moon Rising* (1996); *Viper* (1998) is improvisations with British avant-garde guitarist Derek Bailey.

GUO BROTHERS. The most famous musicians outside of China who play dizi, xiao, and sheng and explore the full spectrum of Chinese music to great effect. *Yuan* (Caroline, 1990) is flute, mouth organ, and oboe music with tasteful electronics geared for the modern world.

CUI JIAN. Jian has captured the imagination of the disenchanted youth with his defiant rock 'and roll, selling more than 10 million records. He gained international attention when he performed at the World Peace Concert in Beijing and received an International Viewers Choice MTV Award in Los Angeles in 1991. *Nothing To My Name* (EMI Hong Kong, 1989).

TANG LIANGXING. Pipa soloist. *High Mountain, Flowing Water* (Shanachie, 1993).

WU MAN. Pipa virtuoso and the most visible Chinese world musician who straddles Western classical and Chinese traditional music perfectly. *Pipa from a Distance* (Naxos, 2003). Traditional sounds mixed with DJs, samples, trombones, and more, a remarkably balanced recording that succeeds on every level; *Chinese Music for the Pipa* (Nimbus, 1993) is an impressive recording debut.

HAO NINGXIN. Traditional music known as *Hakka* focuses on sustained, sliding drone of stringed instruments combined with high-pitched reeds. *Chinese Han Music* (Interra, 1995).

ZHONGXI WU & KARN WI-MIN WONG. *By the River Water* (Global Village, 2001).

LIN YOUREN. *Music for the Qin Zither* (Nimbus, 2001).

LI XIANGTING. Master of the *guquin*, the 7-string Chinese zither. *Chine: L'Art du Qin* (Ocora, 1990); *Soul of China* (Manu, 1994).

INDIA

The Indian subcontinent includes the modern states of India, Pakistan, Bangladesh, Nepal, Sri Lanka, and Kashmir. When the term "*South Asia*" is used, Afghanistan is generally also included. The subcontinent is a regional unit roughly analogous to the European subcontinent or to Southeast Asia in diversity, ecological and cultural coherence, all also containing various peninsulas, islands, and archipelagos.

India—the world's largest democracy—is at the center of world globalization as both a player and a pawn. India is allied with the United States and their former colonial rulers, the United Kingdom, is a strategic ally of the west in the war on terrorism, and an historic opponent of Islamic fundamentalism. Politics aside, India is one of the most complicated and fascinating countries in the world with a rich, ancient cultural history that is second to none. Music is the passion in India, the cultural thread that binds everyone in the country as nowhere else except perhaps Brazil. With a population of more than 1 billion, a great majority of whom are knowledgeable about Indian music, it is no wonder that there are so many genres and artists. Indian music is arguably the first and foremost music in the world music oeuvre in the post World War II era. Long before George Harrison and the Beatles made their connections with Ravi Shankar and Transcendental Meditation, Indian music had permeated western society.

One disturbing development is noticeable on the Indian music scene. The pipeline of great masters produced by the nationwide *gharana* system (regional schools tied to a specific discipline, history, and philosophy of music) is dwindling, with few replacements coming up in the ranks other than the sons and daughters of past masters. Young Indian musicians, like musicians throughout the world, are drawn to the virtual world of the Internet and are becoming victims of the homogenizing effect of globalization.

The scope of Indian world music is so vital and vast that an entire book would not do it justice. This survey will merely skim the surface by enthusiastically attempting to discuss the most important musical genres, artists, and instruments.

CLASSICAL MUSIC

The music of India is one of the oldest unbroken musical traditions in the world, dating back to the Vedas, the ancient scripts of the Hindus. The classical music of India is the first non-European musical art to gain worldwide stature without being absorbed into the commercial styles of the West. The basis of Indian music is *sangeet* (roughly, "music") a combination of vocal music, instrumental music, and dance originally derived from stagecraft. Indian music is based upon *rag*—the melodic form that is loosely analogous to the western scale or mode, arranged in seven notes—and the *tal*, a constantly repeated metrical cycle of beats present in all classical drumming. Volumes have been written about raga and tala. They are at once simple and unimaginably complex. The system of *raga* and *tala* evolved over centuries from the simple folk songs and rhythms of rural village people.

There are two major traditions of Indian classical music: North Indian *Hindustani sangeet* and South Indian *Carnatic sangeet*.

Both traditions have similar systems, but differ in terminology, use of instruments, and practice.

NORTH INDIA

Hindustani Sangeet covers an area from Bangladesh through northern and central India into Pakistan and as far as Afghanistan. This is the music with which Westerners are most familiar, the most widely played outside of the subcontinent. The *Hindustani* system is generally thought to be a combination of traditional Hindu concepts and Persian performance practice. With the emergence of Islamic rule in parts of North India, Hindu music began to absorb musical influences from the Islamic world, primarily from Persia. Amir Khusrau (1253–1325) is credited as the musician who incorporated Persian and Sanskrit, Islamic and Hindu maqam and raga with classical elements to form a new music. He is also credited with developing qawwali and khayal.

Performance differs somewhat between Hindustani and Carnatic music. In the north, music opens with the alap played by a soloist with a tanpura playing the drone. This section reveals the musician's ability. The alap encourages improvisation and builds to a climax. The jor is the next section, a slow movement that increases in pace as the melody is revealed. The music ends and the audience applauds. The gat follows, usually a written section where the pace increases. The climactic jhala is a call-and-response exchange between the players that encourages improvisation.

The major instruments in Hindustani classical music include:

> *Bansuri*: Transverse Bamboo flute the virtuosi select the wood and craft their own instruments;
> *dilruba*: Lap fiddle, bowed string instrument with a resonator;
> *ghugharu*: Bells, also anklets worn by women;
> *harmonium*: European reed organ with hand pumped bellows;
> *santoor*: Hammered zither/dulcimer; 100+ strings pegged and tuned in pairs;
> *maanjira*: Small cymbals;
> *pakhawaj*: Barrel shaped drum of the mridangam family;
> *sarangi*: Fretless bowed instrument, 40 sympathetic strings; very difficult to play; finger nails, not fingers, stop the strings;

sarod: Relative to Afghani rebab, made from teak with goatskin covering the sound box; no frets, 8–10 playing strings, 4 melody, others drone; 12 sympathetic strings; plucked with a wooden or coconut shell plectrum;

shenai: Double reed oboe;

sitar: Made of teak with resonating gourd, 6–7 main strings, 4 for melody, 3 for drone; 9–13 sympathetic causing the jangling sound, 20 moveable frets plucked with a mizrab;

surbahar: Bass sitar;

tabla: Pair of small drums played with the fingertips or palms;

tanpura: A drone, string instrument;

vichitra vina: Lap string instrument with 2 resonators played as a Hawaiian slide guitar.

SOUTH INDIA

Purandardas (1480–1564) is considered the father of *Carnatic* sangeet, credited with the codification of the method of education and as the composer of several thousand songs. Venkat Mukhi Swami (seventeenth century) developed the *melakartu* system for classifying south Indian *rags*. Carnatic music is found in the southern states of Tamil Nadu, Kerala, Andhra Pradesh, and Carnatica.

Carnatic music is based upon a complex system of ragam (rag) and thalam (tal). Ragams are categorized into 72 modes, called *mela*. South Indian scales use chromatic forms not allowed in the north. Varanam is a form used to begin many performances to unfold the various features of the ragam and thalam. The kritis are fixed compositions in the *rag*. The alapana unfolds the *ragam* to the audience and allows the artist to improvise. Notably, Carnatic music has retained its devotional character as an everyday music, untouched by Islamic influence as in the north.

The major instruments in Carnatic classical music include:

damaru: Hourglass drum;

kural: Bamboo flute;

ghatam: Large clay pot, used as percussion; pitch is controlled by closing the hole of the pot by pressing it against the player's stomach as it sits in the player's lap;

gotthuvadyam: A veena with some sympathetic strings;

mridangam: complex 2 headed drum, each played by one hand;

murchang: Jew's harp;

nadaswaram: Large (can be 2 1/2 feet long) double reed, piercing wind instrument;

veena: A lute with 4 playing strings, 3 drones, 24 frets, wood body, resonator, the main Carnatic instrument;

venu: Bamboo flute, similar to the bansuri;

violin: Western fiddle;

tambura (tanbura, tanpura): Four-string drone instrument like a sitar;

thalam (manjira): Small cymbals.

VOCAL MUSIC

There are numerous specific regional and vocal disciplines in Indian music, many related to sacred rituals or deities, some devotional, some singing praise, most about love. These vocal styles are all in many ways similar, with regional and subtle stylistic differences. The most prominent styles internationally are ghazals, thumri, and folk songs. Some of the major styles are:

Bhajan: Popular Hindu religious songs that eulogize Hindu deities;

Dhrupad: Oldest, most sacred Hindustani vocal genre, performed by men accompanied by tanpura and pakhawaj;

Film music: Scores from Mumbai, Bollywood, pop to Ghazal;

Folk songs: The foundation of classical music of all cultures, East and West, is folk music. Unlike classical raga, folk music is confined to short songs, accessible to all;

Ghazal: Means "to talk amorously of Women," sung in Urdu or Persian, influenced by Sufi mystics; much ghazal is based on North Indian ragas;

Khyal: Popular form of North Indian semi-classical vocals, less improvisation than thumri;

Kirtan: Bengali folk song form;

Kriti: Sung in Teluga, Tamil, or Sanskrit, South Indian Carnatic Hindu praise music, usually accompanied by mridangam and tanbura;

Tarana (Tillana): A jazz-like scat singing, used to close a khayal performance;

Ihumri: Popular urban form in north India, light classical, romantic, and devotional sung in Hindi and related to the legend of Krishna and the deity Vishnu. Tabla, tanpura, and sarangi commonly accompany the singer along with violin and harmonium.

The most notable performers of the vocal genres are set forth below in the recommended CD section.

BOLLYWOOD

India's film industry has been centered in Bombay (now Mumbai) for decades; the title Bollywood affectionately alludes to India's attempt to mimic the American movie capital. The music of the films of India is alternately referred to as play back, filmi, or simply Bollywood. The music is the primary vehicle for disseminating popular music in India, listened to by everyone on the subcontinent (Lahore has a minor scene in Pakistan called LaLaWood), and the major artists sell records by the millions.

Despite the prolific rate of moviemaking and the thousands of films churned out by Bollywood, only a select few singers have dominated the business over the last 50 years. Lata Mangeshkar and Asha Bhosle (sisters) absolutely dominate the female vocal scene, often singing multiple parts in movies and rarely allowing anyone else to muscle in on their territory. Only Kavita Krishnamurti is on their level. The men haven't shared the workload either. Mohammed Rafi, Kishore Kumar, and Mukesh monopolized the work until their deaths, and today only Udit Narayan and Kumar Sanu have attained star stature.

Shujaat Hussain Khan was a child prodigy who began playing on a small sitar at age 3. By the time he was 6 he was giving public performances. He represents the seventh generation in an unbroken family line of musical virtuosi. He is the son and disciple of sitar Master Ustad Vilayat Khan and grandson of Ustad Inayat Khan. He is a member of the Imdad Khan gharana and his style of playing is called gayaki ang, which imitates the nuances of the human voice.

Khan's repertoire of ragas includes many obscure ones learned from his family. Shujaat often sings when he plays and recently has been exploring folk music from his native Uttar Pradesh. He sings in both Hindi and Punjabi in a style that is both refined and charming and particularly accessible to Western ears due to the relative brevity of each piece.

Shujaat has toured all over the world for many years and is a regular collaborator with the famed Silk Road Ensemble Ghazal and Iranian Kamencheh star Kayhan Kalhor, appearing on a series of successful recordings for Shanachie. He is also an avid teacher both in India and abroad, currently on the faculty at the University of California at Los Angeles School of the Arts. Shujaat is one of the young masters of Indian music who is keeping the fading classical Art form alive.

RECOMMENDED CDs

BEGUM AKHTAR. The most revered of all ghazal singers who died in 1974; from Uttar Pradesh, her recordings are far too scarce. *Thumri, Sawan, Ghazals* (Music India, 1990); *Malika and Ghazal* (All India Radio, 1982).

NAJMA AKHTAR. Hindustani fusion singer and international star. *Qareeb* (Shanachie, 1987). Qareeb means nearness; a best seller that includes ghazals sung in Urdu.

S. BALACHANDAR. Key figure in Carnatic classical music who played *veena* and a range of other instruments including tabla, harmonium, mridangam, shenai, dilruba, and sita. The veena is a somewhat drier-sounding instrument, plucked much like the sitar, but generally in a slower and more formalized fashion. *Magic Music of India* (World Pacific, 1960); *The Music of India* (Nonesuch Explorer).

BAULS OF BENGAL. The name refers to an itinerant sect of (people) musicians with no caste who play folk music. *Man of Herat* (Amiata, 1998), 3 singers with their ensembles.

V.M. BHATT. Inventor of a nineteen–string, modified lap guitar— three melody, four drone, and twelve sympathetic strings—who blends Hawaiian guitar with sitar, sarod, and veena techniques. He has recorded in the West with Jerry Douglas, Bela Fleck, and Taj Mahal. *Gathering Rain Clouds* (Waterlily, 1993).

TARUN BHATTACHARYA. The most prominent santoor player. *Sargam* (Music of the World, 1995) Santur, shenai, and tabla; sensual and special; *Santoor* (Biswas, 2000).

ASHA BHOSLE. India's greatest filmi singer has recorded over 20,000 songs since Bollywood's inception. *Legacy* (Triloka, 1995) with sarodist Ali Akbar Khan; *The Golden Voice of Bollywood* (Manteca, 2000) is as good a start as any with Moh. Rafi and Kishore Kumar on several cuts; *Rough Guide to Asha Bhosle* (2003), in many guises, the usual great job from the Rough Guide.

ANINDO CHATTERJEE. *Anindo and His Tabla* (Autorec, 1991).

PANDIT HARI PRISAD CHAURASI. The greatest living bansuri artist who actually did not come from a family of musicians. *Call of the Valley*; *Raga Patdip* (Nimbus, 1996); *Rag Kaunsi Kanhra* (Nimbus, 1989).

ZIA MOHIUDDIN DAGAR (1929–1990). Pivotal musician in the process of recording Hindustani music, he played his instrument of choice, the *rudra vina*, the top string instrument in South India's Carnatic school, in a vocal style. *Raga Yaman* (Nimbus, 1991).

KADRI GOLPANATH. Virtuoso saxophonist who adapted his instrument to South Indian music. *Gem Tones* (GlobeStyle, 1999).

SHOBA GURTU. Heir to Begum Akhtar and current Queen of Thumri vocalists as well as a popular radio and TV star in India. *Shoba Gurtu: India* (Times Square, 1989/2002) with sarangi, harmonium, and tabla; *Usfret* (CMP, 1992) her son Trilok's debut.

BHIMSEN JOSHI. One of the great vocalists of Hindustani music. He studied in the kirana gharana with Sawai Gandharva. He possesses a rich, resonant voice that is classical but soulful. *Vocal Phenomenal* (Chhandra Dhara, 1992) is a 2 CD set, one live in Stuttgart.

HARIHARAN. Popular ghazal singer, Hindustani. *Hazir* (Magnasound, 1997) with Zakir Hussein; *Other side of Naushad* (Navras, 1999).

ZAKIR HUSSEIN. After Ravi Shankar, with whom he played for years, Zakir is the most renowned Indian musician outside of India, son of the great Tabla master, Alla Rakha, and a virtuoso in his own right. His career has included fusion projects with musicians from all over the world. *Tabla Duet* (Chhandra Dhara, 1988) with dad Allah Rakha and Sultan Khan on sarangi; *Selects* (Moment, 2002) is a selection of his greatest solos: For tabla aficionados it is the one.

ALI AKBAR KHAN. Master of the sarod, born in Bengali, called the greatest musician in the world by Yehudi Menuhin, five-time Grammy winner, and a national treasure. *Duet* (Delos, 1993) with L. Subramaniam on guitar and Zakir Hussein; *Then and Now* (AMMP, 1955/1990) a great introduction and career perspective; *Signature Series Vol. 1* (AMMP, 1990).

SHUJAAT HUSAN KHAN (See Profile). *Hawa Hawa.* (World Village, 2003). Folk music sung and played by Shujaat in Punjabi and Hindi; *Raga Shahana Kanada* (India Archiv, 1996); *Moon Rise over the Silk Road* (Shanachie, 1999).

SULTAN KHAN. Master and leading proponent of the difficult, bowed sarangi. *Rag Bhupali* (Moment, 1991).

VILAYAT KHAN. One of the greatest Hindustani musicians of the twentieth century, from seven generations of venerable musicians, The late Vilayat (He died in June 2004) and his younger brother Imrat inherited the family musicality. He is known for his vocal style or *gayaki ang* on sitar. *Raga Bhairavi* (India Archive, 1991), mid-morning ragas; *Raga Jaijaivanti* (India Archive, 1989) with tabla player Akam Khan and Idyat Khan on tanpura.

KAVITA KRISHNAMURTY. A current star in Bollywood, but also a talented art singer, married to South Indian violinist L. Subramaniam. *Meera ke Ram* (BMG Crescendo, 1996) contains compositions by Meera, a beautiful recording.

BALAMURALI KRISHNA. Adept *Tillana* singer and Carnatic musician. *Gems of Thyagaraja* (Felmay, 2003) singing compositions from 1767–1864; *Sarvasri: The Beginning* (Orchard, 2000); (Vocal Moment, 1994) hour-long *kriti* in *Lathangi*.

HEMANT KUMAR. Kumar was a fine singer but more influential as a composer, scoring more than 150 Bengali films and 50 Hindi films; he also wrote an estimated 2,000 songs. He first appeared on Indian radio in 1933. *Rare Gems* (EMI, India).

KISHORE KUMAR. One of India's best-loved vocalists, actors, and comedians. He first sang for film in 1948 and developed a relationship with director S.D. Burman, performing over 100 songs in his films. The night before he died of a heart attack in 1987, he recorded a duet with Asha Bhosle. *Retrospect* (EMI, India).

NILADRI KUMAR. Burgeoning star born in Calcutta in 1973, a fifth generation sitarist. *Raga Bilaskhani Todi* (Times, 2000) is youthful and spirited morning raga; *Revelation* (Navras, 2002).

LATA MANGESHKAR. The most prolific filmi singer of all time, revered throughout India. *Memorable Duets* (EMI India, 1994) with Kishore Kumar, Talat Mahmood, Manna Dey.

MALLIKARJUN MANSUR. Master of Hindustani song, who died in 1992. *Khayals* (Dunya, 2003 reissue).

MUKESH. All-time great filmi singer. *Golden Voice of Mukesh* (EMI, India).

UDIT NARAYAN. Filmi singer and heir to the Mohammed Rafi legacy. *Kuch naa Kaho* (RPG, 2003) movie soundtrack, including Kavita Krishnamurty.

MOHAMMED RAFI. The number one male filmi singer of all time, performed an estimated 26,000 songs and was heard in 76 films. Rafi sang in all national languages and genres including ghazals, qawwalis, and bhajans. He died in 1980 at 56 but remains one of the most influential playback singers ever. *Rough Guide to Bollywood Legends: Mohd. Rafi* (2004); *The Golden Collection* (CDF, 1995) is a great collection.

ALLA RAKHA. The tabla master who with Ravi Shankar brought Indian music to the West. *Tabla Duet* (Moment, 1991) with son Zakir Hussein; memorable.

G.S. SACHDEV. Bansuri master. *Full Moon* (Fortuna, 1987) with tanpura and tablas; full moon is a raga played at midnight.

KUMAR SANU. Current male playback star. *Royal Film Hits* (Royal, 1994). Dippy and delightful.

SHAKTI. Fusion supergroup formed in the 1970s with John McLaughlin, Zakir Hussein, and L. Shankar joining forces. *A Handful of Beauty* (Tristar, 1976); *Natural Elements* (Sony, 1976).

ANOUSHKA SHANKAR. Daughter of Ravi (and half-sister of Nora Jones), a rare female allowed into the virtually all-male sitar world who has achieved pop star status. Along with Niladri Kumar, one of the rising stars. *Anourag* (Angel, 2000), with Dad on the final cut.

L. SHANKAR. Carnatic violin virtuoso, fusionist, and charismatic member of fusion group Shakti. *Raga Aberi* (Shanachie, 1991).

LAKSHMI SHANKAR. Semi-classical singer of khayal and bhajan. *Seasons and Time* (Ocora, 1983); *Live in London Vol I.* (Navras, 1992) is widely considered her best; a masterwork.

RAVI SHANKAR. The one and only. *3 Ragas* (Angel, 1956); *India's Master Musician* (World Pacific, 1963) is his first recording in the West, released before the Beatles; *Ragas and Talas* (Angel, 1964) with Alla Rakha.

AHUL KUMAR SHARMA. Young santoor virtuoso. *Music of the Himalayas* (Real World, 2002) is a Sufi maqam, melody from Kashmir, and Kashmir contemporary music.

SHIV KUMAR SHARMA. The leading santoor master and a visionary artist. *Raga Gurjari* (Navras, 1994) is live in a London gallery and special; *Raga Jog* (Ethnic, 1993); *Call of the Valley* (EMI India, 1967/95), Sharma, Chaurasi and Brijbhushan Kabra use their instruments to tell the story of a day in the life of a shepherd in Kashmir using ragas associated with times of the day to advance the dramatic narrative. A must for every music collection of any substance.

L. SUBRAMANIAM. Fusionist and jazz violinist who has collaborated with Stephane Grappelly, Larry Coryell, Sven Amundsen, and others. *Conversations* (Milestone, 1984) with Stephane Grappelly. Carnatic Jazz?

TANJUR VISWANATHAN. The late master of the South Indian bamboo flute, the kural. *Pallavi* (Nonesuch, 1973) an early gem from Nonesuch and one of the first Indian records released in America that did not feature sitar. A young L. Shankar and Viswanathan's brother T. Ranganathan collaborate on violin and mridangam to great effect.

INDONESIA

The most populous Muslim country in the world (with a population of over 200 million) covers an area that would stretch from Ireland to the Caspian Sea. Indonesia contains more than 300 ethnic groups and 3,000 inhabited islands.

Achmed Sukarno was the founder of modern Indonesia following independence in 1949. He was a populist who formed a non-aligned movement of developing countries to forge a "third way" between the spheres of influence of the Soviet Union and the United States. In 1955 he convened the Asia Africa Conference, the first time leaders of the developing world had met to unite for their common interests. The movement espoused respect for human and women's rights, sovereignty, and territorial integrity of all nations, recognition of the equality of all peoples, and settlement of disputes by peaceful means.

When Sukarno began to implement widespread reforms that favored the common man, the United States and most of Western Europe covertly supported his overthrow and the insurgence of General Suharto. In some ways this began the age of globalization, that overused euphemism for "total control of all economies by Western business interests." The truth about Indonesia has been available only since Suharto's fall in 1998 when documents and eyewitness accounts of the mass murder of innocent people became available. It is under this backdrop that one must view modern Indonesia, a country working on its own to be a democracy, at the center of the post 9/11 global conflict.

THE MUSIC

Indonesia's music is as diverse as its population. The best-known genres are Javanese and Balinese gamelan music played on gongs and other metallophones. Solo and group vocal music and instrumental music played on flute, shawm, lutes, zithers, xylophones, and drums is played everywhere. Much of Indonesia's music seems traditional in that it has little or no Western influence. Some genres such as *dangdut* and *kroncong* are popular forms with Western influence, but are sung in local languages and seem traditional.

DANGDUT

This popular genre developed in the underclass in Jakarta in the late 1960s. It mixes Indian, Western, and Middle Eastern music, drawing its audience from lower-class Muslim youth. It expresses the inequities of Indonesian society and includes protest songs. Rhoma Irama is the main star of dangdut. Under General Suharto's rule, Irama was censured for his lyrics (mild by Western standards); after 1998, Irama turned away from his earlier fundamentalism and now supports the current regime. He incorporates Indian *filmi*, rock, and Middle Eastern *shaabi* into his sound. Unlike other national genres, dangdut is dance music for both the performers and the audience, which is mostly male.

KRONCONG (KE-RON-CHON)

The roots of *kroncong* are in Portuguese songs and instruments brought to Indonesia in the late sixteenth century. The genre arose from the lower-class Eurasians (Indonesian/Dutch) living in Batavia in the early 1900s. It was urban folk music with sexually provocative lyrics. The typical ensemble includes violin, guitar, flute, cavaquinhos (ukuleles), cello, and bass. It was the first music taken up by the nascent Indonesian recording industry in the late 1920s. After the expulsion of the Dutch, occupation by Japan during World War II, and during the fight for independence (1945–1949), kroncong songs spoke of revolution and patriotism. Today, the music is losing its following as the youth listen to pop or dangdut, but kroncong maintains a following among the generation now in power, because it was the music of their youth.

JAIPONGAN

Jaipongan is a complex rhythmic dance music from Sunda with no apparent Western influence. It emerged in the mid-1970s in Bandung, the capital of Sundanese Java. The *rebab*, a 2-stringed bowed fiddle, plays the intro as the *kendang*, a large, two-headed barrel drum, plays improvised rhythms in free time underneath whooping cries and strokes of the large gongs, while the *kempul* plays the one-note bass line. Dr. Gugum Gumbira Tirasondjaja developed the genre in the 1960s during Sukarno's drive to highlight indigenous art forms and shun Western influence. The style derives from *Ketuk Tilu,* a local village genre with 3 kettle gongs, rebab, gendang, and a female singer. A five-tone scale with equidistant intervals is used.

GAMELAN

Gamelan is an ensemble of tuned percussion of gongs, xylophones with metal bars, and drums; it can include singers, bamboo flutes, and spike fiddles. Ensembles vary from Java to Bali. Balinese gamelan is louder, harsher, and less refined than Javanese. The large bronze gamelans are common in central Java. *Kempul* are smaller hanging gongs, one for each note of the scale in a large gamelan. Horizontal kettle gongs named *ketuk* and *kenong* are common. Although Java is 90 percent Muslim, the tradition is Hindu-Buddhist. The music is performed in conjunction with poetry, dance, and theatre, including the famous shadow plays—*wayang kulit* —performed with puppets. In Sunda (West Java), Gamelan music is called *dedung.*

KECAK

Bali is Indonesia's greatest tourist attraction, where every local resident is said to be an artist. *Kecak* is the famous Balinese monkey chant where 150 men sit in five or six circles, silently crouching under flickering torches until they begin making a hissing sound. Then, after a slow chant they erupt into the *chak-a-chak-a* sound, imitating the monkey. The kecak is actually the chorus of men. This ritual is derived from the Hindu *Ramayana* legend where a monkey army helps rescue the Queen from the evil King.

Among traditional Indonesian instruments are:

> *suling*: Long straight bamboo flute with 4 or 6 holes;
> *kendang*: Cylindrical drum with each end covered in stretched, taut sheep or goatskin played horizontally while sitting;
> *bonang*: Group of metallic *timbals,* inverted chalices struck with metal hammers or rings wrapped in cotton. Male instruments have a protuberance for tuning;
> *gender*: A group of bronze plates resting on strings stretched between the ends of a wood frame. Thin bamboo resonators

are suspended under the plates and hit with a little mallet; akin to a marimba;

saron: Like the gender, with 6–8 bronze plates;

gong: Two to three metal timbals hung from a trestle;

kempul: Smaller hanging gongs.

RECOMMENDED CDs

PHILIP YAMPOLSKY. His 20 CD compilation of Indonesian Music, recorded in conjunction with Smithsonian Folkways. is a state-of-the-art survey of the music of a country without peer. All the entries are excellent; Alan Lomax would approve.

INDONESIA POPULAR MUSIC 2: Kroncong, Dangdut & Langgam Jawa. Includes four tracks by Rhoma Irama, vocals by Elvy Sukaesih and Lin Sandy, fine orchestration, some Hawaiian style guitar and singing all which conjure sounds from Polynesia and even Ethiopia.

VOLUME 4: MUSIC OF NIAS AND NORTH SUMATRA: Instrumental kendang karo music.

JUGALA ALL STARS. Dr. Tirasondjaja's Jaipongan ensemble. *Jaipongan Java* (GlobeStyle, 1990) with Nuis Komariah singing.

KECAK GANDA SARI: *A Balinese Music Drama* (Bridge, 1990). The first ever recording of a complete Ramayana Monkey Chant, directed by I Gusti Putu Putra. Spiritual, captivating, and scary.

DETTY KURNIA. Pop vocalist who uses western sounds and synthesizers. *Dari Sunda: Woman of the World Vol. 6* (Riverboat, 1995/91) is one of the all-time best selling CDs in Japan.

SABA HABAS MUSTAPA. Born Colin Bass, Saba is a world music raconteur, creator of *3 Mustaphas 3* and promoter of the Jungala All Stars. He combines incongruous genres from all over the world. *Denpasar Moon* (Piranha, 1997), a hit in Southeast Asia.

NASIDA RIA. A nine-woman band that plays *qasidah modern*, a pop interpretation of the Islamic epic that brings archaic values to modern music; now that's a twist. *Keadilan: Qasidah Music from Java* (Piranha, 1997).

JAPAN

The ancient culture of Japan has dominated East Asia for centuries, both militarily and economically. The Japanese have never been content with mere hegemony like their Chinese neighbors. Instead, the Japanese have been imperialists and colonizers throughout history, on a par with the West, while steadfastly remaining xenophobic about their own culture.

Since the humiliating defeat in World War II, the Japanese have completely rebuilt their society. They constitute the second biggest economy in the world and have copied, improved, and advanced the greatest inventions of virtually every pioneer on the planet. In the process they have carefully protected their rich culture, including their music.

The modern Japanese are first and foremost the greatest music lovers and consumers in the world. They are obsessed with American jazz, pop, and rock, and their passion for Brazilian music and tango is unsurpassed anywhere. When it comes to world music however, Japan is not a major player. With the exception of the music from Okinawa, Japan has contributed little to the world music discography in relation to their passion for music.

OKINAWA

The largest of the Ryukyu Islands lies 500 kilometers from the southern tip of Kyushu, the southernmost of the four main islands of Japan. The island has absorbed influences from China, Indonesia, and Micronesia, unlike xenophobic Yamato (the mainland).

Okinawa has been ruled by Japan and China and, after World War II, was occupied by United States forces. The remnants of World War II still abound on Okinawa. Caves where people hid from the United States army at the end of the war, and where many common people died, are intact today. Okinawans feel their island was sacrificed for the rest of Japan during World War II and their music reflects this suffering. Not surprisingly Okinawa is home to Japan's most prominent roots music, the only new music from Japan to make a true impact on the world music scene.

Okinawa has a Southeast Asian feeling to it, its own language, culture, and history that are quite distinct from Yamato. The music also has that familiar sound found in virtually every island culture throughout the world. Whether it is the *morna* of Cape Verde, *son* from Cuba, or *maloya* from La Reunion, there is a strong, almost mysterious affinity among all island music. Something about the sand, the sea, the wind, and the sun clearly binds island cultures around the world, a phenomenon especially apparent in roots and traditional music.

The most prominent folk song genre in Japan is *min'yo*, which are work songs, usually accompanied by *shamisen*, *taiko*, and *shakuhachi*. On Okinawa, the min'yo repertoire is called *shima uta* and the traditional Japanese shamisen is replaced by the smaller *sanshin*, which has a snake skin cover over the sound box. Drums are carried while played on Okinawa, and when struck the sticks are guided away from the drum in a rapid, dramatic movement intended for visual affect and well suited for dance accompaniment.

INSTRUMENTS

Japan's musical instruments are similar in many ways to those found in China, Korea, and other Asian countries, but with their own unique designs and playing styles. The primary instruments are:

- *koto*: Horizontal, 13-stringed plucked zither with a large wooden body;
- *shakuhachi*: Vertical, 5-holed bamboo flute, with ivory mouthpiece; 4 holes on the top, one in the back, with a bowed line and slight tapering away from the root that forms the bell;
- *biwa*: Lute, the *pipa* in China, usually 4 strings; biwas come in many sizes;
- *ogane*: Large bell, used in Buddhist shrines;
- *taiko*: Small barrel-shaped Noh drum;
- *tenpuka*: Small end-blown flute;
- *kokyu*: The only traditional bowed instrument;
- *shamisen*: Three-stringed lute, played with a plectrum, with cat skin/snake skin covering a mulberry or sandalwood body with a thin long neck; the shamsin is a smaller version;
- *binzasara*: Rattle.

CLASSICAL MUSIC

Japan has an ancient classical music tradition explicitly tied to theater, court ceremonies, and religious rituals. The various disciplines and genres are:

- Kabuki accompanies most of Japanese theatrical music and centers on the shamisen.
- *Kagura* is the generic term for all Shinto music and dance. Kagura is both secular and religious (i.e., the music is the same, but the words differ depending on the setting).
- *Nogaku* is the music of the *Noh* drama. The goal of the performance is purely aesthetic and atmospheric, not plot-based as in the West. The slow movements are exactly structured, as is the music. Flute and a variety of drums enter in a proscribed order as the performance unfolds.
- *Gagaku* is court instrumental music. It can be orchestral or chamber, with strings, percussion, and winds. It is elegant and refined, influenced by Chinese, Indian, and Korean music.
- *Shukuhachi* is classical music written for the family of flutes. Shakuhachi is usually the first form of Japanese music studied and appreciated by Westerners. The instrument is made from the root and lower part of the male bamboo plant. *Shaku* is 3 centimeters, 3 millimeters; *hachi* is an additional measure. The standard length is 54.5 centimeters.
- *Biwagaku* is music written for the biwa, the main Japanese lute.

RECOMMENDED CDs

TAKASHI HIRAYASU. Along with Shoukichi Kina, Hirayasu helped bring Western rock and electric instruments to Okinawa's traditional music. *Nankuru Naissa* (Riverboat, 2001) with Bob Brozman; Okinawan folk rock; *Iwkawu* (1991).

JOJI HIROTA. Taiko drum specialist and shakuhachi player with a jazz background. *The Gate* (Real World, 1999) with a string quintet.

HAROUMI HOSONO. Co-leader of the electronica band Yellow Magic Orchestra with Ryiuichi Sakamoto, an eclectic ambient composer and keyboard player. *N.D.E* (PolyGram, 1995) electronics, with Bill Laswell.

SHOUKICHI KINA. Since 1968, when he formed his band Champloose, Kina has provided a musical voice and conscience for Okinawan music. Kina is a talented vocalist and shamisen player, also adept on mandolin and slide and electro-acoustic guitar. *The Music Power from Okinawa* (Globestyle, 1991); *Bloodlines* (Polydor, 1980); *Asia Classics 2; Peppermint Tea House* (Virgin, 1991).

KAZUFUMI MIYAZAWA. Kaz popularized Okinawan music in Japan and South America. He is influenced by Brazilian singers/ songwriters Joyce and Carlinhos Brown, and is popular in Rio and Sao Paolo. *Tropicalism* (2000); *Deeper than Ocean's* (Stern's, 2003); *Okinawa Watashi, No Shima* (Farside, 1998) with his group "Boom," which popularized Okinawan music Internationally.

NENES. Female quartet of singers backed by Sadao China on san-shin, formed in 1990 to make *shima uta* (island songs) accessible to young people. The most successful roots group of all, with lead vocalist Misako Koja. *Akemodoro Unai* (Globestyle, 1998) is Okinawan folk/pop.

RINKEN BAND. Okinawan folk-rock band. *Nifee* (Sony, 1999).

ICHIRO SEKI. Shakuhachi player with a modern edge. *Ichiro Seki Plays Shakuhachi and Presents His Works* (Bamboo, 2001) with arrangements by jazz pianist Ryuichi Sakamoto.

TADASHI TAJIMA. Shakuhachi, a student of Katsuya Yokohama. *Shingetsu* (Music of the World, 1991) is a beautiful recording.

KATSUYA YOKOHAMA. The leading shakuhachi master, one of the last representatives of Japanese traditional music, who also incorporates influences from the West. He is a virtuoso solo performer, and premiered classical composer Toru Takemitsu's *November Steps* with symphony orchestra in 1967. *L'art du Shakuhachi* (Ocora, 1997) solo and duets with disciple, Yoshikazu Iwamoto; *Zen: Katsuya Yokohama Plays Classical* (Wergo, 1988) is a 2 CD recording from 1976; meditative and glorious.

VARIOUS ARTISTS. *The Rough Guide to Okinawa* (2001) is a splendid, state of the art compilation with great notes.

KOREA

Korea is a 4,000-year old culture that is often overshadowed by its Chinese and Japanese neighbors. Korea truly has been the "Hermit Kingdom" through the ages, but it is an extremely sophisticated, resourceful, and inventive culture. Korea developed a printing press long before Europe and boasts one of the most pragmatic alphabets in the world, one that has enabled all Koreans to be literate.

Korea's isolation ended early in the twentieth century when Japanese imperialists colonized the country; Japanese rule ended after World War II. Following the stalemate that was the Korean War, North and South Korea took separate paths; the South has become a global economic powerhouse, while the North hosts an unstable regime that sits atop a growing nuclear arsenal. However, at the dawn of the twenty-first century, communication between South and North has improved, hinting at the possibility of some type of rapprochement.

THE MUSIC

True to its Hermit reputation, Korea has not been truly involved in the world music phenomenon to date. Western classical music, however, borders on an obsession with Koreans both at home and abroad. Whether it is their incredible discipline and fortitude, reverence for the beauty of the music, extremely high aptitude for math, or all of the above, clearly Koreans have excelled in the field of Western Classical music for decades, especially in producing a remarkable number of world-class string players.

CHONG-AK AND SOG-AK

Korea's own musical history dates back to at least the fifth century. Traditional music is divided into two categories: *chong-ak* for the ruling class and *sog-ak* for the common people. Chong-ak was the style performed for the Korean ruling class, and follows the teachings of Confucian philosophy. *A-ak* refers to ritual temple music now performed at Munmyo, the shrine where Confucius and his disciples are honored. *Tang-ak* refers to secular music. *Hyang-ak* is a term that simply means native Korean music. *Sog-ak* music includes Buddhist music, folk songs, farmers music, *nongak* (agricultural music), *pansori* (narrative songs), and *sanjo* (rhythmic instrumental music).

The farmer has had a significant influence and role in the musical history of Korea due to its historically agrarian society. Farmers' music has 12 different rhythmic patterns called *shipich'ae*, which are led by a small gong called *kkwaenggwari*. *Nongak* is a rural form of percussion music, typically played by 20 to 30 performers, usually a farmer's percussion band.

Pansori is vocal and percussive music played by one singer and one drummer who plays the *puk*, a double-headed barrel drum. The lyrics tell one of five different stories, individualized by each performer, often with jokes and audience participation. *Sanjo* is entirely instrumental music that shifts rhythms and melodic modes during the song. Instruments include the *changgo* (drum) set against six fixed forms each played by a melodic instrument, which may include the *kayagum, komungo, taegum, haegum, tanso,* and *p'iri*. *Ppongtchak* is pop developed during the Japanese occupation, which uses double meter as in Japan rather than triple meter as is common in Korea.

THE SONG MOVMENT: NORAE UNDONG

In the early 1980s, the music scene in Korea foresaw the coming break with America currently being advocated by South Korea's youth and progressive politicians. This social-protest song movement became known as *Norae Undong*. The major figure in this style is Kim Min-ki. His music was full of political and social content, attracted activists on college campuses, questioned the American influence in Korea, and advocated rapproachement with the North Koreans.

INSTRUMENTS

The major Korean instruments include:

- ajaeng: Bowed, seven-stringed zither used primarily in court orchestras;
- *changgo*: Hourglass drum, the most frequently used accompaniment in almost all forms of Korean music;
- *chwago*: Medium-size barrel drum hung from a frame used in ensembles or full orchestras;

- *haegum*: Two-stringed fiddle without a fingerboard, held on the left knee and played vertically with a bow;
- *kayagum*: Related to the Chinese *cheng* and the Japanese *koto*; a zither with 12 silk strings;
- *kkwaenggwari*: The smallest gong, struck with a wooden mallet;
- *komungo*: Zither with six strings of twisted silk. The strings are plucked with a bamboo rod (*sultae*) held between the index and middle fingers of the right hand, while the left presses on the strings to produce microtones;
- *nabal*: Metal trumpet without finger holes, used to produce only one sustained tone;
- *nagak*: Conch-shell trumpet, producing only one deep note, used exclusively as a drone;
- *p'iri*: Cylindrical oboe with wide double reed and eight finger holes, a lead instrument that takes the main melody in court music or folk ensembles;
- *p'yon-gyong*: Set of 16 L-shaped slabs of jade stone, counterpart of the bell chimes (p'yonjong);
- *p'yonjong*: Set of 16 chromatically tuned bronze bell chimes hung in an elaborately decorated frame. The bells are the same size and shape but the thickness differs, giving each a different pitch. The player sits behind the instrument on the ground and uses a mallet;
- *pak*: Clapper shaped like a folded fan, consisting of six pieces of wood loosely held together at the upper end by a cord made of deerskin;
- *taegum*: Largest and most representative transverse flute. It has a blowing hole, a hole covered with a thin membrane, six finger holes, and five non-finger holes at the lower end;
- *t'aep'yongso*: Conical wooden oboe, eight finger holes; loud and piercing;
- *tangjok*: Smallest transverse flute, similar to the piccolo;
- *tanso*: Small, notched, vertical bamboo flute with five finger holes; one on the back.

RECOMMENDED CDs

HWANG BYUNG KI. One of Korea's foremost composers and master of the kayagum, who has used the instrument to express his modern compositions. *Silk Road* (Acadia, 1992).

PAK CHONGSON. Classical and court music. *Traditional Korean Music* (Music of the World, 2004). Chongson plays the ajaeng, the 7-stringed, bowed zither.

SAMUL NORI. Traditional percussion ensemble. *Red Sun* (PolyGram, 1994) is a jazzy take highlighting traditional percussion instruments.

MALAYSIA

Situated in Southeast Asia between China and India, Malaysia comprises the Malay Peninsula, which also includes the separate republic of Singapore; and part of the island of Borneo including Sabah, Sarawak, and Brunei. Malaysia was a major shipping center before Islamic rule engulfed the peninsula in the fourteenth century. As usual, the Portuguese were the first Westerners to arrive, followed by the Dutch and eventually the English who were colonial rulers who set up a strong administrative system that has served Malaysia well in the era of globalization.

Malaysia is a mosaic of people who today can boast of a strong economy, stable relations with its neighbors, and the world's tallest building (soon to be eclipsed) in Kuala Lumpur (KL), Malaysia's largest city. Malacca on the west coast is where tradition and ancient culture are most visible, and the island of Borneo is where the oldest indigenous Malayans reside. The Chinese, Indian, and Arab influence is widespread across Malaysia. Singapore, at the southern tip of the peninsula, has become one of the economic centers of the world, an immaculately clean (some say sterile), opulently rich, and westernized metropolis which, along with KL, is the center of world trade in the region.

THE MUSIC

Malaysian music is heavily influenced by neighboring Indonesian and Thai forms, as well as Portuguese and Moorish/Arabic music. The Malays of Kelantan and Terengganu in the northeast are culturally linked to peoples from the South China Sea region. The martial art of *silat* is a branch of self defense also popular among the Malays as an art presentation. Similar to *t'ai chi*, it is a mixture of martial arts, dance, and music accompanied by gongs, drums, and Indian oboes.

Small ensembles called *kertok* perform rhythmic xylophone music. Middle Eastern ghazals are popular on the streets of Kuala Lumpur, especially with the street vendors and buskers. A leading ghazal star is Kamariah Noor.

Ronggeng is folk music from Malacca played with violin, drums, button accordion, and a gong. *Zapin* music and dance is popular throughout Malaysia, usually accompanied by a *gambus*, a six-stringed lute, and drums. *Dondang sayang* is a slow, intense music that mixes influences from China, India, the Middle East, and Portugal. *Kumpulan Sri Maharani* is the leading dongdang sayang ensemble. Indonesian music is extremely popular throughout Malaysia, especially Dangdut (see Indonesia), the Islamic-based pop vocal music championed there by Rhoma Irama.

RECOMMENDED CDs

SHEILA MAJID. Famous pop star who has made a mark in the Asian and Indonesian markets, the first Malaysian to release a compact disk (1987). *Dimensi Baru* (EMI, 1985); *Warna* (EMI, 1987).

SITI NURHALIZA. Popular female singer who uses acoustic accompaniment. *Adiwarna* (Sawah, 1998).

TUSAN PADAN. One of the few, truly traditional musicians to attain any renown outside Malaysia. He played the *sape*, the lute of the *Orang Ulu* tribe of Sarawak. *Masters of the Sarawakian Sape* (Pan, 2000).

P. RAMLEE. Pop singer, actor, director from the 1950s, who westernized *dondang sayang* and gave rise to the modern, local pop scene Iramat and Lagu (1999 reissue). Malaysia's Golden Son.

MONGOLIA/TUVA

Mongolia is a sparsely populated land of 2.5 million people, mostly Buddhists, who inhabit a surface the size of Western Europe stretching from the Asian Steppes to Manchuria, China. In the days of Genghis Khan (thirteenth century), Mongolia ruled the entire region from China to Eastern Europe.

Tuva is a remote corner of Siberia sitting on the Russian-Mongolian border. It first came into existence as a result of the fall of the Soviet

Union. Tuva (formerly part of the Soviet Union and Mongolia) is a culture of herders and hunters who live with and among animals. Their music is used to communicate with the animals and the spirits that they believe inhabit all natural things. Horses, birds, wind, rain, rivers, and grass are elements recreated in Tuvan music.

The late Richard Feynman—author, physicist, philosopher, participant in the Los Alamos project, and one of the true geniuses of the twentieth century (many say the heir to Einstein)—is the one who brought Tuvan throat singing to the attention of the Western music world in 1977. He heard a tape, sent it to his friend, American ethnomusicologist Ted Levin, and the rest is world music history.

THROAT SINGING: XOOMEI

Mongolia and Tuvan music boasts the world's most unusual type of singing called *xoomei* (or *khoomi*), throat singing. The learned technique involves manipulation of the singer's jaw, lips, mouth, and sinuses so as to produce several overtones simultaneously in a low, growling voice akin to the Gyoto Monk chants of Tibet. The music itself is quite simple, with rhythms that mimic horses cantering. With the emergence of world music supergroup Huun Huur Tu, Tuvan throat singing has traveled around the globe, beloved by everyone who hears it.

INSTRUMENTS

The most common instruments heard in Mongolian music include:

- *Morin khuur*: A horse-headed violin played like a cello;
- *Yoochin*: Related to the dulcimer;
- *Thobshuu*: A two-string lute;
- *joochin:* Hammer dulcimer;
- *igil:* Two-string fiddle;
- *doshdpuluur*: Lute.

RECOMMENDED CDs

CHIRGILCHEN. Tuvan group now working in Moscow managed by Alexander Bapa, one of the founders of Huun Huur Tu. *The Wolf and the Kid* (Shanachie, 1996).

EGSCHIGLEN. A classical band affiliated with a conservatory. *Sounds of Mongolia* (Arc, 2001); *Zazal* (Dunya, 2002). More refined than Huun Huur Tu or Yat-Kha.

HUUN HUUR TU. Originally led by singer Kaigal-ool Khovalg and Albert Kuvesin, the name of the band refers to the vertical separation of light rays seen on the grasslands just after sunrise or just before sunset. This is the band that popularized Tuvan throat singing. *60 Horses in My Herd* (Shanachie, 1994); *Orphan's Lament* (Shanachie, 1995) of course it's the throat singing.

IGOR KOSHKENDEY. *Music from Tuva* (Amiata, 1998) accessible, sounds like songs from the Old West.

SAINKHO NAMTCHYLAK. A rare female Tuvan throat singer who mixes traditional instruments and singing with turntables and effects; a cross between Björk and Yoko Ono with a Mongolian bent. *Stepmother City* (Ponderosa, 2002) is accessible and spiritual with duduk, dumbek, shakuhachi flute, slack key guitar, soprano saxophone, loops; beyond eclectic.

PAUL PENA. 1960s blues and R&B artist who went blind and into obscurity for 30 years before he learned Tuvan throat singing from a short wave radio and traveled to Tuva and won the national singing contest. The Documentary film *Ghengis Blues* made from that trip, is a trip, and a must for any music lover. New Train (Hybrid, 2000). Not Tuvan but remarkable.

YAT-KHA. Unlike most of their countrymen, Yat-Kha doesn't want to just keep the past alive; they want to integrate it into a musical future. The guitar plays a very important part, played by bandleader Albert Kuvezin. *Yenisei Punk* (Yat-kha, 2002); *Dalai Beldiri* (RCA, 1999) is ambient.

PAKISTAN

Pakistan is a nation in south-central Asia, loosely divided into four linguistic and cultural regions: Punjab, Sindi, Baluchistan, and the Northwest Frontier. Sind is wholly Pakistani while Baluchis also live in Iran, Punjabi's in India, and the frontier extends to Afghanistan.

Pakistan became an independent nation in 1947, previously comprising most of the Muslim region of India. The word *Pakistan* is an Urdu (the national language) term meaning *land of the pure*. Historically at the crossroads of Asia, Pakistan is aligned with Islamic neighbors Afghanistan and Iran. Since independence, ongoing conflicts with India have maintained extreme tension in the region, especially since Pakistan and India have acquired nuclear capability. At this writing, the dispute over Kashmir had subsided and the two nations were in a ceasefire and negotiating a settlement of many outstanding issues. Pakistan today is a hotbed of Islamic fundamentalism, home to the Madrasas, "schools" that teach nothing but the Koran.

THE MUSIC

The censure of music by Islamism has greatly restricted musicians from performing in Pakistan and music is discouraged except for ceremonial use. As is the case in much of the Muslim world, however, Sufism receives an official exception to the rule. As a result, one of the great musical genres of world music, *Qawwali*, has thrived in Pakistan along with strong folk and classical traditions.

QAWWALI

Qawwali is purported to be the voice of Divine Power, and the term itself means "utterance." It is devotional music of the Sufis, the mystical sect of Islam. The music is thought to elevate the spirit and bring both the artist and audience closer to Allah by inducing a trance-like state. The trance is attained by repetition of words and phrases until all meaning is exhausted and only the form remains and a universal understanding transcending all language, allowing the participants to achieve mystical knowledge.

Qawwali is said to have originated with the founding of the Chisti order of the Sufis in Khorasan, Iran, in the early tenth century and was brought to the subcontinent in the thirteenth century. Traditional qawwali performances are heard at gatherings of the brotherhoods and at shrines. The singer is called the *qawwal*. Traditional ensembles include a vocal soloist, a chorus, several harmoniums (small reed organs), and a *dholak* or *tabla* drum played with the flat hand, unlike the fingertip style of Indian tabla players. The music is performed at all major religious ceremonies and today in many secular settings. Modern qawwali features a rhythmic recitation called Taran, originally used for esoteric religious expression, now a nonsensical singing similar to scat singing in jazz. Traditional languages used include Farsi, *braj bhash* (an ancient form of Hindi), Punjabi, Urdu, and Arabic.

The late Ustad Nusrat Fatch Ali Khan almost single-handedly popularized qawwali in the west and is widely considered to be the greatest exponent of qawwali in the latter part of the twentieth century. Nusrat came from a respected musical family. His father, Ustad Fatch Ali Khan, was a classical musician and master qawwal who exposed Nusrat to Sufi poetry in Farsi, Punjabi, and Urdu at an early age. A 1972 performance at a Sufi festival in Lahore made Nusrat a star. Nusrat's true contribution to the music is that he made radical changes to the classical form, bringing it successfully to a modern audience, synthesizing the old and the new. His passing in 1997 at age 49 resonated throughout the subcontinent.

GHAZALS

Ghazals are love poems sung in Urdu. They are a synthesis of Farsi-language songs from Persia, brought to India by the Mughals and set in their indigenous Indian languages. As a lyric genre, the ghazal has its roots in classical Arabic poetry. Ghazal is an Arabic word that literally means "talking to women." It grew from the Persian *qasida*, a verse form that came to Iran from Arabia around the tenth century BCE.

Ghazals are soothing, lyrical, and lush. A Ghazal is composed of 5–11 rhyming couplets called *sher*. The first verse, called the matla, sets the mood, and each sher is an independent entity. When the couplet reaches the rhyme, it finishes the thought and reveals the beauty of the sher, usually through a modulation.

Other vocal styles from India including *khyal* are prominent in Pakistan as well and are covered in the Indian section.

INSTRUMENTS

Pakistan shares many of the same musical instruments with India (see separate listing). These are among the most common:

- *Dholak*: Double headed drum;
- *Duff:* Handstruck frame drum;

- *Harmonium:* Brought to Pakistan and India by Western missionaries, the free reed keyboard is played by the right hand while the left works the bellows;
- *Idiophones:* Bells, cymbals, clappers, and castanets;
- *Rabab:* A plucked lute, popular in Afghanistan and Baluchistan. The unfretted rabab is a predecessor to the sarod;
- *Sarangi:* Bowed lute;
- *Surna:* Double reed, also known as the *shahna,* a 7–8 hole bamboo instrument;
- *Tabla:* Hand drum.

RECOMMENDED CDs

IQBAL BANO. Fine semi-classical singer specializing in thumri, ghazals, and geets. *Gulistan Vol. 3, 4* (Music Today, 1993); *Ghazals* (Music Today, 1994); backed by Sabir Khan on sarangi and Azhid Khan on harmonium.

JUNOON. Junoon means "obsession" in Urdu. Junoon is a pop-rock band that is loved throughout Pakistan, especially among cricket fanatics. *Azadi* (EMI, 1997). World beat; sufi rock.

MEHDI HASAN. Leading light classical vocalist. *Classical Ghazals* (Navras, 2000/1990) is a triple-CD set that presents a selection of ghazals and other classical song forms such as thumri, dadra, and a Rajasthani folk song.

NOOR JEHAR. Often compared to Lata Mangeshkar, Jehar made her film debut in India in the 1930s. Jehar's vocals were dubbed onto numerous films between 1947 and 1980. *Latest Songs of Noor Jehhan* (EMI Pakistan); *Magic Moments* (EMI India).

NUSRAT ALI FATEH KHAN. One of the giants of world music. *In Concert in Paris: 5 Volumes* (Ocora, 1985/87) is available individually, one of his very best; *Live in London* (Navras, 1989) is a 3 CD set of traditional qawwali; *Shaabaaz* (Caroline, 1992), expanding the boundaries of qawwali; rockin' for the West.

SALAMAT ALI KHAN. When legendary film director Satyajit Ray was selecting singers for his 1958 movie *Jalsaghar,* he picked the young Salamat Ali Khan to sing the khyal parts. The Ali Khan family represents a 500-year lineage from the Shamcharasi

Gharana. Salamat is a legendary vocalist throughout the Indian subcontinent. *Raga Gunkali/Saraswati/Durga* (Nimbus, 1991) is intense and soulful khyal vocals with his sons; *Ragu Megh/Raga Bairagi Bhairav* (Hannibal, 1988/1970) with his late brother Nazakat.

SHAFQAT ALI KHAN. One of the great Salamat's sons. *Sacrifice to Love* (Real World 47707, 1999); *People's Colony No 1* (Real World, 2001); *A Better Destiny* (Real World 10618, 2002).

AZIZ MIAN. Mian expresses the idiom's harder edge, with more recitative, more dramatic diction, and a leaning toward the religious rather than entertainment aspect of the qawwali. Accompaniments include sitar, violin, harmonium, tablas. *Greatist Hits Vol. 1* (Sirocco).

ABIDA PARVEEN. Queen of Sufi mystic singing, one of the most prominent contemporary exponents of the great ghazal and kafi musical styles from the Indian subcontinent. Born in 1954, Abida was initially trained by Ustad Salamat Ali Khan of the Sham Chorasia gharana (school). Abida is not a qawwali singer per se, but gets her devotional inspiration from Sufi poets. *Visal* (World Village, 2002); *Paigham-e-Mohabbat by Muzaffar Ali* (Navras Records); *Jahan-e Khusrau by Muzaffar Ali* (Navras, 2000).

RIZWAN MUAZZAM QAWWALI. These nephews of Nusrat Fateh Ali Khan come from a direct family line of Qawwali vocal music that spans over five centuries. Their inventive reinterpretations of love songs based upon Sufi texts were first showcased in 1998 at the WOMAD Festival in Great Britain. *Sacrifice to Love* (Real World, 1999); *Better Destiny* (Real World, 2002).

SABRI BROTHERS. Pakistan's best known family of devotional singers, hailing from Kalyana in the East Punjab, with over 30 years of singing experience. *Ya Habib* (Real World, 1990); *Ya Mustapha* (Xenophile, 1996); *Jami* (Piranha, 1999); *Qawwali Masterworks* (Piranha, 1993).

SANJEEV AND KARUNA. Ghazal singers who present the art form in a truly accessible manner, especially for westerners. *Inspiration Unfolding* (Times Square, 2001) with Afghan Rabab master Khaled Arman, founder of Radio Kabul and tabla master Ikram Khan.

ZARSANGA. A rare female vocalist from Peshawar. *Songs of the Pashtu* (Long Distance, 1995) Folk songs from the region, parts Afghani, Pakistani, and Iranian in style, backed with rebab and Chants. *Pashtour du Pakistan* (Ocora).

PHILIPPINES

Centuries of Spanish rule had two profound effects on Philippine society: The widespread conversion of the population to Roman Catholicism, and the creation of a landed elite. During colonial rule, the traditional village leaders and chiefs became an elite class of privileged nobility on whom most of the rural population became dependent. A class of tenants without land was created, a division in Philippine society that has been the source of social and political strife ever since. The commercialization of Philippine agriculture and the economic expansion that followed further divided the classes, also giving Chinese mestizo merchants in the provincial centers economic power over the indigenous people.

UNITED STATES INFLUENCE

In April 1898, the United States declared war on Spain. The Battle of Manila Bay was the first hostile engagement of the Spanish-American War, and on May 1, 1898, the United States destroyed the Spanish fleet. Filipino rebels routed the demoralized Spanish forces in the provinces and laid siege to Manila. Independence was proclaimed on June 12, 1898. In truth, Spain ceded the Philippines to the United States, who exercised control over the island nation until well after World War II.

Following true independence in 1962, the Philippines has experienced growing pains as a sovereign nation. Filipinos suffered under the repressive regime of Dictator Ferdinand Marcos, who literally raped the country and left it bankrupt. His democratically elected successor, Corason Aquino, widow of slain populist leader Benigno Aquino, who was shot in the back by Marcos's henchmen, began the road back to spiritual and economic recovery. Today, the Philippines has lessened its long dependency on the United States and enjoys true independence.

THE MUSIC

The Filipino music scene is obsessed with American music and one hears it all over the island. Jazz, rock, hip-hop, and R&B are all the rage. Because of the large segment of the population that speaks English, many top Filipino musicians work in Japan, where they crave the sound of American music sung in English.

There is some traditional music from the islands, mostly from Mindanao, although very little is recorded. In the 1920s, Filipino musicians adapted traditional songs to Western styles resulting in a ballad genre called *kundiman*. In the late 1950s, native performers wrote *Tagalog* (the main language of the Philippines) lyrics for American rock music, resulting in the beginnings of *Pinoy* rock that survives today.

The Philippines musical culture blends Eastern and Western influences. Traditional Philippine music centers on gamelan music played on *kulingtan* gongs, influenced by Indonesia and music derived from the Spanish era. The *git-git* (a violin with strings of human hair) and the *hagalong*, a set of pitched brass or bronze gongs usually played on festive occasions, are traditional instruments still in used on Mindanao.

RECOMMENDED CDs

FREDDIE AGUILAR. The leading musician in Manila and best-known Filipino musician in the world. Aguilar began performing cover songs and original material for United States military personnel stationed on the islands. He wrote several anti-Marcos songs in the 1980s, including *Bayan Ko*, which became the theme song for Cory Aquino's election campaign in 1986. *Freddie Aguilar: Live Vol. 1–3* (Aguilar, 1997).

JOEY AYALA. From Mindanao, Ayala is the one musician who focuses on ethnic Filipino instruments and music, albeit with a rock sensibility. *Lupa't Langit* (Star, 1997). Gongs, lutes, and bamboo flutes combine with electric piano and guitar.

GRACE NONO. Indigenous music doesn't have a wide following in the Philippines, but Grace has incorporated ethnic influences into her music and is the leading female vocalist of the islands. *Tao Music* (Musiko, 1993); *Opo* (Musiko, 1995).

THAILAND

When China was conquered by the Mongols circa 1253, the Thais ("free") fled to Laos, North Vietnam, and modern Thailand. The Thais conquered Cambodia at Angkor in 1431, and were civilized by their Khmers captives. Thailand is bordered by Burma, Laos, Cambodia, and Malaysia and is the only country in Southeast Asia never to have been colonized or taken over by a European or Asian power. Thailand served as a buffer state between British Burma and French Indochina throughout the twentieth century, and, until recently, the music and culture of Thailand has had little Westrn influence.

Formerly known as Siam, Thailand changed its name permanently in 1949. Thailand was loosely aligned with Japan during World War II, but became a United States ally shortly after the war and achieved democracy in 1980 after a series of coups and military rule. Ethnic Thais make up three-quarters of the population but the ethnic Chinese have historically played a significant role in the economy. Music is an integral part of life throughout Thailand, especially in secular and religious ceremonies. Although there is a classical tradition, folk and traditional country genres are the true essence of Thai music. The majority of Thais are Buddhists who revere music as part of their spritual existence.

THE MUSIC

Luk thung is Thailand's ubiquitous country music, which chronicles the life and troubles of the rural population. Luk thung is a recent phenomenon, a popular style based on traditional styles, and developed after World War II. Many luk thung stars come from the central city of Suphanbur, including Pompuang Duangjan, Thailand's most famous and popular female lukthung singer. who died in 1992 at the age of 31.

Mor lam is the predominant folk music from the northeast region of Isan where there is a large Laotian population; mor lam is essntially Latotian music. It is influenced by luk thung but is characterized by rapid-fire, rhythmic pulse played on the khaen, an indigenous bamboo mouth organ that is the signature sound of the genre.

Royal Thai court music has always been important in ceremonies and as entertainment. When the monarchy came to an end in 1932,

Thai classical music was no longer limited to the royal court. Due to a fascination with Western music after World War II, Thai classical music was not widely heard until the 1970s, and now is primarily played at tourist attractions.

Percussion instruments include finger cymbals and larger hand cymbals, castanet-type clappers, the *ranatek* and *ranat thum* (high- and low-pitched xylophones), gongs, and single and double-headed drums.

Woodwind instruments include flute, recorder, the *pinai*, a double-reed instrument similar to an oboe, and the *khaen*, a large bamboo mouth organ with 14 tubes, each containing a small, metal reed. The khaen is the most important instrument in mor lam music of northern Thailand and Laos. It is a relative of the Chinese *sheng*, the *sho* of Japan, and the *saenghwang* of Korea. String instruments include a three-stringed zither, the *phin*, a lute-like guitar, a three-stringed spike fiddle (held vertically), and a hammered dulcimer.

Fixed pitch instruments (xylophones and small gongs) play seven tones to the octave, equidistant, although tuning varies greatly. *Pong lang* is a suspended vertical wooden xylophone whose keys are arranged upside down, with the low notes on the upper end.

The main traditional ensemble is called the *piphat* (pee-PAWT), which includes percussion, cymbals, large gong, drums, and the pinai.

As is the case in much of East Asia, Thailand has a vibrant rock and pop scene that mimics the western genre, replete with electric guitars, trap drums, pop idolatry, and attitude.

RECOMMENDED CDs

CARABOU. Prior to their breakup in the early 1990s, Carabou was one of the most popular groups in Thailand. *Made in Thailand* (1987) contains cryptic attacks on capitalism and the government.

CHAWIWAN DAMNOEN. Isaan's greatest female mor lam singer. *Music of Northeast Thailand; Mo Lam singing of Northeast Thailand* (World Music Library, 1991).

POMPUANG DUANGJAN. Thailand's greatest and most popular singer. *Li Bor Sor: Many Years* (Toplin, 1994).

SAMAN HONGSA. Music from northeast Thailand sung by a husband-and-wife team with traditional instruments but a modern approach. *Isan Slete* (Globestyle).

KHAMVONG INSIXIENGMAI. Melodies from Laos with singers Khamvong Insixiengmai and Thongxhio Manisone supported by khaen, phin (plucked lute) and cymbals. *Bamboo Voices: Folk Music from Laos* (Music of the World, 1999).

FONG NAAM. Pi-pha ensemble started by expatriated American Bruce Gaston. *Nam Hong Funeral Music of Siam* (Nimbus, 1993); *Sleeping Angel* (Nimbus, 1991) is Classical music with a modern sensibility and occasional use of jazz motifs.

ENSEMBLE SI NUAN THUNG PONG. *Chang Saw: Village Music of Northern Thailand* (Pan, 2000).

JINTARA POONLARP. Female mor lam singer with a husky voice, rootsy and real. *Suyasisongolan* (Farside, 1998) is Jintara's rootsiest album.

PORNSACK SONGSAENG. Male mor lam singer. *Saochanganko* (Farside). Phin, gentle grooves, one of Thailand's most popular male singers.

VARIOUS ARTISTS. *Rough Guide to Thailand.* As usual, the most comprehensive review of current Thai music, highlighted by the Thai Elephant Orchestra with actual elephants playing musical instruments with their trunks to remarkable effect, although the group doesn't travel well. *Loyal Court Music of Thailand* (Smithsonian, 1994).

TIBET

Tibet has historically been influenced by three civilizations: Turko-Mongolian, Chinese, and Indian. Its ancient tradition has developed in isolation from the rest of the civilized world, embracing a way of life and a music all its own. Tibet is home to Buddhism, enlightenment, meditation, and a peaceful existence as pure as the snow atop the lofty Himalayas. The Dalai Lama is the spiritual leader of Tibet, the Buddha incarnate and a beloved symbol of nonviolent resistance worldwide. In exile he continues to lead the government from India, spreading Tibet's special message of peace, discipline, and spirituality.

Tibet was almost totally destroyed by the Communist Chinese invasion in 1950 and the struggle continues into the twenty-first century. There once were 6,000 Buddhist monasteries in Tibet; now there are only a few. Much of Tibet's folk and art song history is rapidly vanishing as the Chinese occupation insidiously disassembles Tibetan culture with a clear eye toward eradicating anything Tibetan. Tacky karaoke clubs are the rage in Lhasa, with the usual repertory of Western pop songs.

Tibetan music now comes largely from outside Tibet: from Nepal, Bhutan, Sikkin, and the Ladakh regions of the Himalayas. Nevertheless, music plays an important part in all Tibetan life and has three aspects:

- Folk music, which is part of the daily life of Tibetans.
- Art music, performed by professional musicians and minstrels.
- Sacred chant and instrumental music of the Buddhist liturgy centered in the monasteries..

CHANT

Chant is the music used by monks to recite sacred texts such as the sutras (teachings of Buddha) and the tantras (secret commentaries). Chants are sometimes free but more usually metrical. The close-throated, constricted voice style is common, usually deep in pitch, which is deliberate and contrary to the normal speaking voices of the monks.

Chanting varies from monotone to a melodic style, always based on a mode (from three to seven notes), and is characterized by a glissando effect. Traditional chant is performed by a single monk in private, by a choir of monks, or by laity in services conducted by monks. Chant is usually accompanied by an orchestra (*passim*), which consists exclusively of wind instruments played in pairs, and percussion instruments of indefinite pitch. Stringed instruments are found only in the secular music. The style and nature of Chant varies from one monastery to another. *Gyu-ke* is a tantric chant and *dzoke* is a type of yang chanting emulating the voice of the yak.

FOLK SONGS

Tibetans have songs for many aspects of life, from working to drinking. *Lu* is an ancient tradition, sung a cappella in a high voice.

Nangma and *toshe* are elegant, secular song genres accompanied by lute (dramnyen), dulcimer (gyuimang), and flute (lingbu).

INSTRUMENTS

The most common instruments in Tibetan music include:

- *rgayling*: A double reed, oboe/shawm type instrument that carries the melody in orchestras;
- *damaru*: Hour glass drum now made from wood, but previously made from a human skull;
- *dramnyen*: Lute;
- *drilbu*: A hand bell played with a hand drum;
- *dung:* A long, metal trumpet which played alone or with the orchestra; larger versions are like a didgeridoo;
- *dung-dkar*: A conch shell trumpet, part of the orchestra.
- *gyumang*: Dulcimer;
- *lingbu:* Flute;
- *mkar-rnga*: Gong;
- *piwang*: Fiddle;
- *rgna*: Drum supported on a pole or suspended in a frame, struck with a crooked stick;
- *rkangling*: A short horn now made of metal but formerly made of a human thigh bone;
- *rolmo*: Large cymbals;
- *silnyen*: Small cymbals;

NEW AGE

Before the western notion of new age had developed, Tibet *was* new age. Commercial artists such as Japan's Kitaro have capitalized on the tranquility of the soothing repetition of the Tibetan way. Many CDs listed below may seem "new agey" at first, but upon repeated listening the eloquence of the music comes through.

RECOMMENDED CDs

DADAWA. Rare musical artists from mainland China to release an international vocal album, she draws on Tibetan culture, though she has been called the Chinese Enya. *Voices from the Sky* (Sire, 1988).

DIP TSE CHOK LING MONASTERY. Chanting since the 1700s, now in exile in Dharamsala, India. *Sacred Ceremonies Volume 2: Tantric Hymns of Tibetan Buddhism* (Fortuna/Celest, 1990) is a great recording, as fulfilling as the Gyuto recordings.

CHOYING DROLMA. Daughter of Tibetan exiles in Katmandu, Nepal, who taught mediation, chants, and ceremonies under Tulku Urgyen Rinpoche, and was his personal assistant until his death in 1996. *Cho* (Hannibal, 1997) is chant with synthesizer.

GYUTO MONKS. The Monks from the Gyuto Tantric University fled Tibet with the Dalai Lama and settled in Northern India to work for world peace and freedom for their homeland. They have been chanting in their low, guttural, multi-tonal style since 1474. *Freedom Chants from the Roof of the World* (Rykodisc, 1989) recorded by Mickey Hart.

NAWANG KHECHOG. A monk for 11 years and a hermit for 4, he fled Tibet in 1949. He is a multi-instrumentalist with a pre-new age, new age sound. *Karuna* (Domo, 1995), the title means compassion in Sanskrit, produced by Kitaro; *Sounds of Peace* (Sounds True, 1996).

YUNGCHEN LLAMO. Llamo fled Tibet in 1989, an outspoken advocate for her country and culture, and Tibet's leading female vocalist and a world music star. *Coming Home* (Real World, 1998).

KELSANG CHUKIE TETHON. Beautiful female vocalist who studied at the Tibetan Institute of Performing Arts before expatriating in 1996. Now an activist opposing Chinese hegemony. *Voice from Tara* (Narada, 2004). Highly recommended.

VIETNAM

Ruled by their Chinese archenemies for more than ten centuries, Vietnam is one of the oldest cultures in the world with an ancient musical traditional that emanates from the gorgeous city of Hue, the artistic heart of the country located in central Vietnam. Much of the traditional music has tragically faded into antiquity, a victim of colonization and abuse by the French and political exploitation by the United States of an ancient culture that refused to capitulate to the Western agenda.

Vietnam is a densely populated country—not much larger than New Jersey, it is home to 100 million people—and has recently entered the global economy. Since the opening of the North in the mid-1990s, it has become a hot tourist destination, rife with foreign investment due to the industrious, aggressive, competent nature of the Vietnamese people.

THE MUSIC

Because the separation of classes in Vietnam is minimal, folk and art music share many traits and are more similar to each other than in Western cultures. Generally the folk music is purely vocal and art music both vocal and instrumental. Folk songs are still chanted in the fields, unaccompanied and sung during work.

The only places to hear traditional music in Vietnam are tourist venues. In Hanoi the music can be heard at the renowned Water Puppet Theater, the Cheo Theater, Ho Chi Minh's House on Stilts, at the Temple of Literature, and at a select few restaurants. An official, standardized version of traditional music has been taught at the conservatories in Hanoi and Ho Chi Minh City since the 1970s. Sadly, most of the older, pure traditional styles have passed out of existence without being recorded.

The old capital city *Hue* (hway) is known for its beautiful singing. Singers often accompany themselves using pairs of small teacups as castanets. Visitors to Hue can hear a private concert performed by an ensemble of instrumentalists and singers by taking a moonlight cruise on the Perfume River on a Dragon Boat.

Cai Luoung is a traditional theatre genre dating back only to 1917, based on Vietnamese and French disciplines, which provides a foundation for folk music today. In addition to the traditional music of the Viet majority, there are 53 ethnic minorities, each with their own localized musical traditions, languages, singing styles, and instruments. The Vietnam Musicology Institute's website (listed below) is a good place to explore all the music of Vietnam.

INSTRUMENTS

The *dan bau* (monochord) is the most distinctive Vietnamese traditional instrument. It is a monochord (one-stringed instrument) played by plucking the string at the harmonic nodes, and bending the pitch with a water buffalo horn also known as a "whammy bar." The sound has an inhuman vocal quality and resonates for a long time.

Other traditional instruments include: *dan tranh* (17-string zither); *dan nguyet* (2-string moon lute); *dan nhi* (fiddle); *ken* (oboe); *dan trung* (bamboo xylophone); *ko noi* (stick fiddle); and various drums.

RECOMMENDED CDs

DAN CA. Folksingers of Banar. *Ba Nar* (Vietnam Musicology Institute) Strictly traditional ensemble from the north, with some vocals.

KHAC CHI. A leading, traditional ensemble based in Vancouver, Canada. Named after Ho Khac Chi, a *dàn bau* virtuoso and singer. *Moonlight in Vietnam* (Henry Street, 1997) is music from all over Vietnam, including Xa and Meo in the North. *Spirit of Vietnam* (Jericho Beach, 1999).

NGUYEN LE. Born in Paris, Le is the most visible Vietnamese musician on the world music scene, a prominent guitarist who has worked with Rai Star Cheb Mami, jazz bassist Marc Johnson, drummer Peter Erskine, and others. On *Tales from Vietnam* (Act, 1996) Western Jazz meets Eastern tradition, with Huong Thanh on vocals.

PHONG NGUYEN. Phong plays the dan tranh and dan nguyet. He left Saigon in 1974, moved to France, and studied at the Sorbonne, obtaining a degree in Ethnomusicology in 1982. *Song of the Banyan* (Music of the World, 1997); *Vietnamese Music* (World Music Institute).

THE PERFUME RIVER TRADITIONAL ENSEMBLE. *Music from the Lost Kingdom: Hue Vietnam* (Lyrichord, 1998). Highly recommended.

STILLING TIME. *Stilling Time* (Innova, 1997) with Anh Tu, Lute; Ai Ho, vocals, bells; Mac Thi Cau, Vocals; and Thang Long, reed pipes. Traditional.

HUONG THANH. Excellent traditional female singer making a name in the West. *Moon and Wind* and *Dragonfly* were recorded in Nguyen Le's studio in the Barbes section of Paris. Huong has dual citizenship with France (she has a Corsican grandfather) and settled in Marseilles in 1977.

PHAM DUC THANH. Highly acclaimed dan bau specialist residing in Montreal. *Vietnamese Traditional Music* (Oliver Sudden, 1997); *Vietnamese Traditional Dan Bau Music* (Oliver Sudden, 2002).

COMPILATION. *From Hanoi to Saigon* (Milan, 2001). A sampler of various artists in traditional settings with a few vocal tracks.

WEBSITE: The Vietnam Musicology Institute has numerous CDs and DVDs of traditional music, as well as a museum of instruments. Check: www.vnstyle.vdc.com.vn/vim/english/information/cd.html for detailed information about Vietnamese music.

NORTH AND CENTRAL AMERICA AND THE CARIBBEAN

Antilles	El Salvador	Nicaragua
Belize	Guatemala	Panama
Canada	Haiti	Puerto Rico
Costa Rica	Honduras	Trinidad and Tobago
Cuba	Jamaica	United States
Dominican Republic	Mexico	

In this book, "North America" is rather broadly defined to include Canada, the Caribbean, Central America, Mexico, and the United States. Within these major divisions, we will discuss a wide variety of musical styles and cultures.

CANADA

Canada was settled in the seventeenth and eighteenth century by European colonizers, primarily from Britain and France. It is not surprising, then, that the two most thriving "indigenous" musical traditions are drawn from these cultures: The Scottish/Celtic tradi tions of the Cape Breton-eastern Canadian provinces; and the French traditions of Quebec. However, like the United States, Canada is increasingly becoming a multicultural melting pot, a home to a variety of world music cultures, particularly over the last few decades.

CAPE BRETON AND THE KITCHEN TRADITION

The Celtic presence continues to dominate the eastern provinces of New Brunswick, Newfoundland, and Nova Scotia where the Scots and the Irish have always thrived, particularly in the Cape Breton region, Canada's hotbed for world music.

The Scottish connection to the Cape Breton region of eastern Canada is profound. The Celtic enclave that has made North America home for more than a century is responsible for Canada's most established world music, a distinct brand of Scottish Celtic sound based on a strong fiddling tradition led by Buddy and Natalie MacMaster and Ashley MacIsaac.

QUEBECOIS AND FRENCH CANADIAN FOLK

Quebec is virtually a separate country, not merely in its ongoing political desire to secede from Canada, but in the very depths of its collective French persona. The language, cuisine, music, art, and basic lifestyle in Quebec are more akin to rural France than anywhere else in Canada. From Papineauville in the Laurentians to Montreal; from Magog to Quebec City, the province is staunchly French. If the Iroquois hadn't sided with the English to help defeat them in the northeast, New England might be French today.

The music of Quebec drew only sporadic interest in Canada during the latter part of the twentieth century, but this is all rapidly changing. Spawned by the success of the folk-rock group *La Bottine Souriante* (the Smiling Boot), a plethora of new, mostly young, talented musicians are now playing traditional, folk, and world styles, and the music is evolving by leaps and bounds. While the media is still behind, the region is beginning to get some long deserved attention. Local folk is combined with a Celtic-country style reminiscent of the music of Brittany.

FOLK ROCK

Canada's musical image has been historically tied to its American big brother when it comes to popular music. Joni Mitchell, Neil

Young, Stephen Stills, Levon Helm (and members of the Band), Gordon Lightfoot, the McGarrigle Sisters, and many others are closely associated with the American folk-rock movement of the '1960s and '1970s, and rarely identified as Canadian.

THE CANADIAN WORLD MUSIC SCENE TODAY

Since the early 1980s—thanks to its open immigration policy—Canada has become a home to many world cultures. Enclaves of Eastern Europeans and Middle Easterners have established a stronghold in Toronto and throughout Ontario. The Japanese are increasingly part of the human landscape in British Columbia. As the Canadian melting pot continues to expand, Slavic, Asian, and Middle Eastern Canadians are creating one of the most fertile "new" world music scenes anywhere.

One of the true supergroups on the planet, La Bottine Souriante "does it all—Celtic, Cajun, jazz, reggae, bluegrass, Quebecois; they perform on mandolins, violins, saxophones, brass, accordions, guitars; featuring tight vocal harmonies—with power, style, and élan. The band has the drive of the great Paul Butterfield blues bands of the late '1960s, the polished brass of Blood, Sweat, & Tears, the Celtic sensibility of the Chieftains (with whom they have collaborated), the contemporary swagger of the eclectic French group LoJo, a reverence for the hoedown, and a healthy respect for Serge Gainsbourg.

Led by vocalist/accordionist Yves Lambert (not the Habs hockey player) and foot percussionist Michel Bordeleau (who has recently set out to pursue a solo career), this is a group not to be missed if they come your way. They have been recording for almost 30 years and are still going strong. *La Mistrine*, from 1994, is the North American roots music equivalent of *Sgt. Pepper's Lonely Hearts Club Band*, a groundbreaking, innovative, seminal recording with deft arrangements, moving ballads, virtuoso ensemble work, and that indescribable foot percussion (*à pied*) that distinguishes everything they do. La Bottine has recorded with many world music groups throughout the world, most recently with Basque trikitixa virtuoso Kepa Junkera. They have literally spawned an entire movement of Quebecois/

Acadian bands who have created one of the most vibrant world music scenes in North America.

RECOMMENDED CDs

BE GOOD TANYAS. This hot folk-rock group from Vancouver is only marginally involved with world music, but their sensibility and concept are reaching a world audience. *Chinatown* (Nettwerk, 2003) presents a delightfully depressing, introspective side of the band, with vocals in the style of Alison Krauss.

LA BOTTINE SOURIANTE (See Profile). *La Mistrine* (Mille Pattes, 1994) is their best; *En Spectacle* (Milles Plattes, 1997) is a dazzling journey of musical chicanery, comedy, and swing; *Je Voudrais Changer d'Chapeau* (Rounder, 1989); *Jusqu'aux P'tites Heures* (Mille Pattes, 1991).

ENTOURLOUPE. The "podorhythms"—foot tapping—accordions and fiddles make the style of this veteran outfit irresistible. *Les Choux pis les melons* (Minuit dans la Cuisin, 2000).

MICHAEL FAUBERT & LES CHARBONNIERS/DE L'ENFER (COALMINERS FROM HELL). Faubert fronts a hot band that includes ex-La Bottine members Michel Bordeleau and Andre Marchand. They perform a cappella with only the traditional foot rhythm as accompaniment. *Wo* (LaTribu, 2002).

GENTICORUM. Traditional and *contradance* music is the thing with this eclectic Quebecois group. *Le Galarneau* (Gent, 2002) contains a series of medleys, a concept that is a general style in Quebec, linking tunes and folk songs in one unbroken performance.

MARY JANE LAMOND. Cape Breton's leading Gaelic vocalist. *Suas e!* (Wicklow, 1997).

DANIEL LANOIS. Eclectic producer from Quebec and former colleague of Brian Eno. *For the Beauty of Wynona* (Warner Bros., 1993) contains cajun, rock, and French Canadian ballads; *Acadie* (Opal, 1989) Acadian roots.

ASHLEY MACISAAC. The Cape Breton fiddle wunderkind is now reaching for a more commercial, international audience. *Ashley MacIsaac* (Decca 2003) is Ashley's unabashed foray into the mainstream. *Helter's Celtic* (Loggerhead 1999); *Hi How Are You Today?* (A & M 1995) put him on the map with a heavy metal mentality.

BUDDY MACMASTER. The dean of Cape Breton fiddling (Natalie's uncle) is famed for his interpretation of ancient Scottish tunes. *Cape Breton Tradition* (2000) traditional, straight ahead fiddling.

NATALIE MACMASTER. Cape Breton's leading female fiddler. Along with Ashley MacIsaac, she carries the torch for Cape Breton music throughout the World. *Your Roots are Showing* (Greentrax, 1998) is traditional and straight-ahead.

CHRIS NORMAN. Classically trained flutist extraordinaire from Nova Scotia who performs with Scottish Group Skyedance. *Man with the Wooden Flute* (Dorian, 1992); *The Caledonian Flute* (Boxwood, 2002) a tour de force with pipes, guitar, bass, and drums.

NOROUET. Led by female vocalist Stephanie Lepine, Norouet is a trio (mandolins, feet percussion, guitars, and bouzoukis) that covers Acadian, Irish, Breton, and French Canadian tunes. *Spirale* (Minuit dans, 2002).

LA VENT DU NORD. Touted as a new supergroup, *Le Vent du Nord* is a lyrical band that excels on accordion and the rarely heard Hurdy Gurdy. *Mandite Moisson* (Borealis 2000).

THE CARIBBEAN

Antilles	Jamaica
Cuba	Puerto Rico
Dominican Republic	Trinidad and Tobago
Haiti	

CARIBBEAN MUSICAL HISTORY

Caribbean music history begins with the tradition of indigenous people who inhabited the islands before the arrival of Europeans. Spanish chronicles describe some of the musical practices, including a ceremony known as *areito* in which participants sang and danced in circles around an ensemble playing *slit-drums* (made from hollowed logs), rattles, and other percussion instruments. By 1600, however, most native Caribbean people had perished, along with their music and culture.

Subsequent Caribbean music emerged as a product of the inter-action between African slaves and European settlers. Scholars draw distinctions between *settler* colonies, such as Cuba and Puerto Rico, and *plantation colonies,* such as those in the British West Indies. The settler colonies attracted large numbers of Europeans and hosted lively *Creole* (mixed race) music cultures. With large free black populations and relatively late ongoing imports of slaves, the settler colonies tended to allow for the preservation and continued vitality of neo-African music practices. In the nineteenth century, the local bourgeoisie in these colonies cultivated lively, nationalistic Creole music culture, encompassing such genres as the *habanera* and *danzón.* In the British plantation colonies, cultural repression appears to have been more severe and, because the slave trade ended earlier, neo-African traditions declined faster. Creole bourgeois music failed to evolve in plantation colonies because of the small number of European residents.

In the twentieth century, the advent of the mass media—particu-larly phonograph records and radio broadcasts—stimulated the emergence of commercial dance music styles, often at the expense of traditional folk music. While these new pop styles were influenced by and in competition with popular music from the United States, they nevertheless flourished by combining North American music with local traditions. By the 1920s, Cuban *son,* Trinidadian *calypso,* Dominican *merengue,* and Haitian *méringue* were thriving as distinct local pop idioms. The Cuban-derived *bolero* became popular throughout much of Latin America by the 1940s. In the 1950s, the big-band format was adapted from American jazz and led to Cuban *mambo,* the Dominican urban *merengue,* and the Puerto Rican *plena,* another distinctive Creole style. Calypso was all the rage in the 1950s, brought to international attention by Harry Belafonte and Mickey and Sylvia, and Jamaican *ska* was popular throughout the islands. Similarly, *beguine,* a variation on the European ballroom dance form, held sway in the Antilles.

By the 1960s smaller ensembles were more common as amplifiers and electric instruments became widely available and bandleaders sought to avoid the high cost of maintaining big bands. During this period, the growing communities of Caribbean immigrants in North American cities came to play crucial roles in the evolution of Caribbean popular music. In particular, New York City emerged as a dynamic center for the production and consumption of Latin and West Indian popular music. In the early 1970s, *salsa* emerged as a highly popular reinterpretation of Cuban dance music and Jamaican *reggae* took the world by storm as a derivative of *ska*. In Haiti, *compas* replaced *mirengue*. In Trinidad, *soca* (soul calypso) replaced *calypso* and in the Antilles *zouk* usurped *beguine*.

Leading performers, including salsa singer Rubén Blades in New York and reggae superstar Bob Marley, promoted a sense of sociopolitical idealism, optimism, and activism through the music and their popularity as charismatic stars. The Mighty Sparrow and Lord Kitchener held the same stature in Trinidad and Tobago, albeit in a less overtly political fashion. By the 1990s however, the dominant Latin music genres in the region were the more sentimental, apolitical *salsa romántica* and the generally light-hearted merengue. Similarly, the 1970s style of "roots reggae" or "foundation reggae" gave way in the 1980s to a new style called dance-hall, which featured boasting, erotic, topical lyrics rapped in a semi-melodic style over driving, repetitive rhythms. During the 1990s, a new generation of talented performers emerged from the Caribbean, including Jamaican dance-hall artist Buju Banton and Dominican singer Juan Luis Guerra.

REGGAE AND SALSA

The two most popular and ubiquitous musical genres from the Caribbean are the subject of a plethora of books, articles, documentaries, and treatises so numerous and extensive that salsa and reggae have become huge genres unto themselves. There are encyclopedias on reggae and salsa that alone exceed the collective books in print that survey world music. These are genres with a following and recorded history that approaches that of rock and jazz. We will only be able to briefly discuss the major players in these styles, and refer the reader (in the bibliography) to several excellent books for further study.

ANTILLES

The French Antilles islands of Martinique and Guadalupe are home to the world famous dance-hall music known as *zouk* (zouk literally means "party"), which took Europe by storm in the 1980s and remains the most popular musical form of the Lesser Antilles. As with most Caribbean islands, Guadalupe and Martinique comprise ancestors of African slaves and remnants of their European colonizers. Zouk was born in the late 1970s from a people whose languages are French and Creole, but whose culture is African. In 1946 the islands ceased to be French colonies, although to this day they retain their own French character.

GWO KA, TWI BA, AND THE BIGUINE

Zouk's development can be traced to Guadeloupan *gwo ka* (a rural drum style) and the Martiniquan *tambour* and *twi ba* traditions (drum and bambo percussion). Gwo ka is percussion music with seven basic rhythms and variations. Tambour/twi ba ensembles are the basis of the Martiniquan *biguine.* The biguine was popular in Europe in the 1920s and 1930s as a ballroom dance music performed in legendary Parisian clubs such as the Bal Negre and the Boule Blanche. On its way to the Caribbean it was modernized and adapted for pop audiences and is now know as *biguine moderne.* Prior to the zouk explosion in the 1980s, the biguine was the prominent musical form of the Lesser Antilles, performed by groups that featured clarinet, trombone, banjo, and drums, similar to the format of jazz bands in New Orleans.

Orchestras from Haiti had a profound influence on French Antillean music with *compas* stars such as Weber Sicot and Nemour Jean-Baptiste enjoying widespread popularity throughout the French-speaking Caribbean. *Boleros* and *son* from Cuba were incorporated over time and dominated until the emergence of world music supergroup Kassav in the 1980s.

The Paris-based, 15-piece band Kassav changed the musical landscape of Guadalupe and Martinique beginning in the early 1980s by creating a rhythmic mixture of compás, calypso, funk, rock, and traditional rhythms from the French West Indies. Their popularity and recordings were greatly enhanced by advanced studio technology that was available to them in Paris, which far surpassed the quality of recordings by all other ensembles from the region. When they adopted a nationalistic tone to their pan-Caribbean and pan-African fusions, they became Antillean idols despite being based abroad. Kassav (which is the name of a cocunut and sugar cake) included a *gwo ka* ensemble in its first studio recording, bringing the tradition into urban music for the first time. The band eventually added rock and roll and established *zouk* as a major dance music genre both in the Caribbean and in France. Zouk's star has fallen dramatically in Paris since the heyday of the 1980s, but remains the music of the French Antilles.

DUTCH ANTILLES

The islands of Curacao, Bonaire, Aruba, St. Eustatius, and St. Martin are known for their local rhythms and bands whose music rarely leaves the islands via recordings. Curacao is the most active center for Dutch Antillean music, which borrows from zouk, soca, and merengue. The South American country of Surinam is conceptually part of the Dutch Antilles and features the native *kaseko* music, developed by Surinamese in their native land as well as in the Netherlands. Kaseko is an upbeat African dance genre that utuilizes modern brass and percussion. Leading proponents include William Souvenir, Yakki Famiri, and Carlo Jones.

RECOMMENDED CDs

JOCELYN BEROARD. Kassav's magnetic lead singer is a world music diva. *Siwo* (Sonodisc, 1987).

KALI. Rastafarian proponent of *biguine moderne* began his career in Martinique's finest reggae band, *Sixième Continent,* exploring roots music from the capital of St. Pierre. *Debranch* (Declic, 1995); *Roots* (Philips, 1991); *Racines Vol. 1 & 2* (Hibiscus, 1989).

GIO FORTISSIMO. Popular, talented Curacao band. *Over Drive* (MAT, 1998).

KASSAV. *Zouk Is the Only Medicine We Have* (Greensleeves, 1988); *Eva* (3A, 1982); *Kassav No. 3* (Wotre, 1981).

MALAVOI. A collective of classically trained musicians that has been recording since the late 1960s playing Creolized European dance forms like the quadrille, mazurka, and waltz along with biguine and charanga. *Live au Zenith* (Blue Silver, 1989); *Marronage* (Tinder, 1999); *Matebis* (Declic, 1992).

RALPH THAMAR. The lead singer for the group Malavol, Thamar's own recordings reveal him to be a techno zouk artist with a hard-edged voice. *Caraibes* (Declic 1991).

JOELL URSULL. Former singer in Zouk Machine. *Miyel* (CBS, 1988); *Black French* (TriStar, 1990).

ZOUK MACHINE. Female vocal trio. *Maldon* (Henri Debs, 1988); *Min Ne Nwen* (LisoMusique, 1987).

CUBA

Throughout the twentieth century, the island nation 90 miles south of the United States mainland has been the heart and soul of African music in the Western hemisphere. Accordingly, Cuba holds very special status in the hierarchy of world music. This status paradoxically has been enhanced by its unique sociopolitical existence since the days of the revolution. During Castro's rule, the essence of Cuba's remarkable music has not only survived, but has evolved with virtually no influence from the 800-pound gorilla that is the American music industry. While certain segments of Cuban society fled to Miami or Mexico and continued to produce music, the greatest artists remained on the island maintaining the purity and historical integrity of the traditional music.

Cuban artists have enjoyed widespread popularity throughout Latin America, Europe, and Africa for decades despite going virtually unheard in the United States until 1993. Since the loosening of relations between the United States and Cuba, the island has been invaded by world-music entrepreneurs. As a result, the music is now widely available on the global market backed by United States marketing money and energy. It is all for the good so far; Cuba remains a musical treasure island, a major source of important world music.

AFRO-CUBA

In the late nineteenth century, Cuban music began to combine Yoruban and Santerian religious rituals with West African rhythms and sounds creating forms known as *son, guajira, habanera, bolero, rumba, danzon,* and eventually *salsa.* Except for Belizean *paranda,* a music with virtually no Western influence that is uncannily similar to traditional Cameroonian music, Cuba is the place where the African diaspora has most successfully kept its musical identity intact in the Western Hemisphere.

African slaves were seminal influences in virtually all folk and urban port music that emerged in South America, southern Europe, and the Caribbean in the nineteenth and early twentieth century, but it is in Cuba, more than any other western slave-trading country, where the purest rhythms and spirit of Africa have survived and flourished. More than jazz, tango, fado, flamenco, choro, and samba—all African-*derived* musical forms— Cuban music remains essentially African. Not surprisingly, Cuban music has been highly influential on contemporary African musical styles, a modern day recycling or recapturing of indigenous musical forms.

Cuba's unique stature and relationship to Africa is recognized on both sides of the Atlantic. Early Congolese pop from the 1940s and 1950s leaned on Cuban (i.e., borrowed African) rhythms heavily, particularly adopting the term *rumba.* Recent projects undertaken by numerous African groups have successfully and seamlessly retrieved Cuban sounds in creating modern African world music (see the West African sections). Whatever you call it, wherever it came from, Cuban music is an integral part of the world-music vocabulary.

As the political climate between Cuba and the Untied States continues to defrost, more and more music from the island has become available. Although there has been a large expatriated Cuban population in Florida for over 40 years, their music tends toward salsa and American pop and has distanced itself from the true Cuban persona. It can be great music, but is quite frankly not "the real thing." Castro has always permitted artists to record music, especially in the state operated EGREM studios, and the evolution of the traditional sound has not stopped.

SEPTETO IGNACIO PINEIRO AND SEXTETO HABANERA

Ignacio Pineiro gained his place in Cuban musical history by introducing trumpet to the traditional son bands in the late 1920s, creating a new sonic possibility to accompany the percussion (conga, bongo, djembe) bass-tres (a guitar with three sets of paired strings) format. His innovations immediately caught on, forcing archrival Sexteto Habanera to adapt a similar format. Pineiro was a friend and significant influence on George Gershwin and is a revered figure among the Cuban music cognoscenti. The septeto format remains the classic configuration of Cuban son to this day.

BENY MORE, ARSENIO, AND MAMBO

Beny More was the original "Mambo King," the voice of the music that was to evolve into salsa. He was a fast-living, high-rolling crooner, a slick-dressing teen idol, who died in his early 40s in 1963. His collaborations with pianist/maestro Perez Prado in the mid-1950s (including time in Mexico City) was a partnership that formed the backbone of the mid-century Cuban sound.

Arsenio Rodriguez, the blind tres player, composer and bandleader, is widely considered the most influential figure in the conjunto movement of the late 1940s, an innovator who is credited with starting the mambo form. Rodriguez combined deep-rooted African sounds (his ancestors were Congolese slaves), with sophisticated brass arrangements. Long-time collaborator and legendary trumpeter Felix Chappotin, pianists Lili Martinez, and Ruben Gonzalez (later of Buena Vista Social Club fame) all learned their craft in Arsenio's bands.

CASA DE LA TROVA

The Casa de la Trova phenomenon is Cuba's folk music, born in the foothills of the Sierra Maestra Mountains as a local art form where troubadours brought their music wherever they traveled for work throughout Cuba. The concept set the stage for nueva trova stars Silvio Rodriguez and Pablo Milanes.

Today a series of clubs, cafes, and bodegas feature this traditional music throughout the country, which includes boleros, son, tango, and folk songs. The phenomenon was captured perfectly in the classic *La Bodeguita del Medio* recording from 1957 for the American jazz label Riverside. The recording was made in a coffeehouse in Havana (the title translates as "half a grocery store") with a trio led by the legendary Carlos Puebla, a poet of the revolution and singer/songwriter of the first order.

The Buena Vista Social Club phenomenon, exploitative as some believe it to be, has had the positive effect of exposing the world to Cuban music. Nonesuch's World Circuit label and Ry Cooder are to be credited with marketing genius that perceived a void and jumped in lock, stock, and barrel with an expertly conceived and executed project. The unmatched soul and rhythmic sense of Cuban music is infectious and appealing to even the casual music lover and these recordings capture the essence of the music. With the help of engineer Jerry Boys and a virtuoso ensemble assembled around the elder statesmen, Buena Vista represents music for the ages. Readers must understand however that Buena Vista is only the tip of the iceberg. As great as Ruben Gonzalez, Compay Segundo, Ibrahim Ferrer, and Co. are or were (only Ferrer has survived this writing), they were never the prime movers or innovators either before or after their careers were resurrected by the record and film.

The nueva cancion troubadour Silvio Rodriquez has carried the torch for Cuba since the late 1960s, championing the cause of human rights throughout South America and Europe. He is a national treasure, arguably the most important folk singer from the Spanish-speaking world in the twentieth century. Silvio's masterful recordings from the famed EGREM studios, and later from his own studio in Havana, are now widely available.

Silvio is a Cuban enigma; a musician who prospered economically under Castro, at times playing the role of critic, while remaining in Fidel's good graces. Perhaps it is his magically golden voice, his skill as a tunesmith, and his clever accompaniment on guitar that have made him invulnerable. Along with Pablo Milanes, his long-time collaborator, Silvio is Cuba's most valued musical personality.

Son is the essence of all Cuban and Afro-Cuban music with origins in the city of Oriente in the mountainous eastern part of the country. *Campesina* is country son associated with workers in the 500-year-old sugar cane industry of Cuba. Celina Gonzalez (b.1929) is the leading proponent of campesina and is Cuba's greatest female vocalist. Along with her husband, Reutilio Dominguez, she brought this traditional country style to the world in the early 1950s, incorporating elements of her Nigerian-Yoruban religion, *Santeria*, into the music. She was an active opponent of the corrupt military regimes that ran Cuba before the revolution and remained loyal to Castro even in the most difficult times during and after Soviet support.

Celina's recordings were not available in the United States until quite recently, although she has long been held in high esteem by the rest of Latin America—particularly in Colombia and Venezuela— and Western Europe. Her soothing voice, pure, folksy sound, and effortless delivery are the true essence of rural Cuban music. Celina is *the* female voice that carried the torch for traditional Cuban music long before the Buena Vista Social Club phenomenon.

RECOMMENDED CDs

ORCHESTRA ARAGON. The Duke Ellington Orchestra of *charanga* characterized by melodies in the high register, trilling flute, and lush strings. They were the authors of the first cha cha hit in 1954, *El Bodeguero. Cuban Originals* (BMG, 1999/1954) is arranged by original members violinist Rafael Lay and flutist Ricardo Egues. Felix Chappotin, Sonero Beny More, and Perez Prado all appeared with the band in the 1950s. *La Charanga Eterna* (Lusafrica, 1999) is a 60th anniversary concert. *Heart of Havana* (BMG, 1999/1956).

BUENA VISTA & CO. The initial three World Circuit releases from 1996 are still the best in the series. The late Compay Segundo's "Chan Chan" from *Buena Vista Social Club* sung by Eliades Ochoa is a killer track; *Introducing Ruben Gonzalez* features the octogenarian pianist; *Afro Cuban All-Stars-A todo Cuba le Gusto* may be the best of the lot, with the founders of *Sierra Maestra* in support and Jose Antonio Rodriguez handling the vocals.

CACHAO. Cuba's most influential bassist, uncle of Cachaito. *Cuban Jam Sessions in Miniature* (Panart, 1957). *Havana Descarga "Jam Session"* (BMG).

BOBI CESPEDES. The San Francisco-based singer is a specialist in Santeria and Yoruban inflected spiritual percussion music. *Rezos* (Six Degrees, 2002).

FELIX CHAPPOTIN. Legendary trumpet star. *Tres Soneros del son* (BMG, 1958).

CELIA CRUZ. The late Miami-based diva left Cuba in 1958 never to return and was a salsa star thereafter. *Con la Sonora Matancera* (Tubao, 1998/1953).

FAEZ TRIO. *Casa de la Trova* (Detour, 1997) captures the Faez Sisters, Floriceida and Candida, well into their 70s; soulful, grand-motherly, and charming, accompanied by Trio Miraflores and the legendary Nueva Trova composer/vocalist Daniel Castillo; *La Trova de las Faez* (Detour 2000) features son, bolero, and even a Cobian tango, "Nostalgia."

CELINA GONZALEZ (See Profile). Her best post revolution recording is *Rich Harvest/La Rica Cosech* (Tumi 1996) backed by a great ensemble including laud virtuoso Barbarito Torres. *Rezos y Cantos Guajiros Celina y Reutilio* (Ansonia, 1957).

SEXTETO HABANERA. The definitive son band of the 1920s. *Son Cubano* (Tumbao, 1998) classic reissue from 1924–1927; *75 Years* (Corason, 1995), the current configuration with Trumpet added.

LOS VAN VAN. The group that started the revival on the island in the late 1970s, led by Juan Formell; charanga, son, jazz, and rock create a signature Cuban style. *La Collecion* (BMG, 1996) from 1979 to the mid 1990s; *La Llega* (BMG, 1998).

ORLANDO "MARACA" VALLE. Flute virtuoso, bandleader, and former member of Irakere with Pacquito d'Rivera and Chu Chu Valdes. *Tremenda Rumba* (Ahi-Nama, 2002); *Sonando* (Ahi-Nama, 1998).

MACHITO. Percussionist who helped popularize Afro-Cuban jazz in the 1950s along with Mario Bauza. *Latin Soul Plus Jazz* (Charly, 1957).

PABLO MILANES. Pablo is blessed with a powerful, distinctive operatic voice that Andreas Bocelli obviously copied. He is a legend throughout the Latino world, a Nueva Trova star since the 1960s. *Cancionero* (World Pacific, 1993) is a great compilation; *Lila Vera y Pablo Milanes* (Universal, Cantatour, 1981); *Los Dias De Gloria* (Universal, 1978); *En Vivo en Argentina* (Alfiz, 1987), recorded after the fall of the Junta with Silvio, a gem.

POLO MONTANEZ. (also known as Fernando Borrega Linares). Montanez, who died in a car accident in 2002, was the country singer closest to Celina Gonzalez in style. *Guajira Natural* (Lusafrica, 2000); the posthumously released *Guitarra Mia* (Lusafrica, 2003).

BENY MORE. Mambo pioneer. The place to start is the two volume BMG CD *The Very Best of Beny More*, well produced with 1955–1957 renditions of famous tunes; *From Semilla del son* (BMG, Spain, 1992). Caveat emptor the innumerable "Exitos" and compilations.

ELIADES OCHOA. Guitarist/vocalist and master of the tres, voice on Compay Segundo's *Chan Chan*, and youngest member of the Buena Vista crew. *Sublime Illusion* (Virgin, 1997) is *guajira*, or country son; *Estoy Como Nunca* (Virgin, 2002).

SEPTETO NACIONAL IGNACIO PINEIRO. *Soneros de Cuba* (Real Rhythm, 1998), led by Ignacio E. Ayme; *Sones de mi Habana* (Latino, 1957/1998); *Poetas del son* (2002, Harmonia Mundi). Older recordings under Pineiro's name are all worthwhile.

PEREZ PRADO. Legendary bandleader, pianist, pop star, Mambo King, and Mexican expatriate even before the revolution; an important artist before his schmaltz American popularity subsumed his true talent. *Havana 3 A.M.* (RCA, 1956).

CARLOS PUEBLA. Folk poet/singer/songwriter. *La Bodeguita del Medio* (Riverside, 1958) is one of the truly great folk recordings of all time, a bohemian classic from a bygone era and a must for anyone interested in Nueva Cancion or folk music; a masterpiece.

ARSENIO RODRIGUEZ. *Dundunbanza* (BMG) is a compilation from 1946—1951 and is his most available recording with Chappotin and Martinez shining on many of Rodriguez's compositions.

SILVIO RODRIGUEZ. (See Profile). *Silvio* (Fonomusic, 1992), unaccompanied and stunning; *Te doy una cancion* (Fonomusic, 1975/1998); *Canciones Urgentes* (1991, Luaka Bop) is a great compilation; *Mano e Mano* (BMG, 1991), with Spanish star Luis Eduardo Aute.

GRUPO SIERRA MAESTRA: Juan de Marcos Gonzalez formed Sierra Maestra in 1976 with trumpeter Jesus Alemany, the first post-revolutionary group to reexplore the musical past in Cuba. *Rumberos de la Havana* (Egrem 1991) explores music from the 1920s–1950s and predates the Buena Vista recordings; *Dundunbanza* (World Circuit, 1996); *Tibiri Tibari* (World Circuit, 1997).

TRIO TESIS. Folk artists in the Carlos Puebla mold. *Ritmos de Cuba/Perdidos Dos Passos* (Winter & Winter, 2002), three-part harmony, impeccable tres solos, and old school soneros.

BARBARITO TORRES. The incomparable laud master can be heard on most of the Buena Vista Social Club releases. *Havana Café* (Havana Caliente, 1999).

CARLOS VARELA. Nueva Trova modernist poet and outspoken critic of Castro who gets away with it. Inexplicably, the Bush state department refused him entry to the United States in early 2004. *Jalisco Park* (Eligemen, 1990); *Monedas Al Aire* (QBadisc, 1993).

YUSA. Folksinger in the Nueva Cancion vein. Comparisons to Tracy Chapman and Joan Armitrading are apt. *Yusa* (Tumi, 2002), her debut recording, is full of desire and promise.

DOMINICAN REPUBLIC

After Columbus's landing in 1492, the island of Hispaniola was colonized by Spain. In 1867 the western one-third of the island, now the Republic of Haiti, was ceded to France. The Haitians took over the whole island in 1822, but the Dominican Republic was liberated by Juan Pablo Duarte's forces and became independent in 1861.

Beginning in 1930, the infamous Rafael Trujillo took over in a military coup and ruled by greed, an iron fist, and with little concern for the common man through 1961 when he was assassinated. The Organization of American States stepped in after his assassination and, after a series of military coups, the Dominican Republic survived to become a democracy, albeit an economically impoverished one. The twenty-first century has seen the Dominican tourist trade flourish, but the two most famous exports from the country remain Major League baseball players and merengue.

The Dominican Republic is home to the famous upbeat, dance band music known as *merengue*, the very soul and identity of the island's culture. Merengue is unsyncopated, characterized by an aggressive beat on the 1 and 3, driven by guiros, maracas, accordions, saxophones, and tamburos. The original merengue from the early part of the twentieth century was acoustic with the accordion in the forefront. Modern merengue borrows from salsa, rock, hip-hop, and compas; it is fast paced and sexually explicit, with sardonic lyrics of a political nature the norm.

The origins of merengue are wrought with controversy with differing viewpoints falling squarely on racial lines. Due to a disdain for their Haitian neighbors, Dominicans have bent over backwards to convince themselves that their music is 100 percent Hispanic; however, there is no question that the African influence is profound. One obvious influence is Haitian *mereng,* derived from a fusion of slave music forms and the *contradanza* ballroom music from France. Cuban *danza* is also an influence, again evidencing the African component. The illustrious Dominican composer Julio Alberto Hernandez put it best when he asserted, "While merengue developed from European forms, the music is a syncretic, Afro-Hispanic genre." The arguments about the origins of merengue may never be settled but it seems clear that the music is an amalgamation of several styles, mestizo if you will, and that it expresses the Dominican identity.

As with Argentine tango and its signature instrument, the bandoneon, the presence of the accordion in merengue can be traced to the island's contact with German traders in the nineteenth century.

Bachata belongs to the Latin American musical tradition, typically played by small groups with maracas, claves, bongos, gourds, and scrapers accompanying two guitars. It is related to other romantic Caribbean forms such as Cuban *son* and *guajira* and Mexican *rancheros* and *corridos.* Until the 1980s, bachata was associated with the lower class. Rural party music and the parties themselves were referred to as "bachatas." Despite soaring record sales throughout the country and in the United States, the music received no airplay in Santo Domingo until the 1990s and was rarely featured in major record shops. Only recently, with the overwhelming success of Juan Luis Guerra's classic *Bachata Rosa* has the music become mainstream and acceptable.

Johnny Ventura (born Juan de Dios Ventura Soriano) got his start in the early 1960s and went on to become the Dominican Republic's most famous merengue star, notably incorporating rock and roll, R&B, and salsa into meringue, and replacing the accordion with electric guitar. He is the grand old man of merengue. In 1998 he was elected Mayor of Santo Domingo.

The biggest name on the world music scene today is Juan Luis Guerra, whose popularity and impact on the music of the island has risen to Beatle-esque levels. A Berklee-trained musician, Guerra is a talented singer and composer greatly influenced by the *nueva cancion* movement. His sensibility is more akin to Cuban stars Pablo Milanes and Silvio Rodriguez than to most of his fellow countrymen.

The Dominican Republic has produced a plethora of stars, many of whom have made their mark as salsa musicians in New York, none more so that the great Johnny Pacheco, who was a founding force in the Fania label in the United States in the 1950s. As a pure salsa musician, however, he is outside the purview of this survey.

RECOMMENDED CDs

JOSE ALBERTO ("EL CANARIO"). The people's singer, New York City resident who embellishes his vocals with a signature whistle. *Sueno Contigo* (RMM, 1990).

JOAQUIN DIAZ. Accordion star who plays traditional and folk music similar in style to Tex-Mex music, although at a faster pace and with far more intricate arrangements. *Allegre merengue* (Arhoolie, 2002).

FEFITA LA GRAND. Frenetic, break-neck speed accordionist who has been compared to avant garde jazz trumpeter Don Cherry; an acquired taste. *With Todos Los Hombres son Buenos* (Jose Luis, 1994).

XIOMARA FORTUNA. Female roots singer in the Nueva Trova mold. *Kumbajei* (Circular Moves, 2001).

FULANITO. Drum and bass merengue. *Americanazao* (Cutting, 2001).

JUAN LUIS GUERRA. Bachata star. *Bachata Rosa* (Karen, 1990) won the Latin Grammy; *Arieto* (Karen, 1992) is even better; *Fogarte* (Karen, 1995); *Colleccion Romantica* (Karen, 2000) is a two-disc collection that has it all.

CHICHI PERALTA. Master percussionist fusing tropical rhythms, jazz, merengue, guaguancó, bachata, and vallenato. Formerly with Guerra's super group *4-40*. *De Vuelta al Barrio* (Caiman, 2000).

MILLY QUEZADA. New York-based pop singer. *Tesoros de mi Terra* (Sony, 2000).

FRANCISCO ULLOA. Virtuoso accordionist. *Ultramenrengue* (Globe 1992); *Eres Amor* (Platino, 2001).

WILFREDO VARGAS. The mastermind of the 1980s merengue renaissance is a fine trumpeter, vocalist, arranger, and composer. *Wilfredo 86* (Karen 1986); *Musica* (BMG, 2001); *El Jardinero* (Karen 1993); *Dos Generraciones* (J & N, 2002).

JOHNNY VENTURA. Merengue star. *Y Su Combo* (Kubaney, 1987, reissue), hits from the 1960s; *40th Anniversary* (WEA, 1998) is a review of his recording career.

HAITI

The poorest country in the Western hemisphere has endured decades of military rule by the Papa and Baby Doc Duvalier regimes and most recently has seen democratically elected, albeit corrupt, Jean Baptiste Aristide removed from office under murky circumstances. Haiti is not receiving the aid its Western hemisphere neighbors can and should be supplying. Haitian music is diverse and plentiful and if there were a stable political climate on the island, it would be a major stop on any world music traveler's itinerary.

Haiti is perhaps the purest African culture in the west, steeped in the *voodoo* tradition that derives from Dahomey (now Benin) and West Africa, where music is the medium that takes one from the real world to the spiritual world. Voodoo—vodou in Haiti—means "spirituality," and is the primary religion of Haiti, an amalgam of

West African traditions combined with Catholicism. Although Haiti is predominantly Catholic, it is truly 100 percent voodoo. Voodoo ceremonies in Haiti are conducted in *hounforts*, outdoor temples, and are centered on African drumming, which communicates coded messages to participants and induces trance like chanting. Drumming was a form of language used by slaves to communicate in ways the slave owners could not understand.

PORT-AU-PRINCE

Haiti's capital and largest city rivaled Havana in the 1940s and 1950s as a tourist Mecca and playground for the rich with swank hotels, restaurants, nightclubs, and music. Haiti's musical culture is one of the best-kept secrets of world music, an island whose riches have barely been tapped. Unlike Cuban and Jamaican music, which has had a far-reaching, profound influence on many forms of world music, Haitian music has yet to be widely exported, with only a few groups attaining international fame. *Compas* is the beat now, every bit as infectious and soulful as the *merengue* of the Dominican Republic that shares the island of Hispaniola with Haiti. Compas incorporates genres from all over the Caribbean, including merengue, soca, zouk, salsa, and American jazz. It is a smooth, guitar-based, big-band music made for dancing. The big band sound is a remnant of the United States occupation from 1915–1934, when swing had a big influence on the local music. Nemours Jean Baptiste is credited with creating the sound that became compas with the driving bottom beat and cowbell laced rhythm.

NEW YORK

The Haitian diaspora is strong in Brooklyn, New York, and compas can be heard in many venues in the borough. The disbanded supergroup the Fugees was led by international stars Lauren Hill and Haitian composer/singer/multi-instrumentalist/producer Wyclef Jean. The group featured compas sounds and zouk along with their original brand of soul and hip-hop that greatly impacted the North American recording industry. Jean has gone on to be a giant in the business, a talented engineer, entrepreneur, and gifted musician.

RECOMMENDED CDs

TOTO BISSAINTHE. Expatriated Creole vocalist whose deep sultry voice popularized Haitian music for the international set in the 1960s. *Chante Haiti* (Arion, 1989 reissue) with Marie Claude Benoit and Mariann Matheus; haunting Vodou slave songs; *Haiti: Ti Coca* (World Network, 1994/99) acoustic set with the late Diva.

BOUKMAN EKSPERYANS. The great Haitian band exploded on the scene in the early 1990s combining voodoo and bold protest songs against the military regime; with its masterful arrangements, Boukman Eksperyans is the #1 Haitian world music group. *Vodou Adjae* (Mango, 1991); *Kalfou Danjare* (Mango 1992); *Libete* (Mango, 1994).

BOUKAN GINEN. Spin-off from Boukman, heir to their mantle. *Jou A Rive* (Xenophile, 1995); *Rev An Nou* (Xenophile, 1996).

MAGNUM BAND. High-powered compas from the 1980s. *Adoration* (Mini, 1982).

EMELINE MICHEL. Elegant, sensual New York-based vocalist. *Cordes et Ame* (Cheval de Feu, 2002), produced by Emeline, who is a rarity: A female vocalist from Haiti.

BEETHOVA OBAS. Soft guitars, sexy vocals, and the folk side to Haitian music. *Planet La* (Sachem, 1999) is more bossa nova than compas, an uplifting recording.

DADOU PASQUET. Vocalist/guitarist formerly with Magnum Band. *Dadou en Troubadour* (Creon, 2003).

SYSTEM SOUND. Brooklyn soca band. *Le son Haiti* (Arcade, 1999).

VARIOUS ARTISTS. *Rough Guide to Haiti.* Andy Crenshaw's personal explorations have produced a first-rate compilation.

JAMAICA

Jamaica is the third largest island in the Caribbean after Cuba and Hispaniola. The *Arawak* people first inhabited the island circa 1000 and were the indigenous Jamaicans. When Columbus arrived in

1492, Jamaica became a Spanish colony, and by 1650 the Arawaks had perished, because their immune systems were unable to resist the multiple diseases brought over by the Spaniards.

Following the demise of the Arawaks, African slaves were brought to Jamaica from Ghana, Burkina Faso, and Benin (then Dahomey) for labor. By 1655 the British had taken control of the island, at which time the Spaniards left and released their slaves. Many of the former Spanish-held slaves—called Maroons—fled to the mountains for independence and freedom. Eventually the African population outnumbered the Europeans twenty to one. By 1838, slavery ended and the African influence in Jamaican culture became virtually total. Today 95 percent of the island is of African descent. Modern Jamaica is economically challenged, feeling the effects of stiff competition in the new global economy. In the slave days, sugar and bananas were the economic strengths of Jamaica, but today it is bauxite and tourism.

MARCUS GARVEY, HAILE SELASSIE, AND RASTA

Jamaican-born Marcus Garvey, the so-called father of the "Back to Africa" movement, taught that people of African descent would only find peace, self-expression, dignity, and self-reliance if they embraced their African heritage. Jamaicans took this to heart. Beginning in the early 1930s, Jamaican *Rastafarians* began worshipping Ethiopian Emperor Haile Selassie, focusing on the leader of the one African nation that had never been colonized.

The loudest island in the world is of course most well known (musically) for *reggae* and Bob Marley, one of the most important musical personalities on the planet during the second half of the twentieth century. Reggae is the evolutionary grandson of other Jamaican genres including *mento, ska,* and *rock steady* and has been the subject of innumerable books and reviews, especially since Marley's death from cancer in 1980.

THE MUSIC

In the early part of the twentieth century, a folk music known as *junkanoo* was the main form of Jamaican music. Junkanoo was based on the quadrille (a European dance) and work songs. These forms evolved into Jamaica's seminal genre *mento,* a loose-sounding folk music similar to calypso, which was the first recorded Jamaican music. Mento is still performed, recorded, and released internationally by traditionalist performers, most notably the Jolly Boys

As was the case with much of the Caribbean music immediately after World War II, jazz was the thing in Jamaica. Edward Seaga, later to become president of Jamaica, founded the first recording studios in Kingston in 1958. That same year, Chris Blackwell, a white Jamaican, invested part of his family fortune (the spice merchants Cross & Blackwell) in building the first record plant on the island, his first step on the road to becoming one of the true pioneers of world music as owner and founder of Island and Mango records.

Sound systems—literally portable audio systems brought to dance halls to play records—kick started the Jamaican music boom, at first featuring American R&B and rock and roll. Jamaica's music scene was mired in attempting to cover American hits until Prince Buster (Cecil Campbell) introduced an "after beat" syncopation to mento played by the guitar, the first documented example of the genre to be known as *ska.* Ska combined the catchy backbeat of New Orleans R&B with mento. Mento is affectionately known as the great grandfather of reggae. Duke Reid and Clement Dodd were the two big names whose sound systems exposed the music to the masses.

Ska stressed the 2 and 4 beats over a walking quarter-note bass, with the guitar striking the off beats. Theophilus Beckford is credited with recording the first ska tune *Easy Snapping,* arranged by guitarist Ernest Ranglin, in the early 1950s. This was the music of the Kingston ghetto that arose just before independence from Britain in 1962. Ska grew in the early 1960s and became associated with Rastafarianism. Soon the music began to change with the introduction of slow beats and chants, reflecting a religious tone. The slower version became known as *rock steady,* a more relaxed ska, where the guitar strums only on the 2 and 4 and the bass guitar emphasizes the 1 and 3 beats. In rock steady, drums are less prominent than in ska, because the bass takes over the rhythmic lead.

THE ROOTS OF RAP AND HIP-HOP

Before long a group of dynamic musicians and visionaries began to change and politicize rock steady. Lee "Scratch" Perry stripped away the vocals from the beats that were broadcast at sound-system parties. DJs began "toasting" and "roasting" celebrities at parties with the new beat as background for their humorous ad libs. The DJs' dialogue became increasingly complex and competitive and led to the most innovative, pervasive, commercially successful musical genre on the planet at the end of the twentieth century: Rap, soon to also be known as hip-hop. Legends such as Perry, Toots Hibbert, Alton Ellis, Eric Morris, and the Skatalites were essentially the founders of hip-hop. Later Bob Marley would help change Jamaican music forever, successfully exporting the message and sound that travels under the moniker reggae around the globe where it has morphed and mutated into related forms in Africa, the United States, the United Kingdom, and Brazil.

Known as "the Godfather of Ska," Laurel Aitken was Jamaica's first recording star, one of the first artists to release a ska record and record for the seminal Island label. Born in Cuba in 1927, he moved to his father's native Jamaica in 1938. Aitken developed his style from legendary American jazz singers Louis Jordan and Nat King Cole, also using R&B, calypso, and mento to create his unique, pioneering sound. Due to his popularity in the United Kingdom, he moved to the heavily West Indian Brixton section of London in 1960 and became a star in England. After fading from popularity during the explosive rise of Bob Marley, Aitken made a comeback in the 1980s, working with David Bowie, UB 40, and other United Kingdom stars. He has now settled in as a living legend in his adopted home.

RECOMMENDED CDs

LAUREL AITKEN (See profile). *Pioneer of Jamaican Music, Vol. 1* (reggae Retro, 2000) is a good retrospective.

THEOPILUS BECKFORD. Composer of the classic *Easy Snappin'*, Beckford never equaled the success of his initial big hit, struggling as a session musician for most of his professional life. *Trench Town Ska* (Jamaican Gold, 1999).

ALTON ELLIS. Until Marley came along, Ellis was the #1 Jamaican vocalist, the image of rock steady. *Cry Tough* (Heartbeat, 1993) is an excellent box set; *Sunday Coming* (Heartbeat, 1970);

Soul Groover (Trojan Isle, 1997 reissue), sides from the 1960s–1970s on Duke Reid's label.

JOLLY BOYS. The classic mento group—guitars, banjos, bongos, and good times—no politics, just sex, braggadocio, and drinking. *Pop 'n Mento* (Rykodisc, 1989).

LEE "SCRATCH" PERRY. Mastermind of dub, producer of Bob Marley, eccentric mixologist, and conceptual genius, the Sun Ra of Jamaican music. *Reggae Greats: Lee Perry* (Mango, 1984) with Junior Murvin, Max Romeo, the Heptones; *Open the Gate* (Trojan, 1989).

ERNEST RANGLIN. A pioneering force behind the rise of Caribbean music, guitar virtuoso, and composer, Ranglin's session work at the famed Studio One in Kingston helped give birth to the ska phenomenon. He teamed with Millie Small on the 1963 hit "My Boy Lollipop" and is a vital figure on the international scene. *Memories of Barber Mack* (Polygram, 1998); *Below the Bassline* (Polygram, 1996); *Rock Steady* (2004) a refreshing collaboration with long-time colleague and fellow Jamaican, jazz pianist Monty Alexander.

SKATALITES. Prototype ska band recorded for less than 2 years for Clement Dodd, but were the leaders of pre-reggae party music. *Scattered Lights* (Alligator, 1983); with Don Drummond's trumpet, horns, choruses, and crazy grooves, the one to get; *Greetings from Skamania* (Shanachie, 1996), reformed after 30 years without the late Drummond, a good outing.

TOOTS AND THE MAYTALS. Soul singer Toots was there at the beginning of ska and fostered the move to reggae; the Otis Redding of Ska/reggae. *Funky Kingston* (Trojan, 1973); *In the Dark* (Silverline, 1976); *Live* (Mango, 1980); *Live Hour* (Genes, 1982).

PUERTO RICO

Puerto Rico has been a Commonwealth territory of the United States since 1952, and at times has sought to break away from the United States, most recently in 1999 when statehood was narrowly defeated. The enmity that many Puerto Ricans once harbored for the United States reached its peak in the early 1950s, including the infamous bombings in Washington, D.C., by Puerto Rican nationalists during the Truman administration. Despite recent protests concerning United States test bombing off the coast of the Puerto Rican atoll of Vieques, the island has reluctantly accepted American hegemony, which both protects and inhibits Puerto Rico as a nation and a culture.

Puerto Rico's signature popular music genre, *salsa*, has received exhaustive coverage in countless books and encyclopedias available on the market. We have included a recommended reading list on the genre at the end of this book.

Traditional and folk music from Puerto Rico has had scant international exposure due to the omnipotence of salsa and Puerto Rico's symbiotic relationship with the mighty New York recording scene. Nevertheless, a long folk tradition exists and there are some treasures to be uncovered in Puerto Rico's other music. It is noteworthy that Puerto Rico has a more purely Latino culture than its Dominican and Cuban neighbors. Due to the fact that there were no plantations during the days of slavery, pure African cultural influence is less pronounced in Puerto Rico than in Cuba, Haiti, or the Dominican Republic.

PLENA

The most significant folk genre from Puerto Rico is *plena*, typically associated with the coastal regions of the island. The plena is a narrative song widely thought to have origins in the city of Ponce on the southern coast and examples date back to the late nineteenth century. Plena's roots are in African music and dance, influenced by other Caribbean cultures, and focuses on the life of the peasantry. Spanish musical traditions can be heard in plena and the genre also has many similarities to Mexican corridos, the romances of Spain, calypso from Trinidad, and the merengue of the Dominican Republic.

As rural workers moved to urban areas, plena became a part of the urban cultural life, as is typical of folkloric music everywhere. Once it arrived in the cities, musicians added horns to the sound and improvised call-and-response vocals became part of the genre.

Plena is often referred to as the "living newspaper" because its lyrics deal with events of the day, often in a sarcastic, satirical, and political context. Vocals traditionally consist of a soloist and a call-and-response chorus of two singers who sing harmony an octave above the soloist. *Panderetas* are the most characteristic instruments, drums that keep 2/4 time. The *pandero* is a hand-held drum similar to a tambourine without cymbals. Three panderetas of different sizes and two supporting drums, the *seguidora* for rhythm and the *requinto* for accent, are typical for a *plena* ensemble. Guitars, cuatros, accordions, and harmonicas are also common.

DECIMA AND JIBARO

The *décima* is the root of *jibaro*, Puerto Rico's country music, and a folk style with origins in southern Spain. The songs use ten improvised couplets of eight syllables each, called decimas.

NUEVA CANCION

Puerto Rico has its share of nueva cancion music, allied with nueva trova from Cuba and the South American form. Austin, Texas-based Lourdes Perez is a greatly underappreciated proponent of Puerto Rican nueva cancion.

(*See* Argentina and Chile for a more in depth discussion of nueva cancion.)

RECOMMENDED CDs

ANGEL CARRION. Eclectic composer, poet, guitarist, and singer who blends bossa, plena, reggae, and new song. *Sonidos Urbanos* (Atlas, 2003) includes a clever tune about a visit to the gynecologist.

RAFAEL CORTIJO. The *bomba* and plena traditions of the Puerto Rico's slums were given respectability through the music of Rafael Cortijo, a major artist in the 1950s and 1960s. *El Sueno del Maestro* (Disco Hit, 1980); *16 Exitos* (Discos Fuentes, 1993 reissue).

HACIDO PUNTO N OTRO SON. Tropical bolero group including Silverio Perez. *Ubao Moin* (Artotrax, 1996).

LOURDES PEREZ. Based in Austin, Texas, and a protégé of Mercedes Sosa. *Vestigios* (Vivavoce, 1995) is an obscure little gem.

PLENA LIBRE. Modern plena, with spicy dance beats, a refreshing mix of old and new. *Juntos Y Libre* (Rykolatino, 1999/1994); *Mas Libre* (Rykolatino, 1999).

ISMAEL RIVERA. In 1954, Maelo Rivera and Rafael Cortijo recorded their first hit, *El Bombon de Elena*, bomba and plena. Maelo's voice is extraordinary and he was also a master of Cuban son. *Con todos los Hierro* (Tico, 1967).

TRUCO & ZAPEROCO. Traditional ensemble that play Caribbean Latin music. *Musica Universal* (Red Ink, 2003). Classy arrangements, dance music that is not salsa, ah!

TRINIDAD AND TOBAGO

Trinidad and Tobago's music is rooted in African rhythms, augmented over the past century by American jazz and other Caribbean genres including Haitian *compas*, Dominican *merengue*, and Antillean *zouk*. While most people originally associated calypso with the great Harry Belafonte and his hit records from the 1950s (including the first ever million-selling LP, *Calypso*) the genre dates back to the days of slavery with origins in the controversial minstrelsy tradition.

As is the case with African traditional music, calypso has served as the repository of Trinidad's oral history and culture and has kept the spirit of its people alive in times of strife. Calypso lyrics contain the usual love songs and plaints of the trials and tribulations of love, often with hidden, cryptic lyrics that criticize colonial rulers. It is essentially a folk music that evolved from ditties sung in the local patois into a sophisticated genre containing sociopolitical commentary. Most recently the music has morphed into many forms and now is thought of as party music.

Trinidad, Barbados, and other neighboring Caribbean islands are big on Festival Contests (most notably the National Panorama Competition). Many take place in Port of Spain, Trinidad's capital, where artists win awards and careers are made. Many of the country's popular bands and individual artists achieved their initial renown at such festivals, similar in nature to the festival scene popular in Brazil in the late 1960s and early 1970s, which produced such megastars as Milton Nascimento and Djavan.

SOCA, RAPSO, RAGGA SOCA, AND CHUTNEY

Soca is the name of the modern dance music genre from Trinidad and Tobago, short for "*soul* calypso." It has usurped calypso as the national music. Its birth is credited to Garfield Blackman, also known as Lord Shorty or Lord Ras, who allegedly came upon the fusion in a recording studio in 1973, when he added a few soul riffs into a recording session, also initially using East Indian instruments and rhythms. The intent was to compete with the ubiquitous reggae in light of the fading popularity of calypso. Soca has grown exponentially throughout the Caribbean into party music characterized by big bands with brass, on-stage dancers, strong sexual content, and hot syncopated rhythms.

Rapso is a politicized style of soca, combining hip-hop sensibilities with slower, chant-like vocals, performed unplugged without the big band brass that is soca dance music's calling card. *Ragga soca* is another offshoot, a combination of reggae and soca, distinguishable but familial. *Chutney soca* is a fast-paced genre that contains bawdy lyrics, which, as the name implies, evolved from the large Indian population living in Trinidad and other parts of the Caribbean and northern South America, including Surinam and Guyana.

STEELPAN

The traditional steel pan drums gained popularity during World War II when United States Navy personnel populated parts of the islands. The steel pans originate as large oil drums, which are cut down, coated, and tuned with notes indicated by circles around the inner circumference. Much of the music centers on Carnival, which in Trinidad begins shortly after the new ear and runs through Ash Wednesday.

Although virtually all of the music one hears from Trinidad today is purely popular and despite the fact that much of it is quite derivative of other genres, it has a huge following and a rightful place as part of the world music oeuvre. In Trinidad, the popular music of the people is also their traditional music.

RECOMMENDED CDs

ARROW. The group that gave us "Hot Hot Hot," the national anthem of soca and its best-selling single. *Soca Dance Party*

(Mango, 1990); *Knock Dem Dead* (Mango, 1988); *Soca Savage* (Arrow, 1984).

BURNING FLAMES. High-powered, synth-driven grooves *Dig* (Mango, 1991); *Me not Freard* (BF, 1989).

CALYPSO ROSE. Rare female soca singer and leading diva from Tobago whose gruff voice is her trademark. *Trouble* (Strakers, 1984); *Soca Diva* (Ice, 1994).

LORD KITCHENER. Born Aldwyn Roberts, Lord Kitchener, who died in 2000, spent decades in England where he earned tons of money. Along with the Mighty Sparrow, he is the most important calypso artist of the twentieth century, revered by his progeny. *Master at Work* (Calico, 1985); *Roots of soca* (Charlies, 1984); *67 Kitch* (RCA, 1967).

KROSFAYEH. From Barbados, led by the charismatic Edwin Yearwood. *Ultimate Party–Pump Me Up* (Kalingo, 1997); *Hot Zone* (Kalingo, 1998).

MIGHTY SPARROW. Born Slinger Francisco, the Sparrow and Lord Kitchener are the giants of calypso since World War II. Silky vocals and cryptic lyrics protesting American hegemony characterize his music. *Mighty Sparrow's 25th Anniversary* (Charlies, 1980); *Mighty Sparrow Volume 1* (Ice, 1990).

RENEGADES STEEL ORCHESTRA (AMOCO RENEGADES). Fifteen-piece steel orchestra who play soca, merengue, samba, and calypso, and whose ranks swell to 120 during Carnival. They have toured the world for 40 years, spreading one of the most unique sounds anywhere. *Panorama Saga: Tribute to Jit Samaroo* (Delas, 1995); *While Waiting for Cousteau w/Jean-Michel Jarre* (1989).

DAVID RUDDER. Leading soca star who writes his own tunes. *1990* (Sire, 1990); *Haiti* (Warner, 1988).

LORD (RAS) SHORTY. Born Garfield Blackman, the reputed originator of soca. *Soca Explosion* (Charlies, 1978).

CENTRAL AMERICA

The music of Central America has received the least exposure of any music in the Western Hemisphere. The region in general is rarely in the limelight politically and has suffered a long history of internal turmoil, internecine feuds, civil conflict, and economic strife. Central America has been easy prey for its more powerful neighbors, exploited for its resources, cheap labor, and location ever since it was colonized 500 years ago.

The notable exception to the ongoing hardships in the region is Costa Rica, a nation that does not maintain a standing military, whose economy is sound, tourism thriving, population stable, and whose neutrality rivals Switzerland. In 1987, Costa Rican President Oscar Arias Sanchez garnered world recognition for his work in ending the Nicaraguan civil war. Arias managed to get five Central American presidents to sign his peace plan and he won the Noble Peace prize for his work. Nicaragua today is experiencing relative stability due in large part to his efforts.

THE MUSIC

Belize, Guatemala, Honduras, and Nicaragua have a shared musical heritage, most notably the purely African genre known as *paranda* performed by the Garifuna people who populate these four nations, predominantly in Honduras and Belize. Garifuna live in African-type villages along the coasts, and are unfortunately a dying group. Roots recordings of indigenous and African-descended peoples of Central America have not generally enjoyed the attention lavished on other world folk traditions, but paranda is truly a hidden treasure whose essence is confirmation of the strength, power, and endurance of African culture. Paranda has its roots in Belize, home to Andy Palacios, its leading proponent.

The Garifuna are of Afro-Amerindian descent, a multilingual people who never submitted to slavery. They are direct descendants of Island Caribs and a group of African slaves whose Spanish slave ship crashed near St. Vincent in 1635. The Island Caribs were descendants of the South American Indians known as Arawaks, also the indigenous people of Jamaica before being wiped out there by the Spanish.

Garifuna singing and drumming is percussive, communal, call-and-response music, almost purely African, based in ancestral invocations and spirit possession, as in Cuban *santería*, Haitian *vodou/voodoo*, and Brazilian *candomblé*. It is by far the most African-sounding music in the Western Hemisphere.

Instruments used in Garifuna music include three *garaon* drums: the improvising *primera,* the counter-rhythmic *segunda,* and the bass-line *tercera.* Two strings or wires are stretched over the drumheads to achieve the buzzing sound reminiscent of West African music. Other instruments include claves, bottle percussion, and a variety of shakers and scrapers. Spanish for "carousal," paranda adds guitar to the *garaon* ensemble.

In addition to paranda, there are several regional styles that are also popular. *Punta* rock is an increasingly popular regional dance not dissimilar to Trinidadian Soca. Keyboards, electric bass, brass, and synthesizers round out the standard ensemble. During the 1980s, *La Punta* became popular in Honduras.

Ancient Mayan culture survives most strongly in Guatemala. The marimba (a wooden-keyed xylophone) is the centerpiece of much contemporary Mayan music and has become Guatemala's national instrument. Pre-European Mayan instruments still in use include drums, flutes, ocarinas, whistles, conch-shell horns, string instruments, rattles, shakers, and scrapers.

In Panama, the culture of the Azuero region in the west has come to dominate. This region is inhabited mostly by *mestizos,* persons of mixed African, European, and indigenous ancestry. Panamanian music shares much with its Colombian neighbor, including a penchant for cumbia. The most important native instrument is the *mejorana,* a five-stringed guitar, similar to the Venezuelan cuatro, used to play songs called *torrentes.*

Ruben Blades is the most recognized Panamanian in the world, more than the infamous dictator Manuel Noriega, American baseball legend Rod Carew, or native boxer Roberto Duran. At the beginning of his musical career, Blades gravitated to doo wop before he became a major star in the Fania stable of New York musicians. Ruben has gradually and recently moved toward more eclectic styles and the world music stage.

Blades is truly a renaissance man. He has championed the cause of human rights, education, and democratic values for his native Panama, especially during his historic run for the presidency of Panama in 1994. He is a talented composer, vocalist, movie star, Broadway personality (starring in Paul Simon's ill-fated musical, *The Capeman*), and a citizen of the world with a burning social conscience. Blades is a crusader for the rights of the common man who uses his music to broadcast his message and vision. He is that rare soul who travels well in virtually all social circles, a hero whose message and work continues to carry global impact.

RECOMMENDED CDs

GUILLREMO ANDERSON. From the northern coastal city of La Ceiba in Honduras, Anderson and his band *Ceibana* play Garifuna, reggae, calypso, soca, and rock. *Costa y Calor* (Costa Norte Records, 1999); *Pobre Marinero* (Costa Norte Records, 2001) is an acoustic set.

LOS DEL AZUERO. Folk music from the Azuero peninsula with *mejorana* playing, Afro-Caribbean drumming, and yodeling-type vocals. *Traditional Music of Panama* (Nimbus, 1999).

RUBEN BLADES (See Profile). *Buscando América, with Seis del Solar* (Elektra, 1984). Concept album with gorgeous ballads; *Amor y Control, with son del Solar* (Sony Discos, 1992); *Tiempos* (Sony Discos, 1999). Pan Latin and Brazilian sounds; *Mundo* (Sony Discos, 2002) his best world effort to date; eclectic and hip.

KATIA CARDENAL. During the revolution in Nicaragua, the young Cardenal befriended Silvio Rodriguez and they toured the countryside performing for the poor peasants. *Sueno de una noche verano/A Midsummer Night's Dream* (KKV Norway, 2003). Two of the tracks feature Silvio in duets with Katia, who is backed by a Norwegian trio.

EDITUS. Costa Rican Nueva Cancion Band. *Decada Uno* (Sony, 2001).

TITIMAN FLORES. Punta rocker. *Fedu* (Orchard, 2000) [Belize].

HERMANOS PALACIOS. *Marimba: Music from Nicaragua* (Disco Fenix, 2000).

CARLOS MEJIA GODOY. Nueva cancion artist and political activist. *En Concierto* (Orfeon, 2000). [Nicaragua].

GUARDABARRANCO. Nueva cancion folk group. *Dias de Amar* (Redwood, 1991) [Nicaragua].

GUITARRA ARMADA. Social protest songs from Nicaragua. *Music of the Sandanista Guerillas* (Rounder, 1976).

MOHOBUB. Nicaraguan punta group. *Belizean Punta Rockers Vol. 2* (Orchard, 2001).

ANDY PALACIO. Belizean star of Garifuna. *Keimoun* (Orchard, 2000).

PARANDA. *Africa in Central America*, (Erato Detour, 1998), six Garifuna *paranderos* including Andy Palacios and Jurisino Cayetano. Call-and-response vocals and piercing harmony, the most African sounding music in the Western Hemisphere. A truly important recording.

LOS ROLANDS. Honduran punta group, more soca than paranda. *Los Reyes de la Punta* (Musical, 1991).

VARIOUS ARTISTS. *Music from Guatemala* (Caprice, 1999), a 2-CD compilation that presents a blend of Mayan, African, and European musical traditions. *1955: Songs and Dances of Honduras* (Smithsonian Folkways) is a collection of field recordings from Moses Asch's Folkways label, the recording combines guitar, the three-string *tiple*, violin, maracas, and the marimba. *Rough Guide to the Music of Central America* (Rough Guide, 2001) includes 17 tracks from the region.

MEXICO

From the beginning of the Spanish conquest of Mexico circa 1521, Catholic missionaries were instructed to use and teach music as an aid and tool in the process of conversion of the Aztec Indian population. Aided by the extraordinary musical aptitude of the Indians and the cultural prestige of musicians in native society, the approach formed an early bond between the colonizers and their subjects, which resulted in a rapid, widespread assimilation of Spanish song forms by the Indian population. Liturgical books with music were produced in Mexico as early as 1556 beginning with *Ordinarium*, reputed to be the first book with music printed in the New World.

Mexican/Indian traditional music did not totally lose its identity during Spanish occupation, although the colonizers insisted on conformity with Catholic dogma every step of the way. Native ceremonies relating to the harvest survived and the predominance of traditional flutes and drums remained. The musical form *jarabe,* a couple's dance performed in gala Mexican attire with bright colors, feathers and all, was outlawed by the colonizers but defiantly performed until independence.

Mexican music ultimately is a convergence of Spanish and African forms combined with the indigenous culture, paralleling musical evolution throughout the Americas where slavery and Spanish conquest were part of the equation.

POLITICS

The recent history of Mexico is inextricably entwined with her neighbor to the north, from the Alamo to the Land Grant struggles in New Mexico in the early 1970s to the ubiquitous question of immigration. Due to the opportunistic, at times tolerant, and often duplicitous regimes that have ruled Mexico through the years, the country has been a haven for revolutionaries, political exiles, film-makers, painters, and musicians during the twentieth century. A host of controversial individuals whose lifestyles or political views were not favored in their homeland, including Leon Trotsky, Luis Bunuel, Perez Prado, and Mexican artists Diego Rivera, Frieda Kalho, and Orosco are but a few such names who have found safety in Mexico.

Since the 1970s, Mexico has undergone seismic economic and political change wrought with corruption and plagued by a huge and debilitating drug trade. The rebirth of Pancho Villa's Zapatista movement and its opposition to tyrannical government remains strong today, particularly outside the big cities. Despite the economic boom in certain regions, Mexico remains a poor country with immense political, economic, and social divisions.

THE MUSIC

Ranchera, Son, and Norteno. Following independence, *son* became the heart of Mexican music. Mexican son is quite different from the Cuban version in that it relates specifically to numerous local rural forms including *mariachi* and *sones jaiscienses* from the Jalisco region. Foot-stomping dancing and a quicker-paced tempo are characteristics of the Mexican son tradition. With the revolution in

1910, everything Spanish was initially rejected; European dance styles—the waltz, polkas and mazurkas—became the musical rage. These would eventually mix with the earlier Spanish influences to form several new styles.

As urban areas boomed and the population moved from the country to cities, a new musical form known as *ranchera* developed. It is a bluesy folk music, less complex than son, whose lyrics speak of hard times, betrayal, and poverty while yearning for the good old days of a simple, safe, rural existence; a distant memory for many. *Norteno*, also known as Tex-Mex, began as a music that spoke of the wars with the Anglos in the early nineteenth century when Mexico lost almost half of its territory—California, New Mexico, and Arizona—and many Mexicans became Americans overnight. The musical instruments of the popular Mexican genres began to change during this time with the influx of European immigrants who brought their guitars and accordions. The new instrumentation was adapted to the traditional *corrido* ballads and spawned the conjuntos and Tejano ensembles still popular today both in Mexico and the United States. As trade opened in the late 1800s Mexico also incorporated sounds from South America, most notably the Colombian dance music known as *cumbia*, which is alive and well today in a uniquely Mexican form.

(For more on Norteno, *see* United States Tejano.)

NUEVA CANCION AND EXPATRIATES

Despite its reputation for mariachi, conjunto, cumbia, and ranchera—all local popular forms. Mexico has long been a safe haven for political expatriates and musicians from all corners of the globe. As Castro came to power in the late 1950s, many of the leaders of the Cuban music scene, including Perez Prado, Benny More, and Celia Cruz, moved to Mexico City where they were free to record and continue the evolution of their music (son). Similarly, the politically charged nuevo cancion genre has always maintained a stronghold in Mexico. Until recently the late Amparo "Shelter" Ochoa was Mexico's most important homegrown nueva cancion proponent, but Lila Downs is keeping the tradition intact and expanding Mexican musical horizons (see profile).

There is a new star on the world music horizon from Oaxaca (by way of Minnesota) making waves musically and politically, the multitalented Lila Downs (b.1968). Lila has a stunning, virtuosic instrument for a voice and is a magnetic, theatrical performer. Many readers will recognize her for her role and vocals in the film *Frieda*, about the life and struggles of Frieda Kalho. Lila writes beautiful, soulfully poignant tunes and released three CDs during 2000–2001, all extraordinary. She is an iconoclastic artist who understands how to reach the world market without compromising her art, at once a throwback to the 1960s and a beacon pointing the way in the new millennium.

It is clear that Lila has been influenced by Mercedes Sosa, Lola Beltran, and Woody Guthrie. She is as close as one gets to a modern day troubadour and actively champions the causes of Oaxacan Amerindians and Mexican immigrants in the Untied States. She sings with equal facility in Spanish, English, and her native Zapotec tongue. As fine as her recordings are, Lila must be heard live to be truly appreciated. She is powerhouse on the world music scene, a new international star.

RECOMMENDÏED CDs

LOLA BELTRAN. Lola brought ranchera or mariachi music from the barrios of Mexico to the international stage. *Le Grande* (Warner, 1988); *Grand Exitos* (Sony, 1994) is a two disc greatest hits set.

CAFÉ TACUBA. Popular roots-based ensemble incorporates ranchera, hip-hop, synthesizers, and mariachi. *Tiempo Trans Urrido* (WEA, 2002) is alternative Latin with a street sensibility that rings of modern-day urban Mexico.

LILA DOWNS (See Profile). *Tree of Life* (Narada, 1999) is the CD that first garnered international attention focusing on Lila's Zapotec background. *La Linea* (Narada, 2001) seeks a broader audience, a political recording highlighting the plight of Mexicans crossing the border. An important recording that will appeal to folkies, rockers, and world music fans alike; One Blood—Una Sangra (Narada, 2004)

ANA GABRIEL. Upholding the lineage of her predecessors Lucha Reyes, Lola Beltran, and company, the versatile Ana Gabriel's *Joyas* *de dos Siglos* (Sony, 1998) is unrivaled by other recordings in the ranchera genre.

ASTRID HADAD. Part Lebanese, Mayan, and Mexican, Hadad is the current star of the ranchera genre. Her first recording, *Ay!* (Rounder, 1995), is her best; recorded with the impeccable string band, Los Tarzanes.

EUGENIA LEON. Songwriter and nueva cancion singer. *Norteno* (Universal, 1998); *Elas Cantan Asi* (RCA, 2003).

LLAHSA DE SELA. The reclusive Llahsa's *La Llorona* (Atlantic, 1997) is a seductive recording, a dark take on ranchera with a touch of nueva cancion, French chanteuse, and a little Garbo. She was there before Lila Downs. *The Living Road* (Warner Audiogramme, 2004) is worth the 7-year wait since her first recording; a stunning album.

LOS DE ABAJO. An eclectic band from the streets of Mexico City, on the cutting edge of the world music scene, they play a loose amalgam of ranchera, cumbia, son, hip-hop, funk, soul, salsa, and Mexican folkloric rhythms, artfully arranged, electronically driven, and expertly performed with just the right amount of daring, danger, and taste. *Cybertropic Chilango Power* (Luaka Bop, 2002) is a tour de force best listened to as a whole, effectively transporting the listener to the modern Mexico City streets.

AMPARO OCHOA (Ochoa Shelter). Talented folklorist and nueva cancion singer (1946–1992) who dedicated her life and music to combat the poverty of her people and to support indigenous and women's rights. *Boleros* (Spartacus, 1995); *Corridos Y Canciones* (Discos, 1986/1991); *Trova Yucatan* (Discos Pentagrama, 1983/95); *El Cancionero Popular* (Alerce); *Yo Pienso que a mi Pueblo* (Philips, 1978); *Canta con los Ninos* (Discos Puebla/Philips, 1980).

LUCHA REYES. The first great diva of ranchera. *Serie Platino* (RCA 1964/1998) is a good compilation that probably dates back earlier than 1964; *Mejor de lo Mejor* (RCA 2001 reissue) is a 2-disc set with all her hits; the place to begin.

JUAN REYNOSO. The Paganini of Mexico. A far cry from the typical norteno, ranchero, or mariachi musician, but Mexican through and through. *Genius of Mexico's Tierra Caliente* (Arhoolie 2003 reissue) is from his home region 150 miles southwest of Mexico City; *Plays Sones and Gustos* (Corason, 1993).

UNITED STATES

It is impossible to talk about American "world" music without alluding to the greatest art form to come out of the New World, jazz. The term itself is as inadequate as "world music" or any other label that attempts to collectively categorize and unify an artistic discipline under one heading, but it is an operable term that conveys a specific meaning throughout the world. Thousands of treatises, encyclopedias, biographies, analyses, TV documentaries, and papers devoted to the review, psychoanalysis, historical significance, and social importance of jazz make it a topic beyond the scope of this survey. In an objective, noncommercial sense, jazz is of course America's greatest world music, which has left its indelible mark on world music genres across the six continents.

Similarly, the blues, which is at the very foundation of jazz, is a topic amply covered over the past 50 years, also beyond the purview of this survey. We would love to jump into bluegrass and talk about artists from Bill Monroe to Del McCoury, however, it too is a genre that has been dissected and evaluated elsewhere, innumerable times and to great effect. Ditto American folk. We could wax eloquently about Woody and his children but there just ain't the space since the times have been a changin' so rapidly.

Certain vital, original American music genres have not been exhaustively covered by the media or in books—Cajun/Zydeco, Native American, Hawaiian, and TexMex/Tejana/Norteno—and are touched upon here. Klezmer music, which has its origins in Eastern European *shtetls* and Jewish ghettos, could be placed in any number of countries. Some experts feel klezmer is a Polish music genre; others believe that because it is music of the Jewish diaspora it belongs in the Israel section. In fact, the recent revival of the music began anew in New York in the 1970s and the majority of the leading modern artists are American, hence its inclusion in this section.

KLEZMER

The Renaissance of klezmer music that we hear today is descended from Eastern European Jewish music of the latter part of the nineteenth century. The history of klezmer as a genre however, began at least as early as the fifteenth century when Western European Jews were forced to migrate east due to expulsion, inquisition, and persecution. Russia, Poland, and other governments reluctantly accepted these Jewish immigrants. Although they had lost most of their worldly possessions, they brought their music and language (Yiddish) with them intact.

During the gradual journey east, the music evolved over time, absorbing influences along the way from local folk traditions that the diaspora encountered. Nuances from Galicia, France, Germany, Italy, Hungary, and Romania found their way into the music, enhancing its scope, but it always retained its Jewish character. The klezmorim, as the musicians were called, kept the music alive through oral tradition by passing along the tunes, sung in Yiddish, without notation or scores.

The term klezmer is a combination of two Yiddish words, *kley* meaning "vessel" and *zemer* meaning "song." Despite the long history of the music, the term *klezmer* is a recent phenomenon. It was not coined and applied until the 1930s when it was first used to describe the type of music a Jewish folk musician played, and it did not become widely popular as identifying the genre until the 1970s revival. Before the revival, musicians who played klezmer were said to play "Jewish" or "bulgar" music, a reference to the Jewish dance. Only since the boom of the 1970s has the term *klezmer* gained international recognition as the label for improvised Jewish wedding-jazz-dance music.

Klezmer today most often features the clarinet, which usurped the violin as the lead instrument at the turn of the last century. The violin and clarinet closely mimic the human voice and evoke crying, laughing, aching sounds reminiscent of the Cantor in the synagogue. The combination of instruments used in klezmer ensembles varies, including accordion, piano, bass, guitar, flute, trumpet, and percussion. However, the clarinet and the *fidl* remain the dominant instrumental voices of the music.

Klezmer in the New World has greatly expanded its scope. David Krakauer's reverence for Sidney Bechet, Andy Statman's Coltrane-inspired outings, and Frank London's avant-garde excursions with his many ensembles, including the famous Klezmatics, have transported the genre to new arenas and audiences, while maintaining the integrity of the old style. To a great degree klezmer, as performed today, is a modern genre adopted by premier American (mostly Jewish) and European musicians whose musical soul resides in the 1960s.

An in-depth review of the evolution of the greatest proponents of modern klezmer music reveals an indisputable connection to the Civil Rights and folk movements of the 1960s. That era's love affair both with the American bluegrass cognoscenti and the avant-garde jazz of Ornette Coleman, Cecil Taylor, and John Coltrane is inextricably a part of the modern idiom. Klezmer is the tether from ancient Jewish music to modern American music.

Is David Krakauer the greatest clarinetist in the world? Ivo Papasov, Charlie Neidich, and Andy Statman would protest, but it is a reasonable question. From his roots as an internationally renowned chamber music artist, Krakauer has made a quantum leap musically and artistically that virtually no classical musician before him has ever made—he has remade himself into a world class improviser in a new genre and become a genuine recording star.

Krakauer's work with the renowned Orpheus Chamber Orchestra, the New York Philharmonic, The Metropolitan Opera, and numerous chamber groups was (and is) impressive indeed. His knowledge of jazz, expertise, and love of swing (particularly Sidney Bechet) is formidable. He was a founding member of the Klezmatics and at the forefront of the New American klezmer movement. There is seemingly nothing David can't play well, from Bechet, to Chalkais to Papasov to Stoltzman to John Cage; a rare artist indeed. He has become an in-demand performer in Europe and his recent recording in Krakow, Poland, including the incorporation of rap artists, has moved the genre forward yet another modern step.

RECOMMENDED CDs

NAFTULIE BRANDWEIN. A legend and one of the most soulful clarinetists of the twentieth Century. *King of the Klezmer Clarinet* (Rounder, 1997) is a great recording, thanks to Henry Sapoznik, the tireless champion of the music.

BRAVE OLD WORLD. Revival klezmer group. *Blood Oranges* (Red House, 1997) is a quintessential recording of the new klezmer music, with modern world musical sensibilities. The Yiddish vocals by Michael Alpert make this a very special recording.

BUDOWITZ. Tsimbl, button accordions, and cellos distinguish this talented group. *Mother Tongue* (Koch, 1997) is one of the truly great klezmer recordings of the past 20 years.

DON BYRON. Former member of Boston's Klezmer Conservatory Band, Byron has gone on to become a major international star, an eclectic composer, clarinetist, and bandleader respected as a jazz, klezmer, and classical musician. *Plays the Music of Mickey Katz* (Elektra, 1993) is a tribute to the great Jewish musician/comedian.

ANTHONY COLEMAN. Avant-garde pianist, part of the New York downtown scene. *Sephardic Tinge* (Tzadik, 1995); *Monk and Jelly Roll meet Eastern Europe* (Tzadik, 1998).

GIORA FIEDMAN. Controversial, classically trained clarinetist, born in Argentina, based in Israel; more pop than klez. *Jewish Soul Music* (Hed Arzi, 1973). Magic of Klezmer (Delos, 1986).

DIRE GELT. Italian klezmer group spreading the tradition in Europe and showing that you don't have to be Jewish to play Klezmer. *Sevastopol* (Forrest Hills, 2002).

KAPELYE. Led by multi-instrumentalist/ethnomusicologist/writer/ producer Henry Sapoznik, Kapelye was one of the first bands to record in the new klezmer movement. *Kapeyle's Chicken* (Shanachie, 1987).

KLEZMATICS. The most famous and commercially successful klezmer band in the world, trailblazers for the modern idiom. *Jews with Horns* (Rounder, 1994) has a decidedly downtown New York edge to it; *Possessed* (Xenophile, 1997) is a change in direction:

Clarinetist David Krakauer has been replaced by Matt Darriau, songs with English lyrics by author Toni Kushner, and a tune paying homage to marijuana; *The Well* (Xenophile, 1998) is a thoughtful collaboration with Israeli folk star Chava Alberstein.

KLEZMER CONSERVATORY BAND. A large ensemble modeled on the bands of the 1920s and 1930s; klezmer Swing. *Jumpin' Night in the Garden of Eden* (Rounder, 1988) featuring Don Byron and Frank London.

KLEZMORIM. One of the first groups to make a splash in the revival. *Metropolis* (Flying Fish, 1981).

KHEVRISA. Quintessential classic old form without the adornment and outside influences heard in the modern klezmer movement. *European Klezmer Music* (Smithsonian, 2000) is widely considered to be among the top klezmer recordings of all time.

DAVID KRAKAUER (See Profile). *Klezmer Madness* (Tzadik, 1995) is a tour de force; *Dreams and Prayers of Isaac the Blind* (Nonesuch, 1997) includes the Kronos Quartet and a piece by Argentine Osvaldo Golijov; *Krakauer in Krakow* (Label Bleu, 2004) the artist in his native Poland with Canadian hip-hop artist "Socalled."

KROKE. Chamber ensemble from Krakow. (See Poland section.)

FRANK LONDON. Founding member and soul of the Klezmatics, London has been at the core of the klezmer revival for 20 years, bringing his avant-garde jazz background and worldview to traditional Jewish music. *The Zimros Project* (Traditional Crossroads, 2001) is a work of beauty. London sounds both like a latter-day Dizzy and Miles. The word *Zimros* refers to metrical, hymn-like songs with a poetic liturgical text traditionally sung during and between the three Sabbath meals, a tradition that dates back to the eleventh century; *Nigunim*, (Tzadik, 1999).

SOLOMON AND SOCALLED. *Socalled* is a DJ who has collaborated with Krakauer and London; Sophie Solomon is a violinist, raga-jungle DJ, and founding member of London fusion group Oi Va Voi. *Hip-hop Khasene* (Piranha, 2004), with Krakauer, London, and shtetl MC/Yiddish vocalist Michael Alpert, is an ancient Jewish marriage ritual with old school Yiddish freestylin'.

ANDY STATMAN. From his early roots in bluegrass as one of the greatest mandolin players, Statman moved to Orthodox Judaism and klezmer following the line of Dave Tarras and Naftule Brandwein. He is a true visionary who foresaw the klezmer explosion years before it hit. *Klezmer Music* (Shanachie, 1983); *Between Heaven and Earth* (Shanachie, 1995) is John Coltrane meets Naftule Brandwein, with Banjo star Bela Fleck.

ALICIA SVIGALS. Founding member and former violinist with the Klezmatics. *Fidl* (Traditional Crossroads, 1997) is a pensive, soulful recording reminiscent of a time when the fidl (violin), not the clarinet, was the dominant klezmer voice.

DAVE TARRAS. Klezmer's seminal American legend, a Russian Jew who came to the United States in 1921 and almost single-handedly popularized Eastern European Jewish music in America. *Tanz! With the Musiker Brothers* (Epic Legacy, 1955); *Yiddish American Klezmer Music* (Yazoo, 1992) is a reissue of old 78s from the 1920s to the 1940s.

KLIMPANIA ZELWER. Eclectic new klezmer band from France led by clarinetist and multi instrumentalist Jean-Marc Zelwer. *Daissa* (Le Chant du Monde, 2003). One of the freshest klezmer outings in years; original compositions, santur, accordion, fiddle, derbuka, zarbs, nyckelharpa, some vocals, deft arrangements, and a lot of soul.

CAJUN-ZYDECO

In the seventeenth century, French-speaking Acadians left their Canadian province when conflicts with the French and British forced them to migrate. They eventually settled in Louisiana, where they became known as Cajuns. The region around Lafayette and Lake Charles is home to one of the true world music genres to evolve in the United States. Associated with the Bayou, the music is really from the plains area and fields near Lafayette.

Labels are suspect—as we repeatedly confess on these pages—and there is no better example than the nuanced differences between Zydeco and Cajun. Is Cajun a music played by white bands and Zydeco by Black/Creole bands? Oh, those absurd labels and racial distinctions! Amedee Ardoin, Clifton Chenier, and Buckwheat

Zydeco were Creoles who played Cajun music and Dennis McGee, Michael Doucet, and BeauSoleil are or were French Acadians artists who play Zydeco. However you slice it, it's French, from Louisiana, and mixes the Cajun 2-step, waltzes, a little blues, rock and roll, and R&B. The music is centered on the Accordion and the fiddle, with cooking beats and good times mandatory. Like the cuisine, Louisiana music is a tasty brew like nothing else around.

Led by fiddler and vocalist Michael Doucet, a true Cajunologist, *BeauSoleil*, which means "good sun," is one of the most highly respected cajun bands in the world. A song from the British folk group Fairport Convention, *Cajun Woman*, rekindled Doucet's interest in his native music in the 1960s. He immediately relocated to France where he found the roots of Cajun music were very much alive. He immersed himself in the history and lore of the music and in the mid-1970s joined an improvisational French folk group (Coteau). Upon his return to the United States he received a grant from the NEA and began to uncover old Cajun/Zydeco compositions. He soon formed BeauSoleil with Dennis McGee, Dewey, and Will Balfa, Canray Fontenot, and Bessyl Duhon, some of the finest Cajun musicians on the scene. The band has played on movie soundtracks for *The Big Easy*, *Passion Fish*, and *Belizaire the Cajun*, at jazz and folk festivals around the world, appeared on numerous television shows, and performs regularly on Garrison Keillor's *Prairie Home Companion*.

RECOMMENDED CDs

BUCKWHEAT ZYDECO. Born Stanley Dural, Jr., he began as an organist with Chenier in the 1970s and combined tradition with contemporary sound. *100% Fortified Zydeco* (Blacktop, 1985).

NATHAN ABSHIRE. Cajun who wrote *Pine Grove Blues*, an early standard. *French Blues* (Arhoolie, 1993) from the 1930s, the real deal, imperfect fidelity.

ALPHONSE "BOIS SEC" ARDOIN. Nephew of Amédé and great accordionist who formed the Ardoin Family Band with Dewey

Balfa. *A Couple of Cajuns* (Sonet, 1987), with fiddler Dewey Balfa; *Les Blues du Bayou* (Melodeon, 1967), duets with Conray Fontenot; *Le Musique Creole* (Arhoolie, 1997).

AMÉDÉ ARDOIN (1896–1941). Accordionist and hi-pitched vocalist, the Robert Johnson of Zydeco who laid the foundation for the music. *Louisiana Cajun Music: Vol. 6* (Old Timey, 1983) contains recordings from 1928–1938, including duets with legendary fiddler Dennis McGee (the first interracial recordings of Louisiana folk music); *I'm Never Comin' Back* (Arhoolie, 1995); *Cajun Music: Fais Do Do* (Columbia, 1994), six other tunes with McGee.

BOOZOO CHAVIS. He wrote "Paper in My Shoe" in 1954, the first Zydeco hit. *Zydeco Trail Ride* (Maison de Soul, 1989).

BALFA BROTHERS. Raw Cajun from the older Balfas. *Balfa Brothers Play Traditional Cajun, Vol. 1–2* (Swallow, 1987).

BALFA TOUJOURS. Guitarist Christie Balfa carries on the family tradition. *LaPointe* (Rounder, 1998).

BEAUSOLEIL (See Profile). *Hot Chili Mama* (Arhoolie, 1988); *Bayou Cadillac* (Rounder 1989) includes "Iko Iko," "Bo Diddley," Big Joe Williams' "Baby Don't Go"; *Best of the Crawfish Years: 1985–1991* (Rounder, 2001) is their best compilation and the place to start.

CLIFTON CHENIER (1925–1987). Influenced by Muddy Waters, Fats Domino, and Professor Longhair, Chenier began playing in the early 1950s, and added blues, rock and roll, and R&B to create modern Zydeco. He made the accordion hip in Lafayette, but died just before the music reached national prominence. *Zydeco Dynamite* (Arhoolie, 1960) two-CD classic; *Clifton Chenier Anthology* (Rhino, 1993); *60 Minutes with the King of Zydeco* (Arhoolie, 1988); *Louisiana Blues + 2* (Arhoolie, 1965/91).

CANRAY FONTENOT. One of the finest Cajun fiddlers, friend of Alphonse Ardoin. *La Hot Sauce, Creole Style* (Arhoolie, 1992), with Michael Doucet and Alphonse Ardoin.

BEAU JOCQUE. The biggest zydeco star of the 1990s, the late Beau and his cavernous, booming voice bridged the gap between traditional Creole culture and contemporary music to create a funky, bass-heavy hybrid with mainstream appeal. *Pick Up on This* (Rounder, 1994); *Gonna Take You Downtown* (Rounder, 1996).

EDDIE LEJEUNE. Ardent Cajun traditionalist (no drums), accordionist, and intense vocalist. *It's in the Blood* (Rounder, 1991).

DENNIS MCGEE. Seminal figure and repository of early Acadian, Cajun music, legendary fiddler who recorded from 1929–1934 and set the stage for the music. *Early Recordings* (Morning Star).

QUEEN IDA. First woman to lead a zydeco band, a Cajun musician influenced by Tex-Mex. Ida came to music at middle age, and gained fame through her appearances in the movie *Rumblefish* and on *Saturday Night Live*. *Queen Ida in San Francisco* (Sonet, 1988) is from her adopted hometown, the CD won a Grammy.

ROCKIN' DOPSIE. Born Alton Rubin (1932–1993), he was a star accordionist before appearing on Paul Simon's *Graceland*. *Louisiana Music* (Atlantic, 1991); *Crowned Prince of Zydeco* (Maison de Soul, 1987).

TEJANO–TEX-MEX–CONJUNTO

In 1749, Spain settled the Rio Grande Valley and the Tejano (a Texan of Mexican heritage) was born. *Tejano* also refers to a genre comprising popular and folk music, which has its origins with the Mexicans who settled in Central and South Texas. It is a blend of traditonal Mexican music including *corridos* and *rancheras* and incorporates European styles, including waltz and polka, which were brought to the region by German, Polish, and Czech immigrants at the end of the nineteenth century. Most importantly, these immigrants introduced the accordion, the signature voice of Tejano. It is also called *conjunto*, which means "group" in Spanish. It was not until the Mexican Revolution (1910–1917), however, when the Europeans fled Mexico, that their musical influence was to have a major impact on Tejanos.

Tejano is a cousin to Mexican norteno, although Tejano tends to emphasize the polka beat (2/4) more than the romantic ballads. The standard conjunto unit includes accordion, 12 string guitar (*bajo sexto*), bass, and drums. Narciso Martinez adopted the two button row accordion to the music and is considered the father of conjunto. Flaco (literally, "Skinny") Jimenez became the heir to Narciso, carrying on the tradition and becoming a world music star in the 1980s. As with virtually every North American genre, rock and roll, and country music have influenced norteno, introducing electric guitar and trap drums to the conjunto lineup. Eventually the cheesy 1970s synthesizer craze also corrupted the naturalness of the music as its appeal broadened to include rock and country fans. The late pop star Selena added a Colombian *cumbia* side to the music, which further expanded the audience to South America. Modern Tejano continues to center around the ever-vibrant city of San Antonio, with a strong following in Houston and Austin as well.

RECOMMENDED CDs

LOS ALEGRES DE TERAN. Classic and influential accordion-bajo sexteto duo. *Esto est el Nuestro: Exitos* (EMI, 2001) is a nice compilation of classy and classic norteno and corridos.

RAMON AYALA. Accordionist/singer who also performs with Los Rlampagos conjunto. *20 Exitos* (Sony Discos, 2001) is a nice greatest hits compilation.

TISH HINOJOSA. Folksinger-guitarist from San Antonio with a country bent. More Joan Baez and Emmylou Harris than Lydia Mendoza. *Culture Swing* (Rounder, 1990), with a nod to Bob Wills; *Taos to Tennessee* (Watermelon, 1987) is her debut.

FLACO JIMENEZ. Son of Santiago Jimenez and brother of Santiago, Jr., Flaco is the big name in Tejano. His style is somewhat conservative, "sticking to the rules," so to speak, but he is a classic. *Arriba el Norte* (Rounder, 1988); *Ay te dejo en San Antonio y Mas* (Arhoolie, 1985) is a good starting point.

SANTIAGO JIMENEZ, JR. Flaco's brother who plays more traditionally. *Mero Mero de San Antonio* (Arhoolie, 1990), every facet of the Tex-Mex accordion repertoire is here.

ESTEBAN STEVE JORDAN. Eye patch, long hair, and that avant-garde accordion style set Jordan apart from the rest. *The Many Sounds of Steve Jordan* (Arhoolie, 1985) the "El Corrido de Johnny El Pachuco" track is worth the price of admission.

NARCISO MARTINEZ. Known as the hurricane of the valley (the lower Rio Grande, from Laredo to the Gulf) and the father of conjunto. *El Huracan del Va*lle (Arhoolie, 1977).

RAUL MARTINEZ. Nephew of Narciso and a pioneer accordionist, composer, and singer. *Dueto Alegre* (Arhoolie, 2003) includes sounds from 1948–1956, pure and simple with Bajo Sexteto player and partner Juan Gonzalez.

LYDIA MENDOZA. The first lady of Tejano, who began singing in the late 1920s as part of her family band, Las Hermanas Mendoza. Lydia's rendition of *Mal Hombre* shocked chauvinistic Latin audiences in 1934 with lyrics favoring the female point of view, a nonexistent concept in Tejano at the time. She was "rediscovered" by folklorist/record label owner Chris Strachwitz in the early 1980s, who rereleased her early recordings as well as producing new sessions. *Gloria de Texas* (Arhoolie, 1981); *La Alondra de la Frontera* (Arhoolie, 2001), both sides with Lydia solo on guitar, and the second is live.

EMILIO NAVAIRA. Current singing star who straddles the Tex-Mex line with a country tilt. *El Rey del Rodeo* (RCA, 2000); *Emilo Navaira* (EMI Latin, 1989).

LOS TIGRES DEL NORTE. Based in San Diego and led by the Hernandez brothers; popular, socially aware, and controversial. *Los dos Pleb*es (Fonovisa, 1994); *Corridos Prohibidos* (Fonavisa, 1989) has narcocorridos glorifying the drug trade, but also criticizing corruption.

TEXAS TORNADOES. Supergroup with Flaco Jimenez, Doug Sahm, Augie Meyers, and Freddy Fender. *Texas Tornadoes* (Reprise, 1990) won a Grammy.

BETO VILLA. Orquesta leader and saxophonist who worked with Narciso Martinez and led a big band in the early 1950s. *Father of Orquesta Tejana* (Arhoolie, 1992) is a compilation from 1948–1952.

NATIVE AMERICAN

The United States government has never been able and will never be able to justify the deceit, treachery, and atrocities committed against Native Americans; no number of Casinos, tax breaks, or apologies can make amends. Nonetheless, in the twenty-first century Native Americans, also called First Nations or First Peoples, coexist on their land in an uneasy alliance with their oppressors' progeny and have made great strides in recapturing their complex culture that was virtually made extinct by the first part of the twentieth century.

The history and plight of the Native American has been documented extensively over the past 40 years, and we recommend three special books for those interested: Mari Sandoz's *Crazy Horse*; Ralph K. Andrist's *The Long Death*; and Edmund Wilson's *Apologies to the Iroquois*.

THE MUSIC

The music of Native North Americans is primarily vocal, usually choral, and entirely melodic. There is no harmony or polyphony. There is no true concept of absolute pitch and intonation can appear uncertain. Various drums and rattles are the chief percussion instruments. Wind instruments are mainly flutes and whistles. The flute, represented by the popular southwest icon the *Kokopeli*, is the voice of Native American music. Song is the chief means of communicating with the supernatural, and definite results, such as rain, success in battle, or curing an illness, is expected. Native American songs fall into three categories: Traditional songs handed down from generation to generation; ceremonial and medicine songs; and modern songs, influenced by European culture. Love songs are not common, considered degenerate and from whites by many Native Americans. Many Native American groups consider songs personal property that can be sold, loaned, or inherited, sort of an oral version of the United States Copyright laws. Songs are widely thought to be gifts from the creator and composers "catch" a song in their dreams or through interaction with others. Many song forms employ vocables, phrases, or sounds with no meaning. There are over 500 tribes in North America and it is impractical to review the nuanced differences in their music. In most tribes, songs and dances are included in a variety of harvest festivals, birthing and naming ceremonies, mourning ceremonies, war dances, and hunting dances, each with a proscribed repertoire.

Some notable tribal uses of songs include:

- The Pueblo of the Southwest, including the *Hopi and Zuñi*, have ceremonies centering on the harvest, including green and blue corn dances.

- The *Navajo* call their song and dance ceremonies "ways," which are plays that can last for days and include sand painting and chanting.
- The *Plains* people use the flute regularly and are known for their powwow, major events today that draw dancers and groups from all over the country.
- The songs of the northeast and eastern Woodlands people including the *Seneca* and *Delaware* are often humorous, with a relaxed style of singing and more instrumental accompaniment than in the west.
- In the south, *Choctaw* social dance and song is linked to an athletic event similar to lacrosse (an Indian invention). The music consists of songs for healing, songs by the players, and dance music before and after the game.
- The *Oneidas, Cherokees*, and *Kiowas* enjoy a hymn singing tradition.

RECOMMENDED CDs

BRIAN AKIPA. Sioux flutist whose message is about handing down tradition and giving back to the elders. Mystic Moments (Soar, 1995).

SHARON BURCH. Navajo vocalist and historian. *Yazzie Girl* (Canyon, 1989) a children's album; *Colors of My Heart* (Canyon, 1999) is for mothers and daughters.

COYOTE OLDHAM. Duo of American flutists dedicated to Native American and New Age music. *Tear of the Moon* (Coyote Oldham, 1987); *The Shape of Time* (Coyote Oldham, 1995) is Native American space music for meditation or a planetarium.

JOSEPH FIRE CROW. Traditional Northern Cheyenne flutist. *Northern Cheyenne Flute* (Makoche, 1996) with vocables; mesmerizing.

CISSY GOODEHOUSE. Vocalist and collaborator with Kevin Locke. *Tiwale* (Makoche, 1997).

KEVIN LOCKE (nee Tokeya Inajin). Lakota Sioux who revived the art of the North Plains flute and is adept at hoop dancing.

Dream Catcher (Warner Bros., 1992); *First Flute* (Makoche, 1999), flute, wind, water, and birds.

R. CARLOS NAKAI. Tucson-based multi-instrumentalist and cultural anthropologist of Navajo-Ute descent. He uses synths and writes his own music. His flute recordings are surreal and peaceful. *Ancestral Voices* (Canyon, 1992), serial, spiritual, new age soundscapes with guitarist and string player William Eaton.

ROBBIE ROBERTSON. Legendary superstar, leader of The Band, early Dylan sideman, and film composer (*Raging Bull*) born to Jewish father and a Mohawk mother. He reconnected with his Native American roots with *The Red Road Ensemble: Music for Native Americans* (Capitol, 1994), used for a TV documentary, *Contact from the Underworld of Redboy*.

BUFFY SAINT MARIE. An American icon, a leading voice in the Civil Rights movement of the 1960s, Native American activist, feminist, composer, and provocateur. *It's My Way* (Fontana, 1964) contains her classic protest song "Universal Soldier" and "Now that the Buffalo's Gone." Still her greatest recording; powerful, timely, and gripping 40-odd years later, with Patrick Sky on guitar and jazz bassist Art Davis.

JOANNE SHENENDOAH. Member of the Wolf clan of the Oneida Nation, Iroquois confederacy, and arguably the most prominent Native American artist in the world today, an outspoken advocate for her people. *Orenda* (Silver Wave, 1998) sung in her native tongue; ethereal; *Matriarch* (Silver Wave, 1996), dedicated to the Oneida women, advisors, and counselors to their aggressive males through the ages.

DOUGLAS SPOTTED EAGLE. Flutist/film composer who incorporates synthesizers into Native sounds. *Legend of Flute Boy* (Natural, 1992) is a new age saga.

FLOYD WESTERMAN. Oglala Sioux, outspoken activist, and accomplished guitarist and actor. He was separated from his family as a child, a practice common both in America and in Australia with the Aborigines that is/was calculated by the government to destroy Native Culture forever. *Custer Died for Your Sins* (Red Crow, 1970) contains protest songs; the title is from the Vine Deloria book.

HAWAII

The 50th state is culturally part of Polynesia. It has been a vacation paradise for the rich and famous for a century, home to the greatest surfing culture in the world, and the site of the infamous Pearl Harbor attack on December 7, 1941, which expedited the United States entry into World War II.

THE MUSIC

Hawaii produced one of the earliest forms of world music circa 1916, when the hula and steel guitar sound became popular throughout the United States. Hawaiian music was the bestselling form of music in the United States in the 1920s. The famous hula (dance) and chant (mele), which accompanied the craze, are still found throughout Polynesia.

The instrument most associated with Hawaii is the *ukulele* ("jumping flea" in Hawaiian), which was brought to the islands by Portuguese sailors from Madeira in the 1870s. The ukulele is a relative of the *cavaquinho* and *braguinha,* a small four-stringed instrument, which is a larger version of the cavaquinho (*see* Portugal). Hawaii is also known for its slack key guitar, a style of tuning and playing that developed on the Islands in the early twentieth century. The term *slack key* comes from retuning the instrument (by loosening the strings) so that an open chord is played. A steel bar is used to fret the strings, creating a singing effect. Slack key playing went into remission in the 1960s, but Gabby Pahinui led the revival in the 1970s. The ever-clever and ubiquitous Ry Cooder brought Gabby to public attention from obscurity. The lap steel guitar is also popular in Hawaii. By holding a solid object across the strings while plucking them, a glissando effect is created. The most common drum in Hawaii is called the *pahu,* with a head made of sharkskin and another link to the musical roots of Polynesia.

RECOMMENDED CDs

KEOLA BEAMER. Beamer is a slack key guitar star who has combined the style with modern sounds and stayed current for 30 years. *Wooden Boat* (Windham Hill, 1994).

SONNY CHILLINGWORTH. Slack key player who incorporates Mexican, Latino, and Cowboy music into his act. *Solo Sonny* (Windham Hill, 1994) is soothing and mellow.

ROBI KAHAKALAU. Eclectic female vocalist who sings in Tahitian, Hawaiian, English, and French. *All I Want Is All You Need* (Kanai'a, 2000) is folk rock Hawaii.

ISRAEL "IZ" KAMAKAWIWO OLE. The most popular artist from Hawaii, he died in 1998 at age 38 weighing close to 700 pounds. His music is truly international and is being used in films 6 years after his death. *N dis Life* (Big Boy, 1996); *Ka 'Ano'I* (Tropical Music, 1990).

RAY KANE. Seminal slack key guitarist (b.1925), the elder statesman who has been recording since 1961. *Punahele* (Dancing Cat, 1990); *Master of the Slack Key Guitar* (Rounder, 1988).

LEDWARD KAPAANA'. Slack key disciple of Ray Kane and Gabby Pahinui. *Black Sand* (Dancing Cat, 2000) on George Winston's label.

CYRIL PAHINUI. Son of Gabby and holding the fort in the family slack key tradition. *Night Moon: Po Mahina* (Windham Hill, 1998).

GABBY PAHINUI. Slack key guitar legend. *The Gabby Pahinui Hawaiian Band* (Edsel, 1994). Recorded in North Kona in 1974 with Sonny Chillington, his sons, and a guest spot from Ry Cooder. The one that reignited the Slack Key.

KEAHLI 'I REICHEL. Major voice on the contemporary scene and fine slack key guitarist. *Kawaipunahele* (Punahele, 1994) is chant and traditional; *E O Mai* (Punahele, 1997) has slack key and tasteful vocals.

SOUTH AMERICA

Argentina
Bolivia
Brazil
Chile
Colombia

Ecuador
French Guinea
Guyana
Paraguay
Peru

Suriname
Venezuela
Uruguay

According to recent archaeological, geological, and genetic research, South America is the newest (last) continent to be inhabited by *Homo sapiens*. In many ways it remains the youngest region of the world.

Despite technological and political advances in South America during the past decade, the continent continues to exist in the shadow and under the thumb of the United States and, to a lesser extent, Europe. When it comes to music, however, South America is a major world power, second to none in popularity, influence, and appeal. The variety of Latin musical genres originating from South America is substantial, including tango, milonga, cumbia, paranda, llanero, choro, samba, baio, and vallenato. South America also boasts many unique forms of traditional, folk, and country music that have evolved from Amerindian culture, including the vast array of Andean and

Panpipe Music. The ubiquitous *nueva cancion*—new song—genre is South America's greatest folk music gift to the world.

Although the culture, history, and music of the major South American nations is quite distinct, there is one musical influence that is pervasive and profound throughout the continent: The music of African slaves brought to the New World from the 1500s through the late nineteenth century permeates virtually every genre. The world music of South America is inextricably related to the music of West Africa.

This section of the book focuses on the 10 major countries on the continent, treated here in alphabetical order. The smaller nations of Suriname, French Guinea, and Guyana are covered in the Caribbean section, because of their musical and historical kinship with the island culture of the West Indies.

ARGENTINA

South America's most sophisticated country is an ongoing enigma. Argentina's political legacy in the twentieth century was one of misguided ideals, lost opportunity, squandered wealth, and corrupt governments. The obsessive yearning for recognition in the first world and tying its currency to the dollar in the 1990s led to monetary crises that bankrupted Argentina, which has created a massive depression. Perhaps the crises will lead to true democracy and fiscal responsibility, and allow Argentina to once again compete in the world market as it did in the early part of the twentieth century when Argentina's economic clout rivaled that of France. Only time will tell. Murmurings from Patagonia about secession are not a good sign.

Despite its political history, Argentina possesses great natural riches, is a major world agricultural region, has the most advanced cattle ranching industry in the world, a great winemaking tradition, world class footballers, the best polo players, and a vibrant society of cosmopolitans who boast a style and cache more Western European than South American.

Regardless of her political and economic woes, Argentina is a major force in world music that has given us one of its greatest treasures, tango.

TANGO

As with most indigenous urban port music that emerged during the twentieth century, the roots of tango can be traced to Black slaves who, in this instance, were brought from West Africa to the River Plate during the latter part of the nineteenth century. Tango is a word with a variety of possible origins. Some experts believe it to be derivative of the Yoruban (A West African religion) word *tano*, which slaves used to identify their drums and communicate where music was being played. Others believe the word comes from the Portuguese *tanguera*, meaning "to play." Whatever the origin, it is clear that West African rhythms, dances, and songs were an integral part of the development of the genre. More than 100 years after its creation, tango remains a classic popular music, especially in Buenos Aires where tradition dies hard. The Portenos, as the denizens of the city are called, are passionate about the old music and will not readily countenance change or innovation when it comes to their tradition.

The famed dance music was first transported to Europe by the white slave trade that sailed between Buenos Aires and Marseilles supplying South America with workers and women in a time when Buenos Aires was a major center of world culture and a destination for many Western Europeans seeking to escape the political and social rigidity of their native countries. In the 1920s this cultural exchange made tango the rage in Paris. Americans Vernon and Irene Castle gave tango wider exposure through their performances and the boom became international. It was the great singer and composer Carlos Gardel (who tragically perished in a plane crash in Colombia in 1935), however, who brought tango to worldwide attention by introducing *tango cancion*, a vocal version of the music (see Profile). The music of master tango composers Juan Carlos Cobian, Francisco Canaro, Julio De Caro, Horacio Salgan, Jose Maria Contursi, and lyricist Enrique Cadicamo is still heard throughout Buenos Aires and the recordings of bandleaders Anibal Troilo and Osvaldo Pugliese continue to be popular in Argentina. Tango's stature seems stronger today than ever, enjoying popularity in the theatre, on film, and in clubs throughout the world.

NUEVO TANGO

The indifferent reception Portenos gave to their greatest composer—Astor Piazolla (1921–1992)—during his lifetime exemplifies the stubbornly conservative nature of Argentine society. Father of *nuevo tango*, Piazolla rarely enjoyed a warm welcome in his native land while alive. The tango press continually criticized him for "going too far" much as the jazz establishment rejected Ornette Coleman in the late 1950s. Perhaps they felt Piazzolla sinned by going to study in Paris with the legendary Nadia Boulanger and that his modern approach would ruin their precious music.

In fact, Piazzolla took the tango to lofty musical realms by elevating it from strictly a dance form to performance music for the concert stage. He also introduced group improvisation to a previously strict discipline. With a nudge from the work of seminal pianist Horacio Salgan, who began to stretch the music in the early 1950s, Piazzolla revolutionized tango through his numerous compositions and unparalleled virtuosity on the bandoneon (a small button accordion invented in Germany in the nineteenth century), the signature instrumental voice of the tango. His work is widely considered to be a major contribution to twentieth-century musical literature. Classical orchestras and chamber musicians regularly perform his compositions all over the world.

Piazzolla is revered as a genius and a maestro in the United States, Brazil, Japan, and throughout Europe. He is without question the most important musical force to come from Argentina since Gardel. Since Piazzolla's passing in 1992, his long-time colleague, the virtuoso pianist Pablo Ziegler, has carried the torch for the new tango. Ziegler is exposing the music to a wider audience by incorporating jazz and other world music forms into his own brand of nuevo tango through his compositions and startlingly piano technique.

NUEVA CANCION

Argentina has produced musical forms other than tango, including the rural-based milonga and the country style, accordion-based chamame. The most important other world music form from Argentina, however, is a unique brand of political protest music that emerged in the 1940s. Argentina's long history of dictatorships and human rights abuses throughout much of the twentieth century helped foster *nueva cancion*, a political folk-song movement, which spread throughout South and Central America to parts of Western Europe and North Africa.

Atahualpa Yupanqui (1908–1992) is widely credited as the founder of this unofficial movement. Yupanqui took his name from one of the last-known Incas, and was writing folk songs about the plight of Amerindians as early as 1926. After World War II, he was forced into exile by the censorship of the Peron regimes. His finest compositions were written as an expatriate in Paris in the 1940s where he hung out with Edith Piaf and other postwar bohemian artists, including the great Chilean songwriter-activist Violeta Parra. His music is poetic and provocative. His songs lament the desperation and poverty of rural peasants and cry for respect, independence, and peace. This is the music that spawned the notion that song could serve as a weapon of protest more powerful in combating despots and dictators than the gun. The *nueva cancion* movement used the simple folk song effectively to oppose a seemingly endless number of juntas and dictatorships that plagued South America through the 1980s. Yupanqui's incomparably beautiful, artistic, and politically astute recordings are the place to start in order to understand the genesis, feeling, style, and sensibility of *nueva cancion*.

Yupanqui's progeny and subsequent exponents of *nueva cancion* abound. Argentina's Mercedes Sosa; Chile's Inti Illimani and Victor Jara; Bolivia's Emma Junaro; Cuba's Carlos Puebla, Daniel Castillo, Silvio Rodriguez, and Pablo Milanes; Mexico's Amparo Ochoa; Uruguay's Daniel Viglietti; Portugal's Jose Afonso; Mallorca's Maria del mar Bonet; Catalonia's Lluis Llach; Greece's George Dalaras; and Algerian-Berber Matoub Lounes are all direct descendants of Yupanqui and Parra. These bold artists have followed the tradition as sophisticated composers and performers of protest music. In Cuba the music is called *nueva trova*; in Brazil and Portugal, *nova cancao*. *Nueva cancion* also presaged and fertilized the American folk-protest music that accompanied the Civil Rights movement. Unlike American protest music, however, *nueva cancion* has a political and musical life that survives and thrives today.

The tango did not become truly fashionable until Carlos Gardel and his suave machismo persona emerged in the 1920s. He was one of the first true international superstars of the twentieth century. Born in Toulouse, France, in 1890, Gardel's family moved to Argentina when he was very young and he grew up in the slums of Buenos Aires. With his great voice and good looks, he became a working-class hero at an early age, and his recordings remain the most authoritative examples of classic tango cancion. He transformed tango into a vocal music and has left his eternal stamp on the genre.

Directly because of Gardel, the tango gained such popularity that classical luminaries Igor Stravinsky, Darius Milhaud, and Kurt Weill were inspired to compose classical tango music. Gardel's grave at the famed Chacarita Cemetery in the Recoleta district of Buenos Aires receives more flowers on a daily basis than any other burial site on the planet (yes, more than Elvis). His recordings, initially backed by *orchestra tipicas* of the day, but most often accompanied only by guitar, are widely available today in many configurations. The finest is the 16-disc set (available individually) on the Swiss El Bandoneon label, with detailed notes in Spanish. However, one must be aware of the many poor Gardel recordings on the market, and purchase carefully.

In the land of tango, paradoxically the most beautiful voice from Argentina belongs to the first lady of the *nueva cancion* movement, the remarkable Mercedes Sosa. She has served as the fulcrum for antiwar protest music throughout South America since the 1960s, waging a constant battle against the legacy of injustices perpetrated against her fellow South Americans.

Mercedes was once arrested by the Argentine military, along with half her audience at a concert in 1978, because of her outspoken lyrics. In exile she remained an active voice against the "disappearing" during the military's domestic war against its own people and adamantly opposed the Falkland/Malvinas war. Mercedes has championed the cause of Argentines, Amerindians, and Civil Rights for all of South America using her voice and the stage as her weapons against oppression. Much of her best work, musically and politically, was done while in exile in the 1970s before the change in government in Buenos Aires in 1987. Her exquisite, hauntingly beautiful voice and impeccable choice of material and musical partners places her very high on the overall list of world music singers.

RECOMMENDED CDs

HAYDEE ALBA. *Borges: Milongas y al tangos* (Playasound, 1999), a nueva cancion tango performance with an Edith Piaf accent.

MARCELO ALVAREZ. Leading tenor and opera singer. *Marcelo Alvarez Sings Gardel* backed by Pablo Ziegler (piano), Fernando Suarez-Paz (violin), Hector Console (bass)—3/5 of the classic 1980s Piazzolla Quintet.

CARLOS GARDEL. (See Profile). *Sui Buenos Aires Querido (Vol 1), Criolita Deci que Si (Vol 9), and Gardel en Nueva York (Vol 7)* on El Bandoneon; a good choice for an overview is *The Best of Carlos Gardel* (EMI Hemisphere).

ALFREDO GOBBI: *El violin Romantico del tango* (El Bandoneon), from 1947. Master violinist and composer.

SANDRA LUNA. Recent vocal addition to the nueva tango genre, Sandra is a rising star. *Tango Varon* (World Connection, 2003) covers the 1920s, Gardel, Piazzolla, and originals including candomble percussion. A tasteful acoustic debut.

LITTO NEBBIA: *La Musica Inedita de Enrique Cadicamo* (Melopia, 1994), an instrumental tribute by one of Argentina's leading producers.

NELLY OMAR. *Nelly Omar/Francisco Fiorentino* (El Bandoneon) from 1947 is a gem, recorded under the direction of a young Astor Piazzolla. Nelly is the finest old style female Tango vocalist.

ASTOR PIAZZOLLA. After leaving Anibal Troilo, Astor formed his now legendary quintet in the 1960s; but it is his quintet from the 1980s that brought him international acclaim. He is considered one of the finest Bandoneonists of all time. With the 1980s Quintet: *Tristezas de un Doble A* (Mesidor, 1986); *Zero Hour* (American Clave, 1986); *Camorra* (Nonesuch, 1988 reissue); with the 1960s

Quintet: *Introduction al Angel, Vol. 1; Piazzolla Interprets Piazzolla.*(Melopea, 1963/1993).

OSVALDO PUGLIESE. Essential bandleader and composer in the 1930s and 1940s. *Osvaldo Pugliese, 1947–1949* (El Bandoneon, 1991).

SUSANA RINALDI. *Mi Voz Y Mi Ciudad* (Diapason, 1994), an offbeat cabaret flavored outing with bandoneon and organ.

HORACIO SALGAN. Salgan is the link between classic and nuevo tango. *En Vivo en el Club del Vino*, (WEA, 2000) is a duet recording with guitarist Ubaldi de Lio; *Legendes du tango*, (WEA, 1999) a live set from Paris with the *Quinteto Real.*

DINO SALUZZI. Perhaps the greatest living bandoneonist playing in the milonga tradition; *Cite de la Musica* (ECM, 1998) is his best.

MERCEDES SIMONE. *La Dama del tango* (El Bandoneon, 1993/1928–42).

MERCEDES SOSA. (See Profile). *30 Anos; Gracias a la Vida* (Philips, 1975); *En Vivo Argentina* (Philips, 1982/91) with Leon Geico, Charly Garcia, and Ariel Ramirez; *Mercedes Sosa* (Polygram, 1987).

CHANGO SPASIUK. Spasiuk is the new champion of Chamame, the country music from the northeast of Argentina that incorporates complex African and Spanish rhythms with the local Mbya-Guranai Indian folk tunes. Spasiuk is an accordion whiz, heir to the great Raul Barboza. *The Charm of Chamame* (Weltwinder 2003) includes a guest spot by Mercedes Sosa.

ANIBAL TROILO. *Sur* (El Bandoneon) from 1949 with the great singer Edmundo Rivero; *Del Tempo Guapa* (El Bandoneon) from 1947. Troilo is an all time great composer, leader and Bandoneonist.

ADRIANA VARELA. A current star in Buenos Aires and Spain whose smokey sexy voice is one of our favorites. *Cora Zones per Versas* (Melopea, 1994); *Varela Canta Cadisamo* (Melopea, 1995).

ATAHUALPA YUPANQUI. *30 Ans de Chansons* (Le Chant du Monde, 1997 reissue) is the one to buy first; *Camino del Indio* (compilation from 1942–1944), *La Zamba Perdida* and *Magia de Atahualpa Yupanqui* (an 8 CD set with virtually everything he ever recorded).

PABLO ZIEGLER. *Quintet for New tango* (RCA/BMG, 1999) a tour de force; *Asfalto (BMG, 1997); Bajo Cero* (Khaeon, 2003) with

Walter Castro and Quique Sinesi is gorgeous and peerless as a piano trio recording.

BOLIVIA

La Paz is the highest capital city in the world (12,000+ feet), a mixture of modern technology, breathtaking physical beauty, and ancient Incan culture. The music of the Andes embraces a culture that has survived numerous invasions, but continues to face the harsh realty that is the life of Amerindians forced to integrate into fast-paced Western society on their native soil.

Following the revolution in Bolivia in 1952, the country experienced a period of reform when Amerindians gained many rights, including agricultural reform, the right to vote, and nationalization of the vast mining industry. As peasants moved from rural areas to the cities for work, Quecha, the language of the Incas, and the Incan culture began to be integrated into Bolivian society.

The music of Bolivia speaks of the solitude of the rural existence of the Andean culture, the mystical environment of the region, and its sacred past. Traditional music emerged on the radio circa 1965 when the seminal Andean music group, Los Jairas, brought *folklorica musica* to the urban population, presenting their traditional music in an amalgam of styles, clearly and cleverly geared to the European-based population and its taste. Prior to Los Jairas, middle-class and *mestizo* a cross of (indigenous people with African Slaves) musicians performed most of the music in urban areas, music that did not incorporate Amerindian instruments and tunes. Gilbert Favre and Violeta Parra were creating a similar revolution in Santiago, Chile, at this time as the movement spread throughout the Andes.

Following the lead of Los Jairas, many other Bolivian groups emerged playing music characterized by the mystical sound of the panpipes and quenas (bamboo flutes), singing in both Spanish and Quechan. Inevitably Amerindian music gradually combined with urban dance forms including the *huayno* (also popular in Peru) and *sayas*, a dance with African roots brought to Bolivia in the seventeenth century during the slave trade. *Sayas* are most often performed at carnival with men dressed in full regalia (bells, straw hats, etc.) and are often played by brass bands or folklorica string groups. The music is characterized by a strong drum introduction and repetitive rhythm.

The tune "Llorando se fue," by the popular group K'jarkas is said to have been the basis for the unfortunate lambada craze of the 1980s.

Despite the overwhelming pull from the modern world, Bolivian culture continues to be uniquely Andean in flavor. Ancient mores and customs continue to survive. Traditional clothing is favored, still a trademark. Coca leaves remain important in Andean culture as a part of the diet, not in the processed form so in demand in the contraband global economy, but as a cultural substance; to Bolivians, coca is a sacred plant.

Andean music is performed primarily on the following instruments:

- *Charango*: A ten stringed, mandolin shaped instrument originating after the Spanish invasion. The original charangos were made from the chest of the condor, tortoise, and armadillo shells and clay, but today are made from wood.
- *Zamponas* (also called *sikus*): Panpipes made out of bamboo from the Amazon; the oldest pre-Incan instrument. Today they are played in pairs.
- *Quenas and Quenachu*: Perhaps as old as the *zamponas*, the *quena* is a bamboo flute, end blown, with seven holes.
- *Bombo*: A drum made from llama or sheepskin, played with a mallet.
- *Chajchas*: Sheep or llama hooves twisted together, used as percussion.

RECOMMENDED CDs

LOS K'JARKAS. Los K'jarkas has played a major role in development of educational centers for Andean folk music in Peru, Ecuador, and their native Bolivia. *El Arbol de Mi Destino* (Discolandia, 1992) is a beautiful, sentimental recording; *Cant a la Mujer de Mi Pueblo* (Tumi, 1997) contains "Llorando se fue," the tune that sparked the lambada; *El Amor y la Libertad* (Tumi 1985).

RUMILLAJATA. "City of Stone" in Quechan, Rumillajta makes its own instruments. *Hoja de Coca* (1984, Tumi).

EMMA JUNARO. Nueva cancion singer. *Canta a Matilde Casazola* (Riverboat, 1994) with legendary Uruguayan guitarist Fernando Cabrera.

BRAZIL

Along with American jazz, Brazilian music is the greatest learned popular music of the twentieth century. The catalogue of available Brazilian recordings is extensive, as large as any other world music genre.

As Brazil shed its Portuguese colonizers and abolished slavery in the mid-1800s, its richly diverse musical culture began to gain popularity worldwide. By the end of the nineteenth century, the impact and influence of Brazilian music had outstripped that of the motherland in Europe. *Choro* emerged as Brazil's first international contribution to modern music in the early part of the twentieth century. *Samba,* a more African-based genre created in the urban port cities of Brazil, soon usurped choro's status as the national music. Even more than "futebol," samba remains Brazil's greatest international calling card.

HISTORY AND POLITICS

Throughout the last half of the twentieth century, Brazil was perpetually touted as a country with unlimited potential, a budding giant whose vast natural resources, physical beauty, diverse population, and progressive vision would lead the way to the future. It was a nation that had boldly rejected slavery and paid homage to its African Ancestry while graciously absorbing the best aspects of Portuguese culture. Completion of the futuristic capital city Brasilia in the late 1950s, literally in the middle of nowhere and designed by visionary architect Oscar Neimeyer, seemed to prove that Brazil could do the impossible. For a moment Brazil had arrived and was ready to have lasting impact on the future of world culture, politics, and economics. Somehow the dream has yet to be realized, although the great potential lingers.

As with many countries in South America, Brazil has experienced its share of political turmoil, particularly when a military dictatorship overthrew Kubitcshek's progressive democratic government in the 1960s. Kubitcshek, like his Chilean counterpart Allende, leaned a bit too much toward socialist democracy for the comfort of the economic powers that actually controlled the country. He also had a habit of cavorting with artists and musicians, particularly the *bossa nova* crowd, which eventually contributed to his demise. Repression, censorship, and the loss of important everyday freedoms became the way of life in Brazil following Kubitcshek's ouster. As usual, the artists and musicians led the way in protest.

The openly brazen musical atmosphere prevalent in Brazil before the dictatorship was quickly forced into exile. The *tropicalia* movement, both the musical segment led by Gilberto Gil and Caetano Veloso and the conceptual approach expressed by the Brazilian film and art community, emerged in the late 1960s as the leading form of organized protest against government policies (and against the far left), with a little help from their friends in the United States and United Kingdom. The political climate remained unsteady through the 1970s and into the early 1980s, but the music never stopped, continually evolving overseas and underground.

The current, relative stability of Brazil's economy and government in the new millennium has seen a boom in all forms of Brazilian music. The jury is out on how the 2002 election of Brazil's first "people's President," Lula Silva, will impact the welfare of the country. The initial reports were good as Brazil emerges as a South American power that has maintained stability amidst a sea of war, bankruptcy, and political turmoil in Colombia, Argentina, and Venezuela.

THE SOUNDS OF BRAZIL

The *choro* music of performers Nazareth, Abreu, and Pixinguinha in the early part of the twentieth century represent a style and innovative genius parallel to the early American jazz of Louis Armstrong, Sidney Bechet, Duke Ellington and Fats Waller. It is fascinating to compare the evolution of choro (and Brazilian music in general) from the time of Pixinguinha (Alfredo de Rocha Vianna, Jr.; 1898–1973), with its rapid modulations and melodic leaps, to American jazz and its growth from the time of Armstrong to Ellington. Both African-American musical forms evolved with virtually no cross-pollination until the 1930s, yet the manner of presentation, instrumentation, role of improvisation, relation to popular dance and musical conclusions of choro and early jazz developed along eerily similar lines. After decades of dormancy, choro has enjoyed a renewed worldwide popularity since the mid-1990s.

Samba is Brazil's most classic popular music, also dating back nearly a century. It is characterized by 2/4 meter and interlocking syncopation between melody and accompaniment that, when combined with the Brazilian spirit, produces pure rhythmic magic. Samba arose as Brazil's urban port music, invented by the persecuted, downtrodden workers as a way to express their African culture and as an essential source of dignity and pride. As a basic musical form, samba is to Brazilian music what the blues is to American music.

Samba came to being as a distinct genre in the early part of the twentieth century in Rio de Janeiro. The word itself seems to come from Angola, where "semba" refers to a ritualistic dance involving navel touching that was part of many African circle dances. The music began to coalesce into its own form when slaves and ex-slaves migrated to Rio in the late 1800s following the decline of the tobacco and cocoa plantations in Bahia. The "Law of the Free Womb" (1871), which declared children born to slaves free, and the abolition of slavery circa 1888, also contributed to the influx of slaves into Brazil's capital.

By 1915, a section of Rio called the Praca Onze (eleventh plaza) was almost completely African in its make up. The slave trade had entered Brazil primarily in the city of Salvador in Bahia, but when former slaves became free they migrated to Rio. They kept their musical culture intact by worshiping their African gods (Orishas) and paying homage to them in rituals conducted at the homes of Tias, (aunts), the traditional Bahian matriarchs. In the 1920s the great Batutas (masters) including Pixinguinha, Caninha, Donga, Sinho, Joao da Baiana, and others gathered at the homes of the Tias where the early percussion-based samba was formed. Samba schools (escolas) began around 1928, at first as part of Rio's Carnaval. Today the escolas function throughout the major cities of Brazil as huge corporate entities centering on competitions during Carnival, perhaps the world's wildest, most orgiastic public musical extravaganza.

In the 1930s, a second wave of sambistas comprising mostly white composers including Noel Rosa, Ary Barroso, and Dorival Caymmi, began to write sambas that emphasized melody more than the African-based rhythm of their predecessors. This music became known as *samba-cancao*, and became popular with the middle class. This trend set the stage for the *bossa nova* craze.

The Brazilian musical genre most familiar to the world *is bossa nova*, which began with the work of Tom Jobim, Joao Donato, Johnny Alf, Carlos Lyra, and Joao Gilberto in the mid-1950s. The "new thing" or "way," as the title implies, refined samba much in the same way as the cool sounds of Miles Davis refined jazz. Along with Heitor Villa-Lobos, Antonio Carlos ("Tom") Jobim is the most important composer from Brazil and one of the major composers of popular music and song in the twentieth century, as significant a figure as Cole Porter, Duke Ellington, or George Gershwin. His innovations were greatly influenced by his idol Villa-Lobos and the orchestral style and voicing genius of Debussy. Jobim's break came with the music he wrote for the play *Orfeo Negro*, produced in Paris in 1956. The play became the basis of the classic Camus film *Black Orpheus*, released in 1959, which featured music by Jobim and Luis Bonfa, including Bonfa's classic *Manha de Carnaval*.

Joao Gilberto is the original *voice* of the *bossa nova*, the one most credited with inventing the style. He perfected the concept of *canto faldo*—spoken song—and a style of rhythmic, syncopated guitar playing that was truly revolutionary in the late 1950s, which has become a staple of Brazilian guitar playing ever since. Miles Davis put it best when asked about Joao's singing. He said (to paraphrase): "His voice is so ***ing incredible, I could listen all night to him singing the ***ing phone book." For all its commercialism and overexposure, *bossa nova* remains a permanent part of the vocabulary of pop music throughout the world.

Northeastern *baiao* from the arid *Sertao* region is Brazil's unique form of country music championed by the legendary Luis Gonzaga. The colorful history of baiao musicians includes many outcasts, a penchant for wildly exotic attire, and a roster of notorious cowboy and bandit performers, including some Robin Hood types, who have contributed to the folklore and allure of the repertoire. Baiao often contains raised fourths and flattened sevenths, creating a cadence specific to the Northeast. The accordion is the most prominent instrument, and syncopated rhythm is the thing.

The Musica Popular Brasileira (MPB) tradition championed by Maria Bethania, Joao Bosco, Carlinhos Brown, Chico Buarque, Gal Costa, Djavan, Gilberto Gil, Ivan Lins, Milton Nascimento,

Simone, Caetano Veloso, and their progeny is a topic worthy of a separate treatise. MPB respects and incorporates choro, samba, baiao, frevo, and bossa while continually breaking new musical ground conceptually and sonically. It constitutes the most profound, artfully crafted body of popular world music since the 1960s. Imagine if the greatest tunesmiths from the heyday of Tin Pan Alley continued to expand their repertoire while maintaining the high standards of their writing craft with impeccable taste. Combine the sensibilities of Jimmy Van Heusen, Cole Porter, and Jerome Kern with the vision and performance ability of the Beatles, Smokey Robinson, Joni Mitchell, Bob Dylan, and Stevie Wonder, and you begin to understand the MPB scene in proper context. The giants have not rested on their laurels; they have refused to recycle their art, choosing rather to expand and elevate this unique genre to new heights.

Music sung in the Brazilian-Portuguese dialect has a sensuality and richness unlike any other language. Space constraints make it impossible to do justice to the topic in this survey. For those who become obsessed, we highly recommend Chris McGowan and Ricardo Pessanha's classic *The Brazilian Sound* (ISBN 08230-7673-3), a knowing, loving work that is well-organized and unusually clear and informative.

Along with Milton Nascimento, Gilberto Gil is the true genius of Brazilian music, post bossa. Gil took *bossa nova* and moved it forward, internationalized it, and rocked it, while combating the snobbish left who rejected bossa as commercial and too pop. He also has served in the Brazilian National Congress, been mayor of Salvador, championed political freedom for three decades, and was recently named minister of culture in 2003 by President Lula da Silva, a controversial appointment for the mainstream to say the least. After achieving widespread popularity in the late 1960s, Gil was forced to flee to England in 1970 after being jailed by the Junta for his subversive lyrics. Gil continued to protest and record with Tropicalia cofounder Caetano Veloso and, since his return to Brazil in the early 1970s, has continued to evolve as an artist, composer, and performer.

Milton Nascimento grew up in Minas Geraes, raised by his adoptive parents, where his imagination and creativity was nourished from an early age. He flipped over Joao Gilberto's 1958 recording of Jobim's *Chega de Saudade* and began to pursue his musical calling, moving to Belo Horizonte in 1963 (capital of Minas) where he was exposed to Monk, Mingus, Miles, and Coltrane and began to expand his musical language.

Milton came to prominence in the televised festival contests of the 1960s through interpretations of his songs by Elis Regina. Milton's incredible range, use of falsetto, and reverence for other South American genres instantly distinguished him from all other Brazilian artists. His 1975 collaboration with jazz Saxophonist Wayne Shorter on the *Native Dancer* album changed the way the world listened to jazz forever, serving as North America's first widespread exposure to post-bossa nova Brazilian music.

Nascimento was without question one of the most important musical voices on the planet during the latter half of the twentieth century, an artist of historical importance whose stature is comparable to Bob Marley and Salif Keita.

The late Elis Regina (1945–1982) qualifies as a superstar on anyone's list of singers on the basis of her voice alone, but also because of the important role she played in launching the careers of numerous MPB stars. Elis avoided becoming embroiled in politics at a time when others were forced into exile for protesting the Brazilian dictatorship, but was clearly sympathetic to the cause. She did much to keep the continuity of the music going during the difficult years of the 1970s.

Elis was first and foremost a diva, still revered by most Brazilians for her incredible performances in the festivals of the late 1960s and loved for her many wonderful recordings. Her tragic story, including numerous marriages and a sad, drug-related demise that ended her life in 1982 at age 37, remain a source of pain to this day for the generation of Brazilians who grew up with her music.

Pixinguinha (Alfredo de Rocha Vianna, Jr.; 1898–1973) has a parallel historical stature in Brazilian music to that of Duke Ellington (1898–1974) in jazz. He was the most important band-leader, flutist, saxophonist, and popular Brazilian personality of the first half of the twentieth century, a true pioneer. Pixinguinha's *choros* and *maxixes* are classics of the idiom that have a distinctly Western European harmonic influence combined with an African rhythmic sensibility.

Upon his return from a tour in Paris in 1922, Pixinguinha introduced brass and winds to the music, undoubtedly influenced by the foxtrot orchestras he heard in Europe. His arrangements rival Ellington, Fletcher Henderson, and Jimmy Lunceford in imagination and sophistication, and his compositions rank as some of the best music of the twentieth century. Tunes such as "Um a Zero," "Rosa," "Carinihso," and "Lamentos" are familiar to everyone, by sound if not title. He is one of the forefathers of samba and, along with Ernesto Nazare and Chiquinha Gonzaga, he popularized Choro.

RECOMMENDED CDs

JORGE BEN. An exciting, magnetic live performer who combined funk with quirky writing in the 1970s. *A Tabua Esmeralda* (Philips, 1974); *Ben* (Philips, 1972).

MARIA BETHANIA. Bethania (sister of Caetano Veloso) was the first Brazilian female superstar of the 1960s. She possesses a distinctive, sexy contralto voice and is renowned for interpreting the compositions of upcoming composers. Her voice does not have the range of many other Brazilian singers, but she is the most unique and appealing. *Ambar* (Metro Blue, 1995) is her best; *O Canto Paje* (Verve, 1990); *Memoria da Pele* (Verve, 1988); *Maria* (Buda, 1988); *Alibi* (Philips, 1982) made her an international star.

JOAO BOSCO. Eclectic guitarist, singer song writer with an infec-tious style- a wondrous live performer. *Gagabiro* (Verve, 1984) is his best; *Odile Odila* (Verve), a 1982–1986 compilation; *Da Licenca Meu Senhor* (Sony, 1996).

CARLINHOS BROWN. Along with Chico Cesar, the most vibrant new MPB composer in all of Brazil; *alfagamabetizado* (Metro Blue,

1996) is a masterpiece; *Tribalistas* (EMI, 2002); a collaboration with Arnaldo Altunes and Marisa Monte.

CHICO BUARQUE. A national idol, once equal to Jobim in stature in Brazil. *Album de Teatro* with Edu Lobo (see Lobo); *Chico Buarque de Hollanda* (Polygram, 1966) his debut; *Construcao* (Philips, 1971) is the classic oldie; *Chico Buarque* (Polygram, 1978); *Chico Buarque* (BMG, Ariola, 1987); *As Cidades* (BMG Brasil,1999).

ADRIANA CALCONHOTO. Underrated songwriter with a modern touch and an Edie Brickell quality to her voice. *Fabrica da Poema* (Epic, 1995) features beautiful original compositions and vocals including Gertrude Stein reciting a 2-minute poem!

BETH CARVALHO. Leading female voice of Samba today, carrying the torch for *samba pagode. Brasileira da Gema* (Polygram, 1994) is her best available recording; *De Pe No Chao, Ao Vivo No Olympia* (BMG Ariola, 1991).

DORI CAYMMI. From Brazil's first family of musicians, Dori is one of the country's most important arrangers and musical figures. *Dori Caymmi* (Verve, 1989).

NANA CAYMMI. The musicians' singer. *Voz e Suor* (EMI, 1982) with pianist/arranger Cesar Camargo-Mariano rivals any ballad recording. *Reposta ao Tempo* (EMI, 1998); *O Mare, O Tempo* (Universal, 2002) features Nana singing all Dorival Caymmi tunes.

CHICO CESAR. The diminutive chico is a gifted writer with a knack for intrigue and a unique theatrical sense, always appearing in African Garb and Staff in hand. *Cus Cus Cla* (Velas, 1996) is a fantastic, varied recording of Afro-Brazilian eclectic pop; *Respeitem meus cabelos, broncos* (MZA, 2003) is just as good.

GAL COSTA. Gal is the original Tropicalia Diva, Gil and Velosos's eyes and ears in Brazil during their exile, a National treasury and superb vocalist. *Gal Costa* (Philips, 1969); *Baby Gal* (1985) shows a mature Gal at her peak, *Mina d'agua do meu canto* (1997), compositions of Chico Buarque and Caetano Veloso orchestrated and arranged by cellist Jaques Morelenbaum; *Afoxe e Samba.*

DJAVAN. One of the giants of MPB, his early work is revered by Brazilian musicians. *Flor de Lis,* also known as *Voz e Violao* (1976) is impossible not to love, a true masterpiece; *Coisa de Acender* (Sony, 1991); *Malasia* (Sony, 1996): *Ao Vivo* (Sony, 2001) with a knowledgeable audience singing back-up in tune; *Milagreiro* (Sony, 2002).

MARCIO FARACO. New bossa star based in Paris. *Ciranda* (Universal, 1999).

GILBERTO GIL (See Profile). *Louvacao* (Philips, 1967) Gil's first, a major classic, fresh and alive 40 years later, a peer of *Sgt. Pepper's*; *Expresso 2222* (Universal, 1972); *Realce* (WEA, 1979); *Acoustic* (WEA, 1994); *Quanta* (Mesa, WEA, 1997).

JOAO GILBERTO. The Godfather of bossa nova. *Amoroso/Brasil* is now a double CD (WEA, 1977/80); *Chega de Saudade* (Odeon, 1958) is a classic if you can find it; *Getz/Gilberto* (Verve, 1964) is the one that got us all with Jobim's "The Girl from Ipanema."

ANTONIO CARLOS JOBIM. *Elis & Tom*, (Verve 1974) is Jobim's best work on record, with Elis Regina and the classic *Aguas de Marco*; *Getz/Gilberto* (Verve, 1964); *Passarim* (Verve, 1987); *Orfeu da Conceicao* (Odeon, 1956) with Vinicius de Moraes.

JOYCE. The Cariocan Joni Mitchell; the first female song writer to be recognized as such, a top star going strong for 30 years. *Feminina* (Odeon, 1978) is her classic; *The Essential Joyce 1970–1996* (Mr. Bongo, 1998) is a great compilation; *Language and Love* (Verve, 1991) is in English; *With Banda Maluca, A little bit Crazy* (Far Out, 2003).

IVAN LINS. Power, grace, and masculinity characterize Lins's voice; many of his tunes have become international hits. After Milton & Caetano, he is the biggest International star. *Awa Yio* (Reprise, 1991); *Tribute a Noel Rosa 1 & 2* (Velas, 1996) is a classic; *Jobiando* (Abril, 2001); *Modo Livre* (Philips, 1976).

EDU LOBO. Major voice from the bossa nova era; *Album de Teatro* (BMG, 1982/97); *Corrupcao* (Velas, 1993).

CARLOS LYRA. A peer of Jobim, there at the beginning. *Bossa nova* (Philips, 1960).

SERGIO MENDES. Remains an important figure in MPB. *Brasil '66* (A & M, 1966); *Brasiliero* (Elektra, 1992) with then relative unknowns Carlinhos Brown and Guinga.

MARISA MONTE. The perennial superstar of tomorrow, a versatile singer songwriter. *Mais* (World Pacific, 1991) is her best; *Charcoal and Roses* (Metro Blue, 1994); *Tribalistas* (EMI, 2002).

MILTON NASCIMENTO (see Profile). *Club de Esquina* (World Pacific, 1972) is a landmark event in the history of MPB. *Travessia* (Iris, Harmonia Mundi, 1967/2002), his first; *Geraes* (EMI, 1976) is highlighted by his duet with Mercedes Sosa; *Minas* (EMI, 1977); *Miltons*, (Columbia, 1989) with Herbie Hancock; *Txai* (Columbia, 1990) with a rain forest feeling; *Pieta* (2003) is a surprise comeback.

ROSA PASSOS. Earthy Joao Gilberto influenced vocalist and fine guitarist who recently has risen from obscurity. *Pano Pra Manga* (Velas, 1996) is a special recording on all levels.

LEILA PINHEIRO. Major vocalist and torch bearer for Elis. *Na Ponta da Lingua* (2000), enchanting, sexy, ethereal; *Catavento e Girassol* (1997) is music of Guinga with lyrics by Aldir Blanc.

PIXINGUINHA (see Profile). *100 Anos* (Abril, 1976 reissued) surveys Pixinguinha music from the 1920s to the 1960s. Multi-reed virtuoso Paulo Moura's *Tribute e Pixinguinha* is a tasteful rundown of the classics.

FERNANDA PORTO. Self-styled, modern techno Bossa singer. *Fernanda Porto* (Tama, 2003).

ZIZI POSSI. Eclectic, quirky muse and song stylist always presenting a new twist. *Per Amore*, (Polygram, 1998) is a collection of Neapolitan love songs; *Valsa Brasileira* (Velas, 1988); *Sobre Todos As Coisas* (Eldorado, 1991).

ELIS REGINA (see Profile). *Elis 1974* (Philips) is the best Elis recording with a Cesar Camargo Mariano (her onetime husband) led group. *Essa Mulher* (Philips, 1981 reissue) is a classic; *Elis 1972* (Philips); *Vento de Mayo* (EMI, Hemisphere, 1985 comp); *Elis 1977* (Philips).

MONICA SALMASO. Elegant New York based MPB vocalist (Blue Jackal, 2002) *Voadeira*.

SIMONE. Former model and Olympic basketball star, Simones deep masculine voice is one of the greatest in all Brazil. *Simone ao Vivo* (Polygram, 1997) is fantastic, start to finish; arguably the finest Brazilian release of the past decade; *Seda Pura* (Universal, 2002) is a perfect, recent studio set.

CAETANO VELOSO. Global superstar, tunesmith, and avant-garde lyricist with a João Gilberto influenced vocal style. *Cores Nomes* (Polygram, 1982), *Cinema Transcendental* (Polygram, 1979); *Outras Palavras* (Philips, 1983); *Domingo* (Philips, 1967) with Gal Costa is bossa and precious; *Fina Estampa* (1996) covers classic tunes from eight South American countries with tasteful Jacques Morelenbaum arrangements.

MARTINHO DA VILA. Martinho is the most prominent living sambista and samba composer. His best older works are: *Pelo Telefone* (BMG RCA, 1977); *Canta Canta Minha Gente* (BMG, 1974); *Batuquiero* (RCA, 1987).

PAULINHO DA VIOLA. A national icon and master of the cavaquinho; *Eu Canto Samba* (RCA, 1991) is a must recording for any serious Samba lover.

TOM ZE. Avant-garde Tropicalist-minimalist with a difference, the Anton Webern of Brazilian pop. *Jogos de Amar* (Trama, 2000).

INSTRUMENTALISTS

ASSAD BROTHERS. Fine classical guitarists. *Brasileira* (Nonesuch, 1988) highlights an array of Brazilian composers including Radames Gnatalli, Marlos Nobre, Egberto Gismonti, and Hermeto Pascoal; *Assad Brothers with Nadja Sonnenberg-Salerno* (Nonesuch, 1999).

JACOB DO BANDOLIM. *Jacob do Bandolim Vol. I & II* (Acoustic Discs, 1991/94) from the 1960s, swings like the Django Reinhardt-Stephane Grapelly Hot Club sides from the 1930s.

ELIANE ELIAS. Bill Evans-influenced pianist. *Paulistana* (Blue Note, 1993) shows her at her best.

EGBERTO GISMONTI. Virtuoso pianist and guitarist, Egberto is widely considered one of the greatest musicians in the world. *Sanfona* (ECM, 1981); *Musica de Sobre-vivenca* (ECM, 1993) is his masterpiece; *Dança das Cabecas* (ECM, 1987).

LUIS GONZAGA. Popularized the term and musical form *baiao*. A mythical figure in Brazilian musical history; try *Luis Gonzaga & Humberto Teixeira* (Abril, 1977).

GUINGA. The most significant MPB composer (as opposed to composer/performer) since Jobim. *Cine Baronesa* (Velas, 2001); *Cheio de Dedos* (Velas, 1996).

TONINHO HORTA. Guitarist from the Milton Nascimento branch of MPB, influenced by the great Wes Montgomery. *Diamond Life* (Verve, 1988); *Once I Loved* (Verve, 1992) with the late Billy Higgins.

JAQUES MORELENBAUM. The most in-demand arranger in Brazil today, a virtuoso cellist and eclectic musician; *Quarteto* (Velas, 2000) with the *Jobim-Morelenbaum Quartet*, featuring Tom's son Paulo and grandson Daniel.

PAULO MOURA. Virtuoso clarinetist and saxophonist and an extremely versatile arranger and teacher. *Confusao* (Braziloid, 1987); *Clara Sverner & Paulo Moura Interpretam Pixinguinha* (CBS, 1988).

HERMETO PASCOAL. Joyce actually wrote a tune with lyrics describing how to get to Hermeto's home where musicians make pilgrimages. He is a virtuoso on all reed, brass, guitar, and keyboard instruments, and a master composer. His recordings don't capture his genius, except for *Eu e Els* (2000); *Slaves Mass* (WEA, 1977).

SIVUCA. Accordionist/guitarist from Northeast, long-time cohort of Pascoal, contemporary of Baden Powell and Bola Sete, toured with Miriam Makeba in the 1970s; *Pao Doido* (Kuarup, 1992) is the one to get, with Carlos Lyra on guitar; *Sivuca* (Vanguard, 1973).

TOOTS THIELEMANS. Peer and colleague of Stephane Grappelly in Europe in the late 1940s, the Belgian Harmonica Virtuoso has long-time honorary Brazilian status. *Brazil Project I* (Private Music, 1991) with a dozen stars sitting in is a great record for newcomers to MPB.

CHILE

More than any country in South America, Chile profits from its unique geography. It boasts an extraordinarily long coastline, extending from the Antarctic sea up to the Equator along the Pacific Ocean and is bordered by the Andes mountains to the east. The climate is mostly temperate, and its agricultural assets, particularly its fabulous wine industry, benefit considerably from the natural irrigation of pure water from melting snow.

During the late 1990s and early part of the twenty-first century, Chile developed the most successful and progressive economy in South America. This has of course not always been the case in this most enigmatic of South American nations.

THE MUSIC

Nueva cancion, Allende, and Pinochet. After political stability and a remarkable end to corruption were achieved under the Popular Unity Government of Salvador Allende, the first legitimately elected socialist government in South America (circa 1970), Chile slipped into the heart of political darkness and horror under Gustavo Pinochet. Allende's demise was enhanced by the covert support of the Nixon Administration and the CIA, whose McCarthyist mentality and blind fear of anything that hinted at another Castro led the United States government to commit one of its greatest political blunders in its short international history, backing a ruthless dictator in favor of a genuine patriot and man democratically elected by the people. Pinochet ruled with a corrupt, dogmatic, right-wing iron fist that plagued many nations in South American in the 1960s and 1970s.

In many ways, overthrowing Allende jettisoned a musical movement that would prove to have more impact, substance, and endurance in South and Central American politics than any misguided United States foreign policy. It is in Chile that the *nueva cancion* movement officially planted its roots.

Yupanqui, Violeta Parra, Victor Jara, and Inti Illimani. Taking a lead from Atahualpa Yupanqui's work in the 1940s (see Argentina), Chile's greatest native folk artist, Violeta Parra, brought the *nueva cancion* movement to national attention in the early 1960s with a determined, pacifist defiance to her oppressive government. Like Yupanqui, she collected folk songs from peasants and sang her "new songs" in factories and bohemian clubs, espousing freedom and civil rights for marginalized people. She also pioneered the use of Amerindian instruments in contemporary folk music. Following Parra's untimely death in 1967, the torch of protest was seamlessly inherited by legendary Chilean poet/songwriter Victor Jara, who brought the movement to the international stage.

Jara's charisma, troubadour mentality, and direct manner of communication (with some help from fellow countryman, poet Pablo Neruda) enabled the *nueva cancion* movement to spread throughout South America and the Caribbean. The magical power of song as a weapon against oppression spread further to Western Europe in Portugal and Spain, to Greece, and into North Africa in Algeria. Jara's message was so clear, and his ability to garner support everywhere he traveled so threatening to the Junta, that following the coup d' etat in 1973 Pinochet's henchmen had him brutally murdered and publicly thrown into a soccer stadium in Santiago.

Jara's manifesto for freedom and his struggle were not for naught; his cohorts carry on to this day.

INTI ILLIMANI

Students at the Santiago Technical School created the legendary Chilean roots group Inti Illimani ("Sun God") in 1967. The group was forced into exile when Pinochet took over, but remained politically active as expatriates (living in Rome) for the next 15 years, outspoken ambassadors for Chile. Inti-Illimani is going strong in 2004 with an expanded repertoire and a more sophisticated flute-violin-charango-guitar structure.

RECOMMENDED CDs

GILBERT FAVRE & LOS JAIRAS. Favre is a Swiss-French flutist, and Los Jairas worked with Victor Jara, changing Chilean song forever. *La Flute des Andes* (Musidisc, 1970/1996 reissue); *Lo Mejor de las Jairas* (1974)

INTI-ILLIMANI. Chilean roots group with a political message. *Imaginacion* (Redwood, 1984); *Leyenda* (CBS, 1990), a live set with Paco Pena and John Williams; *Amar de Novo* (Green Linnet, 1999); *Lugares Communes* (Green Linnet, 2003) with a nod to Nina Rota and Peruvian Chabuca Grande.

VICTOR JARA. In 2003, Warner Music (Chile and Argentina) reissued many out-of-print items from its South American archives, including most of the extensive Jara treasury. *Te Recuerdo Amanda; El Compancio; Canciones Postumas;* and *El choro de vivir en paz* are all-important. *Manifesto* (1973) is required listening for all socially conscious music lovers.

VIOLETA PARRA. Parra was an able guitarist (cavaquinho) and effective singer, but her compositions and collections of folk tunes are her legacy. *Antologia* (2003, Warner) contains recordings from 1956–1966, before she committed suicide at the age of 50.

QUILIPAYUN. Political nueva cancion group disbanded in 1990, but an important voice in the movement against Pinochet. *35 Anos* (WEA, 2003).

MAURICIO VENEGAS-ASTORGA. The composer, songwriter, and charango whiz is an ambassador for South American music in Europe. *Ando Cuban* (2002, Tumi), a collaboration with Cuban Nueva Trova Tres player Efrain Rios, combines genres and cultures seamlessly while conveying the truth throughout. No Yo-Yo Ma crossover here.

COLOMBIA

Colombia has a north-south coastline of almost 1,200 miles that includes Andean highlands, a savannah, and a tropical rain forest. English traders, Indians, African slaves, and Spanish settlers all have entered the blood of the Colombian people, a population as varied as any on the continent. Colombia today is a troubled country that has been in a perpetual state of war for decades. Drug cartels, warlords, corruption, poverty, and at times anarchy have characterized the political climate with no end to the senseless killing and hardship in sight. Despite these problems, Colombia's musical heritage is rich and plentiful.

THE MUSIC

Cumbia is a typically Latin music with layered rhythms and syncopation in the melody that has evolved from its birthplace on the Atlantic Coast to become the national music. Originally cumbia was a courtship dance of slaves, performed with only a singer and percussion as accompaniment. It is thought that the name of the music derives from Guinea and its native *gumbe* (cumbe) dance. Cumbia has morphed into a big band style with brass, reeds, electric keyboards, and all the trappings of modern dance music. Its roots are from African Slaves and Indians, and even the European influence that is prevalent in the melodies is actually African, because Spanish music from Granada and the south was greatly influenced by the Moors. Instruments specific to the music include a folk clarinet called the *flauto de millo* and the *gaita*, a long flute.

In the 1940s, cumbia left the countryside and entered urban society. This is when the famous "four square" rhythm, with a loping beat like a horse's trot, entered the genre. In the 1950s, a Cuban influence was introduced into the music, through the radio and recordings released on *Discos Fuentes*, the biggest record label in Colombia, which became immensely popular throughout Latin America. Singer/composer/ producer "Fruko" helped build the popularity of the music in the early 1970s, bringing cumbia permanently under the salsa umbrella and discovering Colombian salsa star Joe Arroyo. Melida Yar Yanguma, (aka *La India Meliyara*), is the star female vocalist.

Vallenato is second only to cumbia in popularity, an accordion-led music of Indian origin from the village of Valledupar, with roots from Barranqjuilla. Over the past several decades, vallenato has incorporated many of the rhythms of cumbia—paseo, puya, merengue, and the fast 6/8 beat—but retains its distinct flavor. The music was traditionally performed with only three instruments; a three-row button accordion, a *guacharaca* scraper, and *caja vallenata* (box drum). Eventually the music added two guitars and the *tiple*, a 12-stringed instrument with 4 groups of 3 strings, similar to the Cuban tres or cuatro. Modern vallenato bands are as big as salsa bands.

Llanera is from the Pacific Coast plains and scrub agricultural region where horse breeding and training is the pride. Llanera from Colombia is similar to that of Venezuela with the harp as the lead voice, usually supported by cuatro, bandola, bandolin, and the small tiple; maracas and violins are also included.

Afro-American music is a phenomenon throughout the continent. *Champeta*, which hails from Cartagena on the Pacific Coast, notably incorporates Congolese, Haitian compass, and ragga, with a decidedly non-Latin feel.

Toto La Momposina is the leading voice of contemporary Colombian roots music. She has studied and performed her native songs and dances for 4 decades and is going strong into the twenty-first century. She is at heart a nueva cancion artist, although her sound and style are more akin to cumbia and dance music than traditional folk.

In 1982 she performed at the Nobel Prize ceremony at the request of her compatriot, novelist Gabriel Garcia Marquez, and then spent four years studying the history of dance at the Sorbonne in Paris. In 1985 she recorded her first album, and in 1991 was invited to perform at WOMAD, subsequently recording for Peter Gabriel's Real World Label. She continues to tour and record as a dedicated ambassador for Colombian music.

RECOMMENDED CDs

JOE ARROYO. Arroyo is a major star who fuses salsa, compas, merengue, reggae, and soca as leader of La Verdad. *Cruzando el Milenio* (Sony, 1999); *La Noche* (World Music Network, 1997), a compilation; *Fuego* (Sonotone, 1993).

YURI BUENAVENTURA. Singer/guitarist/composer in the nueva cancion mold. *Vagabundo* (Universal Latino, 2003).

DIOMEDES DIAZ. Folk singer, vallenato style. The Colombian Simon and Garfunkel. *El Mundo* (Sony, 1987).

ALFREDO GUTIERREZ. Legendary accordionist with Los Corraleros; *El Palito* (RCA, 1956)

LISANDRO MESA. Leading vallenato accordionist and singer, from the west coast. *P'al Mundo* (Faisan, 1996 reissue); *El Mandamas* (Sonolux, 1986).

TOTO LA MOMPOSINA (See Profile). *Toto La Momposina Y Sus Tambores*; *La Candela Viva* (Real World, 1993); *Carmelina* (Indigo, 1996); *Pacanto* (World Village, 2000).

CALIXTO OCHOA. Vocalist and accordionist. *Salsa Cumbia* (Tumi, 1997); *Folclor Costeo Colombia* (Discos Fuentes).

CARLOS VIVES. Soap opera star and heartthrob Carlos is the big name in vallenato. He added electric guitars, drum kits, and modern production to the music. *Classicos de la Provincia* (EMI, 1993) sold a million; *Tierra de Ivido* (EMI, 1995); *Escalona un Canto a la Vida* (EMI, 1992).

LOS HERMANOS ZULETA. Fine vallenato accordion band. *Mananita de Invierno* (Sony, 1993).

Ecuador is perhaps the most picturesque, striking, and purely Indian of the Andean countries. Dense rainforests, volcanic landscapes, spectacular mountain vistas, birds and animals found nowhere else on earth, and of course the Galapagos Islands make Ecuador truly a special place. Quito is the capital, declared by UNESCO as a World Heritage City since 1978, a city that has maintained its colonial charm and diversity.

The music is typically Andean in sound and instrumentation with all forms of Andean pipes—zamponas, quenas, and antaras—prominent. Charangas, guitars, and bandolinas are also part of the sound. As with most South American countries, there is an Afro-Latino musical tradition in Ecuador, based on the west coast, and known as *Esmeraldas*, which is based on West African rhythms. It incorporates call-and-response vocals and the marimba as a replacement for the Mandinkan balafon.

RECOMMENDED CDs

CARMEN GONZALEZ KELZ. Carmen is the closest Ecuador comes to having a world music star. She is involved in *Esmeraldan* culture and sings in a folk style that recalls Toto La Momposina from Colombia. *Andarele* (Triple Earth, 1998); *Caramba* (Network, 2000).

RUMINAHUI ("Stone face"). Ruminahui, from the Quichan, reputedly one of the last Incans to fight the Spanish invaders, is also the name of a Saraguro Indian group formed in the late 1980s. *Saraguro Llactamanta* (1990).

VARIOUS ARTISTS. *Musica de Ecuador*, a compilation of 17 groups including *Los Chagres, Segundo Conejo,* and *Los Tucumbi* on the Caprice label (2002) is a two-disc set and the place to begin to explore the music.

The people of Paraguay have endured repression of their civil liberties since the country's recorded history began, first under Spanish Colonial rule and after independence in 1811 by a series of dictators, despots, and Nazi collaborators. Paraguay sympathized and aided the Axis powers during and after World War II. In 1954, the infamous General Alfredo Stroessner took power and ruled Paraguay for the next 34 years, supported by the United States despite his authoritarian regime, because he was anti-Communist. This duplicitous posture lasted until 1976 when Jimmy Carter's administration exposed Stroessner's regime and the lack of democracy in Paraguay. In 1989 the military overthrew Stroessner's government and in 1992 a new constitution established a democratic system with increased protection of human rights and civil liberties. In 1999 Paraguay continued to move towards cementing its democratic roots with a peaceful transfer of the government to Senate President Luis Gonzalez Macchi, despite endemic fears of a military interference.

THE MUSIC

Paraguayan music comes in two basic forms. *Guarania* is a melodic concert music, which takes its name from the indigenous language in which the Chaco Indians perform a folk and traditional repertoire related to religious rituals. The other popular form is the polka (unrelated to the European polka), a lively dance music that starts with a slow tempo and builds to a crescendo. Paraguayan polka is similar to the *zamba* from northern Argentina.

The main instrument is the harp, which has 36–37 strings and differs in playing method from the chromatic or concert harp. The sound is dependent on the type of wood used, usually from local forests. It is an intrinsic part of Paraguayan culture; families store wood for long periods of time so harps can be made for their children. Guitars, violins, and the bombo (a bass drum) are also prominent.

Paraguayan music has surprisingly little influence from Africa, Brazil, or Argentina, although numerous genres from its neighbors are extremely popular. The music is more European in origin, sung in Guarani or Spanish.

RECOMMENDED CDs

AUGUSTIN BARRIOS (MANGORE). Barrios (1885–1944) was a fine guitarist and the one Paraguayan composer to achieve international recognition in the classical field; "The Paganini of Paraguay" in his day, a peer of Heitor Villa-Lobos. He also wrote numerous folkloric tunes. *From the Jungles of Paraguay* (Arte Nova, 1995) is performed by John Williams.

RAMON ROMERO. Romero is the genius of the Paraguayan harp, now residing in California after 40 years of performance. *Rosas Para Ti* (1994); *Arpa Campesina* (AJR Discos, 2001).

OSCAR BENITO. Leading Paraguayan/Indian harp player from Asuncion who made his break in 1993 at an international competition in Valencia, Spain. *The Paraguayan Harp* (ARC Music, 2003).

VARIOUS ARTISTS. *Paraguay y sus Arpas* (Horizons Vol. 10, ANS Records 1997), performed by Ricardo Gonzales, the place to start to see if this is your cup of tea.

PERU

Long, precipitous coast lines, majestic Andean peaks, mountain lakes, exotic wildlife, ancient Amerindian Culture, and perpetually polarized economic conditions characterize one of South America's most intriguing, ethnically diverse, and mysterious nations. Musically Peru has recently emerged on the world music scene by expanding its traditional Andean image with artists from "Black Peru" enjoying great popularity and success in exposing its original musical forms.

HISTORY AND THE SLAVE TRADE

Peru was the administrative center of virtually all of Spanish South America from the time of the conquest in 1526 through the eighteenth century. Along with Mexico it was the most important colony in the Spanish Empire. Lima, "The City of Kings," began its musical life in the 1600s, boasting a culture and sophistication unequalled anywhere in the Americas at the time and through the end of the eighteenth century.

Peru's history is dominated and eternally tainted by the impact of the slave trade. Unlike the practices in other parts of South and North America where large groups of entire African tribes were transported together, in Peru the Spanish intentionally segregated tribe members from one another in order to discourage rebellion, and to force the slaves to integrate into Spanish culture and to adopt their language. The resultant *Mestizo* culture, a combination of indigenous people and African slaves, developed over the centuries. The Mestizos have been oppressed and systematically segregated and isolated from the wealthy Spanish and Anglo middle class who rule Peru to this day. Lima's Miraflores and beautiful San Isidro districts are bastions of sophisticated, Western culture where the rich and famous cavort in surroundings of unmatched physical splendor while some of the most abject poverty in the Western Hemisphere lies only a few kilometers away.

THE INCAS

Despite continual strong-armed rule by the first world colonizers, Incan culture has survived through the millennia. Both Incan and native Quechan culture permeate much of Peru's history, and it is their legacy and heritage that conjure the world's image of Peru. The ingenuity of terraced agriculture at high altitude, breeding of llamas, alpacas, and vicunas, Andean folkloric art, the phenomenon that is Machu-Pichu, and Andean Pipe music are notable Peruvian accomplishments and landmarks associated with Peru's indigenous people. The strength of the elite, proud Incan culture is considerable.

POLITICS

After the dictatorial Alberto Fujimori's ouster in late 2000, Peru seems to have moved more into the mainstream of the region, notably electing South America's first Amerindian president, Alejandro Toledo, perhaps joining Venezuelan President Chavez's "Axis of Good." Corruption and a poor economy has seen his popularity plummet in 2004.

THE MUSIC OF BLACK PERU

It was not until the international Civil Rights movement of the 1960s that the culture of Black Peru (as distinct from Amerindian or Mestizo) was liberated, at which time their culture and music began to emerge on a broader national and pan-South American stage. Although this music has had a short-lived exposure on the world stage, it is one of the most soulful and unique genres in all of South America.

In the early 1950s, poet/composer/singer Nicodemes Santa Cruz along with the traditional Peruvian group Peru Negra began to expose the music of the ancestors of Peru's slaves as a new musical genre. With its unique hand percussion based on the wooden box called the *cajon* and indigenous forms such as the lando, Black Peruvian music has its own style, sound, and soul, related to Cuban son, Andean music, and Incan folk traditions, but clearly Peruvian. Because of the way African slaves were kept apart from each other when brought to Peru by the slave traders, this music, while African in foundation, is difficult to pigeonhole to a specific African region, making the term "The music of Black Peru" quite apt.

Chabuca Granda is the most important popular Peruvian composer and vocalist of the twentieth century. She was a singer until her 70s, when she began to write in the most popular indigenous form, the *lando*, and is the first native composer to set horns, reeds, and strings to the traditional compositions. Her voicing and arrangements are quite modern (at times dissonant and atonal), always beautiful, and adroitly implemented. She is an important composer who has been greatly overlooked by world music aficionados. Her work was exposed in North America and Europe in the early 1990s on David Byrne's classic *The Soul of Black Peru* compilation and in 1995 on Caetano Veloso's landmark *Fina Estampa*, which used her composition for its title. Chabuca died in 1983, but several valuable recordings of her work both as a singer and composer are available.

RECOMMENDED CDs

SUSANA BACA. Peru's musical ambassador and most famous artist. *Susana Baca* (Luaka Bop, 1997); *Espiritu Vivo* (Luaka Bolo, 2002).

CHABUCA GRANDA (See Profile). *La voz del Peru* (Pampa music); *La Flor de Canela* (Ans); *Chabuca Granda* (RCA, 1977), (aka *Canel, Mariachi, Vargas de Tealitlan*).

TANIA LIBERTAD. Tania has explored folkloric music from all over South America, Central America, and Mexico. *Costa Negra* (World Village, 2002); *El Mismo Pureto* (Orfeon, 2000); *Mexico Lindo Y Querido* (Discos CBS, 1993).

PERU NEGRA. Leading Black Peruvian group founded in 1969, still going strong. *Son de los Diablos; Sangre de un Don* (Times Square, 2001).

VARIOUS ARTISTS. It doesn't get better than the opening track, on David Byrne's *The Soul of Black Peru: Maria Lando,* sung by Susana Baca, composed by Chabuca Granda; a great compilation.

URUGUAY

Spanish settlers began to supplant the indigenous *Charrua* Indians in 1624, and Uruguay today, like neighboring Argentina, is virtually devoid of its native people. Uruguay gained independence from the Spanish Viceroy in 1825 and has been a republic since that date. After decades of military rule, Uruguay regained its civil government in 1985 and has since grown to become one of the most stable economies in South America, with political and labor conditions among the freest on the continent.

Musically, Uruguay is very much tied to its big cousin Argentina. More than half the population resides in and around the capital city of Montevideo, a sister city to Buenos Aires, just across the River Plate. Uruguay has its own brand of tango and milonga, but the influence of Argentine tango is unmistakable. Subtle differences are apparent in the openness of the Uruguayan style when compared with the rigidity of Argentine tango. Uruguay has a strong folk tradition that has been an important part of the nueva cancion movement, and can boast a major international folk icon, Daniel Viglietti.

RECOMMENDED CDs

HUGO FATTORUSSO. Fattoruso hit the New York scene in the late 1960s combining Uruguayan jazz with the sounds of Brazil, which led to work with Milton Nascimento, Djavan, Chico Buarque, and others. *Goldenwings - Magic Time* (Columbia, 1982) shows Hugo's true artistry before he slipped into an insipid Latin jazz style.

VAYO RAIMONDO. Vayo is a singer in the old Edmundo Ribero tango style. *I Am Tango (No Soy Un tango)* (Alula, 2002), is a trio record with bandoneon and guitar. *At the Edge of Night* (Alula, 2003).

RENE MARINO RIVERO. *Bandoneon Pure: Dances of Uruguay* (Smithsonian, 1994) is recommended for the usual Smithsonian attention to the art and for bandoneon lovers.

DANIEL VIGLIETTI. Uruguay's greatest folk singer, outspoken and political with Leonard Cohen style delivery and depth. *Tropicos* (Discemidi, 1972) conducted by Cuban composer Leo Brower with tunes by Chico Buarque, Edu Lobo, Silvio Rodriguez, Pablo Milanes, and an antiwar poem by Bertolt Brecht. *Esdrujulo* (Buda, 1973); *Canciones Para Mi America,* (aka *Desalambra*) (Buda, 1969).

ALFREDO ZITARROSA. Talented vocalist-guitarist carried the torch for Uruguayan traditional folk music abroad until his death in 1989. *Anthologia 1936–1989* (Microton, 1994) covers 1972–1979; *Desde Tacuarendo* (1998) is his other recording available outside of Uruguay.

VENEZUELA

South America's northernmost country is a political, social, and economic enigma. Venezuela's geological landscape includes a large mountainous region, vast plains, dense rain forests, and one truly international city, Caracas. The make-up of Venezuela's population is as diverse as the country's topography. A small segment of the population reaps the benefit of Venezuela's vast oil reserves and can be counted among the world's super rich. Most of the population, however, comprises laborers, peasants, descendants of slaves, and indigenous people who live in the third world, light years away from the privileged Caracas-based jet set. Caracas itself is an overbearing presence in the region that serves as the economic fulcrum and cultural meeting ground for a multitude of Caribbean cultures. Most of the rest of the country remains fixed in the nineteenth century with African and Indian influence profoundly evident.

POLITICS

The controversial President Hugo Chavez has managed to stay in power despite alleged covert efforts from the United States to have him toppled. He fashions himself a "man of the people" and has formed an "Axis of Good" with Brazil's Lulu da Silva, Fidel Castro, and newly elected Ecuadorian President Gutierrez. His tough-guy military persona embodies the stereotype of the quintessential Latin Dictator of a bygone era, but conceals a shrewd, calculating leftist inner soul who has captivated the common man in Venezuela, much to the dismay of the rich, oil-controlling elite.

THE MUSIC

Venezuela's long history of slave trading from the early 1500s until 1834 is quite evident today. When one canvasses the make-up of the population on the long Caribbean coast, African-type villages abound. *Paranda*, a musical form prevalent in Belize, Honduras and Guatemala, remains a vital part of Afro-Venezuelan culture with its unmistakable kinship to indigenous and modern-day music from Cameroon and Benin (formerly Dahomey). Paranda is arguably the purest traditional African style performed in the Western Hemisphere, virtually unaffected or influenced by the two most powerful world music forces on the planet in neighboring Cuba and Brazil.

Llanera, Criollos, Harp Music, and the Cuatro. Llanera is a country-styled traditional form highlighted by the plains harp, heavy on the bass strings, accompanied by guitar, cuatro, percussion, tamboras, scrapers, and a variety of hand percussion instruments. The cuatro rivals the harp as the national instrument. It is a small four-stringed guitar with an earthy light sound, especially in the hands of Cheo Hurtado, the unquestioned master. It is traditional music, extremely popular with the older set; Llanera Criolles refers to the art song form of Llanera, akin to Nueva cancion.

RECOMMENDED CDs

SIMON DIAZ. Diaz is a national figure, folk legend, and composer credited with writing the tune that made the Gypsy Kings famous, "Bombaleo." He is an old school troubadour. *Tonada* (Latin Works, 2002) is a recent set that includes his most famous songs.

IRENE FARRERA. Farrera has resided in the northwestern United States since the early 1980s, but is no stranger in her native Caracas. Her dramatic, contralto voice is intense and infectious. *Serenata* (Paraiso Sonico, 2002) put her on the world music map.

MARCIO GRANADOS. Classically trained flutist and composer. *Amancer* (Hermes, 1995).

HURACAN DE FUEGO. Afro-Venezuelan music. *Agua e Coco* (Nubanegra, 2003).

CHEO HURTADO. Master of the 4-stringed cuatro, Cheo worked as a teacher until 1985, moved to Caracas, and formed *Gurrufio Ensemble* with flutist Luis Julio Toro. *Compadre Pancho* (1996); *Que Te Vaya Bien* (1990); *El Trabadedos* (1996); *Cuatro arpas y un Cuatro* (Tropical Music, 1992/2002); music from the Orinoco River (Ocora, 1997).

OSCAR DE LEON. Vocalist and salsa star Oscar is a *sonero* in the Beny More mold. *Doble Play* (Universal Latino, 2000) was nominated for a Grammy in 2002; *En Nueva York* (RMM, 1997); *Mas Que Amor* (Universal Latino, 2001).

LUIS JULIO TORO. Toro is an accomplished classical flutist. *Ensamble Gurrufio* (1995), features Cheo Hurtado (Cuatro) David Pena (Bass) and Cristobal Soto (Mandolin/Guitarra); *A Dos*.

LILA VERA. Lila is Venezuela's top nueva cancion proponent. *Pablo Milanes con Lila Vera* (1981); Lila can be heard on World Network's Venezuelan Compilation (1997).

AUSTRALIA AND THE
SOUTH PACIFIC

Australia
Fiji
Papua New Guinea
Solomon Islands
New Zealand

It is believed that the first migration to the South Pacific occurred about 30,000 years ago from Southeast Asia with settlements in Papua New Guinea and the Solomon Islands. A second, larger migration left Southeast Asia beginning 3,000 years ago and spread throughout the region, including Polynesia and Micronesia, ending in Hawaii and New Zealand as recently as 1,000 years ago.

Before the arrival of Europeans in the early 1500s, the sea dominated life. South Pacific people had to be adept at navigating the ocean and understanding its intricate system of winds, currents, ocean temperatures, and star patterns. They frequently journeyed between islands for war and trade and survived in the remotest area on the globe.

Today, the region remains the most remote on the planet, and its contribution to the world music scene is not extensive. Although the region is home to some of the oldest instruments in the world, recordings from the South Pacific are indeed sparse, comprising only a few significant artists and several field recordings of note.

AUSTRALIA

Aboriginal life in Australia dates back approximately 40,000 years. Despite numerous theories, it remains a mystery as to how Homo Sapiens traversed the Indonesian Archipelago from Africa, but somehow they did. One thing now seems certain based on the latest genetic scholarship: The aboriginal stone culture's DNA links them to the first South African Man.

Captain Cook claimed the continent for Britain in 1770 and by 1788 the first colony was established in New South Wales. Called the Fatal Shore when it was colonized, the white settlers, many of whom were petty criminals banished to the island from England, met with the realities of a harsh land and few accessible resources. They also encountered indigenous people and for the next 200 years proceeded to take away aboriginal land and suppress their language and cultural identity by committing genocide comparable to White America's treatment of Native Americans in North America.

The world image of Australians today is one of rugged outdoorsmen, extraordinary athletes, fun-loving tough guys who drink unimaginable quantities of beer, entrepreneurial types who are makers of fine wine, and citizens of the world. Many of these images are accurate; Aussies have excelled in sport for 50 years, especially in rugby, swimming, and tennis. The likes of Ruppert Murdoch and Mel Gibson have fostered the image of the capable, strong, indomitable, conservative Aussie.

However, the image is also a deceptive one. Australia remains a far away place in the twenty-first century, despite the Internet and modern technology. The treatment of the aboriginal people has, until very recently, drawn little attention from the outside and the reality of the scandal remains a well-kept secret. Until the late 1990s, the government systematically and forcibly separated aboriginal children from their parents at an early age, placing them in orphanages, allegedly to assimilate them into society. In truth, the government abandoned the children, intentionally perpetuating an apartheid system that differed only in style, but not effect, from that imposed on black South Africans until 1994. One should read John Pilger's *New Rulers of the World* for a truly illuminating discussion of Australian apartheid.

ABORIGINAL AUSTRALIA

Australia's indigenous people occupy the fringes of society, scattered about the country in the least desirable regions. Many have settled in Darwin on the North Coast and in Alice Springs in the center of Australia in the desert. Redfern is the Sydney ghetto where aboriginal Australians live. Their culture has survived, however, and there has been a cultural revival afoot for several years, which constitutes Australia's only world music.

Music, song, and dance remain a very important part of daily aboriginal life and customs. Ceremonies known as *corroborees*, dramatic representations in mime and song of a particular tribe that recall its mythical history, are still conducted. Men dance for hours while women and children sing. Different tribes use various percussion instruments and the ritual varies from tribe to tribe. There is one instrument, however, that is inextricably associated with Aboriginal culture: the *didjeridu*.

THE DIDJERIDU (DIDGERIDOO)

It has been said that the didjeridu is the sound from the center of the earth. Scientists and geologists, who have tried to capture the sound of the earth by lowering microphones as close as they could to the core, claim to have heard a deep drone with a mystical sound. When asked to describe the sound, all the scientists agreed: It sounded like the didjeridu!

The didj, as it is called, is a lip-vibrated aerophone of aboriginal Australia, and is among the oldest musical instruments on earth. It is an end blown instrument, 4–5 feet long with a bore of two or more inches in diameter, made from eucalyptus logs naturally hollowed by termites. Expert locals watch a tree to determine when it is hollowed enough and ready to be cut down. The didj originally came from Queensland in the North of Western Australia, although it is found in many aboriginal regions. It has a stirring, guttural sound that can penetrate the body. It is an aboriginal link to the totems of the past, a sacred instrument. It is said that it takes 40–50 years to learn all the traditional dance rituals that surround the revered instrument. Traditionally, it is played as accompaniment to singing and dancing in sacred ceremonies, and only by men. Players travel with several instruments in different keys, A being the most common; a good player can coax a C flat or C sharp, or even a D, F, or G out of a didj in C.

Playing the didj requires the mastery of circular breathing. Many classical flutists use the technique, which in simple terms means breathing in through the nose while blowing out from the mouth and simultaneously into the instrument. The lips must be relaxed. The amount of air required for the didj is less than one would imagine; roughly what it takes to make a candle flame flicker but not blow out. The didjeridu has become ubiquitous worldwide, showing up on an assortment of Celtic, new age, and fusion recordings.

Australia's vibrant rock and pop scene has incorporated aboriginal music since the early 1990s, since the breakthrough of roots group Yotha Yindi. Rock 'and' roll and reggae have become popular in aboriginal music since the 1980s when Bob Marley's tour left a lasting impact on black Australia. The aboriginal influence is changing the musical landscape down under by incorporating black culture from all over the world into the local music.

RECOMMENDED CDs

ANKALA WORLD ORCHESTRA. *Didje Blows the Games* (Network, 2000) with Janwirri Yiparrka and Mark Atkins.

MARK ATKINS. The leading spokesman for the didj and a master player. *Didjeridu Concerto* (Larriken, 1994), nature is the orchestra: rain, thunderstorm, birds; a truly remarkable recording with literally no discernable break in the drone and music from Atkins' didj for 50 minutes; *Rhythms from the Outer Core* (Network, 1998).

DAVID BLANASI. Blanasi is an elder statesman of the didj from the *Mialli* group in the Northern Territory. *Didjeridu Master* (Big Bang, 2000); *Les Aborigines: Songs and Dances of Northern Australia* (Arion, 1994) is more didj with aboriginal chant vocalist Djoli Laiwanga.

ALAN DARGIN/MICHAL ATHERTON. Inventive didj with Atherton on keyboards. *Cross & Hatch* (Black Sun, 1998).

RUBY HUNTER. The leading female aboriginal singer who was married to Archie Roach. *Thoughts Within* (1994).

SHUSHEELA RAMAN. Born in London to South Indian parents, raised in Australia. *Salt Rain* (Narada, 2001) is global Asian Pop Fusion; *Love Trap* (Narada, 2003) is a truly eclectic side with a classic Mahmoud Ahmed tune, Greek Clarinetist Manos Achalinotopoulos, and Tuvan throat singer Albert Kuvesin.

ARCHIE ROACH. Leading political lyricist and aboriginal rock star who helped expose the aussie practice of "stealing" aboriginal children and placing them in non-indigenous homes. Archie was such a child. *Charcoal Lane* (Hightone, 1992). Rock and soul with political lyrics and a little help from Neil Finn of Crowded House; *Looking for Butter Boy* (Hightone, 1998).

YOTHA YINDI. The most internationally recognized aboriginal band whose importance lies in their fusion of traditional music and performance with rock. *Freedom* (Mushroom, 1994) world beat, not aboriginal.

MELANESIA

Fiji
Papua New Guinea
Solomon Islands

PAPUA NEW GUINEA

Papua New Guinea (PNG) is in the southwest Pacific Ocean and occupies the eastern part of the island of New Guinea, shared by Irian Jaya, which is claimed by Indonesia. It is the most culturally diverse island under one government of all the Pacific Island nations, with more than 500 languages among 5 million people. Until the late nineteenth century, the island experienced no Western influence and parts did not contact the "outside world" until after World War II. PNG was controlled by Portugal and Australia throughout most of the twentieth century and gained independence from Australia in 1976. During World War II, allied soldiers brought Hawaiian and Polynesian popular music to PNG, introducing the guitar, ukulele, and string bands.

The folk music of PNG is similar to that of many aboriginal cultures, featuring a multitude of percussion instruments, flutes, pipes, songs for working, an assortment of ceremonies, and a call-and-response tradition. The focus of the music is on kin groups and entire communities, not individuals. Group events are called *sing-sings* (from Pidgin English), occasions that include complex preparation, elaborate costumes, feathered headdresses, and dancing. The event can be a feast, a purification rite, or a ceremony to denote a young girl's first menstruation.

Instruments include: bamboo Jew's harp; wooden horns (in the Sepik region); *garamut*, a wooden slit drum played by hitting it with two wooden beaters; a one-stringed chordophone made of fibrous roots (played by the Sago people); flutes made of bamboo played transversely, side-blown, or in rare occasions blown through the nose. Sacred flutes are played by two men at a time, and women and non-adult males are forbidden to see them.

Christian missionaries, who invaded in the late 1800s, did not approve of PNG folk music and suppressed it. They introduced hymns and redirected the focus of the indigenous music on the island. Today PNG traditional music is approaching extinction.

SOLOMON ISLANDS

The Solomon Islands are partly in PNG and are a former British protectorate. The *bamboo band* became popular in the 1930s and is the most well known musical style. Bamboo bands include large, horizontal, tuned panpipes played by striking the pipes with a rubber thong beater, much like playing a string bass. Guitar and voice accompany the music, which consists of love and folk songs. Smaller, bundled panpipes are the main instrument of the indigenous people. A unique compositional heritage is prevalent in the villages consisting of songs for birds, frogs, whirring insects, animal cries, water hitting a leaf, the roar of the sea, the crackling of branches, and the like. Each piece becomes associated

with a celebrated musician or village, an aboriginal form of intel
lectual property.

FIJI

The Fiji Islands, independent since 1970, are geographically part of
Melanesia, but musically more akin to Polynesia. The largest island,
Viti Levu, has a musical culture surrounding work and the life cycle
influenced by India, China, and Europe.

Meke is a genre that involves song, dance, and hand gestures used
in group ceremonies and social gatherings where the status of the
dancers, the virility of men, and the grace of women are displayed.
Instruments include: the *dulali,* a nose flute with 5 holes; *derua,* a
bamboo stamping tube, played by beating it on the ground or on
mats; and *bitu sanisani,* a bamboo, end-blown flute. Spear dances,
fan dances, and group *meke* dances are popular. *Vakalutuivoce*—
"dropping the oar"—is a common singing tradition whereby two
people rowing down river sing folk songs in counterpoint. The ceremonial dance and song rituals are also referred to as *sing sing* as
throughout Melanesia.

RECOMMENDED CDs

GEORGE TELEK MAMUA. Popular singer and the one PNG
artist to make a splash in the world music market. *Serious Tam*
(Real World, 2000) is rock and rap.

DAVID BIRDIE AND NOT DROWNING, WAVING. Keyboard
player who incorporates PNG music in his eclectic Aussie band that
brought Telek to world prominence. *Tabaran* (WEA, 1990). Rock
with a PNG approach.

FIELD RECORDINGS: *Sacred Flute Music from New Guinea:
Mandang, Volumes 1 & 2.* Recorded by Ragnar Johnson and Jessica
Mayer in 1976. From the Papua New Guinea north coast, the music
is played on large-bore bamboo flutes that are side blown and almost
6' feet long. The flutes are always played in pairs (male and female).
The flutists play continuous notes, alternating tones, back and forth
almost like a jazz blowing session from the 1940s. The music is used
for male initiation ceremonies and is sacred, intense, and spiritual.

BOSAVI-RAIN FIRST MUSIC FROM PAPUA NEW GUINEA.

Field recording by Steven Feld, 3 CDs (Smithsonian Folkways, 2001). 25 years of in-depth study of the Bosavi people in the southern highlands who live at the base of a volcano and had no contact with the outside world until 1970. The first CD is string band music, which draws on mission hymns approximating a country blues guitar with that shared Island Sound, familiar all over the world. The second disk contains work songs; the third disc is ritual music for funerals and séances.

NEW ZEALAND

One of the most strikingly beautiful places on earth is also the farthest away from the madding crowd, or at least it was until the filming of the *Lord of the Rings* trilogy. New Zealand is an extremely sophisticated English-speaking country with great natural wealth, renowned for its timber industry, shepherding, yachting, the world-class rugby club the All Blacks, outdoor activities, and a booming wine industry.

New Zealand's only world music comes from its indigenous people, the *Maori*. They are Polynesians who have lived in New Zealand since the eleventh century. Their own name is derived from *Ma-Uri*, which means "Children of Heaven." Maori tribal groupings are derived from the people of each canoe that settled in New Zealand centuries ago. Today, the Maori live in Auckland, Wellington, Christ Church, and other big cities, but remain closely connected to their tribes. They have been oppressed by the white colonizers for decades. Since 1995, there has been a significant change in the relationship with the Maori, an increased openness allowing Maori culture its rightful, respected place as New Zealand's native people.

MAORI MUSIC

Maori traditional music is a combination of speech and song known as *Haka*, a call-and-response form with hand clapping and feet stomping as rhythmic percussion. Haka are shouted speeches by men. *Haka Taparahi* are performed without weapons; *haka peruperu* are performed with weapons and associated with war dances.

Waiata is the most popular category of song; laments that are traditionally sung in unison in a group. *Waiata tangi* are laments for the dead, mainly written and performed by women. They can also be modern chants, which speak of the history of a tribe or an individual's place in the social and political structure of the entire society. Because they hold a tribe's history, accuracy in their rendition is essential. In the absence of a written literature, the musical tradition forms a large part of Maori oral literature

INSTRUMENTS

Wind instruments are made from wood, bone, stone, and shells. Three examples are:

- *putorino*: A flute made from wood, decorated with carved patterns and figures. If played by blowing the wider end, it produces a deep tone; if played by blowing across the central hole in the top, it produces a softer tone;
- *pukaea*: A trumpet like instrument, made from wood and ornately decorated, often used as a warning device among tribesmen;
- *koauau*: A wind instrument made of wood, bone, or stone, in a cylindrical shape with three finger holes, blown across the top of one end.

RECOMMENDED CDs

AOTEAROA. With DJ Ngahiwi Apanui and drummer Maaka McGregor, reggae and cutting edge Maori music. *He Waiata Mo Ti Iwi* (Jayrem, 2002).

NGAHIWI APANUI. *E Taunei* (Jayrem, 2003) Haka style maori sound.

TONI HUATA. *Mauri To/Everlasting Force* (WasHuu, 2003). Part Lebanese, part Maori, and a powerful vocalist rooted in Maori chant, produced by Maaka McGregor.

TE VAKA. Electronics mesh with traditional sounds, the pate (log drum), soulful harmonies, and political themes in a Polynesian folk-rock style led by singer songwriter Opetaia Foa'i. *Nukukehe* (2002); *Ki Mua* (Spirit of Play, 1999), political themes about the environment and the evil of missionaries; folk with a Maori feel.

WAI. Producer-arranger Maaka McGregor presents Maori culture in dramatic fashion. *100%* (Jayrem, 2000).

VAROIUS ARTISTS: *Waiata: Music of the Maori* (1999).

GLOSSARY OF GENRES

al Andalousi The Classical Music of the Maghreb was brought from Cordoba, Granada and Sevilla more than 1,000 years ago; called *Gharnata* in Morocco, *Malouf* in Tunisia, and *Ala* in Algeria.

Al jil: A popular form in Egypt, analogous to Algerian Rai.

Axe: Yoruban word meaning "life force," used in Bahian pop music in Brazil.

Bachata: Dominican song style related to other romantic Caribbean forms such as Cuban *son* and *guajira* and Mexican *rancheros* and *corridos*.

Baiao: Country music from Northeastern Brazil, associated with Luis Gonzaga, contains raised fourths and flattened sevenths.

Bal musette: The accordion-based dance music from the early part of the twentieth century in France, originally a piping based music.

Benga: A style of popular music in western Kenya, combining local rhythms with Cuban rumba and Congolese styles.

Bhajan: Popular Hindu religious songs that eulogize Hindu deities.

Biguine: Popular in Europe in the 1920s and 1930s as a ballroom music, modernized and adapted for pop audiences and know as *Biguine Moderne* in Martinique and the Antilles.

Bikoutsi: Cameroon style from the Yaounde Region, the music of the Beti people.

Biwagaku: Music written for the *biwa*, the main Japanese lute.

Blatny Pesny: Russian "delinquent song" depicting the hard life in the Soviet Union in graphic detail.

Bolero: Moderately slow Spanish dance from the 1800s in 3/4, common time, played in flamenco and Cuban music.

Bossa Nova: The "New Thing," Brazil's most popular music, which combines samba and cool jazz, originated with the work of Tom Jobim, Joao Donato, Johnny Alf, Carlos Lyra, and Joao Gilberto in the mid 1950s.

Cai Luoung: Traditional Vietnamese theatre genre dating back to 1917, based on Vietnamese and French disciplines; the foundation for Vietnamese folk music today.

Cajun: Traditional music from Louisiana combining a little two-step, waltz, blues, rock and roll, and R&B, centered on the accordion and the fiddle. Usually associated with white or Creole musicians; *see also* Zydeco.

Calypso: Trinidadian popular song form using slang with accents on the weak syllable, in 2/4 time, highly syncopated and repetitious; the repository of Trinidad's oral history and culture.

Campesina: Country *son* associated with workers in the 500-year-old sugarcane industry of Cuba.

Cante jugo: Deep song, the true essence of flamenco.

Carnatic music: The classical music of South India; also Karnatie.

Celtic: Traditional music from Ireland, Scotland, Wales, Galica, and Bretagne, using fiddles, bagpipes or gaitas, accordions, hand percussion, and performed in native languages including Gaelic (Ireland, Scotland), Bretagne (France), and Gallego (Galica).

Chaabi: Moroccan pop, also in Egypt and throughout North Africa, featuring studio pyrotechnics, dance beats, and modern sounds with allegiance to roots.

Chamame: Country-style accordion music from southern Argentina.

Champeta: Colombian music that incorporates Congolese, compass, and raga, with a decidedly non-Latin feel, derived from West Africa.

Charanga: Cuban big band style characterized by melodies in the high register, trilling flute, and strings; related to the Cha Cha.

Chimurenga: Guitar-driven Afro Pop of Zimbabwe's Shona people, also known as *mbira*.

Chong-ak: Style used for the Korean ruling class, classical music of Korea.

Choro: Brazil's seminal dance form, with distinctly Western European harmonic influence, including waltz and polka, combined with an African rhythmic sensibility.

Compas: Incorporates genres from the Caribbean (Harti) including merengue, soca, zouk, salsa, and American jazz; smooth, guitar-based big band music made for dancing.

Corrido: Mexican ballad form that was the basis of the Norteno and Tejana styles.

Cumbia: Colombian popular dance with layered rhythms and syncopation; originally a courtship dance of slaves; also a similar style from Mexico.

Dangdut: Popular Indonesian genre developed in the underclass in Jakarta in the late 1960s that mixes Indian, Western, and Middle Eastern music; drawing its audience from Muslim youth of the lower-class.

Dhimotika tragoudhia: Greek folk music.

Dhrupad: Oldest most sacred Hindustani vocal genre, performed by men accompanied by *tanpura* and *pakhawaj*.

Dondang sayang: Slow, intense music of Malaysia mixing influences from China, India, the Middle East, and Portugal.

Esmeraldas: Afro-Latino musical tradition in Ecuador.

Fado: Portugal's art song form with lyrics full of regret, mourning, and longing; traditionally accompanied by Guitarra Portuguesa, a 12-stringed guitar, Violao (smaller guitar), and occasionally violin, flute, and accordion.

Fasil: Gypsy music in Turkey.

Filmi: Movie music from Bollywood in India (aka playback or simply Bollywood).

Flamenco: Spain's greatest music and dance form, played on Spanish classical guitar; when sung it is called *cante flamenco* and sung with extreme emotion, accompanied by hand clapping and a chorus of 2–3 singers.

Fuji: A Nigerian Yoruban voice and percussion style popularized by Kolli Barrister and Adewale Ayuba.

Gamelan: Ensemble of tuned percussion of gongs, xylophones with metal bars, and drums from Indonesia; it can include singers, bamboo flutes, and spike fiddles.

Ghazal: Means "to talk amorously of Women" in Urdu or Persian; love songs influenced by Sufi mystics; much Ghazal is based on North Indian Ragas.

Gnawa: Moroccan music of descendants of slaves brought from Mali in the sixteenth century, featuring the stringed *sintir* or *gimbri*; trance-like, used in healing ceremonies.

Griot: West African oral historian/minstrel/storyteller.

Guarania: Melodic concert music from Paraguay.

Gumbe: Related to the Brazilian *samba*, the *morna* of Cape Verde, and the *semba* of Angola, featuring unique West African poly rhythms, non-Portuguese forms; dates back to the 1850s.

Habanera: Cuban dance popular in Spain in the 1900s named after Havana with a 2/4 rhythm like the tango; the basis of son.

Hadra: Part of the ceremony in Tunisian Sufi music.

Haqibah: Harmonic, essentially a capella music from Sudan based on the pentatonic scale.

High Life: Dance music of Ghana from the 1960s, the seminal Afro-World form.

Hindustani Sangeet: *Sangeet* is the word for "music" in India; this refers to North Indian music, covering a region that includes Bangladesh.

Jaipongan: Complex rhythmic dance music from Sunda in Indonesia with no apparent Western influence.

Jit: Zimbabwean dance music characterized by hard, fast percussion, featuring *mbira* and guitar.

Joik: Phonetic poetry music from Samiland consisting mainly of untranslatable vocables and yodeling sounds reminiscent of certain Native American music.

Juju: Popular style featuring Yoruban rhythms and incorporating Western instruments such as the conventional trap drums, pedal steel guitar, keyboards, accordion, along with the African talking drum.

Kabuki: Music to accompany the traditional Japanese theatrical style.

Kabyle: Folk music of the Berbers from the region in Algeria; has political overtones.

Kagura: Generic term for all Shinto music and dance.

Kan ha diskan: Bretagne Celtic vocal music feautring call-and-response singing.

Khyal: Popular form of North Indian semi-classical vocals, has less improvisation than thumri.

Klezmer: Eastern European Jewish wedding music with a jazz flavor, now popular in the Untied States and Europe; the word is a combination of two Yiddish words, *kley* meaning "vessel" and *zemer* meaning "song."

Kriti: South Indian Carnatic Hindu praise music, sung in Teluga, Tamil, or Sanskrit.

Kroncong: Urban folk music with sexually provocative lyrics that arose from the lower-class Eurasians (Indonesian/Dutch) in Batavia, Indonesia in the early 1900s.

Kulning: High-pitched singing form from Sweden.

Kveding: Norwegian vocal style.

Kwela: South African pennywhistle music.

Laiko: Popular Greek music.

Llanera: Country style from Venezuela centered on the plains harp—heavy on the bass strings—accompanied by guitar, cuatro, percussion, tamboras, scrapers, and hand percussion instruments; *llanero*, from the Pacific Coast of Colombia, is similar to Llanera.

Lu: An ancient Tibetan tradition sung a cappella in a high voice.

Luk thung: Thailand's ubiquitous country music, which chronicles the life and troubles of the rural population.

Makossa: Cameroonian dance rhythm from Douala region, associated with Manu Dibango.

Malagasy: A term used to describe many styles throughout the island of Madagascar with a common style and rhythm; the music varies greatly from region to region, defying convenient categorization.

Malouf: Al Andalous in Tunisia.

Maloya: Bluesy form from La Reunion consists predominantly of vocals, sung in creole backed only by percussion; a music that dates back to the chants of the slaves who sang on the sugarcane plantations.

Maracatu: New beat in the northeast of Brazil with march-type rhythms and accents.

Mariachi and son Jalisciense: Music from the Jalisco region of Mexico.

Marrabenta: Mozambique's popular roots-based urban rhythm with salsa, calypso, and merengue influences.

Mbalax (em-Balah): A Senegalese (Wolof) percussion music popularized by Youssou N'Dour using funky Afro-Cuban rhythms and American pop.

Mbaqanga: Also known as Township Jive from South Africa; first popular in the 1960s; Johnny Clegg and the Mahotolla Queens are proponents.

Mbira: The Zimbabwean mbira is a thumb piano with 22–46 metal keys, played with the thumb and right forefinger inside a Zeze, a resonating gourd; *see* Chimurenga.

Mento: Loose-sounding folk music from Jamaica, similar to Calypso; the first recorded Jamaican music.

Merengue: Dominican Republic's main form, unsyncopated, characterized by an aggressive beat on the 1 and 3.

Milonga: Spanish dance form originating in Andalusia, traveled to Argentina; precursor to the tango.

Min'yo: Folk song genre in Japan; work songs, usually accompanied by shamisen, taiko, and shakuhachi.

MPB: Musica Popular Brasileira, catch-all phrase for popular Brazilian music, usually post-bossa nova.

Mor lam: Predominant folk music from the region of Isan in northeastern Thailand where there is a large Laotian population; essentially Latotian music.

Morna: Cape Verdean genre sung in Creole-Portuguese, with folk tunes, guitar, cavaquinho, violin, accordion, and clarinet; Cesaria Evora is the main performer in this style.

Musiqi-e assil: Classical Iranian music.

Nogaku: Music of the Noh drama in Japan.

Norteno: See Tejano

Nova Cancao: Portuguese folk song movement allied with nueva cancion.

Nubian: Music from the Sudan and southern Egypt.

Nueva Cancion: "New Song," political song movement created as protest music by Atahualpa Yupanqui and popular throughout South America.

Nuevo Tango: Tango for the concert hall, not the dance floor; an innovation of Astor Piazzolla.

Organetto: Italian folk music based on accordions and vocals with traditional instruments.

Palm Wine: Sierra Leonese tropical style, with light, airy guitar riffs.

Pansori: Korean vocal and percussive music performed by one singer and one drummer.

Paranda: West African dance and vocal style prevalent in Belize and Central America.

Plena: Narrative song form of Puerto Rico, with origins in the city of Ponce on the southern coast; roots are in African music and dance, influenced by Mexican corridos, meringue, and calypso.

Polska: Folk dance form found in many regions of Sweden.

Qawwali: Devotional music of the Pakistani Sufis, the mystical sect of Islam.

Raga (rag): The melodic form or portion of Indian Classical music; ragam in South India.

Rai: Pop, disco-influenced music from Algeria with roots in Bedoui music from World War II.

Reggae: Jamaican pop dance music, emphasizing the bass, in 4/4 but with the strong beats on the 2 and 4.

Ranchera: A bluesy folk music from Mexico, with lyrics about hard times, betrayal, and poverty, yearning for the good old days.

Rembetika: The most celebrated music of the Greek ports; folk and blues; also rebetika.

Romani: Gypsy music, referring to a wide range of styles from jazz to Eastern European string band music sounding like Klezmer, wedding music, and other forms absorbed wherever gypsies live.

Rumba (rhumba): Lively 2/4 Cuban dance popularized in the 1930s with unexpected accents.

Rumba Gitano: Gypsy rumba from Catalonia, popularized by the Gipsy Kings.

Samba Reggae: A combination of reggae and samba with large drum sections from the *blocos afros* (Carnival associations in Salvador Bahia, Brazil).

Samba: Brazil's most popular traditional form, characterized by 2/4 meter and interlocking syncopation between melody and accompaniment.

Schrammelmusik: Urban folk music from Austria.

Sean-nos: Literally "old style," the most famous traditional style of Irish singing.

Semba: Angola's traditional music; precursor to Brazilain samba.

Sevdalinka: Love song from Bosnia.

Shaabi: Egyptian popular street music of Middle East.

Shakuhachi: Classical music written for the family of flutes in Japan.

Shash Maqam (6 modes): A compendium of instrumental and vocal music that embodies Central Asian poetry and music, linked to the *maqam* tradition of other Islamic countries.

Silat: Branch of self-defense also popular as a Malaysian art presentation, similar to *tai chi*, mixing dance and music accompanied by gongs, drums, and Indian oboes.

Ska: Predecessor to Jamaican reggae that combines the catchy backbeat of New Orleans R&B with mento.

Slack Key: Guitar style from Hawaii featuring open tunings; a steel bar is used to note the strings.

Slattemusikk: Norwegian folk; traditional.

Soca: Soul-calypso style popular in Trinidadian music.

Sog-ak: Korean music for the common people.

Son: The main Cuban form played with percussion (conga, bongo, djembe), bass, tres, and call-and-response vocals; evolved from *danzon*, the main Cuban dance in the 1870s, the musical form that brought African music to the island.

Sonderhoning: Denmark's folk style.

Soukous: Style that is derived from the 1950s Cuban rhumba mixing with zouk and based in the Congo (Zaire), but relocated to Paris.

Sufi: Islamic trance music found throughout the Middle East and South Asia.

Taarab: Tanzania's musical genre, originally simply wedding music sung in Swahili, a blend of African, Indian, and Arabic sonorities based on the island of Zanzibar.

Tala (thalam): The rhythmic part of Indian classical music, a constantly repeated metrical cycle of beats present in all classical drumming.

Tahrir: Iranian singing.

Tango: Traditional, formalized dance music from Buenos Aires and Montevideo, led by bandoneon and derived from the milonga.

Tango Cancion: A vocal version of tango popularized by Carlos Gardel.

Tejano: A blend of traditonal Mexican music including corridos and rancheras that incorporates European waltz and polka, popular and folk music, which has its origins in the Mexicans who settled in central and southern Texas; also called Conjunto; the Mexican version is called Norteno.

Thumri: Popular urban form in North India, light classical, romantic, and devotional music sung in Hindi and related to the legend of Krishna and the deity Vishnu.

Township: Soul, R&B music from South African townships popular in the 1950s–1960s.

Trikitixa: Basque accordion genre from Euskadi (Spain).

Tropicalia: Eclectic pop style and movement from Brazil in the late 1960s.

Vallenato: Popular Colombian music incorporating cumbia, merengue, and the fast 6/8 beat.

Wassoulou: Malian style with an Arabic feel.

Wedding Music: Eastern European genre, traditional music that accompanies the wedding ceremony combining Bulgarian, Turkish, and Rom folk tunes with jazz, always prioritizing improvisation.

Xoomei: The learned technique of throat singing from Tuva and Mongolia that involves manipulation of the singer's jaw, lips, mouth, and sinuses to produce several overtones simultaneously in a low, growling voice.

Ziglibithy: Local tradition of the Bete people with Congolese rhythms to make a new Cote d'Ivoirian music, slower than makossa and characterized by a jerky, almost frenzied rhythm.

Zouk: Creole slang for party; from the Antilles

Zydeco: Louisiana two step technically differentiated from Cajun because it is played by Black Creole bands; see Cajun

BIBLIOGRAPHY

Agawu, Kori. *Representing African Music: Postcolonial Notes, Queries, Positions.* New York: Routledge, 2003.

Ammer, Christine. *Harper Dictionary of Music.* New York: Harper and Row, 1987.

Arnold, Alison. *South Asia: The Indian Subcontinent.* In *The Garland Encyclopedia of World Music, Volume 5.* New York: Garland, 1999.

Azzi, Maria Susan, and Simon Collier. *Le Grand Tango: The Life and Music of Astor Piazzolla.* New York: Oxford University Press, 2000.

Blumenthal, Howard. *The World Music CD Listener's Guide: The Best on CD.* New York: Billboard Books, 1998.

Bohlman, Philip. *World Music: A Very Short Introduction.* New York: Oxford University Press, 2002.

Broughton, Simon, Mark Ellingham, Orla Duane, and James McConniche, editors. *The Rough Guide to World Music, Volumes I and II.* London: Rough Guide Publications, 1999, revised 2000.

Clark, Walter Aaron. *From Tejano to Tango: Latin American Popular Music.* New York: Routledge, 2002.

Clayton, Martin, Richard Middleton, and Trevor Herbert, editors. *The Cultural Study of Music.* New York: Routledge, 2003.

Collier, Simon, with Maria Susana Azzi. *Tango: The Dance, the Song, the Story.* New York: Thames and Hudson, 1995.

Collins, John. *West African Pop Roots*. Philadelphia: Temple University Press, 1992.

Danielson, Virginia, Dwight Reynolds, and Sean Marcus. *The Middle East*. In *The Garland Encyclopedia of World Music, Volume 6*. New York: Routledge, 2001.

Dunne, Christopher. *Brutality Garden: Tropicalia and the Emergence of a Brazilian Counterculture*. Chapel Hill: University of North Carolina Press.

Edwards, Gwynne. *Flamenco!* London: Thames and Hudson, 2000.

Feather, Leonard, and Ira Gitler. *The Biographical Encyclopedia of Jazz* New York: Oxford University Press, 1999.

Fletcher, Peter, and Laurence E.R. Picken. *World Musics in Context: A Comprehensive Survey of the World's Major Musical Cultures*. New York: Oxford University Press, 2004.

Goertzen, Chris, James Porter, and Timothy Rice. *Europe*. In *The Garland Encyclopedia of World Music, Volume 8*. New York: Garland, 1999.

Haas, Karl. *Inside Music*. New York: Anchor Press, 1991.

Hart, Mickey. *Songcatchers: In Search of the World's Music*. Washington, D.C.: National Geographic, 2003.

Hernandez, Deborah Pacini. *Bachata: A Social History of a Dominican Popular Music*. Philadelphia: Temple University Press, 1998.

Jones, Stephen R. *Folk Music of China*. Oxford: Oxford University Press, 1999.

Kaeppler, Adrienne, and J.W. Love. *Australia and the Pacific Islands*. In *The Garland Encyclopedia of World Music, Volume 1*. New York: Garland, 1998.

Keil, Angelika, and Charles Keil. *Bright Balkan Morning*. Middletown, Connecticut: Wesleyan University Press, 2002.

Koskoff, Ellen. *The United States and Canada*. In *The Garland Encyclopedia of World Music, Volume 3*. New York: Routledge, 2000.

Levin, Theodore. *The Hundred Thousand Fools of God*. Indianapolis: Indiana University Press, 1996.

Lornell, Kip, and Anne Rasmussen, editors. *Musics of Multicultural America*. New York: Schirmer Books, 1997.

Malm, William P. *Music Cultures of the Pacific, the Near East, and Asia*, 3rd edition. Upper Saddle River, New Jersey: Prentice Hall, 1996.

Malm, William P. *Traditional Japanese Music and Musical Instruments*. Rutland, Vermont: Kodansha International Press, 2000.

Mathieson, Kenny, editor. *Celtic Music*. London: Backbeat Books, 2001.

McGovern, Adam, editor. *Music Hound: The Essential Album Guide*. Farmington Hills, Michigan: Visible Ink Press, 2000.

McGowan, Chris, and Ricardo Pessanha. *The Brazilian Sound*. Philadelphia: Temple University Press, 1994.

Miller, Terry E., and Sean Williams. *Southeast Asia*. In *The Garland Encyclopedia of World Music, Volume 4*. New York: Garland, 1998.

Mitchell, Tony, editor. *Global Noise: Rap and Hip-Hop outside the USA*. Middletown, Connecticut: Wesleyan University Press, 2002.

Monson, Ingrid, editor. *The African Diaspora: A Musical Perspective*. New York: Routledge, 2003.

Nettl, Bruno, et al. *Excursions in World Music*, 3rd edition. Upper Saddle River, New Jersey: Prentice-Hall, 2000.

Nketia, J.H.Kwabeha. *Music of Africa*. New York: W.W. Norton, 1974.

Olsen, Dale A., and Daniel E. Sheehy. *South America, Mexico, Central America, and the Caribbean*. In *The Garland Encyclopedia of World Music, Volume 2*. New York: Garland, 1998.

Perrone, Charles A., and Christopher Dunn. *Brazilian Popular Music and Globalization*. New York: Routledge, 2001.

Pinker, Steven. *The Language Instinct*. New York: William Morrow, 1994.

Plastino, Goffredo. *Mediterranean Mosaic: Popular Music and Global Sounds*. New York: Routledge, 2002.

Prajanananda, Swami. *Historical Study of Indian Music*. New Delhi: South Asia Books, 2001.

Provine, Robert C., Yoshiko Tokumaru, and J. Lawrence Witzelben. *East Asia: China, Japan, and Korea*. In *The Garland Encyclopedia of World Music, Volume 7*. New York: Routledge, 2001.

Randall, Annie J., editor. *Music, Power, and Politics*. New York: Routledge, 2004.

Rice, Timothy. *May It Fill Your Soul: Experiencing Bulgarian Music*. Chicago: University of Chicago Press, 1994.

Roberts, John Storm. *Black Music of 2 Worlds*, 2nd edition. New York: Schirmer Books, 1998.

Roberts, John Storm. *The Latin Tinge: The Impact of Latin American Music on the United States*, 2nd edition. New York: Oxford, 1999.

Rogovoy, Seth. *The Essential Klezmer*. Chapel Hill, North Carolina: Algonquin Books, 2000.

Roy, Maya. *Cuban Music*. Princeton, New Jersey: Markus Weiner Publishers, 1998.

Sadie, Stanley, editor. *The New Grove Dictionary of Music and Musicians*, 2nd edition. New York: Grove's Dictionaries, 2001.

Sapoznik, Henry. *Klezmer: Jewish Music from Our World to Our World*. New York: Schirmer Books, 2000.

Sawyers, June Skinner. *Celtic Music: A Complete Guide*. Chicago: A Cappella Books, 2001.

Kinzer, Stephen. *Crescent and Star*. New York: Farrar Straus & Giroux, 2001.

Schade-Poulsen, Marc. *Men and Popular Music in Algeria: The Social Significance of Raï*. Austin: University of Texas Press, 1999.

Schnabel, Tom. *Rhythm Planet: The Great World Music Makers*. New York: Universe Books, 1998.

Spencer, Peter. *World Beat: A Listener's Guide to Contemporary World Music on CD*. Chicago: A Cappella Books, 1992.

Stewart, Gary. *Rumba on the River: A History of the Popular Music of the Two Congos*. London: Verso, 2000.

Stone, Ruth M. *Africa*. In *The Garland Encyclopedia of World Music, Volume 1*. New York: Garland, 1997.

Stone, Ruth M. *The World's Music: General Perspectives and Reference Tools*. In *The Garland Encyclopedia of World Music, Volume 10*. New York: Routledge, 2001.

Taylor, Timothy D. *Global Pop: World Music, World Markets*. New York: Routledge, 1997.

Tenaille, Frank. *Music is the Weapon of the Future: 50 Years of Popular African Music*. Chicago, Illinois: Lawrence Hill Books, 2000.

Titon, Jeff Todd, editor. *Worlds of Music: An Introduction to Music of the World's Peoples, Shorter Edition*. New York: Schirmer Books, 2000.

Touma, Habib Hassan. *The Music of the Arabs.* Minneapolis, Minnesota: Hal Leonard, 1996.

Veloso, Caetano. *Tropical Truth: A Story of Music and Revolution in Brazil,* New York: Alfred A Knopf, 2002.

Vernon, Paul. *A History of Fado.* Aldershot, United Kingdom: Ashgate Publishing, 1997.

Warhaft, Gail Holst. *Road to Rembetika—Music of a Greek Sub-Culture: Songs of Love, Sorrow and Hashish,* 3rd edition. Athens, Greece: D. Harvey, 1983.

Waxer, Lisa, editor. *Situating Salsa: Global Markets and Local Meanings in Latin Popular Music.* New York: Routledge, 2002.

Wells, Spencer. *The Journey of Man.* Princeton, New Jersey: Princeton University Press, 2002.

MAGAZINES AND PERIODICALS

fROOTS Magazine, Ian Anderson, editor, (1996–2004), a monthly publication, Southern Rag, Ltd., London, United Kingdom.

Dirty Linen Magazine, Paul Hartman, editor, (2000–2004), a monthly publication, ISSN 1047-4315, Dirty Linen, Ltd., Baltimore, Maryland.

Songlines Magazine, (See Rough Guide), Simon Broughton, editor. (2000–2004).

INDEX